DATE			

THE
M
W
H

Y0-BDX-352

Other Books by Judi Kesselman-Turkel and Franklynn Peterson

Study Smart Series

Secret to Writing Great Papers (Contemporary Books, 1983, Original Title
    Getting It Down, revised ed. University of Wisconsin Press, 2003)
The Grammar Crammer (Contemporary Books, 1982, revised ed. University
    of Wisconsin Press, 2003)
Research Shortcuts (Contemporary Books, 1982, revised ed. University of
    Wisconsin Press, 2003)
Note-Taking Made Easy (Contemporary Books, 1982, revised ed. University of
    Wisconsin Press, 2003)
Test-Taking Strategies (Contemporary Books, 1981, revised ed. University of
    Wisconsin Press, 2004)
Study Smarts (Contemporary Books, 1981, revised ed. University of
    Wisconsin Press, 2004)
Spelling Simplified (Contemporary Books, 1983, revised ed. University of
    Wisconsin Press, 2004)
The Vocabulary Builder (Contemporary Books, 1982, revised ed. University of
    Wisconsin Press, 2004)

Other Co-Authored Books for Adults

The Author's Handbook (Prentice Hall, 1983, revised ed. University of
    Wisconsin Press, 2006)
Good Writing (Franklin Watts, 1981)
Homeowner's Book Of Lists (Contemporary Books, 1981)
The Do-It-Yourself Custom Van Book (Contemporary Books, 1977)
with Dr. Frank Konishi, *Eat Anything Exercise Diet* (William Morrow, 1978)

Co-Authored Books for Children

I Can Use Tools (Elsevier-Nelson/Dutton, 1981)
Vans (Dandelion Press, 1979)

By Judi Kesselman-Turkel

Stopping Out: A Guide To Leaving College and Getting Back In (M. Evans, 1975)

By Franklynn Peterson

with Nancy Selfridge, MD., *Freedom From Fibromyalgia* (Three Rivers Press, 2001)
How to Fix Damn Near Everything (Prentice-Hall, 1977, Wings Press, 1996)
Handbook of Lawn Mower Repair (Hawthorne Books, 1975, revised ed.
    Emerson, 1978, Perigree, 1984)
How To Improve Damn Near Everything Around Your Home (Prentice-Hall, 1981)
Handbook Of Snowmobile Maintenance and Repair (Hawthorn/Dutton, 1979)
Children's Toys You Can Build Yourself (Prentice-Hall, 1978)
The Build-It-Yourself Furniture Catalog (Prentice-Hall, 1976)

THE MAGAZINE WRITER'S HANDBOOK

Second Edition

Franklynn Peterson and
Judi Kesselman-Turkel

The University of Wisconsin Press

The University of Wisconsin Press
1930 Monroe Street
Madison, Wisconsin 53711

www.wisc.edu/wisconsinpress/

3 Henrietta Street
London WC2E 8LU, England

Printed in the United States of America

Library of Congress Cataloging-in-Publication Data
Peterson, Franklynn.
The magazine writer's handbook / by Franklynn Peterson and
Judi Kesselman-Turkel.—2nd ed.
p. cm.
Includes bibliographical references and index.
ISBN 0-299-21494-X (pbk. : alk. paper)
1. Journalism—Authorship—Handbooks, manuals, etc. 2. Feature writing—
Handbooks, manuals, etc. I. Kesselman-Turkel, Judi. II. Title.
PN4775.P436   2005
808'.02—dc22   2005005464

This book is warmly dedicated to our dear friends and fellow writers who gave so freely of their expertise to help us help the next generation of professional freelancers.

CONTENTS

PART III. How to Sell Your Article Ideas

PART IV. How to Write Your Article

PART V. How to Be a Pro

PREFACE TO THE SECOND EDITION

Dear Frank and Judi,

It isn't very often that I come across a book that evokes a spontaneous "I wish I'd written that!" Your *Magazine Writer's Handbook* is one of my favorites. I can't imagine why I never found the book before this year!

Although I already knew practically everything covered, I read the book with interest and enjoyment. And I was grateful to be reminded of some areas I'd half-forgotten. This is a valuable book for the beginner, the intermediate writer, and the well-seasoned professional. The information it contains is outstanding and the writing is superb.

It is with great pleasure that I recommend *The Magazine Writer's Handbook* to my writing classes. I just want to thank you again for doing such a wonderful job.

Cordially,

Louise Purwin Zobel, Professor of Journalism, San José State University, author, *The Travel Writer's Handbook* (Writer's Digest Books); contributor to *Better Homes and Gardens, Bride's Magazine, House Beautiful, Medical Economics, Modern Maturity, Parents Magazine* and newspapers around the country.

This flattering letter arrived in our mail four years after Frank and I first wrote *The Magazine Writer's Handbook.* The funny thing is, we wrote it because we needed a textbook. We'd been teaching courses and seminars in magazine writing, first in New York City and on Long Island and then with the outreach arm of the University of Wisconsin. We'd been looking for a good textbook for serious students, with no luck. Most books on writing didn't even explain what a query is, much less how to write one—and the query is the one tool you need most to sell a magazine article. Few showed how to write a good lead or how to find live experts or interview them once you found them. Not one demonstrated the work that must go into writing a final draft for submission.

So we wrote the book we needed for our courses—and soon began getting heartwarming letters like the one from Louise, reproduced here with her kind permission. To our pride and satisfaction, we heard that other journalism professors were using the book in colleges around the country. We also heard that several top magazine editors were recommending it to favorite novice writers. Long after the first and second editions sold out, we were thrilled when University of Wisconsin Press wanted to publish this updated edition.

Re-reading the prior editions carefully, we've seen little change in magazine publishing in twenty-four years. The only major innovation has been technologic. Computers are here to stay, and they've greatly evolved since the 1982 edition. They're a boon to magazine writers, making short work of sending out many queries on the same topic and making it easy to resell reworked articles many times over.

Since 1982, many magazines have folded and new ones have popped up; some have moved or been bought by other publishers. Editors have retired, moved up on the masthead or jumped to better paying jobs. In their place are new, unseasoned editors full of drive and anxious to discover new writers. In the intervening twenty-four years, several magazines raised their fees to freelancers; others lowered already low fees. A few more fiction markets opened up, but they faded just as fast. Otherwise, every word in the first edition is as true today as when we wrote it.

A lot has changed in our lives, though. Back when *The Magazine Writer's Handbook* and its companion *The Author's Handbook* were first published, Frank and I thought we'd go on writing books and magazine articles forever. In fact, during 1982 we wrote several articles for *Fortune, OMNI* and *Parade* and five more books in our *Study Smart* series for students and others (which has also recently been reprinted by the University of Wisconsin Press).

But by January 1983, we were firmly committed to a new venture. To write those last five books, we had bought two early NEC computers. We learned fast how primitive they were and how incompletely they met manufacturers' promises. We also found out that most people understood nothing about them. So—just as we'd been doing throughout our careers—we decided to interpret *this* new phenomenon to the public.

Frank was way ahead of me. He'd worked as American liaison for a French computer company way back before he became a photojournalist. He understood the technology and some of the lingo. He said we shouldn't write a book. The industry was changing so rapidly, any book we wrote would be out of date before it got published. He ruled out magazine articles for similar reasons. What was left? A newspaper column.

I'd written little for newspapers—a few articles for *The New York Times* and some reviews for a community newspaper. But Frank had put in years as a Sunday supplement writer before we teamed up. "Sure," I said, "why not?"

In the summer of 1982 most folks were buying home Ataris and Commodores to play video games. We felt it was a fad that would fade fast. One of our sons, who's now Architect of Game Technology at Sun Microsystems, made a profitable career proving us wrong. But we decided that longer lasting interest would come from people who could put computers to good business use. We sent a ten-page proposal to all the big newspaper syndicates for a column we christened *The Business Computer.*

The syndicates turned thumbs down. They were betting on video game columns. But we were stubborn. We resolved that if we could convince six newspapers around the country to run our column, we'd sign long-term agreements locking us in. We convinced six editors, began in January 1983, and wrote two columns a week for more than a decade. We discovered that newspaper writing—even of syndicated columns—makes few people rich. But it twice brought us the prestigious National Press Club's Award for Excellence in Consumer Journalism.

Soon after beginning our column, since writers always try to make their research pull in as many assignments as possible, we contracted with a Milwaukee publisher of newsletters for accountants to write and edit a new monthly, *CPA Micro Report.* That contract lasted until 1993, when the publisher sold his company to Harcourt Brace. Feeling that HB's contract offer was tantamount to slavery, we declined it and started our own competing newsletter, *CPA Computer Report.* Once we learned to be entrepreneurs, we attracted and kept a loyal following of public accountants. Instead of having to rely on rich magazine and newspaper publishers for their iffy processing of our hard-earned paychecks, we now rely on steady subscription renewals. By now, writing about computer technology isn't as fast-changing or as challenging as writing about medicine was back when we were strictly freelancers. But we still get to research new topics (which is a lot easier since the Internet came along), to hone words and phrases, and to broadcast our thoughts and ideas to readers who can turn them into reality.

Dear reader, we hope this book will help *you* publish, perfect your craft and delight in the joy of seeing your byline in print. Let us know how you do!

THE
MAGAZINE
WRITER'S
HANDBOOK

Introduction
Three Keys to Successful Magazine Writing

L et's start by offering you the same deal we make with students in our magazine writing courses:

Experience life to the fullest and with a child's questioning mind,
keep setting your discoveries down on paper, and
do it with the professionalism we're going to teach you
. . . and we'll turn you into a professional writer, someone who can sell your articles to first-rank newspapers and national magazines.

We're not promising you'll make your living at it. In the glory days of the mid-1990s, a survey found that full-time writers who worked at it at least forty hours a week averaged only $12,500 a year in income. Only 16 percent earned $30,000 a year or more. In 2002, according to the National Writer's Union, American freelance rates had declined by more than 50 percent since the 1960s. Full-time freelance writers earned, on average, 30 percent less than other equivalently educated workers. Today we can count only a few hundred truly successful full-time freelance magazine writers, not counting the few thousand others who sell an article now and then. But if your goal is to see your name in print, make some money, or let lots of other people in on your wisdom or point of view, the combination of your drive and our direction will surely lead you straight to that elusive brass ring.

A Love Affair with Life

The first ingredient you'll need to succeed is an inquiring mind. Of the several hundred successful magazine writers we know, not one goes through a day without noticing something new or looking at something in a new way. They all constantly ask "Why?" and "How?" and "What next?"

We're just like the rest. Even though we've jotted down enough story ideas to keep us busy the rest of our lives, we leap from our computers at the first sniff of something new or unnoticed. We've traveled through nearly all of the fifty states and into foreign countries just to see what's there. We've been down in coal mines, up in hot-air balloons and open-cockpit biplanes, in jail and on TV.

3

We've questioned Nobel laureates and con artists, movie stars and Bowery bums, then raced home to write down our experiences and impressions.

But inquiry involves more than just physical activity. Most writers are intellectual activists. They keep coming up with ideas for doing things differently or enjoying a better life. We've experienced the thrill of believing in something, writing about it and watching it improve—just a little—the quality of other people's lives. Our articles have helped integrate hospitals in Sunflower County, Mississippi. They've helped save a progressive screening program for North Carolina preschoolers. They've helped find decent housing for the mother of a Vietnam War casualty. They've alerted women and social agencies to a new way of prosecuting rape cases. They've changed the way museums set their entrance fees.

Approach life not as an observer but as a wide-eyed participant, and you'll have grabbed the first key to successful magazine writing.

Time at the Keyboard

When a cousin of ours backpacked through all the countries of Eastern Europe keeping track of her adventures in her diary, her family called her a hippie. When a friend backpacked through all of Eastern Europe and sold articles about his adventures, *his* family introduced him as a magazine writer. He had found the first key to success—the discipline to sit for hours pounding words into modern stone. It's the same secret we'd found early in our own careers.

The two of us combine many decades of making our living as professional magazine writers. Over the years, we've sold several hundred articles to magazines of all sizes and just about all interests (and we've outlasted some of them, too): *Family Circle, Woman's Day, McCall's, House Beautiful, Fortune, Playgirl, Popular Science, Popular Mechanics, Seventeen, Writer's Digest, Science Digest, Omni, Elks, Sepia, Yankee, Family Health, Family Handyman, New York, Chicago, Pageant, Money, Physician's Management, Hospitals,* and many, many more. In addition, we've written twenty books for adults and two for children. Five times in our careers we've received coveted national awards for our hard work: the Brotherhood in Media Award from the National Conference of Christians and Jews, the Journalism Award from the American Optometric Association, the National Press Club's Citation and then First Prize for Excellence in Consumer Journalism, and the Jesse H. Neal Editorial Achievement Award from the American Business Press Association. We didn't start out skilled with words, but after all these years there are few writing problems we can't solve.

Since the early 1970s, we've taken time off from our keyboards to make students like you work hard. In writing classes in New York and Wisconsin, we've told them everything we know about magazine writing, just as we'll be telling you here. But we've also impressed on them, as we will on you, that they could succeed at writing only if they went home and wrote and wrote and wrote.

One of our magazine-writing classes at the University of Wisconsin started out with forty-two adult students all eager to see their work in magazines. After they heard that we demanded an article and a query letter every week, half slowly dropped out. Barely twenty students made it to every class, and only twelve did most assigned writing tasks. But *every one* of those twelve sold an article to a national publication, and two now work full-time at magazine writing.

Holding a daily one-way conversation with a computer screen might be fun for people who don't like other people. But writers are generally among the most gregarious folks on earth. We're no exception. For the reinforcement, as well as the intellectual and professional stimulation, that we get from other writers, we stay active in writers' organizations—especially the American Society of Journalists and Authors, a national group of pros more than fifty years old. Throughout this book we've drawn abundantly on what we've learned from our professional colleagues in the ASJA.

We participate in as many writers' conferences as possible, for a chance to meet fledgling writers. We figure it's part of the dues we owe the people who taught us the tricks of the trade. We're not the only ones who recognize a debt. Fellow ASJA member Alex Haley said at a meeting that he might have stopped writing *Roots* if he hadn't been advised and encouraged by ASJA writers who'd made it. About his success, Alex once told us he hadn't met a single young, aspiring writer who "really was prepared to work five, eight, ten years to achieve it. Most of them seem to have the impression that fame and fortune come quickly—in maybe six months or two years. But the hard, realistic fact is that it is at least as difficult to become a writer as it is to become a surgeon. Hardly anyone who is successful at writing has come to be so without at least a decade of hard, hard work . . . the rejection slips, the psychic put-downs and all the rest of it."

If your goal lies short of becoming another Alex Haley, you may not need a whole decade of preparation. But to succeed at magazine writing, you *will* need to log hundreds of hours at your computer. There's just no other way.

A Professional Outlook

Many people who don't yet think of themselves as professional writers are embarrassed to consider demanding dollars in exchange for words. If you're among those people, we'd like you to engrave—on a placard to be nailed forever above your desk—the following words from a pro:

No man but a blockhead ever wrote except for money.

Samuel Johnson, a father of our country, wrote that. Like us, writing was what he liked best. A lawyer, a senator, a judge and a nominee for our first presidency, he considered it respectable to demand money for anything a publisher thought worth putting in print.

In sports, if you're not paid for what you do, you're dubbed an amateur no matter how long you've been playing or how good you are. The same holds true for writing. Professional writers are not paid *enough* for what they contribute to the commercial successes of the publishers they write for, a fact we'll say more about later. But they are paid, and should be. Begin to demand payment for your words and you'll have unlocked a very important door on your way to developing professionalism.

A mature gentleman who took one of our writing courses had been publishing for years. His scrapbook was bulging with his "letters to the editor," but he'd never collected a penny for any of his writing. We taught him how to package his prose like a pro, and by the fourth session he proudly showed the class his first fifty-dollar check. He was finally on his way to learning what all pros learn: It takes nearly as little time and energy to research and write for a fee as for free.

The fastest way to start getting paid for your prose is to learn to study publications just as thoroughly as a farmer studies the food market before he decides which crops to plant. That's why the first thing we're going to teach you, even before we ask you to write a word, is a thorough understanding of your marketplace.

PART I
The Magazine as Marketplace

1

What a Magazine *Really* Is

MAGAZINE EDITOR, AUTHOR AND FREELANCE WRITER C. P. (Ken) Gilmore had long wanted (like a lot of us) to break into *Reader's Digest.* It's always been one of the highest paying general-circulation magazines. "So," he told us, "I finally spent two weeks studying a year's worth of issues. By the time I was finished, I knew the editors' approach to ideas, subjects they liked and didn't like, how they liked their writers to handle quotes and anecdotes. . . ." As a result, Ken sold an article to *Reader's Digest* with his first query letter—not because he had a great idea but because he knew that an idea is great only if it's sent to the right *market.*

It's this acceptance of the magazine world as a marketplace that separates the pros from the hopefuls who simply choose something they know about, put their knowledge on paper, send it off to a magazine they admire, and wait for the big check to arrive. A pro chooses from two marketing methods:

1. He *studies* a magazine he'd like to write for, *searches* for ideas that are likely to appeal to the magazine's editors, *sells* the best idea via a query letter, *researches* the assigned article's contents, and only then sits down to *write* the article.
2. Or else he *develops* an idea that he feels confident will appeal to particular magazines, *pinpoints* exactly which magazines are likely buyers, *sells* the idea, *researches* the assigned article, and then *writes* it.

Some would-be writers do know that magazines must be studied. But they've never been told *what* to study so they look for all the wrong things. One of our students spent dozens of hours analyzing magazine markets she wanted to crack. She read from cover to cover through *Cosmopolitan, Redbook, McCall's, Ladies' Home Journal* and all the other big women's magazines. When she was finished, she could tell us how long the average article was, whether the magazine preferred long or short sentences, how many articles it ran each month, and which numbers were shown in figures rather than spelled out. She went so far as to count how many cooking features ran in each issue, since she hoped to sell her favorite recipes for a start.

Trouble is, she did all the wrong homework. (1) Details like article length are generally covered in editors' assignment letters to writers. (2) Questions of style for things such as numbers are the copyeditor's responsibility. Writers are not expected to know every magazine's style intimately. (3) The big women's magazines she studied almost never run recipes from nonstaff writers—and she could have discovered that easily if she'd known how.

The first major mistake we see would-be writers make is to turn every idea into an article and try to sell *that* when they should sell an idea first and *then* write it up. We'll cover how to do it right in Part II.

But the second big mistake is to send a potentially great idea to the wrong magazine. To correct that, we're going to devote this entire section to teaching you how to study a magazine the way a professional writer does.

This chapter will explain how to tell one magazine from another and how to find out who its many editors are and what they do. Next you'll learn what to look for when you read a magazine. And Chapter 3 will assist you in picking markets for yourself.

Throughout this entire book we ask you to keep in mind that writing is an art. It requires a personal touch. Here, we can share examples of specific sales techniques and conclusions that have worked for us, our students and our professional friends. But it's important for you to try them just as a jumping-off point. To etch your name in the roster of pros, you're going to have to develop your own techniques and your own style.

Consumer Publications

Of the four kinds of magazines, these are the best known. Their publishers are in business to sell advertising space to manufacturers who want to reach the *consumers* of their products. It is extremely important for the would-be pro to keep in mind that the hefty four-dollar cover price of a magazine like *Playboy* doesn't cover the cost of paper, ink, printing, staff salaries and checks to freelance magazine writers. The sixty thousand dollars and more per page such magazines charge advertisers pays most of the bills.

We can break down consumer magazines into several useful subcategories based on general editorial format.

GENERAL INTEREST MAGAZINES
These publications reach wide audiences with articles of fairly universal appeal. Their circulations range from tens of thousands to millions of readers. We lump into this category even most of the weekly tabloid-format newspapers such as *National Enquirer* and *Antique Trader*.

Reader's Digest is still America's preeminent general interest magazine. Its U.S. edition alone has a circulation of 14 million. A typical issue's topics range from sex (Ed and Sally Kiester's "Sex After 35: Why It's Different, Why It Can Be Better") to war history (Meg Grant's "The Windtalkers"), from advocacy (Sally

Stich's "Making Your Mark in Local Politics," reprinted from *New Choices*) to personalities (Elvis Mitchell's "Bruce Willis: His Way"), from the light ("A Fun Quiz on Humor and Health") to the weighty ("Dancing with Death" by Per Ola and Emily d'Aulaire). On the surface, these articles seem to have nothing in common. But Ken Gilmore was able to make some generalizations about them. With careful study, along with the advice you read in this section, you can too.

Woman's Day is another general interest magazine despite its mostly female readership. A typical issue includes not just recipe, decoration, and housekeeping articles but budget tips, pet news, even automobile advice. Magazines that attempt to attract nearly *all* women or *all* men (such as *Playboy* and *Esquire*) must be classed, from a writer's viewpoint, as magazines of general interest. Personality magazines such as *People* and *TV Guide* belong here too.

SPECIAL INTEREST MAGAZINES

What separates these publications from those above is that, rather than appealing to many kinds of advertisers, they've zeroed in on a narrow range of special advertisers. They've promised those advertisers to appeal to consumers of the advertisers' products. As a result, they ordinarily stay within narrower editorial guidelines.

Generally these magazines cater to their readers' *avocational* passions: *Field & Stream* to hunters and fishers, *Ski* to active or armchair skiers, *Sports Illustrated* to spectator sports fans, *Art & Antiques* to collectors and their suppliers, *Stereophile Magazine* to audio fanatics. Over the years, the number of general interest magazines has declined while more and more special interest magazines keep cropping up.

Don't forget that practically every idea that appeals to readers (and editors) of general interest publications can be adapted to the narrower confines of special interest magazines. While general interest magazines aimed at women over thirty often feature cooking and recipes, why shouldn't *Field & Stream* be interested in how to fillet and fry trout afield, or *Ski* readers be warmed by an article on how to serve up a hot lunch from an insulated backpack during an all-day ski trip?

REGIONALS

Regional magazines are general interest publications for readers who live in a particular area of the country. Most major cities have their own regionals: *New York, Chicago, Boston, Philadelphia, Kansas City, Miami* . . . Broader-based regionals include *Alaska, Arizona Highways, Adirondack Life* and *Wisconsin Trails*. Regionals come and go, most of them publishing on a shoestring and living from one issue to the next. But the smaller regionals that have been around for a decade or more are dependable, fertile markets, hungry for good writers.

To write successfully for a regional, you can choose practically any broad topic you'd see in a general interest magazine. But the article must apply specifically to the region for which it is written. For example, an article for *Wisconsin Trails* might have a regional *slant* (such as "Houdini Was Here" about a Wisconsin town) or use regional *authorities* (such as Wisconsin's Olympic ice skating champ Eric Heiden) or use regional *statistics, anecdotes* and *examples.* Later, we'll explain all these italicized terms in great detail.

Many large newspapers publish their own Sunday magazines. Others distribute *Parade,* a nationally published general interest newspaper supplement, or the newer *USA Weekend.* (As we write, there's talk that Time Inc. will relaunch old *Life Magazine* to compete in this market.) Large newspapers' Sunday magazine sections fit neatly into our regional category, such as those in the *Boston Globe, New York Times* and *Washington Post.* Since they're published weekly instead of monthly, they need more writers with good ideas than the monthlies do. That makes them attractive markets for freelance writers with timely stories to tell.

COMMENTARY

Harper's and *The Atlantic* are two of the better-known magazines devoted almost exclusively to articles of opinion. At times the opinion is bolstered by solid mountains of fact, albeit carefully sifted. At other times the emphasis is on the rhetoric; authoritativeness is stressed less than clever argument. In either case, the viewpoint of the magazine determines whose opinions on what subjects it purchases.

Every magazine in this category does have a definable viewpoint. The magazines cited above sit politically just above the center, seesawing a bit to the mid-right and sort-of-left. *The Progressive, The Nation* and *The New Republic* report on the near-left, while *MotherJones* oversees issues further left. *The New American* and *National Review* are on the solid right. Not all magazines of commentary are politically motivated. The British magazine *Musical Opinion* has been published for over a hundred years. Canada's *Project Magazine* solicits opinions from engineering students. *Business Ethics* reports on businesses' social responsibilities. Like most other publications with under a hundred thousand readers, the smaller opinion magazines pay in chump change or, worse, in copies.

Trade, Technical and Professional Magazines

Many courses in magazine writing still scorn or overlook entirely this broad, very large and important group of publications. Most of them used to pay writers very poorly. Nowadays some are big-time operations—especially the publications for people in businesses and professions. *Beverage Retailer* has a circulation of close to sixty thousand. *Medical Economics* mails to almost 175,000 physicians. The *Corn and Soybean Digest* has nearly two hundred thousand readers a month. Advertisers pay, often handsomely, to appear in these magazines. To guarantee steady readership for the ads, smart publishers rely on professional writers who demand professional rates.

While researching the markets, writers must keep in mind two major distinctions between trade and consumer magazines:

1. Consumer publications generally concentrate on pastime interests of readers, while trades concentrate on their occupations.
2. Although you'll find a great many consumer magazines on your local newsstands, you're not likely to find trade publications there.

The trades are a lucrative market. They're sold almost exclusively by subscription. Some public libraries subscribe to a generous selection, so you may be able to research them at the library near you. Many trade magazines have websites where you may be able to view a sample issue's cover, read some past articles and even download their Guidelines for Writers. If all else fails, write to editors at publications you'd like to write for and ask for a sample copy or two. They're often happy to send them free to any writer who asks.

HOUSE ORGANS

Exxon, Ford, International Paper and many other major corporations used to put up the money for publishing this third category of magazines. They were aimed at employees, stockholders, customers or the general public. They didn't accept advertising from other companies but were themselves a form of low-key advertising designed to impress and inform their readers. Many were handsome—well written, beautifully illustrated and creatively designed. They paid top rates to professional writers.

Alas, almost all of them are dead, victims of easy Internet access and their target readers' information overload. Perhaps they'll revive in another day and age.

Online Magazines

Many Internet publications, also called *e-zines,* solicit submissions from writers. But many expect you to write for glory, not pay, and even those that pay halfway decently are risky markets. In the main, they come and go with such lightning speed, they leave nothing in their wake except angry, unpaid contributors.

As of right now, e-zines that our friends have written for and gotten paid by include *TechnologyReview.com, Weightwatchers.com, the-scientist.com* and *Wired.*

Little and Literary Magazines

Often self-appointed guardians of our literary heritage, these journal-like publications are devoted to short stories, satire, essays, poetry, humor and belles lettres. Their editors make up in enthusiasm what they lack in budget. Mostly they are sponsored by foundations or institutions of learning. They are "little," generally, in two respects: their book-sized pages and the smallness of their circulations. Payment to writers is little, too, often meted out in copies of the issues in which the authors' cherished works appear.

The majority of literary magazines concentrate on fiction and poetry and are, therefore, beyond the scope of this book. Many, however, welcome essays, literary criticism, personal experience of an intellectual nature (such as having discovered a new way of interpreting Joyce's *Ulysses*), as well as sharp reporting about trends or events of current or historic interest.

Some, such as *Antioch Review* and *The American Scholar,* have been around for many years and pay modest honorariums to writers. Others in this category suffer very short lifespans.

Closely akin to literary magazines are the scholarly journals such as *American Sociological Review, American Psychologist, Sewanee Review* and *New England Journal of Medicine.* Most take contributions only from recognized scholars in their fields, so they're not markets for freelance writers. The scholars they publish sometimes even have to pay production costs to get their articles into print. Frequently the only way to find out for sure what a scholarly publication's policy is, is to study its printed or online statement of editorial requirements.

One of our students spent several dollars on postage to learn one very important lesson about the little magazines. He sent some of his articles to high-paying mass circulation magazines. They were promptly rejected because both his ideas and his writing needed lots of polishing. So he sent them to lower-paying general markets that also shipped them back. Figuring, "Well, I won't get paid but I *will* get my name in print," he sent them to what he thought was the bottom of the barrel—the literary magazines. Not only was his work returned, but one editor scrawled a note saying, "Try again when you've learned how to write."

The lesson Jerry finally learned: Never gauge editorial *quality* by editorial *budget.* Study the magazines!

Illus. 1.1. *Sierra* **Magazine Editorial Guidelines**

Sierra is a bimonthly national magazine publishing writing, photography, and art about the natural world. Our readers are environmentally concerned and politically diverse; most are active in the outdoors. We are looking for fine writing that will provoke, entertain, and enlighten this readership.

Though open to new writers, we find ourselves most often working with authors we have sought out or who have worked with us for some time. We ask writers who would like to publish in Sierra to submit written queries; no email queries please. Phone calls are strongly discouraged. If you would like a reply to your query or need your manuscript returned to you, please include a self-addressed stamped envelope. Prospective Sierra writers should familiarize themselves with recent issues of the magazine; for a sample copy, send a self-addressed envelope and a check for $3 payable to Sierra; back issues are included on the Sierra Club's Web site, www.sierraclub.org/sierra/.

Please be patient: Though the editors meet weekly to discuss recently received queries, a response time of from six to eight weeks is usual.

Please do not send slides, prints, or other art work. If photos or illustrations are required for your submission, we will request them when your work is accepted for publication.

Features

Sierra is looking for strong, well-researched, literate writing on significant environmental and conservation issues. Features often focus on aspects of the Sierra Club's conservation work. For more information about issues the Club is currently working on, visit our web site at www.sierraclub.org. Writers should look for ways to cast new light on well-established issues. We look for stories of national or international significance; local issues, while sometimes useful as examples of broader trends, are seldom of interest in themselves. We are always looking for adventure travel pieces that weave events, discoveries, and environmental insights into the narrative. Nonfiction essays on the natural world are welcome, too.

We do not want descriptive wildlife articles, unless larger conservation issues figure strongly in the story. We are not interested in editorials, general essays about environmentalism, or in highly technical writing. We do not publish unsolicited cartoons, poetry, or fiction; please do not submit works in these genres.

Recent feature articles that display the special qualities we look for are "Salmon's Second Coming" by David James Duncan (March/April 2000), "One Man's Wilderness" by Joe Kane (March/April 2000), "How to Heal Our Cities" by David Moberg (May/June 2000), "Where the Caribou Roam" by Reed McManus (July/August 2000), "The New Gold Rush" by Rebecca Solnit (July/August 2000).

Feature length ranges from 1,000 to 3,000 words; payment is from $800 to $3,000, plus negotiated reimbursement for expenses.

Departments

Much of the material in Sierra's departments is written by staff editors and contributing writers. The following sections of the magazine, however, are open to freelancers. Articles are 100–1500 words in length; payment is $100 to $1500 unless otherwise noted. Expenses up to $50 may be paid in some cases.

"Food for Thought" is concerned with what we eat and its connection to the environment. Topics range from drying food for backpacking to bovine growth hormones to the consequences of buying imported produce.

"Good Going" succinctly describes a superlative place, including fascinating environmental and cultural facts, in about 300 words.

"Hearth & Home" offers information and advice on how we can live our environmental principles in our own homes; topics have ranged from composting with worms to building with straw to energy conservation. Articles for this department should be accurate, lively, and helpful (750–1500 words).

"Body Politics" discusses relations between health and environment, often with practical advice on how to avoid health hazards. Articles should be carefully researched (750–1500 words).

"Lay of the Land" focuses on environmental issues of national or international concern. Regional issues are considered when they have national implications. At 500 to 700 words, "Lay of the Land" articles are not sweeping surveys, but tightly focused, provocative, well-researched investigations of environmental issues. Payment varies according to length.

"Mixed Media" features 750-word essays on how media, the arts, and other cultural topics relate to the environment, and also offers short (200–300) word reviews of the books and videos on environmentalism and natural history. (Payment per review is $50).

"Profiles" are 3,000-word biographical sketches of people doing important work to protect the environment. We try to broaden our readers' understanding of the environmental movement with subjects they haven't read about elsewhere: for instance, a pig farmer in Mississippi or an outfitter in Wyoming.

"One Small Step" features the first-person accounts of ordinary folks doing extraordinary things. We publish a 100–150 word quotation from an interview that explains the person's actions, motivations, and impact.

Payment for all articles is on acceptance, which is contingent on a favorable review of the manuscript by our editorial staff, and by knowledgeable outside reviewers, where appropriate. Kill fees are negotiated when a story is assigned.

Address all queries to:
Managing Editor, Sierra magazine
85 Second Street, 2nd Floor
San Francisco, CA 94105

Magazines Are Periodical

When you study magazines as markets, you must keep in mind their periodical nature. Monthly magazines are the norm: *Popular Mechanics, Field & Stream, National Geographic* and *Popular Photography* are familiar examples. We'll devote a major portion of this book to teaching you how to write for and sell to the monthlies.

Some magazines, such as *National Enquirer* and the Sunday newspaper supplements, publish weekly. In terms of writing technique and format, their article requirements are little different from those of the monthlies. But editors of those publications have to have on hand four times as many articles as comparably sized monthlies. This means that, all else being equal, your chances of selling to a weekly periodical may be four times as great as your chances at a monthly. Also, a weekly editor can rush a timely idea into print four times faster than a colleague editing a monthly. That's important to remember when you're marketing ideas that may become outdated quickly.

A few magazines are currently biweekly or semi-monthly, *National Review* and *Fortune,* for example. *Woman's Day* was on a standard monthly schedule in the early 1970s. By the mid-1970s their advertising space was so much in demand that they added a thirteenth "monthly" issue. Right now, they publish seventeen issues a year.

Many house organs and literary magazines appear only quarterly. A few magazines, catering to devotees of seasonal activities, publish on a seasonal schedule. Most publications that focus on snowmobiling, for example, come out only during winter months. *Snow Goer,* for Canadian snowmobilers, publishes four to seven issues a year. *Ski* and *Water Ski* each come out eight times a year. *Notions* publishes quarterly.

There are even a few annuals that qualify as magazine writers' markets. Viking Yacht Company's *Valhalla* and the Saskatchewan Writers Guild's *Spring Magazine* come first to mind.

Aside from the two aspects of periodicity that we've already covered here—the handling of fast-breaking stories and the number of stories editors need to buy each year—timing your submissions depends on knowing in advance what various editors' publication calendars look like. You can make an intelligent guess based on publication frequency. As a rough rule of thumb, assume that editors of monthlies are lining up stories to appear eight issues in the future and editors of weeklies most likely want stories for publication six to eight weeks from now.

Timing is very important. If you submit a New Year's resolution story to a monthly during January, you're more than half a year late or half a year early. Most editors are much too harried to think of buying stories or story ideas they can't think about using until four or more months from now—and few editors' budgets permit them to do it so far in advance. We try to suggest seasonal material to monthly editors six to eight months ahead of publication. We hit editors of most weeklies eight to ten weeks before an upcoming event. If a magazine doesn't publish in May, we don't suggest stories that depend on May Day, Mother's Day, Armed Forces Day, Memorial Day, or Victoria Day in Canada. If a magazine is a quarterly or an annual, we know it rarely considers seasonal material at all. That's how we work; you'll have to figure out what works best for you.

How Magazine Staffs Are Organized

One of the saddest faces we've ever seen was on Susan R., a young student who learned the hard way what magazine organization is all about. She'd had a truly great idea for an article for one of the larger general interest magazines. Not knowing whom to send it to, she'd checked the magazine's *masthead*—the organizational listing found somewhere in every issue of most magazines. Seeing a name listed as contributing editor, Susan assumed that her idea for a contribution ought to go to that person. Months passed and she got no reply. Then one day she saw her idea fleshed out in the magazine, bylined by the contributing editor. "She stole my idea," Susan told us the first day of class.

Some questioning led us to a different conclusion. Susan's letter didn't make it clear that *she* expected to write an article based on her idea. The contributing editor, being just a freelance writer who wrote steadily for the magazine, assumed that the idea was a gift. When we explained what contributing editors do—and don't do—Susan nearly cried at her innocent mistake. The moral: You can't study the masthead until you *know how* to study it.

There are generally two sides to magazine organization. Purely business aspects are the responsibility of a publisher and her staff. This includes buying paper, choosing a printer, hiring typesetters, soliciting advertisements, selling subscriptions, distributing to newsstands, determining how much can be spent—all those details that keep a magazine from going broke.

All the nonadvertising content of the magazine is in the hands of editors. They decide on which freelance articles to run, when to run them, and where to lay them out in the magazine. They order photos and artwork to illustrate articles, create titles for them, write catchy subtitles or *blurbs* (those one- or two-sentence summaries that tease readers into the story), design the cover (often in collaboration with an art director), and handle similar jobs that keep most editors at their desks for fifty or sixty hours a week. In addition, some magazine editors also write one or more articles for each issue. We've both been magazine editors and can attest that most are harried, hassled, and constantly battling deadlines.

At small magazines, there's just one editor and maybe a secretary or assistant. The large-circulation magazines have entire trees of editors. Titles and duties vary according to tradition and whimsy. As Susan discovered, the names and titles of major staff members are usually listed on a masthead, almost always near the front of every issue. In order to publish nearly two hundred pages every four weeks or so, *Ladies' Home Journal,* for example, employs dozens of editors organized into very specific departments. If you can decipher that magazine's editorial maze, you'll be prepared for any you might encounter elsewhere.

At the very top of *Ladies' Home Journal'*s 2004 masthead was Diane Salvatore, Editor-in-Chief. On some other magazine she might be called just Editor. Salvatore is ultimately responsible for the magazine's entire editorial content. Along with that responsibility, she has final power over what articles are assigned, which ones run, and what the writers are paid—although her total expenses for an issue (or a year) must follow the publisher's guidelines. Some editors-in-chief also come up with ideas for articles—though Salvatore delegates a great many responsibilities. She expects executive editor Roberta Capice and creative director Scott Yardley to watch over the execution of all editorial and illustrative matter, including service features and general articles.

Most magazines don't have executive editors or creative directors. The editor (or editor-in-chief) has to cope with administrative matters single-handed.

A great many magazines do have managing editors, a spot filled at *Ladies' Home Journal* in 2004 by Mary Witherall. Briefly, the managing editor does whatever the editor assigns to him. At *Ladies' Home Journal,* it's to oversee deadlines and other day-to-day technical functions of the entire editorial department. Typical functions of other magazines' managing editors include organizing story ideas for discussion at editorial meetings, taking charge of all manuscripts ready to be published, acting as liaison with typesetters and printers, and directing letters and queries to the proper editor.

At *Ladies' Home Journal,* the next lower organizational echelon is filled by the articles director (Margot Gilman, in this case) and her underlings: two deputy articles editors, a health director and an entertainment editor. Under them are a general associate editor and a general assistant editor. Most general nonfiction is assigned, with Witherall's okay, by Gilman or her staff.

Then, *Ladies' Home Journal* has directors, editors and assistants who assume responsibility for smooth issue-by-issue functioning of each department. In 2004, food and entertainment features, for example, were devised, often written, and edited by Jennifer Crutcher Wilkinson and her assistant editor, fashion and beauty features by Carla Engler and her staff, and home-related features (such as "New Ways to Love Your Bed") by Kieran Juska. At other magazines, senior editors (and sometimes other staff members) lend a hand with editing and write *in-house,* or staff-prepared, articles (sometimes called *features*). At many magazines, staff-written articles don't carry a byline.

Ladies' Home Journal, like other huge-circulation magazines, lists its art and photo directors, designers and editors as well as its researchers and editorial production editors. None of these people deals with freelancers except the photo editor or director, who may purchase freelanced photos.

The most shadowy yet vital staff position on any publication is that of editorial assistant. *Ladies' Home Journal* employed three of them in early 2004. At some magazines they're listed on the masthead as editorial associates. In the publishing industry, this entry-level position encompasses chores such as typing, proofreading and acting as gofer. Many editorial assistants, in between handling other responsibilities, act as secretary to someone higher up on the editorial ladder. It's in that capacity that most freelancers encounter them. They rarely have any say in which articles are purchased or assigned to freelancers—though as first readers of the *slush pile,* they often decide whether an unsolicited article or idea gets immediately rejected or passed along to a higher-up. (If you don't think it's fair for a typist to be able to decide if your article idea's worth publishing, become a pro and avoid the slush pile!)

Other titles on the mastheads at *Ladies' Home Journal* and elsewhere are self-explanatory except for editor-at-large and contributing editor. They're so similar we can lump the two. In reality, neither is on the magazine's staff. People with these titles have negotiated formal or informal contracts that call, as a rule, for them to write a at least several articles each year. The magazine may write restrictions into the contracts. Judith Ramsey, one of *Family Circle*'s past editors-at-large, had a contract that permitted her to write for any publication but the competition, *Woman's Day*. Like most people who land such a deal, Judith became editor-at-large after chalking up a long string of successful freelanced articles for *Family Circle*. Unlike most contributing editors, however, Judith also bought ideas or manuscripts from other writers.

What about the many, many magazines whose mastheads display only an editor, an assistant editor, and perhaps an editorial assistant? The editor then has to divide up all the work amongst the three of them. When you see such a short masthead in a hefty magazine, you can be sure that the editors have little time for in-house writing and rewriting. If you write well and have good ideas, you'll be very much in demand there. But be forewarned that the publisher's editorial budget for freelancers is probably as chintzy as his budget for in-house staff.

It's paradoxes like this which help make freelancing the challenge that it is.

2

How to Study
Magazines as Markets

BACK IN OUR EARLY DAYS AS MAGAZINE WRITERS, SOME of our editors used to tell us, "You've gotta write for that Milwaukee beer truck driver," or "You've gotta write for that Milwaukee beer truck driver's wife." In those days, many editors decided who their readers were by the reader mail that rolled in. These days, editors refer with the same degree of passion to the *demographics* they get from computerized readership surveys.

Demographics: Who "The Reader" Is

When Jim Morgan was editor of *TWA Ambassador*, we asked him who read the magazine. He replied, "We're aimed at the traveling executive and professional person, who represents about 80 percent of our audience. We know that 64 percent are men, 71 percent are between the ages of eighteen and forty-nine, 46 percent are college grads, and 43.5 percent have household incomes of twenty-five thousand dollars a year or better." What was the importance of all of those numbers? "You can tell what kind of people those are. You can extrapolate what kind of stories might interest them."

Sitting right next to Jim Morgan at the time was David Williams, then executive editor of *Kiwanis Magazine*. He echoed how important it is for writers to study a magazine's demographics. "The best reader response we've gotten in a long time was with an article called 'Simple Secrets of a Better Lawn'," he said. It made sense, since 82 percent of his readers owned homes—and the grass that went with them. "Just a simple thing like how high do you set the lawnmower blades can fascinate them." You can be sure Dave Williams wanted to hear more ideas from the writer who so cleverly dreamed up that one.

All editors want to buy articles that will interest their readers. They will remember *your* name once you've learned the three steps in using demographics:

1. Identify the type of reader a magazine aims at.
2. Select ideas that appeal right to that reader.

3. Suggest those ideas to the editor—and say why you think they're just right for his or her readers.

If the editor agrees with you, you'll get an assignment.

There are reference books and online sites where you can find some hints at magazine demographics. (The last part of this chapter will introduce you to many of them.) But after using references, you'll still have to decide what kinds of articles each magazine editor believes his particular readers want to read. To tell what the editor himself has concluded from his demographics, study issues of the magazine. As people become top-notch magazine writers, they become top-notch magazine readers and analyzers. You'll go further faster if you learn how to read a magazine right now.

Creative Content Analysis: Cover Lines

Before you even flip open a magazine, carefully read the cover. Cover lines are an editor's best friend. They sell the magazine to newsstand browsers and they make subscribers pick it up before snapping on the TV. That's why the editor features the best articles on the cover and pays more for stories that suggest terse, enticing cover lines. Editors tell us repeatedly that they're looking most of all for ideas that can be cover-lined.

Cover lines tell a clever writer exactly what ideas an editor thinks appeal most to his readers—what ideas he's most in the market for. If you looked at the cover of *Redbook* for October 2003 *(Ill. 2.1)*, could you quickly pick out eight things its editors believed about the magazine and its buyers when they planned the cover? These were the features and taglines that caught our eye:

1. The tagline "balancing family • work • love • time for you" right under the title told us that *Redbook* aims at readers who probably have children at home ("family"), a job ("work") and an adult companion ("love") and who consider themselves very busy people (and thus need "time for you"). The magazine's tagline used to be "the magazine for young women," which meant women under about thirty. Now it's probably aiming to attract women up to forty or even older, which is part of why the publisher changed the tagline. (The demure photo of a woman shows more about who they want to buy the magazine.)

2. The line above the magazine's name—the one that catches folks' eyes on a news rack even if they see little else of the cover—is "Breast Cancer Alert: The Vitamin That Slashes Your Risk." It clued us to the fact that the editors thought health was currently of vital concern to their readers and that promises of beating a bad disease would cause readers to buy this issue. Magazines tend to

Illus. 2.1

vacillate between a preference for promises like this one and gloomy titles ("Beware this" and "The horrors of that"), and for the cover *Redbook* decided to go with an upbeat title instead of the inside-the-book title "Your Scariest Breast Cancer Questions—Answered." Sharp writers stay up-to-date on which mood the editors currently think sells more magazines.

3. The next title down, "Get More Balance In Your Life!" fulfills *Redbook*'s promise (see above) to provide readers with "time for you." They probably hope to assign at least one article on pampering yourself per issue.

4. "New Stress Fixers, Clutter Tamers Inside" actually refers to three separate articles: "Anti-Tired Tactics" (subtitled "What I Do When I'm Too Stressed to Sleep"), "Make Over My Jumbled Jewel Box," and "Stress-Free Zone"—all written by freelancers. If we wanted to crack *Redbook* we'd start files of unique tips for combating stress and clutter.

5. "Love—An Easy Move That Brings You *So* Close" fulfills the magazine's promise to provide articles on love. Inside it's called "Your Redbook Passion Planner." If you can figure out why the word *passion* was avoided on the cover, you'll get another clue to what kind of women *Redbook* wants to attract.

6. Now we come to "349 Money-Saving Secrets" and (in much smaller print) "Great Buys for Tough Times." This title combines the contents of four separate articles in the magazine, "Look 10 Years Younger in 10 Minutes (for under $10)," "Shop Like a Celeb (for a Lot Less)," "Secrets of the Best Bargain Hunters" and "8 Amazing $-Saving Deals!" Numbers—especially big numbers like *349*—are compelling attention-getters. Words like *money-saving*—especially combined with a reminder that the editors know you're having a tough time making ends meet—are a sure-fire magazine seller. *Great buys* alerted a pro that the editors thought it important to aim their tips at a very practical level.

7. *Redbook* put not one but two celebrities' names on the cover—showing that articles about stars still sell lots of magazines. Jackie Kennedy is a perennial favorite—statistics show that her name or photo on a cover still guarantees extra sales. The phrases *shocking new book* and *most private wish* promise salacious news inside about Jackie.

    Note the title "Jewel's Amazing Comeback." *Redbook*'s editors were not as sure their readers would know who Jewel was as who Jackie was. So they added the teasing blurb "'My body was wrecked!' The startling thing she did to get healthy and find *real* happiness." Again, they promise sensational news—about health again, but also about addressing your own needs, an echo of their motto "time for you."

8. Note that we haven't analyzed the prominent cover line "Get More Balance In Your Life!" That's because we couldn't figure out which article in the issue it referred to. The magazine didn't have an article about anything promised by

that title. Did the editors add it because they thought it was a big *Redbook* seller, applicable article or not? Back when we were editors, we would have called that cheating. As freelancers, however, we'd quickly pitch *Redbook* several "startling," "shocking," "risky," "money-saving" or "most private" ideas based specifically on the topic of balancing family, work, love and self-fulfillment — or any combination of the above.

Creative Content Analysis: Stories Already in Print

Writers seldom have direct access to an editor who can tell them what articles the magazine's specifically looking for. Instead, we've learned how to find it out by reading their published articles. We remember Bob Bahr, the prolific author of books ranging from men's health to hibernation, saying, "Skim the bestseller list and you'll find that the top ten are all based on ideas that came along at just the right time." That applies to magazine articles too. But with magazines, your sale also depends on how you approach the idea.

During 1979, country singer Dolly Parton was an idea whose time had come. In June of that year, three magazines arrived in our mailbox that had Dolly Parton cover lines: *Ms., The Country Gentleman* and *Writer's Digest.* The writers of those three pieces (like most pros, we use *article, piece* and *story* interchangeably) must have carefully read past issues of the magazine before querying with the idea of writing about Dolly, because their approaches were as different as the magazines' sets of readers. As a result, the three articles had very little overlapping information.

Margo Jefferson's standard-length article in *Ms.* was titled (most likely by the editors) "Dolly Parton: Bewigged, Bespangled . . . and Proud" and subtitled "I think of Dolly as a genial, playful female impersonator." Its focus was how Dolly exploited her femininity, a *Ms.* kind of topic, and was written in the first person — a common *Ms.* style.

The title and subtitle for Alanna Nash's standard-length article in *The Country Gentleman* played up the same sexual jokes about Parton's parts that Margo Jefferson dumped on in *Ms.* The title was "By Golly, It's Miss Dolly! Great Balls of Fire — Here She Comes Again, Looking Better Than a Body Has a Right To." Ms. Nash stuck to the third person and kept herself out of the article.

For the *Writer's Digest* article, Alanna Nash was again the author. The editor's title, "Goodbye, Dolly!" was followed by a long subtitle that let the reader know that the author had written an unauthorized biography of Dolly. This very long article was in the first person when Ms. Nash talked about researching and writing her book, and in the second person when she offered advice to other authors of unauthorized bios.

These three Parton articles exemplify just a few of the insights you can gain by careful article analysis.

LENGTH

Most editors use two kinds of articles. The first, called *standard length* or *feature length,* can vary from about one thousand to six thousand words depending on the publication. The shorter kind is called a *one-pager, two-pager, short, quickie,* or sometimes even *filler.* Specified length often indicates how much *depth* the editor expects readers to want on the subject. In the *Writer's Digest* Parton piece, it governed how much detail Alanna Nash could include. As a writer in search of assignments, you needn't worry much about length since the editor will generally specify expected length in your letter of assignment.

FIRST, SECOND OR THIRD PERSON

In *Writer's Digest,* Alanna Nash started in the first person. That's what editors there like. But when she got into giving advice, the article switched to second person: "read everything that's ever been written about your subject" and "Don't be afraid to ask other reporters to do a bit of interviewing for you." The same writer's piece in *The Country Gentleman* was entirely third person, which is the way *they* liked it unless the article was bylined by a celebrity or the "expert" giving advice in the story. We know that *Ms.* editors endorsed Jefferson's personal assessment of the Parton phenomenon because they welcomed her first-person approach. That tells us a lot about the editors' likes and dislikes at *Ms.*

By watching for the voice in magazine articles—first, second or third person—you too can gain valuable insight into what approaches the editors like, and into their readers' biases—which become their own biases as editors.

FOCUS AND SLANT

These two terms are quite different in meaning, and we'll explain them more thoroughly in Chapter 6. For now, let's just say that *focus* is the objective aspect of a topic that interests an editor and his readers, and *slant* (also sometimes called *handles* or *angle*) is the subjective approach the writer takes to that topic. An example is the question of Parton's sex appeal (focus) handled unabashedly (slant) by *The Country Gentleman* and a bit disapprovingly (slant) by *Ms.* Focus and slant reveal as much as cover lines do about what editors perceive their readers to be like. For example, in the same issues of the three magazines we've been studying so far, *Writer's Digest* did one piece on the joys (slant) of turning lawyer's jargon into English (topic). *Ms.* took a scathing look (slant) at the right-wing (slant) girls (slant) who were meddling (slant) in the women's movement (topic). *The Country Gentleman* ran a politically conservative (slant) piece entitled "Are Your Property Taxes (topic) Too High (slant)?"

Creative Content Analysis: Ads

In the same three magazine issues studied above, creative reader analysis takes us beyond the covers and articles, to the ads. In many cases the ads give a faster, more graphic picture of a magazine's readers than article content does. The *Country Gentleman* issue we selected, for instance, has a back-cover ad for high-powered rifles and a large ad inside for machine guns. Other ads offer for sale pitchforks, horse pictures, Norman Rockwell reproductions, weather vanes, red suspenders, wheelbarrows, garden supplies, antique supplies and investment opportunities. After a glance at these ads, we can conclude quickly that *The Country Gentleman's* advertisers, the folks who keep the magazine financially alive, believe that in these pages they can reach male, outdoorsy, fairly well off land owners who like the conservative, old-fashioned way of life. You can be sure its editors were eager to provide reading matter that would keep this particular reader group buying their magazine.

This 1979 issue of *Ms.,* on the other hand, features more ads for liquor, cigarettes and cars than we're used to seeing in a women's magazine. From that we conclude that the readers were independent, with some disposable income and a yen for partying.

The *Writer's Digest* ads, at first glance, seem to appeal to professional writers. But let's look more closely. In the issue we've been studying here, we see two full-page ads for writers' schools, two for literary agents who charge reading fees (agents belonging to the professional Society of Authors' Representatives were not permitted to advertise in 1979), and five for "vanity" book publishers (companies you pay to print your books)—all in all, not the kind of ads that established professionals are likely to look at twice. From the ads, the sharp marketing pro would have to conclude that *Writer's Digest* was aimed largely at dilettantes and beginners.

Reference Books about Magazines

Professional magazine writers learn to use every research tool available to help them study their markets thoroughly. How you go about researching magazines depends not only on what tools the Internet and your nearby libraries make available, but on how hard you're willing to work to make it in a field that has little room for the lazy. J. Wandres, who was an editor for *Retirement Living* and then a freelancer for *American Legion, Family Circle, Parade, Saga, TV Guide* and other top magazines, once told us, "When editors say, 'Study the magazine to see what our needs are,' first I go to Bowker's *Magazines for Libraries.* Second,

I go through two issues of *Standard Rate and Data*'s magazine data sourcebook about six months apart to see what growth there has been in a magazine's advertising and circulation, since a magazine that's showing steady growth is one that I'd care to write for. Third, I go to the library and take out a year's issues of the magazine."

J. Wandres was lucky. He lived a few blocks away from the well-stocked Brooklyn Public Library. Our students Phyllis E. and Eileen B. live in rural Beaver Dam, Wisconsin, where the library's hours are as limited as its collection. But like so many states, Wisconsin has an active interlibrary loan program, giving Phyllis and Eileen access to practically any book ever published. It just takes them a little longer to get the books. And like libraries large and small, the Beaver Dam library does have a copy of *Writer's Market,* a professional writer's most-used tool except for the actual magazines. It's published by the same company that brings you *Writer's Digest.*

WRITER'S MARKET

This is a Sears, Roebuck catalog of thousands of the magazines published today: consumer, trade, house organ, Sunday supplement. . . . Also available by subscription as an online database (at www.writersmarket.com) at a cost even starving writers can afford, it lists the name, address and phone number of each magazine and the names of key personnel such as editor, articles editor and photo editor. Each entry offers a few lines of terse information about the magazine's major subject areas, likes, dislikes, seasonal deadlines, etc. *(Ill. 2.2).* Finally, there may be a line or two about payment rates and policies.

The inch or two of space devoted to any one magazine is just enough to whet the serious magazine writer's appetite. Without also studying copies of the magazine, it's seldom enough to initiate a major query letter. But by browsing through *Writer's Market* or trying out the online database, you'll know which magazines seem to be in the right subject and payment range for you. You'll discover the names of magazines you never knew existed. And people we know find that their idea juices often start flowing after a few minutes of reading about editors' needs.

By the way, the publisher's website includes a bevy of useful tools that can help you keep track of your markets and your submissions.

When you can't find copies of a particular magazine at your local library or newsstand, its circulation department will often send you one. Sometimes it's free (especially if it's a trade magazine, house organ, or other smaller magazine whose editors know its copies are hard to find); often it's at cover price (particularly if it's a consumer magazine). *Writer's Market* includes the policy on sample copies for many of its listed magazines.

Illus. 2.2. *Writer's Market* Entry

NATIONAL GEOGRAPHIC TRAVELER $$$$

National Geographic Society   Website: nationalgeographic.com/traveler
1145 17th St. N.W.
Washington D.C. 20036

Contact: Scott Stuckey, or Jonathan Tourtellot, senior editors
Editor: Keith Bellows; Executive Editor: Paul Martin

About NATIONAL GEOGRAPHIC TRAVELER

Magazine
Frequency: 8 times/year

"*National Geographic Traveler* is filled with practical information and detailed maps de-signed to encourage readers to explore and travel. Features domestic and foreign desti-nations, photography, the economics of travel, adventure trips, and weekend getaways to help readers plan a variety of excursions. Our writers need to equip our readers with inspiration to travel. We want lively writing—personal anecdotes with telling details, not an A to Z account of a destination."

Freelance Facts:

90% freelance written
Established: 1984
Circulation: 720,000

Accepts queries by:
• Mail

Responds in 6 weeks to queries.
Responds in 6 weeks to manuscripts.

Pays on acceptance
Publishes manuscript 3–12 months after acceptance.
Byline given.
Offers 30% kill fee.

Sample copy free.
Writer's guidelines for #10 SASE.

Rights purchased:
• One-time rights
• Electronic rights
Editorial lead time 3–12 months.
Submit seasonal material 1 year in advance.

Nonfiction:

Needs:
Essays
General Interest

Historical
How-To
Humor
Inspirational (destinations)
New Product (travel oriented)
Opinion
Personal Experience
Photo Feature
Travel

Does Not Want: "We do not want to see general, impersonal, fact-clogged articles. We do not want to see any articles similar to those we, or our competitors, have run recently."

Buys 80–100 manuscripts/year.
Submission method: Query with published clips
Length: 250–2,500 words.

Pays 50 cents/word minimum.
Pays the expenses of writers on assignment.

Columns & Departments:

Columns open to freelancers: Smart Traveler—Norie Danyliw, editor (travel trends, sources, strategies and solutions); 48 Hours—Susan O'Keefe, editor (the best of a city); Room Check (unique and special places to stay).

Buys 150–200 columns/year.
Submission method: Query with published clips
50 cents/word minimum.

Online Information:

The online magazine carries original content not found in the print edition.
Contact: Tom Giovanni, online editor

Tips:

"Familiarize yourself with our magazine—not only the types of stories we run, but the types of stories we've run in the past. Formulate a story idea, and then send a detailed query, recent clips and contact information to the editor responsible for the section you'd like to be published in." No unsolicited photographs. Will accept unsolicited mss with SASE.

*BOWKER'S NEWS MEDIA DIRECTORY 2003–2004, VOL. 2: MAGAZINES AND
NEWSLETTERS 2004*

This is an expensive multivolume annual reference book designed for public relations executives who want to reach the right editors with their press releases.
The volume devoted to magazines is of value to magazine writers as well. Like
Writer's Market, News Media Directory (formerly called *Working Press of the Nation*) offers thumbnail sketches of each magazine editor's preferences, key editorial personnel, addresses, phone numbers, etc. It doesn't generally include
what editors pay for articles. As we write, the larger libraries are likely to have it
on the shelves—but we expect that Bowker (see www.bowker.com) may soon
phase out the print edition and just keep the database online, selling it by subscription and single-search fees.

STANDARD RATE AND DATA SERVICE

This is a four-volume online directory (see www.srds.com). The volume you'll
want to consult is *Consumer Magazine Advertising Source*—but generally only
large libraries subscribe to it due to its substantial cost and limited appeal. It
keeps advertisers abreast of advertising rates, circulation, and similar information *(Ill. 2.3)*. For larger publications, the editor's name is not listed since the
publisher or ad manager is of more interest to advertising space buyers. It does
offer a professional writer more timely information about circulation than any
other reference tool (address, phone, etc.) since it's constantly updated. And
studying the ad rates and circulation figures can provide a circumstantial peek
at the magazines' financial health.

Illus. 2.3. *Standard Rates and Data, Consumer Magazine Advertising Source* Entry

ESPN—The Magazine

A Buena Vista Magazines, Inc. Publication

Published bi-weekly by Buena Vista Publishing, Inc., 19 E. 34th St., New York, NY 10016. Phone 212-515-1000. Fax 212-515-1275.
URL http://www.bvpublishing.net/

For shipping info., see Print Media Production Source.

PUBLISHER'S EDITORIAL PROFILE

ESPN THE MAGAZINE is written for 18–34 year-old sports fans, with an emphasis on what's coming next; the next star players, rivalries, big events, issues and trends, both on the field and in the lives of today's highest-profile athletes. The magazine features personality profiles with analyses of each coming sport's season and championship playoffs, and in depth features that take readers along on trips into the lifestyles of today's athletes. Coverage focuses on pro and college football and basketball, baseball and hockey, and additionally includes action sports featured in the X Games. For further information go to http://www.srds.com/mediakits/espn/index.htm. Rec'd 10/30/02

1. PERSONNEL

Sr VP, Gen Mgr—Geoff Reiss.
Sr VP, Sales & Mktg—Andrew Sippel.
VP, Pub—Chris Collins.
Mktg Dir—David Lehmkuhl.
David.Lehmkuhl@espn3.com
Assoc Dir, Mktg—Cathy P. Martin.

2. REPRESENTATIVES and/or BRANCH OFFICES

•New York, NY 10016—Chris Collins, chris.collins@espn3.com, Pub, 19 East 34th Street. Phone 212-515-1136.
•Southfield (Detroit), MI 48075—Chris Marcangelo, chris.marcangelo@espn3.com, 1000 Town Center, 28th Floor, Ste 2839. Phone 248-359-1169. Fax 248-350-8531.
•Chicago, IL 60610—Chris Schuba, schuba@schubaco.com, Publisher's Rep, 500 N. Dearborn, Ste. 510. Phone 312-604-0350. Fax 312-604-0360.
•San Francisco, CA 94133—John Handley, john.handley@espn3.com, 50 Osgood Pl, Ste 340. Phone 415-318-1812. Fax 415-434-0396.
•Newport Beach, CA 92660 (Los Angeles)—Don Reis, don.reis@espn3.com, 500 Newport Center, Ste 950. Phone 949-721-8044. Fax 949-721-8120.

3. COMMISSION AND CASH DISCOUNT

15% to recognized agencies. Net 30 days.

ADVERTISING RATES

Effective 1-1-03   Confirmed 6-03

5. BLACK/WHITE RATES

	1 ti	3 ti	6 ti	12 ti	18 ti
1 page	108,000.	104,760.	102,600.	97,200.	93,950.
¾ page	99,360.	96,380.	94,400.	89,425.	86,235.
½ page	74,520.	72,280.	70,790.	67,065.	64,830.

16. ISSUE AND CLOSING DATES

Published bi-weekly.

Issue:	On sale	Closing
Jan 6/03	12/25	12/6
Jan 20/03	1/8	12/20
Feb 3/03	1/22	1/3
Feb 17/03	2/5	1/17
Mar 3/03	2/19	1/31
Mar 17/03	3/5	2/14
Mar 31/03	3/19	2/28
Apr 14/03	4/2	3/14
Apr 28/03	4/16	3/28
May 12/03	4/30	4/11
May 26/03	5/14	4/25
Jun 9/03	5/28	5/9
Jun 23/03	6/11	5/23
Jul 7/03	6/25	6/6
Jul 21/03	7/9	6/20
Aug 4/03	7/23	7/3
Aug 18/03	8/6	7/18
Sep 1/03	8/20	8/1
Sep 15/03	9/3	8/15
Sep 29/03	9/17	8/29
Oct 13/03	10/1	9/12
Oct 27/03	10/15	9/26
Nov 10/03	10/29	10/10
Nov 24/03	11/12	10/24
Dec 8/03	11/26	11/7
Dec 22/03	12/10	11/21

SPECIAL FEATURE ISSUES

Jan 6/03—College Bowl Preview; Action Sports.

Jan 20/03—NFL Playoff Preview.

Feb 3/03—Super Bowl XXXVII Preview; Winter X Games Preview; Francise Rankings.

Feb 17/03—NASCAR Preview.

Mar 3/03—Action Sports.

Mar 17/03—Sprint Training.

Mar 31/03—NCAA Tournament Preview; ESPN The Magazine Fifth Anniversary.

Apr 14/03—MLB Preview; NHL Playoff Preview; Masters Golf Tournament Preview.

Apr 28/03—NBA Playoff Preview; NFL Draft Preview.

May 12/03—NHL Conference Preview; NBA Round 2.

May 26/03—NBA Semifinals; WNBA; Indy 500 Preview; Global Preview.

Jun 9/03—US Open Golf; NHL Finals Preview.

Jun 23/03—NBA Draft; NBA Finals.

Jul 7/03—Wimbledon Preview; Action Sports.

Jul 21/03—MLB All Star Preview; British Open Golf Preview.

Aug 4/03—ESPN Sports Nation; NFL Training Camp.

Aug 18/03—X Games IX Preview; PGA Golf Preview; "The Life" Summer Special.

Sep 1/03—College Football Preview; US Open Tennis Preview.

Sep 15/03—NFL Preview.

Sep 29/03—Late Season Baseball; Action Sports.

Oct 13/03—NHL Preview; MLB Playoff Preview.

Oct 27/03—World Series Preview; Midnight Madness.

Nov 10/03—NBA Preview.

Nov 24/03—College Basketball Preview.

Dec 8/03—NFL Coverage; Action Sports.

Dec 22/03—Next 2004.

18. CIRCULATION

View detailed ABC Audit Report   (Requires: Adobe Acrobat Reader)

Established 1998. Single copy 3.99; per year 26.00.

Summary data—for detail see Publisher's Statement.

A.B.C. 12-31-02 (6 mos. aver.—Magazine Form)

Tot. Pd	(Subs)	(Single)	(Assoc)
1,550,138	1,507,335	42,803	. . .

Average Non-Analyzed Non-Paid Circulation (not incl. above):

Total 61,095

TERRITORIAL DISTRIBUTION Nov 25/02–1,552,492

N.Eng.	Mid.Atl.	E.N.Cen.	W.N.Cen.	S.Atl.	E.S.Cen
95,848	229,847	279,488	144,367	276,593	82,297

TERRITORIAL DISTRIBUTION Nov 25/02-1,552,492

W.S.Cen.	Mtn. St.	Pac St.	Canada	Foreign	Other
128,961	96,847	209,016	4,425	1,683	3,120

Advertising rate base: 1,500,000.

% above/below rate base: 3.3.

Publisher states: Effective with January 1, 2004 issue, guaranteed net paid circulation average of 1,750,000.

ULRICH'S, GALE'S, ETC.

Libraries that can afford it subscribe to Bowker's *Ulrich's Periodicals Directory* online (www.ulrichsweb.com) and/or purchase *Gale Directory of Publications and Broadcast Media* (www.galegroup.com). Like us, librarians use them as guides to periodicals. Ulrich's can be searched by topic, title, language and more, and now includes listings for e-zines. Gale *(Ill. 2.4)* is principally organized by state and city of publication and shows the publication's address, phone, fax number and e-mail address and names of key personnel including editors, sometimes with their email addresses.

Illus. 2.4. *Gale Directory of Publications and Broadcast Media* Entries

10944 Indianapolis Woman
Weiss Communications
6081 E. 82nd St., Ste. 401phone 317-585-5858
Indianapolis, IN 46250
  Magazine for women living in and around Indianapolis. **Founded:** 1984. **Freq.** Monthly. **Print Method:** Web press. **Trim Size:** 8 1/8 x 10 7/8. **Key Personnel:** Delores Wright, Editor; Paula Cook, Advertising Mgr. **ISSN:** 0897-0211. **Subscription Rates:** $12.47 individuals. **Remarks:** Accepts advertising.
Ad rates: BW $1,120   **Circ:** Non-paid 58,227
4C $1,650
    10945 Indy's Child
    Indy's Child, Inc.
    836 E. 64th St.   Phone: (317) 722-8500
    Indianapolis, IN 46220   Fax: (317) 722-8510
    Publication E-mail: indyschild@indyschild.com
    Magazine covering parenting news. **Founded:** 1984. **Freq:** Monthly. **Print Method:** Web press. **Trim Size:** 11 x 13½. **Cols./Page:** 4. **Col. Width:** 2⅜ inches. **Col Depth:** 12½ inches. **Key Personnel:** Gregory P. Wynne, Publisher; Anne-Marie Damier, Pres. and Editor, editor@indyschild.com. **Subscription Rates:** $18. **Remarks:** Accepts advertising. **URL:** http://www/indyschild.com
Ad Rates: BW: $2,040   Circ: Free 60,000
                 4C: $2,440   Paid: 100
PCI: $39.25

The annual *International Directory of Little Magazines and Small Presses (Ill. 2.5)* and *Directory of Small Press/Magazine Editors and Publishers* provide names and addresses for a slew of sometimes hard-to-find publications, and many useful details about editorial needs and practices. They can currently be purchased for under thirty dollars apiece at Amazon.com, but since most little magazines come and go very quickly, you're best off researching these directories at a local library.

Your library may also hold or subscribe to *The Standard Periodical Directory,* which has circulation, advertising, production and list rental data for more than seventy-five thousand North American magazines, newsletters, newspapers, journals and directories.

Illus. 2.5. *International Directory of Little Magazines and Small Presses* **Entries**

SEMIOTEXT(E), Autonomedia, Inc., Semiotext Foreign Agents Books Series, Sylvere Lotringer, Jim Fleming, PO Box 568, Brooklyn, NY 11211, 718-963-2603, e-Mail semiotexte@aol.com. 1974. "Do not solicit submissions" circ. 6M. 2/yr. Pub'd 2 issues 2001; expects 2 issues 2002, 2 issues 2003. sub price: $16; per copy: varies; sample: $12. Discounts: trade 40%, distributors 50%. 350 pp; 6x10; of. Publishes 2% of manuscripts submitted. Payment: varies. Copyrighted, reverts to author. Pub's reviews.

SENECA REVIEW, Deborah Tall, Editor; John D'Agata, Associate Editor for Creative Nonfiction, Hobart & William Smith colleges, Geneva, NY 14456, 315-781-3392, Fax 315-781-3348, senecareview@hws.edu. 1970. Poetry, articles, interviews, criticism, long poems. circ: 1M. 2/yr. Pub'd 2 issues 2001, expects 2 issues 2002, 2 issues 2003. sub price $1, $20/2 years; per copy: $7; sample: $7. Back issues: $7. Discounts: 40% trade for stores. 100pp; 8½ x5½; lp. Reporting time: 10–14 weeks. Simultaneous submissions accepted: no. Publishes 1% of manuscripts submitted. Payment: 2 copies and a 2-year subscription. Copyrighted, reverts to author. Ads: $75, special small press rates, exchange. CLMP, NYSSPA.

3

How to Pick
the Right Magazines
to Be Your Markets

AUTHOR AND MAGAZINE WRITER SALLY WENDKOS OLDS has long been able to just about choose a magazine and land an assignment there. But it wasn't always that way. Sally says she got started "when I was working for a civil rights organization in Chicago. Civil rights was very new then, so I wrote up what we were doing, sent it to a church publication, and they ran it. They didn't pay me a cent but they gave me a hundred free copies of the issue."

That "sale" was all Sally needed. "After that, my cycle was to write and learn, write and learn." Partly, she learned in a Chicago writers' workshop. Mostly, she learned by writing for the smaller markets until she got good at it and then for middle markets (such as regional editions of *McCall's* and *Good Housekeeping*) until she knew how to turn out material they would accept without several revisions. Then, finally, she wrote regularly for top-paying magazines.

It's a slow but sure path most professional writers have trod.

Markets Beginners Should Avoid

The late, great Mort Weisinger used to urge us, when we ourselves were climbing from small to middle markets, "Start at the top. It's as easy to write for a thousand bucks as for a hundred." That was true when Mort got started in the 1940s. The first part's still true: the writing's the same. It's the chance of getting your idea noticed that's changed since then. "We get twelve hundred unsolicited manuscripts and queries every month," *Family Circle*'s former articles editor Bobbie Ashby warned at a writers' conference. "On top of that, we get several hundred story ideas from writers we have already worked with. So the competition here is very tough."

At the same large writers' conference, Roy Herbert, *Reader's Digest*'s managing editor at the time, listed the three ingredients he and other *Digest* editors looked for: quality of the writing, quality of the research, and quality of the basic idea—"and that's the toughest of the three. You must really know your market and tailor each suggestion to the magazine."

Ideal Markets for Aspiring Writers

Some kids collect stamps, coins or beer cans. By the time coauthor Franklynn Peterson graduated from high school, he had collected a thick stack of printed rejection slips from *Reader's Digest, Saturday Evening Post, The New Yorker, Esquire* and similar biggies. When Frank decided to start earning his living at writing, however, he approached it the way any young person should approach a career—by working his way up. Being interested in social activism, the place he decided to start was a social-activist weekly magazine called *Avé Maria.*

Frank's first query to *Avé Maria* suggested he take a critical look at twentieth-century high-rise apartment buildings through the allegorical eyes of a twenty-first century archaeologist who's discovered their ruins. It was a trifle lofty for the down-to-earth magazine, and editor and publisher Monsignor John Reedy wrote back two pages explaining that gently.

Feeling encouraged by that personal rejection, Frank queried *Avé Maria's* managing editor Dan Griffin about a civil rights organization in Louisiana that used guns to protect civil rights demonstrators. He'd earlier received turndowns on that idea from *Look, Life,* and *Ebony,* no doubt because the editors were afraid (rightly so) that Frank lacked the experience to turn in a polished story. But *Avé Maria* took a chance, assigning the article. Frank wrote it. They paid him seventy-five dollars. Then Dan edited the manuscript into a far better story than the original.

Reading the printed version taught Frank a lot about writing for magazines. By the end of his first year, he was selling at least one story a month to *Avé Maria*—without lots of editorial revisions.

Dan Griffin needed Frank's stories to fill up his magazine with lively ideas as much as Frank needed Dan's editing, guidance and checks. Both were shooting for bigger places than *Avé Maria*. But they both knew that they had to master their trades first.

Dan Griffin moved on to the International desk at the *Washington Post*. Frank moved on, too. When he queried *Science & Mechanics* about hot-air ballooning—an undiscovered sport back then—he'd learned how to pick an appropriate focus for a story idea. He got the assignment, and because he'd also learned well enough how to write a basic magazine story, it reaped a $250 check. *Science & Mechanics'* editor put Frank through another apprenticeship, this time in picking story ideas slanted to the magazine's market. Before long, Frank was cashing one or two of their checks every month.

From *Science & Mechanics,* the editor who bought Frank's ballooning story moved up to best-seller lists; he was Lawrence Sanders, author of top novels beginning with *The Anderson Tapes.* And Frank, a bit older and much wiser, landed solidly in a couple of $400 to $500 markets. It's how most pros we know worked their way up to fees they could survive on. It's probably the best way for you, too.

Pros Sell Ideas

So far, we've mentioned only one article that was sold after it was written—and that was Sally Olds's first one. All our other anecdotes so far tell about how writers sold *ideas.* That's the professional way. Professional writers think in terms of selling ideas, and most professional editors think in terms of buying them.

Of course, there's a catch to this method: If an editor assigns a story based on an idea, she assumes that the turned-in story will also be acceptable. If it isn't, the writer most likely will lose all or most of his payment—and part of his reputation as well.

We're going to devote all of Part II to selling article ideas. For now let's concentrate on how pros match up good ideas with appropriate magazines.

First, let's briefly define what an article idea is to a writer.

1. It's a subject worth writing about for a thousand or more words. (Even most shorties are worth at least a thousand words. They're just very tightly written to cut down the verbiage to 750 words or less.)
2. It's got a narrow enough focus so that almost everything important and interesting about it can be said in a few thousand words.
3. It appeals to the narrow interests of an individual magazine's readers.
4. It has something new to say.

As we said in a previous chapter, there are two ways that pros go at marketing ideas. Sometimes they come up with exciting ideas and then search for one or more magazines that assign articles based on those ideas. Other times, with a magazine already in mind—either a steady market or a market they'd like to add to their list—they brainstorm for appropriate ideas.

How to Pinpoint Magazines for Your Story Ideas

Eve Merriam, prolific author of adult nonfiction books and articles, children's books, plays and poems, once told us she was sometimes assigned an article based on an *editor's* idea. But most of the time, "I am on a soapbox for something that's captured my attention and try to persuade an editor that his magazine should offer a forum for the idea. It may be something as frivolous as forecasting the next turn in fashion or as serious as an analysis of changing patterns in family life by an examination of what several hundred American middle-class children think of working mothers." But how does a writer decide which editor to try to convince that her idea's worth a forum?

Here's how it's been done by Bill Nelson, a freelance writer and former articles editor of the *Milwaukee Journal's Insight* magazine. He'd keep a mental file of ideas he'd like to write about (or had already written about once). Then he'd spend one day a month at the library researching to pinpoint five new markets for his ideas. Bill studied magazines pretty much the way we advised you to in the last chapter. "In fifteen minutes to a half hour, I had a pretty good idea of the pulse and personality of the publication." He jotted down his assessments in his marketing notebook along with appropriate names and addresses. One February day, his market research netted Bill $795.60 in story sales.

His first sale for the day's work came about because Bill glanced once more through *Reader's Digest,* a magazine he'd read a thousand times. Now he noticed their one-page features for the first time. He had recently written a short feature for a Wisconsin newspaper about the famed Burlington Liars Club. Two months after "library day," Bill was cashing a $400 *Digest* check for "The Truth About the Liars Club."

Bill also researched markets that day for a photo essay he was working on, which lamented the passage of windmills from rural America. At the library he scoured *Magazine of the Midlands* (a Sunday supplement to the *Omaha World-Herald*) and *Prairie Farmer,* both strong markets for rural pieces. Bill also saw that the "People" page in *The Christian Science Monitor* ran occasional glances at contemporary Americana. He sold the windmill yarn to all three noncompeting markets for a total of $150—not a lot, even back then, but enough to pay the electricity bill.

Bill had always wanted to write the hair-raising saga of life with his feisty foster son Kevin. That afternoon he identified *The Lutheran* and *Catholic Digest* as likely markets for the story. Two weeks later *The Lutheran* bought his domestic adventure piece. A year later, *Catholic Digest* reprinted it from *The Lutheran,* the two sales adding another $85 to Bill's "library day" proceeds.

Many writers like to jot their early-stage ideas down in lists or on index cards. Other writers find it limiting. Like Bill Nelson, they outline each idea loosely in their heads and then spontaneously reshape its emphasis or choose specific aspects that match the idea to the special demands of a chosen market.

No matter how good an idea is, it's almost impossible to sell it to a magazine that pays its staff to develop articles in that subject area. The arts and crafts, recipe, and needlework sections of many large magazines are written almost exclusively in-house. You can quickly spot situations like that by comparing bylines, if they exist, to names on the masthead. If cooking articles are not bylined—or bylined by the cooking editor or her staff—there's small chance of selling your recipes to that magazine. If major articles have no byline, they *probably* are staff-written, but this rule isn't hard and fast.

When matching an idea to a market, always compare its masthead entries to names of the authors who wrote that magazine's articles about similar subjects. Submit your idea first, as a rule, to magazines that use lots of freelance contributions in that subject area. You *can* occasionally break into a magazine that relies on staff writers for that subject, but it's a tough route.

For every rule in this business, there's an exception. Deanne Raffel is one of this rule's exceptions. An avid do-it-yourselfer, she decided to turn what she'd learned about remodeling her own home into a monthly column. She suggested it to *House & Garden,* which had plenty of staff writers in that subject area. But Deanne stressed that she could provide a woman's touch to home repair and that was something new back then. Deanne's "House Craft" column became a steady feature in *House & Garden.*

How to Develop Ideas for Your Chosen Markets

Beginners are often at a loss for what to write about. In our classes we hear, "I don't know anything but mothering and I can't even qualify as an expert on that," or, "I press buttons all day but I'll be darned if I want to write about that." What can beginners write about? Here's what we assign to our students:

1. Go through the magazines you like to read and find five (or more) articles you enjoyed and could have written yourself. Ask yourself how you would have written them differently. Develop ideas based on those differences.
2. Read your newspapers for ideas. Clip every article that sparks your interest. Ask yourself how you could turn each subject into magazine format and length.
3. Notice, as you go through your day, the things that make you react emotionally. Does the mail carrier never get there on time? Are the flowers in your neighbor's yard extra bright this year? Does the third cup of coffee taste worse than the first? Ask yourself why. The answer is probably an article idea.
4. List all the things you'd really like to know more about. You're not the only one. Each is an article idea.

Once you develop these four tips into habits, finding ideas will come easy.

Unlike so many beginners, professional writers are rarely at a loss for ideas. How often a bunch of us have sat around over a glass of something cool and mused that we ought to form a corporation to sell unused ideas to fledgling writers! At a dollar an idea, our Ideas Unlimited would generate millions.

Frankly, we pros need to start with thousands of ideas a year just to come up with enough assignments to pay the bills, because what we'd like to write about isn't necessarily what the magazines are looking for. Some magazines we want to write for because we can count on them for steady income; others we attempt to crack because of their pay scale, their prestige, or simply the challenge of that particular market.

Editor Pamela Fiori once told us, "The most frequently heard word around the editorial staff of *Travel+Leisure* is: 'No.' Conservatively speaking, we say no fifty times a day: on the phone, in person, and by letter." When Bonnie Remsberg was launching her long career, she mailed out twelve to fifteen query letters for every assignment she got. Without a fertile supply of ideas, magazine writers are doomed to destitution.

A few decades ago, Frank wrote twenty to twenty-five stories a year for a syndicate of Sunday newspaper magazines. They depended on him for timely articles. He depended on them for income. During their peak advertising seasons, he was expected to write a story every week. He had to come up with—or at least help develop—most of the story ideas. That meant weekly brainstorming sessions with his editor, the late Don Feitel. Here's the give-and-take of one session.

Frank knew the newspaper group liked dramatic personal sagas set in traditional blue-collar American situations. So, "What about a family of steel mill workers?" he began.

"What about 'em?" Don retorted.

"They're in Pittsburgh. It's hot work. It's well paid. It's dangerous. . . ."

"So?"

"Well then, how about a family of dairy farmers?"

"What about 'em?"

"Well, for the first time in the family's history, they're able to make a good living from dairy farming."

"Okay, that's a handle. Go find a family."

"Is it an assignment?"

"Yes."

That would be easy. Frank's uncle was a prospering dairy farmer in northern Wisconsin. But he tried for more assignments while he was on a roll. "How about coal mining?"

"What about it?"

"Why not a story about a modern coal miner?"

"What about him?"

"He's caught between the company and the union."

"Yah, but that's not enough for a story. We need a handle."

"Like what?"

"Like the third generation in a coal mining family."

"If we find one, do we get the story?"

"Yup, we'll call it 'Three Generations in the Mine.'"

It took Frank a year to locate a third-generation mining family, and then only by one of those breaks that make all writers believe in luck. It turned into one of the most touching stories Frank was ever privileged to write.

Like so many publications, this newspaper/magazine group wanted more consumer information articles than it could get. It especially needed unusual approaches and eye-catching titles. Most writers' suggestions fell short of the mark. In hunting out story ideas for them, Frank didn't look for importance or even freshness of information as much as for drama. While everybody else was writing about how consumers can do their own doctoring, he wrote "The Dangers of Self-Medication." Every spring, consumer magazines run something about buying lawnmowers. He pitched and wrote, "Beware the Lawn Mower." While other writers encouraged creative hobbies, he wrote "The Hazards of Hobbies."

At Christmas, everybody wrote about toys. Frank asked what happens to battery-powered toys *after* Christmas. The result was an exposé of how batteries are marketed: "The Caustic Truth About Batteries."

Most magazines feel obliged to run some seasonal material. After a few years on the job, editors run out of fresh-sounding ideas for Christmas. Frank's newspaper group editor was no exception. One year Frank wrote up the coldest spot in the nation, the next the snowiest. What next?

Well, there was this northern Wisconsin town that was red-light district from one end to the other all during summer tourist season. What went on there in the depths of winter? He called the article "There's No Hot Time In This Old Town Till Spring." Feitel loved it.

Frank knew that editors—and readers—love predictions. So in "Where Are the Snows of Nexteryear" he predicted (with help from the federal government's weather and climate experts) how much colder the United States was becoming and how fast, and on which states the big snows would fall. Of course, climate warming later proved him wrong—but that was well after he cashed the syndicate's check.

Frank did the prediction bit again the next year. Thanks to the nation's number one weather expert, an M.I.T. professor, he predicted we were in for a record cold winter. Title: "It's Going to Be a Red Flannel Winter." Based on the expert's prognostications, he even sketched maps showing how much colder various parts of the country would be and where the heaviest snows would fall. The story incorporated practically every ingredient editors love. The only hitch occurred months after the story was written and paid for. Turned out, the expert had been one year premature in slipping half the country's readers into red flannels. The article ran in Sunday magazines all over the U.S. during one of the warmest winter days in history.

It's stories like the last two that make us glad we're writers. Since Frank quoted weather experts, he could sit at his desk and chuckle about meteorological miscues. If *he'd* been the expert, he might have been out of a job.

PART II
The Article as Marketable Property

4

There's More to Writing Than Typing

L IKE A MERRY-GO-ROUND, THE FIELD OF WRITING RARELY stands still. While Part I's guidelines for studying markets will always be true, the conclusions you reach today about a particular market may be out-dated by next year. Learning everything that's important to become a successful magazine writer is like photographing all of a merry-go-round: There's no logi-cal beginning to the subject. You have to take it all in before any of the parts fit properly into place.

Some teachers jump on at the writing stage. First they help students learn how to write articles. Then they show the various kinds of markets, if any, that exist for the students' articles. Since we're convinced that people take our courses primarily because they want to appear in print, we start by discussing the mar-kets, as we did in Part I. Without a market, no matter how exciting the idea or how beautiful the execution, your article won't get published.

In Part II, we still won't have you writing finished copy. First, we feel, you have to learn to visualize your magazine articles from the same perspective that works for successful magazine writers and editors. You'll need this skill so you can judge whether your ideas are salable and can present them so they will sell.

The one activity most novices associate with writing—the actual appli-cation of words to paper—takes up relatively little time in a professional mag-azine writer's work week. Author Flora Davis, who also wrote regularly for *Redbook* and *Women's Day* (and taught writing and journalism at the New School for Social Research and Fordham University), told us she usually spent four to six weeks on an article, generally with at least two articles in the works at one time. And even though Flora carefully wrote and rewrote, she logged in little more than a quarter of her time at the keyboard. "I spend a heavy amount of time on research," Flora told us. "That's where I get my psychic rewards." Although we never kept a log of our hours—that's too bureaucratic for most freelance writers—when we wrote magazine articles regularly before becoming publishers ourselves, we spent barely half our working time at our keyboards and half of *that* time writing query letters.

For the series of forty-odd monthly articles we wrote for *Physician's Management,* for example, we had to interview fifty doctors each month. The interviews took up three or four working days on the telephone. Organizing our research took several hours. The writing was done in eight hours or less of actual keyboard time, with an evening in between for absorbing and reconsidering the unedited draft.

For some articles, we've spent just an hour on the phone and half an hour at the library; the writing took a lot longer than that. But for most articles, you'll probably spend a week or more chasing down information for each two or three days of writing time. Then, of course, don't forget to add in the hours—often days—spent selling the article idea.

We've found that most people who want to be writers want to spend as little time as possible selling. We've organized this book to help you accomplish that goal. Part I, which concentrated on magazines as markets, should have helped you pick salable article ideas. But an idea is only the bare bones of what magazine editors want to know before they'll buy. Even though a pro rarely writes any article until after landing an assignment, he does know a great deal about every article he wants to sell and eventually to write. He decides in advance which of the various *formats* can best show off his idea (Chapter 5 takes care of this). He finds a simple *focus* and a suitable *slant* to the idea. He singles out a possible *lead* (all covered in Chapter 6). He does preliminary research (Chapter 11) to ensure that he can deliver what he intends to promise. Then, when *querying* an editor (explained in Chapter 9), he shows off his mastery of the *techniques* (detailed in Chapter 7) that make articles leap off the printed page.

All these devices work to the writer's advantage. Just as corporations have developed standard ways to organize personnel, magazines have developed standard ways to organize words and ideas. You'd be labeling yourself less than professional if you were to write to an editor, for example:

> I want to tell you what's wrong with school buses. I want to investigate why they don't put seat belts inside and I want to ask mechanics how often the buses leave the garage with defective brakes and bald tires. I want to check the driving records of men and women who drive them. My article will alert parents to the dangers their children face every morning on the way to school.

A pro might write instead:

> I'm planning an exposé on school buses that documents drivers' poor driving records, bald tires, questionable brakes and lack of seat belts. My digging may make parents nervous when they kiss Sis or Junior good-bye, but I've located organizations and officials who are working on solutions, and concerned parents can join them.

The second paragraph uses about twenty fewer words—important in a field where tight writing is revered. But the second paragraph includes two additional important ideas. First, it mentions the point that you'll provide more than just your say-so. Second, it incorporates *exposé,* a word that signals to editors that you promise a lot of hard-nosed investigation into what's dangerous about school buses and writing that's highly dramatic. The editor knows all that without your having to say it because the professional writer and editor speak a special vocabulary.

The instinctive writer discovers this vocabulary—formats, pegs, elements, techniques—and the rituals of magazine writing by trial and error, reinventing the wheel as he learns his craft. But they're just as standard as chemical formulas and, as you'll see, can be learned quickly and easily once they're understood.

5

Ten Standard Article Formats

BEFORE YOU SUGGEST YOUR FIRST IDEA TO AN EDITOR, you have to know what format it needs and which elements and techniques that format requires. More than half a century ago, the late Beatrice Schapper, in her classic book *How to Make Money Writing Magazine Articles,* listed nineteen article formats linked to subject matter and another fifteen formats linked to treatment. We've reorganized her topics into ten standard article formats, and we'll provide at least one example of each so you can study and learn from them.

The examples, excerpted from archetypal published articles, are all bylined here except for those written by one or both of us. They will be referred to again later in the book. Learn their formats, and you can talk and think like a pro.

The How-To

This is one of the easiest types of article to sell—and write, too. There must be thousands published every month because nearly every consumer magazine uses them.

"Build Your Own Luxurious Plastic Furniture," which we've reproduced in part *(Ill. 5.1),* is written in classic how-to style. It opens with a *rousing promise:* you too can build the elegant, expensive-looking plastic furniture then making a comeback in retro home design. It describes the *materials and tools* needed, and finally it moves into *step-by-step directions* for building actual furniture. In the exposition—which is one of the three writing techniques that we'll explain in Chapter 7—we balance the article's *point of view* by covering some of raw plastic's shortcomings—it scratches and it's expensive. We also, at the end, tell readers how to locate suppliers of material in their local phone directories and, in case that fails, the name and address of a company that would mail them information and supplies. Editors who publish how-to's like to see as many of these elements as possible worked into their articles—a promise of success, step-by-step instructions, warnings and self-help lists. *Family Handyman*'s editor Gene Schnaser must have found everything he wanted. He published this article exactly as we wrote it and invited us to submit more story ideas.

Illus. 5.1. First How-to Excerpt

Build Your Own Luxurious Plastic Furniture

If a home handyman finds a lovely-to-look-at but expensive piece of wooden furniture, he'll try to build one just like it and usually he achieves a neat creation. Wood has always been a favorite of do-it-yourselfers. Plastics, however, being relatively new, still frighten a great many people. But working with plastic is in many ways easier than working with wood, once you learn the basic differences.

By the time you've finished this short article, you'll know these differences. Better still, you'll know how to build the luxurious $575 shelves for about $150 (closer to $100 if you shop carefully; closer to $200 if you take the easy way out). You'll be able to build the $100 coffee table for $10 to $15.

The Materials
Furniture shown here is built from a clear acrylic type of plastic sold under brand names such as Plexiglas, Lucite and Acrylite. Acrylic plastic is just as clear and sparkling as glass, yet it is incredibly hard to break. It comes in sheets of various thicknesses. The thicker your plastic, the more luxurious your finished furniture will look.

However, price is a big factor too. Acrylic plastics aren't cheap. So in designing the furniture here we've kept thickness to a minimum.

Acrylic plastics scratch more easily than glass. That's the major problem you'll find in building and enjoying furniture like this. However, even glass will scratch if you slide gritty or sharp-edged metal or glass objects over it. With plastic you can do something about the scratches; with glass you can't. If you do happen to get a scratch on some highly visible part of your plastic furniture, you can buff it out.

Most acrylic plastic you find on the market is sandwiched between lightly glued protective papers. Leave the paper in place while you're working to avoid scratches.

Tools and Methods
You can cut acrylic plastics with any saw that cuts soft metal—hacksaw, coping saw, saber saw or circular saw. However, when you're building furniture such as the two items shown here, many local plastics suppliers will cut pieces to size if you don't ask for too many different-sized cuts.

Cut with the finest-toothed blade you have available, be sure it's sharp, and use the slowest speed possible. You have to be sure that your blade is cutting through the plastic and not melting its way along. Best approach of all is to buy an acrylic-cutting blade for your saw.

How-to's can be about *physical actions:* how to build plastic furniture, extra closet space, bird houses . . . how to fix cars, bikes, refrigerators . . . how to make fancy pies, strawberry shortcake, lined drapes for the living room. . . . But they can also be about *intangible actions* that improve our mundane lives or provide guidelines for once-in-a-lifetime events: how to save money, find a job, pick a husband, choose a divorce lawyer, sue a doctor, drive safely. . . . Judi's article "12 Ways to Get More out of Studying" *(Ill. 5.2)* is also written in classic how-to format.

Illus. 5.2. Second How-to Excerpt

12 Ways to Get More Out of Studying

Effective studying is the one element guaranteed to produce good grades in school. But it's ironic that the one thing almost never taught in school is how to study effectively.

For example, an important part of studying is note-taking, yet few students receive any instruction in this skill. At best you are told simply, "You had better take notes," but not given any advice on what to record or how to use the material as a learning tool.

Fortunately reliable data on how to study does exist. It has been demonstrated scientifically that one method of note-taking is better than others and that there are routes to more effective reviewing, memorizing and textbook reading as well. Following are twelve proven steps you can take to improve your study habits. We guarantee that if you really use them, your grades will go up.

1. Use behavior modification on yourself
It works. Remember Pavlov's dogs, salivat-ing every time they heard a bell ring? Just as association worked with them, it also can work with you. If you attempt, as nearly as possible, to study the same subject at the same time in the same place each day, you will find after a very short while that when you get to that time and place you're automatically in the subject groove. Train your brain to think French on a time-place cue, and it will no longer take you ten minutes a day to get in the French mood. Not only will you save the time and emotional energy you once needed to psych yourself up to French or whatever else, but the experts say you'll also remember more of what you're studying!

2. Don't spend more than an hour at a time on one subject
In fact, if you're doing straight memorization, don't spend more than twenty to thirty minutes. First, when you're under an imposed time restriction, you use the time more efficiently. (Have you noticed how much studying you manage to cram

into the day before the big exam? That's why it's called cramming.)

Second, psychologists say that you learn best in short takes. (Also remember that two or three hours of study without noise or other distractions is more effective than ten hours trying to work amid bedlam.) In fact, studies have shown that as much is learned in four one-hour sessions distributed over four days as in one marathon six-hour session. That's because between study times, while you're sleeping or eating or reading a novel, your mind subconsciously works on absorbing what you've learned. So it counts as study time too.

Keep in mind that when you're memorizing, whether it's math formulas or a foreign language or names and dates, you're doing much more real learning more quickly than when you're reading a social studies text or an English essay.

When writing about *physical actions,* how-to's are almost always organized in time sequence. Readers must follow directions in order or they won't get the promised results. When writing about *intangible actions,* it may be harder to decide which comes first—though even here, a good how-to almost organizes itself. Sometimes it progresses from the general act to the specific, or from easy to hard. Sometimes the most interesting points are interspersed with less interesting ones, to keep the reader moving along. The *Seventeen* article combines techniques. Whichever organization you choose, you must choose consciously and carefully to achieve a well-written how-to.

How-to's should be kept as simple as possible. Readers (and editors) look first of all for easy-to-follow instructions. Intricate organization and flowery language only get in the way. Readers want *reassurance* that what you're advising them to do is within reach, *proofs and promises* that lead them to anticipate with pleasure the finished product or action, and *referrals* for required supplies or additional information. It's better by far to leave the readers wishing you'd said more (especially if you tell them where to find out more) than to have them wishing you'd stopped three hundred words ago.

How-to articles should be as short or as long as your subject requires—no longer, no shorter. Editors can be counted on to know how much information on the topic the magazine's readers want. They'll provide you with guidelines as part of the article assignment. For *House Beautiful* we wrote five hundred words on how to buy lumber and, for *Popular Electronics,* five hundred words on how to build a simple record stand. On the other hand, our *Popular Science* story about how do-it-yourselfers can add dormers to their houses required four thousand words.

The Profile and Interview

These are popular twin formats, found in a majority of consumer magazines and a large proportion of trades. You have to be careful with them because they look deceptively simple. Students stumble repeatedly before understanding the elements that make them come alive for the reader.

First, it's important to comprehend the difference between the two terms. A *profile* is simply a prose sketch of one or more aspects of someone's personality or life. (Don't try to reveal the *whole* person or tell the *whole* life story. Nobody can be revealed totally in article length.) Pros often call a profile of a celebrity a *personality profile* or a *personality piece*. Editors rarely publish profiles of anyone who is not considered celebrated or otherwise outstanding by the publication's readership.

To research a profile, the writer usually interviews the subject and, often, other people—spouses, managers, coworkers, children, neighbors—anyone whose observations provide further insight into the aspects he wants to reveal. Good writers rarely limit themselves to interviews. They draw on newspaper clippings, previous magazine stories, books, and anything else that provides anecdotes, suggests clues to the subject, or sparks questions for follow-up during the interview. But the profile ordinarily relies heavily on the interview and is most often written up using the interview's time and place as the frame of reference and the subject as the story's organizing backbone.

Many people use *profile* and *interview* interchangeably when referring to article format. The two are slightly different. Unlike the profile, which is written in conventional article style, the interview often mimics the actual give-and-take of a live interview by using a question-and-answer format, called Q&A by the pros. Q&A has become popular with editors. It looks embarrassingly simple to write but is far more difficult to bring off than you might think.

The benchmark of Q&As is *Playboy*'s regular feature "The Playboy Interview," which has been going strong for over thirty-five years. In it, a person of some national importance is explored in great depth through probing questions and carefully edited answers *(Ill. 5.3)*. A while back, Barry Golson, then editor of the *Playboy* interviews, explained to us the work that goes into these seemingly off-the-cuff Q&As. Barry selected each subject interviewed during his reign, either himself or from a writer's query. Then he asked the writer (or a likely candidate for doing the interview, if the idea was developed *in-house*) to show him between a hundred and five hundred questions in advance. Then Golson discussed all aspects of the subject with the writer to select the questions to ask. Only then did the writer's first face-to-face meeting with the interviewee take place. Usually thirty to forty hours of taped interview sessions were expected of the writer, from which the spontaneous-looking published Q&A was pieced together. Golson said, "We make no bones that a *Playboy* interview is a serious discussion put together from various tapes to retain the flavor and integrity of the original conversations. A conversation as you hear it can *never* be printed verbatim."

Illus. 5.3. Interview Excerpt

(This excerpt from The Playboy Interview with Dr. Edward Teller, who's been called "father of the hydrogen bomb," comes from an interview that took place within five days of the nuclear accident at the Three Mile Island plant near Harrisburg, Pennsylvania.)

PLAYBOY: What do you make of this catastrophe?

TELLER: I would not call it a catastrophe; I would not call it a disaster; I would not call it an accident. I would call it a malfunction.

If I undertake something really dangerous, such as driving a car, and the car stops and I can't make it work, but no one is hurt, that is called a malfunction. If someone is hurt, that is called an accident. In the Three Mile Island malfunction, no one was hurt.

PLAYBOY: But there is great fear that people will be hurt in the future.

TELLER: I am very confident that no one will be hurt. Should I be invited to visit there, I would do so, and I wouldn't feel like a hero, as I have every confidence that I would be all right.

In the functioning of many reactors, health-damaging accidents have been avoided. There is no exception. It just so happens that the antinuclear movement, lacking a real accident, has latched on to this one, promoting it into something that it isn't.

PLAYBOY: Nevertheless, it is the most serious malfunction—if that's what you want to call it—that has occurred so far.

TELLER: Indeed. I estimate that the financial damage will be even greater than it was in the Browns Ferry malfunction, which cost $120,000,000. My hunch is this will cost even more.

PLAYBOY: For which, of course, the utilities' customers will be paying.

TELLER: If we don't have nuclear reactors, the utilities' customers will be paying much more, because even counting in these costs for shutdowns, nuclear reactors are still cheaper than the next cheapest source of electricity, coal, and much cheaper than oil or gas.

A $500,000,000 loss, while it may hurt the customers in the long run, has an immediate and severe impact on the utility concerned; it will suffer loss, compared with other utilities. Therefore, the utility has the most direct financial interest in seeing that such a malfunction never occurs again. Right now, there are enormous numbers of responsible engineers who are carefully analyzing the questions: What has gone wrong and what other things may still go wrong? When the story is over, we will know how this kind of nuclear plant might malfunction, and therefore, we will know more about how to keep it safe. Utilities will be more careful in seeing that every component is safe, that instruments are employed in the reactor that will appropriately inform the operators, so that wrong judgments can be avoided. They will train operators to avoid mistakes that may have been made here. So, as a net result, we will have bought added safety for our money, without sacrificing human life or human health.

There are many degrees of variation between the strict interview format and the classic profile. Sometimes a writer incorporates his questions into an article's text instead of standing them starkly aloof as in the *Playboy* format. Sometimes he leaves out his questions, narrating just the answers. Answers may be quoted exactly, with comment or without, or interpreted through the writer's words.

Interviews may cover many aspects of a person, jumping from topic to topic without the need for transitions. Profiles, as a rule, focus on a single major aspect of the subject's experience. When Judi profiled Lynn Redgrave for *Weight Watchers Magazine (Ill. 5.4),* she built the story around one theme. The editor highlighted it in the article's subtitle: "Growing Up Fat with the Fabulous Redgraves." Judi's article deals mostly with Lynn's childhood but covers almost nothing beyond its food- and weight-connected aspects. Lynn's equally famous older sister Vanessa fits into the story too, but only in terms of *her* eating problems while they were growing up. Later in the article, Judi talks about Lynn's acting career—but again she sticks to its weight-related aspects.

Illus. 5.4. Profile Excerpt

Ladies and Gentlemen . . .
Meet the Girl Who Made It
as a Fat Movie Star

"I was a food junky," Lynn Redgrave announces.

She sits across from us, all sleek and attractive, her long bony arms obvious proof of the fact that her past lies far behind.

Behind—but not forgotten. "The pain, the hysteria, the self-hate—they're things you never forget," she admits, emotion softening her clipped British accent.

Lynn Redgrave made it as movie star on her fat. In *Georgy Girl,* as the overstuffed English bird who can't attract her own man but gets a friend's cast-off on his rebound, she won an Academy Award nomination in 1967. And now, padded all over for the title role in the Broadway play *My Fat Friend,* she's having to relive every night that fat-girl feeling again. "The only consolation," she says, "is that by the end of the play, I've shed 60 pounds and am my thin self again."

She clasps the tips of her long fingers, crosses her long legs at the knees and sighs. "If anybody had offered me this play six years ago, I would have said, 'Play a fat girl? I can't, cannot do it. I cannot go through that again.' It's only because I haven't been a fat girl for years, and have some distance from my pain, that I could take it on at all now."

Anger, aggression, pain, hysteria, hate. It was all there, from the time Lynn was 13 or 14. She hadn't always been fat. In fact, born in 1943, in the midst of the bombings on England during the second World War, Lynn came into the arms of her actor-parents enormously anemic, with huge calcium and iron deficiencies.

"When my mother was pregnant with me, people were uninformed about iron and vitamins. Food rationing was on. We were allowed one egg a week, and, of course, my 3-year-old brother Corin and my 6-year-old sister Vanessa got to share it. Of meat, I think you were each permitted two ounces a week, and, of course, extra milk was unheard-of. Oh, I was born a good size and the right weight, but I was always so tired as a baby, I literally couldn't take a walk." Whenever Nanny took the children out to the park, Lynn had to be pushed in a stroller—right up until the age of 6. She was tall and straight, but she couldn't manage the few blocks under her own steam.

But then the war was over, and gradually food became more plentiful and nutritional knowledge began filtering down to the local doctors. "By the time I was 7 or 8, they were feeding me full of pills and of eggs from chickens Nanny kept in the garden, and by the time I was 8 or 9, I was packing in the starchy foods and getting quite chubby."

We've picked up a random stack of old magazines to demonstrate, just by their cover lines, the important point that a good personality piece captures a single major theme or *focus*. In each case, we've underlined the key words that tell the theme:

Ladies' Home Journal
 "John Travolta: A <u>Career in Crisis</u>"
 "Barbara Walters Takes You <u>Behind the Scenes</u> of Her TV Triumphs"
 "Shirley MacLaine: Warren Beatty Is <u>Looking for a Woman</u> Like Me"
McCalls
 "Dinah Shore: How to <u>Look Your Best</u> All Your Life"
 "Kristy McNichol: Her <u>Real 'Family'</u> Is Stranger than TV"
Good Housekeeping
 "Jackie Kennedy <u>at 50</u>"
 "Michael Landon: 'How <u>I Got Back the Daughter</u> I Lost'"

As we said before, most published profiles are about celebrities or outstanding persons. But the rule isn't hard and fast. The same technique—singling out aspects of a person that illuminate a central theme—can be used with utterly unknown people. *Reader's Digest* often runs articles of this type.

When Frank wanted to expose the continuing miseries of coal mining, as mentioned in Chapter 3, he chose the profile, not the exposé, as his format. He found a Pennsylvania coal miner whose father and grandfather had been miners too, a man whose name hadn't been in print since a local newspaper had reported his marriage many, many years earlier. Then he spent two days interviewing the miner, his father, his son (who was about to become the fourth generation of miners), and others important to the story. Frank wrote the article just as if it were about a celebrity. The only difference was its treatment by the Sunday newspapers that ran his story. They headlined the subject's occupation instead of his name: "The Miners: Been Down So Long" *(Ill. 5.5).*

Illus. 5.5. Profile Excerpt

The Miners: Been Down So Long

As an occupation, coal mining has taken its lumps ever since the Industrial Revolution set men to attacking underground seams of black coal to feed the machines that make things. From the once green valleys of Wales to the eroded hills of Appalachia, coal miners have endured deprivation and danger as a steady diet. In lore as in life, a miner's lot has been described as 16 tons of debt-ridden existence with disaster and black lung disease as companions. Bad enough, they say, for a man who can't scratch out a living otherwise, but a foolish choice for a job if he can drive a truck or sell shoes.

Yet, mine crews around Western Pennsylvania don't suffer from a labor shortage, and the interesting fact is that now, possibly for the first time, a miner can make a decent living. There is also a proud tradition that goes with coal mining. Call it coal dust in the blood or a dogged determination to follow a trade, the fact is that new coal miners tend to come from the families of old miners. The Guza family of Amity, Pa., reflects this tradition for four generations. They've got complaints against the system, of course. Volumes of them. But the mine is their life, and they don't ask for much more than steady employment at fair wages.

Back in the early 1900s, when a German immigrant named Daniel Guza went to work in the coal pit at Marianna, Pa., miners were paid $2 for a 12-hour day. To old Daniel, whose specialty was erecting oak timbers to shore up tunnel roofs, it seemed foolish after a while to have a healthy, half-grown son just sitting around the house. So he got a job in the mine for his son. Soon, young Frank learned to handle the mules that pulled carts of coal out of the mine. "It was considered a good job," recalls the son, who's retired now, "because the mine bosses cared more then about mules than men. The mules, after all, cost $100 or so."

Perhaps it's the stories told on wintry evenings that set a youngster's course. Frank's son, Francis, who's 48 now, grew up on tales of muscle pitted against rock, of John Henry-type achievements with shovel or pick. He knows by heart the details of the great disaster at the Marianna in '07, when a short circuit in an electric cable ignited a gas pocket, blew up the mine, and killed more than 100 men. Long before Francis graduated from high school, he was determined to be a miner, like his father, maybe even a mite better one. It didn't seem to him, he recalls now, there was another choice worth considering.

The Informative Article

All articles give information, of course, but this format emphasizes information for its own sake. It uses expository writing, anecdotes, quotes, facts, figures— any of the journalistic and literary techniques that we will examine in Chapter 7—to inform readers about a subject they want to know about. Some magazines, especially the big women's publications, have adopted the term *service article* to include both the how-to's and this format, which we probably could have labeled the *what-to, why-to and when-to*.

Science magazines lean heavily on this format to relay new developments. Health magazines use it to talk about diseases (while they use how-to's to talk about regimens for better health). Sports magazines use it to tell readers about great salmon streams in the Northwest. Business magazines rely on it to reveal trends. With a bit of scanning, you can spot it in almost any magazine you pick up.

The informative article, like the how-to, has to be organized logically. Sometimes chronological order is possible; most often, it moves from major point to next logical major point. The best writers instinctively find a subject's logical progression. But the knack can be developed by writing, rewriting, testing alternate organizations and judging them critically.

Like the how-to and the profile, the informative article must concentrate on one unique aspect of the subject—in editorial jargon, the *focus* or *handle*.

Illus. 5.6. Informative Excerpt

Tornado Factory

On April 3, 1974, one of the most ferocious tornado storms ever to hit the United States screamed across the Midwest. By the time the winds died down, more than 148 separate twisters had bulldozed a path through 13 states—killing at least 300, injuring thousands, and destroying several billion dollars' worth of property.

Despite its ferocity, that storm may mark the first step toward the taming of tornadoes. For as the winds subsided, meteorologists at Purdue University learned that Wally Hubbard, an Indianapolis TV cameraman, had taken some remarkable movies of the storm.

Driving home from an assignment, Hubbard spotted a twister several miles away. Steadying his camera against the car, he filmed the twister as it approached— and as it swept by him, barely a mile away, Hubbard took some of the clearest films ever made of tornadoes. More importantly, his lens captured one of the twisters breaking up into four separate cones, all of them barking and biting as they sped counterclockwise around the spot where the single funnel had vanished. For the first time, the Purdue meteorologists had documentary proof to back up what many had suspected—that a tornado, especially a highly destructive one, often has several cones rampaging in concert.

Some 9,000 people have been killed by tornadoes in the United States in the past 50 years, according to Dr. Waltraud A. R. Brinkmann, geoscientist at the University of Wisconsin. And property damage averages between $200- and $300-million a year.

Despite such visible devastation, until very recently tornadoes have remained an enigma to weather scientists. Part of the reason is their utter unpredictability. Even fulltime tornado scientists, who strive mightily to be where the tornadoes are, consider themselves lucky if they observe two a year.

And with winds of 200 mph or more and a funnel that spans two miles across and often stretches 10 miles up into the sky, tornadoes don't lend themselves to easy study. So when Purdue meteorologists saw Hubbard's breakthrough films, plus the many still photos that had been taken during that April storm, they decided on an alternative to field study. Professors Ernest M. Agee, Christopher R. Church, and John T. Snow started to build themselves a tornado-making machine right in their laboratory.

The handle of the "Tornado Factory" article we wrote for *Popular Science (Ill. 5.6)* was the aspect of *tornadoes* (the subject) that focused on *why-to:* why tornadoes behave the way they do, as understood by Purdue University's tornado scientists who built a giant tornado simulator inside their lab. It employed *anecdotes* such as the one about the TV reporter who photographed the 1974 tornado, *quoted* experts such as Dr. Brinkmann (even though we didn't put quotation marks around her figures), and also used *exposition.* For *Family Health (Ill. 5.7)* we again wove *anecdotes* (such as the opening story about Wade Barnes) and *exposition* into an *informative* article about a new piece of medical hardware. The *handle* was: do our hospitals really need this expensive new piece of equipment? It was a *why-to,* though it also answered other questions.

Illus. 5.7. Informative Excerpt

Miracle Machine

Wade Barnes is a big, likable, middle-aged man who used to make television commercials before he became a successful New York real estate dealer. Despite the pressure of his current job, he is usually in excellent health—except for periodic, but painful, gallstone attacks. The last time he had one, the standard gallbladder dye tests failed to produce positive findings and Barnes's doctor, concerned about ulcers or colitis, ordered a complete GI, or gastrointestinal, series. Barnes obediently swallowed some evil-tasting liquid barium and posed in a variety of uncomfortable positions as technicians took x-rays of the thick fluid passing through his intestinal tract.

When the radiologist examined the x-rays, he suddenly became less interested in Barnes's gallbladder than in a peculiar shadow he spotted on the pancreas. He told Barnes's doctor, "I don't like it. Looks like there might be something growing in there." The physician passed the bad news on to Wade Barnes. *Something growing? Cancer!* was Barnes's first, frightened thought.

But how were they to find out for sure? X-rays, like the ones Barnes had just had, can hint at a pancreatic growth, but cannot define it. The reason? Unlike bone and other hard body tissues, which reflect radiation onto an x-ray plate, soft body tissues, such as the internal organs; absorb almost uniform amounts of radiation. Thus, the differences between diseased and healthy tissues in an organ like the pancreas will be barely distinguishable even to a specialist's trained eye. Barnes would have to undergo risky, expensive and painful exploratory surgery so that a doctor would see with his own eyes if there was, indeed, a growth.

Fortunately, however, Barnes was acquainted with a team of radiologists who had recently bought themselves a fancy new machine that was capable of taking readable x-ray pictures of parts of the body never clearly photographed before. Barnes called the radiologists at their Queens, New York, office and asked if their machine could help him. He was told it could, so he made an appointment.

The doctors, however, couldn't see him for two weeks and, during that time, Barnes lived with fear of the disease and apprehension about the complicated new machine that would determine his fate. His nervousness didn't abate when he walked into the scanning room, changed into a paper examining gown, and was asked to lie on a table and insert the lower half of his body through a donut-like ring and into a huge, rectangular steel device. He was prepared for the worst—certainly for more discomfort than a GI series.

Instead, as the noisy machine started up and the rectangle began clicking and circling around his stomach like a robot from some science fiction novel, the only discomforts Barnes experienced were those of having to remain motionless for several minutes at a time and of holding his arms stiffly behind his head. After half an hour, the technician who'd helped him onto the table helped him off. It was all over and, by the time Barnes had dressed, the radiologists, Drs. Herbert Rabiner and Jeffrey Kaplan, were ready for him. "Wade," Dr. Rabiner said, "there isn't a thing wrong with your pancreas. It looks as healthy as mine."

The machine that saved Wade Barnes from exploratory surgery is called a CT or CAT whole body scanner. (There are also scanners designed to photograph only the head or the torso; the whole body scanner, however, does both.) The initials stand for Computed Tomography or Computerized Axial Tomography, different terms for the same process. The computing is done by minicomputers similar to the ones used in rocket ships. The word axial refers to the fact that, unlike conventional x-rays that produce a two-dimensional, lengthwise picture, CT scanners use the patient as an axis and rotate the machine around him. The result: a crosscut image. And tomography is a Greek word meaning "to write a slice," which is exactly what the CT scanner does—it writes a detailed description of what a thin slice of the patient would look like if a doctor could section him the way a cook slices tomatoes.

But when Barnes had his pancreas scanned, he wasn't even poked. Instead, the CT scanner made a series of 180 degree arcs around his stomach, pausing every so often to direct a tiny amount of radiation—no greater than that of conventional x-rays—through him. The x-rays were then fed through an electric eye into a computer terminal, where the information was translated into a front-to-back photo of the inside of Barnes's torso, as well as a numerical print-out and a magnetic tape to be filed for future reference.

Within seconds, a slice of Wade Barnes could be viewed on a TV screen—either in black-and-white or, with the press of a button, in psychedelic colors. His pancreas, his stomach and his backbone and spinal cord were all clearly distinguishable. And with assurance of 95 percent accuracy, the radiologists could tell Barnes that his pancreas was not malformed, that it was not diseased and that there were no blood clots or other foreign bodies that shouldn't be there. Only surgery could give more precise information—but that, fortunately, was no longer necessary.

The CT scanner can bring to light organs other than the pancreas, too. It can examine the liver for hematomas (tumors containing effused blood). It can detect benign cysts in the kidneys, which can then be drained to cure the patient without surgery. And it can show the extent of cancerous tumors and ascertain whether or nor they've spread. For example, after an ordinary chest x-ray, one patient was told that she had a lung tumor. An operation would have followed almost automatically, except that a CT scan revealed that the tumor had spread to the chest wall, making surgery useless. Although the woman wasn't cured, at least she was spared a needless operation.

Surgery isn't the only unpleasant diagnostic tool that CT can replace.

A patient suspected of colonic tumors, polyps or diverticula (sacs produced by abnormal protrusions through organ walls) may be scanned instead of having to take an uncomfortable barium enema. Scanning is also a possible alternative to tests involving the injection of dyes or radioactive materials via painful catheterization of the artery that supplies blood to the liver, pancreas, spleen or kidneys. (Sometimes dyes are used in conjunction with CT scanning but, on those occasions, comparatively small amounts are administered by simple needle injections.)

Valuable as it is, CT body scanning is only a babe-in-the-woods compared to its older sibling, CT head scanning, which has revolutionized the diagnosis and treatment of brain disorders.

Until seven years ago, a doctor had few alternatives—none of them pleasant—if he wanted to find out what was happening in the soft tissues hidden behind a patient's skull. He could order an encephalogram, a technique that involves forcing air into the patient's brain to outline the convoluted tissues on an x-ray plate. (The patient would . . . .
continued in Ill. 7.1

In writing informative articles, you should be prepared to answer those classic canons of journalism: who, what, why, when, where and how. Occasionally, these articles end with brief how-to sections or referral lists so that an ambitious, inquisitive reader might investigate further. We've added how-to's to many of our stories for *Popular Science* and to articles on such topics as rape (listing crisis centers), alcoholism (listing helping agencies) and test-wiseness (listing books that provide more information). Many editors love to receive extra tidbits that add to the service aspect of articles and often treat them as *boxes* or *sidebars*.

When we tackled geodesic-dome homes for *Popular Science,* we stuck almost entirely to the handle of what was *new and exciting* about the subject, since the magazine had done dome stories almost biennially since Buckminster Fuller invented the concept. As you can see in the article's ending *(Ill. 5.8),* we were able to carve the story almost entirely from anecdotes and quotes, using exposition merely to glue the other elements together. At the end, as we'd promised the editors, we offered a central source of additional practical information. We also prepared a list of more than two dozen dome home manufacturers' addresses so readers could write for help in buying their own domes. Editors wisely sidebarred the list, setting it apart from the story, because a long list of facts, simply facts, makes for boring reading. And the first commandment for good writers and editors has always been: keep it exciting.

(Wondering about the phrase *[PS, Sept. '72]* in the illustration's second paragraph? It refers to an article in a past issue and was inserted by the editor.)

The Exposé

One specific kind of informational article has evolved into a separate format with its own structure: the exposé (a word often written without the accent that reminds us to pronounce the final *e* as *ay*). *Exposé* writers use *investigative reporting,* which is simply research for facts that will hopefully shock the readers.

Illus. 5.8. Informative Excerpt

There are two basic construction methods in use today among dome suppliers. The hub-and-strut method is closest to the early Buckminster Fuller models. Conceptually it's very much like building with Tinker Toys. A steel hub, typically a short length of a six-inch pipe, is bolted to a collection of 2 x 6 pine struts that fan out until they link up to other struts via other hubs. The network of resulting triangles curves gracefully into the famous dome shape.

Stresses from the weight of the hubs, struts, snow, wind, and other building loads are evenly distributed through the network, coming finally to rest on the ground. Alternately, the dome can be set upon a foundation of poured concrete, cement blocks, or specially treated wood [PS, Sept. '72]. Some domes are built on top of risers that increase the height of the outside walls.

The second basic dome construction method uses the panelized approach. This hybrid technique combines the early Fuller concept and traditional frame carpentry. Buckminster Fuller approves of the method.

Wisconsin dome manufacturer Ray Shultis explains how his version of the panelized dome developed: "My dad got interested in domes five years ago, and he took me along. But about all that anybody knew about domes back then was in *Dome Book I* and *Dome Book II,* produced by the counter-culture. So our first dome came right out of *Dome Book II.* It was nice, but it was also too hard for your ordinary building contractor to work with. So I spent 18 months educating myself about the math and design of domes. And we redesigned our dome so it fits into the experience of your ordinary frame carpenter."

Four times better

Says Bob Koger, a Florida architect who's collaborated on Shultis' design: "We've designed our domes to be four times better than the building codes require. We have them out for third-party testing now, and when the results are in, we won't have to go through so much red tape at local building departments."

An informal survey of building departments finds that inspectors are willing to okay domes, but many of them do want to see studs every 16 inches like the old frame construction. A Madison, Wis., building code supervisor chuckled as he said the major problem he'd have with domes was deciding where the roof (requiring 30-pound snow-load capacity) ended and the wall (requiring only a 20-pound wind load capacity) began! He added, "I don't see any problems that can't be tackled easily."

The U.S. Department of Housing and Urban Development is starting to okay the structural soundness of a few dome manufacturers' designs. HUD approval is generally required before an FHA-insured home mortgage is possible.

You can get more information by writing the National Assn. of Dome Manufacturers (Suite 470, 1701 Lake Ave., Glenview, Ill. 60025) or by contacting individual manufacturers below. [A list of names and addresses follows.]

Too many would-be exposé writers think their jobs are done at that, but it's really only a first step. The exposé writer must (1) *present* the facts in a way that shocks readers, (2) stay carefully within the bounds of accuracy, and (3) hedge discreetly when necessary to avoid needless libel suits or nasty letters to the editor.

Not much exposé research is of the mind-boggling Woodward-and-Bernstein variety. Exposés of Watergate magnitude generate newspaper headlines and laudatory pickup stories by other writers. But startling statistics, authoritative quotes and shocking anecdotes work well for stories with more modest pretensions as long as they add to the exposé's end result: to shock. Since early efforts in your writing career will probably be confined to exposés that don't shake the world, we'll work with such examples here.

"The Skateboard Menace," an article Judi prepared for Family *Health* magazine *(Ill. 5.9),* highlighted what was then a new fad. It exposed the broken bones, torn muscles, concussions and fatalities that had occurred. In among the exposition for parents who didn't yet know a skateboard from a Ouija board, Judi strung out statistic after statistic, anecdote after anecdote, each more shocking than the last.

Judi researched the story by asking selected police and medical officials about skateboarding problems. She asked skateboard officials about them, too. Among newspaper archives, friends and acquaintances (quoted in the article), she found dozens of horror stories. She studied medical journals and authoritative accident statistic compilations. She didn't discover anything press-stopping (skateboards had not become the number one crippler of children), but her classic exposé-writing skills shocked parents nonetheless. Let's pinpoint these techniques.

In Judi's *lead* paragraph, she establishes skateboarding as a big and growing hobby and a multimillion-dollar business, thus providing *framework of magnitude*. After all, unless skateboards are used by a significant part of the population, the dangers—no matter how great—are of insignificant concern. Then she quickly (first full paragraph on the article's second page) introduces *statistics* that show the *reason for concern*. Notice that Dr. Coll, her *authority*, doesn't actually say that 20 percent of all accidents are caused by skateboarding. He says, in fact, that in a *typical weekend* (typical, of course, being whatever the doctor and author choose to call it) 20 percent of *only certain accidents* are from skateboarding. But as worded, the *quote* shocks the quick reader. That's what readers like—and pros always try to engage the reader.

Later Judi offers another *statistic*. She mentions that, thanks to polyurethane wheels, skateboards can hit fifty miles an hour. Do they ever attain that neck-breaking speed on neighborhood sidewalks? Judi sidesteps the question, qualifying her figure by saying, "on a race track."

Editors and readers alike want to look into the future. Judi found figures for the previous year's skateboard accidents—27,522. But what about the *coming* year? No way to know for sure, of course. Instead, Judi informally surveyed several hospitals. She wrote that in three months this year they had patched up as many skateboarders as in the previous twelve months. Quick readers would conclude that there could be four times as many accidents this year. They could be right. A pro never ever fudges on statistics—but she does learn to use them to best effect. In the hands of the good exposé writer, they are a powerful device.

Illus. 5.9. First Exposé Excerpt

The Skateboard Menace

Business is booming for orthopedists all over the country this year. Broken wrists, splintered elbows and smashed ankles are just three common hazards of the reborn skateboard craze.

Skateboarding became a short-lived fad about 10 years ago, when out-of-season surfers attached roller-skate wheels to their surfboards and took to the hilly roads. As other young people took up the sport, manufacturers began to offer mass-produced skateboards. But as quickly as the fad blossomed, its popularity faded.

Two years ago, a California enthusiast tried something new: He screwed a set of new polyurethane wheels to an old board, achieving a faster, smoother, quieter ride. Almost instantly, a whole new generation of skateboarders emerged, and this time close to 150 manufacturers undertook to meet their needs. Today, skateboarding is a multimillion dollar business. In June, 26 top skateboarders met in New York to vie for $7,000 in prizes at the first World Masters Invitational competition, and in September the first open World Invitational meet will take place in California—with a

$50,000 purse! At least one magazine for skateboarders or "hot doggers" is being published, the first skateboard movies are making the rounds and a TV series is in preparation. *Newsweek* magazine estimates that between 6 and 10 million Americans are now on the boards.

But for most of these fans, generally boys in their teens and preteens, skateboarding is neither business nor semi-pro sport; it is a popular neighborhood pastime—and a very dangerous one. As Dr. Geoffrey Coll, orthopedic resident at Long Island Jewish/Hillside Medical Center in New York, says, "The year before last we saw no skateboard injuries in emergency orthopedics. Last year I remember only one or two. This year the numbers are significant: Out of twenty bad strains, sprains and broken bones in a typical weekend, I'd estimate that 20 percent are from skateboard accidents. And," he pointed out, "I only see the more serious injuries. Minor scrapes and bruises are treated by the interns in our general emergency room."

Little accidents happen mostly to beginners, according to a Great Neck, New York, pediatrician. "The novices are cautious at first. They choose their roads carefully and avoid dangerous tricks. They fall on their fannies or scrape their hands and knees, but, in general, they get no more banged up than beginning bicyclists. When they think they've mastered the boards, that's when they start taking chances and really hurt themselves."

A Long Island policeman reports that people are complaining about teenagers trespassing upon neighbors' drained swimming pools to "ride" them. In this gravity-defying trick, picked up from a California skateboard movie, necessary momentum is gained to make the skateboard wheels cling to the curved upper sides of the pool, while the rider spins dizzily atop—or, more accurately, aside—his board. So many children perform "nose wheelies" and "tail wheelies" (tipping back or front) that some skateboards are now being manufactured with snubbed noses and flipped-up tails.

Tricks like these were not possible a decade ago, when skateboards were made of wood and wheels were steel or clay. Today's good-quality boards are flexible fiber glass, aluminum or Lucite, and boast sophisticated "trucks," the mechanisms to which wheels are attached. The polyurethane wheels themselves provide the remarkable traction necessary for "riding" pools, and on a race track can carry their passengers as fast as 50 miles per hour.

Since mechanical advancements make it possible for almost any experienced skateboarder to do some fancy tricks, in-

tense pressure insures that youngsters will try. In fact, a cult glamorizing both risk and pain is rapidly developing around the sport. According to the code, if you haven't been badly hurt at least once, you haven't attempted a really difficult trick. "Wiping out is considered neat," explains Bill Colvard, a salesman in the Durham, North Carolina K-Mart sports department, where skateboards are the season's biggest-selling merchandise. "A kid who's experienced the pain of skateboarding is really big stuff. His image is definitely enhanced."

Enhancing or not, a wipe out can be a serious matter. In New Haven, Connecticut, a young teen's braces cut right through his lip; a Chicago youth, swerving to avoid a dog, collided with a parked car and broke both knee caps. In Haverstraw, New York, a high school junior struck a rut and wound up hospitalized for two days with a concussion. Severe scrapes and bruises are common enough to be referred to as "road rash," and so many youngsters have suffered arm injuries that, according to *The Physician and Sportsmedicine* magazine, doctors now call a shattering of the olecranon, "skateboard elbow." At least two fatalities have been recorded in California, and on a national level, skateboards caused a spectacular 27,522 injuries requiring hospital treatment in 1975—a record that promoted them from eighth to third place in accident frequency for all children's toys (except for bicycles, which are in an accident class by themselves). A recent three-month survey showed more skateboard casualties in some hospitals than in an earlier twelve-month period.

Another modest exposé, reprinted here in part, shows that almost no topic is outside the purview of this journalistic technique. In "Household Hotlines" *(Ill. 5.10)*, an attempt to scare people into being careful with extension cords, Frank's lead sentence tries to scare, stating that every year there are *hundreds* of serious fires resulting in *millions of dollars* of damage (*framework of magnitude* and *reason for concern* all rolled into one). It also states that deaths occur, although not in every fire. Frank could have used precise statistics. He had them on hand. But numbers like 257 and $2,475,620 would have slowed down the reader's eye, generating less shock.

In the last line of the first paragraph, Frank creatively uses National Fire Protection Association figures. Instead of writing, "Extension cords cause X many fires, TVs Y many fires, and microwave ovens Z many fires," or, "Extension cords cause one-fourth as many fires as all appliances put together," he sums up all these statistics. The lowly extension cord, he writes, "is the most dangerous electrical item in common use." You too will be able to select and present facts with maximum impact after you cut your piranha teeth on a few exposés.

Illus. 5.10. Second Exposé Excerpt

Household Hotlines

Every year hundreds of serious fires resulting in deaths and millions of dollars of damage can be traced to faulty extension cords or their improper use. Innumerable incidents involving these connectors go unreported. They include minor fires, major scares and damage to household furnishings and appliances. Damage and tragedies caused by the innocent-looking extension cord have increased to such an extent that now it is the most dangerous electrical item in common use, according to figures compiled by the National Fire Protection Association.

Basically extension cords become dangerous under three conditions: when they are old; when they are used permanently; when they are overloaded.

In Washington, D.C., a mother wanted a reading light for her side of the bed. She found an old extension cord and ran it under the bed to a wall outlet. Months later, the forgotten old cord overheated or shorted, ignited the bedding and mattress, and in the fire which resulted the family's five children perished.

The National Fire Protection Association (NFPA), a major spokesman in the electrical safety field, warns that extension cords must never be used near combustible materials such as a mattress or clothing. They advise that before using any extension cord, "look for frayed, broken or brittle insulation," all of which can lead to shorts which generate such intense heat that fabrics can be ignited in seconds.

A Seal Pleasant, Md., family's TV was connected to a cord which often sent out a shower of sparks when somebody stepped on it. Early one morning, a six-year-old son went down to the living room and tried to get the TV and extension cord to work. Sparks ignited the living room draperies. Before the morning was over, $16,000 in fire damage had been done to the house. The mother and two children died.

The Maryland family, among its other misjudgments, had also violated the National Electric Code (NEC) by using an extension cord as a permanent installation. Most insurance companies follow the NEC in making electrical safety inspections. The Code recommends that extension cords be avoided whenever possible and forbids their use for anything other than strictly temporary jobs.

Used Permanently

An extension cord was wedged into an out-of-the-way crack under the stove in a Maywood, Ill., kitchen. A combination of wear and heat gradually destroyed the extension cord's insulation. When it short-circuited one night, three children died in their upstairs bedroom because of the ensuing fire. The mother and two other children escaped with injuries.

Heat and most chemicals are murder on extension cord insulation. Electrical cords should never be used near radiators, heat pipes, stoves or even near the back or bottom of TV sets which also generate considerable heat. And if a cord is going to be used near moisture (such as in a damp basement or outdoors) or near oil (such as in the kitchen or a garage), the NFPA recommends that you "use only cords marked water-resistant or oil-resistant."

Overloaded

During a chilly November night in Stillwater, Okla., a college fraternity hooked up a 1650 watt electric heater to an ordinary light extension cord. To keep members from tripping over the cord, it was laid under a rug in the bedroom. During the night, the small cord which was forced to handle too large an electrical load overheated and set fire to the rug. Fortunately, an automatic alarm system alerted fraternity brothers in time to escape, but $600 in damages resulted.

"Portable electric heaters need special extension cords designed to carry heavier loads," says the NFPA. Most common cords are made of number 18 size wire and should not carry more than 700 watts of power, according to the NFPA. Heaters, toasters, broilers, vaporizers and similar home gadgets require more than 700 watts of power. It is safest not to use any extension cord with heaters and such appliances. But if you feel that you must, buy a heavy-duty extension cord made of wire large enough to handle the load. Every extension cord on sale should be clearly marked with a label designating the maximum electrical load it can safely handle.

Human Interest Articles: The Personal Experience, Reminiscence and As-Told-To

One of our students set out to write about a weight-reduction program fairly new to Milwaukee. He decided that the liveliest way was to tell how it helped him shed forty-seven pounds and then add enough facts to help readers who wanted to do likewise. The *Milwaukee Sentinel* feature editor agreed. We've reproduced the first part of John's "Food Greaser Loses 47 Pounds" *(Ill. 5.11)* so you can see for yourself how well his personal experience piece succeeded.

Illus. 5.11. First Personal Experience Excerpt

Food Greaser Loses 47 Pounds

by John L. Hirsh

I used to be a greaser. A food greaser.

On a typical day I ate several quarter pounders with cheese, extra crispy fried chicken, deep dish pizza and a couple of ham sandwiches. In between, I kept myself going with refined sugar products. I munched chocolate bars with almonds, sweet rolls and cream filled cupcakes.

My stomach started to jam up against the steering wheel of my car. Then my stomach began to rebel. To neutralize the acid and gas, I gobbled Rolaids, Alka 2, Tums and Pepto Bismol—whatever was handiest.

When I walked a block or two, I'd huff and puff and say, "I have this asthma condition, you know."

At 5 foot 10½ inches, I weighed close to 250. On some days I denied every pound of it to myself. On others I decided it was really macho to be that heavy.

Being a food greaser also led me to the dentist's chair. My teeth were rotting. I had to have root canal work and new fillings.

The incredible pain I suffered convinced me that I had to get some grease relief. I had to abandon "gut bombs" and sugar. I had to start eating the right food. I had to go on a . . . on a . . . on a diet.

BUT WHICH ONE? There are so many. And each is different.

The "more of" diets suggested an increase in wine, liquor, vegetables, lollipops, ice cream, candy or liquid protein. The "less of" programs recommended no breakfasts, no meat, virtual starvation or just plain wiring the mouth shut.

About a year ago, when I was in a pharmacy buying a chocolate bar with almonds, I made the decision to "degrease." Spotting *Consumer Guide to Rating the Diets* by Theodore Berland helped me make that decision. I checked to see which diets rated high. Based on Berland's criteria of high protein, a maximum of 30% fat (mostly unsaturated), low carbohydrates and sugar, he gave a four star rating to 21 programs. Of the top three programs, two had branches here—Weight Watches and Diet Workshop.

I had tried to lose weight in groups before. I'd been moderately successful, once almost going below 200, but the "confession" aspect of the meetings turned me off. I always *knew* I was doing things wrong. What I wanted now was a program to change my behavior.

I REVIEWED Berland's book again, discovering that Diet Workshop could tell me what to eat, how to use behavior modification principles, and I liked its emphasis on exercise. Eleven months ago I joined Diet Workshop. I lost and I won.

I had been a member of Weight Watchers in 1974 and then again in 1976. As to which is better—Weight Watchers or Diet Workshop—I can only say that it really depends upon you and the group leader. What follows is my experience with Diet Workshop.

A good diet, I discovered, does NOT reduce the amount of food. It teaches you HOW to eat and WHAT to eat. It changes your lifestyle. I was amazed at the quantity of food I could eat. I learned about low fat meats which I had never heard of or was too poor to buy: antelope, buffalo, caribou, venison, elk, goat, moose, pheasant, quail, squab, squid, tripe, finnan haddie, chicken haddie, butterfish.

I learned that I could eat high fat proteins—beef or frankfurters—only three times a week. At first I splurged once a month and ate sirloin steak. Then I learned that I could lose weight faster by eliminating beef from my diet altogether.

FOR BREAKFAST I got an egg and toast on one day, cheese and cereal on others. Never having thought of cheese as breakfast food, I soon discovered delicious varieties like gouda, edam and ricotta.

I also could eat five fruits a day including bananas, cantaloupe, peaches, pears, plums, raspberries and strawberries.

I got to eat as much as I wanted of asparagus, bean sprouts, broccoli, cabbage, celery, chard, cucumber, endive, lettuce, mushrooms, onions, radishes, spinach or zucchini. But I was limited daily to 4 ounces or one-half cup of artichokes, brussels sprouts, carrots, eggplant, kohlrabi, peas, pumpkin, squash or tomato.

Occasionally, as a bonus, I could substitute frozen yogurt or ice milk (from stores like Dairy Queen or Boy Blue) as a 4 ounce substitute for an 8 ounce milk requirement. Best of all, I learned I could drink up to 1 ounce of liquor or 3 ounces of wine two or three times a week!

The personal experience story combines some elements of both the profile and the informative article. It is usually organized chronologically and highlights an aspect of a person. It's even possible to do exposés and how-to's based on personal experience. Do a personal how-to, for example, if you've learned how to build a Saran Wrap flying machine and are willing to share your unique techniques with other readers. Do a personal exposé cum personality profile if a KKK Grand Dragon locked you in a bathroom with Richard Pryor's ghost for eighteen hours, during which Pryor told you one bad joke after another. If you could expose southern public restrooms and Richard Pryor's humor all in the first person, you'd have a selling article for sure.

A majority of students begin by trying to crank out a personal experience story. Some, we're sure, do it because they think it's the easiest kind of format. But we get the haunting feeling that many enroll in writing courses simply to learn how to get their letters to the world published. The number one requirement for selling a personal experience story is not that you want to *write* it, but that enough people want to *read* it. In short, you have to have had a personal experience that's different in some substantial way from the day-to-day lives of quiet desperation that Thoreau felt most people live.

For the same reason, reminiscences don't sell either, except sometimes locally for a few dollars. (Reminiscences, for the uninitiated, are bundles of at least several personal experiences.)

How many of us can survive enough falls off twenty-eight-story buildings, or recover from enough near-fatal illnesses, to make a living writing personal-experience articles? The pros who do make a living at it write about *somebody else's* tragedies and triumphs. Sometimes the person who's lived the experience gets the entire byline. Other times the actual author is listed second: "as told to . . ." Rarely can the author count on a traditional byline—usually only for articles involving celebrities.

The dean of personal experience storytellers was Terry Morris, an early, beloved president of the American Society of Journalists and Authors. Way back in 1950, Terry abandoned short-story writing in favor of human-interest magazine articles about people in crisis. Her genius for telling a touching story carried over from fiction to nonfiction. She sold her very first two articles to *Cosmopolitan* and *McCall's* early in 1951.

Terry's all-time favorite was "Please Don't Lose Faith in Me," an as-told-to article written from the viewpoint of the mother of a schizophrenic son. We've reproduced the beginning *(Ill. 5.12)* so you can study how a master molds somebody else's personal experience.

Illus. 5.12. Second Personal Experience Excerpt

On Sunday, rain or shine, my husband and I drive twenty-five miles through a pleasant countryside to visit our first-born, our son Jamie. Jamie is 30 years old. If he should ever again, by the grace of God, raise his head and stand erect he would measure six feet two inches. He has broad shoulders, a lean waist, and the strong, bold features of a man of decision. Looking at him we see what he might have been—but what he is not and never will be.

The Essay or Personal Opinion

Back when Judi was tending both her first two sons' intellectual curiosity and the family's tight budget, New York City museums initiated a not entirely voluntary "contribution" fee. Judi got angry. Rather than write a letter to the editor, she typed her thoughts in personal opinion article format. *The New York Times* not only published it but paid her for it because she had put into strong words an opinion many of its readers agreed with *(Ill. 5.13).*

Illus. 5.13. Personal Opinion Excerpt

It Costs Too Much To Go to a Museum

So the museums are doing poorly, are they? Well, I'm secretly glad to hear it. I've been doing poorly myself ever since they slammed their doors on me and my children several years ago.

I used to think that the Metropolitan and the Natural History museums were *my* museums. When I was a youngster growing up in lower-middle-class Brooklyn, those museums were where our family went on glorious excursions to New York. The dinosaurs in the cavernous halls are linked forever with the double-decker Fifth Avenue busses among my earliest memories. When I began traveling the subways alone, I met friends from the Bronx in the Egyptian tomb at the Metropolitan and we wandered the other corridors until we knew them by heart.

A school trip introduced me to the Museum of Modern Art, and I loved its paintings. But its entry fee, then 50 cents, was for the most part beyond my means. When I did splurge for a ticket, I felt like a poor relation in its intimate rooms—tolerated, but not really welcome. (These days, a visit to MOMA with my two sons would set me back $3.50 in all, so we're still poor relations.)

Then I married and moved to Manhattan to bring up my children on the borders of Central Park. I counted pennies while my first child was in the stroller. In the Museum of Natural History, I discovered, they allowed me in with the stroller, and on weekdays when the halls were empty of all but school groups, I'd push my son around the museum. When he was very young, there were the stuffed animals; he'd look and I'd explain what the placards said.

Later on we graduated to the snakes and turtles in the live-animal room, the Indian displays, the oil rig, the nature hall, and the fine new Hall of Man. By then he was out of the stroller and his little brother was in it. I had widened his horizons to the Metropolitan, starting with the "Knights in Shining Armor." Then the Metropolitan opened its Children's Wing, with a ground-level door through which the Wing welcomed my stroller.

The children grew, our mobility increased and we widened our horizons to include all the exhibits of both museums. A yearly trip to the Guggenheim consisted of taking the elevator to the top and then chasing after the kids as they alternated a happy run down the ramp with an occasional long visit with a piece of art whose color or form caught their happy eyes. That delighted romp down the ramp was itself worth the 50-cent admission price: it reinforced their observations that pleasure went with art.

For the most part, however, even as we grew more affluent we ignored the museums that charged admission.

Just as your personal experience stories have to involve some experience that a great many people want to read about, your personal opinion article must contain opinions on a subject of consequence to thousands of people. As a rule, national magazines publish relatively few personal opinion articles, and then almost exclusively on vital national issues written by people of national stature. Local editors are more likely to publish opinions by local writers on subjects of local or national importance.

The essay, classically, is a carefully constructed opinion piece in which *all* the facts, arguments and conclusions are filtered through the author's unconcealed (and at times quite opinionated) viewpoint. This genre does not represent a substantial market for pros. If you want to pursue it, we suggest you reread Chapter 1's comments on magazines of commentary and study the publications mentioned there.

Humor and Satire

There's nothing funny about humor. It's tough work. Most editors we've met tell us they'd like to see more humor coming across their desks but they haven't seen much good humor yet. What is—or is not—funny is very subjective and always changing.

Humor can be applied to any of the other standard magazine formats. A humorous personal experience is out-and-out humor. A humorous exposé, a humorous how-to, a humorous interview and so forth often turn into *satire. The Onion,* a free national weekly in tabloid format, thrives on satire.

You may have considered writing humor because even your mother laughs at your jokes. In that case, we suggest you try writing movies or TV sitcoms. There's bigger money and a greater market. If you're set on writing magazine humor, who are we to stand in your way? Write it and send it out. Unlike most other formats, you can't sell humor based on ideas alone. You must mail the finished article to an editor and hope she thinks it's funny too.

Because we believe humor is such a specialized, hard-to-sell field, we don't include an example here.

The Inspirational

In a sense, one could call the inspirational article a form of how-to. It tells readers how to *feel good* or how to *do good things:* how to feel good about themselves, how to do well at selling vacuum cleaners, how and why to lead more exemplary lives. Most inspirationals are personal experiences. They weave the experience of some person, celebrity or not, around a moral message.

Many people automatically associate inspirational stories with religious magazines. Those publications do, in fact, buy lots of inspirationals. But business, civic and other magazines use them, too *(Ill. 5.14).*

Illus. 5.14. Inspirational Article Excerpt

One Teacher's Triumph

by Paul Martin

The school day at Westside Preparatory School sometimes starts as early as 7:30 in the morning. The students' rigorous work schedule includes recitation of passages from Shakespeare, Kipling and Emerson, discussions of Socrates. Grammar-school youngsters write themes about Sophocles and Dostoevski's *The Brothers Karamazov* that reveal a grasp of abstract concepts. Spelling and grammar are accurate.

An expensive private institution in Shaker Heights or Scarsdale? Not at all. It's a one-room school at 3819 West Adams Street on Chicago's tough west side. Students range in age from 5 to 12, and their enthusiasm for knowledge is the inspiration of a remarkable woman—Marva Collins.

Westside Prep opened three and one-half years ago, the vision of Collins who was "fed up after 14 years of teaching in the Chicago public schools." Using the family savings, her husband, Clarence, remodeled the second floor of their two-family home, and the school opened in September 1975. It began with 6 neighborhood youngsters and grew to 14 by the end of the year. Today 31 students attend Westside Prep.

With boundless energy, Marva Collins encourages, jokes, cajoles and inspires her young scholars, telling them to sit up straight, speak up, look people in the eye and pay attention. While one group masters a drill in a workbook, another group of children receives personal instruction from her.

Marva Collins fosters a strong sense of individual responsibility among her students. "Success doesn't come to you," she declares. "You go to it. You don't buy it with Green Stamps. There's no paycheck until the work is done. You don't get a report card unless all the homework is in. Every moment here is going to be used."

The techniques for writing inspirationals are little different from those used to write profiles or personal experience articles. In each of those other formats, writers concentrate on a single topic; in the inspirational, the *focus* is always the inspirational point that you (or your editor) want to make.

Markets for inspirational articles are bountiful.

Payment, as a rule, isn't.

The Historical Article

Many beginning writers see this as a separate article format from the informative, profile or personal experience article. They come to us—those who are too shy to want to tell all in a personal experience story—and say that they want to tell all about this or that legendary character who lived in their neck of the woods or this or that legendary event that happened nearby. It's a noble venture, to be sure, but generally a futile one unless your daddy grew up with the likes of Jesse James or John Dillinger and has a steel-trap memory.

A historical article won't sell if it's *only* about something that happened a long time ago. It must also meet all the criteria we detailed earlier for profile, personal experience and informative articles. (History can also be fodder for humor.) It must, therefore:

> tell about events or people of interest to thousands or even millions of readers,
> focus on a single aspect of the subject,
> be organized logically (usually chronologically in this case),
> tell readers (and editors) something substantial they didn't already know,
> and tell it in an exciting fashion.

To have discovered some previously unheard-of person or event is *not* reason enough to write a historical article—not if you expect to see it published. If that previously unheard-of person or event involved something terribly funny, dangerous or historically significant, then you might be able to sell the piece.

When Frank was researching cartoonists, he discovered Louis Raemaekers. Attracted to the man's art and his caustic perspective on World War I, he started collecting Raemaekers's lithographed cartoons. Suddenly it occurred to him that if he'd never known about Raemaekers before, maybe a lot of readers didn't either. That proved true—but it wasn't salable. What *was* salable was Frank's unearthing the fact that many credited the little-known artist with having started Belgium's involvement in World War I. Because Raemaekers fit the requirements for a historical article, Frank was able to sell a story with this angle to *Mankind* magazine.

The national history magazines such as *History* and *American Heritage,* and the regional magazines of history, are natural buyers for historicals—but they're an overcrowded marketplace. Magazines of more general interest also buy history if its subject fits into a publication's framework. When Frank re-read Jules Verne's *From the Earth to the Moon* and noticed many parallels to real rocket launches, he sold *Science & Mechanics* "Who Planned Apollo II, Von Braun or Verne?" *(Ill. 5.15).*

Illus. 5.15. First Historical Article Excerpt

Who Planned Apollo II, Von Braun or Verne?

The space vehicle was just a nautical mile or two in the distance. All hearts on deck of the recovery ship paused for the duration of this momentous voyage. Breathing stopped as the small boats put out for the craft just returned from its trip around the moon. The Pacific Ocean itself seemed subdued and awestruck.

And as one recovery boat drew near, all ears cocked to catch a sound of life. What momentous scientific lore would the three intrepid space travelers be discussing at a moment such as this?

"Queen! How is that for high?" a nasal voice broke the calm with its twang.

It was followed by an even shriller response, cloaked in a bit of an accent. "King! My brave Mac! How is that for high?"

"Ace!" came still a third response. "Dear friends, how is that for high?"

High-Low-Jack! The three astronauts were so preoccupied with their game of high-low-jack they hadn't noticed the recovery vessels steaming toward them. A rousing game of cards was quite a fitting ending for a space voyage conjectured back in 1865 by none other than Jules Verne.

On their way to the moon, Verne managed to stow some very exquisite chow on board the space capsule *Columbiad,* including bottles of vintage wine like Chateau Yques and Clos de Vougeot. When Aldrin, Collins and Armstrong set out a century later for the same celestial body, the menu was hardly less exquisite than Jules Verne concocted for his three imaginary astronauts.

Colonel Collins, for instance, radioed back: "My compliments to the chef. That salmon salad is outstanding." Scalloped potatoes, shrimp cocktail and butterscotch pudding accompanied the three 20th century hardies on their way, but no wine. And no deck of cards.

In researching another story, Frank discovered an obscure but well-documented old book telling about African explorers who'd made it to America before Columbus. From that start, he discovered twenty-three other explorers who had probably touched North America before old Chris. That year, editors at the Metropolitan Sunday Newspaper Group presented a unique Columbus Day offering: "Goodby, Columbus, To No. 1" *(Ill. 5.16)*.

Illus. 5.16. Second Historical Article Excerpt

Goodby, Columbus, To No. 1

Everybody knows Columbus discovered America, and the year was 1492. But was he the first "foreigner" to land in the New World or was he, as some historians reckon, about the 25th to discover America? And there are always new claims popping up, like Chinese claims of landings somewhere in Mexico around the year 1 A.D., and reports of various Polynesian drifters who might have gone eastward beyond Hawaii.

Since Columbus Day is near, it might be interesting to put together some of the accounts of prior discovery, which are more or less documented by more or less responsible sources.

The Vikings landed in the New World five centuries before Columbus. Eric the Red, former bodyguard to the Norwegian King, had a fight with his boss and fled to Iceland. From there, he sailed westward in 982, landing on then virgin Greenland. Like Columbus, Eric thought himself the first man to set foot in North America.

In 986, a Viking named Bjarni Herjulfsson made a wrong turn on his way to join Eric in Greenland and sailed all the way to Cape Cod before turning back. Seventeen years later, Leif Ericson, Eric's son, borrowed Bjarni's boat and led an expedition which landed on Nantucket. Leif wanted to settle there eventually but died before he could return from his Viking homeland.

Eric the Red's other son, Thorwald Ericsson, also borrowed Bjarni's boat and spent several happy years living among friends he took with him to Nantucket. The Ericsson family really didn't have to borrow boats, being well-to-do, but the Norsemen were a superstitious lot. Since Bjarni's boat had made the trip once, the sailors decided fate would guide it there again. And it did. In 1007, Thorwald's luck finally ran out when he was slain by unfriendly Indians.

Right where Wall Street is today,

Thorfinn Karlsefni, another Norwegian, formed in 1010 what he hoped would be a permanent colony. A son, Snorri, was born there a year later. However, in 1014 Wall Street went through such a rough winter that the Viking settlers decided to seek better environs.

Other Vikings, including a Norwegian bishop no less, visited various parts of New York, Rhode Island, Massachusetts and Nova Scotia right up to the time of Columbus. In 1362, a group of 30 Norwegian and Swedish hunters actually made it as far as Kensington, Minnesota, a part of the country still inhabited by latter-day Norwegians and Swedes. In 1898, a Minnesotan discovered "the Kensington Stone," a rocky tablet on which was inscribed accounts of the hardships the 14th Century settlers faced.

Irish fishermen reached the North American fishing banks in 1150, whereas their English counterparts didn't make it for another 330 years. Thomas Lloyd of Bristol, after finding good fishing in the New World, decided to make annual trips there between 1482 and 1491.

The Roundup

The roundup is a *collection,* really, of bits and pieces of information or anecdotes or quotations or opinions or recipes or anything else *from many sources* all tied together *with one theme.* We've reproduced pages from two of our own roundups as *(Ills. 5.17 and 5.18).*

Illus. 5.17. First Roundup Excerpt

10 Questions Patients Are Afraid to Ask About Cancer

When Duke University of North Carolina plugged in its statewide Cancer Hotline last May—the first widespread information service of its kind in the nation—it was immediately deluged with phone calls. Within the first few months there emerged a pattern of most-frequently asked questions: by and large, these were all ones the callers felt they couldn't ask their physicians.

Duke's Cancer Hotline is an offshoot of its Comprehensive Cancer Center, one of 17 federally funded ones established by the 1974 Amendment to the National Cancer Act. Through outreach programs to the surrounding communities, these Centers attempt to help the public understand and deal more effectively with cancer.

A number of the Centers have Hotlines, but Duke's is the first to serve an entire state. It is also the first to insist that a Center physician approve every answer.

The Hotline personnel at Duke discovered that ten kinds of questions head the most-frequently-asked list, and that in many cases it is the anonymity of the phone call that permits people to express the fears and overcome the shyness that prevents them from going right to their doctors with these problems.

These ten questions may be the very ones your patients don't want to ask you.

1. "Is cancer contagious?"
Many patients don't really understand what cancer is. But they feel they ought to, so they're too shy to admit their ignorance to their doctors. The misapprehension that cancer is contagious is due to the oft-quoted statistics about a person's being more likely to get cancer if a family member had the disease. An all-too-frequent question to the Hotline is, "A family member has cancer. What can the rest of us do to avoid it?"

2. "How rapid is 'rapid growth'?"
People speak of cancer as if it were one disease with one cure, while it is, of course, many kinds of diseases, each with its own pattern and each requiring unique treatment. For example, very few people realize that there are 42 different kinds of cells in the lungs alone, and that each kind can go haywire in its growth to make 42 different kinds of lung cancers; or that cancers of the blood and lymph systems are very different from bone cell cancers.

People are also confused about the role of cell growth in cancer. People hear talk of "growing cells" and "abnormal cell growth" in cancerous tissue, and many assume that all cell growth—certainly all abnormal cell growth—means cancer. The doctor must take the time to educate his patients so they understand that all our cells are constantly growing and that there are always a few abnormal cells in the body which are ordinarily destroyed by the body itself without outside intervention. The patient should understand what we mean when we say "uncontrolled growth" when referring to cancer.

Illus. 5.18. Second Roundup Excerpt (in the form of captions under photos)

High Schools of the Stars

Goldie Hawn
"All through high school I spent every afternoon in dance classes. I was a late bloomer, and not so pretty as my sister. I never clowned for my friends, and almost never had a date. I was—well, sort of small, underdeveloped. Boys didn't ask me out. Not that I really wanted to go, I wasn't really ready for it, but, uh, I sure wanted them to ask me."

Sally Struthers
"I overdid it in high school. I was an honor student, president of the girls' league, and head cheerleader. I would devise all the yells for our school events, even the wrestling matches. The thing I'm most proud of was forming the first girls' track team—we were so good, some of our girls even went to the junior Olympics. I also worked as a waitress after school, and

clerked in the drugstore on Saturdays. Why did I cram so much in? Well, I guess the busier you are, the less time you have to spend alone."

Muhammad Ali

"In high school the kids sometimes would make fun of me because I said I wanted to be a champion fighter. I guess I always liked attention and publicity; even then. I used to race the school bus 28 blocks, and beat it, that kind of thing. I guess I became the most popular kid in Central High School . . . but I was not the best student, because I saw fast there was no future for me in a high school education. As a matter of fact, I graduated with the lowest marks possible, not because I didn't study—which I didn't—but because I had other things to do. Boxing, for example, which even then made me feel like somebody different. I knew a lot of guys who had diplomas who were just laying around in the streets."

Peter Nero

"In four years at Music and Art, I once figured out, I rode 61,000 subway stops from Brooklyn to Harlem—and it was worth every stop. I'd leave home before seven in the morning, run three blocks to the elevated subway, and when I'd get to the end of the second block, if I saw that the train coming from the other direction hadn't reached the station yet, I knew I was going to make my train. If I missed that train, I knew I'd be late to school. School and subways, it was all tied together, an hour to get there and an hour to get home every day. They used to expect us to do three hours' homework and two hours' practicing our instrument each evening, and in addition I was earning money accompanying dance classes three times a week, three hours a night at 13 or 14, so high school was one long memory of being tired."

Editors love the roundup for three reasons:

1. It can often play up the *magic of numbers* in its title and on a cover line. The March 10, 2004, issue of *Parenting* magazine has two articles that depend on numbers: "10 Great Life Shapers" and "24 Easy Ways to Make Your Day Simpler." The October 2003 *Redbook* cover that we analyzed in Chapter 2 *(Ill. 2.1)* boasts "349 Money-Saving Secrets."

2. It can often play up the *magic of big names.* Our roundup for *Swank* magazine reproduced here, using quotes as captions for photos of the "High Schools of the Stars" *(Ill. 5.18),* dropped nine celebrities' names.

3. It can often play up the *magic of graphics and interesting layouts.* Although a flashy layout meant absolutely nothing to the doctor-readers of *Practical Psychology for Physicians,* to the editor of *Swank* the graphics were as important as the words. In fact, our assignment included getting pictures of the stars' high school buildings.

Writers, too, love a roundup—for the modest amount of writing time it takes to collect the same fee as any other article. (We find that a writer trying to produce a profile can consume days trying to coax a few hours from a celebrity who's hot at the moment. When you're doing a roundup, it's easy to get a star's public relations firm to come up with the few appropriate lines you need.) But, as with every pot of gold, there is a hidden crack. Good ideas for roundups are tough to keep dreaming up. That's because they have to stand the tests we laid down earlier for profiles, how-to's and informative articles. The numbers aspect can be used only to enhance an already salable idea.

The Photo Story

This is a bonus to our Ten Standard Formats. So many writers these days pack cameras alongside their portable computers that we think you ought to keep the photo story in mind as part of your marketing armada. Technically, it isn't a genre all by itself; it can be a personality piece, a bit of an exposé, a graphic approach to history, humor . . .

In this format, the writing is often less important than the photos—although no editor will object to good writing. But the photos themselves have to satisfy all the requirements for a good article. You must create a lead photo that hooks the reader and sets a tone for the rest of the photos. Your pictures have to be organized logically. The story has to have a concluding photo too.

When we suggested to *Popular Science* an article showing how homeowners could avoid painting their palaces more than once every ten years, the editors liked the idea. But, they suggested, instead of supplying the information first in words and again in pictures, why not do it only once through pictures with comprehensive captions? The result, our first pictorial how-to story, satisfied all the criteria of a how-to from the lead photo showing lab research underway down to the happy-ending photo of the almost completely painted house. Technical requirements preclude our reproducing the article here, but you can find it back in the May 1979 issue of *Popular Science*.

We don't have space here to cover photography thoroughly, and we've found that different photo editors have different requirements for photo submission. So we'll limit ourselves to a few of the major problems we've seen in the way beginners handle photo stories.

First, if your editor asks for digital photo submission your first question has to be, "Should I e-mail them to you or store them on a CD-ROM?" If the latter, you can set your camera to generate TIFF images because you can cram a hundred five-megabyte TIFF photos onto one CD. By e-mail, some editors may want compressed JPG files.

Second, with black-and-white photos, the 8 × 10-inch single-weight glossy or double-weight semigloss print is *the* standard. While some magazines accept smaller prints, submitting them is a giveaway that you're an amateur. With color, transparencies (35mm and 2¼-inch sizes) are standard; color prints are almost always the mark of an amateur.

Have the transparencies mounted in cardboard and slip the cardboard mounts into plastic protectors. With 35mm slides, the twenty-to-a-page plastic protector is standard. Be sure your name and a caption are on each slide. Some writers just number the slides and submit separate caption sheets keyed to the numbers. Ideally, you should do *both*.

Having been editors, we know the mayhem that prevails in editors' offices. So we always submit captions in duplicate (for black-and-white as well as color). We create a sheet of captions, and print three copies. We submit the original captions in manuscript format on 8½ × 11-inch paper. For black-and-white, we cut up the second copy and fasten each caption to the back of the appropriate picture with rubber cement or double-sided tape. (Regular Scotch tape is taboo. After a few years in the files, it sticks to the face of adjoining prints.) For color we submit the first and second copies, both uncut and keyed to numbers or letters penned on the photo sheets. The third copy goes into our file in case the editor loses the other two sets. After all, one way of advancing in this crazy career is to recognize that editors have problems too and to encourage them to rely on you to solve some of them.

6

The Four Elements
of a Good Article

IT MAY SEEM CONTRADICTORY THAT IN THIS BOOK FOR free spirits and idealists, we keep telling you, "Do this, don't do that." But the fact is, a set of classic article formats, elements and techniques has evolved over the years. Using them works to the advantage of everybody—writer, editor, reader. It makes writing—as well as reading—fun, fast and unfailing. It helps writer and reader walk together on familiar ground.

In your reading, you may never have consciously identified the four elements found in almost every good magazine article: lead, topic sentence, body, ending. But they're there. Most pros find it almost obligatory to use all four elements in all their articles, although any literary rule can be broken successfully by a pro who's studied her craft.

As an introduction to your study of the four elements, let's look at the reproduced part of the "Female Alcoholics" article Judi wrote for *New Dawn* magazine *(Ill. 6.1)*. As you read it, see if you can intuitively answer the following questions. Compare your answers with ours, provided at the end of this chapter.

1. How does Judi get the readers' attention and make them want to read her article?
2. What is the article about?
3. What approach does Judi take to the topic?
4. Where does Judi state her topic and slant?
5. What device does Judi use to lead the reader to want to know more about her topic?

Illus. 6.1. Article Lead, Topic Sentence, and Beginning of Body

Marie Neenan was a trusted legal secretary. She handled confidential files, important memos, and even, at times, large amounts of money. Her bosses never knew that sometimes she worked in a total blackout, unable to remember afterward what she'd done in her alcoholic stupor.

Pat Frye seemed like any other young mother, wheeling her baby carriage to the corner deli to have lunch with a friend. But that lunch was often four hours long and almost totally beer, and then she'd *weave* her carriage home, not wheel it.

These women are alcoholics. Although

they haven't touched a drop in more than a decade, they know that they are uncontrollably addicted to alcohol—that one sip of anything harder than a Coke might send them right back to the hell out of which they dragged themselves.

Women alcoholics have always been around. It may be worse nowadays; one study suggests that the number of *known* female alcoholics has doubled in the last thirty years. Or it may be simply that women aren't hiding at home so much anymore—that, as alcoholism counselor Ruth Maxwell (formerly with the Smithers Alcoholism Rehabilitation Center of Roosevelt Hospital in New York, and now a consultant to business and industry in setting up alcoholism pretreatment programs) suggests, now that women are working more, they are more easily recognized. At any rate, it's now an accepted fact that *just as many women are prone to alcoholism as are men.* Since one out of ten is an alcoholic, it may have already enmeshed *four million women* including you or your best friend. And the only way to defend against its ravages is to understand what it is and how it affects us.

The Lead

If you were to launch an expensive research project to locate the single trait that predicts the success of a magazine writer's career, we bet you'd find that trait to be the caliber of the writer's leads. The lead is built into the very first one or more paragraphs of an article. It's the article's jumping-off point, the bait that hooks both reader *and* editor into reading on into your story. A good lead (sometimes called a *hook*) is the best selling tool there is. It usually makes its sales pitch in one or more of three ways:

It brings a subject to life for the reader.
It intrigues, excites or startles the reader.
It appeals to the reader's emotions.

We can still tell you how we stumbled onto each of our best leads. We still wince remembering the story or two we turned in without a great lead, after every trick in the book failed to produce a beginning that grabbed and shook. Every professional magazine writer we know can pick up an article and know instinctively, "That's a great lead!" or "Boy, what a washout of a lead!" But ask precisely why it's great or a washout and you're likely to hear a minute of unbroken stammering.

Don't ask most fine writers *how* to create a great lead, either. Most likely, they do it instinctively. We've grabbed a random stack of old magazines and, leafing through them, found ten articles by writer friends—all members of the American Society of Journalists and Authors—whose fine leads continue to illustrate the various approaches that can be taken. (If you want to know what the editors ended up titling the articles, check the end of the chapter.)

APPROACH 1—BRING THE SUBJECT TO LIFE

The easiest way to get the reader involved in your subject is to bring it to life for him. The writer's tool for doing that is most often the *anecdote,* a little story that illustrates one of the article's points.

So many top writers lead off with an anecdote that we like to think of it as the magician's rabbit of our profession. In Judi's article on female alcoholics *(Ill. 6.1),* her first three paragraphs seem to be about two women whom almost none of the readers has ever heard of. Yet readers know instinctively that the article is not about either woman per se; that their stories are a lively, personal, exciting way to get Judi's article rolling. Being experienced, Judi knows she'll hook her readers with that lead, that they'll read further to learn more about Marie and Pat.

Flora Davis's *Woman's Day* piece on how to cope with stress *(Ill. 6.2),* Lee Edson's true-life drama about an infant burn victim *(Ill. 6.3),* and Jack Galub's very practical information about how to prevent drowning *(Ill. 6.4)* all make effective use of anecdotes for leads.

A lead can include one anecdote or several. Often, the writer chooses the most dramatic examples uncovered by research. That's the case in Jack's lead but not in Flora's. She opted not for drama but for greatest likelihood of grabbing the average reader's attention. And Lee was bound by the need to use almost strictly chronological organization. Still, he pulled off a beginning that grabs. In all three examples, the selected leads do the job of bringing the subjects—stress, burns, drowning—vividly to life. They say, "It's happened to somebody." They imply, "It could happen to you."

Illus. 6.2. First Lead

By Flora Davis

Sarah has a job on Wall Street that's one long crisis from nine to five. By the end of the week she's worn out. Her husband is worried about her and wants Sarah to look for less demanding work. "He says I'm under too much pressure," she said, "and that stress can make you sick. But I love my job. I don't want to give it up."

Like so many people, Sarah wants it all: a life crammed to the brim with work, family, fun. And like others, she's concerned about stress. In recent years researchers have concluded that stress can contribute to various medical problems—heart disease, high blood pressure, ulcers, asthma, headaches and more. Even the common cold is sometimes included in the list. The theory is that stress breaks down your natural defenses so you fall prey to every virus that comes along.

Illus. 6.3. Second Lead

By Lee Edson

It was a snowy January morning in 1978. Having been up most of the night, Linda Short could barely keep her eyes open, but she would not give in to sleep as she watched over her eight-year-old daughter, Rena. The child was swathed in blankets in the emergency ward at Dorchester General Hospital in Maryland. The young resident doctor and local pediatrician who examined Rena agreed that the little girl needed to be moved immediately to a larger facility—to Baltimore City Hospital.

The doctors tried not to upset Linda (she had already been through an overwhelming ordeal), but they felt they had to be truthful. "Rena is badly burned," they told her. "If she lives two weeks, she may make it, but she'll be lucky to live two weeks."

Linda looked down at the tiny discolored doll that was her daughter. In her overfatigued state, different images came and went. Some were dreamlike; others, she knew, were all too real.

Illus. 6.4. Third Lead with Topic Sentence

By Jack Galub

The child was found unconscious in a backyard pool. She had been underwater for possibly 15 minutes. Resuscitation efforts failed. But minutes after being given up for dead, the drowned two-year-old began to breathe. Sixteen hours later, she recognized her mother and spoke to her. A two-year follow-up showed the child growing normally, with no sign of brain damage.

An 18-year-old drove off a country road and crashed to the bottom of a 10-foot-deep, iced-over pond. Lifted out of the water 38 minutes later, he gasped spontaneously despite no detectable life signs. Intensive resuscitation efforts by a team of doctors started his heart beating. After two weeks, he returned to college, continuing as an A student.

These lives were saved by the "mammalian diving reflex"—an involuntary reaction developed by whales, seals, porpoises, sea lions and other animals that remain under water for extended periods of time. The reflex is present in all mammals, and recent discoveries confirm that it can operate in some human beings, especially those under age 20 when they are plunged facedown into cold water.

While the reflex is operating, water does not enter the lungs; blood circulates slowly between the brain, lungs and heart. A person undergoing the reflex may give every physical appearance of being dead—no discernible pulse, no breathing, blue skin, pupils dilated—and yet may not be dead. And such a person may be revived with *no lasting impairment of mind or body* after a much longer period than has been expected.

Such new knowledge has stimulated an intensive study of water-related accidents and has led to important new first-aid rules for drowning victims.

APPROACH 2——INTRIGUE, EXCITE, OR STARTLE THE READER

Nothing hooks readers faster than a question that asks something they've always wondered about. Next best is to ask something they've never wondered about in such a way that they suddenly wonder *why* they never wondered about it. In general, people are accustomed to looking for answers in their magazine reading. They seem to pay special attention when confronted with a question in an article's lead.

National writing award-winner Bonnie Remsberg begins her classic *Ladies' Home Journal* article *(Ill. 6.5)*—whose title promises answers about love and sex for the reader—with a question asking why couples rarely talk about sex. Her lead segues into her topic when she asks three more questions. Is it effective? We sure think so.

Illus. 6.5. Fourth Lead and Topic Sentence

By Bonnie Remsberg

Why is it so often true that the most intimate side of the relationship between a woman and a man is the one they talk about least? A tricky question, almost certainly with as many answers as there are marriages. But the fact remains that most couples, even when the marriage seems fine, can talk about everything—except their love life. Things can go along quite well this way for as long as both partners feel satisfied. But what if one or both of them want things to be different? How can they solve a problem they can't talk about?

To meet the needs of men and women who want their lovemaking to be the best it can be, a new breed of specialist has emerged—the sex therapist. Sex therapists, some of whom are psychologists, some psychiatrists, some gynecologists, are treating couples of all ages who have all kinds of sex problems. And they're doing so with great success.

What, the *Journal* wondered, are these experts learning, not only about troubled marriages, but about flourishing ones as well? What, specifically, leads people to seek their help? And in what ways can the knowledge and expertise of reputable sex therapists benefit even the most contented couple? To find out, we initiated a cross-country search to talk to, and learn from, the leading practitioners of this new, important and growing field.

Claire Safran starts her lead with three questions, writing for *Redbook (Ill. 6.6),* a magazine where she was once an editor and whose audience she therefore knew well. She could be sure these were questions her readers asked their own children. Why? Because she'd seen lots of parents play this game.

Illus. 6.6. Fifth Lead with Topic Sentence and Beginning of Body

By Claire Safran

"Where are your eyes? Your nose? Your toes?" In the little games we parents play with our young children we teach them about their bodies. In the ways we dress them, clean them, comfort them and hold them, we show them how highly we value and how deeply we care for those bodies.

And that is sex education—or the simplest and most important part of sex education. A mother may not think of it that way, but her hugs and kisses are the ABC's of the physiology of sex, a child's early lessons in physical pleasure and in feeling good about her body. The free flow of affection between parent and child is also a course in the sociology of sex, in what loving, caring and relating are all about.

There are other parts of the curriculum, though, and few people are at ease with all of them. The burgeoning sexuality of young children is rarely talked about. When it is discussed, there is confusion about what it means and how to deal with it. So a mother may feel uncomfortable, oddly disturbed in spite of all she's read, when she sees her young son exploring his body. Or a father may half enjoy, half worry about the ways his little daughter flirts with him. Even for parents who feel free and uninhibited in their own sexuality, the notion of their child as a sexual being can be discomfiting.

Today it is especially difficult for parents to be sex educators. Social change is everywhere. New ideas clamor to be sorted out. Old rules are challenged. For parents who want to raise their children to be at ease with their sexuality, there are few models to follow.

Across the country, doctors have as many questions as parents do, and they are finding many of the answers in a growing body of neonatal research. In recent years pediatricians, psychiatrists and researchers have been interviewing parents in depth and observing young children at their most intimate, unguarded moments. They are trying to fill in one of the last great gaps in our knowledge of human sexuality— the sexual behavior and feelings of young children. And many of the answers to parents' and doctors' questions can be found in the new insights researchers now have about what is *natural*.

It is helpful to know how the drama of sexuality unfolds for most children.

The scenario of sexuality begins at birth, if not before. Feeding, cuddling, touching and being touched—these activities may not seem strictly "sexual" but they are the ways a child learns to feel comfortable—or uncomfortable—about her body and her identity. According to Dr. Veronica B. Tisza, lecturer in psychiatry at

Harvard Medical School, "If parents don't hug, hold and admire the child with their hands, their eyes, their mouths, then the child may be deprived in a number of ways, including sexually."

Readers, editors, and even writers like to puzzle over paradoxes of all kinds. These, too, make intriguing leads. Alan Haas's *Science Digest* paradox is posed in question form *(Ill. 6.7)*. His lead also startles the reader with facts and figures—in this case, large sums of money. After doing all his research, the New York pro organized his article on antique cars so that his flashiest data could be shown off up front. Then he used both question and startling statement to hook his readers into wanting to know more.

Illus. 6.7. Sixth Lead with Topic Sentence and Beginning of Body

By Alan D. Haas

If you had purchased it in 1972 for $50,000 you could have sold it currently for $235,000. What is it?

A Picasso or other modern painting? A Russian sable fur, a rare diamond or postage stamp, a mansion in Beverly Hills, several gold bricks?

No; none of these. The answer: an eight-cylinder, 1932 Duesenberg Phaeton SJ-261 vintage automobile, sold at auction in the Midwest for this astonishing price—highest dollars ever paid for a classic American car.

According to Frank (Skip) Marketti, director of the Auburn-Cord-Duesenberg Museum in Auburn, Indiana, where the auction took place, "Duesenbergs have increased at least 20 percent in value each year for the past ten years." This particular Duesenberg appreciated even more because its owner, Ed Lucas, an engineer in Detroit, spent thousands of hours lovingly restoring it to its original beauty.

What was formerly a hobby, the collecting of Locomobiles, Cords, Bugattis, Isotta Fraschinis, for the pleasure of owning, tinkering with, or simply admiring these splendid machines of the past, has, in the past decade, become a bonanza for knowledgeable car freaks.

For instance: A 1928 Mercedes-Benz SSK roadster worth $25,000 in 1968 would, in today's market, bring around $200,000. A 1925 Isotta Fraschini Type 8A Tourer, with a value of 38,500 a decade ago, would fetch $80,000 now.

The late Marvin Grosswirth's use of paradox *(Ill. 6.8)*, in his *Science Digest* article (one of a series he developed explaining little understood popular terms), is straightforward intrigue. Marvin knew that most people don't know much about osteopaths—which is why he suggested the story to editor Daniel

Button in the first place. To hook his readers, he startled them with three simple paradoxes. His three-paragraph lead looks so obvious it seems anyone could have written it; yet it took a top pro to recognize instinctively that within all the data he had collected about osteopaths there lay three paradoxes that would make any reader want to know more.

Illus. 6.8. Seventh Lead with Topic Sentence

By Marvin Grosswirth

An osteopath is a fully recognized, fully licensed physician—but he is not an M.D.

He has been trained in the art of manipulative therapy—but he is not a chiropractor.

The number of osteopaths increases every year—but they are nevertheless in danger of becoming invisible.

Approximately ten percent of all people who visit physicians' offices go to osteopaths, but many of them are unaware of any difference between a Doctor of Medicine (M.D.) and a Doctor of Osteopathy (D.O.) But there is one, and the osteopathic profession is determined to preserve it.

Basically, that difference may be described as the allopathic approach to medicine as compared to the holistic approach. *Allopathic* medicine—practiced by most M.D.'s—treats a particular disease or condition. *Holistic* medicine treats the entire organism.

A really powerful quote can also make an exciting, intriguing article lead. David Zimmerman chose a mother's candid remarks about her test-tube baby to lead off his *Woman's Day* article *(Ill. 6.9)*. David couldn't have dreamed up an opening more dramatic than this mother's quote. But it took a sensitive writer to give the quote its context—and its excitement—by artfully adding the phrase "first baby ever conceived outside a woman's body."

Illus. 6.9. Eighth Lead with Topic Sentence

By David Zimmerman

"Dear God, she's so lovely," exulted Lesley Brown, as she held her daughter, Louise, the first baby ever conceived outside a woman's body. "She's so beautiful, and she's mine!"

For Lesley, Louise's birth last July is a personal miracle. Without *in vitro fertilization,* the so-called test-tube baby procedure through which Louise was conceived in a laboratory dish, Lesley was hopelessly infertile. She lacks fallopian tubes, the organs in which conception normally occurs.

The birth of baby Louise has wider meaning, however. The in vitro method is one of three dramatic experimental procedures that represent a scientific revolution in the treatment of infertility. They offer real hope, for the first time, that millions of childless women one day will carry and deliver babies of their own.

APPROACH 3—APPEAL DIRECTLY TO THE READER'S EMOTIONS

Though both foregoing types of leads appeal to the reader's emotions, neither is a direct appeal. But look at Michael Frome's *Woman's Day* travel story *(Ill. 6.10)*. Mike chose to begin his article ostensibly by appealing to the reader's *interest* in being like "women on the go." But read more closely; his appeal is to her *concern* about traveling alone. Appeal to the emotions, Mike knew, is much more of a hook than appeal to intellectual interest.

His second paragraph reinforces the concern he has generated by flashing specific visual images of conceivable situations—a sick friend far away, a business trip, a prize vacation, a dream getaway from women's cares and concerns. Notice the hidden emotional appeal of all these instances. It's all part of his lead.

Illus. 6.10. Ninth Lead

By Michael Frome

Like practically every woman on the go these days, at some time or other you may find yourself traveling alone.

You may be called to stay with a sick friend or a relative in a distant state. Or you may be sent out of town by your company on a ten-day business trip. Or your husband may be tied up with work just when you win a free ticket to Tijuana. Or you may just plain want to throw caution—cooking, cleaning, dirty dishes and diapers—to the wind and find out once and for all what it's really like to wing it on your own.

What's standing in your way? Nothing, according to travel experts, who maintain that with the new liberated attitudes and lifestyles—not to mention the growing number of singles across the country (close to forty-four million, according to latest totals, or about one fifth of all households)—more and more women are not merely traveling on their own, but wondering why it took them so long to give it a try.

The advantages, of course, are obvious. You can move at your own pace, shopping and sightseeing at will, waking up at the crack of dawn or sleeping late till noon, without having to worry about keeping someone else waiting or, worse yet, having to wait yourself. If you've always wanted to see New York and your husband has his eye on Los Angeles, you can both get your wish: Split for a week, then when you get back, put your heads together over a cup of coffee and compare notes.

If you've never had to learn about financial matters, you can get a first-hand crack at making reservations, booking flights, renting cars, using credit cards and tipping that will stand you in good stead not just when you're out on the road but once you get home. And best of all, you can acquire a new sense of independence, a stronger self-confidence and a broader range of experience and friendships that should endure for the rest of your life.

The Topic Sentence

It is important to let readers know early just what you plan to talk about in your article so they don't expect something more or something different from what you're prepared to deliver. Disappointing readers—especially disappointing editor-readers—leads to loss of sales. The place to announce (or imply) your topic is in your topic sentence, which almost always comes right after the lead.

We mentioned in Chapter 2 that there are two aspects to every topic. The *focus,* or objective parameter, is always part of the topic sentence. The *slant,* or subjective approach—your point of view toward the topic—may be stated in the topic sentence, or implied there, or not even mentioned at all but revealed between the lines as the article unfolds.

A topic sentence may be a phrase or it may be several sentences long. It can be as simple and obvious as the "now I will talk about" topic sentences in your school essays, or it can be disguised in a quote, question or statistic. It may be smoothly sewn onto the end of the lead, stand by itself, or begin the next paragraph. In some magazines it's echoed in the title; in other magazines the title may have nothing to do with it. (We stripped the editors' titles from these excerpts so that you wouldn't be falsely led into believing they echoed the articles' topic sentences.)

Novice writers whose titles contain their topics often forget to include a topic sentence. Pros, who know that editors often change titles, leave nothing to chance.

In Judi's article on female alcoholism *(Ill. 6.1),* her topic sentence is found in the first part of her fourth paragraph. It narrows the focus from alcoholism (too broad a topic for three thousand words) to female alcoholism (still a broad topic) and further to "what it is and how it affects us." It also promises to help readers "to defend against its ravages"—the *slant.* By telling readers, right after they're hooked, precisely what they're getting into, she avoids having to explain the purpose for each of her many statements and examples as they are introduced in the body of her article. And readers, spared from having to wade through dull, repetitive exposition, can still follow her points readily. Unless Judi tells them otherwise, they will know that every one of her sentences refers to what female alcoholism is and how it affects them so they can guard against it.

In every article shown in our discussion of leads, the author uses some kind of topic sentence. Studying them reveals several different techniques for weaving them smoothly into the text.

Claire Safran *(Ill. 6.6)* has a long lead in which she says parents do give their children some basic sex education. But then she uses a paradox ("The burgeoning sexuality of young children is rarely talked about") for transition into her topic sentence: "It is helpful to know how the drama of *sexuality unfolds for most children*" (the topic and focus).

Often the topic sentence is contained in a separate paragraph. In his traveling-alone article *(Ill. 6.10)*, Mike Frome does the unorthodox. He postpones that paragraph for several more hundred words. If you look up his article (see the end of this chapter for reference data) it's the paragraph beginning, "Planning a trip alone, in short, calls for some groundwork." For Frome, this long postponement works. For novices, it's a risky procedure.

Alan Haas *(Ill. 6.7)* uses a full sentence for his topic sentence beginning "What was formerly a hobby, the collecting of Locomobiles" and ending with exactly what it is about those old gas buggies (his focus) he's chosen to highlight: "a bonanza for knowledgeable car freaks" (his slant).

Marvin Grosswirth's and David Zimmerman's topic sentences are simple, obvious and straightforward. They limit the focus of the topics about to be discussed so they're manageable yet lively. David's topic sentence *(Ill. 6.9)* says he'll show "three dramatic experimental procedures that represent a scientific revolution in the treatment of infertility." He sets the slant of the article, too: "They offer real hope." Marvin's, after stating that people don't know if there's a difference between an M.D. and a O.D. *(Ill. 6.8)*, adds his slant: "but there is one" and the rest of his article explains that big difference.

In her love-and-sex-questions article *(Ill. 6.5)*, Bonnie Remsberg needs a very long topic paragraph to establish her framework. Instead of cutting corners (and possibly leaving her readers uncertain of the article's parameters), she prevents the long paragraph from getting dull by casting her slant into questions, a sure-fire device for exciting readers. She begins, "*What*, the Journal wondered, *are these experts learning,* not only about troubled marriages, but about flourishing ones as well?" After posing two more topic questions, Bonnie promises readers they'll get the answers if they read on. But she does it with the subtlety of a real pro: "To find out, we initiated a cross-country search to talk to, and learn from, the leading practitioners of this new, important and growing field" (sex therapy, which is the topic).

For her lead *(Ill. 6.2)*, Flora Davis uses an anecdote: the story of Sarah. Her topic sentence has to change the focus of readers' attention from Sarah to the entire, loosely defined population included in her story about stress. See how smoothly she makes the transition while establishing the parameters of her story.

We've underlined the transition: "<u>Like so many people</u>, Sarah wants it all: a life crammed to the brim. . . . And <u>like others</u>, she's concerned about stress." Topic and slant are the part not underlined: living a full life while managing stress.

Jack Galub's one-page water safety article *(Ill. 6.2)* opens with two anecdotes that lead into a long explanation of the "new knowledge" he wants readers to understand, because their acceptance of "new knowledge" paves the way for his topic sentence. It's the last part of the last sentence in his long introduction: "important new first-aid rules [topic] for drowning victims [slant]." Why not just offer his water-safety tips with no lead and no topic sentence? Because without the focus given by the topic sentence and the illustrations offered in the lead, the reader may well take a fast peek, think, "There's nothing here I didn't already know," and flip the page. (If the editor thinks the reader will do that with *your* article, he won't run it in the first place.)

The Body: Development of Your Slant

To comprehend fully how you get meat onto the body of an article—that long section between beginning and end—you must understand the techniques that every professional writer learns to use. A thorough explanation takes up all of Chapter 7. Here we'll explain in depth just that elusive quality so many beginners have trouble tying down—the article's *slant*.

We defined slant along with focus when discussing the topic sentence because, as we said, it's sometimes summed up there. However, when it comes to writing the body, there's no choice for the writer: the slant must pervade its every paragraph.

Because the novice confuses slant and focus, we'll redefine them once again:

Focus is *what* you're writing about. It's sometimes called the *handle* or *theme*.
Slant (sometimes called *approach*) is *how* you write about it. It's the author's viewpoint and it's essential to every article.

But if an author slants an article, what happens to objectivity, that foremost essential of good writing?

To answer that, we must define *objectivity* more precisely than it's been defined in school. Objectivity in magazine writing is not the bland, unbiased presentation of both sides of every issue. Objectivity is, instead, fairness, the sharing with readers of viewpoints opposing the writer's own *where they are significant*. (Obviously, they are more significant when dealing with whether children should be taught about sex than when writing about your depressing trip to China.) It permits readers to disagree with the author's viewpoint—but lets readers know clearly what that viewpoint is.

Many people become writers because they want to make their viewpoints more widely known. Most of us choose article slants that coincide with our viewpoints. However, even when we suggest an article about which we have no strong viewpoint, we make value judgments throughout: what's to be included and what left out, what's to be highlighted as more important and what given little space, what's to be dramatized and what merely announced. The basis for our value judgments—our slant—must, in all fairness, be shared with our readers. In marketing our idea, we must recognize that its slant is as important to the editor as the topic itself. He may not want an article whose slant—too radical or too conservative—will anger his readers.

When we wrote about new developments in geodesic-dome housing for *Popular Science (Ill. 5.8)*, we had no strong feelings for or against dome homes. *Should we allow dome homes or not?* was not a social issue. Still, after doing our preliminary research, we formed several subjective criteria that carried over into our query and then into our article. We gave greater emphasis to contractor-built domes than to do-it-yourself dome kits. We pointed out that building departments were finally okaying domes rather than relating incidents where domes were running into code problems. We chose to include, albeit with an editorial grain of salt, the anecdotes, unsubstantiated by scientific research, suggesting that domes are cheaper to heat than traditional houses. We signaled our slant in the last line of our lead-cum-topic paragraph. After warning of our provisos—"Thus far, however, the geodesic dome has proved too kinky to appeal to the masses of home buyers, too unproven to merit mortgages from conservative bankers, too unorthodox to satisfy zoning and building codes"—we announced our hopeful, optimistic, yet vaguely hesitant slant: "But now all that may be changing."

When we sold *Popular Science* on the dome-home story idea, we let them know our slant. We opened the query with, "Until we went to two home shows in the area recently, we never realized how readily available—and practical—the Bucky Fuller dome home has become." Further on we focused our stance more: "Frankly, they're not for just anybody. . . . They seem ideal for a second home, or a first home for the artsy or environment-oriented small family; for a home that you need erected in a hurry, or a place you can enjoy with a minimum of overhead." When *Popular Science* assigned the article, they knew not only what facts and figures we intended to present, but also the sort of coloration our presentation would have.

Pro or con? Moderate or extreme? Reasoned or impassioned? Writers don't often tell editors baldly, "My slant will be . . ." but they make that slant clear when marketing. We're sure that clarifying our slant impressed *Popular Science* a great deal more than just writing, "We'd like to tell your readers about dome homes."

One time in particular, our slant was crucial to a sale. A lawyer we knew was advocating that rape victims immediately hire lawyers, a radical idea at the time. Any editor hearing that focus without our slant would have figured the lawyer was being self-serving and would have refused the article. In our query to *Viva's* Ernie Baxter, we spelled out that our slant was twofold: to help put more rapists behind bars and to help ease some of the agony of rape victims. It was exactly the slant Ernie needed to be able to run an article on rape. Imagine how readers would have received that article if it had "objectively" given the rapists' side of the story equal space.

The Ending

When you've said everything there is to say, it's not enough simply to stop writing. When the time comes to end your article, it's important to create a proper *ending*—the fourth essential element in a magazine article.

The ending leaves readers feeling that the article has come to a successful, satisfying conclusion. This is not to say that you must save your conclusions about your subject for the ending. The general pros and cons of your topic are most often suggested by the focus and slant messages of your topic paragraph. The ending is a reiteration, a summation, or even in some cases a statement that there is more to be learned or to be said than the reader has been told.

But we can save a full treatment of endings until we get into Chapter 13, and a full-blown discussion of the mechanics of writing an article. In selling your idea, you'll rarely need to discuss how it's going to end.

Answers to 5 Questions Regarding Ill. 6.1

1. By describing two ordinary young women who sometimes do strange things.
2. The topic is alcoholism in women.
3. The slant is how to defend against it by understanding what it is and how it affects us.
4. Topic and slant are stated at the end of the excerpt.
5. Judi uses two anecdotes, statistics and a quotation from an authority.

Titles of Articles Illustrated in This Chapter

Ill. 6.1 "Female Alcoholics," *New Dawn,* October 1976.
Ill. 6.2. "How to Live with STRESS and Thrive," *Woman's Day,* May 22, 1979.
Ill. 6.3. "Doctors Call Her the Miracle Girl," *Family Circle,* June 26, 1979.

Ill. 6.4. "Summer Water Safety—Amazing New Facts That Can Save Your Life," *Family Circle,* June 26, 1979.

Ill. 6.5. "Love and Sex: The 10 Most Often Asked Questions," *Ladies Home Journal,* July 1979.

Ill. 6.6. "How Children Feel About Their Bodies," *Redbook,* June 1979.

Ill. 6.7. "For Fun and Profit (Lots) Buy That Bonanza V8 Convertible or a '55 Goldmine Coupe," *Science Digest.* March 1979.

Ill. 6.8. "What Is a . . . Doctor of Osteopathy?" *Science Digest,* March 1979.

Ill. 6.9. "Are Test-Tube Babies the Answer for the Childless?" *Woman's Day,* May 22, 1979.

Ill. 6.10. "Traveling Alone," *Woman's Day,* August 7, 1979.

7

The Three Standard
Writing Techniques

NOW THAT YOU KNOW THERE ARE ONLY FOUR ELE-
ments to every article—lead, topic sentence, body and ending—we
hope you are beginning to see the skeleton of every article you read (and write).
To put some flesh on that skeleton, the magazine writer can use only three basic techniques, the same three available to nonfiction book authors, short-story
writers and novelists: anecdote, quotation and exposition.

When an author sees something happen and narrates it for readers, that's
an *anecdote,* the magazine writer's name for narration. When an author hears
something worth repeating and repeats it in writing, that's a *quotation,* the magazine writer's equivalent of dialogue. When an author *thinks* something and
reports it to readers, backing it up with facts to prove it, that's *exposition.*

Anecdotes

Everybody loves a good story. Who can pass up a chance to hear a juicy tale
about the next-door neighbors? And what's more exciting than a small bit of innocent eavesdropping? In lively magazine writing, too, little narratives—anecdotes—provide the juice. They are used with abundance in nearly every standard magazine format.

Many of our students start out confused not only about how to use anecdotes but about how to recognize them. So let's lead off with a good working
definition.

> An anecdote is a complete story in miniature.
> It has a beginning and an ending.
> It takes place in a particular setting and that scene usually has to be described in
> brief.
> It depicts a real person or real people.
> Time passes or the people move about.
> Something happens to the people—or they make something happen.
> The setting, action, dialogue and/or narrative contained in the anecdote make a
> point that belongs in the article.

The anecdote is the second most useful tool of a successful magazine writer. (The first is the lead. Writers are fond of anecdotal leads because they know that the combination is a powerhouse.) Effectively used, it *takes the place* of exposition, which is the laying out of your facts. It not only whets reader interest by spinning a yarn about interesting people in interesting settings doing interesting things, but it conveys some of the information the reader needs in order to understand the point of your article. If, instead of writing that Mount Kilimanjaro is nineteen thousand feet high, you tell readers about a sixteen-year-old cheerleader from Secaucus, New Jersey, who climbed all nineteen thousand feet of that mountain to deliver homemade brownies to a guru, the reader is much more likely to remember that mountain's height. If you tell how a machine saved a person's life, that's a story that will glue readers to the page. If you merely describe the dials and wires inside the machine, that's no story at all.

Two chapters ago, we reproduced the first two pages of our *Family Health* story on CAT scanners *(Ill. 5.7)* as an example of the informative article format. Our article had to inform the reader about price, size, theory of operation, duration of a scan and medical benefits. Most important, though, the article had to grab readers and hold them. So we put absolutely every piece of information into a beginning anecdote that told the experience of one man. Just look at how much we got across: that CAT scanners are new, that CAT scanning is painless, that traditional X-rays have trouble distinguishing between healthy and diseased soft tissue—and why. We also told what the machine looks like and gave a patient's-eye view of how it works.

We've reproduced some pages from the same CAT scanner article *(Ill. 7.1)*, bracketed each of the anecdotes and marked them *A* for Anecdote in the margin. The first anecdote relates how the machine was developed. The next describes the plight of thirty children born too soon to benefit from CAT scanners but promises the possible prevention of similar misery in children born today. That mini-story also tells the reader that there are several forms of infant brain damage. The third anecdote is a true, dramatic story about a four-year-old boy whose brain has been saved by a scan. (Notice the interweaving of hard facts about radiation danger in using CATs.)

Anecdote number four isn't just a story about a boy in a life-and-death drama: it informs about the CAT's TV screen as well as its computer printout capabilities. Then it tells just how precisely a CAT can measure the position of tumors. Our final anecdote on the reproduced pages explains that the CAT works in conjunction with surgeons for on-the-spot emergency operations. But that fact is narrated via the drama of a stroke victim's brush with death.

Check how many of an anecdote's attributes, described at the beginning of this section, each of our anecdotes has. Then reread the anecdotes, but this time keep in mind what an anecdote is *not* (see p. 103). Our students often have trouble figuring that out, too.

Illus. 7.1. Use of Anecdotes

suffer excruciating headaches for days afterward.) He could perform an angiogram by injecting dye into the arteries that supply blood to the brain—a procedure that sometimes triggered convulsions, stroke or even death. Or, if he was associated with a major research center or teaching hospital, he could request what was then called a brain scan. With this method, radioactive liquid, injected into the brain, is charted as it makes its way through the soft tissues. Not only are these techniques painful and/or dangerous, but they cannot be counted on to detect anything more subtle than a major stroke or a large tumor.

For years, medical researchers had played with the idea of a device that could collect a series of soft tissue x-ray pictures, and with the aid of computers capable of differentiating minute shadings, combine them into a well-visualized "slice." Little had come of it beyond one experimental machine that worked too slowly and projected too much radiation to be practical. But [in 1970 an English scientist, Godfrey Hounsfield, who had been working on a CT scanner for three years, turned on his brand-new machine in a London hospital—and 20 minutes later gave the startled doctors mankind's first clear, detailed look at a tumor deep within the interior of an uncut human brain.]

Three years later, improved, faster-operating versions of Hounsfield's invention—capable of illuminating for the first

A

time the soft tissues of the eyes, nasal passages and larynx—were introduced to American hospitals and laboratories and hailed as wonder tools.

According to Dr. Marvin E. Haskin, chairman of diagnostic radiology at Hahnemann Medical College and Hospital of Philadelphia: "The head scanner brings medicine out of the dark ages. Now we not only can look directly at the brain but we can do it so easily and safely that even a newborn infant can be scanned. With CT, we have picked up correctable abnormalities in children as young as four days old."

Dr. Haskin and his team of radiologists at Hahnemann have done much of the pioneer work in brain scanning and have written definitive medical texts on the subject. Since July 1974, when their hospital purchased a head scanner, they have examined over 6,000 patients, many of them youngsters.

Haskin's associate, Dr. Patricia D. Laffey, chief of Hahnemann's section on noninvasive imaging, department of diagnostic radiology, sees many of the pediatric patients. [Recently, she examined a four-year-old boy who was behaving erratically following a fall and a sudden blackout. Positioning the child in her scanner, she discovered not only the blocked brain ventricle (cavity) that had caused the boy's blackout but a benign tumor the size of a tomato that nobody had known about.] Had the child not been scanned, the tumor could have gone undetected until it

Q

A

caused irreparable brain damage. The boy might have grown up deformed or retarded—or he might not have grown up at all.

Q

"As a result of our scan," Dr. Laffey says, "the doctors knew just where to operate to remove the tumor." And, after the operation, a follow-up scan made sure the entire growth had been removed. The small amount of x-ray exposure each CT series entailed—about as much as a den-

Q

tist's x-ray—seemed a reasonable risk to take in return for what Laffey calls "every chance of complete recovery."

Scanning also led Drs. Laffey and Haskin to discover a surprising number of cases in which children, diagnosed as retarded, turned out to have unsuspected brain tumors or hydrocephalus (water on the brain). [They promptly arranged to

A

scan 30 children from St. Elizabeth's Home, a school for the educable and trainable retarded in West Philadelphia. Fully 20 percent of the youngsters—a much higher figure than anticipated—were found to have tumors, cysts, water on the brain, congenital malformations or structural abnormalities that could have caused the mental problems.] Unfortunately, the diagnoses were made too late to help most of the St. Elizabeth children. But Haskin feels that, as head scanners become more accessible, many similarly afflicted youngster will be discovered in time to be treated. "My experience has convinced me

Q

that every hospital with a patient load of over 100 should have a head scanner," Haskins says.

Dr. Stephen Rothman, director of computerized tomography at Yale New Haven Hospital in Connecticut, agrees.

Q+A

[He recalls the case of Chuck, a little boy whose only symptom was that he "behaved strangely." When Dr. Rothman settled Chuck into the head scanner, the TV screen promptly revealed a benign tumor as large as a grapefruit.] "I not only could tell the surgeon there was an operable tumor but from the computer printout which provides exact positions to within a millimeter—I could tell him just where the tumor was placed," Rothman says.

Q

"Today Chuck is alive and normal, but he would have had a dim prognosis before CT scanners came along."

Even more dramatic was the case of the adult patient rushed to Yale New Haven's emergency room with a stroke. [As the staff worked over the 50-year-old man, his vital signs deteriorated rapidly. Then, on impulse, the doctors rushed him to radiology, and shifted him to the CT scan table. While residents stood by, Dr. Rothman set his instruments in motion, and in less than a minute a "slice" of the dying patient's head appeared on the TV screen. Clearly visible were the eyes, both sides of the

A

brain and the ventricles containing the cerebrospinal fluid that transports nutrients to the brain and toxic materials away from it.

Dr. Rothman's trained eye isolated the problem at once: A blood vessel in the brain had burst and was bleeding into a ventricle. The surgeon watched closely as Rothman pinpointed the endangered area. Right there in the CT scan room, the surgeon drilled a hole through the man's skull, inserted a needle and drained the cavity.] "If that ventricle had filled with blood," Rothman says, "the patient would have died within minutes. Instead, he left the hospital some days later, completely well."

"After I did a thousand head scans I was excited by the tool," Dr. Haskin says. "Now that I've done six thousand, I'm six times more excited—and that's rare in medicine. This machine is revealing pathology we could only guess at before. And although no indirect diagnostic tool is 100 percent accurate, the CT scanner's record of 95 percent accuracy makes it 25 percent better than any other radiologic instrument!"

So enthusiastic is Haskin that he recommends a head scan if any of the following symptoms occur: sudden-onset recurrent headaches, seizures, sudden and continued behavior changes, concussion, sudden . . . .

An anecdote is not:

a quotation in which an expert (or nonexpert) gives information or talks about something that happened;

a mini-story that duplicates information already given through exposition;

a mini-story spliced into the article simply to offer readers relief from straight, tiring exposition.

We know several writers who, while researching, put each anecdote they find on a single 3 × 5 card. To organize the article, they group their note cards into a logical layout. To complete the article, they just fill in the transitions and generalizations. That's how vital you should make anecdotes to your own writing if you plan to make it professionally.

Obviously, then, a large part of your article research should be the constant search for anecdotes. How should you go about this? One way is through interviews, to which we devote all of Chapter 12. When you ask people to provide you with *anecdotes,* they may not understand what you're talking about. But if you ask, instead, for *examples,* you'll get the same thing.

For our CAT scanner article, for example, we interviewed Dr. Laffey for facts and opinions—but we were also looking for anecdotes. Like most scientists, she was accustomed to speaking in terms of the specific example. When she'd state a fact or figure, we'd ask, "Give us an example," and, "What's another example?" That's how she came up with the story of the four-year-old boy that gave the article so much pathos.

Another way to get true, exciting, believable and informative anecdotes is to tell all your friends what you're writing about. You'd be surprised how many people have had experiences with your topic that they're dying to share. For a while, Judi was regularly doing features for *Playgirl* on contemporary subjects such as how to choose a divorce lawyer, how to handle a love affair, how to be assertive, how to avoid on-the-job molestation. As each new article idea was assigned to her, Judi would ask friends about their experiences and whether they knew anybody else who might share similar experiences. No matter how personal the subject of her article, she always came up with half a dozen solid anecdotes within her circle of acquaintances plus leads to another half dozen.

Judi didn't name names in *Playgirl,* which is one reason her friends didn't hesitate to tell all. If your article is on a sensitive subject, your editor (and your readers) won't expect your personal confidants' full names. As long as your anecdotes have the ring of truth—achieved by getting all the details and making the reader see them too—nobody will doubt your word that "Janice P., who lives in a quiet suburb of Madison, Wisconsin, has been secretly plotting her husband's death for six years now." The only time you weaken an anecdote by not using complete, authentic names is when those names would be easily recognized by your average reader. In an article on the hazards of living together, an anecdote about the damages actor Lee Marvin had to pay his ex-mate kept readers more interested than an anecdote about anonymous Joe Blow's or Lee M.'s troubles. (Until you've built a reputation for yourself, editors may insist on being told your sources' full names and addresses for verification. But they'll promise not to reveal the identities.)

Well, if you don't need a full name, what's to keep you from making up an anecdote if it's harmless and illustrates the point? That's a question our students ask repeatedly. And we answer repeatedly, "Try it!" You'll find that making up a believable setting, history, experience and voice of a fictitious character is much harder to pull off than getting on the phone and locating a real anecdote. Besides, the fictions you create are never as farfetched as the truth. In faking an anecdote about a man who studied books to trim his waistline, would you think to give intimate details about the improvement in his sex life? Or in faking an anecdote about a prominent southern mayor, would you insert the way he'd "gotten a girl in trouble" in his younger days? These and other stranger-than-fiction anecdotes rewarded our for-real research efforts.

Calling themselves *new journalists,* some writers openly (and sometimes not so openly) invent settings, people and situations. As expected, the people described sound like stick figures and the articles fall flat. The true "new journalists" use real people involved in real happenings. Sometimes these writers set their subjects in their natural milieus even though the interview may have taken place somewhere else. That might be considered invention. But it works, because during the interview, as a rule, the successful journalist—old or new—has solicited enough facts to reconstruct the subject's natural habitat. In fact, the technique is not new at all.

Sometimes it's acceptable to amalgamate anecdotes. One magazine editor wanted a piece about a hooker's daily life. A noted writer who got the assignment researched prostitution without uncovering any one hooker with a long enough memorable story. With the editor's blessing, the author amalgamated parts of the lives of various prostitutes she had interviewed until she'd fashioned one helluva hooker. She chose so artfully amongst her anecdotal data that very few people suspected her super-hooker was about as real as James Bond. The magazine did not point out the amalgamation. Did readers believe it anyway? Sure, because it had the ring of truth. (The editor who told us this anecdote asked that we uphold the fiction. That's why we haven't included any identifying data.)

Judith Ramsey was faced with a similar dilemma while preparing a *Family Circle* article on incest. It was a new and rather touchy subject for that magazine. Judith and her editors realized they could show its ramifications most effectively through one family's saga. But no family had experienced everything they wanted to say in the article. So Judith amalgamated experiences of several families and wrote her touching article as if it were about one family. Then, at the end of the article, *Family Circle* editors—unlike the editor in the above example—told readers how the piece had evolved. Both editors' solutions were acceptable because they didn't weaken the article or suggest factual untruths.

Manipulating anecdotes is controversial. For some editors, it's taboo. Our philosophy on controversial techniques is simple: When in doubt, tell the editor in advance what you're doing and tell the reader in print what you've done.

Quotes

We suspect that three-quarters of all grammar school teachers don't know a quotation mark (") from an exclamation point (!). Since so many of our students mistake the one for the other, they must be mislearning in some standard place such as grammar school. They insist on dropping in exclamation points at the ends of sentences they began hoping to initiate a great deal of excitement but ended suspecting they'd failed. They slap " " around ideas which they suspect won't stir up much excitement, hoping to achieve some of the magic they've heard resides in quotes.

There's no magic inherent in either exclamation points or quotation marks. They do not cause excitement in themselves. They do not conceal boring, hackneyed writing. Exclamation points indicate strong emotion and should be practically nonexistent in professional magazine writing. Quotation marks around phrases or sentences indicate *only* that the words between them have been borrowed.

The reason people think quotes are a magic device for lifting an article out of the mud is that anecdotes often quote the words of people involved in the actions. A good anecdote, we saw before, is an exciting literary technique, one that you should strive to use. But it is not the quoted dialogue in anecdotes that makes them anecdotal. It is the action. The entire lengthy first anecdote in the CAT scanner article *(Ill. 5.7)* contains only two very short quotes.

If there is no action—if nothing is happening except for the transfer of information, experience or opinion, and if the words in the transfer were borrowed from someone else—the information is not an anecdote but a quote. We put quotations around borrowed words to show that they are secondhand.

Just as you must learn to choose among possible anecdotes, you must learn to choose *only* quotes that will make your article exciting. Improperly used quotations say as much about your writing as improper table manners say about your upbringing. They may say, for instance, that you lack the confidence or originality to draw conclusions on your own. They may smack suspiciously of name-dropping or of padding a poorly prepared outline. Here's how noted language authority H. W. Fowler put it in his classic *Modern English Usage:*

> A writer expresses himself in words that have been used before because they give his meaning better than he can give it himself, or because they are beautiful or witty, or because he expects them to touch a chord or association in his reader, or because he wishes to show that he is learned or well read. Quotations due to the last motive are invariably ill advised. The discerning reader detects it and is contemptuous; the undiscerning is perhaps impressed, but even then is at the same time repelled, pretentious quotations being the surest road to tedium. The less experienced a writer is, and therefore on the whole the less well read he is also, the more he is tempted to this error. The experienced knows he had better avoid it; and the well-read, aware that he could quote if he would, is not afraid that readers will think he cannot.

There! Now, did our long quotation of Fowler's words—carefully chosen, artfully turned, and written by the greatest of authorities—quicken the pace of our chapter, or even enlighten you more than our previous summation? What's more, if we have not already convinced you not to misuse quotations, would our borrowing from Fowler really help our cause?

Here are some guidelines for using quotations so they support your writing, not get in its way.

FOR AUTHORITY

Use a quote when you need the voice of authority—and when that voice can't be incorporated into an anecdote or paraphrased more clearly and more interestingly.

In *Ill. 7.1,* where we marked anecdotes in a section of our *Family Health* article, we also marked several places where we needed an authoritative voice to make a generalization or offer an opinion. For example, it would not have been nearly as convincing for two journalists to have concluded what Dr. Marvin E. Haskin concluded in the first quote: "The head scanner brings medicine out of the dark ages" and it's much more convincing if Dr. Rothman himself describes a patient as "behaving strangely" than if we were to take the phrase out of quotes.

On the controversial question of who should own CAT scanners, we wanted to share Haskin's expert assessment and make it clear that it was only his opinion, not fact. Again we put his words between quotes: "My experience has convinced me that every hospital with a patient load of over 100 should have a head scanner." Notice how we incorporated clearly into his quote the basis of his opinion: his experience.

We used our third Haskin quote in the article as shorthand to cite the authority for some exciting data we wanted the reader to know: "the CT scanner's record of 95 percent accuracy makes it 25 percent better than any other radiologic instrument."

We quoted Haskin once more on the reproduced page, this time on the subject of when CAT scans should be the preferred diagnostic tool. It's a recommendation better made by doctors than by writers, especially if the publication is *Family Health*. Notice, however, that there are no quotation marks around this quote. That's because it often takes doctors—and Haskin proved no exception—a lot of words to offer advice like this. They use half a dozen qualifiers before every noun and half a dozen more after every verb. We attributed the recommendation, giving him credit for the basic idea. But because he would have said it differently, we omitted the quotation marks. (Another example of that is in *Ill. 6.1,* Judi's article on female alcoholics. She credited Ruth Maxwell as the authority for her information, but calculatingly paraphrased because quoting Ms. Maxwell exactly the way she offered the information would have slowed the story.)

FOR TONE OF VOICE

Use a quote when someone's exact way of saying something is important to the point or the coloration of your article.

Judi tape-recorded her interview with actress Lynn Redgrave *(Ill. 5.4)* because she knew in advance she wanted her article to capture Lynn's British speech inflections. But when she used Lynn's quotes—and she used them extensively—it was not *only* to show off Ms. Redgrave's inflections. The quoted material had to contribute to the article's flow. In addition to *flavor*, it had to add *information* about Lynn's weight problem. Here are two examples from unreproduced portions of the article:

> "I assumed that if I got thin, I wouldn't be funny anymore. It was a lot of rubbish, but it was a great cop-out."
>
> "I had three complete wardrobes—and then my last resort, a shifty dress that covered all of me when nothing else would."

Judi also seized the chance to point out the actress's flair for storytelling by incorporating one long quote:

> "We would sit on this beach in Majorca and we'd eat ice creams and such, and whenever I'd get depressed and say, 'Listen, girls, I've got to lose weight because I've got a job next month,' they'd say, 'Ah, darling, you're having such a good time—and you look lovely in that suntan.' Well, I wanted to believe it. And it's really true what they say about Spanish guys being more likely to pinch your bottom if you're fat."

But did this *just* tell a story and show Britishisms? No, it also added pathos, humor and a telling glimpse at Lynn's self-evaluation.

Judi chose her quotes to make this article's point. She had so many leftover quotes that made *other* points, she was able to sell an entirely different article about Lynn to Canada's *Chatelaine* magazine. Her choices for *Weight Watchers,* out of the hour-long taped interview, included many *picture words,* as you can see in the excerpted sentences—thin, three wardrobes, eating ice cream on a beach in Majorca, lovely suntan—so her readers had something to look at, not simply to listen to.

One of our students interviewed a local judge, a woman whom she very much admired. But an early draft of her profile rendered the jurist an injustice by quoting her:

> Judge B———is an accessible person: "I think it is very important that the people who come into these courts feel that this is not an aloof, distant, impatient or crabby person who doesn't care about their case, because their case to them is the most important thing at that moment in their lives, or they wouldn't be there. So it is very important to me that they feel they have got a judge listening to them and is trying to figure out why their case is unique and really willing to hear why it is unique. Whether or not they win or lose, they feel if they have had that kind of a hearing, most people, even if they lose, go out satisfied with the process and the system."

Clearly, if the student kept the quote, she needed to clean up the judge's way of speaking, and we cover the ethics of that more extensively in Chapter 12. The important point here is that she should have left out most or all of this quotation. It *rambles* and *reiterates* and doesn't make an *authoritative* statement. It shows only the judge's own biased *estimation* of her accessibility and of whether people in the courtroom get a fair hearing. Moreover, her words—at least as quoted—aren't colorful or memorable and give us no clue to what she's *really* like. The way the quote is used only *weakens* the writer's argument. We told our student to sit in the courtroom and see for herself what people did there that would lead readers to conclude what she wanted them to, and then go back to her keyboard to paint a picture of what she saw.

OUT OF NECESSITY

Use a quote if that's the only way there is to present the information. When Metropolitan Sunday Newspaper Group assigned Frank an article they later entitled "The Nightmare of Nuclear Blackmail," he had to keep his own conflicted viewpoint meticulously out of the way. In addition, due to the subject's highly technical nature and the fact that much of the useful information was classified, Frank was obliged to let the ten experts he queried speak in their own words. Most answered in writing. A few insisted that not a single word of what they'd written, not even a punctuation mark, be changed.

What could be done to save the article from the inevitable boredom created by unliterary people giving dry facts about technical matters? First of all, Frank asked all the experts ten identical questions. Next he sorted the answers, choosing the most significant responses for each question. From those, he singled out the one or two answers for each question that could be presented in the liveliest fashion. Finally, Frank organized the story to incorporate *every* expert and to answer *every* question. In all, he used *barely 4 percent* of all the words his experts had contributed. He made the best of one of the worst possible ways to have to write an article.

Frank's result (part of which is reproduced as *Ill. 7.2*) wouldn't win any literary prizes. But it is a highly authoritative look at a timely subject that makes effective use of quotes.

Illus. 7.2. Use of Quotes

The Nightmare of Nuclear Blackmail

Anybody who's seen a TV crime show could make up a likely scenario about a band of criminals, terrorists or crackpots who put together their own A-bomb and threaten to use it for whatever kind of blackmail they have in mind.

Already, students at MIT and the University of Iowa have talked about A-bombs they designed themselves. And the FBI admits it has investigated several nuclear threats, which to date have all been proven hoaxes.

But around the globe, the haunting question remains: Will homemade or stolen nuclear devices become the terror weapons of the future?

The possibility of this happening drew strong opinions from a panel of experts whose divergent views ranged from alarming to comforting. Some even felt that any publicity on the subject would excite sick minds. All, however, agreed that enough technical literature about A-bombs has been declassified so that there are no secrets left about how to build a simple one, in theory at least. (An H-bomb is considered too far-fetched to worry about for several reasons including the fact that you'd have to start with a workable A-bomb.)

For instance, it's public knowledge that there were about 132 pounds of uranium in the bomb dropped on Hiroshima and it exploded with the force of 13,000 tons of TNT! Almost nothing is left to the imagination, too, in how it was put together and how its mechanisms worked.

As to the difficulties involved, veteran A-bomb designer Theodore B. Taylor feels uncomfortably certain that a clandestine A-bomb small enough to fit into the trunk of a compact could be built today.

Taylor, who worked at Los Alamos from 1949 to 1956 designing both baby and super-bombs and has been a consultant to the U.S. Air Force, thinks that anybody who's very knowledgeable in physics could blueprint an A-bomb from what he could learn in libraries.

Obtaining proper materials, Taylor believes, is the hard part.

After that, says he, "It is possible for an extra-ordinary individual or a few people to construct a workable nuclear device in a modestly equipped basement workshop. No exotic tools are required, but certain manual skills are necessary. Many nuclear physicists I know couldn't even fix a plugged sink, so they'd probably need help from skilled craftsmen."

Once the bomb is made, Taylor adds, "It's relatively easy to detonate a home-made nuclear device. Ordinary high explosives are required. But if somebody got just a little clumsy in working on the thing—a very real possibility for beginners—they'd probably end up very dead."

Gen. Edward B. Giller (U.S.A.F. Ret.) is deputy assistant administrator for national security at the Energy Research and Development Administration (ERDA), one of the two agencies formed out of the old Atomic Energy Commission. Previously, he worked for the AEC and he's one of the most widely known authorities in the field of nuclear security. We asked him, "Do you think a small group could assemble all the needed ingredients and then build an A-bomb?"

Gen. Giller said, "I'm under the impression that the detonators and wires and things that people use in hard rock mining would be the easiest to use in detonating the high explosives you need in any atomic bomb. But it's a very risky business. If the high explosives go off by mistake, there's going to be one hell of a hole in the ground, much bigger than some of the explosions today's terrorists have had.

"It's much different than the pipe bomb business. The amount of high explosives used in pipe bombs is peanuts compared to the amount of explosives you'd have to play with in building a nuclear device. You've got to manhandle a lot of explosives in a way that I for one would never care to do.

"Our agency's position is that we do

recognize it's within the capabilities of dedicated, fearless, technical people to conceive a bomb design and survive to the point where they've fabricated it. But both we and they would be unsure whether it would actually give a nuclear explosion if they detonated their bomb. A lot would depend on their background, their dedication and their facilities.

"We can't say it can't be done. We can't say it can be done. So we address ourselves to protecting against the loss of nuclear material. I don't want to lose any of the stuff, now or ever. I couldn't take any comfort in trying to evaluate somebody's machine shop expertise or educational level in trying to help me with the problem I might face if somebody does acquire nuclear material illegally."

George Day is editor of the Bulletin of the Atomic Scientists, which for many years has provided a forum for top people in nuclear research. We asked him, "Where would terrorists or criminals be likely to obtain enough uranium or plutonium to build an A-bomb?"

Day replied, "In the process of producing electric power in nuclear generators, plutonium is formed as a by-product inside the nuclear reactor's fuel rods. But in that form, it's so radioactive that you'd be dead before you got it home. So that part of the plutonium life cycle is not particularly vulnerable to groups eager to build a bomb.

"However, used-up fuel rods are hauled to reprocessing plants. There the plutonium is chemically separated out. It ends up as a relatively stable powder. It's not even dangerously radioactive right then. And that's when plutonium is most vulnerable to theft."

Exposition

The only other technique available to magazine writers, in addition to quotes and anecdotes, is exposition. It's simply the presentation of your thoughts with the data that back them up. The thoughts are offered in *generalizations* of fact and opinion, about which we'll have more to say in Chapter 8. The backups are all the specifics—dates and statistics, definitions and concrete examples—that prove the generalizations without the need to call on other people's experiences (anecdotes) or authority (quotes).

Most of our students come to us knowing all the fundamentals of expository writing that they have to know (except how to make it colorful). It's the only nonfiction writing they've been taught in college and high school. All those "compare and contrast" essays have prepared them to find facts and figures and to pepper their papers with lots of convincing examples. Mostly, our job is to make students *avoid* exposition wherever possible, substituting anecdotes and lively, pertinent quotes.

Some articles, especially how-to's, don't lend themselves to anecdotes and quotes. They become entirely exposition. One easy way to keep the reader interested is to speak to him directly (see *Ill. 5.1,* our plastic-furniture article, for the use of *you*). In addition, keep in mind that when you use expository writing, it can and should be as vivid as your quotes and anecdotes. Vivid exposition seems so difficult for beginners to achieve that all of Chapter 13 shows how to make words work for you. A small portion of our long cancer-immunology article illustrates what we always strive for—and sometimes achieve:

> Why do people get cancer at all?
>
> Stated most simply, it is for approximately the same reason that, when a flu epidemic hits, some people contract flu but most others don't. No one has been able to calculate how many mutated cells a normal body destroys before they develop into cancer, but the odds appear to be very, very much in favor of your staying healthy.
>
> Working with American Cancer Society figures, we have extrapolated that on the average, the odds actually are 350 to 1 that you are immune to cancer at this moment. And if you are under 55 years old and are a nonsmoker, the odds are more like 650 to 1 in your favor.
>
> A number of factors enable cancer occasionally to outwit the immune-surveillance network. One factor is that a certain amount of time is needed to mount a strong defense. Even though, as one experimenter found, in fifteen days your body could make 1000 different cells from one cell through consecutive mutations, what happens if none of those 1000 new antigen codes is the right one? The cancer would itself keep growing, of course.

All we had to work with, in writing the above, was a stack of statistics and dull research reports. By using the expository devices we'll explain in Chapter 13, we were able to convert them into a salable article.

8

The Five Commandments No Pro Forgets

NOVICES WHO THINK THE LOGIC OF PUTTING TOgether a complete magazine article is self-evident ought to read the Constitution of the United States of America. Its copywriters, the likes of Benjamin Franklin, Alexander Hamilton and Thomas Jefferson, didn't notice until it was already enacted that they'd left out all the important guarantees of personal freedom which led them to found the United States in the first place.

They had the luxury of quickly drafting ten amendments. If you're that far off the mark, no editor will allow you a rewrite.

There are five commandments that every pro makes part of his consciousness in order to avoid a blooper like the one our foundering fathers made. They are:

> Make your point and prove it.
> Offer generalizations but avoid generalities.
> Separate fact from opinion.
> Locate universal images and experiences.
> Above all, entertain.

Make Your Point—and Prove It

We can't tell you how often we've polished off a first draft, beaming at how cleverly we'd uncovered an unknown fact and sketched in a breathtaking anecdote, only to be pulled up short, maybe days later, to realize that in our excitement we'd *missed making the point* of our article.

Missing the point can kill article ideas as well as finished manuscripts. If you don't clearly identify what you want to write about when you first outline your article for an editor, you'll probably miss getting the assignment. If you do get it, you may discover after weeks of work that the story won't hold together. Or, having found a point, you may turn it in—and have it tossed back because the editor thought you had a different point in mind.

The main point of your article is usually in your topic sentence. It includes your focus and your slant. When you've finished writing the first draft, check back to that topic sentence and make sure that what you've written after it backs up what you started out to write. Your ending, of course, must be about your main point. But that's not all. All your evidence in the article's body—your quotes, anecdotes and exposition—must keep building up the validity of your main point. And your slant must never veer from its original point of view.

For some subjects, you will have to consider both the point and its counterpoint. But editors usually expect you to present a well-established case favoring one side or the other. The only exception is when you are specifically assigned to explore a controversial issue while remaining neutral. (This, by the way, is one of the trickiest pieces a pro can undertake. If you think it's easy, just try it.)

Let's look again at our CAT scanner story for *Family Health (Ill. 5.7 and Ill. 7.1)*. We were assigned to research the controversy over whether hospitals really needed CATs. The question, it turned out, had two aspects: medical value and cost. The only opposition we found to the CATs' medical value came from a lightweight, a technician trained in traditional X-ray methods. She told us dozens of things wrong with the scanners, but it turned out she worked at the other end of the hospital and knew less about scanners than we did. On a hunch that she was probably afraid of being displaced by the CAT, we left her opinion out of the finished article. We did present both sides as to whether CATs cost too much because both opinions were expressed by experts. However, our digging turned up information that convinced *us* that, in most instances, CATs were worth the cost. We weren't able to present all our technical backup data; as it was, the article ran longer than the assignment called for. But we did let readers know the decision we'd reached. And we designed the article to thrust home that positive viewpoint from beginning to end.

The main point of Frank's article "The Nightmare of Nuclear Blackmail" *(Ill. 7.2)* was that the threat of somebody's building an A-bomb represented a genuine nightmare to nuclear security people and to concerned scientists. That was his working title; that was his lead; and his selection and placement of data and opinion relentlessly led the reader to that conclusion.

Let's look at the beginning of that article. First Frank presented a former A-bomb designer's opinion that it's easy to design a bomb but tough—although possible—to assemble one. Next, one of the people responsible for U.S. nuclear security vacillated on whether it is possible for terrorists to get the materials for a bomb. His statement, which he qualified in order to deny Frank's premise, actually *supported* the article's contention that the "nightmare" isn't farfetched. Strengthening the premise was the authority's concern about keeping plutonium out of the hands of would-be bomb makers. By following with a quote from the editor of *Bulletin of the Atomic Scientists,* who said that the nuclear reactor industry soon will produce easy-to-get plutonium, he made nightmare into plausible reality.

At first it might seem that Frank should have chosen the more dramatic slant that terrorists *will* build a clandestine A-bomb, no doubt about it. But if he had, fairness would have obliged him to give substantial space to solid and respected representatives of the opposing viewpoint. The same resources who were willing to say that bomb building is *possible* would have argued that it would never happen—and he would have been forced to give their opinions full weight. Then, his arbitrary conclusion that terrorists *will* build a bomb would have been suspect. By choosing a less dramatic point to make, Frank was able to make it unequivocally—and because he proved it solidly, he actually produced a more dramatic article.

Generalize, but Don't Use Generalities

We don't often rely on dictionary definitions, since most words have several subtly different meanings and depend on context for complete definition. But the two words *generalize* and *generalities* throw so many would-be writers we'll call on all the ammunition we can find:

> Generalize: *active verb;* to derive or induce a general conception or principle from
> particulars; to draw a general conclusion from; to give general applicability to.
> Generality: *noun;* total applicability; a vague or inadequate statement.

It is the good writer's primary job to find interesting situations, study them, evaluate them and finally draw general conclusions about them. In the most successful articles, situational data are presented to the reader and most of the generalizations are left for the reader to make. Sometimes, however, a generalization is necessary. In that case, it should always have, directly preceding or following, the specifics that back it up. The writer who makes *generalities* instead of leading the reader to *generalizations* is not doing his job.

Here is a generality:

> We studied the Jones, Smith, Watson, Johnson, Olson, and Rogers families and concluded that residents of Shaker Haunts Houses are pretty decent poker players, lousy backgammon players, and let their kids throw Frisbees on the front lawn.

Now here is a generalization, followed by the situational specifics that support it:

> The Watsons are typical of families residing in Shaker Haunts Houses. They manage to win a few dollars at Friday-night nickel-stakes neighborhood poker games, but lose it all at Saturday-night backgammon club. Sundays, they try to mow the lawn. It isn't easy, since Shaker Haunts is the local Frisbee-tossing arena.

The first example is inadequate—dry and devoid of humanity. The second example is vivid and personal. There's no doubt which will more quickly catch the reader's attention and remain longer in the memory.

Let's take an example from a student's article. His premise was that a guerrilla war is being fought between smokers and nonsmokers. At one point in the article, he wrote:

> In public accommodations, nonsmokers are less and less being discriminated against as greater numbers of nonsmoking sections are being established.

There's a generality for you! How much less discrimination? How many greater numbers? Which public accommodations? Instead of relying on weak generalities, he should have created a line or two of expository specifics and let the readers make the generalization. We'll assume his research was deep enough to get the facts that led him to this conclusion. (It's the *poor* writer who solidifies his conclusions before he checks them out and then arms himself with backup data.) Let's use hypothetical data to show how the writer might have more effectively convinced the reader.

> In public places such as restaurants, retail stores, elevators, buses, and airplanes, nonsmokers are breathing easier. So far, twenty-seven states have enacted laws that require nonsmoking sections in specific public areas; and in 1979, federal laws outlawed smoking on interstate buses, trains and planes.

(This is a good place to point out that the good writer *always* chooses his words carefully to mean what he wants to say. The student used "public accommodations," a term limited mainly to hotels and restaurants, when he meant "public places." And his article nowhere proved, with evidence, that nonsmokers were ever *discriminated against* as that term is properly used.)

Look at another paragraph from the same article. See how many generalities you can spot and how many misuses of the language. (There are a lot of trite phrases, too.)

> Smoking did in fact for a period of time become such an emotional issue that children and parents would have bitter quarrels over the smoking habits of parents. Husbands and wives at times would become angered beyond despair at the disagreements generated in households where one person was a militant nonsmoker and the other a militant smoker.

Intended here was the generalization that families were *torn apart by the smoking issue.* Instead, generality was piled upon generality: "Children and parents" and "husbands and wives" apply to nearly everybody on earth. There are two likely reasons for this: one, that he hadn't done enough research to back up his hunches; the other, that he hadn't yet learned the power of using anecdotes, quotes, facts and figures to bolster his generalization. We'd rewrite the above paragraph so it limits the generalization just to families housing nonsmokers along with smokers, and use specific examples to make our points. But our rewrite is a generalization, not a generality, for another reason: because it paints a *general* principle derived from particular examples.

> When a smoker lives with a nonsmoker, the living isn't easy. Ned and Ellie, for example, had smoked all their lives. Suddenly their two teenaged children began to harass them like angry parents every time Ned or Ellie would light up. They began a guerrilla war, too, soaking cigarettes in soapy water, putting chalk in the filters, dumping unopened packs in the toilet tank. The tension became so keen that Ned and Ellie's smoking practically doubled. In the case of Ernie the smoker and his wife Susan the militant nonsmoker, the attacks were more subtle. Susan would only make nasty remarks in front of friends. Ernie retaliated by refusing to entertain or go visiting, and the couple only saved their marriage by . . .

When in doubt, the safest way to be sure your writing makes meaningful generalizations, not meaningless generalities, is to examine your qualifiers. Do you use lots of *for examples*? That's good. Do you use lots of *mosts* and *manys*, *somes* and *alls*? That's bad.

Separate Fact from Opinion

The necessity for separating fact from opinion ought to be self-evident. Unfortunately, we've seen many fine stories fall apart when their authors attempted to substantiate their generalizations with opinions instead of facts.

If an economist tells you that the gross national product is $47 billion, and you or he verifies the figure, that's a fact. (If he says it's $47 billion and it isn't verified, it may be an *incorrect* fact.) But if the economist says it ought to be $47 billion, no matter how many others concur, it's still an opinion, not a fact. You may overlook that important difference as you rush toward a deadline, but your editors and readers will know it's opinion. And if you treat it as a fact, they'll mistrust your credibility throughout the rest of the article.

The easiest way to signal opinion is with qualifiers—such words as *most, some, possibly, probably, can* and *may*. But carefully selected nouns and verbs can also do the job. When we wrote about cancer immunology for *Science Digest*, credibility was a big factor since the article's point of view was at odds with the public's. One section of the article answered the question, "Are viruses a cause of cancer?" There, it was especially important to separate fact from opinion. For opinion, we selected nouns and verbs, as well as qualifiers, that signal opinion. We'll underline them throughout the following extracts.

You <u>may</u> have <u>heard</u> that viruses cause cancer. <u>Suggested</u> by researchers as a <u>question</u>—not an answer—some years ago, this <u>theory</u> quickly was <u>espoused</u> by physicians, patients, and especially the popular press. It was a pleasant <u>theory</u> to believe; if a virus caused cancer, an inoculation that <u>would</u> prevent or cure it <u>just had to be</u> around the corner.

For matters of fact, we used words that left no doubt as to their factuality. Later in the virus section we wrote:

A virus has the ability to sneak in beside a normal cell's DNA and unite with it at a point or two where the DNA is particularly vulnerable. Aided by enzymes, the virus then alters the composition of the normal cell's DNA.

There's no equivocation in those two sentences.

An author has to make the point she sets out to make. Our point was the opinion, based on our research back then, that viruses rarely if ever cause cancer. So we proceeded to lay out the facts behind our opinions, but we took care to label every tentative conclusion with a qualifier:

Many private physicians <u>still support</u> the viruses-cause-cancer <u>theory</u>. And some clinical researchers are <u>still searching</u> for viruses that can link to human cancer. But <u>almost</u> without exception, the basic scientists we interviewed and those whose papers we studied <u>doubt</u> that viruses are (or <u>will ever</u> be found to be) a <u>significant</u> cause of human cancer. Dr. Temin states simply, "<u>Most</u> human cancers <u>appear to</u> result from genetic changes that are not a result of viral infection."

Incidentally, we'd earlier identified Dr. Temin as a Nobel laureate for his work on viruses in cancer. So it was not chance that led to our choosing his quote to settle the argument we fastidiously composed from irrefutable facts laced with strong, authoritatively held opinions.

Try doing the following to the above paragraph:

Add a summary statement of Temin's conclusion without qualifying it.
Change the quote to state the same conclusion without qualification.

Note how, if we try to color the opinions of our experts or state opinion as fact, we lose credibility and, in doing so, lose our argument.

Locate Universal Images and Experiences

Many beginning writers fail to use universal images or single out universal experiences. They choose examples they understand, forgetting that it's the *reader's* comprehension they need. When a student wanted to put down a much-touted tourist attraction, she wrote:

> The beautiful oriental dolls were so out of place I wondered if one might not mistake them for Bucky Badger dolls.

Bucky Badger dolls? Many residents of Wisconsin know what she meant, since Bucky is the University of Wisconsin's mascot. But the image makes no sense to readers in the other forty-nine states. If she hopes to sell nationally, this writer had better keep *all* her potential readers in mind.

Another student set out to write an angry article on the lack of rights for women in Brazil. For her lead, she deliberately chose to use the images most Americans see when that country is mentioned:

> When one speaks of Brazil, the mind's eye sees Carnaval, samba, and sandy beaches filled with beautiful women.

Then she introduced her topic:

> Next to the beaches, women are the second biggest tourist resource, making Carnaval a mammoth and even more X-rated version of New Orleans' Mardi Gras.

She called forth pictures stored in the heads of most readers, and based her new information and conclusions on those familiar old images.

"How do you know," we're often asked, "what is and what isn't a common experience?" Our best answer is, either write for the people you associate with or associate with the people you want to write for. And read a lot. Learn the same things your readers learn. Even beginning writers know that, when communicating with third graders, words like "philistine" and "plebeian" are out and concepts like euthanasia and adultery are probably beyond the readers' imagination. The fact that good writing must be based on universal images leads us to recommend that beginning writers write for magazines they like to read—and on subjects they like to read about. If you do that, you'll start out with a useful set of images in your head that closely matches the set in your readers' heads.

We could now compose for you a list of six hundred universal concepts common to the majority of *Popular Mechanics* readers, and another list for *Playgirl* readers. But our lists would do you no good because three hundred of those images will change as trends change, becoming outmoded within a few years. Half the fun of vivid writing is spotting the changes in readers' image banks. The other half is using old images to create new ones that may become commonly accepted. We found two clever examples of that in a 1930 issue of *National Geographic*. The author, Frederick Simpich, obviously had a lot of fun orchestrating these images about one of New York City's most mundane statistics:

Can you imagine a man nearly a mile tall, with a mouth a hundred feet wide? A man who could wade across Lake Superior, which is 1,000 feet deep, and get wet only up to his knees? Such a monster, drinking night and day, could just about consume New York's water supply. On a hot day the city uses one billion gallons. There are less than two billion people on earth; so that is more than half a gallon for every person.

Simpich even played word games in this piece to help his readers grasp monumental quantities:

But how much food of all kinds does New York eat—it and its environs served by delivery wagons?

Nobody knows exactly. Experts have estimated it at about 10,000,000,000 pounds a year. "How much is that?" you ask? Well, 5,000,000 tons. Neither does that mean anything.

More then, than is consumed each year by all the standing armies of the world.

Entertain

After just reprinting those seventy-odd-year-old excerpts, it seems redundant to mention that good writing has to entertain. But it's a point overlooked by most beginners. Successful writers know that they're in show biz. This doesn't mean they can't be journalists. It doesn't mean they can't write informative, useful, exploratory, inciting, or touching articles. In fact, to get into print we *need* to write informative, useful, exploratory, inciting, and touching articles, and use journalistic techniques in doing so. But our articles must also be lively, fast-paced, and to the point. We must never bore. We must always keep our reader begging for more until our very last line.

In order to entertain readers, you don't have to keep 'em laughing, or even smiling. If you've watched a TV soap opera, you know that entertainment can come from having emotions stroked and tear glands exercised. If you've seen a TV documentary, you're aware that most do not document at all but dramatize, even sensationalize. Even the TV news entertains with its short, chatty, heavily illustrated segments. People aren't used to thinking of the daily newspaper as entertainment, but even the once-staid *New York Times* conceded that its business is entertainment and long ago changed its style accordingly. The underpinning of the magazine business, too, is entertainment, short and simple.

Not even business trade journals are read only for serious knowledge. Take, for example, the journal *Physician's Management.* We wrote a regular monthly feature, "PhoneScan," for it for several years. It was read by two hundred thousand successful doctors each month—read closely enough to keep advertisers renewing their contracts. If our articles had run in a newspaper, they might have been called gossip. They informed about trends, but by way of lively quotes and anecdotes from fifty randomly chosen physicians each month. If we had begun to turn in "PhoneScans" that informed with statistics and medical jargon instead of with the most entertaining quotes and anecdotes we could find, we'd have been tossed out of the magazine instead of winning awards for our pieces.

When we wrote our long, technical article on cancer for *Science Digest*, we had to take into account readers' biases. The widespread fear of cancer made any levity on the subject taboo. How did we entertain in this tricky subject area? Here's the picture we created for the cell-by-cell drama we discovered:

It's dark. Somewhere deep inside your body a T-cell is on patrol, outfoxing the darkness with hundreds of sensitive tentacles that instantly identify the shape of every cell it encounters. As long as the T-cells patrol, every other cell can go about its individual job without worry.

Suddenly the T-cell tenses because its stubby tentacles brush against a strangely shaped cell. It doesn't belong there. It's a runaway cell that, left to its selfish devices, would become a tumor crowding nearby cells and robbing them of nourishment.

Instantly the T-cell patrol sends out an alarm, a special bit of protein excreted only in emergencies. That alerts the body's soldiers, the Killer-cells, and their not-so-smart but hard-working helpers, the macrophage cells. Yet, even before help arrives, the T-cell attacks, attaching itself to the tumor cell.

The T-cell is no match for the young giant. But within three minutes, several Killer-cells and macrophages have sped to the scene. Together they unite into an antibody. Plunging against the tumor cell, the warriors rip at the invader's protective cell membrane.

Ten minutes later, the barrier is breached, the tumor cell disintegrates, and the triumphant cells slowly move away.

PART III
How to Sell Your Article Ideas

9

How to Write a Dynamite Query Letter

I N CASE ONE OF OUR MORE IMPORTANT MESSAGES HAS somehow eluded you, we'll repeat it: If you want to be a magazine writer you have to face the fact that you are in the business of selling. The query letter (short for letter of inquiry) is the usual way in which authors sell their products—articles—to their customers—editors.

Like the magazine article itself, the query letter has evolved its own standard format. Many authors work out their personal variations, and no doubt you'll come up with your own touches. But if you want to appear to be a professional writer, you'd better include certain uniform information that editors expect to see. The best query letters are sales letters with everything presented deliberately in the way most likely to sell the idea.

Many beginning writers in our classes fooled editors into thinking they'd had long experience in article writing, and therefore could be trusted with hefty assignments, simply by learning to write professional-quality query letters. Then their only concern was to avoid suggesting articles too difficult for a novice to deliver. Judi herself learned how to write a selling query letter before she'd fully mastered the art of article writing. Her first sale was to *Good Housekeeping,* which had to pay her a $300 kill fee for an unusable article on school counselors that, she realized years later, sounded more like a term paper than a magazine piece. When she got over her embarrassment, she aimed her next batch of queries at magazines that demanded less professionalism of their writers.

Format

We use the term *query letter* because most editors want queries from writers with whom they aren't on a first-name basis in the form of single-spaced business letters, double-spaced between paragraphs for easy scanning. Once an editor knows you, he may prefer e-mailed queries. If he does, he may even suggest it without your asking.

In times long gone, queries were often called outlines and written as double-spaced synopses. You may still hear somebody using the term *story outline,* which was borrowed from fiction writers in that period of magazine history. The story outline was useful way back when there were at least half a dozen very similar general interest magazines around (for example, *Life, Look, Saturday Evening Post, Coronet,* and *Pageant*). Writers could send the same outline to each of them in turn. But for nearly half a century, every magazine has been targeted to a slightly different audience, and each editor likes to feel that her authors take the trouble to tailor suggestions to her own magazine's peculiarities. By writing your query in letter format, you will give her the warm feeling that the idea has been especially developed with her magazine in mind.

If one query is turned down, the wily writer, of course, leaves in applicable segments when editing it to create a new version for a different editor. But we've found that, even in sections left nearly as-is, we make changes as we sharpen the focus or find better ways to express ourselves.

Unless it is utterly, honestly, journalistically impossible, limit your query letter to *one single-spaced page.* ONE PAGE! Editors are very busy people and hate to read long letters. They don't give long ones any more time than short ones, only less attention. Worse, they assume that—barring any obvious extenuating circumstances—if you can't say what's important in one page, you probably don't have a clear enough handle on the idea. Our experience supports the assumption.

Don't create a fancy letterhead or add do-dads to catch the attention of the editor. It could seem to smack of amateurism. (Early on, Frank adorned his letterhead with a cute clip showing a writer on an ostrich, pen in hand. He dropped it as soon as he became confident that he didn't need a drawing to announce his profession.) Simply make sure to print your query on white or light-colored 8½ × 11-inch paper and to put your name, address, phone number and e-mail address (if you have one) at the top. When Judi sends queries, she adds a footer showing the team's important associations and national writing awards but keeps it in a quiet 12-point type:

> Members, American Society of Journalists and Authors, Authors Guild. National writing awards: National Press Club, National Conference of Christians and Jews, American Business Press Association, American Optometric Association

Frank, however, rarely adds the footer. It doesn't seem to make much difference.

Center your query (top to bottom) and make it look as attractive and businesslike as possible. Leave left- and right-hand margins wide enough for the editor's assistants or associates to comment. Make sure your type looks sharp and dark; if needed, change your printer's setting from *draft* to *text* and replace your black ink cartridge. We save each query as a separate file (in a folder called *mag queries*) since each one's slightly different from the others, and name them with a shorthand working title, the publication's name and the date we sent the query, such as *Test Tips Self032204.doc* (for *Self* magazine) and *Date Rape MedEcon010906.doc* (for *Medical Economics*).

Salutation

Address your query letter to a real, living, breathing, working, thinking, buying editor at the magazine you've singled out. Otherwise your idea will probably be relegated to the lowest person on the totem pole. (Chapter 3 dealt with how to pick both magazines and editors.) Just as writing magazine articles is a highly personal endeavor, so is editing magazines. Like writers, editors have egos, and you should not risk offending an editor by misspelling her name, using the wrong form of address, or getting the name of her magazine incorrect.

Your salutation should be "Dear Mr. So-and-So," or "Dear Ms. So-and-So" unless you know that the editor prefers to be addressed as Mrs. or Miss. Using first names, unless you're genuinely on a first-name basis, is as taboo as addressing by first name the personnel director you've never met at a company where you're applying for a job. It's possible to develop a first-name relationship by mail. In fact, there are many editors we've never met personally whom we address "Dear Bob," or "Dear Sally," and who write to us as "Dear Judi," and "Dear Frank." Our rule is to wait until the editor has used our first names before we use his.

Title, Topic, Slant

Editors like to think about ideas in terms of titles. If you have what you consider a super title, or even a good, catchy, fairly short title, it's great to start off with a bang by giving the title first:

Re: "How to Make Dynamite in a Backyard Barbecue"

Some writers prefer to work the title into the letter's opening paragraph.

If your title doesn't completely spell out your suggested article's focus and slant (see Chapter 6), you should try to work them into the first paragraph. In the classic query letter, therefore, by the end of the first paragraph the editor should have a concise but sharp understanding of the specific idea you are proposing, the *slant* you propose to take and, if you have one, a suggested title.

Illus. 9.1. First Successful Query Letter

(date)
Mr. Ernest Baxter
VIVA
909 Third Avenue
New York, NY 10022

Dear Mr. Baxter,

How about this article:

HOW TO KEEP RAPISTS FROM GETTING OFF SCOT FREE

If you like, this can be an as-told-to bylined by the attorney whose plan it is. He's Neil Comer, ex-professor of law at the U. of Minnesota and now in private practice in New York. If so, we could call it:

YOU'RE HELPING ME FREE YOUR OWN RAPIST

Neil has gotten rapists off. He'd rather not, but these people have come to him for defense, and the women in the cases have, through their ignorance of the law, made his job easy. We'll document these cases, and then we'll present Neil's plan for preventing the freeing of rapists. In essence, it calls for calling a lawyer before you talk to the police. Get the lawyer to escort you through the station house, the hospital, the D.A. and courtroom maze. Have the lawyer make sure the cops take down your statement showing how much force was used (usually they jot down only the personally titillating elements of your case). Have the lawyer insure that your rights are protected; you can be sure the rapist has a lawyer protecting his rights.

Besides being well-credentialed and articulate, Neil is young (not over 40, I think) and very good looking. We could shoot some photos of the attorney in court if you like.

I enclose Xeroxes of articles of mine which ran in Playgirl. The Divorce article was reprinted by Educational TV's Consumer Survival Kit (expurgated, of course). I also write for Seventeen, Parade, Family Weekly, Modern Maturity, the New York Times, Chatelaine, Barrister, Change . . .

I look forward to hearing from you.

Sincerely,
Judi R. Kesselman

Why the Reader Wants to Read about It; Why the Editor Wants to Print It

Using everything you learned about marketing in Part I and Part II, your second paragraph should concisely tell the editor why his audience wants to read about the idea you're proposing. If you can't come up with a selling answer, you're trying to sell to the wrong magazine. It's not enough to simply say—as so many students do—"This is something your readers will really want to read about." Here's where you have to tailor the idea to your market. You must convince the editor that you know his audience's specific interests and, knowing them, are sure your idea will cater to them. For example, if you're suggesting an article on job hunting to *Seventeen* and you have authoritative evidence that teenage females are terrified of looking for their first jobs because they're afraid to have anyone know they don't know the first thing about it, cite your fact and the evidence. Since *Seventeen* caters to young females likely to be looking for first jobs, it will be obvious to the editor that you know that his magazine and your idea are made for each other.

If you're writing to Jack Brockley, Managing Editor of *Kiwanis Magazine,* and one of the principals of your story is a VIP in a local Kiwanis club, say so. But don't let tangential facts provide your only rationale for querying that magazine. Brockley would be more receptive to hearing about a new home maintenance wrinkle with no ties to Kiwanis (since almost 80 percent of his readers own homes) than about a Kiwanis member who has done nothing more interesting to readers than undergo fourteen ingrown-toenail operations.

Aside from showing the editor why his readers will want to read your suggested article, your second, third, and maybe even fourth paragraphs should show why he needs to publish it. Convince him by answering the following questions:

WHAT'S BEEN WRITTEN ON THE TOPIC BEFORE?

Many editors feel it's your responsibility to tell them whether competing or major noncompeting magazines have run similar ideas within the past several years—and how the printed articles differ in general terms from what you are suggesting. A hunt through *Reader's Guide to Periodical Literature (RGPL)* is one fast way to find out, although it doesn't list every major publication and none if any of the online ones. If you use the print edition, be sure to check the latest supplements and make a note of how current the most recent data really are.

Just because a similar idea has appeared in print, it won't rule out yours, especially if you can demonstrate a new handle. But it's important that you let the editor know you're aware of what's in print, and that you explain why you still feel certain your idea is right for her magazine at this time. If you've done your homework and aren't afraid to admit that the subject has been tackled before,

Illus. 9.2. Second Successful Query Letter

(date)
Mr. Don Feitel, Editor
Metropolitan Sunday Newspaper Group
260 Madison Avenue
New York, New York 10016

Dear Don:

QUERY: Don't Catch the Bad Food Flu!

One half of all cases of flu and those minor but distressing ailments we chalk up as a "virus" are probably cases of food poisoning. That's the word from Dr. Howard Bauman, a respected bacteriologist and vice president for science and technology at the Pillsbury Company in Minneapolis.

Bowman's 50 percent figure isn't something developed from a recent survey of minor illnesses that will soon appear in print all over. Doctors just don't take time out to study ordinary "flu" and ordinary "virus." Bauman bases his conclusion on a rule of thumb which a lot of experienced MDs and food scientists have developed over the years. It's a figure we can make stick. And if anything, the incidence of food poisoning is on the increase.

To supplement Bauman's expertise, we'll work in facts, opinions, guidelines, and anecdotes from MDs and food scientists as well as professors of home economics who are themselves starting to pay attention to this problem.

Today's homemaker just doesn't know how to handle food the way Grandma did! A few chief culprits are. . . .

. . . cooking food at too low a temperature (we'll give guidelines)

. . . keeping frozen foods on hand too long (guidelines)

. . . canning without knowing how (guides here too)

. . . not chilling big pots of food before storing them

. . . not covering food (the air is full of potentially harmful bacteria and spores)

. . . using cutting boards that absorb bacteria from one food and pass them on to others

. . . not knowing fish and chicken are particularly dangerous due to salmonella

. . . not knowing microwave ovens require special attention

We can cover, as pleasantly as possible, symptoms of major forms of food poisoning and how they differ from real flu and real virus infections. We'll leave readers with the pleasant food for thought that, after a few changes in kitchen routine, they can cut their family's flu and virus rate in half. How's that for a service piece?

Very Cordially,
Franklynn Peterson

your genuine confidence that the idea is still right for her publication can be contagious. On the other hand, if you say *Reader's Guide* shows nothing has ever been written in widely read magazines about left-handed mousetraps, and the editor read all about them in *Newsweek* six months ago, no matter how hard you pitch your idea, she may be wary of your research ability—with good reason.

WHAT'S NEW ABOUT THE SUBJECT?

While many editors feel obliged to run Thanksgiving pieces every November and Christmas pieces every December, they still want to know what's new about your Christmas tree or turkey story idea. Have you found previously suppressed evidence that St. Nicholas was really a dirty old man? Or can you show how to make fifty different and original tree decorations from soda pop bottle caps? Addressed to the right editor, these are salable ideas. Taking a new focus or a new slant on an old topic is a favorite device of many old pros.

Even on a heavily reworked subject, editors welcome queries that offer a new slant. Just when everybody assumed there wasn't a single new wrinkle to report on Jackie Kennedy Onassis, a bunch of enterprising writers noticed that May 19, 2004, was the tenth anniversary of her death. They all suggested anniversary articles on Jackie to their favorite editors, whose readers, they knew, were still eager to read about her. That added yet another dozen Jackie stories to the thousands already published. We bet that for issues appearing on the fiftieth anniversary of John F. Kennedy's death (November 22, 2013), editors will avidly welcome queries that suggest a new slant to the Kennedy story.

ARE PICTURES AVAILABLE?

Many magazines rely heavily on graphics. Editors at big-ticket magazines—the ones paying well over $1,500 for a story—let their art directors worry about getting and paying for pictures. Editors elsewhere often consider picture possibilities at the time they consider article assignments. So if pictures are likely to be an important aspect of your story, and if you know they're readily available or you can provide professional-quality illustrations yourself, it can't hurt to say so. But don't send photos or any other artwork with your query letter.

Who Are the Authorities?

Aside from wanting to know the uniqueness of your suggested idea, the editor wants to be sure you're genuinely able to produce a usable article if he assigns it. Unless he knows you by reputation, he needs to be convinced that you're enough of a hard-nosed researcher to come up with the kind of authoritative information that most magazines demand. Therefore, the classic query letter—even

Illus. 9.3. Even Pros Get Rejection Slips in Answer to Query Letters

(date)

Ms. Mary Cantwell

Senior Editor, Mademoiselle

350 Madison Avenue, NY 10017

Dear Ms. Cantwell,

> MADEMOISELLE
>
> *350 Madison Avenue, New York, N.Y. 10017*
>
> Our many thanks for your inquiry. Although the idea is not quite right for us, we appreciate your thinking of MADEMOISELLE.
>
> Features Editor

Can you use an article we title:

Are you setting yourself up for rape?

Males in social situations are almost always on the make—and they insist on making the assumption that the women who flirt with them are, too. We have quotes to that effect by a male judge in California, a male lecturer on the psychology of the sex offender, and a male reporter.

More women are raped by men they know than by men they don't know. We have statistics and quotes to that effect from researchers and women in crisis centers.

By trusting casual male acquaintances, women sometimes put themselves in situations where they seem to be inviting rape—and often enough, the "invitation" is acted on. We have anecdotes that are poignant revelations by women who have learned that lesson.

The article we propose to write for you makes the above points and ends by giving 5 Rules to Avoid Rapes by Acquaintances:

1—In every male-female situation, do what's best, wisest, and most comfortable for you.

2—Don't accept any favors from males without first finding out what favors they want in return—or making it clear there'll be no favors given.

3—Learn to recognize the situations males consider to be sexual and stay out of them unless you want sex.

etc.

We have published in PLAYGIRL, McCALL'S, VIVA, SEVENTEEN, and many others. A sample of our writing is enclosed.

Sincerely,

Judi R. Kesselman and Franklynn Peterson

from well-established pros—summarizes where the suggested article's facts, figures and opinions will come from.

If you're the principal source of information, you'd better come up with impressive personal credentials on the suggested topic. If you're pitching yourself as the authority for information that usually requires professional expertise (for example, medical, financial, child psychology, or employment advice), you'd better be a pro in that field. But if it's a craft idea, simply having successfully made the project is usually credential enough.

Here's a query letter written by a former student *(Ill. 9.4)*. Notice that she didn't claim to be an expert on how to make banners. She didn't have to. The editors who were interested in her idea—and she's sold it several times since—were convinced that if her local church hung her banners, it was proof enough that they were up to snuff.

This was a fine query letter for a beginner, but there were weak spots that could benefit from revision. We pointed them out to our student and, with our suggested revisions, her query sold. We've numbered the lines so you can follow our suggestions:

> Line 2: Change "great" to "cheap." That's your selling point. Do put it in the title. Also, say "banners." You're suggesting many designs.
>
> Line 3: Change "are" to "keep." Stronger verb. Delete "a supply of." Extraneous words.
>
> Line 4: Unless you mean "only," don't say it. There may be other troubles too. Change "have" to "buy expensive." Isn't that your point?
>
> Line 5: Delete "on hand." Extraneous.
>
> Line 6: Change "are used" to "are dragged out." Stronger verb.
>
> Line 8: Delete "I think" and "would like to know" and substitute "Let's tell your readers" etc. Notice how much stronger a positive statement is. Avoid "I think" at all costs.
>
> Line 9: Change "using" to "that combine" for a clearer statement.
>
> Line 10: Delete "This would be": sounds extraneous and unsure.
>
> Line 11: Delete "It" and the period to make one sentence.
>
> Line 12: Change "could" to "will" for a stronger statement. Don't say "any or all of." The editor wants to know now what you plan to deliver. Don't seem to vacillate or hedge. "Size": do you mean "sizes you can make them in" or what? Say it with enough words so the editor doesn't have to guess.
>
> Line 13: "Where and how to hang": is this an important point? Are these banners hung differently from others? Do they need special care? Your inclusion of this phrase without explanation, and in a position of priority in terms of order, would make me wary if I were the editor. It probably should be mentioned last and with an explanation.

Illus. 9.4. Student's Query Letter That Sold When Corrected

(date)
Ms. Doloris Kanten
Lutheran Brotherhood Bond
701 2nd Ave. So.
Minneapolis, MN 55402

Dear Ms. Kanten,

1   Could you use an article like this?

2   HOW TO CREATE A GREAT NEW BANNER FOR EVERY OCCASION

3   Most churches are accumulating a supply of
4   banners. The only trouble is, once you have banners
5   on hand you are stuck with them. The same banners
6   are used week after week and year after year.
7   Bright and bold decorations become "same old stuff."

8   I think your readers would like to know how to
9   make throw-away banners using permanent backs with
10   disposable designs in front. This would be a step
11   by step explanation of the throw-away idea. It
12   could include any or all of the following: size;
13   where and how to hang; how to finish off the back;
14   material to use for backs and fronts; idea sources;
15   how to apply designs and the advantages of these
16   throw-aways. I could arrange for photos of our
17   banner collection and the banner makers at work.

18   My only credentials are a desire to share a
19   good idea and lots of experience in making such
20   banners.

21   Hope you like the idea.

                 Sincerely,
                 (Sig.)
                 Mrs. Connie Scharlau
                 Route X
                 Arcadia, Wisconsin 54612

Line 14: "Idea sources": this is also unclear and needs more words.

Line 15: "The advantages": this should come first or second in your listing, as it's very important.

Lines 16 and 17: Good!

Lines 18, 19, and 20: Be sure of yourself, not self-negating. I would say instead: "I have had lots of experience in making such banners and would like to share it with your readers."

Line 21: Not really needed. If you run out of space on one page after your changes are made, you can leave it out.

When it comes to being expert enough in some field to be the sole authority behind an article, most of our students, we find, can offer national magazines only marginal personal qualifications. Even lower-paying national magazines do want some voice of authority—several voices if the idea is important or controversial or if the magazine is paying what it considers a good fee. When in doubt, bring in backup authorities.

An authority, of course, is someone who is defined as an authority. Anybody who is the first to do something new, whether it's using alcohol as auto power or baking mixless cakes, is automatically an authority. Anyone who has studied under the primary authority is usually considered an authority, as is anyone paid to make decisions based on his authority. Volunteers can also be authorities, provided they have been given titles (such as Governor's Adviser on Women's Affairs) or won awards (such as First Prize for Rose Raising at the Dane County Fair). For some stories, a local authority is perfectly acceptable. For other stories, you will need to choose people whose expertise, unlike our rose expert's, is not limited to a particular locale.

Authorities are not difficult to find even if you live away from the coastal centers of intellectual swarm. Look for them in colleges, junior colleges, trade schools, local corporations, local hospitals, local trade or professional associations and government agencies—and in scholarly journals in your library and in online searches. These days it isn't hard or even expensive to interview a number of authorities in distant locations by telephone or e-mail. (In Chapter 11 we'll discuss such research techniques in detail.)

Why You're Qualified to Write the Article

Writers, not just their authorities, need credentials. The editor reading your query letter will look for signs of your writing professionalism. There are three ways you can illustrate a substantial degree of professionalism *even in your first query.*

Illus. 9.5. Barbara Gibbons' "Letter That Launched My Professional Career"

barbara gibbons

(date)
Arthur M. Hettich, Editor
Family Circle
488 Madison Avenue
New York, New York

Dear Mr. Hettich:

I'm a former newspaper editor and fashion copywriter who has been teaching a very unusual group of adult classes for the past several months. The subject is "Creative Low Calorie Cooking."

This course was born out of my own experience with dieting. (I can't.) It wasn't until I started to "de-calorize" all my family's favorite foods that I succeeded in bringing my weight from 208 to 125 . . . where it's been for the past six years, without dieting!

These classes have been unbelievably successful, far beyond my wildest hopes. Each averages around 45 women . . . all ages, sizes and backgrounds. Before beginning these classes the sum total of my public speaking was getting a word in edgewise at dinner, but I guess my enthusiasm carries me through because my students really love it. I have a long waiting list, plus stacks of letters from women begging me to make room for them.

Which brings me to the point of this letter. I think that a regular monthly column on low-calorie cooking ideas would be a very popular feature in Family Circle . . . and I would like to write it. I don't mean yet another diet or nutrition column but one that takes a positive approach, with lots of recipes that only seem fattening!

I'm sure that your first thought for such a column would be to have it staff written or bylined by a name cookbook author. Let me explain why I sincerely believe that I would do a far better job. I know this subject better than anybody. Anybody. Because I don't just write about low-calorie cooking, I cook this way. For myself and my family, everyday for the past six years. I've read just about everything in print on the subject . . . all the great imaginative ideas, plus the so-called low-calorie recipes that are simply slick translations of standard recipes with some skim milk and saccharin thrown in. And I've taught this topic to hundreds of women. I know what they'll accept and what they won't . . . priceless experience you don't get at the keyboard.

Beyond possessing the skill and subject knowledge to write this column, I also have the energy and enthusiasm to promote it . . . to speak to women's groups or make TV or radio appearances. I've got a good story to tell and women want to hear it.

I do hope you'll share my eagerness. I'm enclosing some columns I wrote for local newspapers for my course plus some clippings and my resumé. I'd like very much to talk with Family Circle about it.

Thank you,
Barbara Gibbons

The first way is to write a dynamite query letter—the hallmark of a real pro. If you offer an exciting article idea, if you clearly delineate exactly what it is you'll concentrate on (focus and slant), if you spell out why the idea matches the editor's audience, if you single out qualified experts, if you show some writing ability, and if you accomplish this all within the confines of a single page, your letter will stand out from among the flood of second-rate queries and the editor will assume you're a pro.

The second way is to play up, near the end of your letter, any writing credentials you've accumulated. For instance, if you're proposing an article about teenage stress to *Seventeen* and you've written about teenage problems and mental health for markets such as your local newspaper's Sunday magazine, we suggest saying, "I've written about teen problems and mental health for regional magazines." If, instead, you've sold articles on gardening to *Elks* and on house plants to *Lady's Circle,* you could type, "I've written for such national magazines as *Lady's Circle* and *Elks.*"

There's something about writers—even those who can turn somebody else's rusty tin lean-to into a palace in print—that freezes their keystrokes when it comes to shedding a line of light on themselves. Don't let it happen to you, even if you have to go through twenty-seven drafts until you finally arrive at a suitable, accurate, but sufficiently laudatory sentence or two of credentials. It's important. If you get stuck, ask somebody else to draft the honors for you.

On the other hand, if you don't have any credentials to speak of, don't make them up. Don't mention, either, that you write a mimeographed PTA newsletter or once had a letter to the editor printed in the *Wisconsin Rapids Daily Tribune.* It's better to say nothing than to list among your credentials a market that's obviously amateur. And never, ever mention college or adult ed writing courses, or relatives who write or edit.

You may laugh at this list of don'ts, but we've found examples of every item in one or another student's first query letter.

The third way to demonstrate your writing credentials to a queried editor is to enclose photocopies showing a published article or two. This device has become a standard and important asset in making a sale. We've been at this exciting business for many decades and we still maintain a file of *tearsheets* (published articles we can photocopy and submit with query letters to editors who haven't bought from us recently). We try to send an article that's similar in subject or style to what we're suggesting. If you don't have anything similar, send along the best you have in print even if your only credit is a newspaper article. It proves, as nothing else can, that you really are publishable. If your byline isn't on the article (as sometimes happens with students who write first for local publications), send it anyway. No editor will doubt a piece is yours if you say it is. Rare is the writer with so little vanity he'll take credit for something he hasn't written. If you're so unethical as to send an unbylined article that was really written by Nat Hentoff, you'd better be able to deliver an article as fine as Nat would have turned in.

If you have never had an article professionally printed in a newspaper or magazine, do *not* send photocopies of articles from amateur club newsletters, college papers or the like. It's better to send nothing but a high-powered query letter.

Self-addressed Stamped Envelopes

Another courtesy that writers traditionally show editors is to enclose a self-addressed stamped envelope (SASE) with every query. But it's not just for courtesy alone that we enclose ours. We hope the SASE will encourage the editor to respond as quickly as possible, since he can simply jot down a quick "thanks but no thanks" on our original letter and slip that into our SASE. (Yes, we get rejections. Most pros average about one sale out of every ten to twenty queries.) Having been editors who've worked our own way through tottering stacks of mail, trying to answer all the queries quickly but thoughtfully, we can attest to how much extra time it seems to take to key in and print out a reply envelope.

Most editors use a standard form for all their rejections. Some are kind enough to scribble, "Let's see more ideas" on the form if a writer seems promising. If you get a personalized rejection, assume that you've sparked true interest and quickly send off another query.

When an editor has good news—an assignment—generally he'll stop to compose a personal assignment letter or e-mail. More about that in the next chapter.

Among established writers, one school of opinion contends that enclosing an SASE brands one a beginner. It's true that most editors don't expect frequent contributors to attach SASEs to their queries. Some editors don't expect SASEs from anyone who has sold anything to them, even one short piece—in fact, some prefer to get and answer these queries by e-mail. Trouble is, it's hard to know in advance which editors will recognize your name when they see it. When in doubt—which is much of the time—we stick in an SASE. It doesn't hurt our pride a bit, and it sometimes seems to get a quicker response.

Marks of an Amateur

There's some mysterious force that urges fledgling writers to stamp "Beware! Amateur writer at play!" all over their query letters. Aside from the points we've already covered, here is a list of some of the more obvious giveaways to avoid:

Colored paper. White 8½ × 11-inch paper is standard, everything else suspect.

Colored type. Black is standard, the blacker the better.

Schooling. Editors don't want to know where you've gone to school or even *if* you've gone. (The major exception is if you're suggesting an article for a scholarly publication.)

Appraisals of your writing skills by other editors, teachers or your mother.

Ultimatums. If your idea is clearly timely—that is, if long delay makes it unsalable—a fast answer is essential. In that case, an editor won't mind if you suggest that you'll assume they're not interested unless you hear by a certain date. We've recently discovered that a better way of putting it is to ensure *exclusivity* until that certain date. It means the same thing, but it sounds much nicer. (In the next chapter we'll discuss timing of queries and requeries.)

Pictures. Unless you're suggesting an idea that demands a photo story, don't send photos. If you want to write about something but don't trust yourself to describe it excitingly enough in your query letter, enclosing a snapshot may only convince the editor not to trust you with the article assignment.

10

Sales Tactics

S OME OF US CAN SELL SHOES OR VACUUM CLEANERS OR encyclopedias or cosmetics for a living. Others can't.

But almost without exception, every full-time freelance magazine writer has to be a salesman for his article ideas or he won't be able to write for magazines.

Back in the good old days, agents would handle magazine writers, making submissions to the likes of *Life, Reader's Digest, Liberty, American Mercury* and *Look*. In those days, postage stamps cost three cents and the *Digest* paid $2,200. Now postage is more than ten times that, but the *Digest* stopped climbing at about $4,500 and it's still among the best-paying markets.

Few agents bother to try to sell magazine articles these days, even for writers whose books they handle. But this new arrangement is really preferable to the old because magazines are a fast-paced communication medium. If editors and writers work out story ideas directly, with no agent to slow things down, the process usually moves along more smoothly.

The idea that a writer must be a salesman first of all is anathema to some of the more idealistic novices we've met. But article selling has nothing in common with the glib, high-pressure, memorized patter of a foot-in-the-door magazine subscription peddler. Editors don't expect, or even want, patter. Their doors won't slam, having been propped permanently open years ago by stacks of their boss's old magazines. Besides, if your ideas are sound and your presentation to the point, you're in a seller's market. Editors will welcome the chance to buy from you.

This doesn't mean that if you simply zip off a bunch of query letters you'll be deluged with prompt answers. Editors, as we've said before, are busy people. Sometimes their replies are excruciatingly slow. And when they reject perfectly fine ideas, they rarely take time to explain why. All these problems in communication raise immediate questions for people breaking into the field. We'll answer some of the most frequent.

Will Editors Steal My Ideas?

No!

Well, hardly ever. We can *prove* it happened to us once but that was many years ago by a flamboyant radical magazine out to conquer exploitation. We *suspect* it happened two other times. With more than six decades of experience between us, that makes less than one in a thousand purloined ideas. Those are better risks than in most professions.

Editors learn very quickly that it rarely pays to steal an idea. No matter how large or small a magazine, what its editor pays its writers is a tiny part of the overall budget. Comptrollers couldn't notice the savings earned by stealing one idea a month and having it staff-written. If an editor steals it to give to a writer friend, he stands to gain almost nothing but headaches. First, there's the chance of getting a reputation for absconding with ideas. That's dangerous in a small, gossipy profession like this. More to the point, it's very tough for one writer to do justice to somebody else's idea. The driving excitement, commitment, and basic knowledge of the subject are all missing, and it shows in the manuscript. Editors quickly learn that the best article comes from the writer who suggested the idea.

There's another reason editors rarely steal ideas. Beginning writers think ideas are hard to come by because they haven't learned to recognize them quickly. Pros have more ideas than they can handle; we have several folders full of ideas we can't get to. Editors generate more ideas than *they* can get to. On top of that, they're bombarded every day with still more ideas.

Editors tell us that most good ideas seem to have their *time.* Several writers offer the same—or very similar—ideas almost concurrently. What leads an editor to choose one writer from among the several? If she's worked with one of them before, she knows he can deliver. If another's query is the most exciting, she might choose him.

Why do we even bother to include this question of idea stealing under sales tactics? Because we've seen so many beginning writers paralyze themselves through misbegotten fear of having their ideas stolen. They hold back information in their query letters, trying to make it tough for an editor to learn enough so he can misappropriate the story. In doing so, they only ensure the editor's not getting enough of a feel for the idea. They hide away their most precious ideas in file drawers to await the day when they've made it and their brainchildren become unsnatchable. By that time those well-hidden ideas are stale and unexciting.

Besides, writers who hold back good ideas have small chance of making it. It's tough enough to make a living in this field even when you push your very best ideas.

How Long Should I Wait for a Reply to My Query?

How patient are you?

Many editors say it takes up to six weeks before they can get replies back. Some of our faster-paced colleagues allow them much less time. Vic Cox, for example, politely mentions in query letters that in approximately two weeks the idea will be sent to another editor. He told us, "I've been an editor. I know that if an editor likes the idea, he'll be back within that time anyway."

There is no hard-and-fast rule about how long to wait for a reply. Even the same editor takes longer at certain times during the year (especially when summer vacations and Christmas parties intervene) or at certain times of the month (especially going-to-press time). From our own experience, and having picked the brains of friends, we tend to give editors a month with our ideas. To an editor who's assigned us work in the recent past, we may send a copy of our query with a short, polite note (by mail or e-mail) asking if maybe it got lost somewhere along the way.

There's no law that says you have to wait for a reply to one query before you send out another for the same idea. You can set your lag time at two or three weeks if you like. If you've received no reply to a query letter by then, draft another one to an editor at another magazine.

You're not obliged to let the first editor know that you're sending the idea to a second editor. Editors don't, as a rule, take kindly to notes that sound like ultimatums or the work of a dilettante. What happens, you're sure to ask, if queried editor number two agrees to buy your story, and then editor number one finally gets back to you with a go-ahead? Assuming you haven't already told editor number two you'll accept his assignment, you could take the best offer. If you must refuse editor number two's offer, explain that an editor who was offered the story earlier belatedly got back to you with an okay. If you must refuse editor number one's offer, explain that he answered your query after you'd given up hearing from him and had pitched it elsewhere.

This kind of situation doesn't happen very often, but it did to us on one occasion. Editor number one, who lost out on the idea for having dallied so long, took the news graciously, as we expected he would. He's our friend to this day and has never stopped buying stories from us. In fact, we're sure his answers to our queries started coming back a little faster than they did before the incident.

Can I Submit the Same Idea to Several Editors at One Time?

Yes and no.

There was a time when magazine writing was a slower-paced profession. Dozens of magazines ran general interest articles. They'd publish a story on darn near any subject as long as the writing was exciting. Now magazines are quite topical and the topics come and go—quickly, at times. So writers have to get their ideas into print while they're still timely.

In those slower-paced, less news-oriented days, magazine writers used to query only one editor at a time. If the first editor didn't buy, an idea would often be equally timeless the day it landed on a second, third, or fourth editor's desk. Many editors in this business still prefer that old way. Many of that breed feel they're in fierce competition with magazines similar to theirs. They nurture the hope that an exclusive on your ideas will give them a competitive edge. Others like to feel they're the only editor you want to write for, forgetting that a year's writing fees from them may not even cover your rent.

Until literary agents introduced the book auction, book editors also expected one-at-a-time queries. Now multiple submissions of book proposals are increasingly the rule. (For more about *that,* see our companion book *Authors Handbook.*) Magazine writers, too, are pushing toward multiple query submissions. Here are some guidelines based on the pros' collective experience.

FOR QUERYING IDEAS THAT HAVE TIME VALUE

If you have a hot idea—one that will lose its value if it isn't in print soon—and it's one you think several magazines might buy but you're not yet a name writer, first draft a punchy, well-documented query letter. Then, we suggest from personal experience, do one of three things:

Send it to all the editors you've selected, all at the same time. Somewhere prominent in each letter, ask for a prompt response due to the topicality of your idea. (You can even risk raising a few editorial hackles by suggesting a reasonable date by which you'd like a yes or no.) Mention in the query letter that the idea is being sent to several publishers "because time is of the essence" in getting the story in print.

Not all our colleagues agree with this approach. They feel it will weaken the chance of a sale to an editor prejudiced against multiple submissions. They recommend sending the query to one editor at a time, starting at the top of your list and working down to the lower-paying or less prestigious magazines. If you do that, include a statement that you're sending the idea to just that editor but that since it has time value you can keep it exclusive just so long. (We usually offer several weeks of exclusivity.) When your deadline arrives—assuming you haven't heard by then—simply mail out a new query to the next editor on your list.

A third way that it's possible to sell a hot idea is by phone or e-mail. We'll cover that next in this chapter. But keep in mind that many periodicals have long lead times—often as long as six months—and while newspapers stop the presses all the time, it's rare for a magazine to get anything into print in less than three months from the time it's written.

FOR QUERYING IDEAS WITHOUT TIME VALUE

If you have an idea that's very exciting to you but obviously won't become quickly dated, you can't so easily hurry editors into fast responses no matter how eager you are to get started with research and writing. In this situation, many of our colleagues simply create slightly different slants for each of several editors, don't mention they're making multiple simultaneous submissions, and mail them all at once. Beginners, so delightfully full of hope, fear that every editor on their list will offer an assignment. Take it from us old-timers: It rarely happens.

In case more than one editor does give you an okay and the slants of your letters overlap, we counsel taking the best offer. It's true, you risk alienating an editor, but in our experience it's a very small risk and well worth it. Editors are well aware of (and many even sympathize with) the hustling required to make a living as a freelance writer. Some of our best writer friends have been—and will again be—editors.

FOR QUERYING THE SAME IDEA TO MAGAZINES WITH DIFFERENT AUDIENCES

If you have an idea that appeals to several completely different groups of readers, you are legally and ethically free to send exactly the same idea simultaneously to the magazines that reach those readers. Your only constraints are to make sure the readers of those magazines don't overlap and to make it clear that you're selling each editor *one-time rights*. Julian Block, who specializes in short tax-tip articles, often sells not just the same idea, but the same identical article, to publications like *Electrical Contractor, Dental Economics,* and *Successful Farming.* He tells each editor that what's for sale is not *first publication rights* but *one-time serial rights exclusive to your special audience.* Most editors of narrowly targeted publications welcome simultaneous submissions because they know they can generally buy one-time rights for less than first rights. (Chapter 15 explains *rights* in depth.)

Is It Okay to Phone or E-mail an Editor?

Sure, if you have a good reason. By "good reason" we mean something the *editor* thinks is a good reason. Here are three common reasons writers use for calling or e-mailing editors that editors almost *never* see as good reason.

THE IDEA IS TOUGH TO EXPLAIN IN WRITING

Tell that to an editor and you're sure to promote molehills of confidence in your ability to commit any assigned idea to paper.

I DON'T HAVE TIME TO WRITE A QUERY

That's *your* problem! Since you're selling and the editor's buying, you'd better keep *her* problems in mind. It takes much more of her time to talk on the phone or pick your e-mail out of the spam pile than to skim your query letter.

I WANT TO GET TO KNOW THE EDITOR BETTER

So do hundreds of other writers. Most editors try to avoid phone calls from them all and end up hating the ones who do get through no matter how nice their phone voices are. Read the magazine and get to know the editor by his editorial tastes.

Here are what the typical editor generally considers valid reasons for accepting your call or answering your email:

> He asked you to phone or e-mail.
>
> You have corresponded with him for many months. He has definitely encouraged you to continue suggesting ideas (not simply been polite). You can, and will, query in writing with an idea you have but your idea has six different slants, all perfectly salable. You want to get his input into which slant to take.
>
> You have a genuinely hot topic that could vanish before your query letter makes the rounds. This can't be an idea that depends on today's headlines because that will be old hat by the time most weekly and monthly magazines can whip it into print. But it may be a topic for which your access to a key resource is about to vanish. Let's say Robert Redgrave is in town to visit a long-lost sister, you've been promised an interview, and he's leaving town tomorrow noon. Even in this situation, you'd better be prepared to outline appropriate writing credentials for the editor to whom you pitch the story over the phone or in e-mail. Enough editors have been bamboozled into making assignments to non-writers who talk an exciting game that all editors are cautious about this way of doing business.

Can I Drop in to See an Editor?

Sure, under the right conditions. But unless you're a well-known pro, there are probably only two right conditions. Don't be like our naïve Wisconsin student who announced one day she was going to New York to "see the editors." She thought that if she could talk her way into an editor's office, he'd hand her an assignment and she'd at last crack the national markets. But she'd never queried those editors, so they'd never seen her name or her credentials, which consisted of bylines in a few local publications. And when she e-mailed for appointments, she had no firm story ideas in mind to offer them. The editors politely declined to see her. She should have figured out that if they took time to chat with every would-be professional, they'd have no time to put out their magazines.

A lot of beginners also pick up the idea that in order to make it as a magazine writer, you've got to live in New York City. They must think there are lots of late-night clubs where all the editors hang out awarding assignments. True, editors attend their share of literary cocktail parties and writers' club meetings, but they go to relax just like everybody else. It's considered gauche to button-hole them there to pitch article ideas.

While we were living, working and partying in New York City and met lots of editors socially and at ASJA meetings, we generally kept to the mails our initial business contacts with them. After we moved to the Midwest and were rare visitors incapable of becoming nuisances, the editors we had written for shuffled appointments to see us. Rarely, we also set up appointments with editors who didn't know us, since face-to-face talks can pinpoint a publication's changing interests faster than trial-and-error query letters. But it helped that by then we had a lot of impressive tearsheets to flash.

So we'll agree that it is sometimes appropriate to suggest visiting an editor if you're traveling and plan to be in the city where the magazine is edited. But unless the editor knows you by reputation, write first to ask if you can visit, include a few brief sample article suggestions and, assuming you have some, mention writing credentials at magazines similar in stature.

The best occasion for seeing an editor in person is if he suggests it. Even if it isn't convenient, you should try to make the visit. Although most editors are accustomed to looking at the world through a computer monitor, some enjoy face-to-face contact with writers who they feel can benefit from personal guidance. A request that you come in and talk is solid indication of interest in your writing. (Assuming it's your writing that's on the agenda. A student of ours had been querying an editor regularly and had finally sold a slightly salacious article. He asked her out to dinner and she went, envisioning his proposal of several assignments, maybe even a steady monthly column. What she got was another kind of proposition. But that's a rare situation.)

What Does an Assignment Look Like?

Most of them look like a lot of red tape and deadlines.

We've reproduced a couple of our assignment letters and contracts so you can see what some of them look like. There are certain standard elements, but not all assignment letters contain them all. Also, some letters are brief but are attached to contracts that require the author's signature. The assignment, whether in letter or contract form, contains such clauses and conditions as:

PAYMENT

That's one of the more important things to tie down before beginning the assignment. If it isn't in the assignment letter, ask what it is. If you agreed on a fee over the phone but it isn't mentioned in the assignment letter, respond with your

Illus. 10.1. Assignment Letter

seventeen

320 PARK AVENUE
NEW YORK, NY 10022
212-759-8100
Judi R. Kesselman
16 Pont Street
Great Neck, New York 10021

Dear Judi.

Your outline looks good and we would like you to go ahead with the article HOW TO IMPROVE YOUR TEST SCORES.

We will pay $550 for a mutually satisfactory article of approximately 2,000 words. Our reject fee is one quarter of the total offered. Please let me know what sort of deadline would be agreeable to you.

We will pay receipted expenses up to $75, so keep a record of long distance calls, gas used when doing research, etc., for we will need an itemized accounting in order to reimburse you. If you exceed that amount, let me know.

This can be a very useful article for our audience and we'll look forward to seeing it.

Sincerely,
Annette Grant
General Features and Fiction
Editor
AG:ds

own letter accepting the assignment and stating the agreed-upon fee. If the editor doesn't write back saying, "Hey, that's not what we agreed on," then the fee is as legally binding as if it were in the original assignment letter.

With most magazines, the fee quoted in the assignment letter is pretty well fixed in the editor's mind. But if it's negotiable, the only time you can negotiate is *before* you turn in the assignment. (See Chapter 16 for more on the economics of writing.)

Ill. 10.2. Assignment Contract

13-30 Corporation
Assignment Confirmation and Agreement to Transfer
Publication Rights

TO: Judi Kesselman and Franklynn Peterson
3006 Gregory St.
Madison, Wisconsin 53711

FROM: Don Akchin
Associate Editor

This agreement confirms your assignment, and defines the rights and duties
of both you as author and 13-30 Corporation as publisher.

1.   Confirmation of Assignment
You agree to research and write an article on __job hunting__ for the
upcoming edition of __18 Almanac__. The article will run approximately __3,000__ words and will be due in 13-30 Corporation's offices
on __June 11__.

The fee for your article will be __$1,000.00__. 13-30 Corporation
makes every effort to pay writers within three weeks of submission of manuscripts in satisfactory form, and guarantees that writers will be paid no later
than the last printer deadline for the magazine named above.

In the event that the draft first submitted to us is unsatisfactory, you agree to
revise and rewrite the article as required. If the revised or rewritten draft of
the article is unsatisfactory (as determined by the associate editor) 13-30
Corporation will pay you a kill fee of one-third the agreed-upon writer's fee.

In addition to your writer's fee, 13-30 Corporation agrees to reimburse you
for reasonable travel and telephone expenses incurred in connection with
this article. Such expenses are not to exceed __$50.00__ and you must
provide us with copies of receipts or bills in order to be reimbursed.

2.   Warranty of Material
You warrant that the article you submit to 13-30 Corporation is original,
that you are the sole author and owner of the article and all rights to that article, that it has never before been published, and that it contains no unlawful or infringing matter. In the event that certain parts of the article <u>have</u>
been previously published (including tables, charts or graphics), you guaran-

tee that permission has been obtained for publication in 13-30 magazines, and you will submit to 13-30 Corporation a copy of the permission document and information for credit lines.

3.   Transfer of Publication Rights

You grant to 13-30 Corporation exclusive First North American Serial Rights to the article described above for use in a 13-30 publication. In addition, you grant 13-30 Corporation the right to produce and distribute reprints of the article and the right to grant reprint permission to other publishers. In the event that 13-30 Corporation receives requests to reprint or translate your article, you will receive 50 percent of the permission fee charged, if any. In addition, you agree to grant, for a mutually satisfactory fee, 13-30 Corporation the right to use all or part of your article in other 13-30 publications. If at all possible, however, you will be given an opportunity to update and recheck your article for accuracy.

You retain all other rights of copyright to your work. (Note that you retain these rights to the original manuscript, not to the edited version.)

4.   Editing and Publication Decisions

You agree that your article will be subject to editing by 13-30 Corporation, and that we cannot guarantee publication. However, in the event that your satisfactory manuscript is not published in the magazine named above, 13-30 Corporation will pay you the agreed-upon writer's fee, and retain First North American Serial Rights to publish that article for one year. After this time, you are free to market your manuscript elsewhere.

5.   Signature and Personal Data

Please sign and date this agreement and return one copy to 13-30 Corporation immediately. If two authors are involved, both signatures are required on this agreement. In order to issue payment to you, we will also need your Social Security Number. This information will be considered strictly confidential.

If you have any questions about the terms of this agreement, please contact me.

DEADLINE

Many editors plan their assignments with specific issues in mind. Your editor may be counting on your story for the next issue he's putting together. Even if he isn't, he probably knows that most writers work best when they shoot for deadlines. Unless you've worked with a particular editor before, you won't know for sure which reason governs his assigned deadline. So *meet your deadlines.* If you find the deadline unrealistic for some reason, let the editor know *as soon as you can.* That's the professional way of doing business.

LENGTH

The editor suggests the length of your article to fit his magazine's needs. Some editors expect fairly strict adherence to this figure; they block out a certain amount of space for each article. If it comes in much too long or too short, they have to do heavy editing, ask for a rewrite, or juggle space allocations. If they've got enough extra manuscripts on file, they may even reject your article.

Other editors are more casual. They give suggested lengths and accept the fact that most writers turn in three or four extra pages. There's really no way to tell how a particular editor feels until you've worked with him. The safest approach is to be sure, as you write your first draft, that you cover all important points with as much depth as each deserves. If the first draft you knock out looks as if it may be more than 25 percent above or 5 percent below the suggested length, warn by phone or letter. (Editors figure cutting is always easier than thinking up new copy to add.) If you don't get specific instructions or negative feedback, assume your new length is acceptable.

CONTENT

The editor may point out certain elements she particularly wants to see in the article, as well as material she'd like excluded. She may restructure your slant if she thinks her emphasis works better than yours. This may be because she understands her readers better than you do, or because she's interested in only part of your overall idea, or because she wants more of an overview than you suggested. Most editors are sticklers in this area. If they say they want a topic or slant covered in your story, they expect to see it covered. If they say they don't want it covered, they don't.

Like other points in the assignment letter, suggestions for content are negotiable. If you think the editor's approach may cause problems for you or your story, say so immediately. The smoothest way to raise the subject is by asking the editor for her thinking behind the approach that bothers you. After that, explain the problems you're having with it: "I see it a bit differently" or "I don't think I can get access to information that will substantiate that." She may convince you that her approach will work, she may alter her approach, or she may have a report about it on her desk that hasn't been published yet. The best way to handle a question about content is by phone. It's one time an editor will be grateful you called.

Illus. 10.3. Assignment Letter with Helpful Guidelines to Author from Editor

PLAYGIRL INC. 1801 CENTURY PARK EAST, CENTURY CITY. SUITE 2300 LOS ANGELES, CALIFORNIA 90067 213 553-8006

Ms. Judi Kesselman
106 South Middle Neck Road
Great Neck, LI 11021

Dear Judi:

This is to confirm your assignment to do an article for Playgirl about Hit-and-Run Lovers, the men who take you to bed and whom you never hear from again. As we discussed they are a proliferating breed, and every woman on the scene, unless she is extremely cautious, will run into one or more of them. Most women are left unhappy by this kind of man. And generally they are left wondering "What did I do wrong?" "Did he find me unattractive?" etc. etc. Probably she did nothing wrong. These guys are that way for other reasons—and the reasons are what we want to uncover in this article. From shrinks and men of this kind, find out their motivations, hang-ups, etc. Of course, you must have women talking about their experiences and reactions, and you will supply the usual anecdotes. In the end the reader should understand the warning signs in order to avoid or be prepared for a man who is a hit-and-run lover. Also find out if there is any behavior on a woman's part that encourages this, or attracts this kind of man.

In passing you might mention the increase of women who hit and run as well—but that most women still don't and are left saddened by such encounters.

Payment will be $750. Deadline as we agreed is November 22. The piece should be about 3,000 words. Kill fee is one-quarter.

My best to you as always.

Sincerely,
Carol Botwin
Articles Editor

CB:rg

RIGHTS

Under the copyright law you own your story, every last well-chosen word in it. The magazine is obliged to buy from you the right to publish it. We'll devote considerable space in Chapter 15 to which rights you should sell and which rights the magazine's publisher wants to buy. For now, keep in mind that this aspect of the assignment is also negotiable.

KILL FEE

This is writers' jargon for a *money guarantee.* The better magazines guarantee professional writers that they'll be paid something no matter what may go wrong between getting the assignment and seeing the story in print. And hundreds of things can go wrong. The profile's subject may die or be sent to jail in disgrace, the magazine's competition may come out with a story on the same topic before you turn yours in, promises of information may fail to materialize, the FDA may discover that the face cream you planned to write about causes stuttering, or all of the above.

It never ceases to amaze us how poorly communications professionals communicate with each other. On occasion, the editor who assigns the story may have a prose picture in mind that's totally different from the one in your head. In such a situation, your assigned story will be turned down—with regret, to be sure, but turned down nonetheless. It's happened to us with more frequency than any of the foregoing occurrences.

If your letter of assignment contains provisions for a kill fee or guarantee, you'll be paid something for your efforts even if the editor can't run your piece. Kill fees vary from about one-fifth to one-third and rarely even one-half of the fee you would have been paid if everything had gone as hoped. Usually the killed article reverts to you and you can attempt to place it elsewhere. We were able to turn around an article killed by *Parade* and sell it to short-lived *Vital* magazine. Most articles, however, are written with a specific readership in mind and can't be resold so easily.

A kill fee can be a two-edged sword. It allows editors to kill articles simply because they're sorry they assigned them. We got three memorable kill fees in our careers. The first, Judi received when *Good Housekeeping* decided that even heavy editing couldn't save her first-ever investigative article. It was justified. She had no idea how to write a professional magazine piece.

But in 1977, Judi pitched *Playgirl* "the first-ever article for a popular magazine" on date rape. When she turned it in, the editor killed it because of cold feet about being thrust in the forefront of a fight to stop something still publicly considered "the woman's fault." And in the early '80s, good old *Good Housekeeping* sent us a kill fee instead of publishing what we hoped would be the first-ever popular article exposing the facts that teenagers get adult-type depression and that tested medications could alleviate it. Despite our well-documented personal experience and our many quotes and anecdotes from well-credentialed authorities, the magazine's sole independent expert (an East-coast child psychologist who thrived on selling years of therapy sessions) convinced them the science in the piece was suspect.

We still grieve at having those two pieces killed. Professional writers are never eager to accept a kill fee. Not only is it poor pay for the time and energy spent, but any rejection makes writers feel they failed to deliver. Still, we like to get assignments that contain guarantees. They are concrete assurances that the editor is serious about wanting the story and will most likely help patch up what's wrong with it if it misses the mark. When an editor pays a kill fee, he has nothing tangible to show for the money. Rather than explain the kill fee to the bookkeeper, he'd prefer to work a bit to save the article.

You're not likely to be given guarantees for your early assignments, although Judi got one her first time out. But keep them in mind because as you build your reputation, you'll not only get them but find they're often negotiable. There's very little in magazine writing that's not negotiable except for strict compliance with the highest professional standards.

PART IV
How to Write Your Article

11

Research, Research, Research

Before *READER'S DIGEST* PUBLISHED AN ARTICLE MEN-
tioning that George Washington stood six feet three and a half inches in
his size thirteen boots, editorial researcher Nina Georges-Picot was assigned as
its fact-checker. She wondered if old George really owned boots that big. But
how to find out? First she pored over the New York Public Library's sixteen volumes about Washington. Nothing. Next she studied books, letters and diaries
of Washington's associates. None of them cared a whit about George's shoe size.
The ardent fact finder called Mount Vernon, where somebody knew about a
statue in the Richmond, Virginia, state capitol building that was made entirely
from plaster casts of Washington's body. Ms. Georges-Picot called Richmond
and prevailed on the building's superintendent to measure George's feet. With
boots on, the right foot was ten and seven-eighths inches long, the left eleven
inches—a man's size eight boot. If one can believe the accuracy of the measurement, that's a long way from size thirteen.

George Washington's boot size may seem entirely too trivial to have been
worth so much of the *Reader's Digest* researcher's time. But the writer who evi-
dently was caught with the wrong information in his article probably doesn't
think so. We hope he went back and double-checked because, if the researcher
was right, that tiny foot on such a big man could make a peg for another George
Washington article.

A good magazine article must entertain. Some of the entertainment is
dished out from a service of catchy facts, figures and formulations. As our anecdote about Washington's boot size illustrates, they'd all better come from authoritative sources, sources that can be trusted to be accurate and precise.

The facts should be not only accurate but plentiful. When we were
editors, some of the dreariest stories we rejected were ones in which the authors tried to stretch too little research across too many pages. Many writers
we know spend as much time at their local libraries as they do at their keyboards. We make it a rule always to collect more information than we think
we're going to use, so we can choose the best and the most apropos in making
our points. We think of ourselves not as composers, but as arrangers who
assemble other people's themes and counterpoints until they match the available
instruments.

A Fact Is Only as Good as Its Source

There are at least three practical reasons why writers should stick to dependable sources *and keep track of what they are:*

IT'S MORE EFFICIENT

Let's say that you're researching a story about the shrinking job market. From a chart of statistics, you extrapolate that the number of U.S. workers over sixteen is projected to increase by only about 7½ percent over the next dozen years. Then, while organizing or writing the article, you decide it will be more effective to count only the number of workers over age twenty-one. You'll waste a lot of time relocating your information unless you also made note of your source: a report from the Bureau of Labor Statistics that you found on the Internet at ftp://ftp.bls.gov/pub/special.requests/ep/labor.force/clfa1050.txt. (If we find the information in a printed source, not online, we jot down the title, call number and name of the library unless we used only one library in researching the article.)

IT'S MORE BELIEVABLE

One author writes, "We can expect a labor force increase of only 7½ percent over the next dozen years." Another writes, "The latest report from the Bureau of Labor Statistics projected a labor force increase of only 7½ percent over the next dozen years—an average of about half a percent a year." Which sounds more like a fact? Which sounds more dramatic? If the source of your fact is authoritative, its mention lends credibility.

IT'S SAFER

If you say that we're adding jobs at an average of only a half percent a year, without saying how or where you got your numbers, in effect you're personally vouching for the statement's accuracy. If, instead, you include the specific source of your data, you are reporting it. Aside from being more authoritative, it also leaves you practically in the clear if somebody else got the numbers wrong. As we saw in the example about George Washington's boots, a fact is no better than its source.

There are two basic kinds of sources. If you get your information directly from trustworthy sources (from the expert's mouth, as it were) that's a primary source. If, instead, you take the information from a newspaper story, article, book, movie or online report you're using a *secondary* source. This distinction is not merely academic, as all too many writers have learned the hard way— notably Jason Blair, the *New York Times* reporter who was caught taking other writers' in-print anecdotes without correctly attributing the source, and Doris Kearns Goodwin, who (in her own words) "failed to provide quotation marks for phrases that I had taken verbatim" from someone else's book. After *The Nation* published an article by columnist Eric Alterman, it had to run the apology, "When this column was originally published, a fact-checking error caused the word 'owner' to be removed from a reference to the Jewish 'owner-editors' of *U.S. News & World Report* and *The New Republic.* This may have made it appear as if Alterman was addressing the issue of Jewish 'editors' in general with regard to media coverage and Israel, rather than merely the two men he cited." Sloppy fact checkers have lost their jobs over smaller errors than these. Likewise, sloppy writers have lost dependable markets.

At this point, you're probably expecting a repeat of a rather standard lecture: Get Your Facts Straight. But we assume that every nonfiction writer starts with that premise. What isn't so obvious to a beginner—and unfortunately to some more advanced writers, too—is that we can't accomplish that goal 100 percent of the time. We don't all have staff positions at plush publications that let us spend hours verifying the size of Washington's feet. We can't all afford the time it would take to check the primary source of every useful statement we encounter. As we've seen, not even *The Nation* gets all its facts straight before publication. But we do follow these three guidelines:

> Whenever possible, we start right at the primary source.
> When we're using a secondary source, we try to double-check with an *independent* secondary source.
> We always report our information accurately and, unless there's an overriding reason, identify our source in print or, at least, in the notes we keep long after the article's been published.

There are five reliability checks against which you should measure the facts you research. Use at least one of them to assess every piece of information you encounter—but keep in mind that no measure is foolproof.

ACCURACY

If you see an event happen and report it carefully, you and your readers assume you've also reported it accurately. But six eyewitnesses to any accident may in reality render six conflicting reports, and six polls may phrase the same general question slightly differently. So an "accurate report" may not always reflect everyone's truth. Total accuracy is seldom achieved.

AUTHENTICITY

Not to be confused with accuracy, authenticity is what you get automatically from a primary source. It comes from the horse's mouth—the logical, natural origin for the chosen information. You can present it as the source's statement, but it isn't the same as verified fact.

The best case for showing the distinction between authenticity and accuracy is that of the Pentagon. It's about the only team in town that has accurate information about U.S. missile strength. When it's asking for money, it claims there aren't enough missiles; when it brags about the good job it's doing, there are suddenly more than enough missiles planted in the ground. Sharp writers make it clear that statements about missile-strength coming from the Pentagon are authentic, but they don't make claims about the statements' accuracy.

CREDIBILITY

The source's way of telling his facts and backing them up, or his proven track record, may lead you to conclude that the source is credible. This suggests that his facts can be believed. So *that's* how to present the information to your readers—with "I believe" or "he believes" stated or implied.

PLAUSIBILITY

If a fact simply makes sense to you on the face of it, it will hopefully make sense to other people. That's how we'd write it—not as verified fact but as plausible consideration.

CORROBORATION

If you obtain information from a separate, also believable source that verifies or substantiates the first source's facts, and tell your readers how you've verified it, they will rarely question that it's indeed a fact. Corroboration is the professional writer's strongest ally—and three witnesses is always five times better than just two.

The Perils of Internet Research

As we showed in Chapter 1, the Internet is filled with ready-done research about everything under the sun, much of it free for the taking. We were able to update 90 percent of this book just by looking things up online from our desk. If you haven't selected the search engine you prefer (we still like Google) and learned its rules and shortcuts for using key words and doing advanced searches most effectively, do it now.

Some search engines are useful for special searches even when they're not best for everything. Lycos, unlike Google, lets you specify whether to find what you're looking for in text on the site or in the site's name (URL). The National Library of Medicine's *Medline* and *Premedline* databases are excellent search tools for finding health-related authorities and authoritative information.

In any search, choosing the right key words is the key to fast success, though

Google's internal list of synonyms makes the job a bit easier. When we looked up *search* + *"key word"* in Google, it found 753,000 hits (website pages where the two appeared together). When we typed in *"search engine"* + *"key words"* + *"Web search"* + *tips* and used Advanced Search to request pages updated in the last three months, it narrowed the results to about 650 hits, a number we could reasonably scan in a few minutes. (It helps if you opt to see fifty results on a page, not ten, since you'll usually find what you need within the first fifty or one hundred results if the engine is good.) On the other hand, guard against narrowing your choices so much that you block out half of what you're looking for.

If you need detailed help learning how to use key words and search rules, you can find it by typing *"search engine"* + *"key words"* + *"Web search"* + *tips* as key words in your favorite search engine.

Bear in mind that a lot of what's offered as fact on the Internet has been poorly researched and may be untrue. Also, since some sites try to disguise opinion as fact, make sure you get independent authoritative corroboration for every "fact" you decide to use in an article—and then be sure to cite its sources so that readers can decide if it's true. Also, if you copy more than a phrase from a source, be careful not to tread on anyone's copyright or to overstep the limits of fair use *(see Chapter 15).*

Finding Treasure in the Library

Every year or so we used to teach a short course in research techniques for professionals in many fields, and the session we spent in the reference room of the University of Wisconsin Memorial Library boggled most of our students' minds. The amazed response was, "We never dreamed there were all these tools to meet our specific needs."

A good library is a primary depository of *secondary sources* and a useful lead to primary data as well. Surprisingly, we've found that its untariffed wealth is sadly untapped by beginning writers. A typical nonfiction novice enters the local public library, heads for the card catalog or computerized index, looks up the subject, checks out available books and calls it a day. But books are rarely useful to any magazine writer other than a history buff. By the time a book is written, printed, and tucked away on a library shelf, its information is usually at least a couple of years old. Smarter beginners add *Reader's Guide to Periodical Literature* (RGPL) to the search. But by the time a magazine writer gets an assignment, does her research, turns in the completed story, the editors find space for it, it's published, *RGPL* indexers index it, and *RGPL* is printed or put online, *that* information is likely to be a year old.

Books and general interest magazine articles *can* be useful for providing an overview of the subject you're researching, especially if it's one you're not terribly familiar with. If you're doing a low-budget research job for a magazine that knows it can't pay for (and therefore can't demand) exhaustive research, books and popular magazines are often a quick route to information, examples, and maybe anecdotes too. But even in that situation, your editor will expect more than just a rehash of what his readers have already read. Here's how to get it from the library.

THE LIBRARIAN

Right after God created angels, She made librarians. Your first contact after you take off your coat should be with a reference librarian. Say precisely what it is you're looking for, and why.

Not: "Something on cars."

Instead: "Something very current about pollution-control systems on diesel cars for a *Popular Auto Magazine* article that I'm researching."

Not: "A book about protein."

Instead: "Whatever is very new about high-protein diets and especially their hazards. I'd like to do an exposé on them for *Fat Prevention Magazine.*"

Great Neck, New York, librarian Elsa Resnick told us about a man who came in one morning and asked for "information about the old West." At the end of the day he was still searching through mountains of books and magazines. Starting a conversation, she found out all he wanted was an early map. Within five minutes she'd found what he was looking for.

As you become more familiar with your own library, you'll learn where all useful volumes are kept. But in some libraries, the most useful ones are *behind* the reference librarian's desk. As the librarians become more familiar with you, they'll probably feed you tips about what's back there—and about new reference tools as they come in.

THE REFERENCE COLLECTION

In most libraries, the tools designed for researchers are set aside as reference collections. In some libraries they are centrally located, sometimes filling entire rooms. In others, each division maintains its own collection. Some libraries allow a few of these books to be checked out; others insist that all must be used on library grounds. (The Great Neck library where Judi researched her book *Stopping Out* had a marvelous system of permitting overnight check-outs from after 5 P.M. to 9 A.M. the next morning. That way, the books were always there for researchers while the library was open, but could be taken home by late owls and deadline beaters.)

How does a professional magazine writer use the reference collection? Let's say you need current information on the ancient art of enameling. Your library might have a book or two that covers the topic. You might also find a popular article or two by using *RGPL* and other useful guides to current periodicals. But you still might not have all the information you'd like, and you might want to interview experts for livelier material. If your reference room has, for instance, *A Directory for Information Resources in the United States: Social Sciences,* published by the National Referral Center of the Library of Congress, that volume's index will steer you to entry number 1877, the Department of Industries of the National Museum of History and Technology, which is an unbiased, authoritative source of information on, among other things, "use of enamels from ancient times to the present." The entry gives its address and phone number; to obtain additional information you need only write or phone.

No matter how abstruse the subject, it's rare that a well-stocked library reference collection doesn't have, if not information, at least a solid lead to information sources. As we said before, the keeper of these nuggets is the librarian. We've found that the tougher the questions, the happier most librarians are to work on them for you.

PERIODICALS

Many libraries maintain their magazine collections in their reference departments. Others keep them separate. Popular periodicals are indexed in *RGPL* and such. Some professional and scholarly periodicals are indexed online, on the publisher's website. Others are indexed in *Education Index, Sociology Index, Index Medicus* and the like (*see below*). For the freelance magazine writer, these academic periodicals offer valuable keys to current thinking and the latest research. Some libraries' collections of both general and technical periodicals are extensive; others are inadequate for our needs. But most now have interloan facilities for getting needed periodicals within a week or two, and many libraries maintain subscription lists of the holdings of other libraries in the state. (We'll explain interloan further at the end of this section.)

INDEXES AND ABSTRACTS

These readers' guides to professional journals are published by professional societies and by companies catering to the needs of the various professions. One of those needs is quick access to research data. Therefore, a great many professional journals and their matching abstracts or indexes are on library shelves, if not online, within a few months after the scientists have completed their research papers. For the magazine writer, timeliness is assured.

Aside from new, un-dog-eared facts and figures, the journals also provide leads to the papers' authors, the people doing the most current research, whom you can reach by mail, e-mail or telephone for the most up-to-date information, interpretation and opinion. The journals usually note their authors' professional addresses.

An *index* is simply a categorized listing of article titles or topics plus authors' names. You can find journal articles on your topic by first locating the general subject in the index and then singling out the titles that seem most appropriate. With your list of article titles, journal names and page numbers, you can skim the journals in your library's periodical collection (or through interloan) to pick out what you need.

An *abstract* does everything that an index does. In addition, it includes a thumbnail summation of the salient points covered by each indexed article. The summations generally save having to skim dozens of articles to locate the two or three that are right on target. Sometimes the abstracts are comprehensive enough that, depending on how much detail you require, you can work from *them* and not have to read the articles at all.

Keep in mind that many libraries are linked up to subscription Internet services that most individual writers can't afford, such as *Proquest,* which links you to regional and national newspaper indexes and includes many articles in full text, and *ReferenceUSA Business,* a directory of about twelve million U.S. businesses of all sizes that can be searched by phone number, address, CEO, estimated sales and much more. We can access these and other services from our desk just by surfing to our local library's website and clicking on the service we want to use.

INTERLIBRARY LOAN

Years ago librarians realized that even the best-budgeted libraries were not going to be able to purchase every book published. Eager to provide users with complete facilities, they developed interlibrary loan systems. Depending on which locality or state you live in, you may have easy access to almost any nonrare book and periodical in almost any public or academic library in the U.S. Many states maintain special central collections of books that are mailed to smaller libraries on request. Even part of the Library of Congress's collection is kept busy circulating to libraries across the country. When you get into a major research project—better still, before you get into it—ask your librarian about interlibrary loan procedures.

Most people are aware of the local public library or, in the case of larger cities, the library system that serves them. But there are a great many other kinds of libraries available to serious magazine researchers. Many specialized libraries are indexed in the *Directory of Special Libraries and Information Centers,* which reference librarians can steer you to.

COLLEGE LIBRARIES

Your nearest college or university no doubt has a library. The larger the institution, the larger its collection, as a rule. Most publicly run colleges permit citizens of the state or city free use of library facilities, although a nominal deposit may be required to check out books. Many private colleges allow outsiders to use libraries, although there's sometimes a fee for the privilege. You won't know unless you ask.

Most colleges have more than one library, a fact that many writers overlook. At the University of Wisconsin, for example, Memorial Library is the major library. But the Schools of Engineering, Medicine and Agriculture each have their own large library as well. A number of individual departments such as Geology and African American Studies maintain smaller, specialized libraries whose administrators know their respective fields intimately and can be valuable guides to resources and to authoritative people.

CORPORATE LIBRARIES

Albany Molecular Research, Inc.'s Corporate Library in Illinois, keeps all census data for Cook County, Illinois. The library of pharmaceutical company Berlix, Inc., a New Jersey Schering affiliate, keeps a well-maintained database of its holdings for its business and therapeutic research staffs. Land O'Lakes's corporate library has books, tapes and journals its employees can search via the Internet—and you can search, with easily obtained permission, if you're near their Minnesota headquarters. A great many other corporations maintain in-house libraries for staff research, and most of them permit limited access for folks researching magazine articles on their special interests.

TRADE ASSOCIATIONS

Darn near every association of professionals, businesses and activists from the Administrative Management Society in Pennsylvania to Zero Population Growth, Inc., in Washington, D.C., maintains a library. Most of them feel it's part of their mandate to help you research articles in their fields of interest. Check your library's index to these special libraries.

NEWSPAPER MORGUES

Ever dramatic, newspapers have always called their libraries morgues. Invariably crammed between the boiler room and the coal bin, they used to include 143 filing cabinets, two shopworn tables and four intelligent and eager employees who'd clip and file every article and photo in their newspapers by topic and name. Most morgues switched by the 1980s to microfiche, and by the millennium they were using computer disks or tapes. If you want to find out how many different businesses a local hustler has defrauded, first check out the morgue. Very few newspapers refuse access to magazine writers. Some also handle short questions by phone and answer requests for photocopies, usually for a fee. Many now open their files via the Internet.

How to Locate and Work with Primary-Resource People

Plenty of fine stories have been written from secondary sources. But the *big* stories, the *better paying* ones, and the vast majority of the articles pegged on *new* data hinge on writers' using primary sources—getting facts, figures, anecdotes and quotes right from the experts.

Most novices have little trouble locating primary sources. Their biggest slip-ups come from using only sources that can be reached with local phone calls. It's important to realize, if you're writing for a national publication, that its editors look for nationally distributed experts. We're now living in Madison, Wisconsin, and we could locate dozens of experts on almost anything at the University of Wisconsin. But we're forever quoting experts in Minnesota, Virginia, Indiana, Texas, Pennsylvania, New York, Maine and California to make the editorial point that our articles are national in scope.

The most convenient way to get information from distant sources is by telephone. It's a lot cheaper than many writers realize. We currently pay seven cents a minute for long-distance calls within the U.S. To research one article we called:

New York City, 20 minutes:	$1.40
Macon, Georgia, 30 minutes:	2.10
Anchorage, Alaska, 30 minutes:	2.10
Jamaica, West Indies, 21 minutes:	13.50
Total:	$19.10

With good interview techniques, you can elicit a lot of facts and figures in twenty minutes; we figure thirty minutes on the phone is equivalent to an hour and a half face to face since people usually give us their full attention in a phone call. (We'll discuss interview techniques in the next chapter. Nearly all of them apply to telephone interviews as well as in-person ones.)

Results you get by mail may not arrive as fast nor always be as quotable, but for some projects it's the preferred way. Jack Harrison Pollack, who was a Senate committee investigator before he became a prolific magazine writer and author of best-sellers *Earl Warren: The Judge Who Changed America* and *Dr. Sam,* reduced his by-mail research to a form letter for most projects. But to every copy he appended a short handwritten note. To the form letter researching his Earl Warren book, he attached, "My apologies for this form letter. I'm trying to meet a deadline." Important people understand deadlines, so Jack had no trouble getting replies. "Even Haldeman and Ehrlichman wrote from jail," he told us. "Supreme Court judges, college professors, presidents' wives, all answered promptly."

When Judi was researching her first book, *Stopping Out,* she needed to know the attitudes of members of law- and medical-school admissions committees toward applicants who'd taken time out from college. She wrote to committee chairpeople at forty-seven representative schools, describing the purpose of her project and listing the four specific questions for which she needed answers. She enclosed a stamped, self-addressed envelope with each letter, and was rewarded with twenty-one responses that included several good quotes she could use verbatim in the book.

Today, e-mail can often take the place of postal mail. But be aware that people tend to be less precise in e-mail than in typed letters.

To be successful at researching by mail:

Address the letter to a real, live person.

Tell why you need the information.

Tell how the information will be used. (Is it background? Are you asking permission to quote it?)

Ask specific questions. If there's more than one, number the questions. Don't expect more than a few words for each answer, though you may be pleasantly surprised.

Refer to your deadline. Allow at least a week for reply after the letter is received.

Keep it businesslike and short—no more than one page.

Enclose a stamped self-addressed envelope but also invite replies by fax or to your e-mail address.

Where do professional writers get the names, addresses and phone numbers of primary sources? Here are just a few of our own favorite aids:

WHO'S WHO AND OTHER BIOGRAPHICAL DIRECTORIES

Almost every field of endeavor—science, medicine, psychology, even journalism—has its own biographical directory. Often addresses and phone numbers—at work or at home—are included along with achievements. Many libraries maintain at least small collections of these tools in their reference sections. Even home addresses of the movie stars are listed in some (though the best way to get to celebrities is through their agents or public relations representatives).

COLLEGE AND UNIVERSITY WEBSITES

Many college websites contain department listings and catalogs that show who's teaching the topics of our articles. It's a good bet that these people are authoritative and up to date. College websites also usually include personnel directories that show the professors' titles, e-mail addresses and where-to-mail-to information. (Some public relations departments of the larger colleges also prepare directories of experts and mail them free to writers who request them. We'll soon discuss these folks in greater detail.)

JOURNAL ARTICLES

After reading a particularly useful article on our subject, we get in touch with its author at the institution listed (along with his name and title) at the beginning or end of the article.

SOURCES FROM PREVIOUS ARTICLES

Even if an expert used in a previous article isn't exactly right for our new project, she often has friends where she works who are. It takes only an e-mail or a brief phone call to ask her to suggest an expert. (This is a particularly valuable way to sneak past red tape when using sources employed by the government or by large, careful companies. Make sure to ask your old source if you can use her name as a referral when you contact the new source.)

TRADE ASSOCIATIONS

Most trade associations' managing directors know which member companies have the most accessible experts; many volunteer to contact the companies and ask the experts to call us. Often, they phone at their own expense.

PUBLIC RELATIONS OFFICES

Manufacturers and sellers of everything from nuts to education, hospital care, and peace are all out to promote their products. Many produce packets of information for writers (press kits and press releases) and for the general public (pamphlets, booklets and such). They are often useful in researching articles and are usually yours for the asking. In addition, every fair-sized company, association and university—even some professionals such as doctors and dentists—hire public relations specialists whose job is to make your research task easier if it will conceivably get their products' or organizations' names into print. Sometimes these people are staff members; often they are in outside agencies.

Simply write, phone or e-mail an organization's public relations office, public information officer, community relations person, promotions director, corporate communications office, or the agency that handles its public relations (the organization's switchboard usually has the name, phone number and e-mail address), and say, "We need an expert on . . . for an article we're preparing for *Fortune* magazine." The P.R. department usually asks the best authority it can find to call you back at its expense.

It is important that you pay particular attention to evaluating the credibility of information provided by public relations people. Keep in mind that they are hired to promote the images of their employers. It would be unrealistic to expect a P.R. employee to volunteer data that reflect badly on his boss or client. You can often get information from him that is not entirely favorable to the employer, but you'll probably have to ask for it.

Because of the credibility gap, editors are not fond of having writers quote public relations people.

There are public relations subtleties even some pros don't know. We writers learned a new wrinkle at one ASJA meeting, where a P.R. representative revealed that his firm employs writers to shill for manufacturers on radio and TV. As an example, he mentioned a woman who had written a book on toys. "She has been touring for us for four years. We pay her *per diem* plus all her expenses. We smooth the way and book appearances for her . . . as an author and an authority on toys. Of course, she happens to be traveling with our toys. When she talks about a good or a bad toy, the good toy is ours."

FEDERAL, STATE, AND LOCAL GOVERNMENTS

One of the largest sources of primary (as well as secondary) information is the feds. The *U.S. Government Manual,* a guide to that bureaucratic morass, can be searched online (at http://www.gpoaccess.gov/gmanual/) and at most libraries. It also includes information on quasi-official agencies, international organizations in which the United States participates, and a slew of boards, commissions and committees. Detailed though it is, it just touches the tip of the information iceberg. The names listed in the manual tend to be department heads and sub-heads who will refer you to knowledgeable subalterns.

For quotable facts and figures, no library (except the Library of Congress) contains as much up-to-date and often practical data as the huge library of publications ground out by the U.S. Government Printing Office, stored in pamphlets and available on microfiche by depositories in selected libraries in every state. You can search the GPO's website (www.gpoaccess.gov) to see if there are pamphlets that apply to your topic, and you can order them at that website, too. Novices quickly learn that most of this material is uncopyrighted and can be lifted whole; what most don't realize is that every once in a while, the preparer of the pamphlet or chart received permission to use something already copyrighted. Unless you are sure that the government is the author, you cannot safely assume that anything emanating from the GPO is in the public domain.

State governments inevitably have matrices of informed individuals tucked into their political superstructures. If you can locate them—generally via departmental public information—they're ready sources of up-to-date information and leads to other sources. Larger local governments have good resource people too.

In using government sources, keep in mind your readership as well as the scope of your subject. Quotes from a federal official have fairly universal applicability, so if a Department of Agriculture expert on green potatoes talks about green potatoes, you're safe using his quotes and data to make nationwide generalizations. However, if you opt for a state agriculture official as your authority, her comments on green potatoes may be valid only for her region of the country.

Nowadays, readers don't entirely trust government sources. When it comes to potatoes, weather and census figures, you're on sure footing. But start to build an argument in an area such as employment, taxes or housing that relies for its documentation on government figures and government officials' opinions, and you may be in big trouble. To play it safe, answer in advance whether, if you were *reading* instead of *writing* the article, you'd have much confidence in the information's bearer. If not, maybe you need to turn to the private or academic sector for input. This is just one more situation where the sharp writer has to be careful not to think *for* his readers, but to think *like* them.

Power Interviewing

THE INTERVIEW IS ONE OF THE WRITER'S MOST EFFECTIVE research techniques. Yet the rookie writer seldom interviews well or makes sharp use of the interview's results. Much of this ineffectiveness, we're convinced, comes from not appreciating the six different kinds of objective and subjective things to look for during even a short interview.

Six Article Ingredients to Get from Any Interview

Don't waste your interviews. In every interview, go after as many of these six ingredients as you can. We've annotated part of an article by Frank *(Ill. 12.1)* so you can see where the six kinds of input his interviews gave him fit into place.

Illus. 12.1. Six Kinds of Information Gleaned from Interviews

The Arm Bone's Connected to the Microphone

Inventors and hobbyists who spend years perfecting the proverbial better mousetrap have a staunch ally in the new but highly respected field of biomedical engineering. Its specialists look over the paraphernalia and techniques of medical procedures and seek to develop better tools for doing things. A leading research center in this field is at Vanderbilt University in Nashville, where Paul King, a Ph.D. in engineering, runs a special biomedical engineering program in cooperation with university medics. [His students are both ③ graduate engineers and undergraduates bent

on continuing in this field or specializing in medicine.]

Of late, Vandy's biomedics have come up with some fascinating cures for longstanding bottlenecks in medical technology. [When physicians at the Vanderbilt hospital described to Prof. King how difficult it was to pinpoint the precise location ① of a brain tumor, he eagerly set his engineers to tackle the problem.] With X-rays, it's often hard to differentiate between a tumor and healthy brain tissue, so [for many years doctors injected patients with a radioactive substance which is absorbed ②

171

by the tumor.] However, [all the various X-ray machines proved too imprecise to ① come closer than an inch or so away from the actual site of the buried growth.] Finding the exact position of a brain tumor can be a clear-cut matter of life or death since the brain cannot tolerate much exploratory surgery.

[Prof. King and colleagues designed a ① type of camera which can zero in on the radioactive substance that has been imbedded deep inside the brain, via the circulatory system. The result is a picture of the tumor's location, accurate to within ¼ of an inch. This newly developed camera is called a Tomographic Scanner, a special form of X-ray device which gives a more precise picture by bringing the area under examination into focus while leaving the adjoining tissues fuzzy.] ["The first version ⑥ of our Tomo Scanner is like a Model-T Ford," says Prof. King,] pointing to a new, more sophisticated version being erected by his students.

The new Vanderbilt Tomo Scanner uses 12 lead cylinders, plus steel and aluminum hardware. It all adds up to [a 500-③ pound device which, despite its size, can be easily positioned around a patient's head.] [In two minutes, a patient can have ① his condition diagnosed at a cost that is considerably cheaper than X-ray analysis.]

[These days, Vanderbilt's graduate stu-② dents in biomedical engineering, Leslie Hightower and Norton Busby, are inviting friends into their lab to be hit on the elbow with an electrified version of a doctor's ① rubber hammer.] [The engineers want to determine how fast sound can travel thru a healthy bone.] [Prof. King explains that ⑤ the project was requested by Dr. John Con-

nolly, an assistant professor of orthopedic surgery at Vanderbilt, who often takes engineers with him when making hospital rounds.]

[Dr. Connolly, and other orthopedists, want to know how well a bone is knitting, ① information X-rays cannot give adequately. Prof. King and Busby and Hightower tried various ways of finding measurable differences between bones that are healed and those still in the healing process, and the progress of healing, as well as determining if a bone is broken at all. Their solution involves a new use of sound waves.] [For instance, a patient with a broken arm bone is fitted with a microphone ② at the wrist. A doctor, outfitted with an electrified version of an orthopedic rubber hammer, taps the patient on the elbow and watches the results on a TV-type screen. The screen instantly displays three types of data which will vary, depending upon how completely the fracture has healed.] [Sound waves travel faster in a solid bone than in a broken bone, and that's one of the three ① measurements. A broken bone vibrates at a higher frequency than a fully mended one, so frequency is another measurement shown on the screen. But the vibrations of the broken bone are less regular than a solid or well healed bone, which is the third quality displayed instantly on the screen.

Once Prof. King's sound wave device is perfected, a physician will be able to assess accurately the state of a broken bone in under a minute, a process which now can involve hours of clinical diagnosis.]

Another branch of medicine to benefit Tr. from Vanderbilt's engineers is ophthalmology. [Doctors, engineers, and even two

③ psychologists have gathered in the basement biomedical engineering lab] to design new ways to study the eyes. [Vision may be our most important sense, but laymen ① would be shocked to find out how little basic information actually is known about the eyes and why they function. For instance, from two to five per cent of all people suffer from a condition called amblyopia ("lazy eye") which can cause many physical and psychological problems if not corrected early in life. But ophthalmologists have been stymied in positively diagnosing the condition in children too young to cooperate with a complicated examination.] Vanderbilt's engineers have de-
[Tr.] veloped a workshop full of devices which can analyze eyes without a subject's need to cooperate. [Among the devices is a set of glasses with two tiny lights and two tiny ③ photoelectric sensors attached, all of which are so miniaturized that a patient would hardly notice them.] [The photoelectric information is fed by electricity to a com- ① puter which then gives the appropriate diagnosis.]

[Dr. Robert Fox, a psychologist, and ⑤ Dr. John Bourne, an electrical engineer—] [both of them under thirty years old—] ③ [have had this project funded by grants from the National Science Foundation, ① the National Institutes of Health and other organizations concerned not only with eyes but also kidneys, cancer, nerves, and arthritis.]

["The challenge of the space age is not lost on the medical profession," says Dr. ⑥ Connolly. "It has created, however, an interstiture of learning for which the field of biomedical engineering has had to be developed. The end result is that medicine with its new technological aids will rapidly fill a lot of old knowledge gaps."]

---

1. INFORMATION.

Books and magazines are okay for looking up facts and figures, but by the time they're in print, they're dated. Few editors buy a story from somebody who turns in stale facts. On the other hand, most editors place great stock in writers who consistently submit information that has never been published anywhere before.

Facts, figures, observations, guidelines, and similar data can't be more current than when they're gleaned directly from a person who's doing vital research or making important decisions on the topic of your projected article. In Frank's article for Metropolitan Sunday Newspapers *(Ill. 12.1)*, *every* fact and *every* figure came from an interview. Frank had to do it that way because most of the medical hardware he was writing about was too new to have been written about anywhere else.

2. ANECDOTES

Exciting writing is built on exciting anecdotes, so the good interviewer always listens for them. A really sharp interviewer also listens for clues to experiences that could make lively anecdotes. Then he directs his subject to "Give me an example" or "Tell me about a time when that actually happened."

In the interview leading to the marked examples in our illustration, at first Professor King simply described the results of his work, a piece of metal, not how he achieved those results. Only when Frank prodded the inventor to recap what had transpired along the way did he offer an anecdote about why the machine had been needed, how it had been invented, and what it did. True, it's not the world's most exciting anecdote, but it is more interesting to read than just a description of the end product.

3. DESCRIPTION

You can't interview in a vacuum. We all want to view the subject—whether machine or person—in some kind of real-life setting that magazine readers can relate to. If the article you're researching through interviews is about a person, you may want to point out the special things about his office or apartment that reflect his personality. If the article is about a technological breakthrough, as in the case of Frank's reprinted piece, it helps readers visualize your points if you tell them what the equipment and labs look like.

During his interviews for "The Arm Bone's Connected to the Microphone," Frank jotted down notes so he could later recreate the following descriptions: (1) the size and complexity of the Tomographic Scanner, (2) the fact that the lab is in a basement at Vanderbilt University, (3) the youth of the behavioral and physical scientists cooperating on those projects.

4. AMBIENCE

Is the subject you're interviewing entirely on the level, or is this person puffing up her accomplishments? Does the office look like that of a corporation that's really earning $27 million in profits a year? Do these researchers take themselves superseriously, or do they paste intemperate cartoons onto expensive lab equipment? All these and dozens of other subjective clues and hunches make up the atmosphere that colors a writer's viewpoint. They will color yours. If you go into an interview consciously prepared to jot down clues to ambience instead of just permitting yourself to pick up unconscious "feelings" you can't substantiate, you'll be a better writer for it. You'll have something tangible to pass on to readers.

You have to look closely to find clues to the ambience Frank felt at the Vanderbilt University biomedical engineering lab, but they're there. One clue is that nobody smiles as he speaks. Frank is telling readers that these fellows take themselves seriously. Even Professor King isn't painted with a grin as he says that an early version of his Tomographic Scanner is "like a Model-T Ford."

Frank rated the biomedical engineers highly. How do you know that for sure? Because he connects practically no qualifiers to the information they gave him. If, for example, he had thought an engineer was overenthusiastic in saying, "In two minutes, a patient can have his condition diagnosed at a cost that is considerably cheaper than X-ray analysis," Frank could have either put quotes around the sentence and added *the engineer believes,* or displayed doubt by reporting with qualifiers: "*Usually* in *about* two minutes a patient can have his condition diagnosed for *somewhat less* than common X-ray analysis."

5. LEADS TO ADDITIONAL RESOURCE PEOPLE

Who should know better than one expert on your topic who the other major experts are? Make it a habit, during interviews, not only to find out *what* your interviewee knows on the topic of the day, but *who* he knows who can offer additional information. Also ask him to recommend important books or journals on your topic.

At Vanderbilt University, for instance, the public information office steered Frank to Dr. King and Dr. Fox. By asking them for more leads, Frank found Dr. Connolly and Dr. Bourne.

When Terry Morris was preparing an important *McCall's* story about the romantic life of Stalin's daughter Svetlana, she convinced the magazine that the real story lay in India. (It was the birthplace of Svetlana's husband.) When Terry stepped off the plane in New Delhi, her ticket paid for by *McCall's,* she had leads to only two resource people in the entire subcontinent. She parlayed her two contacts by asking each interviewee to suggest at least one more person for her to see. When she boarded the plane for New York, her attaché case was bulging. *McCall's* felt amply rewarded for its investment when Terry turned in an article bursting with information and anecdotes that no other writer had been able to get.

Hal Higdon told us that when he was in a number of small towns researching the Leopold and Loeb murder case, he made it a point to interview the towns' librarians. First of all, many of them personally knew the people involved. Second, they provided easy access to others who could offer insight into the tragedy.

6. QUOTES

The least important purpose for most interviews should be to gather passages to repeat verbatim in your articles. The overuse of quotes is a common error of beginning writers.

There are just three major occasions when interview material should end up as quotations in your article:

1. When the interviewee's use of language is particularly picturesque *and* sharing it with your readers adds to the point of the story. *Both* criteria must be present.

Picturesque language alone is not enough. Dr. King's "Model-T" quote in the article is an example of this double use.

2. When it is important for written information—especially interpretive information—to come from an obviously authoritative voice. Remember that this works only if your reader knows the voice is authoritative. You've got to make your authority's credentials clear to the reader. Dr. Connolly's quote at the end of Frank's article shows this second type of use.

3. When you want to insert an opinion or point of view that the reader may quibble with if it's merely your unauthoritative opinion. This use of quotes is particularly useful if the opinion is not a popular one. When readers see the quotation marks, they get a clear and quick signal that your viewpoint has been interrupted and another, perhaps contradictory, viewpoint has temporarily taken over.

What Exactly Is a Quote?

Even a direct quote is not always what it seems, despite the definition that has been advanced by English teachers. At the risk of their enmity we'll share the way most working writers we know use quotes from interviews with live sources: They generally rewrite awkward words, phrases and sentences, being careful never to change the meaning or the speaking pattern of the source, and place *that* within quotation marks. The information and opinions in the quotes come directly from the attributed sources—but they rarely duplicate each and every word that the sources used.

It is always more important to write what your source *meant* to say than to quote his exact words. Let's suppose John Dean was told that President Nixon was about to bug his inner office, and two writers heard Dean's offended reaction. One sent in the story with Dean's precise words: "Dean said, 'I'd like him to do it.'" The other wrote, "Dean said, 'I'd like to see him do it.'" Which reporter would Dean think was quoting him correctly? Of course, it's the one who made it clear what Dean meant. A good writer makes the *sense* of her interviewee's words accurate, not necessarily the exact language of those words. It is, in fact, dishonest to quote precisely if you know that it gives a false impression of what the person really meant.

This definition of direct quote helps solve one dilemma that almost every experienced magazine writer faces time and again: You interview a person with one idea firmly in mind. Then, after more research, your theme or point of view shifts slightly. Now the interviewee's responses are no longer precisely in context. If you quote the person's exact *words,* you may find they no longer represent his exact *ideas.*

This working definition also simplifies the interviewer's job, because in most situations a pro's note-taking gets the gist but not all the words of a person's thoughts. If, in reviewing her notes, an experienced writer wants to quote a thought directly, she often bridges the gap with words the interviewee would have said in the appropriate time and place.

Only once in our decades of writing has a subject later claimed, "I didn't say that." In that particular case, we *had* transferred his exact words from our notes to our manuscript. People recall their own precise words as rarely as interviewers remember them. It's their exact ideas that you'd better get right.

Academics troubled by our pragmatic definition of *direct quote,* which forces writers to think at least as much as their interview subjects, will find little comfort in the next refinement we'll detail: A quote may be the words a subject wishes he had said.

Very few people speak in a style that reads as if it expresses precise or exciting thoughts. Most tend to be tentative, internally contradictory, ungrammatical, and either overly choppy or overly long-winded. One of the easiest ways to make your interviewee appear illiterate is to quote her exact spoken words.

Sometimes a writer does want to make the point that the interviewee's speech patterns are illiterate, picturesque or disjointed. Then he copies the words exactly and quotes them without cosmetic improvement. But in most cases it is the essence of a thought, not the manner in which it's delivered, that's important. When a good writer cleans up mistakes in grammar and word usage, the interviewee is always grateful for the courtesy. In fact, people who are interviewed frequently expect writers to make them sound educated and may be indignant at anybody who seems to ridicule them by printing their exact off-the-cuff words.

What if you interview someone who has trouble saying what she really means? The ideas may all be present, but the presentation so poor you can't extract a good quote even by cleaning up the fuzzy language. In a case like that, the experienced interviewer listens for quotable ideas. When we hear one that's good but not said well enough to make exciting reading, we prompt the interviewee with: "Do you mean to say . . . ?" and then, on the spot, rephrase the material so it can be used in our article. If the interviewee says, "Yes," then we feel we've received permission to write the quote the way we said it and attribute our restatement to the source of the idea.

Were the working definition of the quote not so vital to tenderfoot writers, we might not have dwelled on it so frankly. By revealing what is not common knowledge, we're inviting caustic comments from self-styled media critics and from folks who were taught in journalism school (and may be teaching it there now) that true journalistic integrity calls for parroting words exactly, their meaning be damned. We want to stress, especially to those people, that we cannot condone writers who invent quotations from whole cloth, who put words into unwilling mouths, or who in any substantive manner alter the true meaning of what a person has to say. Ethics aside, such perversions invite libel suits, and justly so. But the opposite is equally unethical—and equally libelous—as shown in our anecdote about the hypothetical writer who misrepresented what John Dean said while reporting his words precisely.

Should I Use a Voice Recorder?

The hardware of our profession is much less important than the skills we hone. Still, one question beginners always ask us is whether they ought to use a voice recorder for live interviews. We answer, "Never use one unless you're convinced it's the only way to get what you need." We've interviewed hundreds of people during our careers and we stopped using recorders long ago.

In deciding whether to record, keep in mind that almost every interview contains at least six kinds of input to go after. Only two—quotes and anecdotes—can be captured digitally. Even then, you can't capture a quote's context, only its words. Ambience is tough to record. So are scenic descriptions, unless you add them afterwards. You can record facts, figures and leads to other sources, but you'll get easy access to the data only after you convert it to readable format.

Technical errors are rife: Batteries go dead, memory runs out, fire engine sirens cover the most important phrases. We're sure you can supply your own horror stories. Technical problems aside, there are practical questions to answer:

WILL THE PERSON INTERVIEWED BE AT EASE?
In this era of electronic journalism, many people are comfortable with voice recorders. Still, we feel it's important to ask permission first of anyone you plan to record. (In some states, it's the law.)

WILL *YOU* BE AT EASE?
If you're forever fiddling with a switch, you'll end up nervous—and so will your subject. The alternative—letting the recorder run from start to end of the interview—results in a lot of irrelevant recording. Here are some technical tips based on many authors' sad experiences:

> Buy a recorder with a high quality microphone. Don't chintz or you'll be sorry.
> Be sure you know how to work the recorder, especially if you're counting on voice activation.
> Be sure it's working and the batteries are fresh. Take along spare batteries anyway.

Be sure you have enough free memory to last the entire interview even if it takes twice as long as expected.

Set up some foolproof gimmick for knowing when the memory chip is full unless your recorder features a built-in signal.

Sit as close to your subject as practical, to minimize voice-muddling room noise and echo. If your interviewee's voice is soft, raise high the recording volume.

Even if you've taken every precaution, you still might want to cross your fingers—and take backup notes. During the most important interview of your life, your recorder is sure to give you trouble. Back in the days of tape recorders, we assigned a young writer to interview Alex Haley. Murphy's Law prevailed, of course. His second tape turned out blank. Having relied entirely on his recorder, all the writer could do was drop Haley an S.O.S. and pray. Happily Haley phoned and said, "Come on over and this time use *my* recorder." The author of *Roots* then admitted having recorder failures in his own career.

Your subject might not be that indulgent.

WILL YOUR MIND WANDER?

Many writers are less alert to answers when they're confident that the recorder is taking down everything. They miss important afterthoughts that might clue them into asking unprepared questions. It's *those* questions that unearth new facts and closely guarded attitudes.

WILL TURNING THE RECORDING INTO USABLE FORMAT BE A TERRIBLE CHORE?

Once the interview is recorded, a best-selling (or independently wealthy) writer can sometimes have it converted by someone else into usable format. But if you've got a mumbler for a subject, you may get a recording that's nearly worth-less unless you convert it yourself—and can *that* kill time! Also, if you interview a subject who rambles, or if you like to invite rambling, relying on a recorder ensures a monumental job.

ARE YOU PRONE TO EDIT INSTEAD OF WRITE?

Many articles based on interviews read as if they were cut-and-paste jobs. The creative input, the writer's interpretation, just isn't there. If you find yourself cutting and pasting transcripts and just inserting transitions, hoping that'll turn them into articles, you should seriously consider losing your recorder.

AFRAID YOU CAN'T TRUST YOUR MEMORY?

Playboy magazine used to insist that all its interviewers use recorders; no assign-ment was given without that understanding. Still, the famous *Playboy* quote in which then President-to-be Jimmy Carter admitted to having lusted in his heart was written from memory. Carter didn't make that remark until after the machine was packed away and the *Playboy* entourage was on its way out the door.

Many years ago Frank had a standing magazine assignment: If he ever managed to interview the at-times reclusive Professor Marshall McLuhan, he would be paid well for an article entitled "Marshall McLuhan, What're You Doing Now?" *(Ill. 12.2)*. On a trip to Toronto, he finally wangled an hour with the media guru. McLuhan specified right up front: no recorders. Not even any note-taking was permitted. Right afterward, Frank had to hop a cab to the airport and a plane back to New York. All the while, his feverish pen recreated the interview from memory. By the time he touched down, his first draft was finished.

Our best advice is to try interviewing without any props before you learn to rely on them. Given a chance (and a bit of on-the-job training), your memory will serve you better than you think. That and your eyes, your pen and your pad are all the tools you'll need to successfully handle most interviews.

Illus. 12.2. Interview without Recorder or Notepad

Marshall McLuhan Is Still A-Doin'

When the Guru of Media was spreading his message to an audience at Princeton recently, a streaker ran through the hall yelling the once familiar intellectual query— "Marshall McLuhan, what are you doing?"

Chuckling as he relates the story, McLuhan says, "That streaker knows best what I'm doing. I'm trying to strip away the facade of life in America and see what the ground beneath actually looks like."

This observation is remarkably clear in comparison to McLuhan's usual pronouncements. Several dozen articles, a few books, at least two films and endless debates have attempted to interpret what McLuhan really meant.

Even the public relations director at the University of Toronto, with which McLuhan is affiliated, says: "He doesn't tell us what he's doing. It's just as well. We wouldn't understand it anyway."

McLuhan, one of the most prominent names on the cocktail party circuit of the 1960s, has almost vanished from the discussion scene. His ideas, however, have been entombed in millions of copies of books in which, among other things, he talks about the imminent demise of books at the hand of television.

Those who remember McLuhan at all recall him as the "medium-is-the-message" man. That was from the first chapter of his epic *Understanding Media* and the basis for a pun, another book, *The Medium is the Massage*.

"I'm sorry I even used those terms," McLuhan says today. "That's all some people remember about those whole books. It singles out the media for special attention when they're really just one more institution working tirelessly at making everybody anonymous, just like government, big business and education.

"The streakers," says McLuhan, "were just a spontaneous cry for recognition in this individual-less age we live in. By removing his clothes, the streaker adds further to the illusion of anonymity. To make their point, they have to appear totally anonymous."

At 63, McLuhan is as fast as ever at drawing conclusions. "Nobody recognizes the individual today," he says. "But it's a strange anonymity. There is no privacy in our own homes. TV barges in day or night, friends call or come over, solicitors invade the home. Interruptions are the rule. People have to get out of their home to find privacy today. And that search for a moment's privacy outside our home leads to some terribly interesting phenomena," McLuhan notes, obviously warming to a new idea of his.

"We don't want waiters to talk to us in restaurants, because we go there to find privacy. People in the street shouldn't talk to us either. The car is about the biggest way people seek some privacy from their overly stimulating way of life. They get into their automobiles, where there's a lot of space around them, roll up the windows, turn on the music and air conditioner. And at last they're alone. That's why the small, personalized, form-fitting European kind of car will never catch on in the U.S.A. or Canada. And that's why mass transit systems are doomed—there's not enough privacy there.

"People actually have to go to work to find privacy," McLuhan insists from his carriage house converted into offices on the edge of the University of Toronto. "Most people need only a telephone or a few tools for their work. They could communicate to work instead of transport themselves to work if they had enough privacy at home. But even that's breaking down now. The coffee break broke down the privacy of the office. It was a revolution and marked the end of the work system as it used to be."

Consistently, there is no sign of a coffee pot or water cooler in McLuhan's global headquarters. Nor TV. Not even a tiny transistor radio. To hear this self-admitted eccentric hold forth about revolution in social practices and rebellion of the mind might lead to the suspicion that McLuhan is another of those radicals hoping to tilt the government off its hinges. Yet during the red-tinged 1930s, when he taught at the University of Wisconsin, Herbert Marshall McLuhan opted to join the Roman Catholic Church while fellow intellectuals were joining the Communist Party.

Son of an actor-mother and insurance salesman-father, McLuhan has mastered the dramatic art of selling his interpretations of social events to the intellectual community. He began by claiming to be an expert on the arcane works of Irish author James Joyce. Since nobody else really understood some of this stuff who could dispute McLuhan's claim to expertise?

"I'm still mainly a professor of English literature. All of my media studies began from that," says McLuhan. "At best, my medium and message research was a hobby."

It turned out to be quite a hobby. Book royalties have garnered over $250,000 for him; his lecture agent can command fees of around $1,500 for appearances at seats of learning and tries to get $1,000 even for an interview with the prophet.

McLuhan claims that he writes very little about American society and the media because he's hot on the trail of new interpretations of James Joyce's *Finnegans Wake*. To friends or colleagues passing through town, however, he's still willing to spin a few yarns about the passing of American life as it used to be.

"This is the age of Acoustic Man," McLuhan declares. "While scholars and the media are busy talking about what they believe is a new thing—the Visual Man—they're too late as usual. Society has moved at the speed of light past Visual Man and into something new. It's just as well, really, because our visual environment has become overpolluted with atrocious houses, visually vicious ads and sensory-insulting industrialization.

"Rock and roll killed the visual electric media," McLuhan says quietly. "By the time most people realize intellectually that the Acoustic Man is hear—er, here—he'll be gone and something else will have taken its place."

It really isn't necessary to understand what an Acoustic Man is . . . McLuhan however, does offer a partial explanation. "Acoustic Man harkens back to the tribalized age when people could only communicate orally. There wasn't any printing and certainly no electric media. It started as a language of grunts and groans, just like rock and roll. Moral standards in a tribal community are very high at a national level. But personally, they're very, very low. That's what we see all around us today.

"President Nixon is a Visual Man,"

says McLuhan. "He can't understand our Acoustic Age. That's why he's having so much trouble with this Watergate thing. He made the blunder of translating his acoustic materials (that's McLuhanese for "the tapes") into visual materials ("the transcripts," in other words). But visual materials are open to all kinds of interpretation, some of them favorable and some of them hostile.

"I think President Nixon is a sincere person doing only what all of his predecessors did. But now we're in an Acoustic Age, it's a tribalized sort of existence. Tribal Man won't allow a government leader to help his family or friends. He can help only the public at large, only the tribe, so to speak. But everybody else in the tribe is not only allowed to help family and friends, it's expected." McLuhan unfolds his morning paper to show that Canada, too, has a government leader in trouble because of the changing moral values of Acoustic Man. The Canadian, it seems, awarded government contracts to family members.

"The whole Watergate episode actually unfolded in a single Sunday evening," McLuhan insists. "All the rest of this is just writing footnotes to keep the government and media busy. I fully expect that President Nixon will be sacrificed. Tribal Acoustic Man demands it. He violated their new sense of national moral standards, even though at a personal level most Acoustic Men do the same things themselves as they criticize the President for doing."

McLuhan's tribe includes his son Eric, an artist, and a secretary who all share the quaint carriage house plastered with posters, cartoons and clippings from the newspapers and magazines which McLuhan says are extinct—they just don't know it yet! A former darling of the hot and cold media who popularized his wit and wisdom, McLuhan himself is risking extinction. His tomes are sold now mainly as textbooks in the history of communications, and reporters rarely use the well-worn path to his carriage house door.

Dressed with the studied casual air of a country gentleman in corduroy and tweed, McLuhan tops his slender frame with unruly, gray strands which he seldom cuts any more. But he does quickly push his chair back with one self-conscious hand whenever a camera appears. He obviously enjoyed his fling at muddying the media waters. But right now he's more intrigued with studying James Joyce anew, and perhaps getting back to literary scholarship, which is, after all, his admitted specialty.

As he shows a guest out the front door of the carriage house, he warns about the mud out front caused by a water main break. It reminds him of a significant line from Joyce, "The mud is thickest from where it's thrown."

He smiles enigmatically, and you leave feeling sure he said something profound—until you try to decide just what he meant. . . .

The Eleven Commandments of Power Interviewing

Too many beginning interviewers—and a lot of experienced TV "hosts"—let their subjects wander off the track, sometimes deliberately, ignoring a question. They don't know how to practice the craft of power interviewing. In teaching young writers, we learned to sum up the basics of take-charge interviewing in eleven easy-to-remember commandments. Once adapted to your style and personality, they will keep you in control of your interviews. For a first-rate lesson, compare their use by a skilled interviewer such as Charlie Rose or Barbara Walters with any interview by a late-night show-biz host like Jay Leno.

DEFINE THE PURPOSE OF YOUR INTERVIEW

You must know concretely why the interview is taking place *before* it takes place or you'll end up with a conversation instead of an interview. It helps if you run through the six article ingredients that interviews offer and figure out how much of each ingredient you can expect to get. Usually it's helpful to let your subject know concretely, in advance, what you're looking for. Most people want to help. They may prepare charts or find papers that make their points better than their words. They may remember anecdotes at leisure that last-minute questioning doesn't call to mind. They may simply pull together some of their muddled thoughts.

Even if you're on a tough investigative assignment for which you must track down an elusive character, it's wise to let her know, once she's found, why you want to interview her. It's a safe bet that she'll know, anyway, pretty much what you're looking for.

Draw up a list of questions that need answering. Use it as a guide, not a bible. Make sure to get them all answered, but *be prepared to ask other questions that are suggested in the course of your interview.* We used to call this practice "digging" and it's the commandment least practiced by today's average interviewer. We've watched a lot of opportunities for a "scoop" fly by because the interviewer was concentrating more on the paper holding his next question than on the half-answer or evasion he was getting to the current question.

DO SOME BACKGROUND RESEARCH

If you know something about the topic and the person before the interview begins, your prepared questions will display intelligence instead of ignorance. They'll elicit more thoughtful, less simplistic answers. An easy and useful place to do backgrounders is online. (Chapter 11 is full of tips for doing this research.)

Knowing the spelling of your subject's name and her title in advance is a must. (You can get them from the secretary.) If she has written books, articles or published papers, be familiar with them so you don't ask questions they already answered—or, if you deliberately ask some, you can refer to the answer she's already published. Mentioning that you've read something appropriate by or about her may reward you with an easier interview.

If you're researching a technical topic, become passingly familiar with the field's vocabulary before the interview. Nothing sours an interview more than to have a professor take five minutes to explain his findings in detail, only to have the interviewer say, "I lost you after the first minute. What's the meaning of interface?"

When Frank first interviewed Nobel prizewinner Howard Temin for his cancer article excerpted in Chapter 7, Dr. Temin spoke in science-speak, using terms and concepts way over Frank's head. Frank stopped him ten minutes into the interview, explained the problem, and asked if he could come back and resume the interview after doing some more research. Dr. Temin was so pleased at Frank's honesty, in the second interview he made sure to explain any concept or term he thought a layman might not know.

MAKE THE RIGHT IMPRESSION

Review your background notes and your questions in advance. List questions in the order in which they can be most logically answered. Get to the interview on time. (We try to arrive five minutes ahead of time. It shows that we're there on business, not for a social call.) Look, and feel, like you're ready. Dress appropriately; jeans that give you credibility in one office, destroy it in another. When in doubt, dress conservatively. Take a pad to jot down important numbers, not loose paper. Take two pens so when the first one dries up, you'll still have one working.

GET TO THE POINT

Begin the interview in a cordial yet businesslike manner. We know a lot of old pros suggest you start like a peddler, with talk about sports or the weather. But we believe it relaxes a nervous subject (and novice interviewer) if you get right to what you're there for.

Don't be vague. Don't let the interviewee be vague either. Be sure her answers are to the point or ask the question again, adding that the first answer wasn't quite specific enough. Be sure you stay on point; few things make a busy subject more fidgety than an interviewer who beats around the bush or can't keep to the topic at hand.

Don't ask complex, multifaceted questions. Most people think and speak one thought at a time. But *do* (to reiterate the point we made earlier) *be prepared to ask other questions that are suggested in the course of your interview.*

BE SENSITIVE ABOUT RAPPORT WITH YOUR SUBJECT

Tune in to the interviewee. Don't take out a cigarette or stick of gum unless he smokes or chews first. He may hate smokers or gum chewers, and then where are you? On the other hand, if you're offered a cup of coffee or a smoke, it may be a clue that a break is needed.

It's okay to acknowledge that you know you're inflicting some strain. But don't ever think you need to apologize for it. If you've done your job right, he's known in advance what you're after and has agreed to see you about it—even if reluctantly. If the strain is due to *information* you're bringing out (or struggling to bring out), it isn't your fault.

If the strain is due to your ineptness or impoliteness, that *is* your fault.

SAVE SENSITIVE OR EMBARRASSING QUESTIONS FOR LATE IN THE INTERVIEW

There are two major reasons for adopting this stance. The first is practical: If you get booted out for asking impertinent questions, at least you've managed to get some information; moreover, it sometimes makes a dramatic point to say in an article that you interviewed the subject but got tossed out for asking about closeted skeletons. Second, during the early part of the interview you can assess whether you're getting candid answers; that's something you'll have to know during the tougher give-and-take.

However, don't shift gears consciously for incisive questions, or in other ways signal that you feel it's time for the really tough stuff. The more matter-of-fact your questions, the more matter-of-factly the subject will answer.

Don't save tough questions for too late. If you do, your interviewee might do a quick, "Oh, I'd love to answer that but our time is up. Isn't that a shame?"

Above all, don't feel you have to be a nice guy and avoid touchy, controversial, embarrassing, nosy or probing questions. If they're needed in your pursuit of information for a story, it's your duty to ask them and unprofessional not to. Keep your fact-finding responsibility as a writer in mind and you'll be surprised at how easily even impertinent questions will be answered.

One *Playboy* interviewer was bothered by the fact that while every Barbra Streisand article sounded nice-nice, people who worked with her complained how difficult she was. So in his interview with her he fired off, point-blank, "Why are you such a bitch?" Stunned by his honesty, Barbra talked for six candid hours about how the media had misinterpreted her entirely. According to *Playboy*'s interview editor Barry Golson, "It was a great interview."

When Terry Brunner was executive director of the Better Government Association (a citizen's watchdog organization in Chicago), his technique when dealing with a hostile subject was to accuse him of a dozen different foul deeds. Terry told us, "Sometimes he'll deny one or two but not attempt to deny the others." It's devices like that which enabled Terry to help convict Mafia members and corrupt police officers. If you routinely interview shady characters, you might give the device a try. But for most interviews, honest, straightforward, tireless questioning—whether it's "Where were you born?" or "Why did you disappear with the document?"—pays off most consistently.

VERIFY WHAT THE SUBJECT IS TELLING YOU

Investigative assignments require interviewers to attempt to check the accuracy of everything they're told. Everyone knows that who remembers Woodward and Bernstein. What beginners don't know is that every interviewer can spot-check, during the interview, whether he's hearing the subject accurately—and whether he's getting the truth. Basically there are three ways to verify information obtained through interviews.

Corroboration is backup proof of the honesty or accuracy of your interview subject's statements. You can corroborate a statement by going independently to a separate resource person or by asking your subject to provide proof. Of course, corroboration is no more than corroboration: if everybody is lying or in error, you still may not have the truth. (That's why we always name, in print, the source of statements that aren't self-evident fact.)

Internal checks are simple to make if you think quickly enough. At two or more points during the interview, ask questions that should elicit identical information. If you get it, the subject's probably telling the truth and you're hearing it right. If the answers differ, you'll have to find out—with more questioning or with independent corroboration—if you heard wrong or were told wrong.

External checks are only a bit different. Ask one or more questions to which you already know the answer, probably through background research. If the subject's answer checks out, you've got verification of what he's saying and what you're hearing. If it doesn't, you're in the same spot as with internal checks.

LISTEN TO WHAT YOUR SUBJECT IS SAYING

Here's a third reminder: If you work only from a list of prepared questions you may miss a lot of very valuable information. If you are lucky enough to be interviewing someone who plunges into new ground—or are skillful enough to lead there—and you aren't clever enough to follow up with more questions in that direction, take up a pastime other than freelance writing. We will never forget, as long as we live, the transcript of an interview one writer sent us (in our days as editors) in which controversial basketball great Kareem Abdul-Jabbar ended an answer about how poorly he ate in his youth by saying, "But that wasn't the worst of my problems." The novice writer plunged right ahead with his next prepared question, "Do you eat well now?" At that instant Abdul-Jabbar had been ready to reveal something special about his childhood. The writer muffed a possible scoop.

KEEP YOUR MOUTH SHUT

A subject cannot give you information while your own voice is in gear. Self-evident? Yet it's overlooked by countless interviewers who monopolize their interview time. A good interviewer is a great listener. There are so few good listeners around nowadays that if you can be one, you're practically guaranteed a great interview.

On many occasions we've actually used silence as a device. We'd just sit quietly, not speaking, not asking another question, waiting to see what the subject would say spontaneously. Often it's been a surprising elaboration on the last question we asked. That's because the subject didn't know how much we knew, felt we could evaluate the answers better than we actually could, and—eager to stay clear of trouble—tried to explain the response more fully.

Barry Golson's favorite example of the value of silence is when one *Playboy* interviewer asked Mel Brooks how he would describe himself. Brooks groaned and said, "How can I answer that?" There was a pause, Golson told us, and the interviewer knew enough to wait it out. "Then Brooks said: 'Well, I'm six-two, blond, blue-eyed and have a physique like Robert Redford. . . .' and he was off into one of the funniest answers we ever had."

END WITH AN OPEN-ENDED QUESTION

Two of our favorite endings are "Is there something I didn't ask that you think I should have?" and "Have we covered everything now?"

EASE OFF BEFORE LEAVING

If you feel obliged to chat, this is the time for it. First of all, it's nice to part on a cordial note. Then, too, some people react entirely differently when the pressure's off. It's not just Jimmy Carter who mumbled his most quotable words after the recorder was switched off. We've gotten some doozies after packing away our pens. It wasn't until after Frank stopped his interview and started taking photographs that Notre Dame's Father Hesburgh finally revealed his real feelings about President Nixon, who'd just fired him from the Civil Rights Commission. And after Frank interviewed the lawyer who'd first argued for desegregation for a twentieth-anniversary article about the Brown v. Board of Education decision, they were walking together to their cars when the lawyer volunteered that he'd just filed a friend-of-the-court brief that supported separate but equal schools.

So just because you've eased off your pressure on the subject near the end of your visit, don't lose your own alertness. Some valuable information often changes hands even when the interviewee has stopped noticing you and wished you well.

> The subject may pull out the file he slipped into a desk drawer when you walked in. What's in it?
> He starts returning the urgent phone call he wouldn't take while you were on the job. Who's it to?
> He puts on a pair of thick eyeglasses. What does that say about him?

Leaving on a cordial note has another purpose too. You should try to leave the door open for a follow-up phone call in case you missed something important or need points clarified. Other questions may occur to you after you do more research or start writing.

The Telephone or E-mail Interview

We can't hope to cover in one chapter all the bases that professional writers have to run when using interviews to research their stories. We've concentrated mainly on pointers needed by writers early in their careers. We have one last reminder: Stay aware of how many different forms the interview can take.

Classically, a writer phones for an appointment, shows up at the appointed time and place for a face-to-face talk, then goes back to his own office and incorporates the formal interview into his story. These days, however, interviews are commonly done on the telephone or, after initial written or phoned agreement, by e-mail. With just an electronic connection between you and the subject, you won't be able to *see* her office setting, face and clothes. But in a phone call you can tell from her voice how seriously she treats the topic you're discussing and whether she's hedging or sharing information straight out. Humor, anger, sarcasm, cynicism, wistfulness—all transmit well over telephone lines, giving busy interviewers the chance to gather factual material for stories in a minimum of time.

The telephone interview isn't always the first choice of writers. But it is often a necessary expedient. For instance, when Terry Morris was researching her *McCall's* scoop on Svetlana Stalin, she interviewed face to face most major personalities involved. Svetlana herself was kept off limits by lawyers for the publishers of her memoirs. Terry did entice Svetlana into permitting a courtesy phone call, however, and she managed to extend the chat into a thirty-minute interview. It not only answered many of her research questions but, equally important, lent enormous credibility to Terry's story in *McCall's*.

Whether to get your first-hand information by mail, e-mail, phone or personal interview often depends on the depth of response you need. Mailed and e-mailed replies are usually superficial and should be used only when you can ask questions that elicit exactly what you're looking for. (They should also be short and limited to just a few easy questions. Last month, a novice hoping to write a history of fan magazines e-mailed Judi a long, open-ended list of questions about her fan mag editing days. Needing several days to type even perfunctory answers, Judi still hasn't found the time for it.) Phone interviews are always more pliable than mail or e-mail—and able to elicit deeper and clearer responses. Face-to-face interviews are, of course, best by far.

13

Writing the First Draft

WHEN ASKED AT A WRITERS' CONFERENCE WHAT SHE liked most about writing, Bonnie Remsberg quickly replied, "Having written." Those words have been said by many writers. There's no magic and very little glamour in writing an article, only hard work that demands unrelieved concentration. Few writers work in sunny picture-windowed offices, simply because the distractions become overwhelming.

When small groups of professional writers gather, we inevitably share with each other the latest ploys for procrastinating when there's a manuscript to be written. Shopping for the family's groceries, reorganizing the files, writing personal letters, sharpening pencils, reading books, doing extraneous research . . . they've all been tried. The two of us like to write query letters as a form of procrastination, albeit an often profitable one. You'll have to find your own favorites—and your own way to discipline yourself into gluing the seat of your pants to a chair for as many hours as it takes to write what has to be written. Take heart; it's the first draft that's the hardest.

We've already taken a long, hard look at the elements and techniques that belong in that first draft. Now let's concentrate on the moves that braid them into a strong article.

Find the Point

One of a writer's trip-ups, in getting a story written, is becoming so involved in orchestrating the wealth of statistics, anecdotes, and quotes he discovers in his research that he overlooks or drifts away from the story's purpose. In your query letter you promised the editor an article that presents a particular slant on a specific topic. If the editor is to okay your finished story, you must deliver substantially on your promise.

When your research is completed, go over it all with your article's original proposal in front of you. Does the information you found match what you expected to find? Do you have the kinds of experts you promised? Are your anecdotes and quotes strong enough to make the points you have to make? In short, do the extensive data in your files fully paint in the sketchy picture you drew in your query? If they deviate markedly into a new slant, you'd better discuss your changed overview with the editor. If they're close enough, rivet the story's underlying purpose to your consciousness and plunge ahead.

Organize

You can jot down a formal outline, or make just a few notes. But whichever works best for you, you must begin with an unclouded perspective on exactly how you'll organize your article's first draft. That perspective may change once you've got your first draft keyed in. You may see relationships that weren't clear until you wrote down your ideas. You may discover that an anecdote fits better in a different place, or leads to a different conclusion than you thought it did. But unless you begin with a plan, you'll come out with a hodgepodge of long notes instead of a first draft.

Very often the subject matter itself dictates the most logical sequence for writing it up. Some articles beg chronological or step-by-step organization. Often you must impose logical order on your ideas such as a point-by-point sequence or a succession of pros and cons. Many articles include several types of organization, but in those cases there is still, as a rule, one main organizational pattern that weaves from start to finish.

CHRONOLOGICAL ORGANIZATION

Just before the twentieth anniversary of the famed Brown v. Board of Education decision, Frank headed for Topeka to interview people who'd been involved in that landmark desegregation case. When he sat down to write his first draft, there was no doubt in his mind how the story would be organized. It fit neatly into one of the easiest formats to work with, chronology.

Judi's article "Miss Lynn Redgrave" *(Ill. 5.4)* is the story of growing up fat. Chronologically was an obvious way to tell it. John Hirsh's article "Food Greaser Loses 47 Pounds" *(Ill. 5.11)*, talks about growing thin. It too lends itself to chronology. Judi's "It Costs Too Much to Go to a Museum" *(Ill. 5.13)* tucks a long chronology of events between its lead and its ending.

Do-it-yourself articles, too, are naturals for chronological organization: first you do that, then you do this, and finally you do something else. The exact order is dictated by the sequence readers must follow in duplicating the project. It helps, of course, if you've done the thing you're writing about (or something like it). Then you'll have no doubts as to the correct sequence.

Our "Build Your Own Luxurious Plastic Furniture" *(Ill. 5.1)* is organized in order of the jobs to be done: getting the materials, collecting the tools, cutting the plastic, making the holes, polishing the cuts and holes, gluing the pieces together, and so forth.

POINT-BY-POINT ORGANIZATION

Even when the various topics you plan to write about don't fall into chronological sequence, you still have to arrange them sensibly so that readers follow easily from topic to topic. Some arrangements to consider are:

> from the general point to its specific aspects
> from easy concepts to the more difficult ones
> from the least controversial to the most controversial
> from the least complicated to the most complicated
> from the theoretical to the practical.

Sometimes several techniques are combined. For example, you may decide to move from the least to the most controversial points and, within each point, from the theoretical to practical examples. The reader is able to follow much more easily if you stick to one pattern than if you sometimes reverse the pattern (going, for example, from the theoretical to the practical within one large topic and from the practical to the theoretical within the next).

In our article excerpt on house calls reproduced from *Practical Psychology for Physicians (Ill. 13.1)*, the seven conclusions that governed our organization could have fit together in several ways. We laid them out so the article began with generalized conclusions arranged chronologically: "Most doctors develop guidelines for deciding when a house call is necessary" (decisions about future visits), and "Most doctors feel they can't practice good medicine on a house call" (on-the-scene decisions). Then we moved to conclusions that became more directive. Our conclusion number seven, "When care is taken to educate patients, they are actually surprised when you do suggest a house call," is a refinement of conclusion number six, "Patient education lessens the house call problem."

Illus. 13.1. Point-by-Point Organization

Are House Calls Ever Necessary?
A Survey of Current Practices

Among the arsenal of treatment techniques which the practicing physician has at his disposal, the house call creates perhaps the greatest dilemma. The AMA has no official position on its value or use. Medical schools generally don't counsel practitioners-in-training on its advisability, suggesting only that those who prefer not to make a house call should make *that* their policy right from their first day in practice.

The general feeling in the medical community seems to be that patients want house calls too often, and for no good medical reason. Patients, on the other hand, sometimes complain that doctors never make home visits, even when a person is dying.

To help determine just where the truth lies, this team of reporters surveyed 25 primary-care physicians randomly chosen from a geographic cross-section of large cities and small towns. From these interviews we were able to form seven general conclusions with regard to house call policy.

Conclusion One: *Most doctors develop guidelines for deciding when a house call is necessary.*

It's a rare doctor who *never* makes a house call. Every doctor in our survey said he would respond to a call from an elderly or severely disabled longstanding patient who had no easy means of transportation to the office or hospital. But the majority reported that they rarely make house calls, now that most people have cars to bring them to where services are available.

Each physician's house call guidelines are slightly different. Some doctors go out if, on phone evaluation, it seems like an emergency. Others visit the home only if it *isn't* a real emergency; for crisis situations, they feel, an ambulance or rescue unit could bring the patient to the hospital much faster than they could get to the home. This is especially true if the symp-toms suggest a heart attack, but the preponderant feeling is that for any emergency it's better to examine in a setting where testing and medicating resources are available.

Now that it is generally accepted that fresh air won't exacerbate even a fever of 105°, a good number of doctors said, they make house calls more for the patient's convenience than for rendering emergency care. "I cannot think of any medical indications for making a house call," one physician stated flatly. Others said they use the house call for follow-up after hospitalization, and for the critically ill who couldn't be placed in a hospital.

One doctor attempts to save his patients the expense of ambulance service by first calling at the house to decide if it is, in fact, "as serious as they thought." This physician told of one instance where he visited a patient to convince her that the hospital was indeed the best place for her. "An elderly woman, she had been convinced hospitals were only for dying," he said. On the other hand, several doctors feel the house call is abused by family members who are too lazy or reluctant to miss work to bring the patient in. After meeting a few such cases, these physicians tended to sharply limit their house call practices.

Conclusion Two: *Most doctors feel they can't practice good medicine on a house call.*

Quite a number of doctors feel, as one expressed it, "Too many things are missed when you're having to examine a patient under poor light, bending by a bedside that's too low to get at the patient, with all the . . ."

In using a point-by-point organization, it isn't necessary to number the points as we did for *Practical Psychology for Physicians*. But it's a handy device. *(See also Ill. 5.2, "12 Ways to Get More Out of Studying," and Ill. 5.17, "10 Questions Patients Are Afraid to Ask About Cancer.")* If the topic paragraph tells the reader to expect x points to follow, numbering them makes for fast and easy transition.

In our "Reasoned Strategy Prevails as You Battle the Odds" article for *Science Digest (Ill. 13.2)*, we had only a casual organizational outline in mind before tackling the first draft: show why we're writing about war gaming; define it; tell who plays it, how it's played, and why. Since it was strictly an informative article, the journalistic who-what-why-when-where-how organization could be juggled for the smoothest flow of ideas. Articles like this one can be written without advance outlining once you find the knack. Others, like the house calls article, demand rigorous planning. (It's a worthwhile exercise to read entirely through the entire articles reproduced in part in Illustrations 5.2, 5.5, 5.6, 5.8, 5.9, 5.10, and 5.17—all organized point by point—to see if you can uncover the outlines behind the finished products.) They're on our website www.booksthatteach.com.

Illus. 13.2. Point-by-Point Organization

Reasoned Strategy Prevails as You Battle the Odds

Lee's infantry are hard on the heels of his cavalry that have just ridden through the streets of Gettysburg, swords flailing. Meade's infantry are dropping their muskets and fleeing. Union artillery are pointed the wrong way and Lincoln may have to surrender to the Confederacy at any minute.

Given some lucky rolls of the dice and smarter leadership than some of Lee's original generals displayed, *it could happen today*—in any of today's war games that not only realistically restage battles such as the U.S. Civil War, but fight wars in space or Middle Earth.

Hobbyists of all ages are turning by the thousands to war gaming. War gaming companies put the number of hardcore war gamers in the U.S. at half a million— "and growing geometrically." The rate of increase in Canada is believed to be at least as great. In England, 4 percent of the population plays war games, making it the largest indoor sport there. Those figures don't include the less fanatic war gamers who indulge occasionally in some battle that happened years ago—or hasn't yet taken place. The half a dozen war gaming companies sell some 2 million games a year, costing $8 million retail.

Topic sentence

Don't let the name "war gaming" scare you off. Actually, the entire basis is the science of probabilities. The appellation is an old, unfortunate one that people who market war gaming equipment are trying to replace with "adventure gaming" or "fantasy gaming." Stendahl, in his 1830 classic *The Red and the Black,* told of an imperial general who passed time between battles playing war games. And H. G. Wells in his 1913 book, *Little Wars,* used war gaming in his plot.

Wars with soldiers and guns and battles—*strategy and tactics war games*—are still around, and preferred by many en-

Tr.

thusiasts. But new since the 1960s are the *role playing, fantasy war games.* These include marches by elves and dwarves against dragons and giants, all straight out of Tolkien's *Lord of the Rings* and similar adult fairy tales. Or "Star Wars" characters struggling to outmaneuver each other at Warp-3 speeds. Or Earp and Holliday drawing to see who wins a trip to Boot Hill.

Reformed Computer Addicts

Tr.

Nowadays, war games are the sport of many cured computer junkies. In short, war games are a humanized version of the computer-vs.-man strategy games. The players, making an algorithm of an entire war, first devise a set of parameters for their game, then a game board, and finally a comprehensive set of characteristics for the "men" involved in the game. Probability plays a key role in deciding moves, but instead of pushing computer buttons, the players use a set of dice with, variously, 4, 6, 8, 12, and 20 sides.

One of the most popular role-playing war games today is "Dungeons and Dragons"—"D&D" to aficionados. In it, lovers of Tolkien and western mythology each actually choose a mythical character to portray—elf, dwarf, cleric, wizard, hobbit, thief. . . . But the characters have to be chosen after chance rolls of three 6-sided dice describe their strengths and weaknesses.

High *strength* ratings are helpful for fighters who take on giants and dragons. *Intelligence* and *wisdom* scores of 13 or more are needed by clerics and magic workers. Everybody can use hefty *constitution* ratings to endure damp dungeons and hot-breathed dragons. *Dexterity* upwards of 13 helps to dodge weapons and monsters. Not everybody needs high *charisma* points, but when an elf is defeated by a witch, if he has an 18 charisma rating she'll keep him around as a lover instead of turning him into a frog. As is true in most similar war games, "D&D" players roll dice at the start to determine how many *hit points* they have, or how severe a hit from a spear, stone, or magic spell they can withstand. Dice also decide how much wealth a character begins with.

Then, unlike "Monopoly" and similar board games in which players compete against one another, in fantasy games the players compete against mathematical probabilities, using their own reasoning powers. The goal is to avoid point-losing pitfalls at the hands of dragons and evil wizards while trying to accumulate points through experience, finding treasure, and out-maneuvering the bad guys.

PRO VS. CON ORGANIZATION

An extension of point-by-point organization, this one could be called "point by counterpoint." It's especially useful when organizing material presenting both sides of several different topics. In researching her article on how to select a divorce lawyer, written originally for *Playgirl (Ill. 13.3)*—and reprinted (with its lead hacked off and minor changes in language) by the Maryland Center for Public Broadcasting—Judi concluded that none of the lawyer types she found was all good or all bad. So she laid out her story to show both the pros and the cons. But she also used a point-by-point organization and, toward the end, a chronological one.

Illus. 13.3. Pro vs. Con Organization

The Divorce Game

There are over 260,000 lawyers in the U.S. and every lawyer is a general practitioner: in theory, he's supposed to be able to handle every type of legal work. In reality, the men who want to do corporate law start out employed by businesses, the men who want criminal law join the D.A.'s staff right from law school, and many of the people who open an office immediately drift into handling divorces.

Nobody has ever counted how many actual divorce lawyers there are. In small towns, matrimonials are merely one facet of almost every G.P.'s practice; it's only in large cities and densely populated suburbs that "divorce lawyers" per se are found.

Most divorce specialists have two things in common. First of all, they're combatants: they enjoy slugging it out with an opponent, although some like a courtroom battle whereas others prefer to fence toward an out-of-court settlement. "They're taught in school that divorce is an adversary contest and their entire stance is in terms of 'our side' and 'their side,'" one lawyer told me.

Second, most of them have an extremely old-fashioned attitude toward women. They've hatched this attitude in law school, where there are few women among faculty or students. They've nurtured it in the course of their practice, because most male clients have already had some dealings with lawyers and appear smart and cool, while most women come in green, ask the wrong questions, and tend to "tell all" emotionally. The lawyers think in terms of "handling" these "frail nincompoops." Many lawyers "handle" them no more patronizingly than they've been "handled" for years by the banker and the plumber. But there are three types of tacticians to beware of.

First there's the *Lover Boy*—the kind who uses words or sexual insinuations. Attorney Joan Goldberg of New York, says: "A woman feels ambivalent about her divorce, and emotionally upset, and the lawyer is often the first person she's been able to trust in years. These male lawyers take advantage of the dependence."

Tr.

Topic sentence

Then there's *Big Daddy* lawyer, graying or balding on top, who says "call me counselor" and proceeds to counsel you on everything from your self-image ("You're young; go out, have a good time") to your image of your husband ("He's a sick, horrible, selfish man. How could you have lived with him for so long?"). Remember that most legal counselors have never taken a psychology course. In emotional areas, their advice is no better than your mother's.

Many men have the ability to change from Big Daddies to Lover Boys or vice versa: they're the *Chameleons*. Sometimes it takes several visits: somewhere along the way, they cross the line from fondness to fondling. Others are quick-change artists.

A *Chameleon* will often try to psych out a potential client and give her the father image or sexual overtones he thinks she's looking for. Even nonchameleons tend to assume that all women are emotional creeps while men are clear-headed and businesslike—even though attorney William Gold has found, "Men frequently are just as hysterical as women are supposed to be, with just as much rejection and hurt coming through and just as many phone calls at three A.M."

In addition to how they relate to women, divorce lawyers can be understood in terms of how they do their job. There are two distinct types, the *Classy Character* and the *Lone Wolf*.

The Classy Character is a partner in a middle-to-large-sized firm. He speaks well and smoothly, dresses with conservative elan, usually smokes a pipe, and has a clean, airy office. It's impressive, but keep in mind that appearances don't count: what counts is what he can do for you, and what it'll cost.

The Classy Character has lots of legal secretaries to do your paperwork, lots of clerks to read your files, and lots of young assistants to research applicable rulings and appear in court on routine matters. Since your fee is determined not only by the time spent on your case, but also by whether Mr. Class or his less expensive assistant puts in the time, your divorce may cost less than you'd think. In addition, he usually likes to settle out of court, so he'll tend to avoid antagonizing the opposition. . . . .

When you're dealing with nebulous subjects, it's important to make them as graphic and as quickly distinguishable as possible for the reader (and editor). The names Judi gave to divorce lawyers were mostly her own invention, triggered by discovering a newspaper article that referred to one advocate as a "bomber." The careful researcher picks up a lot more than just facts and figures.

Pick Out and Write the Lead

In Chapter 6, we spent a great deal of time discussing what leads do, in theory, for your article. (You might want to review that section before you go on.) Now you've actually got to choose a lead. The most vital part of the story, it's also the place where beginning writers most often get bogged down. They try one approach after another, discard them all, and finally end up staring at a blank screen. They let the lead lead them instead of the other way around.

Once you really know what a lead is and does, it often jumps right off your notepad and hits you in the face. As you become more experienced, you find yourself recognizing a lead statistic, quote or anecdote that appears during an interview or one that pops up in your research. For instance, when Judi was interviewing actress Lynn Redgrave for her *Weight Watchers* article *(Ill. 5.4)*, and Lynn said, "I was a food junky," Judi knew instantly that the quote would be her lead.

At other times, writers have to work a little harder to find the most exciting hook. Here are some questions pros ask themselves when hunting through their notes for the best possible lead.

CAN YOU STATE A PARADOX IN THE TOPIC?

That's what Judi did in her study article for *Seventeen (Ill. 5.2):* "Effective studying is the one element guaranteed to produce good grades in school. But it's ironic that the one thing almost never taught in school is how to study effectively."

That's what we did in our *Family Handyman* article about how to build plastic furniture *(Ill. 5.1):* "Wood has always been a favorite of do-it-yourselfers. Plastics, however, being relatively new, still frighten a great many people. But working with plastic is in many ways easier than . . ."

CAN YOU FIND A PROVOCATIVE QUESTION ABOUT THE TOPIC THAT'S GUARANTEED TO GRAB READERS' ATTENTION?

Judi opened her museum-for-pay essay in *The New York Times (Ill. 5.13)* by asking, "So the museums are doing poorly, are they?" *(See also Ills. 6.5, 6.6, and 6.7.)*

IS SOME FACT ABOUT THE TOPIC DRAMATIC ENOUGH ALL BY ITSELF TO SERVE AS A LEAD?

In his extension-cord exposé for the Sunday Newspapers syndicate *(Ill. 5.10)* Franklynn began, "Every year hundreds of serious fires resulting in deaths and millions of dollars of damage can be traced to faulty extension cords or their improper use."

In her skateboard exposé for *Family Health (Ill. 5.9)* Judi opened with, "Business is booming for orthopedists all over the country this year. Broken wrists, splintered elbows and smashed ankles are just three common hazards of the reborn skateboard craze."

IS THERE ONE ANECDOTE ABOUT THE TOPIC SO DRAMATIC OR
EXEMPLARY THAT IT MAKES AN EFFECTIVE LEAD?
Our tornado story for *Popular Science (Ill. 5.6)* began: "On April 3, 1974, one
of the most ferocious tornado storms ever to hit the United States screamed
across the Midwest. By the time the winds died down, more than 148 separate
twisters had bulldozed a path through 13 states—killing at least 300, injuring
thousands, and destroying several billion dollars' worth of property."

In the CAT scanner article for *Family Health (Ill. 5.7)* we opened with a
long anecdote about a likable man who'd been spared pain because of the new
machine.

IS THERE SOME WAY TO OPEN BY IMMEDIATELY INVOLVING THE
READERS IN THE TOPIC?
That's what we did in our *Popular Science* article on painting *(Ill. 5.19)*: "If
you, like most home-owners, dread the next time your house needs an exterior
paint job, take heart!" Mike Frome did likewise in his "Traveling Alone" piece
for *Woman's Day (Ill. 6.10)*.

So many people with backgrounds in newspaper writing try to make it in
the world of magazines that we have to warn you: A good lead for a news article
almost never works as a magazine lead. Journalism schools teach newspaper
reporters to tell the whole story in miniature in the opening paragraph. In magazine writing, we want to show only enough of our hand in the opening play to
keep the reader in the game. We give him a peek at our best card as a teaser and
reveal the rest, little by little, only after he's hooked.

Write the Body, Using Transitions and Subtopic Sentences

Once you have chosen your lead and written it, we hope you'll follow it with a
smooth transition into a topic sentence (or phrase or paragraph). (If you're
stymied on the lead, choose any lead at all for the time being and move on. This
is only your first draft, and as you write it the best lead will reveal itself.) We covered topic sentences fully in Chapter 6, so we'll plunge right into your next writing job—the body of the article.

It's important to write the major portion of your article as quickly and
straightforwardly as possible. Arky (Arturo F.) Gonzalez put it the best we've
heard. He said that in the first draft, he'd try to get the Christmas tree up as
fast as he could, even if he knew it was not completely straight. Once the tree
was up, it was easier and more satisfying to add the tinsel, lights and baubles of
good writing.

But even in your first draft, when you're finished dealing with your first point, you shouldn't abruptly begin point two. You must warn readers with a transition, and then mark each new point with its own subtopic sentence (or phrase or several sentences). If you've spent a page or two writing about the care and cultivation of apple trees, it may seem self-evident that you're switching to a page or two about pear trees. But that's only because you know how you've organized your notes. If you lose readers while they try to figure out where your new point began and what it is, you may never get them back.

In general, the greater the shift in context, the more obvious your transitions and subtopic sentences have to be. If you're switching from Jonathan apple trees to Macintosh, you might end the last Jonathan paragraph with "that's why Jonathans are so easy to pick," and simply begin the next paragraph with "Macintosh [the topic], on the other hand [the transition]." Dozens of other short phrases also work as simple transitions: *however, but, in addition, unlike, at other times. . . .*

In the left column of the second page of the "House Calls" article *(Ill. 13.1)*, we've marked with *Tr.* a transition that introduces, at the end of one point (emergency care), the subject of the next point (nonemergency care). If you can find a noun or strong verb common to both subtopics, that's an effective shortcut for transitioning.

More radical changes in context demand more obvious transitions. Often they flow from some words in the last sentence of the previous subtopic right through the sentence or two that introduces the next one. In Judi's divorce lawyer article *(Ill. 13.3)*, we've marked three transitions. The first, in the right column on page 196, seems a simple one provided by the word *but* and directly followed by the next topic sentence: "there are three types of tacticians to beware of." It's actually not as simplistic as it looks. The beginning writer might have made this sentence the beginning of a new paragraph. By tying it in at the end of the old one, Judi heightened the reader's sense of transition. She felt that was needed because the tie between the two points was really very tenuous. She could have written more of a transition and solved the problem that way. But she decided that the reader's interest was great enough to carry him along. What do you think?

In the ninth paragraph, Judi uses one sentence to provide a transition ("In addition to how they relate to women") *and* to introduce a new subtopic ("divorce lawyers can be understood in terms of how they do their job"). But she immediately follows with another transition ("There are two distinct types") to introduce her sub-subtopics ("the Classy Character and the Lone Wolf"). Then she immediately begins elaborating on her first sub-subtopic, the Classy Character.

For the war-gaming article *(Ill. 13.2)*, we were obliged to pack a lot of information into a relatively short assigned length. So we worked with sparse transitions and subtopic phrases. At the end of our fifth paragraph, the transition phrase "But new since the 1960s" directs the reader's attention away from historic aspects of war gaming and into the present. We offer two sentences' worth of what's new and use the transition "Nowadays" to move through "computer junkies" to the mathematical basis of the pastime. Sparse though they are, our transitions lead readers through our organizational network.

Write with Subheads Wherever Possible

A great many magazines use subheads—bold type that breaks up articles into short units. These subheads are usually used as graphic devices, not editorial ones. Their approximate placement is suggested by the artist who lays out the page, often without having even read the article. Therefore, the subheads don't always divide subtopics exactly the way the writer might divide them.

Many writers include subheads in their finished manuscripts anyway. We generally do, except when writing for magazines that never use them. The subheads (such as "Reformed Computer Addicts" in Ill. 3.2) are a quick way for editors, as well as writers, to see logical progressions and to locate the article's various subtopics. For beginners, they are as helpful as curve-speed signs are to drivers on strange roads. We suggest you insert them as regularly as you can.

But never use subheads to substitute for transitions and subtopic sentences. An article must be able to stand on its own without them. If subheads that get dropped onto the editing-room floor leave you without transitions, some editor is going to have to compose some for you. He may not enjoy it a bit. In our experience, we've found that editors seldom mind crossing out, but usually resent taking the time to bridge your gaps.

End with a Bang

By now we assume you're all the way through your first draft, right up to the ending. But even if you've said it all, you can't just stop writing. You must bring the article to a definite conclusion that leaves the reader satisfied that you've delivered what your topic sentence promised.

Endings don't have to be long; they seldom are. But they do have to be included. Here, too, is where the magazine article differs greatly from the newspaper article, which often just tails off after the last point is made.

There are as many ways to create a good ending as there are ways to create a good lead. And there's some similarity between the two devices. Here are several of the more common ways to end.

SUM UP

Pick a line or two that neatly wraps up the entire subject with a note of finality for readers.

The *Practical Psychology for Physicians* article on "House Calls" *(Ill. 13.1)* ends by summing up the seven conclusions—its seven subtopics—into one general rule: Have a fair and consistent policy:

> Despite all of the public criticism of medicine today, the uselessness of most house calls is understood and accepted if your policy is consistent and fair.

"The Miners" article *(Ill. 5.5)* ends by summing up the topic, stated as "the mine is their life," with statement and quote:

> When employment at the mine opened again . . . he leaped at it. "I packed away all his white shirts and striped ties. . . . They're still in the closet. Guess we haven't even opened the box in years."

HARKEN BACK TO THE LEAD

Judi begins her Lynn Redgrave interview for *Weight Watchers Magazine (Ill. 5.4)* with Lynn's line, "I was a food junky." In ending, she picks a matching quote: "It's not hard to be sensible about food . . . because I'm not hooked on it any more."

John Hirsh begins his article *(Ill. 5.11)* with the word "greaser." His ending picks up that word from the lead (and the editor liked it so much, he put it in the title):

> I feel more awake than ever before. And I can jog almost 30 minutes at a clip which is pretty good for a greaser who couldn't walk one block without feeling totally exhausted.

Judi's "Museum" article's *(Ill. 6.13)* ending echoes the "slammed door" image of her lead with "open doors" and "turnstiles" in her ending:

> Can't the city's Cultural Affairs Bureau find some way to open the doors to these children again? Or are they planning to put turnstiles at the entrances to playgrounds next?

END ON AN IRONIC NOTE

After spending a few thousand words warning about the skateboard menace for *Family Health (Ill. 5.9),* Judi ends ironically:

> And don't mention this consoling thought to anyone under 21: If the fad lasts as long as it did the last time around, it'll be gone by this time next year!

In our war-gaming article *(Ill. 13.2),* the concluding irony is aimed at one variation of the pastime:

One company, Flying Buffalo, Inc., has run computer war games by mail for years now, but they've stayed rather small. Without rolling a 12-sided die, the odds are strong that war-gamers who've tasted the kibbitzing and improvising that go on with living, breathing partners are not likely to wave a white flag after a frontal assault by some punch-card general.

OFFER SOURCES FOR MORE INFORMATION

In a way, this device doesn't end the story at all, but encourages readers to continue it on their own. In her study techniques article *(Ill. 5.2)* Judi ends:

> For more information on studying, consult the following books: *How to Study in College,* second edition, by . . . and *How to Study,* second edition, by. . . . Both, available in paperback.

Our *Family Handyman* story on how to build plastic furniture *(Ill. 5.1)* ends in similar fashion:

> For 75 cents, Rohm and Haas Company, Dept. FH, APO Box 9730, Philadelphia, Pa. 19140, will send you all of the following literature: (1) Do-It-Yourself with Plexiglas, (2) How to Install Plexiglas for Safety Glazing, (3) Project Plans Mail Order Catalog, (4) Approved Tools for Working with Plexiglas Mail Order Catalog and (5) List of Approved Plexiglas Distributors.

Often, the writer or editor tacks this ending onto one of the other endings. At the end of John Hirsh's "Greaser" article *(Ill. 5.11)* the editor plugged an accompanying article:

> Some of my recipes which have helped me drop my weight can be found on page 7 of this section.

If you don't like that ending, write one yourself. In fact, try writing new leads, topic sentences, transitions and endings for some of the articles we've looked at, or for others. You'll soon find your own unique way of putting your ideas on paper—the way that works best for you.

You'll know you've succeeded the day someone finally says, on first meeting you, "I read your article in my favorite magazine and loved your style."

14

Good Writing = Rewriting

U NLESS YOU'RE A CLOSET SHAKESPEARE, YOUR WORDS will *never* fall onto the paper just right on your first try. There are too many words in the language, too many shades of meaning, too many opportunities to be just a bit more precise or effective. Your first try should never be shipped off to a waiting editor. Would-be writers who make that mistake become has-beens before they ever break into the field.

Magazine writing is in no way like writing for a large newspaper, where a rewrite department is part of the staff. This field demands a honed and polished finished product. Of course, any good editor can edit drivel into finished prose. But he won't—that's not his job. If you want to make it as a magazine writer, you must learn to be your own editor.

We've been in this business for a long time, with hundreds of published magazine articles, twenty-two books, and two decades of writing, editing and publishing a monthly trade newsletter. Yet we still go through a minimum of two heavy edits on everything we write. In our early days, we needed four or five drafts to get an article right. We don't expect we'll ever be able to turn in unrevised manuscripts that give us the pride of ownership that makes all of writing's headaches worthwhile. We now prefer to make our first run at editing on the computer and our last with a pen, but we still habitually slog through several drafts.

If you organize your article tightly before you begin, and cover almost every salient point on the first run-through, maybe you'll be able to carefully write your first draft, cut and paste, and make final corrections all on the computer. On the other hand, you might be one of those writers whose first drafts are little more than loosely organized scraps of thought. In that case, you'll probably need a second run-through to take you down the plotted channel, a third go-round on the computer, and then a meticulous pen editing of bumps and dips before you're ready to call your work finished. If you're a true writer, we'll wager that even after you print out your final draft you'll tinker here and there before it's mailed or e-mailed.

A few beginners put off submission by polishing past the point of shine. They rub away at each and every word and end by wearing off the spontaneous flow of thought that is the real object of writing. It's important to keep in mind that *every* word need not be the best possible word. But if you are to successfully conquer the challenge of writing for magazines, you must develop the skill of recognizing good writing in other articles and in your own. More important, you must develop the discipline required to turn in an article that represents your best current writing.

Perhaps if we share with you *our* thoughts as we edited a manuscript's first draft, you can start studying your own manuscripts like an editor.

Good Writing = Good Editing

Illustration 14.1, taken from our own files, is a page of a brief article we wrote for a regional magazine. It's the first of a series of restaurant reviews, and had to establish our credentials and objectivity. The first draft, reproduced here, is not bad—but it's not good enough. In *Illustration 14.2,* you can see how we edited the rough draft. The editing was slow and painstaking; usually editing takes us more time than the rough draft we write at full speed to get our ideas down on paper.

When we felt the manuscript was sufficiently ready *(Ill. 14.2),* we went through again, making even more little improvements *(Ill. 14.3).* We printed that out, penned in a few polishing touches and, certain now that the article said what we wanted it to, we mailed it off.

Let's look first at the purpose for each paragraph in our example.

> *Paragraph 1:* The primary purpose is to provide a lead. Since this is a local maga-
> zine, we've chosen to tease readers into wanting to know how cosmopolitan
> big-timers rate their restaurants. A secondary purpose is to establish our cre-
> dentials as big-timers. It fits easily into our lead, and we get it done in the
> very first sentence. A third, even more subtle, purpose—to establish objectiv-
> ity without seeming snobbish—we tried to handle in the next two sentences.
> The final sentence is a transition and the topic of the article: several restaurant
> reviews.
>
> *Paragraph 2:* Our purpose here is to review one restaurant in particular without
> wasting any time. We use specific examples (the second sentence) and com-
> parison (the third sentence) to make the point—that this is a good restau-
> rant—in the liveliest yet tersest way.

In the first draft, we quickly put down the words and phrases that popped into our heads. We knew they wouldn't survive intact into the final draft. But we knew that we'd never get to a final draft if we didn't start out with some approximation of our thoughts on paper.

The next illustration *(Ill. 14.2)* shows our actual editing of the first draft. To take you through our editing thoughts line by line, we've numbered each line so you can follow along.

Illus. 14.1. First Page of Unedited First Draft

Since we travel so much as writers, we've
grown to appreciate Madison's unique position as
a homey place to live, where people of all sorts
are free to enjoy a very high standard of living
at a relatively low cost of living. Nowhere is
that reflected more dramatically than in Madison's
retsaurants.

While we were visiting Madison with an eye
to moving here, imagine our delight at discovering
l'Etoile where we were served like royalty a duck
lavished with orange sauce, sipped the finest wine
reasonable money could buy, overlooked the calories
in fresh torte, and nearly fell over when the bill
came to almost $20. Only a month earlier we'd
enjoyed truly comparable splendor at New York's
famed Algonquin where the tab ran up to almost 3
times l'Etoile's!

Line 1: "As writers" is too general. "Freelance writers in search of articles of national interest" is more specific, more vivid, and more credible.

Lines 1 and 2: The purpose of the article is to discuss the restaurant dining we do (more often and in more places than most of this article's readers) as travelers, not writers. So we switched around the two clauses so "freelance writers" fits into an introductory phrase while the more important "we travel" becomes the sentence's subject and verb.

Line 1: Whoops! We'd forgotten to include the article's topic—the point of "we travel"—in our opening. We didn't want readers to be misled, even for a moment, into thinking the article had to do with writing or travel. We quickly edited in "and we eat out a lot."

Lines 2 and 3: We tied the third sentence to the second with the thought "appreciate." We could have made it more evident by saying, "We especially appreciate," but didn't want to be top-heavy with "appreciation." Apple-polishing, we figured, was fine from us outsiders; bowing and scraping was not. We chose "pleased" instead.

Lines 3, 4, and 5: That we live in Madison—the region covered by the magazine—is important to help readers identify with us. But "homey place to live" is off the topic, so out it went. Also, comparing "high standard of living" to "low cost of living" is too clichéd for comfort. We chose more straightforward language.

    Notice the progression in organization, from sentence to sentence, from the general "many things" to the more specific "good living" to the most specific "restaurants."

Line 6: A noun's missing here—not a crucial oversight. Many magazine editors would not have paused to insert one, but it caught our attention because, as originally drafted, that sentence was arhythmic. Add "fact" and it's got rhythm. We could have chosen from many other nouns, any one of which would have been appropriate. But if we'd selected a more noticeable one, such as "merge" or "amalgamation," it would have shifted some impact from the two more important parts of that sentence, "dramatically" and "Madison's restaurants."

Line 10: "served like royalty a duck lavished with" is too awkward to ignore. We knew it stuck out when we were typing the first draft, but at that point our emphasis was on getting the ideas down on paper. And it's good we didn't take the time to change it then. While editing this portion, we had more than mere clumsy writing in mind.

Lines 8, 9, and 10: In the first draft, we deliberately put in first position "While we were visiting Madison" to transition from the previous paragraph to this one. Then we saw a chance to sew up neatly our own transition from living in New York City to living in Madison by adding the phrase "with an eye to moving

Illus. 14.2. Page of Edited First Draft

As free-lance writess in search of articles

(and eat out alot)

of national interest, a great deal Since we moved to Madison

~~Since~~ we travel ~~so much as writers~~, we've

many things about this lovely city. We are especially

grown to appreciate ~~Madison's unque position as~~

pleased to find that people here

~~a homey place to live, where people of all sorts~~

good

~~are free~~ to enjoy ~~a very high standard of~~ living

at ~~a~~ relatively low cost. ~~of living.~~ Nowhere is

fact

that reflected more dramatically than in Madison's

retsaurants.

first (like gastronomic kings)

~~In fact, one of the reasons~~ We knew we could live

~~While we were visiting Madison with an eye~~

in Madison when, ~~we~~ on a visit from New York City, we

~~to moving here, imagine our delight at~~ discover~~ing~~ed

(In the little second-floor restaurant overlooking the Capitol,

dined on

L'Etoile, ~~where~~ we ~~were served like~~ royalty, ~~a~~ duck

lovingly ~~we~~ the best house

lavished with orange sauce, sipped ~~the finest~~ wine,

~~we~~ consumed ~~the lovingly~~

~~reasonable money could buy, overlooked the calories~~

~~prepared~~ baked ~~we~~ grinned from ear to ear at the less-than-

~~in~~ fresh torte, and ~~nearly fell over when the bill~~

$20 bill for two.

~~came to almost $20~~. Only a month earlier we'd

a feast ~~dining~~

enjoyed ~~truly~~ comparable ~~splendor~~ at New York's

only there had run SP

famed Algonquin, ~~where~~ the tab ~~ran up~~ to almost (3)

L'Et

times ~~E'T~~oile's!

here." During editing, however, we decided that we really didn't have to include minutiae such as "with an eye to moving here" since obviously we were here; we'd said so in paragraph one. Out it went. We kept "Madison" in our rewritten sentence as a bridge from the "Madison" in the previous paragraph's last sentence. But we also carefully laid out all the information we wanted in this sentence.

Most beginning writers would have cast that sentence this way: *We first knew we could live like gastronomic kings in Madison when we discovered l'Etoile on a visit from New York City.* Why did we make a complex sentence of it instead? Because we wanted to save our most dramatic revelation for the end. If you give away your punch line at the start of a story, why should your friends listen to the rest of the joke? The same applies, in a general sense, to sentences and paragraphs as well as entire stories. We wanted "l'Etoile" to be our punch line. It's the topic we were about to discuss over the next several paragraphs. So we reversed the positions of "on a visit from New York City" and "l'Etoile."

Lines 8 and 10: The first draft hadn't taken time to set the scene at all. So we edited in a very short picture of what l'Etoile looks like. We also edited in "live like gastronomic kings" to underline the topic of our article, restaurants, providing a second bridge from paragraph one.

Line 10: In the haste of getting the first draft onto paper, we'd cast this sentence with an inactive verb: "we were served." But to create exciting reading, you need active verbs. So we reworked the sentence so that, instead of passively watching the duck being served to us, we actively dined on it. Still later, if you compare that line to our final draft, we crossed out "dined" and substituted the more explicit, and point-making, "feasted." By using the simple expedient of a specific, active, exciting verb, we were able to eliminate adjectives and adverbs and still create the same mood as in our first draft. Contrary to what your English teachers told you, adjectives and adverbs often get in the way of exciting writing. If you link explicit, active verbs to explicit, vivid nouns, you won't have to prop up weak sentences with extraneous modifiers.

Line 11: However, here we actually added a modifier, the adverb "lovingly" before "lavished." First of all, the alliteration is fun. Second, the word is anything but extraneous. It makes an entirely separate point on its own, showing the manner in which the whole staff at l'Etoile approaches food.

Line 13: Notice here how easy it is to cross out one cliché, "nearly fell over," only to substitute another, "grinned from ear to ear." Fortunately, we corrected that slipup in our final draft. Also notice our struggle over how to describe the wine and the reasonable price we paid for it. The first draft's elusive "sipped the finest wine reasonable money could buy" evolved to "sipped a wine as good as any." That wasn't at all accurate (if compared to a seventy-four dollar bottle of Dom Perignon, for example), so we struck it, too. Then we remembered that the paragraph's purpose was to show the reasonable price we paid for an outstanding meal. We weren't setting out to criticize individual menu items, so we

Illus. 14.3. Final Draft with Last Polishing

As free-lance writers in search of articles

of national interest, we travel a great deal and

eat out a lot. Since we moved to Madison we've grown

to appreciate many things about this lovely city. We

are especially pleased to find that people here

enjoy good living at relatively low cost. Nowhere is

that fact reflected more dramatically than in

Madison's restaurants.

We first knew we could live like gastronomic

kings in Madison when, on a visit from New York City,

we discovered L'Etoile. In the little second-floor

restaurant overlooking the Capitol, we ^feasted ~~dined~~ on duck

lovingly lavished with orange sauce, sipped the best

house wine, ~~consumed~~ tasted ~~nibbled~~ fresh-baked tortes -- and grinned

~~from ear to ear~~ with pleasure at the less-than-$20 ~~bill~~ tab for two.

Only a month earlier we'd enjoyed a comparable ~~feast~~ banquet

at New York's famed Algonquin -- ~~only~~ but there the ~~tab~~ bill

had run to almost three times L'Etoile's.

didn't have to deal with details about the wine at all. Simplicity prevailed over superlatives and we ended up with "sipped the best house wine."

Lines 16 and 17: Here we deliberately left in two far-from-extraneous adjectives. For accuracy, we had to say that what we'd eaten at the Algonquin Hotel's restaurant was "comparable" in quality; otherwise our price comparison wouldn't have held water. We kept "famed" before Algonquin so that Madison's readers—not, as a whole, nationwide travelers—would know immediately that the Algonquin is a good many notches above Howard Johnson's.

Lines 13 and 16: At the last minute, we switched around "tab" and "bill" so line 15 of the final draft gained a pleasant alliteration, "less-than-$20 tab for two," without in any way diminishing the overall impact of line 17.

Line 17: It took us until the very last minute to take a swipe at that exclamation point. If the sentence itself didn't excite the reader, a tiny blob of ink wouldn't either.

As you may have noticed from other examples in the book, this puffery-loaded article is unlike our usual writing style. That's because, in studying the magazine, we discovered that its readers expected a light, flighty, filigreed style. As we said in Chapter 2, write for the readers and you won't go wrong.

A Checklist for Editing Manuscripts

It's easier to learn good editing on somebody else's manuscripts. We suggest you practice editing your kids' school papers, your friends' letters and your spouse's business reports. Then attack your own sloppy first drafts again. By the time you've become a bloodthirsty editor of your own writing, you will instinctively reach for a pen every time your eyes spot something to read—even when you pick up a letter from the folks back home.

To start you thinking like an editor, we've selected unedited pages from three different manuscripts. When you think you've got them whipped into fine shape, compare your editing to ours, which we've reproduced at the end of this chapter. If your changes don't match ours, don't automatically assume that yours are wrong. Editing, like writing, is a personal art, and there are a hundred right ways of doing it. Did you fix a few things we didn't bother with? Did you pick up the same clumsinesses we zeroed in on? See if your corrections are worse or better than ours.

Eventually you'll develop a mental checklist of problems to look for when editing your manuscripts. At risk of having you edit *this* book first, here's a condensation of our own long list. Most items can be summed up in one underlying principle: *good writing is simple writing.* Forget the notion that published writers take basic notions and opaque them with eloquent words and convoluted sentences. Truly good writers take eloquent ideas and make them readable, understandable, even enjoyable, through carefully selected everyday words.

SELECT VIVID NOUNS

The subjects and objects of your sentences must paint pictures in readers' minds. Don't write about a *horse* if *stallion* is more accurate. Don't choose *cat* when *Persian kitten* is what you have in mind. Given a choice, would you look first at a *picture* or a *tintype*? Pick explicit nouns that don't require adjectives to clarify their meanings.

CHOOSE ACTIVE, EXPLICIT VERBS

Make your subjects *do something* by choosing active verbs: *prance, dance, enhance, romance.* If you insert the passive voice too often—*was carried* away, *is being* lifted, *was improved, is being* put to sleep—your subjects will feel passive too. And so will your readers.

Choose, too, the verbs that most explicitly show the actions you're thinking of. Do you mean *grab, grip* or *grapple with*? Do you say *like* when you mean to say *prefer, admire* or *enjoy*?

STICK TO SIMPLE TENSES

Whenever possible, use the *simple present tense* unless the *simple past tense* is more accurate. The *future* and *conditional* tenses (such as "he would fly") tend to undermine the author's sense of authority; readers suspect people who forever hedge with *coulds* and *shoulds*. And *has beens* and *had beens* are hard to follow.

WEIGH ADJECTIVES AND ADVERBS

Adverbs and adjectives slow down the pace of reading. They dilute the impact of nouns and verbs. They diminish the author's authority, since people are trained to suspect a fact accompanied by a string of modifiers.

Here's an example of adjective overuse, from a student's first draft:

> When my *four-year-old* daughter *gently* slipped her mother's cigarette from its *familiar* pack, placed it *jauntily* at the edge of her mouth, and said, "Hey, Dad, howya doin'?" I entered the final phase of a *long, too* drawn out *personal* battle against smoking.

All the italicized words are extraneous. Read the sentence without them and see for yourself.

Here's a fact that loses credibility due to the author's timidity:

> Entering college freshmen, on the whole, are often prone to develop homesickness.

A confident writer simply says, "College freshmen often become homesick."

Ill. 14.4. Pages of First Draft for *You* to Practice Editing (Later, Compare to Our Editing in Ill. 14.6)

> At Christmas, every bdy wrote about toys. But we asked,
> what ~~ahaatx~~ happens to all of those damned battery powered
> toys <u>after</u> Christmas. And ~~wxakaxx~~ we wrote an expose about
> how batteries are marketed: "The caustic truth about
> batteries." ~~/When/everybody/was/~~ While all of our friends were encouraging people to get
> themselves ~~x~~ creative ~~hobby,~~ hobbies we wrote "The Hazards of
> Hobbies."
>
> Every magazine feels obliged to run some seasonal material.
> And after a few years on the job, editors find Christmas
> and similar editorial holiday issues to be more and more
> depressing as fresh ideas get harder and harder to find.
> Our newspaper group editor was no exception. One year
> we did the coldest spot ôn the nation, then next the snowiest.
> What next? Well, there was a northern Wisconsin town
> that was red-light district from one end to the other all
> summer. What went on there in the depths of winter?
>
> "Where are the snows of nexteryear?" predicted
> with help from the federal government's/climate ~~and~~ weather and
> experts, how much colder the U.S. was becoming, and
> how fast, and ~~where~~ on which états the big snows would fall, and so on.
> Editors -- and there readers -- love predictions.
>
> Next year we predicted, thanks ~~ka~~the nation's
> #1 weahter wexpert, an M.I.T. professor, that we were about
> to have a record cold winter: "It's going to be a red
> flannel winter." We even sketched maps, based on the
> expert's prognotications, showing how much colder various
> parts of the country would be and where the heaviest
> snows would fall. It was a marvelôus story. ~~ixwaxx~~

++Sometimes the person who lived the experience gets the entire by-line. Other times, the actual author is listed second: "As told to....." Rarely, usually only in articles involving celebrities, does the author get t~~he~~traditional by-line.

R~~i~~~~c~~k~~i~~~~n~~g~~x~~~~u~~p~~x~~~~t~~~~h~~~~e~~~~x~~~~e~~~~n~~~~x~~~~x~~~~e~~~~n~~~~t~~~~x~~READER's~~x~~DIGEST~~x~~~~w~~~~e~~~~x~~~~f~~~~i~~~~n~~d~~

~~p~~~~e~~~~r~~~~s~~~~o~~~~n~~~~a~~~~l~~~~x~~~~e~~~~x~~~~p~~~~e~~~~r~~~~i~~~~e~~~~n~~~~c~~~~e~~~~s~~~~x~~~~s~~~~t~~~~o~~~~r~~~~i~~~~e~~~~s~~

How many of us can survive enough falls off 28
                                          near
storie buildings, or ~~r~~~~e~~~~r~~~~e~~x recover from enough/fatal

illnesses, to make a living at writing personal experience

articles? So, the pros who make at living at writing

personal experience stories write about some body else's

tragedies and triumphs. ++~~P~~~~r~~~~o~~~~b~~~~a~~~~b~~~~l~~~~y~~ the dean of personal
                    must be
experience story tellers ~~i~~~~s~~ Terry Morris, one-time

president of the American Society of Journalists and

Authors and ~~p~~~~r~~~~o~~~~f~~~~i~~ ~~p~~~~r~~~~o~~~~f~~~~i~~ prolific pagazine writers.
        abandoned
She ~~s~~~~w~~~~i~~~~t~~~~c~~~~h~~~~e~~~~d~~, about 1950, ~~f~~~~r~~~~o~~~~m~~ writing short stories

in favor of human interest magazine articles about people

in crisis. But she never abandoned her gift for

telling a touching story, so she sold her first two

artgicles to COSMOPOLITAN and McCALL'S early in 1951.

Terry's all-time favorite was "Please don't lose faith
                              from the viewpoint of
in Me" an as-told-to article ~~b~~~~y~~ the mother of a
                son.
schizophrenic ~~s~~~~o~~~~n~~~~x~~~~t~~~~h~~~~a~~~~t~~ McCALL's ran it ~~i~~~~n~~ July 1953;

we've reprinted the first page nearby~~x~~ so you can

study how a master handles somebody else's personal experience.

6.11 The Photo story

This is a bonus! The photo story ~~kan~~ technically

isn't a genre all by itself since it can be used

as a form of personality piece, a bit of an expose,

a graphic side to history, humor,... And in photo

stories, the writing is often less important than the
    although no editor will object to your writing.well.
photos // But so many writers these days pack a camera

alongside their typewriter, that we think writers ought

to keep the photo story in mind as part of their
    ing
market/armada.

The photo story has to satisfy all of the requires
                         create
for a good story.~~xx~~ you must ~~have~~ a lead photo, that

gets the reader hooked on your photo story and seta a

tone for the rest. Your pictures have to be organized

chrono~~xxixx~~logically or logically. The story has to

have an ending or conclusion. (In a later chapter we'll

discuss tehnical aspects such as size, presentation,

quality, etc.)

When we suggested to POPULAR SCIENCE that we ~~ka~~ could

do an article about how home owners can paint their

palace ~~x~~only once every 10 years, the ~~dix~~ editors liked the

idea. We knew they would~~X~~! But they suggested, instead
    giving
of ~~telling~~ the information once in words and again in

pictures, why not do it only once, through pictures with

comprehensive captions. The result was our first pictorial

how-to story.

Some modifiers sneak in by force of habit. We've seen them so often with certain nouns we forget they don't always belong together: *golden opportunity, the right answers, pretty close, force of habit.* Here's our rule for determining whether a modifier is needed: If the word adds meaning to only one other word, such as an adjective making a noun more precise or vivid, we try to cross them *both* out and look for a more explicit word. If the modifier adds substantial meaning to the entire sentence—better still, to the entire paragraph—we leave it in.

CONSIDER CLICHÉS
Clichés are not all taboo. The proper time to use one is when you want to make your idea sound familiar, commonplace, or old hat. The improper time is when you're trying for a vivid way to make your point.

ALWAYS AVOID JARGON
If the readers for whom you are writing understood the jargon, it wouldn't be jargon.

We know that the inventors of jargon words and phrases (such as *interpersonal communication* for conversation, and *overachiever* for someone who's been underrated in the first place) claim that their coinages clarify meaning and express subtle nuances. But some would-be writers hide their insecurity or lack of research behind these words. And jargon merely makes their writing bad.

VARY SENTENCE LENGTH
Make sentences as long as you need to, as short as you want. But don't make them all the same length. Many teachers try to convince beginning writers that short sentences are required for clear writing. But the fact is, we can relate complex ideas to one another most clearly in complex sentences. Carefully written, they're no harder to read than short sentences.

DON'T HAMSTRING YOUR PARAGRAPHS
You already have a natural rhythm to your paragraphs. Some are long, some short, depending on how much you have to say within them. Consciously trying to write only very short paragraphs, as some journalism teachers suggest, defeats the purpose of paragraphing. Paragraphs organize ideas into readable compartments, which are then linked together with transitions. If you arbitrarily chop up your articles, it will be hard to follow your thoughts and to know when a new thought appears. You'll leave readers wondering just when you've hopped from one idea to another and just how all your ideas relate.

Nonetheless, it is important to recognize that magazine paragraphs are, as a rule, shorter than book paragraphs and longer than newspaper paragraphs— and that a magazine's readers' average educational level often determines that magazine's average paragraph length. If you don't want your paragraphs arbitrarily chopped up for you, study the market your article is aimed at.

ERADICATE CUTESINESS

We all have fun hammering out clever turns of phrase that show off our normally hidden genius. Unfortunately, anything that makes the reader notice *the writing* instead of *what is written about* is distracting. And that's bad writing.

Nearly every beginning writer has to find a personal way to cope with cutesiness. When Frank was getting started, he'd go through every manuscript and cross out ten of his choicest expressions. That way, unless he'd had a particularly trite day at the keyboard, most cutesiness was extracted. Most of it turned out to be irrelevant anyway.

CUT AND PASTE

Until computers invaded our lives, two of the writer's most useful tools were scissors and a roll of Scotch tape. We used them often to cut up the first draft, subtopic by subtopic and paragraph by paragraph, and then tape it back together in a more logical or more exciting sequence.

With computers, it's a lot easier. Writing in Microsoft Word, we can just highlight a section, hit the F2 key, and move any phrase, sentence or paragraph wherever we like. We can read it at once in its new context and, if the new placement isn't better, click the Undo icon and try somewhere else.

Sometimes we can't see a better arrangement of our words until we've printed out the manuscript. A computer screen holds only a few readable paragraphs. It's hard to keep in mind what you've read two screens ago. All sorts of problems in arrangement sometimes show up only when we have a whole set of pages in hand. So we never consider our manuscript finished after its first print-out. Usually, at least one sentence or paragraph needs to be circled and penciled, "Move to page x," with a complementary reminder on page x to "Insert from page y."

In cutting and pasting, it's often necessary to add or delete transitions between newly joined portions. That's all part of good writing.

A Reference Shelf of Writing Basics

Within the limited confines of a single chapter, we can't begin a thorough treatment of how to write correct English. We must presume that you already know how. If you need more help, we recommend our textbook *Good Writing,* which has hundreds of illustrations and self-help exercises. For quick summations, keep Strunk and White's *Elements of Style* near at hand.

A good, up-to-date dictionary is also a must. First, make sure you keep your word processor's spelling checker set to Check Spelling As You Type. (If you don't know where the option's located, look up *check spelling* in the program's Help screens.) We also keep our e-mailer's spelling checker on full-time. Also, we keep a printed dictionary available. (The computer dictionaries we've looked at are barebones compared to the in-print *Webster's Collegiate*.) An important use for the dictionary is to find the correct spelling for a homonym your word processor's spelling checker can't find, such as whether it's *its* or *it's, ad* or *add, he lead* or *he led*. A much less important use, for writers, is to look up the meaning of a word they're not sure of. Our rule is that if *we* aren't sure of its meaning, our readers probably won't be sure, either, so it's much better to substitute a word we know.

For the spelling of technical terms, we use an online search engine, typing in the word or phrase we're searching for and then the word *definition*. Among the choices our search engine shows us, we're careful to select the most authoritative source.

When you're looking for exactly the right words to use in your articles, a dictionary is not much help. For the noun that shows precisely what you want the reader to see, or the active verb that's so on-target you don't need modifiers, the writer's best friend is a thesaurus. If you've never used the thesaurus bundled in your word processor, start at once. Let's assume you're writing an article involving a *sort of lovable* character, but you need a more explicit, shorter way of describing him. Look at the choices for *lovable* in Microsoft Word's thesaurus: *endearing, adorable, enchanting, attractive, delightful, affable, congenial, amiable, cute*. If you don't find the right word there, you can click on the choice *despicable (antonym)* and get even more suggestions plus a suggestion to check its antonym *admirable*. By doing that, we got eight more suggestions to choose from.

The best thesaurus is the one that's fastest and easiest to use. That's why we recommend using the one your word processor has even though it's not half as complete as a paper-bound thesaurus.

If you want other opinions than ours on how to write for magazines, the best book we know is *The ASJA Guide to Freelance Writing: A Professional Guide to the Business for Nonfiction Writers of All Experience Levels,* edited by Timothy Harper and published by St. Martins Press in 2003. Eleven top magazine writers share their experiences and freely offer their advice on everything from querying editors to writing for the Internet.

If you need more help with research sources and skills, we'd like to point you to our book *Research Shortcuts* (Revised Edition, University of Wisconsin Press, 2003). It includes all the fine points in our tried-and-true research techniques. If you still have trouble organizing your articles, pick up another of our books in the same series, *Secrets to Writing Great Papers* (University of Wisconsin Press, 2003). Both books can be ordered from the publisher (www.wisc.edu/wisconsinpress), from Amazon, or from our own website (www.booksthatteach.com). And for help finding secondary markets for those photos you take for your travel stories, Rohn Engh's *Sell and Resell Your Photos* (5th edition, Writers Digest Books, 2003) is excellent.

Writer's Digest's website (www.writersdigest.com/101sites/) keeps an excellent listing called "The 101 Best Websites for Writers," where you'll find leads to many useful online resources.

How to Prepare Your Final Manuscript

Many editors prefer article submissions on disk. Some even like to have them e-mailed. If your editor requests one or the other, ask if there are special guidelines to follow. If you mail a disk, be sure to affix a label with your name, address and phone number, the article's name and the rights being sold *(for which see Chapter 15)*. If he asks you to submit your article on paper, print it out for submission the way nearly all other professional magazine writers print theirs. That way, the editor will assume that yours is from a professional, too.

Use only 8½ × 11 white paper, preferably twenty-pound bond so it holds up through several readings on the subway or commuter train.

Don't use obviously expensive paper (with an inlaid pattern, gaudy watermark, or such).

Print only on one side of the paper.

Double-space your article and leave enough room in the margins (at least 1½ inches on the left and 1 inch on the right) for the editor and her associates to write comments. A margin of at least 1 inch at top and bottom, and several inches between your first page's identifying data and your title is usual *(Ill. 14.5)*.

Indent paragraphs five spaces. (Some editors also still prefer two spaces between sentences, though most word processors assume you only want one space.)

Don't footnote unless the magazine usually prints footnotes, and don't indent for long quotations unless it's the magazine's normal style.

Even if your computer offers all kinds of fancy fonts, don't use any for any manuscript. If you're not given any guidance, stick with Times New Roman. Don't use bold type either, although you can feel free to use italics or underline—both mean the same thing to production folks.

Put a copyright notice *(see Chapter 15)* and your name, address and telephone number in the upper left-hand corner of your manuscript's first page.

Don't put a lot of space between the title and your first paragraph or put just the title on page one. A title page that contains nothing but your identification and your article's title is for books and classroom essays.

Put the article's title (or an abbreviated version) and the page number at the top of each page except page 1. (The word processor's *Insert header* tool is great for doing this.)

You can fold a manuscript that's no more than four pages long, and mail it in a regular business envelope. Mail all others flat. Cardboard isn't necessary unless you're mailing illustrations at the same time.

Send assigned (even assigned-on-spec) stories by first-class mail. Mark "assigned manuscript" on the top of the first page and in the lower right- or left-hand corner of your envelope. This is to keep your prodigy from accidentally ending up on the slush pile of unsolicited manuscripts. (Note that we also add a reminder of what rights are being sold. More on that in Chapter 15.)

Not every editor insists on such rigid rules, but we assume that our professionalism is weighed by the care we take with our submissions. We do always read and correct even our final drafts. Editors appreciate small signs of careful, thoughtful proofreading and infinitely prefer an occasional smudge or crossed-out word to misspellings and the misuse of grammar and punctuation.

We've reproduced the first two pages of one of our manuscripts *(Ill. 14.5)* so you can see for yourself what ours look like when we submit them.

Three Edited Manuscripts

On the pages 223 to 225, fully edited, are the three manuscript pages that were reproduced for you a few pages ago. See if you can find the reason for every change we made. It's really true that every time you edit someone else's manuscript you polish your own writing just a little more.

Commonly Used Proofreaders' Marks

Learn these marks and use them in making final changes in your manuscripts. They're almost universally used by writers and editors in passing along copy changes. (Notice that for many of these marks, you mark the copy one way and then put another explanatory mark in the margin. For instance, to set a group of capital letters in small letters [lower case], you circle the group in the manuscript and write *lc* in the left-hand margin. To center a line, you put a bracket at the left *and* one at the right of your copy.)

Illus. 14.5. First Two Pages of Manuscript Formatted for Submission

© 2004
P/K ASSOCIATES INC.
xxxx Gregory Street
Madison, Wisconsin 53711
(608) xxx-xxxx

Assigned article
First North American
serial rights only

Surfing for Free Help Is Easy

Some of the sharpest advice from your fellow accountants is available free, and it's just a couple of mouse
clicks away. If you haven't sampled an Internet news group
or haven't tried one since the clunky old DOS-era BBS
bulletin boards, you're in for a treat.

The obvious use for these newsgroups and informative websites is to help you find answers to technical questions about an accounting problem or program. But it also
pays to just hang around and join discussions. It keeps you
in touch with others in the profession, shows what they're
thinking and doing, and provides feedback on what you're
thinking of doing.

How to join a group

Joining a newsgroup is easy. Launch the "News Reader" tool in Outlook, Outlook Express or your other email software. (In Outlook click the View menu, point to Go To and click News.) Set up your ISP's news server (usually news.[ISP].com or .net). Clicking on it should bring up the question, "Do you want to download a directory of all the newsgroups?" You may need to cull from thousands of names but you can search the list by keywords such as *accounting.* The most suitable groups often begin with *alt, biz,* or *comp.*

For groups you want to try, click on "subscribe" to add their names to your Enroll list. (Don't add too many. Real benefit comes only from consistently reading what other subscribers on a particular list have to say.) Before you click to Enroll, delete from the list all groups that seem irrelevant to your needs.

Most groups use news server software to post messages and responses in well-organized, timesaving displays. You can click on a thread (jargon for "topic") to scan all questions, comments and answers concerning the first message posted in the thread—or you can just read specific messages within a thread.

Some groups don't post threads but email all submitted questions

Illus. 14.6. Edited Manuscript Pages. Compare to Ill. 14.4.

At Christmas, everybody wrote about toys. But we asked,
what happens to all of those damned battery powered
toys after Christmas. And we wrote an expose about
how batteries are marketed: "The caustic truth about
batteries." While all of our friends were encouraging people to find
hobbies,
themselves a creative hobby, we wrote "The Hazards of
Hobbies."

Most magazines feel obliged to run some seasonal material.
And after a few years on the job, editors find Christmas run out of fresh-sounding ideas.
and similar editorial holiday issues to be more and more
depressing as fresh ideas get harder and harder to find.
Our newspaper group editor was no exception. One year we
did the coldest spot in the nation, then next the snowiest.
What next? Well, there was a northern Wisconsin town
that was red light district from one end to the other all during
summer. What went on there in the depths of winter? 's tourist season. We called the article,——.

"Where are the snows of next year?" predicted
weather and
with help from the federal government's/climate and
experts, how much colder the U.S. was becoming, and
on which states
how fast, and where the big snows would fall, and so on.
Then, too is
Editors--and there readers -- love predictions.
to
Next year we predicted thanks to the nation's
#1 weather expert, an M.I.T. professor, that we were about
Title:
to have a record cold winter. "It's going to be a red
flannel winter." We even sketched maps, based on the
expert's that ed
prophs prognostications, showing how much colder various
parts of the country would be and where the heaviest
snows would fall. It was a marvelous story.

& we did the prediction bit again

++Sometimes the person who's lived the experience gets the entire by-line.

Other times, the actual author is listed second: "As told to...." Rarely, ~~m~~

for
usually only ~~in~~ articles involving celebrities, ~~does~~ can the author ~~get~~ count on a traditional

by-line.

~~picking~~ ~~up~~ ~~the~~ ~~someone~~ ~~READERS~~ ~~DIGEST~~ ~~we~~ ~~find~~

~~personal~~ ~~experience~~ ~~stories~~

How many of us can survive enough falls off 28

near
stori~~e~~s buildings, or ~~xxxxx~~ recover from enough/fatal

illnesses, to make a living at writing personal experience

do   it a
articles? So, the pros who make ~~at~~ living ~~at writing~~

~~personal experience stories~~ write about some body else's

⊕
tragedies and triumphs. ~~Xxhax~~ The dean of personal

must be magazine writer
experience story tellers is Terry Morris, one-time

president of the American Society of Journalists and

Authors ~~and~~ ~~prolixxprofi~~ ~~prolific magazine writers.~~

Terry abandoned
~~the~~ ~~wildwood,~~ about 1950, ~~from~~ (writing) shortstor~~ies~~

in favor   human-interest magazine articles about people

Her genius for
in crisis. ~~But she never abandoned her gift for~~

carried over from fiction to non-fiction and
telling a touching story, ~~so~~ she sold her first two

artgicles to COSMOPOLITAN and McCALL'S early in 1951. Not a bad

beginning!
^Terry's all-time favorite ~~was~~ "Please don't lose faith

from the viewpoint of
in Me" an as-told-to article by the mother of a

son.
schizophrenic ~~xxxxxxx~~ McCALL'S ran it in July 1953;

we've reprinted the first page nearby so you can

can molds
study how a master ~~handles~~ somebody else's personal experience.

6.11 The Photo story

to be added to our 10 standard formats.

This is a bonus! The photo story ~~xxx~~ technically

isn't a genre all by itself, ~~since~~ it can be ~~used~~

~~as a form of~~ ^a personality piece, a bit of an expose,

a graphic ~~side~~ ^approach to history, humor,... ~~And~~ ^But in photo

stories, the writing is often less important than the

although no editor will object to ~~your~~ *^good writing.* ~~well~~

photos. ~~¶ But~~ So many writers these days pack a camera

alongside the~~ir~~ typewriter, ~~that~~ we think ~~writers~~ ^you ought

to keep the photo story in mind as part of ~~their~~ ^your

~~ing~~

~~market/armada.~~

The photo~~s~~ story, ^in a photo ha~~s~~ to satisfy all of the requirements ~~themselves~~

create

for a good story, ~~xx~~ You must ~~have~~ ^have a lead photo, that

^which are detailed in chapter ___.

gets the reader hooked ~~on your photo story~~ and sets a

of the photos.

tone for the rest, Your pictures have to be organized

~~chronologically logically~~ or logically. The story has to

have ~~an ending or~~ concludion. (In a later chapter we'll

of submitting photos

discuss te~~h~~nical aspects ^such as size, ~~presentation,~~

quality, etc.)

When we suggested to POPULAR SCIENCE ~~that we do could~~

showing that *need*

~~do~~ an article ^about ~~how~~ home owners ~~can~~ paint their

palace~~s~~ ~~x~~ only once every 10 years, the ~~xix~~ editors liked the

idea. ~~We knew they would!!~~ But, they suggested, instead

giving supplying *once*

of ~~telling~~ the information once in words and ^again in

pictures, why not do it only once, through pictures with

comprehensive captions. The result was our first pictorial

how-to story.

Illus. 14.7. Proofreaders' Marks

MARK	EXPLANATION	EXAMPLE	MARK	EXPLANATION	EXAMPLE
✄	Take out this character	The proofs	↑	Raise up	The proof
ʌ/ong	Insert word shown	The proof	↓	Lower	The proof
ʌ oo	Insert these characters	The prf	←	Move left	← The proof
#	Insert space	Theproof	→	Move right	The proof
eq. #	Even out the spacing	The proof of a	‖	Align lines	The boy The proof The gauge
less #	Make less space between words	The proof of	⊙	Insert period	The proof
⌣	Close spacing	The proof	↗	Insert comma	The proof
∿	Transpose	The is in proof	⊙	Insert colon	The proof
wf	Wrong font	The proofs of	⌃	Insert semicolon	The proof
lc	Change to lower case	The PROof	⌄	Insert apostrophe	The proofs
sc	Change to small capitals	The proof	" / "	Insert quotation marks	The proof
cap	Capitalize	the proof	=	Insert hyphen	A proof mark
ital	Change to italics	The proof	⌄²	Insert superscript	A², B, C²
rom	Change to Roman	The proof	⌃	Insert subscript	H₂O
bf	Change to bold	The proof	ʌ!	Insert exclamation mark	The proof
stet	Let it stand as originally written	The proof	ʌ?	Insert question mark	the proof
sp	Spell out	King Geo.	[/]	Insert brackets	The proof
?	Query for editor	The proof	(/)	Insert parentheses	the proof
⫿	Indent paragraph	The proof	⌐ₙ	Insert 1-en dash (hyphen)	Proof mark
⫿	Start new paragraph	end. The proof	⌐ₘ	Insert 1-em dash	Proof that
run on	No paragraph (run on)	end. The proof	c /)	Insert single quote	The proof
⌐	Set as a new line	the proof. Next	⸋/ʌ/e	Several corrections	All it's prof neds

PART V
How to Be a Pro

The Writer and the Law

F ROM THE CLASSES WE'VE TAUGHT, WORKSHOPS WE'VE
given, and writers' conferences we've participated in, we know that year-
ling writers are full of questions about the law. Copyright, libel, taxes, privacy,
slander, defamation, contracts—they want to know it all. They think that it's all
vital to their careers as writers.

When you get right down to it, though, the law seldom affects writers
except in several limited ways:

> You should know about libel and privacy laws in order to write defensible articles.
>
> You need to know a smattering of facts about copyright law.
>
> You must live with the tax laws, like it or not.

Libel

To paraphrase a definition from Harold Nelson and Dwight Teeter's textbook
Law of Mass Communications, libel is defamation that occurs by written communication and exposes a person to hatred, ridicule, or contempt, lowers him
in the esteem of his fellows, causes him to be shunned, or injures him in his business or calling. (Defamation is, in legal jargon, any intentional false communication that injures another person's good name or reputation.) Statutes on libel
vary from state to state, and judicial precedents waver from decade to decade,
but this definition is pretty standard.

Not many years ago, we warned students that people were suing for libel
at the drop of a hat. Nowadays the pendulum has swung back to the point
where, to deliberately libel somebody, you'd almost have to hire a good lawyer
as co-author. When we write about people or institutions, we don't have to be
quite so cautious.

Libel concerns writers for two reasons: First of all, in almost every libel
lawsuit, the publisher isn't the only one threatened; the author is too. Second,
you can't count on publishers to know what is and what is not libelous. You can't
even count on them to hire lawyers to read your manuscripts for libel. They may
send controversial manuscripts out for legal opinions, but it's not necessarily the
controversial pieces that give the most problems.

For instance, a while ago we were assigned a simple, uncontroversial bread-
and-butter piece about dome homes. We weren't thinking consciously about

libel at any time during the research and writing that went into it. Yet just after the issue with our article hit the newsstands, the magazine received an envelope containing two complaint letters. One was from an executive of a building company not even mentioned in the story, threatening to sue if not given space in a forthcoming issue to say that he took serious exception to a quoted statement from one of our experts. He claimed we had cast doubt on his professionalism since he belonged to the large builders' association an expert had taken issue with in the article.

We paid little attention to the executive's letter because a journalist cannot libel an individual simply by referring to a large group he belongs to. (On the other hand, if we'd said that most magicians in Chicago were perverts, and there were only three magicians in Chicago, any one of them might have been able to sue us for libel because the odds would be two out of three that we were referring to her.)

The other letter in the envelope, however, was from an expert we'd interviewed by phone and quoted in the article. We knew that *he* might have cause for a libel suit if we'd really made the mistakes he claimed we'd made and, in doing so, had damaged his reputation. The most important of his claims was that we'd misquoted him badly. Since the best defense against most libel actions is the truth, we knew we could undercut his claim if we could establish that what we wrote was reasonably accurate.

It turned out, our professional instincts had literally saved the day for us and for the magazine. Without planning it that way, we had covered every opening through which a libel action could be pursued.

First, when we pulled out the story file, sure enough, there in our notes was the *exact* quote—so it passed the accuracy test. (Frankly, not every quote in print so closely matches our notes as his did. God smiled on us that day.)

But *context* figures into acts of libel, too. If we'd put his words into a context that changed their meaning, he still might have had a case. Happily, our notes even showed context. They established that we'd been talking to the expert about the precise topic that contained his quote. So we could prove we'd neither misquoted him nor quoted him out of context. (Or so we could claim. If it went to court, so far the case would be his word against our word and our notes.)

But the expert also wrote, in his letter via the executive, that he didn't remember talking to us and, if he had, certainly he hadn't spoken for publication. Again our thorough files saved the day. First, our telephone bill for the proper month established that we'd received a collect phone call from the appropriate city on the very *date* we'd scribbled at the top of our notes—and *always* do. The call lasted twenty-three minutes, so he certainly hadn't called to say, "Leave me alone." Then, our notes for the day before the interview showed a phone call to the public relations office at the expert's employer. Alongside the phone number were the names of two experts the public relations department had recommended, one of them our potential plaintiff.

We called the public relations office again, and they remembered telling the expert why he was to call us—to be quoted in an article.

So far, so good. If we went to trial, we could establish that the conversation took place, that the expert knew why it took place, and that we'd quoted him accurately according to our notes.

But we still weren't home free. At that point we had to face one of the trickier and fastest-changing parts of libel law: the definitions of *public* figures and *private* figures. If our expert were deemed a public figure, he'd not only have to prove that we'd misquoted him, but that we'd done it with malice—a word commonly defined as *reckless disregard of the truth*. If he were a private figure, then *we* might have to prove that we hadn't been negligent: that we had exercised reasonable care in attempting to determine the truth of what we'd said in print. This could have applied even to the truth of what we claimed the expert had said.

People are considered private figures if they don't seek publicity, don't do things that affect the public at large, and don't affect the news which reaches the public. However, private figures can become limited public figures under libel law when they intrude or allow themselves to be intruded into newsworthy events. Under that definition, it is entirely possible that our expert would have been called a public figure by the trial judge, getting us off the hook of having to prove that we weren't negligent. The trouble was, a lot of time and money would have been wasted getting to that day in court. And what if the judge had decided the expert was a private figure?

Again our professional instincts backed us up. There seemed to be three facts in the quoted statement that the expert said were not facts. Checking our notes, we reassured ourselves and the magazine that, on each of the three points, we'd interviewed two other people besides the expert to check his accuracy. Our notes had preserved the names, titles, phone numbers, and comments of the six people who verified the information in the expert's quote. No reasonable judge should have said we'd exercised less than reasonable care in attempting to discover the truth. (We don't always triple-check every statement, but our instincts at the time had told us that some of the expert's statements might be opinion rather than fact, and we'd wanted to find out which were which.)

There was still one nagging matter left, and there wasn't much we could do about it. Despite all our care and accuracy, the expert could still claim that we had damaged his reputation. True, he wouldn't have had a strong case, considering how well we'd covered every other aspect of libel law. But he could have brought in the disgruntled executive, who might have said he thought less of him as a result of our article. So we asked the head of the public relations office at the expert's employer what she thought of the article. She said it was excellent and volunteered that the quote in question showed high character on the part of the expert and not ill repute. We asked the head of the product's trade association for comment; he said that over ten thousand people had liked the article well enough to write in for more data. (He even volunteered to go into court on our side if the matter came to that.)

Breathing a sigh of relief, we passed on to the magazine's lawyers photocopies of everything we'd dug up. The complainers folded their tents, and that was that.

Privacy

People have the right to be left alone as long as they keep themselves from becoming public figures. Somebody who is not newsworthy *at the moment,* who is not a government official, and who doesn't comment publicly or for publication about anything of any sort of public concern, has the right not to be quoted, pictured or named in publications.

This has potentially serious ramifications for most writers. Every time you ask somebody—your neighbor or a total stranger—how she raises her kids, and then quote her in print, you are beyond a doubt invading her privacy unless she's given you permission to (1) interview her, (2) quote her and (3) use her name in your article. How can you be sure that in six months, when she sees your published story and reads what she said earlier about her lousy brats, she'll remember that she gave you broad consent? The fact is, you can't unless you had her sign a release. Using such a release is not standard operating procedure for journalists at the moment, but it may become common if the privacy pendulum swings against us.

To date, the most serious privacy cases against magazines to reach the courts have involved people who were once in the news but had faded from the public eye. One, for example, was instituted against *Reader's Digest* by a onetime truck hijacker who said that he'd gone straight for eleven years by the time his name was smeared by a *Digest* article on hijacking. Another was brought by a man who'd been a math prodigy and, at the age of sixteen, had lectured to eminent mathematicians amid great publicity. *The New Yorker* profiled the grown-up math genius twenty-five years later, saying he was living in a seedy flat and was employed at menial labor. In both cases the courts sided with the magazines and authors, saying, in essence, "Once a public figure, always a public figure *to some extent.*" In the latter case, the judge wrote:

At least we would permit limited scrutiny of the "private" life of any person who has achieved, or has had thrust upon him, the questionable and indefinable status of "public figure."

Sports Illustrated once profiled a body surfer who granted the writers long interviews and many photos. In the court's eyes, that constituted his consent to the story's being published. But just before publication, the surfer learned that there were some aspects of the story he didn't want published. He withdrew his consent. *Sports Illustrated,* on their lawyers' advice, ran the story anyway and lost its day in court. The judge wrote that if consent is withdrawn prior to publication, "the consequent publicity is without consent."

On appeal, the judge gave *Sports Illustrated* a limited reprieve: It didn't have to pay damages to the body surfer. But the rest of that judge's decision haunts journalists, publishers, and constitutional lawyers to this day, since there's no telling when it will be used as precedent to decide another privacy case:

> In determining what is a matter of legitimate public interest, account must be taken of the customs and conventions of the community and in the last analysis what is proper becomes a matter of the community mores. The line is to be drawn when the publicity ceases to be the giving of information to which the public is entitled, and becomes a morbid and sensational prying into public lives for its own sake, with which a reasonable member of the public, with decent standards, would say that he had no concern. *(Virgil v. Time Inc., 527 F. 2nd 1122. 1124; 9th Cir. 1975)*

In light of decisions such as those just quoted, a noted literary lawyer advised us once at an ASJA meeting to ask anyone we interview for any article to sign and date a simple release form like this one:

> I hereby consent to publication of the interview conducted by . . . on . . . and consent to its publication by . . . and its subsidiaries throughout the world.

There's no doubt that using a release form for all of our face-to-face interviews would be a fine safeguard. But we haven't started using them. None of our colleagues has either—that we know. It must be because, in the past, we enjoyed the give and take of trust that went with being a magazine writer. Maybe it's romantic—but most professional writers are exactly that.

Copyright

There are at least two reasons to know rudimentary copyright law: (1) to understand your rights so you can maximize your protection and your income from those rights; (2) to understand how much of somebody else's copyrighted writing you can incorporate into your own.

As drafted by Congress, the 1976 Copyright Act is simple and straightforward. Freely interpreted in the offices of various magazine publishers, it seems complicated and deals harshly with the rights of writers. So when you are looking for information about Copyright Act provisions, choose your sources carefully. Make sure they're not biased against you.

As Congress drafted it, the 1976 act grants an immediate, automatic, and almost unlimited copyright on your work the instant you write it. To protect it, you do *not* have to register your article before publication with the U.S. Copyright Office and you do *not* have to type a copyright notice on your manuscript (although it doesn't hurt if you do). When your work is *published,* a copyright notice such as *Copyright © 1984 George Washington* must be printed in the proper location. The general notice that a publisher prints near the front of the magazine protects *your* own copyright in *your* own article.

The copyright law is very protective of creators of artistic works of all sorts—poets, magazine writers, book authors, online scribblers, lyricists, painters, sculptors, even composers of heavy metal music. First of all, if publication takes place without a copyright notice, the law allows five years for you to correct the error. Second, you don't lose copyright protection if you don't fill out the Copyright Office's forms—although you can't sue for infringement until you do fill them in. Third, the 1976 law makes it clear that you may sell bits and pieces of your overall copyright.

Which piece of your copyright should you attempt to sell to a magazine? Only a license to publish your article once. You can even limit that license to first publication in North America. (U.S. publishers sell enough copies of their magazines in Canada that *first North American serial rights* are sold instead of only *first U.S. serial rights.*) That way, you can also sell *first Australian serial rights* and *first German serial rights.*

Let's assume that, as a pro, you sell only first North American serial rights to the first buyer of your article. This means simply that the magazine that "buys your story" actually buys only the right to be the first magazine (serial) to publish it. As soon as it has enjoyed that right—when your story has appeared between its covers—you can then sell *second publication rights,* often called *reprint rights,* to however many other magazines or newspapers you're lucky enough to interest in your article. You can also sell *one-time rights,* the right to publish an article once.

Julian Block, tax lawyer-cum-writer, has done this all through his lucrative writing career. He told us about a hundred-word article he wrote on how long to keep tax records in case the IRS audits your returns. "I've sold that one at least sixteen times for payments ranging from $200 to $15." Julian simply mails a printout of his original manuscript with a short covering letter offering one-time rights and asking how much the editor will pay for the material. In his covering letter Julian explains that if the publication buys it, he will not sell any rights in his offered article to any *competing* publication. By that, the industry means any publication that tries to attract approximately the same demographic or geographic readership. (For instance, *Woman's Day* competes with *Family Circle* and *Newsweek* competes with *Time.*) So far, the tax records article has appeared in magazines for druggists, undertakers, dairy farmers, electrical contractors, people who manage warehouses, truck drivers and auto repair shop owners.

While it's true that Julian has chalked up more *one-time rights* sales than anybody we know, many pros count on selling articles more than once. The rate a magazine pays for one-time or reprint (sometimes called *second*) rights is generally lower than its rate for first serial rights, but it's not always something to sneeze at. Judi sold a reprint of her $600 study-tips article (originally written for *Seventeen*) for $500 to *Nutshell,* for $250 to an Australian magazine, and for $150 for use in a textbook. One of our students sold her story about a new rescue tool to the *Milwaukee Journal's Insight* magazine for $50 and then sold its reprint to *Elks* for $200.

To protect your interests, as well as to alert publishers that you know the value of what you are protecting, it's a good idea to observe certain formalities. First, at the top of the first page of every manuscript, you can type *Copyright* © followed by the year, followed by your name. Example: *Copyright © 1984 George Washington.* Also, you can type *First North American serial rights for sale* unless you've already sold those rights, in which case you specify the rights you are currently selling.

The first page of a manuscript has traditionally doubled as something of an invoice between writer and publisher. But it's not a very good medium. The better way for you to alert publishers that you know your rights and expect to have them respected is to submit a formal invoice with every assigned article. This is typical of the language we use on our invoices:

> A license for first North American serial rights to my Copyright © 2005 article "How I Became a Billionaire" will be granted to *MadCap Magazine* upon payment of $1,000.

The principal hitch in the 1976 copyright law is a provision known as "work for hire." It defines the only area in which the author is not the owner of his work's copyright. In its major use—and also its clearest use—"work for hire" applies to staff employees. If you punch a clock at *Time* magazine and write an article for it, Time Inc. owns the copyright.

But the definitions section of the 1976 copyright law includes a second, more controversial meaning for the term "work for hire":

> a work specially ordered or commissioned for use as a contribution to a collective work . . . if the parties expressly agree in a written instrument signed by them that the work shall be considered a work made for hire. *(17 U.S. C. 101)*

What's at stake is this: If you write an article and, either openly or unknowingly, let it pass to a publisher as a work made for hire, the publisher will own 100 percent of the copyright. You will not be able to sell or control the sale of reprint rights to other magazines or websites. You will not be able to sell or control the sale of reprint rights to book publishers. You will not be able to sell or control the sale of your article to makers of a film, play, film script or TV show. You may not even be able to stop your publisher from printing the article on T-shirts. You will need the rights holder's permission to post it on your own website!

To prevent transfer of rights without your knowledge, copyright statutes are very explicit about how your work becomes a "work made for hire": First, it has to be specially ordered or commissioned for use as a contribution to a collective work—and most magazine assignments are just that. In addition, both you and the publisher—or his representative, the editor—have to agree *in writing* that it is a work made for hire; both of you have to sign the agreement. And third, since the statute uses the word *expressly,* whatever document you and the publisher sign must not beat around the bush; it must state clearly that the purpose of the paper being signed is to transform your article into a work made for hire. (This is just one reason to read carefully any written letter or contract your publisher asks you to sign before you cash your check for an assignment.)

Magazines have come up with a relatively new tactic for grabbing more of your copyright than you want to license. Their written agreement buys first rights—and adds a clause allowing them to reuse the work in perpetuity in various media. You may still technically own your article, but the publisher may continue to re-use it whenever it wishes for no additional fee. If you don't want that to happen, cross out the clause (and initial the change) before returning the signed contract. It's a new wrinkle on the ancient trick of sending checks with rubber-stamped notations on the backs that say something to the effect that they are buying *all rights*—a term left over from the pre-1976 copyright law. Folks who still use these stamps must believe that your signing the check endorses "work made for hire" status. Both the U.S. Register of Copyright we spoke with and an eminent UCLA law professor we double-checked with tell us it's not true.

If you receive a check marked "all rights" or "for hire," the most forthright thing to do is to return it and demand a new one without the rubber stamp.

With our steady markets, we've done that on a number of occasions. But when you're dealing with magazines, a check in hand is usually worth two in the mail. Another action you can take is to cross out the rubber-stamped nonsense, endorse the check, and deposit it. We've done this on a number of occasions too. We've also, when whim has overtaken us, simply changed "all rights" into "no rights." Nobody—certainly not the bank—seems to know or care about a check-editing job. Even under the pre-1976 copyright law—which gave less protection to writers—we collected from one magazine publisher who sold unowned reprint rights for our articles to an encyclopedia. Every one of this publisher's checks had contained the "all rights" rubber stamp; we'd crossed them all out. Since our case never went to trial, we can't tell you what the judge would have said. But we did enjoy depositing the offending publisher's non-rubber-stamped settlement check for several thousand dollars.

A third recourse you may have is to deposit your check without signing it. Many banks accept such an arrangement, although you may have to remind the teller if your bank has that policy. We're not sure whether this is better or worse than the second method, and lawyers we've asked won't venture an opinion.

So far there have been few significant tests of the 1976 copyright law's "work for hire" provisions as they apply to freelance writers, though there have been many involving musicians and record companies. The U.S. Copyright Office used to be in the forefront in protecting all authors' rights under the law, but that's changing. The ASJA and the Writer's Union are just two groups trying to put more spunk in their members when it comes to defending their copyrights.

Protecting your copyright has become extremely important since publishers discovered they could sell copies of past issues and individual articles over the Internet. They don't seem to understand yet that buying first rights doesn't mean buying Internet rights. But that may change after an $18 million settlement was awarded to us and our colleagues this year (2005) as the result of a combined class action suit against publishers who included the New York Times, Time Inc. and the Wall Street Journal and database companies including Dow Jones Interactive, Knight-Ridder, Lexis-Nexis, Proquest and West Group.

We were among just twenty-one individual writers named in the suit filed on behalf of colleagues whose stories appeared in these companies' online databases without our consent after all we'd sold was the right to publish once. The action's attorneys asked to name us because, unlike most freelancers, we had incontrovertible proofs that these companies had cheated us. We'd always stated, in letters of agreement or directly on the manuscript's first page, that all we were selling was first rights. And we had actually spent the money to register some of our purloined articles with the Copyright Office (mostly, we admit, to protect rights in our syndicated newspaper column). The settlement agreement rewarded each of our timely copyright filings with twenty-five times as much settlement money as our non-filed articles could collect. The aggregate could pay for a nice trip to exotic places. (*Settlement In Re Literary Works In Electronic Databases Copyright Litigation, MDL No. 1379* [S.D.N.Y.]; *combined from the following suits: Literary Works in Electronic Databases Copyrights Litigation,* MDL No. 1379 [S.D.N.Y.]; *The Authors Guild, Inc., et al., v. The Dialog Corp., et al.,* Dkt. No. 00-CV-6049 [S.D.N.Y.]; *Posner, et al., v. The Gale Group Inc.,* Dkt. No. 00-CV-7376 [S.D.N.Y.]; *Laney, et al., v. Dow Jones & Co. Inc., et al.,* Dkt. No. 00-CV-769 [S.D.N.Y.]; RRM (D. Del.); *and The Authors Guild, Inc., et al. v. The New York Times Company,* Dkt. No. 01-CV-6032 [S.D.N.Y.].)

Fair Use

This is the second area under copyright law that is of concern to magazine writers. Fair use does not deal with your copyright but with *somebody else's* copyright on words you want to use. The Copyright Law allows any writer (and anyone else) to publish parts of copyrighted works without having to get permission—within reason:

> You cannot, without permission, copy so much of somebody else's work that you diminish its commercial value.
>
> You should not, even with permission, copy somebody else's work without crediting its author.

Incorporating a paragraph without permission from another author's twelve-page article into your own ten-page article (if the author is credited) would probably be considered fair use. Copying anyone's five pages of words in print in your ten-page article (even with complete attribution) would probably *not* be considered fair use. But as you can see, what is fair is left pretty much to your discretion—and to the judge's if the original author wants to challenge you after the fact.

In general, if we're writing about a particular subject and a brief excerpt from something copyrighted by another author definitely figures into the subject, we feel safe using it. But we use it sparingly, with credit, and only if it's the best literary device we know of to make the point we have to make. We don't copy somebody else's words out of laziness and we never copy surreptitiously. If we want to copy more than a brief excerpt, we always request a letter granting permission.

It's important here to remember that copyright protects words—specific words and the sequence in which they're used. Ideas, concepts, philosophies, facts, observations, and similar cerebrations are not protected by copyright *so long as we don't use the author's words in restating them.* We always do credit another author whose intellectual observations or conclusions we borrow and put in our own words, but only out of fair play, not because of fair use constraints.

A Journalist's Code of Ethics

The Society of American Business Editors and Writers, the Society of Professional Journalists (composed mostly of newspaper writers), the Association of Business Writers, American Business Media, the American Association of Travel Writers and the Association of Healthcare Journalists all have written Codes of Ethics for their members. Over the years, the American Society of Journalists and Authors also evolved a Code of Ethics that it hoped would govern relations between magazine writers and editors. Though the ASJA no longer prints the Code in its Member Directory or keeps it on the ASJA website (probably because most publishers refuse to agree to many of its provisions), we think it still has great relevance in showing what professional writers feel would be fair treatment from magazine publishers. So, with permission, we've copied that Code of Ethics here in its entirety *(Ill. 15.1).*

Ill. 15.1. Code of Ethics and Fair Practices

PREAMBLE

Over the years, an unwritten code governing editor-writer relationship has arisen. The American Society of Journalists and Authors has compiled the major principles and practices of that code that are generally recognized as fair and equitable.

The ASJA has also established a Committee on Editor-Writer Relations to investigate and mediate disagreements brought before it, either by members or by editors. In its activity this committee shall rely on the following guidelines.

1. Truthfulness, Accuracy, Editing

The writer shall at all times perform professionally and to the best of his or her ability, assuming primary responsibility for truth and accuracy. No writer shall deliberately write into an article a dishonest, distorted or inaccurate statement.

Editors may correct or delete copy for purposes of style, grammar, conciseness or arrangement, but may not change the intent or sense without the writer's permission.

2. Sources

A writer shall be prepared to support all statements made in his or her manuscripts, if requested. It is understood, however, that the publisher shall respect any and all promises of confidentiality made by the writer in obtaining information.

3. Ideas

An idea shall be defined not as a subject alone but as a subject combined with an approach. A writer shall be considered to have a proprietary right to an idea suggested to an editor and to have priority in the development of it.

4. Acceptance of an Assignment

A request from an editor that the writer proceed with an idea, however worded and whether oral or written, shall be considered an assignment. (The word "assignment" here is understood to mean a definite order for an article.) It shall be the obligation of the writer to proceed as rapidly as possible toward the completion of an assignment, to meet a deadline mutually agreed upon, and not to agree to unreasonable deadlines.

5. Conflict of Interest

The writer shall reveal to the editor, before acceptance of any assignment, any actual or potential conflict of interest, including but not limited to any financial interest in any product, firm, or commercial venture relating to the subject of the article.

6. Report on Assignment

If in the course of research or during the writing of the article, the writer concludes that the assignment will not result in a satisfactory article, he or she shall be obliged to so inform the editor.

7. Withdrawal

Should a disagreement arise between the editor and writer as to the merit or handling of an assignment, the editor may remove the writer on payment of mutually satisfactory compensation for the effort already expended, or the writer may withdraw without compensation and, if the idea for the assignment originated with the writer, may take the idea elsewhere without penalty.

8. Agreements

The practice of written confirmation of all agreements between editors and writers is strongly recommended, and such confirmation may originate with the editor, the writer, or an agent. Such a memorandum of confirmation should list all aspects of the assignment including subject, approach, length, special instructions, payments, deadline, and kill fee (if any). Failing prompt contradictory response to such a memorandum, both parties are entitled to assume that the terms set forth therein are binding.

9. Rewriting

No writer's work shall be rewritten without his or her advance consent. If an editor requests a writer to rewrite a manuscript, the writer shall be obliged to do so but shall alternatively be entitled to withdraw the manuscript and offer it elsewhere.

10. Bylines

Lacking any stipulation to the contrary, a byline is the author's unquestioned right. All advertisements of the article should also carry the author's name. If an author's byline is omitted from a published article, no matter what the cause or reason, the publisher shall be liable to compensate the author financially for the omission.

11. Updating

If delay in publication necessitates extensive updating of an article, such updating shall he done by the author, to whom additional compensation shall be paid.

12. Reversion of Rights

A writer is not paid by money alone. Part of the writer's compensation is the intangible value of timely publication. Consequently, if after six months the publisher has nor scheduled an article for publication, or within twelve months has not published an article, the manuscript and all rights therein should revert to the author without penalty or cost to the author.

13. Payment for Assignments

An assignment presumes an obligation upon the publisher to pay for the writer's work upon satisfactory completion of the assignment, according to the agreed terms. Should a manuscript that has been accepted, orally or in writing, by a publisher or any representative or employee of the publisher, later be deemed unacceptable, the publisher shall nevertheless be obliged to pay the writer in full according to the agreed terms.

If an editor withdraws or terminates an assignment, due to no fault of the writer, after work has begun but prior to completion of the manuscript, the writer is entitled to compensation for work already put in; such compensation shall be negotiated between editor and author and shall be commensurate with the amount of work already completed. If a completed assignment is not acceptable, due to no fault of the writer, the writer is nevertheless entitled to payment; such payment, in common practice, has varied from half the agreed-upon price to the full amount of that price.

14. Time of Payments

The writer is entitled to payment for an accepted article within ten days of delivery. No article payment should ever be subject to publication.

15. Expenses

Unless otherwise stipulated by the editor at the time of an assignment, a writer shall assume that normal, out-of-pocket expenses will be reimbursed by the publisher. Any extraordinary expenses anticipated by the writer shall he discussed with the editor prior to incurring them.

16. Insurance

A magazine that gives a writer an assignment involving any extraordinary hazard shall insure the writer against death or disability during the course of travel or the hazard, or, failing that, shall honor the cost of such temporary insurance as an expense account item.

17. Loss of Personal Belongings

If, as a result of circumstances or events directly connected with a perilous assignment and due to no fault of the writer, a writer suffers loss of personal belongings or professional equipment or incurs bodily injury, the publisher shall compensate the writer in full.

18. Copyright, Additional Rights

It shall be understood, unless otherwise stipulated in writing, that sale of an article manuscript entitles the purchaser to first North American publication rights only, and that all other rights are retained by the author. Under no circumstances shall an independent writer be required to sign a so-called "all rights transferred" or "work made for hire" agreement as a condition of assignment, of payment, or of publication.

19. Reprints

All revenues from reprints shall revert to the author exclusively, and it is incumbent upon a publication to refer all requests for reprint to the author. The author has a right to charge for such reprints and must request that the original publication be credited.

20. Agents

According to the Society of Authors' Representatives, the accepted fee for an agent's services has long been ten percent of the writer's receipts, except for foreign rights representation. An agent may not represent editors or publishers. In the absence of any agreement to the contrary, a writer shall not he obliged to pay an agent a fee on work negotiated, accomplished and paid for without the assistance of the agent.

21. TV and Radio Promotion

The writer is entitled to be paid for personal participation in TV or radio programs promoting periodicals in which the writer's work appears.

22. Indemnity

No writer should be obliged to indemnify any magazine or book publisher against any claim, actions, or proceedings arising from an article or book.

23. Proofs

The editor shall submit edited proofs of the author's work to the author for approval, sufficiently in advance of publication that any errors may be brought to the editor's attention. If for any reason a publication is unable to so deliver or transmit proofs to the author, the author is entitled to review the proofs in the publication's office.

Taxes

It's a lost cause to point out that governments used to support their artists instead of the other way round. Or to add that freelancers enjoy neither the lobby of big business nor the protective paternalism the government sometimes gives to small business. Nonetheless, many tax law provisions have been interpreted to help us in our continuing struggle to keep groceries on the table.

Be forewarned that, since full-time freelancers are as rare as bald eagles, you may have to teach your local tax auditor how his provisions apply to us.

In the first place, every full-time professional freelance writer has to accept—and potentially make a doubting tax auditor understand—the principle that nearly everything we do is potentially income-producing. Two examples that often happen to us can make our point:

> You're at a party and somebody says, as they so often do, "Hey, you oughtta do a story about . . . ," and the story makes you money. Since you have to pay tax on the money, you are within your rights deducting the cost of giving and going to parties if you find they sometimes lead to article sales.

> You travel to North Dakota on what you've told the kids is a vacation. But on the trip, you take pictures of buffalo that end up eventually in a story for a travel magazine; and a character you meet talks about uranium mining and you sell his profile to a company-sponsored magazine. Since you sure are required to pay taxes on income from resulting articles and photos, you are within your rights to deduct most of your trip's cost (but not your wife's or your kids' costs if they can be separated from yours).

The principle you must keep in mind, as a full-time freelance magazine writer, is *intent*. If you can show that you consistently go to parties intending to find article material, that's all the law really asks for. The same for your trips. The fact that you pay taxes on the income resulting from the parties and trips, *before* being audited, helps to document your honest intent. And keeping records of story ideas developed at parties and on trips—or during other forms of research—backs up your serious intent.

Part-time magazine writers can take part-time advantage of expense deduction. The key philosophical point there again is intent. You have to have offered for sale the stories for which you ran up research and writing expenses. You do not have to have sold, only offered for sale. There are limitations on how many years in a row you can claim to have lost money on your writing profession—spent more than you took in—but rules on this change, so you'll have to research what's applicable when you need to know.

As important as your intent—which you can demonstrate only circumstantially—are your records. You have to prove *where* every penny of your expense money went, *why* it went, *when, how much,* and *to whom.* Last we checked, Uncle Sam accepted paper records and computer diary entries as sufficient proof for most individual expenses below seventy-five dollars. But check on current regulations for this changing guideline. In whatever accounting, diary or calendar software you choose to use, make a habit of jotting down notes about stories you're working on, people you're meeting, trips you're taking, money you're spending. You'd be surprised how fuzzy your memory gets about why you went to Hawaii, what you did there, what you wrote about it afterward, and who published (or refused to publish) it. If you keep the log on computer, be sure to cut a disk for each year's expenses and keep it with your tax records.

Writers, like all other professionals, have to hold on to their records until there's no chance the IRS wants to see them. If you buy a house or condominium apartment to use as your office and depreciate it over thirty years, you must keep all pertinent records for thirty years plus *at least* the three years during which the IRS can audit your tax returns after the thirtieth year. Julian Block, noted tax writer, recommends that you routinely hold on to *all* records for at least three years after you've used them in filing a tax return. That includes letters offering magazine articles for sale. How else will you substantiate that you were in the business of selling the articles for which you claimed expense deductions?

An accountant may be able to help you. But we've tried a number of different accountants, all highly recommended by lawyers and business friends, and so far we haven't found any who could cope with the peculiarities of the business of freelance writing. Julian warns, "The IRS is one place to get information, but be aware that you can't absolutely rely on them. Even in the IRS's own book, *Your Federal Income Tax,* mistakes are inevitable, and the IRS is not bound by them."

You may have to apply your research skills to answering your tax questions, as we've done most of the time we've been in doubt. We locate books and articles with tax (and other) advice for businesses, and tailor the tips to our own peculiar craft. Although it's worked for us so far, we're a long way from writing a book called *Tax Tips for Freelance Writers.* Maybe you can write that one.

Economics:
The 3 Rs of Writing

I T OUGHT TO BE OBVIOUS THAT IF YOU WANT TO BE A PRO-
fessional magazine writer instead of a dilettante, economics will have to
be on your mind as often as exposition, collecting money as often as quoting
experts. But most beginners seem to have grown up on ancient movies in which
well-groomed authors are wined and dined by fat cats or kept by sex-starved
debutantes. Alas, when the house lights go up, it isn't that way at all.

Being a professional writer means unflinchingly balancing income against
expenditures. Weighing the caché of a byline in low-paying *American Journalism Review* or *Christian Science Monitor* against the comfort of a well-paid but
unbylined piece in *UAW-GM People.* Recycling sixteen different excuses that keep
the lights turned on until the check comes from the corporation whose million-
dollar computer had its monthly "breakdown." Telling the kids their bikes will
arrive a little late this Christmas because, after paying bonuses to salaried staff,
the magazine can't pay until January for the story you turned in last September.
If that's the life you're prepared to lead, and if you promise us—here and now—
that you'll try to go at it with your eyes wide open, we'll share with you the real
facts of economic life for the professional writer. We've boiled them down to
three Rs: rates, recycling and reality.

Rates: The First R

The income you get from writing is the assets side of your writing ledger. Once
you've decided to write professionally, you must also decide to maximize that
income. There are several ways to accomplish that.

One, of course, is to move as quickly as possible from lower-paying magazine markets into higher-paying ones. But there are limitations to this route.
First, you can't count on moving into a higher-paying bracket until you've
honed your skills at the lower level. That takes time and perseverance. Second,
as you move progressively toward higher and higher paying magazines, the number of other writers trying to sell to the same markets increases geometrically.

That means your ideas will have to be more unique (an oxymoron almost everywhere but in freelance writing), and also more uniquely presented, than those of writers who got there first and know the ropes better than you.

Keep in mind that almost every magazine writer who is selling to high-paying markets today started at lower paying ones. It'll help you stay the course.

A second way to earn more money from your writing is to make sure that the magazines you write for steadily raise the rates they pay you. This shouldn't seem controversial in the least, but it is in many circles. Some magazine publishers believe that even writers who do dependable, consistently top-notch jobs never deserve raises.

But you do deserve raises. After you successfully complete several articles for one magazine, you're worth a great deal more money to that editor. First, she probably has to spend less of her time editing your articles now that you've learned the magazine's style. Second, if you've proven dependable by delivering articles in publishable shape when you promised to deliver them, she doesn't need to buy inventory as insurance against missed deadlines or copy that skirts the mark. Isn't that worth a higher rate of pay? We think so, and it's a question you ought to put to any editor who insists on paying you the same rate for your fourth story as your first.

As the cost of living goes up—and, along with it, the value of your time and the cost of your overhead—you may think you're entitled to cost-of-living raises. In magazine publishing, that's such a radical idea we'd be run out of the editor's office for hinting at it.

Don't expect to get *any* raise unless you ask for it. Then, don't ever make your request sound tentative or outrageous. If you seem unsure of yourself, you're inviting a turndown. In all our years of writing for a living, we've never lost an assignment from one of our regular markets for having asked for more money. We've often won the raise we said we deserved. And when we haven't, often as not we've left the editor feeling he ought to have a talk with the publisher about a bigger editorial budget.

In the area of money, the editor is rarely the ultimate culprit. Her freelance budget is passed down from the publisher's office. It is usually the tiniest slice of the cost of putting out the magazine, coming way behind printing and distribution costs, office overhead and salaries. Publishers, who often know little about either editing or writing, usually think they could churn out their magazines single-handed if they had the time. They also believe every writer is either independently wealthy or a moonlighter knocking out assignments as a break from a high-paying nine-to-five job. As good businessmen, they raise their advertising rates and cover prices to pay for printing hikes, paper hikes, postage hikes and the office staff's cost-of-living increases. But they don't hike their freelance budgets because there's little pressure from freelancers to do so. It's as simple as that!

Within the confines of editorial budgets, some editors make it a policy to pay a single set fee for all articles of a certain type. But others have flexible rates, paying more when they're forced to and less to writers who'll work for less. You won't know which policy prevails until you start asking for the additional money you deserve.

HOW DO YOU FIND OUT A MAGAZINE'S RATES?

In considering which markets to try to write for, it helps if you know in advance the approximate rate each of them generally pays. Of all the reference books and websites we discussed in Chapter 3, only *Writer's Market* includes entries about current fees. But its information is compiled from questionnaires returned by magazine editors, so each fee entry is as inflated or deflated as the individual editor wants it to be.

Both *Writer's Digest* and *The Writer* magazines include some information about pay rates in their articles and columns. In general, fees listed there are fairly accurate for first articles published in low-end markets—but they're often understated for articles by regular contributors or experienced pros, especially for work published in high-paying magazines.

Most of our most accurate information about fees comes from other professional writers. In our get-togethers, we often trade rate information along with other professional tips. The ASJA's newsletter devotes several pages each month to an exchange of the latest magazine rates, and a members-only page on its online database lets members search fees actually received by other members within the last five or more years from specific magazines. These are just two important benefits of belonging to that organization of professional writers. The National Writers Union (http://www.nwu.org) also provides its members with online information about pay rates. It, too, goes to bat for writers in so many other ways, it's an organization well worth joining.

Another benefit of belonging to writers' organizations such as the ASJA, the National Writers Union, the Society of American Travel Writers, the Society of American Business Editors and Writers, the Outdoor Writers Association of America, and similar national and local clusters of professional and near-professional writers, is reinforcement: a feeling that you're not in this alone. It helps to hear how others have tackled problems you're facing today; it's encouraging to learn that old pros were greenhorns once; it's bolstering to know that your peers are pushing for more money too. Names and addresses of writers' organizations can be found in *Literary Market Place, Writer's Market,* and online in links from sites like http://www.internet-resources.com/writers/.

In 1974, in a bold step forward, the ASJA developed and published a schedule of recommended minimum rates. Based partly on what freelancers had been paid back in the fifties, and realistically factoring in about half of the annual cost-of-living increase until then, it gave younger writers something to shoot for and older pros an established benchmark, and it alerted publishers that writers were becoming more assertive. Unfortunately, the New York State Attorney General's office decided that the schedule represented price fixing. (Don't we wish!) The ASJA agreed to stop recommending minimum rates and immediately stopped publishing its recommendations. Fortunately, the schedule appeared once in an uncopyrighted publication so we can personally, without the ASJA's blessing, update that guide's recommendations by factoring in the Bureau of Labor Statistics' assumption that what cost $1 on average in 1971 now costs $4.60. So here, presented just as a guideline, as a basis for negotiating with magazine editors, are the minimum rates we think publishers ought to pay and writers ought to expect to receive for professional work.

Recommended minimum rates based on type of magazine:

1. For trade publications, regional and Sunday magazines outside of the main metropolitan areas, and national magazines of special interest and/or low circulation (such as *American Grocer, Madison Magazine* and *Art and Antiques*): 92 cents per word

2. For national consumer magazines of under three million circulation (including publications like *Harper's, Ebony,* and *Men's Health*): $2.30 per word

3. For national consumer magazines of over three million circulation (such as *Modern Maturity, Woman's Day, Reader's Digest* and *Playboy*) and other prestigious magazines of special interest (such as *The New Yorker* and *Travel and Leisure*): $4.60 per word

Recommended minimum rates based on time (usually requested for articles that require much more research time than writing time):

Daily: $920 plus out-of-pocket expenses.

Weekly: $3,450 plus out-of-pocket expenses.

Note: per-word rates are based on assigned article length. Standard magazine articles run 2,500 to 3,000 words; shorts, 1,000 to 1,500 words. ASJA's policy has always been payment on acceptance.

The regularly updated book *National Writers Union Freelance Writers' Guide,* edited by James Waller, includes actual rates reported by the Union's freelance members and can be purchased even by nonmembers at their online store. It is an interesting, if often dispiriting, exercise to compare prevailing rates with the above suggested minimums. By and large, fees have stayed steady since the 1970s at about half of professional freelancers' hoped-for minimums.

COLLECTING MONEY

On days when we're particularly cynical and a young writer tells us, "I just sold an article to a magazine," we feel like answering, "Don't count on it until you can eat it." Having sold the article is all too often just the first step in a lengthy, complicated ritual.

A great many young writers don't understand why a magazine that's part of a multibillion-dollar conglomerate should deliberately delay payment of a paltry sum for months and months. We'll explain. If a magazine owes a writer a thousand dollars for an article, and holds the money for three months longer in a savings account, it earns about five dollars interest. That's hardly worthwhile. But multiply the saving by 100 magazine articles, 50 cartoons, 75 photographs, 6 tons of coated paper, 500 pounds of printer ink and 10 gross of pens . . . then you start to see some conglomerate-sized earnings from nothing but slowing the outgoing part of the cash flow.

We don't know how U.S. Steel reacts when General Motors put off paying it several million dollars for months at a time, but we know the frustration we feel when a multibillion-dollar publishing conglomerate owes us a thousand dollars that's long past due. Yet in all our years, we still haven't encountered any surefire magic for prying loose the money owed us any sooner than the company wants to let go of it, other than by constantly nagging the bookkeeper until she wants us off her back. If we nag the editor until *she* wants us off her back, we may lose the market. (It actually happened to us with a notoriously slow-paying magazine in the health field.)

We try to stay out of situations that threaten to involve delayed payments. When we first do business with a magazine, we inquire about the payment schedule. When we discuss fees, we emphasize that the rate is predicated on prompt payment. We always send an invoice with our manuscript. If we don't get our check on time—we consider roughly a month time enough—we remind the editor of the promise of quick pay. Sometimes we remind him more emphatically a week or two later. But we have to weigh the time spent trying to collect a fee with the time we could be writing.

Before deciding how vigorously to go about collecting what's due you, you must answer two important questions on the magazine's behalf. (1) Did your article, as submitted, really deliver writing that was up to the magazine's standards? (2) Did it deliver what the query promised or the assignment letter demanded? If it didn't do both, it's going to require a rewrite, either by you or by the editor. Barring a formal agreement to the contrary, it's fair for the editor to expect the rewrite to be completed before the check is made out. On the other hand, it's equally fair for the editor to permit *you* one chance at the rewrite and to get you started on it within a month.

In our experience, the need for a rewrite has more often been due to an editor's faulty communication of what he expects than to our out-and-out failure to deliver what we thought was expected. That's why we try to discuss any assignment with its editor before we begin writing. But even that's not foolproof.

There isn't much you can do, realistically, about collecting money from slow-paying magazines, though writers are sometimes driven to great lengths. An ASJA member once flew all the way from his home in England to Indianapolis to collect a long overdue check. But that was because he was fighting mad and knew he could cover his trip expenses in the New World with other, more easily collected sales.

One early December, when half a dozen major publishers owed *us* all together a fairly large sum of money—and some had owed it much too long—we designed a pre-Christmas card. We listed the money due, from whom, and for how long. We ended the card, "Merry Christmas?" and mailed a copy to each editor on the list, every president of their companies, and several publishing trade magazines. Before Christmas we'd collected every penny—and had also been blacklisted by two of the magazines, probably because we'd embarrassed them to their peers. Interestingly, those were the two who'd held on to our money the longest.

Murray Teigh Bloom, who headed the ASJA's writer-editor relations committee for many, many years, has helped scores of writers resolve conflicts with editors. Most have been over uncollected money—and most, Murray found, "involved $500 or under pieces. Also, most of these complaints are directed against magazines the writer has not dealt with before. He's gotten a lead, someone may have told him the magazine is buying, and he makes some kind of negotiation." A lot of these assignments are for publishers just starting out or just holding their own at the bottom of the market.

Murray drives home his point by comparing the writing life to a cocktail party. What would you do, he asks, if you found a good listener there, spewed all you knew about Alaska, and after ten minutes your new-found buddy said, "By the way, could you lend me three hundred bucks?" "You'd ease away, naturally," Murray says. "But the writer confronted with the $500 assignment from a new magazine doesn't leave. He does the piece even though he doesn't know anything about the person he's giving the $500 property to."

What *should* you do when you're faced with writing for a new publication? As a tenderfoot, it may happen to you often. Murray's recommendation: "The first time out with a new market, especially when there's $500 or less involved, it would be wise to ask for half the fee up front."

Fee advances (retainers) are common in advertising, public relations, music, art, law and other fields. But it's rare for a magazine to give a rookie writer part of the fee when an assignment is made. This logical—and needed—extension of the kill fee (discussed in Chapter 10) is just a dream for most professional magazine writers. When you're just getting started, it's unlikely that you can negotiate a kill fee, let alone money up front. But *do* begin to ask for both kinds of payment just as swiftly as you can.

Early in our careers, we began submitting an invoice for the agreed-upon fee (plus our expenses, if any) with every assigned manuscript we mailed. We're in business and submitting invoices is a businesslike way of showing that there's money due. Editors tell us they appreciate receiving invoices because it saves their having to make out vouchers to start the payment process, and we're overjoyed at the thought that it may speed up our checks.

Sometimes, especially if we're working with a trade magazine, our invoice borrows a merchandising concept by offering a small discount for prompt payment and by demanding interest for payment made after thirty days:

> 2 percent discount ten days;
> net thirty days;
> a charge of 1 ½ percent per month interest if paid after thirty days.

Only twice have editors complained about the discount and interest provisions, and neither of them was a problem payer anyway. Seldom are publishers well enough organized to get payments through within ten days, but if they do, they're welcome to the 2 percent. After thirty days expire, if we're the least bit anxious about payment, we photocopy our copy of the invoice, type in the interest that's accumulated, and mail it to the slow payer. It's one of the finest collection tools we've ever found, though there's rarely payment of interest due.

If all else fails, you can sue. Sometimes just the threat of suit is sufficient. Most cities now have small-claims courts, which writers have successfully used to collect money owed them. But as a rule, an action must be taken in the city where the magazine is published, so if they're in New York, the local Peoria small-claims court probably can't help you.

Unless you have a letter of assignment it's tough, although never impossible, to collect even in small-claims court. So get each assignment in writing. If the editor gives it to you over the phone, ask him to confirm it by follow-up letter. If he doesn't, *you* should send the letter. Spell out what you understand the assignment to be along with payment, deadline, kill fee, and anything else you've agreed on. End by writing, "Unless I hear otherwise, I'll understand that these are the terms of the assignment."

A number of magazines make collection nearly impossible by promising to pay you when the article's published. It sounds like a fair arrangement for a publisher with limited resources, but think about it from the writer's viewpoint. You agree to offer a publisher your research and writing talents. In addition, if you promise first serial rights, you agree not to offer your article to any other magazine until this one has published it. In return, the publisher agrees to *nothing* except that, if he should ever run the article, he will pay you for it. He may run it immediately or it may simply sit in the file indefinitely—unprinted, unpaid-for, almost untouchable by you unless you've planned ahead.

We don't deal with publishers who pay on publication ("on pub") for first rights. (We don't even offer them pay-on-pub *second* or *reprint* rights, since we feel that publishing a magazine at the writer's expense is unconscionable.) But if you feel you must, at the very least get an understanding in writing of the most distant acceptable publication date. If your work hasn't appeared in print by then, and you haven't been paid, you will be free to offer it elsewhere.

"On spec" is another term loosely bandied about by editors. In simple terms, it means that you may never be able to collect what's due you for your work. "Spec" is short for "speculation." Technically, every assignment that doesn't include a kill fee provision is on spec. The editor may like your idea, believe you can write it up suitably, and expect to pay you when the job is done; if it turns out you can't write it up suitably, even after a rewrite, only a rare editor pays for the useless sheaf of papers you've turned in.

Why, then, do some editors answer a query letter with a letter agreeing to assign your suggested article on spec? To us, it signals their doubt that the work will ever be publishable in their pages. Judging by young writers who've shared their heartbreaks with us after writing on spec, we must conclude that they're saying, "I doubt that your article idea or your article-writing abilities will make it in my market but if you want to submit anyway, I'll read it." On spec *always* means they feel free to return it without comment and without any payment.

Beginning writers often do have to write articles on speculative go-aheads. It's hard to expect financially strapped editors to take chances on unproven authors. On the other hand, while you're proving yourself, realistically assess whether an on-spec assignment's possible return is worth the probable investment.

EXPENSES

Traditionally, the fee agreed on for an article is payment for time spent *creating the article* despite the fiction that editors buy a commodity—*x* words. The magazine ought to pay extra for out-of-pocket expenses you incur doing research. Editors often feel it's a courtesy they should not extend to beginners, but they're more amenable to paying expenses than to promising kill fees.

Allowable expenses can include long-distance phone calls, travel to interviews, books, research, download charges and similar necessities. For big assignments, travel to distant places and hotel expenses are often covered. It's important for you discuss in advance the extent to which a magazine is willing to pay your expenses. Some have monetary limits; others limit the kinds of items they'll reimburse.

When you ask an editor to cover expenses, you're not asking the magazine for a handout. So don't ever hesitate to raise the matter when talking money at the time you get an assignment. Like all the other terms, get it spelled out in writing in advance.

Once a magazine agrees to pay for expenses, you are always expected to submit an itemized accounting with the manuscript (or shortly thereafter). Most magazines expect receipts that verify major expenses. (Send copies so your originals don't get lost on somebody's desk.)

Recycling: The Second R

This is the liability side of the writing ledger. If we could just sit at our computers all day and turn out page after page of magazine prose, our standards of living would rise astronomically. However, we must do a lot of research to find salable ideas, sell them, and then examine them more fully. Beginning writers, especially, often sell article proposals for what seems like a fair price—and then discover that doing them justice takes overwhelming research time.

When we weigh the pros and cons of a particular idea, we try to estimate how much research is demanded. If it seems a lot compared to the payment we can expect from its likely markets, we scratch the idea if we can't cut down on our research time. (We suggested some ways in Chapter 11.) But we often choose another option. We find ways to expand the expensive research into several article sales.

SELLING REPRINTS

In Chapter 15, we showed how your copyright can be divided into many salable pieces. Each sale of a piece of that copyright can bring in additional money. Peddling first rights to a tangible piece of property to more than one buyer is illegal, of course. But your writing is intellectual property, and you're not selling the property, but the *right* for a magazine to copy your creation. It's perfectly legal for you to sell other rights.

Magazines are not the only markets for reprints and second rights sales. Newspapers sometimes buy them, and educational book publishers make wide use of them for reading supplements and anthologies. Magazines and newspapers published outside the United States are good reprint markets for many pros. It's normally tough for United States-based writers to sell to most European, African, South African and Asian publishers because of prohibitive postage costs (though some foreign publishers accept e-mail queries). But a number of agencies specialize in marketing foreign rights to articles, and you'll find them listed in *Writer's Market* and *Literary Market Place*. Typically the agency takes up to 50 percent of whatever sales it generates, but since the transaction invests very little of your money and time, the split is usually worthwhile.

SELLING SPIN-OFFS

Unlike many of our colleagues, we place the selling of *reprint rights* at the end of our recycling spectrum. We find it more enjoyable, and usually more lucrative, to sell spin-offs.

Most novice writers, we've found, think of their files full of research in terms too narrow to derive maximum income. Once they've submitted an article, they deep-six their files. Professionals, on the other hand, know that reusing the research is the most obvious, most direct, and often the least time-consuming way to make another sale. They peddle *spin-offs*.

The spin-off relies on your file, crammed full of research notes from a completed story, to help create another article with a slightly different focus or slant pegged to a magazine that doesn't compete with the first one. You probably don't have to do much, if any, new research for the second story. You do have to sell it and then write it. Both take time, but on stories for which you've already done most of the research, it's time well spent.

How different do spin-off stories have to be? Norman Lobsenz, long a high-paid freelancer for top women's magazines, told us, "For *Woman's Day*, I did an article called, 'What Makes a Marriage Happy?' It came about when we were talking about the fact that people who are unhappy can tell you exactly why yet people who are happy rarely can. By analyzing what *unhappy* people complain of, that article looked into what presumably goes into a happy marriage. Then, for *Modern Bride*, I turned the idea around, asking, 'How Do You Know That Your Marriage Will Be Happy?' and wrote about what the experts said made a marriage happy, not unhappy."

But Norman managed to sell slight shifts in emphasis all the time. "A piece I might do for *Woman's Day* or *McCall's* could often be reslanted for a bridal magazine or for *Modern Maturity*. All I'd be doing was changing the age angle on it."

You may find that some parts of your first article fit neatly into the second article, as is. Can you copy them whole? Legally, the answer is almost always yes; after all, you have the same right to *fair use* of your material as any other writer. (See Chapter 15.) But from a practical perspective, some editors feel cheated if the exact anecdote in an article you sold them appears around the same time in an article you've sold to another magazine. The prudent approach, therefore, is to ask editor number one's blessing and to alert editor number two to the prior sale. Norman Lobsenz echoes, "It's not only vital to be scrupulously ethical, it's sensible because you don't want to antagonize a major market by incorrectly using something in a minor market." We've adhered to that policy, haven't been turned down, and find that editors appreciate our openness.

SELLING SIDETRACKS

Unlike some of our friends, we never hire college students to do our research. For one thing, we believe people don't catch all of a story's fine points unless they research it as well as write it. For another, while doing research for one story, we usually find leads to at least two new story angles and a substantial part of the research we did for the first article fits nicely into the subject areas of stories number two and three. That saves our having to chalk up much research time for the two sidetrack articles. Less time outlay means more profit. Without such down-to-earth considerations, writers can't make it as freelancers.

Beginning writers, we've found, hesitate to use any of the research referred to in story number one when preparing stories two and three. They believe that in buying the first article, the publisher has bought your research time as well as its fruits. This just isn't true. Even if you sold "all rights," all you've sold is the right to publish the *words* in your article. The ideas you picked up remain your intellectual property, whether in your head or your file of notes. And *information* can be used by anyone. It's in the public domain. Information cannot be copyrighted, only words.

SELLING EXPERTISE

Our final way of recycling research is a Chinese-restaurant approach. Writers tend to concentrate on one or several areas of interest. In those areas, their continual research eventually makes them experts to some degree. Within the confines of their expertise, each new story sold can draw two pages of notes from column A, three pages of concepts from column B and, to complete the article, a column C of new research that updates the subject.

Some freelancers make their marks primarily in one or two areas of specialized interest—Julian Block in taxes, Normal Lobsenz in marriage life-styles, Suzanne Loebl in medicine, Hal Higdon in sports, Lee Edson in science, Mark Sosin in the outdoors. Other freelancers think of themselves as generalists. We used to be generalists until we started writing exclusively about technology. Writing about whatever suited our shifting fancies led to our being considered medical specialists at *McCall's*, education specialists at *Seventeen*, popular psychology specialists at *Playgirl*, obesity specialists at *Weight Watchers*, home improvement specialists at *Popular Science*, and life-style specialists at *Physician's Management*—although we've also written about the law, science, movie stars, government and how to catch fish. We never called ourselves specialists in querying any of these magazines. They simply began to count on our expertise in the subjects we pitched to them. If you sell and deliver a well-researched article on any particular subject, you almost immediately acquire a reputation with that magazine—and its competitors—as an expert in that field. There is one subject that, frankly, we're tired of writing about. But because we're considered experts, assignments keep coming in—and the income gives us freedom to investigate new subjects.

The Big R: Reality

Magazine writing can be as glittery and glamorous as any profession this side of Hollywood. It's a sure ego boost to be seen on television sagely discussing the fine points of your latest article. And the head swells measurably every time a trade association bestows its annual gold-plated journalism award on you for promoting its cause. But glitter sticks to the teeth when you try to ingest it, and glamour doesn't cook up well in a stew pot. Landlords don't take bylines in lieu of rent. Children have trouble enjoying Mommy on TV with holes in their sneakers. Next year, all those plastic-encapsulated awards will be just more knickknacks to dust.

At the beginning of this book we quoted Alex Haley as having said, "It is at least as difficult to become a writer as a surgeon." By now you're probably convinced of that. But there's a subtler aspect to Alex's comparison. As magazine writers, we take the lives of our readers into our hands every time we touch our computer keys. We advise them about life and love, explain death and health, counsel on diets and exercise, help raise their children, offer comfort to their parents. We teach them to connect homemade lighting fixtures onto potentially deadly wires without harming themselves or the fixtures. We send them into their gardens, onto their roofs, into strange and distant lands. If we've learned our craft, remembered our ethics, adhered to our sense of responsibility, readers come away happier, healthier, wealthier and wiser. But if we slip up, we cause mayhem—not only to readers but to magazines that depend on our articles to sell their advertising pages.

Yet publishers who wouldn't think of striking bargains with the white-frocked surgeons about to operate on them, daily invent schemes for bargaining down the demands of writers. We're not sure which is more unconscionable, publishers who train their editors to cry poverty or writers who are content to do the same.

The reality of writing as a profession is that you need money to stay alive. You need enough income so you and your kids can lead a middle-class existence like the readers you write for. You need money to cover your own medical plans and your own Social Security (forget pensions!). You need cash in the bank to tide you over the months when every expert you need to talk to is out of town and every editor you know got up on the wrong side of the bed. You need assets to plunge recklessly into the kind of far-fetched research that Betty Friedan did on her own time and money to produce not just a magazine story for *Esquire* but the book that grew out of it, *The Feminine Mystique*—a book which is still improving women's lives in much of the world.

Some people might say we're ending on a soapbox, advocating a writers' revolution. Others might say we're raising consciousness. The way we see it, we're just letting you know that there's more to being a pro than learning your craft. You also have to learn your worth, and then communicate that to the editors with whom you do business.

ILLUSTRATION CREDITS

1.1. Copyright © Sierra.
2.2. *Writer's Market.* Copyright © 2004 F&W Publications Inc.
2.3. *Standard Rates and Data, Consumer Magazine Advertising Source.* Copyright © 2004 SRDS Media Solutions.
2.4. *Gale Directory of Publications and Broadcast Media,* Edition 136. Copyright © 2002 Thomson Gale.
2.5. *International Directory of Little Magazines and Small Presses,* 38th Annual Edition. Copyright © 2003 Dustbooks.
5.1. *Family Handyman,* July-August 1977. Copyright © 1977 P/K Associates, Inc.
5.2. *Seventeen,* Sept. 1976. Copyright © 1976 Judi R. Kesselman.
5.3. *Playboy* Interview with Dr. Edward Teller, August 1979. Copyright © 1979, *Playboy.*
5.4. *Weight Watchers,* August 1974. Copyright © 1974 Judi R. Kesselman.
5.5. *Chicago Tribune Magazine,* April 16, 1972. Copyright © 1972 Franklynn Peterson.
5.6. *Popular Science;* July 1978. Copyright © 1978 P/K Associates, Inc.
5.7. *Family Health,* January 1977. Copyright © 1977 Judi R. Kesselman and Franklynn Peterson.
5.8. *Popular Science,* April 1979. Copyright © 1979 P/K Associates, Inc.
5.9. *Family Health,* August 1976. Copyright © 1978 Judi R. Kesselman.
5.10. *Cincinnati Enquirer Magazine,* December 9, 1973. Copyright © 1973 Franklynn Peterson.
5.11. *Milwaukee Sentinel,* January 11, 1979. Copyright © 1979 The Sentinel Corporation.
5.12. *McCall's,* July, 1953. Copyright © 1953 Terry Morris.
5.13. *The New York Times,* November 11, 1973. Copyright © 1973 Judi R. Kesselman.
5.14. *Success Unlimited,* February 1980. Copyright © 1980 Paul Martin.
5.15. *Science & Mechanics,* March 1971. Copyright ©1971 Franklynn Peterson.
5.16. *Columbus Dispatch Sunday Magazine.* October 7, 1973. Copyright © 1973 Franklynn Peterson.

5.17. *Practical Psychology for Physicians,* September 1976. Copyright © 1976 Judi R. Kesselman and Franklynn Peterson.

5.18. *Swank,* October 1976. Copyright©1976 Franklynn Peterson and Judi R. Kesselman.

6.1. "Female Alcoholics," *New Dawn,* October 1976. Copyright © 1976 Judi R. Kesselman.

6.2. "How to Live with STRESS and Thrive," *Woman's Day,* May 22, 1979. Copyright © 1979 Flora Davis.

6.3. "Doctors Call Her the Miracle Girl," *Family Circle,* June 26, 1979. Copyright © 1979 Lee Edson.

6.4. "Summer Water Safety—Amazing New Facts That Can Save Your Life," *Family Circle,* June 26, 1979. Copyright © 1979 Jack Galub.

6.5. "Love and Sex: The 10 Most Often Asked Questions," *Ladies Home Journal,* July 1979. Copyright © 1979 Bonnie Rernsberg.

6.6. "How Children Feel About Their Bodies," *Redbook,* June 1979. Copyright © 1979 The Redbook Publishing Company.

6.7. "For Fun and Profit (Lots) Buy That Bonanza V8 Convertible or a '55 Goldmine Coupe," *Science Digest,* March 1979. Copyright © 1979 Alan D. Haas.

6.8. "What Is a . . . Doctor of Osteopathy?" *Science Digest,* March 1979. Copyright © 1979 Marvin Grosswirth.

6.9. "Are Test-Tube Babies the Answer for the Childless?" *Woman's Day,* May 22, 1979. Copyright ©1979 David Zimmerman.

6.10. "Traveling Alone," *Woman's Day,* August 7, 1979. Copyright © 1979 Michael Frome.

7.1. *Family Health,* January 1977. Copyright © 1977. Judi R. Kesselman and Franklynn Peterson.

7.2. *Oklahoma City Oklahoman Orbit Magazine,* September 21, 1975. Copyright © 1975 Franklynn Peterson.

9.5. Copyright © 1974 Barbara Gibbons.

12.1. *Chicago Tribune Magazine,* September 24, 1972. Copyright © 1972 Franklynn Peterson.

12.2. *The Memphis Commercial Appeal Mid-South Magazine,* July 28, 1974. Copyright © 1974 Franklynn Peterson.

13.1. *Practical Psychology for Physicians,* August 1976. Copyright © 1976 Judi R. Kesselman and Franklynn Peterson.

13.2. *Science Digest,* April 1978. Copyright © 1978 P/K Associates, Inc.

13.3. *Playgirl,* October 1975. Copyright © 1975 Judi R. Kesselman.

INDEX

PRINCIPLES & PRACTICES OF
LASER
TECHNOLOGY

PRINCIPLES & PRACTICES OF
LASER
TECHNOLOGY

BY HRAND M. MUNCHERYAN
B. SC., E. E., M. SC.

TAB BOOKS Inc.
BLUE RIDGE SUMMIT, PA. 17214

FIRST EDITION

FIRST PRINTING

Copyright © 1983 by TAB BOOKS Inc.

Printed in the United States of America

Library of Congress Cataloging in Publication Data

Muncheryan, Hrand M.
    Principles and practice of laser technology.

    Includes index.
    1. Lasers. I. Title.
TA1675.M863   1983   621.36′6   82-19289
ISBN 0-8306-0129-5
ISBN 0-8306-1529-6 (pbk.)

Contents

Introduction

In writing *Principles and Practice of Laser Technology,* I have attempted to supply a unified account of the present-day knowledge of lasers and their applications in varied professional and industrial fields. Such fields include laser physics, laser-processing industry, medical and dental instrumentations by lasers, military weapon and security tactics, aerial and fiberoptic communications, metrology, and related disciplines. As in other fields of science, laser technology has advanced to a stage where empirical methods of learning the basic concepts no longer are acceptable to the industry or biomedical profession now actively engaged in the constructive implementation of laser beams. The physical phenomena that pertain to geometrical optics, radiation, and interferometry have become fundamental to the comprehensive learning of this efflorescent science of radiation.

This book is devoted to the teaching of the principles and practices of laser technology at a first- or second-year undergraduate level curriculum and, where applicable, at senior high-school level where the student is familiar with basic algebra and trigonometry. For those engineers and scientists who are advanced in laser technology, this book will serve to review their knowledge by answering the questions and solving the problems at the end of each chapter, and further, it will provide them with new directions for the technical advancement of their companies. The text is written in language that is easily understandable by the self-learning individual who wants to advance his knowledge of lasers by digging into the depths of this science and finding the answers to his dormant questions from concepts treated in the gradually more difficult chapters which are evolved from the fundamental principles presented in the earlier chapters.

The various subjects discussed in this book are carefully developed to offer a strong and basic optical-background education coupled with radiation concepts to help you acquire an exact and comprehensive knowledge of laser generation, system development, operation, and applications in the varied branches of industry, military, and the biomedical profession. Some of the more difficult but practical concepts delineated by the equations are worked out in the pertinent chapters to facilitate the understanding and learning of the technology by the novice as well as the professional. The present curriculum in this book is intended to offer the prospective laser worker the theoretical background coupled with practical work. This is achieved by structuring and conditioning your knowledge to adapt yourself to the industry's needs. The book is particularly suitable for use as instructional reference material by the professional who desires to broaden his knowledge in laser technology, and thereby to guide him in the designing and developing of laser equipment of his own innovation.

The present course of instruction contained in this book will also be suitable to train high-grade technicians preparatory to becoming associate engineers in laser developmental work. The material is organized and presented in a manner whereby you are progressively introduced to increasingly more complex systems. Furthermore, to implement these instructions in an effective and practical fashion, I have refrained from the use of highly mathematical expressions in the treatment of the various subjects in this book. However, of necessity, several expressions of higher mathematics are used in a simplified manner to present the theoretical essentials to the reader in order to consolidate his practical knowledge based on applicable precepts.

While I have emphasized the design and development of laser equipment and its manipulations, particular endeavor has been made to present the associated theoretical considerations necessary for intelligent applications of the procedures discussed. There is sufficient essential information for the reader to make a sagacious choice of alternative systems or methods, when he is formally engaged in the laser field.

With the beginning of a new era for the concerted use of various types of laser beams in medical and dental instrumentations, I have selected particular subjects and discussed them in an effort to stimulate the thinking of the reader. There is a great need for the design and development of medical and dental instrumentation systems and accessories. These will, in course of time, become just as commonplace as metal processing laser systems which are now playing important roles in the manufacturing, construction, and the military, and even in home security devices. From that standpoint, I have given some exemplary devices and medical cases for which pertinent laser equipment is direly needed at the present time.

The appendices contain a table of chemical elements and their characteristics, electrical units and their equivalents, international units of measurement, and the names and addresses of laser and laser-oriented companies, listing the important products they manufacture. Another appendix is devoted to auxiliary references categorized for finding the specialized subject matter from which the reader may want to acquire additional information.

I wish to acknowledge my indebtedness to those many institutions and manufacturers who have furnished some of the illustrations of their equipment, together with technical data on their more recent research and developments. I am particularly appreciative of the photographs of the Laser Fence, specifically prepared for inclusion in this book, by the United States Air Force Public Affairs Office, Hanscom AFB, Massachusetts.

Chapter 1
Introduction to Lasers

Technically, a laser is a device for producing electromagnetic radiation, the same as light, but of considerably higher radiant energy. The word "laser" is an acronym derived from "light amplification by stimulated emission of radiation," and is generally used in referring either to the radiation or the device that produces it. Laser radiation can be produced in the spectral ranges from ultraviolet, through visible, to infrared radiation. The laser generator is an optionally active medium confined in an optical cavity located between two reflecting surfaces. The generated light oscillates in this cavity and becomes amplified by the cumulative increase of the light by reflection between the reflectors. The amplified light possesses the characteristics of a monochromatic radiation, high radiant intensity, and directionality; it is projected through air or space in a pencil beam. The lasing (active) medium may be a gas, a solid, or a liquid.

The wavelengths of lasers differ from those of light waves in that for each type of laser radiation there is, practically speaking, only one wavelength and one frequency range, neglecting harmonic wavelengths, and frequency-multiplied radiations produced artificially. This characteristic makes the radiation coherent and monochromatic, with all emission wave amplitudes in phase with each other. Thus, such a radiation is easily adaptable to convergence to a sharp focus without a fuzzy peripheral area about the focus, as usually produced by ordinary light. Since it is the focus of the laser radiation that is generally used in industry and medical work, this characteristic of sharpness of focus of the beam makes it ideal for cutting, drilling, and welding materials.

GENERATION OF LASER RADIATION

There are several methods of producing laser radiation. One way is to pass a heavy current through the active medium. Another method is to illuminate the active medium using a high-intensity light source. A third way is the use of microwave radiation to stimulate the active medium to radiation; the last method is not used as frequently as the other two methods. One simple method is to fill an electric discharge tube with a mixture of helium and neon, and to apply a high voltage across the tube to ionize the gas within the tube, whereupon the familiar red fluorescent light appears from the tube, shown in Fig. 1-1. This light, as seen decorating store fronts, is not a laser light and its intensity is not comparative to the high-energy laser radiation. In order to obtain a laser radiation from such a discharge tube, the ends of the tube must be provided with mirrors facing each other in parallel relation. The electrodes of such a tube are either a ring type or are disposed in the wall of the tube adjacent the ends, so that while the electric discharge occurs between the electrodes the column of light between the mirrors is free to oscillate (reflect) back and forth between the mirrors to become amplified.

During the oscillation of the light, from one mirror to the other, the *light quanta*, known as *photons*, collide with the electrons of the gaseous atoms excited due to the energy of the applied voltage on the tube. The collision of electrons with the photons transfer *photonic energy* to the electrons causing them to radiate with the same frequency and wavelength of the photon in the encounter. This action increases the number of photons in the discharge tube by the cumulative actions of the other photons oscillating between the mirrors, thus amplifying the intensity of the oscillating light. Consequently, the radiation from the discharge tube is the familiar laser radiation.

If the mirrors are 100 percent reflective, the photonic energy in the discharge tube may increase to such an extent as to cause the eventual destruction of the discharge tube by the formation of an intense heat within the tube. To avoid this condition, as well as permitting the radiation (laser) within the tube to be projected to the exterior of the tube, one of the mirrors is made about 40 to 50 percent transmissive and the other is made nearly 100 percent reflective. The partially transmissive mirror is known as the output

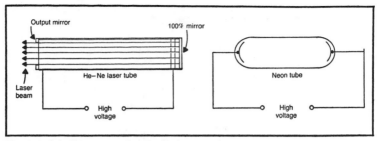

Fig. 1-1. A helium-neon electric discharge tube.

mirror, and the accumulated photon radiation within the tube projects through this output mirror. Since the (resonant) cavity in which the laser radiation is produced is of capillary type (small diameter), the projected radiation is a pencil beam of a diameter equal to the optical aperture of the tube. This aperture is generally equal to the diameter of the capillary, using a few millimeters in diameter. Thus, from a helium-neon (He-Ne) laser tube, one obtains an intense red light beam of extreme directionality.

The second method is to illuminate the active medium with a high-intensity flashlamp or mercury arc lamp. In this case, the active medium is a highly transparent, cylindrical rod made of sapphire, glass, or yttrium-aluminum-garnet (YAG) doped with an ionizable material. For example, when sapphire is doped with a small percentage of chromium oxide it becomes a ruby laser rod; glass or YAG when doped with neodymium becomes a neodymium-YAG (Nd-YAG) laser, rod, or neodymium-glass laser (Nd-glass). These laser rods are known as solid-state lasing elements and are optically pumped (energized) by means of a flashlamp.

The rod receives its excitation energy from the illuminating photons, which couple with the electrons of the excited dopant atoms in the lasing rod. The dopant content of the laser rod varies from 0.5 percent to about 3 percent. The flashlamp is usually made of a quartz tube filled with xenon gas and has nonreactive metal electrodes at each end impressed with a high-voltage direct current, as illustrated in Fig. 1-2. This type of laser radiation is usually in the pulsing mode due to the pulsing radiation given off from the flashlamp. The laser is produced only when a pulsed radiation is incident on the rod from the flashlamp. When a tungsten-arc-type lamp is used for optically pumping the laser rod, the radiation could be produced continuously. The ends of the laser rods are highly polished and coated with a reflecting material, such as silver, gold,

3

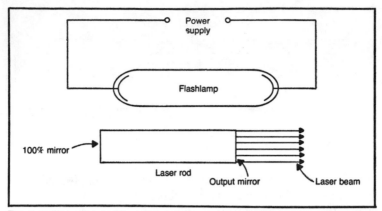

Fig. 1-2. The scheme of a solid-state laser rod radiation.

rhodium, or magnesium fluoride (MgF_2). Because the end surfaces are made precisely parallel to each other, the emission of pumped photons is amplified by the oscillation of the photons between the reflecting surfaces (mirrors). One end of the rod is made semitransparent, controlled by the thickness of the coating and the other end is made 100 percent reflective by the increased amount of coating on that end.

A third type of laser device is a semiconductor diode, which is built with a pn junction at which the laser radiation is produced when a forward current is passed across the junction. There are several types of semiconductor laser diodes, the most common of which is the gallium arsenide (GaAs) diode. This diode emits at wavelengths between 8,200 and 9,050 angstroms. The active junction is formed by two surfaces, a p-type active surface and an n-type active surface, as shown in Fig. 1-3. The current flow across the diode junction is from the n-type active surface to the p-type active surface layer. The space between the two active layers forms a discharge cavity. When a forward current of 100 milliamperes or more is applied across the junction, electrons are discharged in the cavity and radiate in the infrared spectrum. The radiation fans out from the junction to the exterior and must be collimated for any given application. Recently, one manufacturer produced a laser diode whose emitted radiation is collimated by means of built-in optics.

The liquid-type laser consists of a organic dye dissolved in an alcoholic solvent in a definite molar concentration. A molar solution of a dye contains one molecular weight of the dye in 1 liter of the (alcoholic) solution. The emission from this solution occurs when the solution is placed in a small-diameter glass tube and illuminated by an intense light, which may be either continuous or pulsing. While the radiation from a dye solution is not as intense as that emitted by any of the solid-state laser rods, because the radiation can be easily tuned to emit different wavelengths it has many applications in industry and in academic circles.

OPTICAL ELEMENTS USED IN LASER SYSTEMS

The optical elements that are used in controlling the profile of the projected laser beams consist of optical lenses, prisms, mirrors, etalons, and beam splitters made of these or variations of these elements. The commonest lenses are biconvex, planoconvex, biconcave, and planoconcave. Other lenses are meniscus type, cylindrical type, and spherical type in general. The mirrors are front surface coated or back-surface coated and are either flat, spherical, or parabolic, although other shapes are also possible and are used in laser work. The prisms used in laser work vary in their angular shapes from a right-angle prism to very thin apex prisms, or etalons which reduce the output linewidth of the radiation. These optical elements will be fully discussed under pertinent headings in various sections or chapters, as their applications are discussed.

Figures 1-4 through 1-9 illustrate the various configurations of the optical elements used in laser work. The convex lenses are used to converge a collimated (parallel) laser beam and concave lenses to

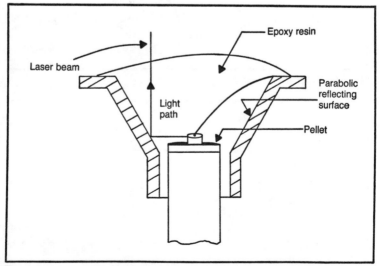

Fig. 1-3. A schematic drawing of a semiconductor laser diode.

5

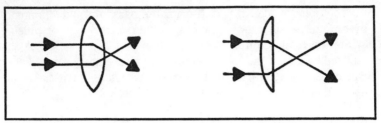

Fig. 1-4. Convex lenses.

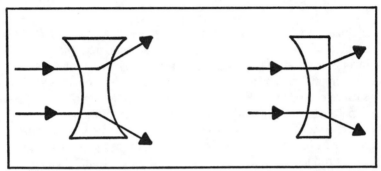

Fig. 1-5. Concave lenses.

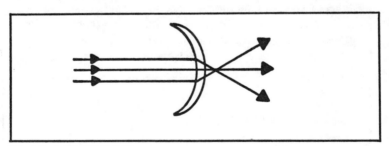

Fig. 1-6. A meniscus lens.

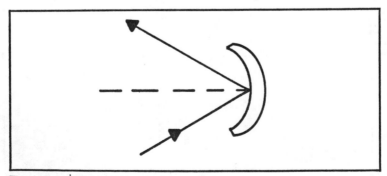

Fig. 1-7. A spherical mirror.

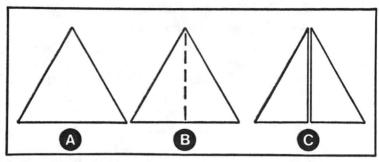

Fig. 1-8. Various types of prisms.

diverge a collimated beam incident normal to the optical axis. The meniscus lens, when positioned with its convex surface against the laser beam, minimizes the spherical aberration in an optical projection system. Spherical concave mirrors come in various focal lengths and are used, in a resonant cavity, to collimate or direct the laser beam to the output mirror; they are coated on their first surfaces.

Prisms are also produced in various shapes and are generally used to disperse a laser beam that contains more than one wavelength (harmonics). The Brewster-angle prism, Fig. 1-8A is chosen for use in a resonant cavity for tuning a dye laser or an ion laser, which contains several harmonics in its bandwidth. Tuning is achieved by rotating the prism on an axis, with the laser beam incident on one of the equalateral surfaces. When a Brewster-angle prism is slit, as shown by dotted line in Fig. 1-8B, two Littrow prisms are formed, Fig. 1-8C, which are used for dispersing multiline (multiple wavelength) laser beams. An etalon, shown in Fig. 1-9, is a form of prism, as illustrated, that is placed in an optical cavity, with the laser beam passing through it, to reduce the spectral bandwidth of a dye laser beam.

Fig. 1-9. Configuration of an etalon.

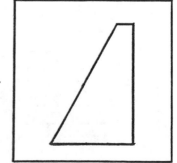

GEOMETRY OF LASER-BEAM PROJECTIONS

Laser-Beam Reflections and Refractions

A laser beam can be reflected from one or more reflecting surfaces during its transmission from the source to its destination. The reflecting surface can be either flat or curved. The reflector may be either a highly polish metal surface or it may be made of transparent glass or plastic coated on either the front surface (first surface) or back surface (second surface). The coating consists of a highly brilliant metallic deposit or a dielectric material, such as MgF_2. In total reflection of a laser beam from a surface, the first-surface-coated mirror is preferred, because there occurs no ghost reflections as it would when the second surface is coated. This phenomenon is illustrated in Figs. 1-10A and B.

It will be noted from Fig. 1-10A that as the beam reflects from the first surface of the mirror (M_1) it produces no ghost reflection like that shown in Fig. 1-10B. Thus, when a laser beam is to be reflected from a surface, as in bending at 90° in a welding or drilling machine, before it becomes incident on the object to be processed, the first-surface mirror must be used to obtain a sharp focus or point of incidence. Furthermore, as illustrated in Fig. 1-10A, the angle of incidence (i) and the angle of reflection (r) are equal; this is shown by the broken line drawn normal (perpendicular) to the surface of the mirror.

In Fig. 1-11, a laser beam becomes incident at an angle i on the surface of water contained in a glass vessel designated by C. Since water has a higher optical density than air, as the beam enters the water it bends toward the normal N in water due to the slowing down of the speed of laser lights in the higher optical density medium (water in this case). As the beam emerges from the trans-

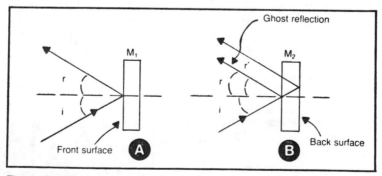

Fig. 1-10. Mirror coatings, (A) first surface coated, and (B) second surface coated.

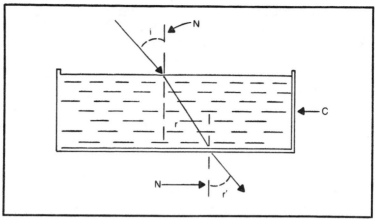

Fig. 1-11. View illustrating refraction of a laser beam in passing through water.

parent vessel C it bends away from the normal, and proceeds in the same direction as the incident laser beam, making an angle equal to the angle of incidence (i) of the laser beam on the surface of water. The bending of the laser beam in going from one transparent medium to another transparent medium of different optical density is called refraction, and the angle at which the beam bends with respect to the normal is known as the angle of refraction. Thus, it may be stated that when a laser beam passes from a medium of greater optical density to one of smaller optical density, the beam bends away from the normal, and as the beam passes from a medium of lower optical density to one of higher optical density the beam bends toward the normal, provided that the beam is not incident on the surface normal (perpendicular) to it.

A relationship exists between the angle of incidence and the angle of refraction, which may be given as:

$$\frac{\text{Sin } i}{\text{Sin } r} = n \qquad \textbf{(Equation 1-1)}$$

where, n is known as the index of refraction of the medium penetrated by the beam after incidence on its surface at an angle other than the normal.

The refractive characteristic of e medium traversed by a laser beam is utilized in fabricating lenses of different configurations, such as convex lenses or concave lenses, in which a laser bends toward the thicker portion of the lens. For instance, in e biconvex or planoconvex lens, the beam, as it emerges from the lens, bends toward the thicker central part of the lens. Thus, such a lens is known as the focusing or converging lens. When the beam passes through a biconcave or planoconcave lens, it bends toward the peripheral thicker section of the lens, as the beam leaves the lens. Such a lens is known as diverging lens. Accordingly, the converging lens is used to focus the beam on a material for cutting, drilling, or welding. The diverging lens is used for diverging the beam in holographic work, or for collimating the beam in conjunction with the use of a converging lens, as will be discussed in a later section.

Collimation of a Laser Beam

In order to collimate a pencil beam of laser radiation at an expanded diameter, two lenses are required. One of the lenses must be preferably a biconcave lens and the other a biconvex lens. The laser beam emergent from the exit port of the laser-generating cavity, known as the resonant cavity, is first brought into incidence on the biconcave lens, which expands the beam diameter and projects the beam on a biconvex lens, which collimates the beam, as shown in Fig. 1-12. In order that a beam collimation can be achieved, the distance between the optical planes between the two lenses L_1 and L_2 must be equal to the focal length (f) of the biconvex lens L_2; otherwise no collimation occurs.

The collimated laser beam can be focused with precision on an object, such as for cutting, drilling, or welding of a metal or plastic object, by the use of a biconvex or planoconvex lens, as illustrated in Fig. 1-13. In this case, a second convex lens (L_3) may be positioned at any distance from the first convex lens L_2, within a reasonable distance. Also, the collimated laser beam can be projected to long distance in air, for instance, up to 50 kilometers in clear weather, although other factors, such as dispersion due to refraction from contaminants in air may prevent the beam from remaining collimated up to its destination. However, this problem has not been too

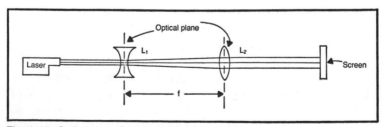

Fig. 1-12. Collimation of an expanded laser beam.

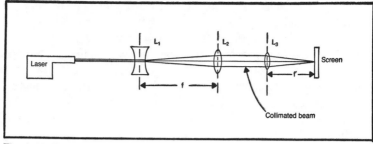

Fig. 1-13. Focusing of a collimated laser beam.

significant in using a collimated beam in rangefinders used for moderate distances, in the line of sight of the laser system.

Laser-Beam Splitting

A laser beam can be split into two or more beams by the use of various optical elements, such as precisely ground and polished glass or plastic plates, optical prisms, and semitransmissive mirrors. Several methods of splitting a laser beam are illustrated in Figs. 1-14A through C. The splitting of the beam by means of a glass or plastic plate is accomplished by positioning the plate at a 45° angle with respect to the beam axis, although other angles are also possible. In the case of a cube splitter, the cube is formed by two right-angle prisms with their bases cemented together with an optically transparent balsam. The beam is projected perpendicularly to one of the short sides of the prism and at a 45° angle to the bases of the prisms, as shown in Fig. 1-14B. If the thickness of the balsam cement is regulated so that it is 50 percent transmissive,

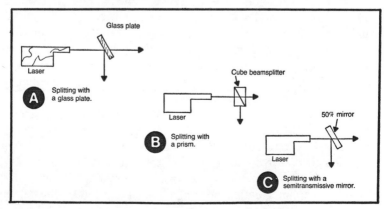

Fig. 1-14. Laser-beam splitting schemes.

then the split beams will have equal intensities. Furthermore, in order to eliminate reflections from both the entrance and exit surfaces of the cube prism, these surfaces are treated with a thin layer of spectrally flat antireflection coating. Figure 1-14C illustrates the most common beam splitter, whose front surface is coated with a dielectric material, such as MgF_2 in increments of ¼-wavelength layers to the desired degree of transmissivity. The number of coatings can be deposited in such a way that the intensity of the transmitted beam can equal to the reflected beam intensity. Still another method of splitting with a prism, commonly used in chemical analysis instruments, is to direct the laser beam perpendicularly to the apex of a wedge prism, so that the beam will be split as if by a knife edge into two equal to unequal intensity beams, as desired.

LASER SYSTEM CONSTRUCTION

Since there are numerous laser systems, designs, and constructions, only a few important representative systems will be described to illustrate their construction and operation. Beginning with the simplest system, the gas laser, it consists of an electric discharge tube containing one or more inert gases which are excited to laser emission by passing through the tube a high-voltage current. As described earlier, the two mirrors located at the opposite ends of the discharge tube reflect the generated radiation within the tube back and forth to increase the photon emission by stimulating the excited inert gas atoms. The beam is projected through the tube and to its exterior in a pencil beam, as illustrated in Fig. 2-1 and described in the succeeding text.

A typical solid-state laser system is shown in Fig. 1-15, which is a commercially available welder and driller. Figure 1-16 is a very simplified electric circuit diagram of a pulse solid-state laser system. It will be noted in this diagram that the system consists of a laser-generating element (L) such as a ruby or Nd-YAG laser rod, a laser-exciting flashlamp (F) a power supply consisting of a voltage-amplifying and rectifying subsystem, and a control system for adjusting the amount of power to be applied to the flashlamp and hence the energy of the laser radiation to be produced. In order to obtain a continuous operation from the system, a cooling system is also provided to cool the flashlamp and the laser rod. The cooling medium may be either a gas or water circulating through the chamber containing both the lasing element and the flashlamp, as illustrated in the figure.

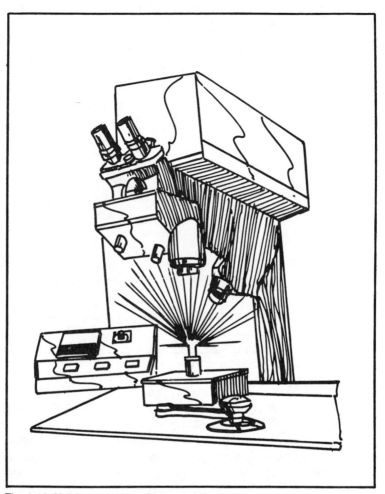

Fig. 1-15. Holobeam laser welder and driller.

The operation of the system shown in Fig. 1-16 consists of applying a 115 to 120 volt alternating current to a variable step-up transformer (T), whose high-voltage coil is connected across a rectifying bridge circuit (R). The output of the bridge is connected to a pulse-forming RC (resistor-capacitor) network having RC sections with control switches. Each section may be made to develop an equal amount of energy in joules, in accordance with the following relation:

$$P = \frac{CV^2}{2} \times n \qquad \text{(Equation 1-2)}$$

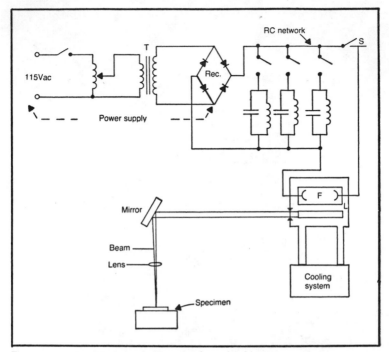

Fig. 1-16. A simplified circuit diagram of a pulsed laser.

in which, P is the total electric energy in joules, C is the capacitance in microfarads of each RC section, V is the voltage in kilovolts, and n is the number of RC sections energized in the network circuit.

For example, if the power supply is controlled from the instrument panel to furnish 4,000 volts dc to each RC section containing 200 microfarads, and out of four exemplary sections given in the figure only two RC sections were energized, then the pulsing power developed in the two RC sections may be calculated as:

$$P = \frac{200 \times 4^2 \times 2}{2}$$
$$= 200 \times 16 = 3200 \text{ joules.}$$

While there are a number of factors that enter into the exact production of laser emission from the lasing element, a practical and rough approximation can be made by the use of the following equation:

$$J = (3200 - 320) \times 0.004 \text{ (average)}$$
$$= 11.52 \text{ joules.}$$

14

An accurate method of laser emission would be to make a direct measurement of the emitted radiation, using a radiometer or power meter. The manufacturer usually makes a graph, using different applied voltages in increments versus laser output as measured by a radiometer. From this graph, one may select the required voltage to produce a desired laser radiation in joules.

The method of energy transfer from the flashlamp to the lasing rod is as follows: the intense greenish light from a xenon flashlamp consists of high-energy photons which upon incidence on the lasing rod excite the chromium ions in the dopant Cr_2O_3 (chromium oxide) to move to higher energy levels. This action causes some of the extranuclear electrons in the dopant atoms to absorb photonic energy from the photon-electron encounter. The energy-recipient electrons then radiate with the same frequency as that of the incident photons, thus increasing the number of photons in the reasonant cavity (in active medium). As the newly formed photons together with the incident photons oscillate between the mirrors at the ends of the rod, additional photos are formed. This is known as *stimulated emission* of photons (radiation). When the energy of the oscillating photons exceeds the resonant cavity threshold, an avalanche of photons projects out of the partially mirrored end of the rod, producing the familiar red laser beam from the ruby rod. The radiation energy from the rod may be given as:

$$\text{Photonic Energy} = h\nu = \frac{hc}{\gamma} \text{ ergs} \qquad \textbf{(Equation 1-3)}$$

where, h is Planck's constant equal to 6.625×10^{-27} erg-second, v is the frequency of the photon, c is the speed of light in centimeters, and λ is the wavelength of the photons in angstroms (converted to centimeters during calculation).

From Equation 1-3, it will be readily seen that the shorter the wavelength of a photon the greater is its energy. Also, the greater the photonic energy the higher is its frequency. Thus, the ultraviolet radiation from, for instance, an argon laser has the greatest frequency and hence the greatest energy, and the infrared laser radiation has the lowest frequency and thus the smallest energy in the laser radiation spectrum. However, with increased number of photons in the infrared spectrum, one may obtain much higher total energy from infrared-producing atoms than those producing ultraviolet radiation; here, the intensity is the determining factor. The total energy of the laser then will depend on the amount of emission (intensity) of the active medium.

Much of the flashlamp energy expended in producing laser radiation is in the form of heat, which, when absorbed in the lasing element, reduces the efficiency of laser production very rapidly unless the heat is removed from the system as fast as it forms in the resonant cavity and its surroundings. As an illustration, let us take a case in which the flashlamp of a certain solid-state laser system receives an energy input of 250 joules at a repetition rate of 10 pulses per minute. The total energy received by the flashlamp in one minute will be 2,500 joules (roughly equal to 625 calories). If the above system, including the flashlamp and the solid-state laser element, weighs one kilogram (1,000 grams) and has an average specific heat of 0.016 cal/gm, the thermal capacity of the system will be 16 calories. If the system started operation from a room temperature of 25° C, the final temperature of the system will be approximately 25 + 38 = 63 °C, since the temperature rise is 625/16, equals roughly 38.

A temperature of 63 °C will considerably reduce the emission efficiency of the laser generation and, if continued for sometime, the lasing element may cease emitting and may even crack due to the elevated temperature. For this reason, the lasing system together with its flashlamp must be cooled continuously to retain the efficiency of emission of the laser element. The cooling is accomplished generally by circulating deionized water through the system at a rate from 0.5 to 2 gallons per minute, depending on the power rating of the laser system.

HANDLING LASER SYSTEMS AND SAFETY RULES

There are three types of precautions that can be exercised in handling laser equipment. They are precautions of handling optical elements, precautions against electrical shock, and precautions against exposure to laser radiations.

Handling Optical Elements

Lenses, prisms, and mirrors have optically ground and polished surfaces generally coated with an antireflective material such as MgF_2. The surfaces are vulnerable to rough handling, such as scratching them inadvertently by using a cleaning cloth that may contain dust or fine-grain contaminants. Touching the surfaces with fingers at times causes the surface of the lens or the mirror to become contaminated, which, when left unattended for a time, may cause deterioration of the surface coating. This coating is a very thin layer of metal or dielectric deposit, which is also used for antireflection of rays from the surface. The following precautions are necessary in handling lenses, prisms, and mirrors.

■ All optical-element surfaces must be dusted off and fingerprints removed with a soft cloth or lens tissue before using them. There should be no fingerprints on them in the first place, because the elements should be held by their edges or peripheries.

■ All lenses, prisms, and mirrors and wedges should be identified, after cleaning, with a label on the box or container, stating the diameter, focal length, and the type of lens, and similarly for the mirrors and prisms.

■ Some lenses, prisms, and etalons used in a laser laboratory may have been made of plastic and for that reason no solvents, such as methanol or ethanol, should be used when cleaning them, unless they are marked clearly as "glass" on the containers.

■ When not in use, all optical elements comprising lenses, mirrors, prisms, etalons, beam expanders, optical filters, spatial filters, and other optical accessories should be carefully wrapped in optical tissue paper and boxed, with accurate labels on the boxes.

Precautions Against Electrical Shock

As already discussed, all laser equipment operates at high voltage, regardless of the intensity of the laser emission from them. Accordingly, the following precautions should be taken when handling laser systems:

■ The beginner should familiarize himself with the laser system circuits and should know definitely where the high-voltage points are in order to avoid them, while the system is operating.

■ While the laser system is in operation, no bare wires in the circuit should be touched, except by means of well-insulated probes for measurement purposes.

■ For repair work, the laser system should be turned off and, if the system contains any capacitive network, the capacitors must be discharged to ground by means of heavily insulated jumpers before any work is undertaken.

■ All laser systems should be securely grounded by the use of a three-pronged plug or by grounding the system with a cable to a cold water pipe.

■ Prior to starting the laser equipment, all safety interlocks should be checked to ensure their proper contact; if the safety interlocks are found defective, they should be immediately repaired before the power is turned on.

■ The operator of the equipment should never leave the laboratory without an attendant in charge or without shutting down the power to the equipment.

■ He-Ne, CO_2, argon or similar plasma tubes are apt to implode if they are damaged or cracked by rough handling. Thus, these plasma tubes should be carefully handled to prevent damage. Any evidence of a crack or severe scratch on the tube would make the tube vulnerable to shock and vibration, and hence to damage by implosion during operation. Therefore, when there is an evidence of damage on the tube, it should be removed from the circuit.

Precautions Against Exposure to Laser Radiations

Laser beams of any type should be considered hazardous to the body when it is exposed to the radiation. Even the radiation from a gallium arsenide diode (which emits less than a milliwatt generally) should be avoided. The Bureau of Radiological Health (BRH) and Laser Institute of America (LIA) have developed the following general classifications for all types of laser devices. They are:

Class I—Exempt Laser Systems. Class I lasers are considered nonhazardous to the body areas vulnerable to the action by laser radiations. An example of such a laser is gallium arsenide (GaAs), whose spectral wavelengths range from 8,200 to 9,050 angstroms.

Class II—Low-Power Lasers. Class II lasers emit power less than 1 milliwatt; these lasers can produce retinal injury when the radiation from them is viewed directly, or indirectly as by reflections from bright surfaces. The system must be provided with a pilot light and a shutter; the shutter is used when the system is in a quiescent operational state. The system must bear a *Caution* label.

Class III Lasers. Class III lasers are classified into IIIa and IIIb categories. The He-Ne lasers which do not emit more than 4 milliwatts are included in Class IIIa group; they are highly hazardous to the eye. The system must bear a Caution label. Class IIIb lasers are those that emit between 4 to 50 milliwatts of radiation power. The system of this category must be provided with a pilot light, a shutter, and a *Danger* label on the equipment.

Class IV Lasers. Lasers in this category emit radiations up to 50 watts; such lasers are CO_2, Nd-YAG, Nd- glass and the like. Either the direct rays or the reflections from such lasers are very dangerous to the eye and certain other areas that may become exposed to the radiation for a nominal period. A *Danger* label must be provided on the system.

Class V Lasers. These lasers are very high power systems and are enclosed at all times. No stray radiation should leak from the enclosure. The safety interlocks should be examined from time to time to see that they are firmly fitted and no damage exists. While no particular label has been prescribed by BRH or LIA for these systems, it will be wise to place a *Danger* sign on the system.

My own safety rule is to be *Cautious* when handling any power-level laser equipment and to avoid viewing the direct or reflected rays from any type of laser equipment. System labels, classifications, or other signs of caution may have fallen off or worn out so that they are not readable. Safety goggles prescribed by BRH or LIA should be used at all times when in doubt of the rating of the laser equipment. Even a visitor to the laboratory where a laser system is in operation should be provided with proper precautions or goggles when the system operator considers it to be necessary.

Rules, regulations, and even the classifications of the laser systems may be changed or modified from time to time by the BRH, LIA or other laser agencies responsible for the safety rules. Accordingly, the operator of a laser system must feel it his responsibility to be provided with the latest safety rules and regulations. These are available from the BRH and LIA at all times. The safety rules may be obtained by writing to one or both of the following agencies:

Bureau of Radiological Health (BRH)
Rockville, Maryland 20852

Laser Institute of America
4100 Executive Park Drive
Cincinnati, Ohio 45241

TRIGONOMETRIC FUNCTIONS

In the chapters that follow, we will occasionally use a few of the trigonometric functions that will be found useful in solving problems related to laser beam propagation, reflection, refraction, and beam intensities. The reader not familiar with these functions will find them easy to learn and utilize in cases where other methods would not be as simple to use and to obtain solutions to the problems in hand. These functions are sine, cosine, tangent, cotentent, secant, and cosecant. To simplify our learning, the first four functions, that are used here occasionally, will be explained in this section.

For simplification, we may take up the case of measuring a distance from the laser source, which is projecting a pencil beam to a target at the desired distance. Two marks, for example C and N, about two meters apart, are made on the target. First the beam is focused on C and then on N. The angle θ through which the beam was rotated is measured. Then, by using a relationship selected from the following trigonometric functions, we can calculate the distance D between the source S and the Target C.

(1) Sine   — Sin θ = R/A = Cos (90° − θ)
(2) Cosine   — Cos θ = D/A = Sin (90° − θ)
(3) Tangent   — Tan θ = R/D = Cot (90° − θ)
(4) Cotangent — Cot θ = D/R = Tan (90° − θ)

In the triangle SCN shown in Fig. 1-17, we may use the tangent relationship in which we obtain:

$$\text{Tan } \theta = R/D$$
$$D = R/\text{Tan } \theta$$

or,

in which, R is 2 meters, and the angle θ as measured is 20°. The tangent of the angle 20° (as looked up in any physics handbook) is 0.3640. Therefore, the distance D is calculated as:

$$D = \frac{200 \text{ cm}}{0.3640}$$
$$= 500 \text{ cm (approx.)}$$

In a second example, assume that the intensity of laser radiation at r is 80 watts/cm². What will be the intensity at R, if r is located one-half way between C and S?

$$\text{Tan } \theta = r/\tfrac{1}{2}D = 2r/D$$

Since r is equal to ½R, then its numerical value is 100 cm, and D is 550 cm., we have:

$$r = D \text{ Tan } \theta/2 = 100 \text{ cm.}$$

Since the areas of circles 1 and 2 are inversely proportional to the respective intensities, we may equate the areas of the two circles as follows:

$$\frac{\pi R^2}{\pi r^2} = \frac{80 \text{ watts/cm}^2}{X}$$

where, X is the unknown intensity at R.

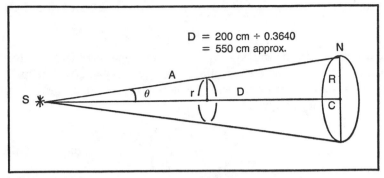

Fig. 1-17. Using trigonometry to measure distance.

Then:

$$X = \frac{80 \text{ watts/cm}^2 \times \pi r^2}{\pi R^2}$$

$$= \frac{80 \text{ watts/}(100)^2}{(200)^2}$$

$$= \frac{8 \times 10^5 \text{ watts/cm}^2}{(200)^2}$$

$$= \frac{8 \times 10^5}{4 \times 10^4}$$

$$= 20 \text{ watts/cm}^2.$$

The last problem proves that the intensities at r and R are inversely proportional to their respective areas. Furthermore, it is shown that when the distance from a reference point is doubled, the intensity of radiation becomes one-fourth, and when it is tripled, the intensity falls to one-ninth of that at the reference point, the point r in this case. This relation holds, however, for only diverging beams from a point source.

LENS MAGNIFICATION AND FOCAL LENGTH

The magnifying power of a lens is a function of its focal length and is commonly expressed in diopters. A lens having one diopter has a focal length of one meter. The focal length of a lens depends on the curvature of the lens as well as on the index of refraction of the lens material. The greater the curvature of a lens the shorter is its focal length and the greater is its magnifying power. Thus, writing an equation for the lens magnifying power, we have:

$$D = \frac{1 \text{ meter}}{f} \qquad \text{(Equation 1-4)}$$

and,
$$f = \frac{1 \text{ meter}}{D} \qquad \textbf{(Equation 1-5)}$$

where, D is the magnifying power of the lens and f is its focal length.

An equation expressing the focal length of a lens with respect to its radii of curvature and the index of refraction of the lens material may be given as:

$$\frac{1}{f} = (n - 1)\left[\frac{1}{r_1} + \frac{1}{r_2}\right] \qquad \textbf{(Equation 1-6)}$$

and,
$$f = \frac{1}{(n-1)\left[\dfrac{1}{r_1} + \dfrac{1}{r_2}\right]} \qquad \textbf{(Equation 1-7)}$$

where, n is the index of refraction of the lens material, r_1 is the curvature of one surface of the lens, and r_2 is the curvature of the opposite surface of the lens. These equations are related to a convex lens, and for a concave lens, the positive sign becomes a negative sign.

Questions and Problems

1-1. What is a laser? How does the radiation from a laser differ from ordinary light rays? What is an optically active medium? What is a monochromatic radiation? State the types of active mediums for the generation of laser radiation.

1-2. If two laser beams are in phase, what characteristics in the two beams make them similar? Why can one focus a laser beam to a sharp point? Discuss the reasons. To what type of industrial operations does sharpness of focus make the laser beam adaptable? Discuss.

1-3. State the method of producing a laser beam. Discuss why an ordinary neon light tube cannot produce a laser beam. What elements are necessary to achieve stimulated radiation from a neon tube? What design of electrodes should be used in a neon gas tube for the production of a laser beam?

1-4. What action in an electric discharge tube causes the amplification of the photons? Discuss. What are the surface coatings used in laser generating feedback elements made of? What is the difference between the rear reflecting mirror and the output mirror? Can metallic mirror surfaces be used in laser feedback mirrors?

What material is used to prevent the degradation of the metallic mirror deposit? Can that material be used as a mirror? Discuss.

1-5. What is the mechanism of photon production in a gas-filled laser tube? How can laser action be produced in a ruby cylinder? How does a ruby receive its energy to emit radiation? What is the energy source called? Should the source of energy be equal, greater, or less than the energy required to produce photons in ruby? Why? Discuss.

1-6. What other active medium rods besides ruby can produce laser radiation? Is their energy emission process the same or different from that of ruby? Can ruby be used continuously to produce laser radiation? Can it be used in the pulsing mode? Which mode is more characteristic to ruby? Discuss.

1-7. What is a dopant? Approximately what percentage of dopant is used in ruby? In Nd-YAG? Nd-glass? What type of illumination is used for the continuous emission of a laser? What type of illumination is used for pulsing-mode emission? How does laser light oscillation occur in a ruby rod, Nd-YAG rod, or Nd-glass rod? What elements are used to cause oscillation of laser light in these rods?

1-8. What is a semiconductor diode laser? How is it constructed? What is a pn junction? In what spectrum is the light emitted from a diode laser? Compared with a He-Ne emission, how strong is the emission from a laser diode? What is the most common laser diode? In what systems is it generally used? Discuss.

1-9. What is a forward bias current in a diode? About how much is the threshold current of a laser diode? What does a threshold current mean? Would the threshold current be the same or different for different laser diodes? Why? Discuss. What is the spectral range of a GaAs diode?

1-10. How is a liquid dye laser excited to emission of radiation? What is a liquid dye laser? How is it made? In what proportion is the dye mixed with its solvent? In what mode can a dye laser operate? Is the dye stationary or in motion? What is the reason for your last answer?

1-11. Name some of the optical elements used in a laser system and state their functions. Certain optical elements have front-surface coatings. What is the nature of the coating? What is the reason for coating the optical element on its front surface? On the back surface? Which one is used in bending a laser beam? How do you produce a laser-beam focus with a mirror?

1-12. A laser beam becomes incident on the surface of a liquid at an angle of 45° (with respect to the normal) to the surface. In the liquid, the beam bends toward the normal at an angle of 40°. What is the index of refraction of the liquid?

1-13. When a laser beam passes through a convex lens perpendicularly to the optical plane, in what direction does it bend? In what direction does the beam bend if it passes through a concave lens? In what direction does the beam bend when it passes through a prism? Which wavelength bends the most, when a beam of white light passes through a prism? Discuss. Why?

1-14. What is meant by the collimation of a laser beam? What types of lenses are used to collimate a laser beam? What is the distance relationship between the lenses used? How many lenses and what types are used in collimating, and focusing a laser beam? In what order are they placed in the beam with respect to the central ray?

1-15. Give several methods for splitting a laser beam. Do you use a second-surface-coated optical element for splitting a laser beam? Why? Discuss. How is a cube beam splitter used? How does its efficiency of splitting a beam compare with other beam splitters? Give a few applications for beam splitters.

1-16. In what two modes do laser systems generally operate? Why should a cooling system be used in a laser system? When does a laser system not require a cooling system? When does one use a capacitive network in a laser system? What is a capacitive network? Discuss.

1-17. A certain laser system has seven sections in its capacitive network, each section having a capacitance of 200 microfarads. If four of the capacitive sections are energized at a voltage of 1,000 volts for a certain laser processing technique, how much energy will be developed in this technique? If each pulse is 100-milliseconds long, what is the power rating of the laser system?

1-18. What must be the applied energy in joules on a capacitive network so that a pulse of 18 joules of laser can be produced? If this energy is expended in 1/20th of a second, what is the rating of the laser system in watts?

1-19. If the wavelength of a photon is 6,000 angstroms, what is its frequency in hertz? Which wavelengths have higher frequencies, ultraviolet or infrared? How does the efficiency of laser emission vary with temperature? Give reasons and discuss your answer.

1-20. What types of precautions are there in handling laser equipment? What precautions would you take before leaving the laboratory where you have been operating a high-power laser system? When would you pull out the electric plug from its socket? Under what conditions? Carbon dioxide laser radiation is invisible; would you need any safety goggles while using a carbon dioxide laser beam in the laboratory? Why? Discuss.

1-21. A diverging laser beam was measured at one meter from its source and was found to be 30 watts per square centimeter. The same beam was also measured at distances of 2 meters and 3 meters. What would be the intensities of the laser beam at the 2 and 3 meter distances from the source?

1-22. A diverging laser beam is incident perpendicularly on a wall and illuminates a circular area having a diameter of 40 centimeters. If the triangle formed by the source, the center of the circle, and the periphery of the circle has an included angle, near the source, of 30°, what is the distance between the source and the center of the circle?

1-23. What is the magnifying power of the lens whose focal length is 10 centimeters? What is the focal length of a convex lens whose magnifying power is 20 diopters? What is the focal length of a biconvex lens whose refractive index is 1.50 and its radii of curvatures are 6 centimeters and 8 centimeters?

Chapter 2
Laser Radiation Principles

An atom may be generally considered to be the smallest particle of matter exhibiting all of the characteristics of that particular type of matter. Matter, as referred to here, means one of the naturally occurring 92 or more elements contained in the periodic table. Since this book is not intended to teach a course in chemistry, we shall give only a brief outline of the chemical elements and pass on to the activity of some of the selected elements which are playing important roles in the formation of laser radiation under specific conditions. Furthermore, the intent of our discussion is to concentrate on the dynamic state of the atom rather than the static state, which is the concern of the chemist. The dynamic model of an atom is fashioned after the physicist's concept of material particles in activity as noted in the emission of radiations from them. In discussing the structure of an atom model of a state having no motion, it is assumed that the atom is isolated from all external influences. An atom of such a character has definite physical and chemical properties in a given element and is considered to be electrically neutral.

STRUCTURE OF AN ATOM

A typical atom consists of a nucleus containing one or more neutrons, protons, and other nuclear structures, such as positrons, nutrinos, etc., with which our work will not be concerned. The neutrons and neutral particles, and it is believed that a neutron may be a combination of a proton and an electron, although they have not yet been isolated from a neutron. A proton is a positively charged particle that always remains in the nucleus. The nucleus is surrounded by one or more planetary orbits, in which negatively charged particles known as electrons are confined in definite numbers when the atom is in a neutral or at ground state. The electrons are dynamic and move from one orbit to another when energized by an electrical force. The combination of neutrons and protons form the atomic weight of the atom, and since there are more than 90 naturally found elements, each element has a definite weight depending on the number of nuclear structures (protons and neutrons). When all the elements are arranged sequentially by their atomic weights, from the lightest to the heaviest, and are numbered progressively from the lightest to the heaviest element, they can be assigned atomic numbers and identified by these numbers. For instance, the hydrogen atom is the lightest element and has an atomic number of 1, sodium is the eleventh heaviest element and has an atomic number of 11, sulfur has an atomic number of 16, mercury has an atomic number of 80, and so forth to the last and heaviest element. In arbitrarily numbering these elements from the lightest to the heaviest element, it is also found that the atomic number of an element is equal to the number of protons in the nucleus, or to the number of electrons in the orbits at the ground state of an atom.

From experimental observations, as proceeded along the successive elements from hydrogen to the heaviest element, periodically occurring monatomic gaseous elements will be encountered. These elements generally do not enter into any stable chemical combination with other elements and, therefore, are known as inert gases. They are: helium, neon, argon, krypton, xenon, and niton (radon). It must be pointed out here while these gases are ordinarily nonreactive, when they are used in laser resonant environment in an electric field and in presence of halogens, such as chlorine, fluorine, bromine, or iodine in specific conditions, they do enter into temporary combination with these elements and produce very useful and powerful laser radiations, about which we will learn in the ensuing sections; such lasers are known as excimers. In the inert gases, the extranuclear electrons in the outermost orbit of an atom complete the number of electrons that can be held in that orbit, usually two electrons in the helium atom and eight in the other inert gases. When the outermost orbit of an atom is not complete, then that atom can enter into a chemical reaction with another atom. In the chemical reaction, the atoms react in such a manner that in the combined atoms the outermost orbits are completed by the mutual sharing by the reacting atoms of their valency electrons.

The combining property of an atom with another atom is determined by the number of electrons occupying the outermost orbit at ground state. These electrons are known as *valency electrons*. The property of an atom of intersharing electrons with other atoms in a chemical reaction is known as the *valence* of that atom. The valence of an atom, then, is dependent on the number of electrons in its outermost orbit. For example, suppose we take two different atoms whose outermost orbits could contain only eight electrons and no more when completed in a chemical reaction. Let us further assume that one of the atoms has three electrons on its outermost orbit (a valence of 3) in a normal state, and a second atom has five electrons in its outermost orbit in a normal state. When these two atoms combine chemically, the two atoms share their electrons so that their outermost orbits are complete, in doing so, each atom assumes an inert-gas-like outermost orbit, and the chemical combination is a stable bond between them, forming a compound.

In the study of laser radiation, the valance electrons are important because they are the ones that become ionized first in an electric discharge tube, such as in a helium-neon or mercury-vapor tube, and produce light by radiation. The atoms of He-Ne, argon, krypton, or other gases in a discharge tube become ionized upon application of a high-voltage current through the tube. The emission of radiation occurs when the electrons recombine with the excited atoms that have lost electrons. In the recombination, those electrons that are accelerated toward the nucleus radiate, giving off a photon of light per electron. This is known as an electronic transition from a level of higher energy to one of lower energy. The frequency of the emitted photon depends upon the energy expended during the radiation, as given by Equation 2-1.

RADIATIVE TRANSITIONS IN EXCITED ATOMS

In an atom at ground (neutral) state, the extranuclear electrons are at the lowest quantum energy state. However, when the atom gains energy, such as from a thermal environment, electric field, or by absorption of photonic energy (from illumination), the electrons move to higher energy levels. An electron, however, cannot remain stationary in a higher energy level and tends to fall back to its original energy state. When this occurs, the electron gives up its energy by radiating a photon with an energy equal to that it has gained. Therefore, the higher the energy the electron has gained in moving to a higher energy level the higher is the frequency of the photon which it emits. Photonic energy (also known as quantum energy) may be given by the term hf, in which h is a constant and f is the frequency of the photon.

In an electric discharge tube containing a gas and having been impressed with a voltage (V), the energy gained by the extranuclear electron can be given as $\frac{1}{2}mv^2$, its kinetic energy. If all the kinetic energy of the electron is converted into a radiation energy for emission of a photon, then we may equate the relation between the kinetic energy and the photonic energy as follows:

$$\frac{1}{2}mv^2 = hf \qquad \text{(Equation 2-1)}$$

where, the energy of each term is given in ergs, and m is the mass of the electron equal to 9.107×10^{-28} gram, v is the electron velocity in centimeters, h is Planck's constant (equal to 6.6234×10^{-27} erg-second), and f is the frequency of the photon emitted. This type of energy transition is known as spontaneous emission of radiation.

While spontaneous emission of radiation gives us a basis for studying laser radiations, the radiation itself is not a stimulated emission, because there is no stimulative energy involved in the process. A stimulated emission of radiation occurs when a quantum of energy (photon) excites an electron to radiate with the same frequency, and hence with the same wavelength, of the exciting photon. This can occur only when a photon of energy becomes incident on an electron of an excited atom in an electric field, where the electron has moved to a higher energy level and imparts its photonic energy to the electron. Because of the feedback mechanism of the mirrors in the resonant cavity, the photons thus produced oscillate between the feedback mirrors, producing additional photons from electrons to the excited atoms. This process is known as *stimulated emission of radiation*, which is the laser radiation we have been studying. Thus, the photon resulting from this stimulated emission has the same frequency, wavelength, phase profile, and direction of propagation as the photon that triggers the newly formed photon. These two photons now proceed on their way to trigger more photons from electrically excited atoms. Consequently, we not only have a stimulated emission but also amplification of photons, or simply an amplification of radiation intensity. This latter state of affairs is commonly termed as "population inversion." I do not prefer to use the latter two words in future discussions, because (1) they are not definitive of the mechanism of stimulated radiation, and (2) they have the connotation of degeneration of human population. It is possible that for lack of better terminology these two words may be sustained in laser literature.

ELECTRICAL CHARACTERISTICS OF ATOMS

It has already been shown that an atom is electrically neutral at ground state, when it has an equal number of electrons in its orbits and protons in its nucleus. But, an atom may acquire a charge when the number of electrons in the orbits is increased or decreased with respect to its normal structure. The atom becomes negatively charged when it gains one or more electrons in excess of its normal number of electrons in the orbits; and, it acquires a positive charge by losing one or more electrons when it is ionized. Thus, the process in which an atom acquires an electrical charge is known as ionization. The acquisition of an electrical charge may be achieved by the atom in a magnetic field, electrolytic solution, or in an electric discharge tube. The negative charges from such atoms when made to travel through a suitable metallic conductor constitute a current of electricity.

Unit Quantity of Electricity

In a metallic conductor, the planetary (orbital) electrons are easily dissociated from the atom under a magnetic field, such as in an electric generator, in which two types of electric charges are produced, a positive charge and a negative charge. The positive charges remain stationary when the electrons leave the atoms. Thus, the only charges that can move are the electrons known as free electrons, under the magnetic influence of the generator's magnetic poles. The faster the generator's coil rotates between the magnetic poles, the greater the electric current produced. Since the magnetic poles separate the electrons from the positively charged protons, one end of the conductor coil becomes strongly charged with positive charges and the other end becomes equally charged with a negative charge. This effect produces an electrical potential difference (voltage) between the two ends of the conductor coil located between the magnetic poles. This difference of potential, known as the voltage, drives the current (electrons) through the conductor coil. It is thus seen that a potential and a current are produced simultaneously in the electric generator. However, the amount of current that can be obtained from a generator depends on the resistance offered to the flow of current in the generator coil. This resistance is known as ohmage. Accordingly, to produce a flow of current in a conductor, one can see that a voltage has to exist between the ends of the conductor to drive the electrons (current). If the resistance in the conductor is small then a large current can be transmitted through the conductor with a given voltage. If the resistance is large, then relatively less current can be carried through the conductor by the same voltage.

As we have already seen, the electron is the smallest unit of electricity obtainable and has an estimated charge of 4.8×10^{-10} electrostatic units (esu). Approximately 10^{19} electrons are equivalent to 1 coulomb, as given by the expression,

$$Q = It \qquad \text{(Equation 2-2)}$$

where, Q is the charge in coulombs, I is the current in amperes, and t is the time in seconds that the current is produced. Thus, a current of 1 ampere is made up of 10^{19} electrons flowing per second.

Electrical Units of Measurement

This section is intended for those who need a refresher study of the electrical units of measurement. The electrical units used to measure electrical parameters are: ampere, volt, and ohm. To relate these units to each other, we may state that an ampere is the amount of current that can be driven in a metallic conductor by a potential of 1 volt against a resistance of 1 ohm in the conductor. Putting this relation in an equation form, we have:

$$V = IR \qquad \text{(Equation 2-3)}$$

where V is the potential in volts, I is the current in amperes, and r is the resistance in ohms. For example; How much voltage will be necessary to transmit a current of 25 amperes through a conductor having a resistance of 16 ohms?

$$V = IR = 25 \times 16$$
$$= 400 \text{ volts.}$$

Another example: How much current can be transmitted through a conductor having a resistance of 12 ohms and impressed with a voltage of 240 volts? From Equation 2-3, we may write:

$$I = \frac{V}{R} \qquad \text{(Equation 2-4)}$$

$$\text{and, } I = \frac{240}{12}$$

$$= 20 \text{ amperes.}$$

In laser work, there are other electrical units that are used to express the amount of electricity, laser intensity, laser energy, in integers, multiples of integers, and fractions of integers. For example: A watt of electrical power is equal to current times the voltage. A kilovolt is 1,000 volts and a milliampere is 1/1,000 ampere; when these two quantities are multiplied by each other the resultant is 1 watt. A microampere is one-millionth of an ampere. The power conducted in an electrical conductor is given by:

$$P = IV = I^2R \qquad \textbf{Equation 2-5)}$$

where, P is the rate of power consumption per second, and is given in watts, and the term I^2R is derived by substitution of V for IR.

The energy flow per second is the joule, which is equal to Pt, where, t is the time in seconds. For example: If a current of 25 milliamperes flows through a transmitting wire having a resistance of 4 ohms, (a) what is the voltage to drive this current? (b) At what power is the current being transmitted through the transmitting wire? (c) How many joules are being produced if the current flows for 40 seconds?

(a) $V = IR = 0.025 \times 4 = 0.1$ volt.
(b) $P = VI = 0.1 \times 0.025 = 0.0025$ watt.
    $= I^2R = (0.025)^2 \times 4 = 0.0025$ watt.
    $= 2.5$ milliwatts.
(c) $J = P \times t = 0.0025 \times 40 = 0.1$ joule.
    $= 100$ millijoules.

The commonly used units in expressing laser power and energy are: kilowatt, milliwatt, watt, kilojoule, joule, and millijoule. In addition, the term watt per square centimeter and its multiple kilowatts per square centimeter are used to express the intensity of laser radiation. Other electrical and measurement quantities are also used, and we shall study them in the pertinent sections in the ensuing chapters.

RADIATION FROM ATOMS

Atoms may become excited in an electric field and produce electromagnetic radiations, whose optical spectrum ranges from cosmic rays to electric waves. About midway between these two extremes are the ultraviolet, visible, and infrared radiations with which we will associate our discussions throughout this book. As we have seen in the earlier sections of this book, when a high voltage is applied across an electric discharge tube filled with an ionizable gas or vapor, the atoms become dissociated into positive and negative charges known as ions, the positive ions being the ionized atoms and the negative ions being the electrons that are disrupted from the atoms. An atom which has thus "lost" one or more electrons from its structure is unstable and tends to regain its original, neutral state. In doing so, it must gain electrons. As the electrons return to the atom, they release or expend their energies gained from the electric field and radiate, as they accelerate toward the nucleus of the atom to become located in extranuclear orbits. The character of this radiation depends on the energy with which the electrons radiate. The higher the energy of the electron the higher is the frequency of the radiation which it produces, and the shorter is the wavelength of the photon thus produced.

The shorter-wavelength radiation falls in the spectrum toward the ultraviolet end of the laser radiation and the longer-wavelength radiation falls in the infrared end of the laser spectrum, with which we will associate ourselves in our study. The ultraviolet radiation having short wavelengths is invisible to the eye and the infrared radiation having very long wavelengths is also invisible to the eye. Only medium wavelengths between the two invisible radiations are visible. The visible spectrum extends from about 3,900 angstroms to about 8,500 angstroms, although some authors would prefer to assign the visible spectrum to the range between 4,000 to 7,5000 angstroms. There are no distinct boundaries between where the ultraviolet starts and where it ends; in the same manner, there is no distinct boundary between the infrared and the visible spectrum. These spectra overlap each other at the boundary regions.

LASER SYSTEMS

The following describes different types of laser systems.

Gas Lasers and Excimers

Laser systems that produce radiations in a gaseous medium enclosed in an electric discharge tube are generally known as gas lasers. These lasers employ neon, helium, argon, krypton, xenon and interim, unstable compounds of these elements. These compounds are ArF, XeF, KrF, XeBr, HF-DF, etc., and are known as excimers. These compounds are formed in an electric discharge tube in an electric field, and after radiation they dissociate into their elemental forms. However, in the form of excimer lasers, they produce very intense and important radiations that are used even in experiments of atomic fusion. The gas lasers produce radiation by ionization and emission of photons, as in an ordinary neon tube we see on store fronts. However, in addition to emission of photons, the laser tube is designed so that the photons are reflected from one end of the tube to the other. In their oscillation between the ends of the tube, the photons encounter excited atoms in the gaseous medium and produce additional photons from the accelerated electrons of the excited atoms, thus amplifying the intensity of the photon radiation.

A simplified diagram of the gaseous laser discharge tube is shown in Fig. 2-1, in which the tube T is filled with a mixture of neon and helium gases. The electrodes of the tube are ring-shaped to allow the radiation to be projected against the mirrors M_1 and M_2. The emitted photons oscillate between the mirrors and in their traverse through the tube from one mirror to the other, the photons collide with the electrons of the excited atoms in the tube and stimulate the electrons in encounter to emission of photons of the same energy as the colliding photons. This action produces a radiation with photons having the same wavelengths and frequencies, so that an almost monochromatic radiation is created in the tube. However, as mentioned earlier, one of the mirrors is coated with a reflecting material that reflects 100 percent of the radiation to the other mirror. The other mirror, known as the output mirror, is only partially coated, so that it is about 40 to 50 percent light transmissive. Thus, when the radiation in the laser tube reaches a threshold stage, an avalanche of photons project out of the tube through the output mirror. This projecting beam is the stimulated radiation or simply the laser radiation. The beam issuing from the exit port has a beam diameter almost equal to the internal diameter of the laser tube, whose dimension is just a few millimeters. The emission is dominantly of a wavelength of 6,328 angstroms, although weak harmonic wavelengths are also produced at 1,152 and 3,391 angstroms. The laser operates continuously, with some versions made to operate modulated, such as for communication.

In order that an ionization occurs in an atom confined in a discharge tube, an electron in the outer quantum level must receive a threshold energy required to remove the electron from its normal quantum level. This energy is known as the work function and is

34

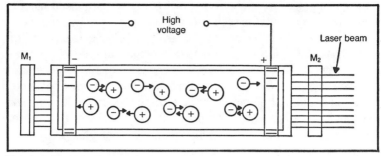

Fig. 2-1. Simplified diagram of a He-Ne laser.

usually expressed as ϕ equal to Ve/300 electron volts. If the applied voltage on the tube is V_o, then the energy gained by the electron will be equal to $V_o e/300$, where e is the charge on the electron equal to 4.80×10^{-10} esu, and 300 is a conversion factor from electrostatic volts to practical volts. The kinetic energy of the electron in the electric field will be:

$$\tfrac{1}{2}mv^2 = V_o e/300 - Ve/300 = V_o e/300 - \phi \quad \textbf{(Equation 2-6)}$$

The velocity of the electron in the discharge tube may be given as:

$$\tfrac{1}{2}mv^2 = V_o e/300 - Ve/300$$

and, $$V = \sqrt{\frac{2e(V_o - V)}{300m}} \quad \textbf{(Equation 2-7)}$$

The voltage (V) in the above equations represents the ionization potential of the gas. For helium, the ionization potential is 20.55 volts and for neon it is 16.58 volts. As should be evident, the higher ionization potential for helium is due to its ionizable electron being much closer to the influence of the positive proton charge in the nucleus than that of the neon atom, in which the ionizing electron is farther from the influence of the corresponding nuclear protonic charge.

The inert-gas lasers, such as argon, krypton, and xenon operate continuously, although some operate pulsed, too. They possess multiline outputs ranging from ultraviolet to the visible spectrum. These lasers can be made to emit selectively their harmonic lines by the use of optical elements, such as etalons and prisms. Other gases, such as nitrogen, and ammonia gas, can also produce lasers. Nitrogen lasers are also used to pump dye lasers in the pulsed mode. The gaseous excimer lasers operate in the pulsed mode at reasonably high outputs in the ultraviolet spectrum. Excimers emit in the range of 1,930 angstroms for ArF to 3,540 angstroms for XeF; NeF has been observed to emit at 1,080 angstroms, overlapping the long-wavelength x-ray radiation spectrum. Up to 100 joules of laser energy have been obtained from these excimers. It must be pointed out that the lasting elements in the excimer lasers are very poisonous and, therefore, they are mixed in hermetically sealed vessels and led to the ionization chamber in a continuous flow.

Solid-State Lasers

Solid-state lasers are ruby, Nd-YAG, Nd-Glass, holmium-doped YLF, erbium-doped YLF, alexandrite, and the like. The principal output line of ruby is 6,940 angstroms, for Nd-YAG it is 10,640 angstroms, for holmium-doped YLF it is 20,600 angstroms, for Nd-glass it is 10,640, and for erbium-doped YLF laser the emission is at 8,500 and 17,300 angstroms. Alexandrite emits between 7,300 and 7,800 angstroms multimode. Various versions of these laser operate at TEM_{oo} and in pulsed mode at various wavelengths. All solid-state lasers are pumped optically by the use of either a xenon flashlamp or a tungsten-arc lamp. The dopant contents of these lasers vary from 1 to about 3 percent, and the ionization of the dopants occur by optical coupling of the flashlamp or arc-lamp photons.

The optical pumps usually consist of a quartz tube containing xenon gas with nonreactive metal electrodes, such as stainless steel, aluminum, or the like. A tungsten-halogen-arc lamp is also used by some manufacturers to excite the Nd-YAG to emission. The output from a ruby laser is from 1 to 50 joules per pulse per second, or variation thereof. Nd-YAG lasers operate continuous-wave and pulsed at repetition rates of 50 or more hertz. Nd-glass laser and YLF lasers operate pulsed. One other recent laser is the F-center laser, which is tunable and its active medium is a crystal defect containing electrons. The emission occurs at the quantum energy levels in the defect sites. They operate TEM_{oo} and multimode at 23,000 to 33,000 angstroms and at 24,000 to 32,000 angstroms, all in the far infrared.

A very simplified scheme showing the optical pumping of a solid-state laser is given in Fig. 2-2. In this figure, F is a flashlamp energized by a high-voltage power supply PS. The radiation from the flashlamp is a blue-green illumination of much higher energy than the photons emitted by either ruby or Nd-YAG laser. The laser

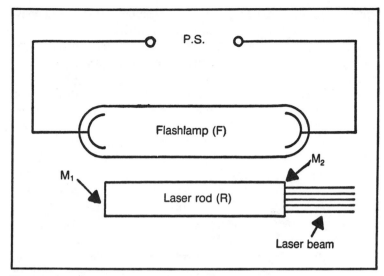

Fig. 2-2. Simplified diagram of a solid-state laser generation.

rod R is coated at each end with a reflecting material, such as silver, gold, or MgF_2. The reflector M_1 is coated heavily so that all photons incident on it are reflected within the rod to reflector M_2 and back to M_1 and so on. The reflector M_2, the output mirror, is coated thinly so that it can transmit about 40 to 50 percent of the radiation to the exterior of the rod. When the flashlamp is triggered by switching on the high-voltage current, instantly a laser beam is projected from the output mirror (exit port) from the rod. The time between the oscillation of the photons and their projection to the exterior of the rod takes only microseconds or less. The diameter of the laser beam is the same as the exit port diameter, which may be slightly smaller than the diameter of the rod because of the optical mounts at the exit end of the system.

Diode Lasers

A diode laser, also known as an injection laser, is a semiconductor diode having a pn junction and emitting laser radiation when the diode is forward biased with a current above the threshold of the pn junction material. There are several types of laser diodes, the most commonly used being the gallium arsenide (GaAs) diode, which emits in the infrared spectrum in the range of 8,200 to 9,050 angstroms. These diodes can operate at room temperature and can be modulated; for this reason, they find much use in the communication field. The diodes can be constructed to emit peak powers in tens of watts in the pulsing mode; they can operate in continuous-wave mode at lower power within milliwatt levels.

The direction of forward current flow is from the n-type layer to the p-type layer in the pn junction, when a current of 100 milliamperes (threshold current) or more is applied across the junction operating analogous to a resonant cavity (Fig. 2-3). Both GaAs and its modified form GaAlAs can operate continuously in applications such as high-frequency analog and digital modulation, in videodisk, and in fiberoptic communication systems. The modulation can be achieved either electro-optically, optically, or electro-acoustically.

The pumping action in these diodes occurs by the injection of carriers from the n-type layer to the receptors in the p-type layer at the junction. The chip of a GaAs/diode consists of the p and n type GaAs active elements included between two GaAlAs layers, with a gap of less than a micron between them. The two p and n active layers form the parallel mirrors of a resonant cavity and have reasonably high reflectivity, to an extent of about 30 percent or more. The diodes behave like an ordinary light-emitting diode when biased with a current below the threshold level. But, when the threshold level of current (or more) is transmitted through it, the diode emits laser radiation in the range recited above. The emission wavelength of a diode laser can be varied by modifying the mixture of the active layer at the pn junction; this is achieved by the addition of indium and phosphorus ions in specific amounts, as well be described in a later section.

Liquid Dye Lasers

In dye lasers, the active medium is an organic dye dissolved in an organic solvent, such as ethanol, and the solution thus prepared is optically clear. The advantages of dye solution lasers is that they can be tuned to various wavelengths in the range of 1,900 through 11,000 angstroms by using different types of dyes in solution. The solutions are optically pumped by flashlamps, nitrogen laser, argon laser, Nd-YAG laser, ruby laser, krypton laser, and ionic copper laser. Various dye solutions have different affinities for coupling with the optical pump illumination; therefore, no one pump can be generally used for all types of dye lasers. The manufacturer who fabricates the dyes has prepared tables showing the solvent for the dye, the optical pump to be used, and the wavelengths that can be produced by the particular dye and its tunable range. Some dyes operate more efficiently when operated in the pulsing mode and others operate in the continuous mode. Several companies, such as

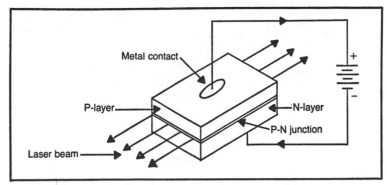

Fig. 2-3. Schematic diagram of a GaAs diode.

Eastman Kodak, and Exciton Chemical Corporation, manufacture dyes for use in laser work.

A large number of companies, such as Coherent, Spectra-Physics, Lexel, Phase-R, Lambda Physics, Molecron and others manufacture various types of dye laser systems, which are generally tunable to various wavelengths and are operated either pulsed or in the continuous-wave mode. Pulsed lasers are found to emit laser radiations in broader range and have much higher power than continuous-wave lasers. While the continuous-wave dye lasers are limited in their tuning range, they can produce narrow linewidths at greater stability than pulsed lasers.

The principal applications of dye lasers are in the medical field requiring tunable ultraviolet rays, in Raman spectroscopic work, in physics and chemistry laboratories for experimental work, in the atomic spectroscopy to map hiperfine transitions, and in isotope separation. A simplified diagram of a dye laser is shown in Fig. 2-4, in which the dye solution flows continuously through the resonant cavity. The system also shows an etalon for selecting the wavelength desired, and external mirrors for photonic feedback. A more sophisticated dye laser system will be discussed in Chapter 6.

Questions and Problems

2-1. What is an atom? Describe the structure of an atom. Differentiate atomic weight from atomic number. What are extranuclear electrons? If an atom loses one or more extranuclear electrons, does it become another type of atom? What does it become? What is it called?

2-2. If an atom loses a proton in a nuclear reaction, what becomes of the atom? Does it also lose an electron? From what part of the atom does it lose an electron, if any? Does the atom become

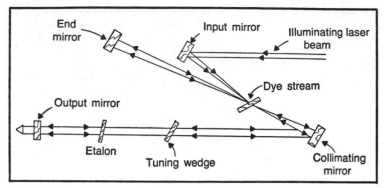

Fig. 2-4. Schematic diagram of a dye laser.

another atom of different atomic weight? Can this occur in a chemical laboratory routine reaction? Discuss.

2-3. What part of the atom characterizes its ability to enter into a chemical reaction? Do inert gases enter into any chemical reaction in ordinary chemical reactions? Why? Do the inert gases enter into a chemical reaction in an electric discharge tube? What types of elements can combine with inert gases? Is this combination stable? Discuss.

2-4. How does one obtain electricity from atoms? Describe one method by which electricity is produced. What constitutes electricity? What are positive charges in an electric field? Do positive charges move in an electric wire? Do positive charges move in an electrolytic solution? How fast can electrons move in a metallic electric conductor?

2-5. On what factor does the amount of electricity produced in an electric generator depend? What is an ampere? What is a volt? What is an ohm? What is a watt? What is a joule? What is a coulomb? What is power? What is energy? State the units by which an electric power can be expressed. State a unit by which electric energy is expressed. How do you convert power to energy units?

2-6. If a certain electric light bulb uses 150 watts at 1.5 amperes, what is the voltage of the current furnished to the electric bulb? What is the resistance of the light bulb? If the light bulb is operated for 20 seconds, how many joules are produced?

2-7. How is radiation emitted from atoms? In what different ways can one obtain radiation from atoms? What is that radiation? In a neon display tube, how does the light get its red color? Is light produced in the nucleus or in the extranuclear region? What structure or entity is responsible for emission of light?

2-8. What is a photon? Does it have any energy? If so, from where does it get that energy? Can a proton produce a photon? If two electrons are lost from a neutral atom in an electric discharge tube, what becomes of the atom? Can the atom in this condition move in the electric discharge tube? If it does, in what direction does it move? In what direction does the electron move? Does the electric current flow in the same direction as the electron or does it flow along the same direction as the ionized atoms?

2-9. What are gas lasers? Describe several of them. What is an excimer? How is an excimer formed? Is an excimer a chemically stable compound? What one factor is responsible for the production of stimulated radiation? What will that radiation be called? What is the difference between a stimulated radiation and a spontaneous radiation? Is the latter radiation a type of laser? Discuss.

2-10. What are mirrors used for in a gas discharge tube? Can external mirrors be used in a solid-state laser system? Can a solid-state lasing element be used without external mirrors? Explain how? How are the two mirrors in a resonant cavity constructed? From which end does the laser radiation project to the exterior of the laser tube? What causes the atoms in a gas discharge tube to become excited? Is an excited atom an ionized atom? Discuss.

2-11. When atoms are excited, what becomes of the extranuclear electrons? Do the extranuclear electrons radiate? From what source do the electrons in a discharge tube obtain their radiation energy? Can an applied voltage on an electric discharge tube containing an ionizable gas produce radiation? Is this radiation spontaneous or stimulated, if the tube contains no mirrors? Explain.

2-12. What is ionization potential? What is threshold potential? Which potential removes the electron from the atom? Which potential is responsible for the electron to radiate? Does the photon produced in this action have an energy equal to the applied voltage times the charge on the electron? Explain how energy transition occurs.

2-13. An electron in an electric discharge tube acquires an energy of $\frac{1}{2}mv^2$. If this electron collides with an atom and transfers its entire energy to the atom at ground state, what becomes of the energy if a quantum of light is produced in the tube? Discuss in terms of the energy absorbed and energy utilized in producing a quantum of light. What is the energy unit in this transition?

2-14. Under what energy condition can an ultraviolet light be produced? Visible light be produced? Infrared light be produced? If these lights were laser radiations, what two characteristics differentiate one light from the other? Which radiation will have the shortest wavelength? Why? Discuss.

2-15. What is a diode laser? How is it constructed? How does it operate? Compared with an average He-Ne laser output, how energetic is the radiation from a diode laser? In what spectral range does a GaAs diode laser operate? What is GaAs diode usually used for? Can GaAs operate continuously? Can it operate modulated? How? Explain.

2-16. What is an optical pump? What does it consist of? Is the radiation from the optical pump greater, equal, or smaller than the laser radiation it produces? Why? Discuss. Can the optical pump be operated in the pulsing mode? Can it be in the continuous-wave mode? What types of lasers can be produced by the continuous-wave type and by the pulsed operative type optical pumps? What is an F-center laser? Discuss.

2-17. In a liquid dye solution, how can one obtain laser radiation from it? Explain its operation. Can a dye laser be used for welding, drilling, and cutting metals? What type of laser radiation is the most suitable for metalworking? Why? Explain. What type of laser is best suited to fiberoptic communication work? Why is that laser which you named chosen for that operation? Explain.

2-18. An electron travelling in a discharge tube gains an energy of $\frac{1}{2}mv^2$ ergs and produces a photon of equal energy. If the frequency of the photon thus produced is 5×10^{14}, what is its wavelength? What is the velocity of the electron before radiation? Neglect any energy used as threshold.

2-19. Write an equation for wavelengths, when the mass of the electron and its velocity is given. Write an equation for wavelength when the applied voltage, threshold energy, and Planck's constant are given.

Chapter 3
Ionic and Molecular Laser Systems

By far the most widely used laser systems are those that contain an ionizable gas as an active medium. Among these gases are: helium, neon, argon, krypton, xenon, carbon dioxide, carbon monoxide, nitrogen, hydrogen, and combinations of these gases with other gaseous elements, such as fluorine, chlorine, and liquid bromine. The laser output from these gases varies from less than a milliwatt to kilowatts, depending on the type of gas used. Among the gas laser systems, helium-neon (He-Ne) combination possibly leads the others in number manufactured and of applications because of their ease of manufacture, relatively low cost, and safety of handling. A He-Ne emits in the visible at a principal wavelength of 6,328 angstroms, and harmonic wavelengths of 11,520 and 33,910 angstroms in the infrared range; the latter lasers are not as prevalent as the principal-wavelength version. Thousands of hours of operation can be achieved with He-Ne laser systems and, because of their narrow beam characteristics and intense red color which is easily visible to the eye, they have many applications in industry, the biomedical field, and in the research laboratory.

All lasers are polarized to some extent, either linearly or randomly. However, they can be polarized in any version desired by the use of optical elements, such as etalons, filters, fresnel mirrors, neutral polarizers, and other reflecting surfaces built into the laser system. Linearly polarized lasers are preferred when the beam is to be used in modulation of voice and data, in precision measurements, holography, and character recognition, because beam fluctuations are reduced to a minimum in a linearly polarized laser beam. The control of the beam is also relatively easy by the use of external polarizers or retarder elements. Of course, if the laser beam is to be applied in an alignment system, quality control work, or similar operations, polarization is not of special concern. The environmental operations of these systems vary between $-10°C$ to $+60°C$. The gaseous lasers are the most versatile systems that are used in the near ultraviolet, visible, and infrared regions of the electromagnetic spectrum.

The carbon dioxide laser is the leading contender of all the molecular lasers for commercial use. Two versions of the system are available: one version is a sealed-in gas tube and the other is a continuously flowing gas in traverse respect to the optical axis and at right angles to the electric field. Both types operate in continuous-wave or pulsed mode at TEM_{oo}, and emit from less than one millijoule to several kilojoules. The applications of the carbon dioxide lasers range from tunable spectroscopy to materials processing. The carbon monoxide (CO) also lases but its applications have remained in the laboratory thus far, possibly because of its toxicity.

ION LASER SYSTEMS

An ion laser system contains for its active element an ionized gas, such as neon, argon, krypton, xenon, and metal-vapor types such as helium-cadmium vapor, helium-selenium vapor, copper vapor, etc. These lasers generally operate at the TEM_{oo} mode, both pulsed and in continuous-wave modes; however, ion lasers generally sold on the market are argon or krypton, which can operate in both single-line and multiline modes, meaning one wavelength or more than one wavelength mode. Argon ion lasers emit the highest visible power levels in the multiline mode, within the spectral range of 4,550 to 5,145 angstroms, with power rating of 15 watts to more than 40 watts. Argon laser can also produce ultraviolet rays at 3,300 to 3,600 anstroms in doubly ionized transitions requiring higher input current levels than that for the visible multiline lasers in their commercial versions. Ion lasers are produced commercially by a number of companies, such as Coherent Corporation, Spectra-Physics, Lexel, American Laser Corporation, and others.

Krypton laser can produce wavelengths in the range from 3,300 angstroms in the ultraviolet to 7,990 angstroms in the near infrared at TEM_{oo} mode. In a mixture of argon and krypton, the laser can emit from 3,300 to 10,900 anstroms both in the TEM_{oo} mode and in multimode; the power output could range up to 5 watts. The krypton lasers have the ability to produce more laser power in the red spectrum than the He-Ne, ruby, and similar lasers, and the krypton discharge tube is only one-half as long as the He-Ne tube. Furthermore, krypton has the best performance of all. These lasers possess both amplitude and frequency stability dominant in low power ion lasers.

In Fig. 3-1, an ordinary neon discharge tube is shown in which the neon gas becomes ionized into positively charged neon ions and negatively charged electrons. The electrons move from the cathode to the anode, and the positive ions move from the anode to the cathode, the current flow being from the cathode to the anode. As the high voltage is applied across the discharge tube, the atoms in the neighborhood of the cathode become ionized by receiving energy from the incoming current. The extranuclear electrons in the atoms are the first ones to be isolated from the atoms, leaving the atoms charged positively. Thus, the ions move in opposite directions, and in their traverse along the tube they encounter other atoms and impart their energy to those atoms, exciting them to higher-energy states. As the atoms regain their original energy state, they give off photons with frequencies dependent on the energy transitions. As long as the high voltage is sustained across the tube, the process continues by the ionization of the atoms and the recombinations of the electrons with the positive ions. In doing so, the electrons are accelerated toward the ionic nucleus. An electron accelerated radially to the atom must radiate. This radiation is known as spontaneous radiation and no laser is produced.

If the electric discharge system shown in Fig. 3-1 is constructed so that its cathode and anode (electrodes) are made ringshaped and the ends of the tube are provided with mirrors facing

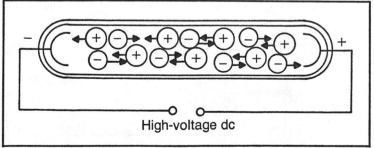

Fig. 3-1. A simplified diagram of a neon gas discharge tube.

each other in perfect parallelism, as illustrated in Fig. 3-2, then the emitted photons can oscillate from one mirror to the other. During this oscillation, the photons encounter excited atoms in the gaseous medium and transfer their energies to the electrons disrupted from the excited atoms, whereupon the electrons fall back to their stationary states in the atoms, radiating photos with energies significantly equal to the energies of the colliding photons. This action is known, in the literature, as population inversion; that is, it is a stimulated emission of radiation. This latter concept follows a precept which states that the photonic energy causes the atoms to acquire higher quantrum states from which they return to the ground state giving off stimulated radiation. The flaw in these two words (population inversion) is that it fails to explain how the atoms are excited to the higher energy quantum states. In any case, the explanation of a stimulated radiation is that there is a photonic energy transition to excited atoms which emit a radiation with wavelengths equal to the radiation energy of the transferring photons by a process of stimulation.

The mechanism of excitation and cumulative production of radiation from an active medium may be given by the expression:

$$N = N_o e^{ax} \qquad \textbf{(Equation 3-1)}$$

in which, N_o is the initial number of photons in the discharge tube, N is the cumulative number of photons produced after stimulation and amplification in the discharge tube, e is the base of the Napierian logarithms, a is the coefficient of ionization of the active-medium atoms, and x is the space traversed by the energy-transferring photons in the discharge tube.

The most vital part of an ion laser is its plasma tube. The design and quality of construction of this tube directly influences the performance and reliability of the laser system. The earlier plasma tubes were made of pyrex or quartz because of its hardness among

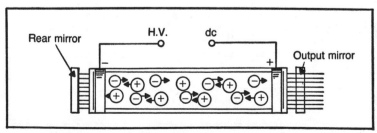

Fig. 3-2. Production of stimulated radiation.

glass materials. However, in course of time, the inside wall of the bore became eroded by the bombardment of the gaseous ions and the tube required frequent filling with the active gas because of leakage and heat preservation, although for low-power He-Ne lasers these problems have not been of much concern. However, for high-power gas tubes, such as a carbon dioxide laser tube, a new material, beryllium oxide (BeO) is used for the capillary bore of the tube in which the gas is in continuous motion. This material imparts high reliability and fail-safe performance of the laser by its being rugged and having high thermal conductivity. Thus, the heat dissipation is efficiently achieved, permitting the tube to operate relatively cool to retain laser emission efficiency. The beryllium-equipped laser plasma tubes have very low internal bore-surface erosion and the tube does not require refilling for as long a period as 10,000 hours or more of operation.

The plasma tube is mounted on a low thermal expansion (thermostable) resonator framework made of either quartz or Invar. Such a structure offers good optical stability of the beam, with power levels from milliwatt to kilowatts with low optical noise, which may run in the neighborhood of plus or minus 0.2 percent. Consequently, ion plasma laser systems have the capability of providing a diverse range of wavelengths and ease of control, at various combinations of power levels. There are a number of manufacturers of ion lasers, and among them are Hughes Aircraft, Spectra-Physics, Coherent Corporation, American Laser Corporation, Liconix Corporation, and many more. Liconix does further specialize in the manufacture of helium-cadmium lasers.

A standard He-Ne laser system manufactured by Hughes Aircraft Company is shown in Fig. 3-3, in which the power supply is a separate unit from the laserhead, which is the cylindrical black module. These lasers provide linearly polarized outputs; the HP series have a linear polarization ratio of 1000:1 and the LF and LC series have a ratio of 500:1. As stated earlier, the polarization characteristic of a plasma tube permits better control of the tube output intensity and its use with different types of modulators especially those for communication work.

One other important characteristic required of a plasma tube is low divergence, thus permitting the beam to travel long distances before the pencil narrow beam profile begins to expand. The Hughes laser beam begins with a beam waist at the exit port profile and gradually diverges dependent on the beam waist diameter; the larger beam waist diameter produces a slowly diverging beam at

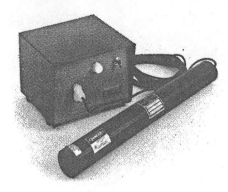

Fig. 3-3. Hughes He-Ne standard laser system (LF series).

long distances. An equation expressing the beam divergence versus distance prepared by Hughes for their He-Ne laser systems is given as:

$$d = d_o (1 + 6.492 \times 10^{-9} D^2/d_o^4)^{1/2} \quad \textbf{(Equation 3-2)}$$

where, d is the beam diameter at a distance D from the exit port, d_o is the diameter of the beam at the exit port or aperture. This equation applies to He-Ne lasers emitting at 6,328 angstroms. For carbon dioxide plasma lasers, the equation is slightly modified as:

$$d = d_o (1 + 1.82 \times 10^{-6} D^2/d_o^4)^{1/2} \quad \textbf{(Equation 3-3)}$$

Of course, to retain divergence to a minimum, a beam collimator could be used. A beam collimator usually expands the beam first to a desired diameter and then collimates the beam. For instance, if a beam expander has expanded the laser beam 10 times, then the collimated beam expands more slowly as it proceeds from the exit port. The graph drawn for Hughes lasers shown in Fig. 3-4 shows that for one type of collimator, Model 3970H used with the laser system Model 3076H, a very low beam divergence can be achieved.

The laser-beam divergence of any laser system is generally given in the manufacturer's technical bulletin, so that the diameter of the beam at any distance from the exit port can be calculated as follows:

$$d = S\phi + d_a \quad \textbf{(Equation 3-4)}$$

where, d is the diameter in centimeters of the diverged beam at the distance S in centimeters, ϕ is the beam divergence in radians, and d_a is the diameter of the optical aperture (beam exit port) in centimeters.

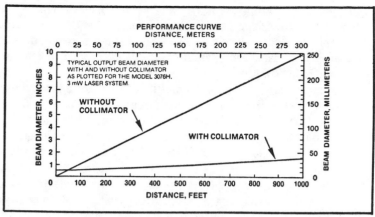

Fig. 3-4. Hughes He-NE laser performance curve.

Another ion laser, which is manufactured by Lexel Corporation, deserves our study because of its technological approach to advanced laser developments. These lasers include both argon and krypton types. They produce a variety of wavelengths at high-power levels, from ultraviolet, through visible, to near infrared portion of the electromagnetic spectrum. The argon lasers manufactured by Lexel have very high levels of visible radiation in the wavelength range of blue and green. As will be seen from Table 3-1, the argon laser emits a multiline spectrum from 5,145 angstroms to 4,579 angstroms, the most used wavelengths being from 5,145 angstroms in the green and 4,880 angstroms in the blue. By changing the resonant cavity mirrors, a radiation of 10,900 angstroms may

Table 3-1. Wavelengths Given in Percent of Total Power.*

Wavelength (Angstroms)	Percent of Total Power
5145	43
5017	5
4965	12
4880	20
4765	12
4579	8

* Taken from Lexel Corporation's product brochure.

be obtained from the system. When a current higher than the normal biasing current is impressed on the discharge tube, the argon atoms doubly ionize and produce ultraviolet rays in their stimulated transitions. A schematic representation of the laserhead in multiline operation is shown in Fig. 3-5.

An ion laser is inherently a multiline laser, since it contains in its beam spectrum multiple wavelengths in different proportions, as shown in Table 3-1. The radiation can be obtained either as a single beam or it can be separated into its component wavelengths by means of a prism located externally to the plasma tube. The feedback mirrors are aligned externally to the plasma tube; the rear reflector is 100 percent reflective while the output reflector (transmitter) is 35 to 50 percent transmissive, thus transmitting most of the stimulated emission to the exterior of the plasma tube. With a standard mirror coating, the argon output consists of six different discrete wavelengths, as given in Table 3-1.

Krypton ion lasers, on the other hand, can be made to emit wavelengths through the entire visible spectrum, the red wavelengths 6,471 and 6,764 angstroms being the most prominent and yielding the best radiation performance. The power rating of the krypton lasers are based on the 6,471 angstrom wavelength output, because at that wavelength the gas can produce the highest amount of red radiation from the plasma tube.

When a single-line monochromatic wavelength is required for a particular type of work, it will be best to select a single-line (single-frequency) beam using a prism between the Brewster window and the rear high reflector, shown in Fig. 3-6, since the power available to the outside of the plasma tube will be greater than when a single beam from the tube is separated externally into multilines.

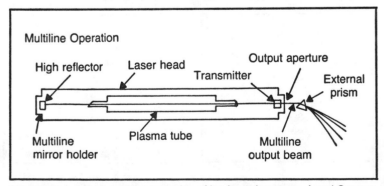

Fig. 3-5. Scheme of multiline operation of ion laser (courtesy - Lexel Corporation).

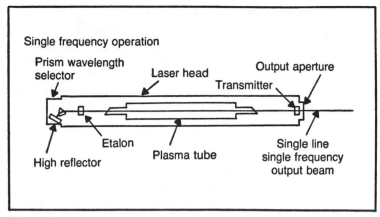

Fig. 3-6. Single-line plasma tube operation.

In the single-line operation, only one wavelength will be separated from the beam and will produce the lasing action. In this way, the wavelength selector prism will also permit the tuning of the entire laser beam wavelengths selectively. Both the argon and krypton lasers manufactured by Lexel operate in the fundamental mode of TEM_{oo} with Gaussian power distribution; this yields the smallest beam diameter and hence small beam divergence. The Gaussian laser beam is measured at $1/e^2$ power points which correspond to the diameter of an optical aperture stop that will transmit 86.5 percent of the laser power incident on the output mirror from the plasma tube. The Lexel ion lasers operate at nominal beam diameters of 0.9 to 1.3 millimeters, depending on the model. The beam divergence varies from 0.6 to 1.2 milliradians respectively from argon to krypton models. The beam polarization ratio is 100:1 in the vertical vector. The lasers are powered by 120 Vac and 240 Vac at 50/60 Hz and 3 phase, Y- or delta-connected, dependent on the model type.

MOLECULAR LASER SYSTEMS

Molecular laser systems are those whose active media are molecules. The active media comprise: carbon dioxide (CO_2), carbon monoxide (CO), ammonia (NH_3), deuterium-tritium (DT_2) and the like. The most commercially important of these lasers is the carbon dioxide laser. Although the name may imply that the gas is possibly pure CO_2 gas, for best efficiency of performance, the gas is used in combination with other gases. The mixture consists of 4.5 parts of CO_2 13.5 parts of nitrogen, and 82 parts of helium. The

51

mixture emits at the 10.640 angstrom wavelengths. Because a very high-power laser output can be obtained from the laser, it is used in industry for cutting, drilling, and welding thick metallic materials. It is also used in cutting textile and cloths, measuring atmospheric pollutants, spectroscopy of otherwise inaccessible spectral regions, and recently in atomic fusion experiments. For medical surgery work, carbon dioxide gas is the prime candidate for incising and coagulating various organic tissues, such as the stomach, liver, kidney, brain, or heart, because of its high compatibility of absorption by blood-forming or blood-transmitting vessels.

While ion lasers are excited axially to the optical resonant cavity, the CO_2 lasing elements find the greatest efficiency of emission in becoming excited transversely to the current flow in the discharge tube; the process is known as "transversely excited at atmospheric pressure" (TEA). The TEA CO_2 laser can be operated continuously and pulsed. In the pulsing mode, it can emit kilojoules of energy per pulse, and in the continuous mode, terawatts of peak power can be obtained from it. The TEA lasers can also optically pump other molecular gases such as N_2, CO, HF, N_2O, and excimer lasers such as HeF, KrF, ArF, ArBr, and the like.

Carbon dioxide lasers are produced in a sealed-in form or a continuously flowing as form, the latter emitting a more powerful laser beam than the former type, which is ordinarily used in the laboratory and for cutting thin sheets of plastic or metal foils. Because the flowing-gas-type laser operates at 10 atmospheres of pressure or higher, a continuous tuning of the laser beam for more than 2,000 different spectral wavelengths is possible. The power output of this system generally depends on the length of the discharge tube, and a power of 10 kilowatts per meter length is not unusual to achieve from routinely manufactured laser systems. up to 15 kilowatts per meter of discharge length has been reported by AVCO Everrett Corporation.

The Model 3038H has a minimum laser power output of 1 watt at a wavelength of 10,600 angstroms (Fig. 3-7). Its beam diameter is 1.4 millimeters and has a beam divergence of 10 milliradians. The beam is randomly polarized and has a lifetime of more than 500 hours. The system operates from a 117 Vac, 50/60 Hertz alternating current source. The applications for this laser system are: fusing optical fibers for communication cables, microdrilling holes and welding plastics, etching and marking thermoplastic materials and parts, and microelectronic device resistor trimming. Other applications include the use of the beam as an infrared beacon, in plasma diagnosis, medical surgery, optical radar, and spectroscopy.

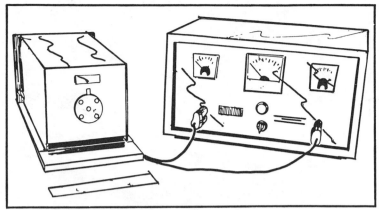

Fig. 3-7. Hughes waveguide CO_2 laser system Model 3038H.

Another versatile CO_2 sealed-off tube laser is one manufactured by Spectra-Physics, shown in Fig. 3-8. This system is suited to applications requiring a single line or tunable CO_2 laser. The active medium discharge cavity is made of fused quartz with zinc selenide (ZnSe) Brewster windows and feedback mirrors. The water-cooled sealed-off construction of the laser active cavity results in long-term stability of the optical frequency, unlike certain instability characteristics arising in systems having flowing gas CO_2 gas. The cavity length is adjusted to operate without regard to temperature fluctuations in the coolant.

The CO_2 laser system operates in single TEM_{00} mode, with the beam vertically polarized, at a wavelength of 10,600 angstroms nominal. The output powers of this model series range from 3 to 8 watts. The beam diameter is from nominal 4 to 5 millimeters for the higher-power laser tubes. The beam divergence is less than 4 milliradians for the nominal power systems and less than 3.5 milliradians for the high-power systems. The optical cavity length for the lower-power systems is 45 centimeters and for higher-power lasers it is 77 centimeters. By tuning one version, Model C950, over the 150 megahertz linewidth, the Doppler shifts corresponding to moving target speeds of up to 0.5 kilometer/second can be measured, according to the manufacturer. The cooling requirements for this series is flowing water at ¼ gallons/minute, the power supply for the lower laser-power systems furnishes 300 watts from a 115 Vac, 50/60 Hz alternating current source. For the higher-power systems, the power requirement is 600 watts, 115 Vac, 50/60 Hz.

The applications for the Model C900H series include heterodyne communications and measurements where good fre-

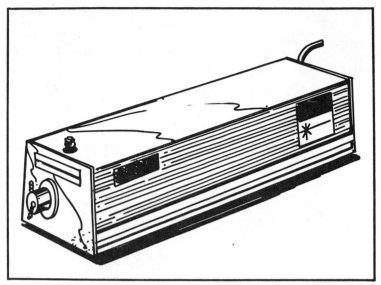

Fig. 3-8. Spectra-Physics series C900 CO_2 sealed-off tube laser.

quency stability is required, and atmospheric transmission and turbulence studies where tunability of the system can provide data at several wavelengths. It is also applicable to pollution monitoring and detection, which is achieved by the use of isotopes to match the particular absorption lines of gases emitting from 9-micron to 11.4-micron particulates, Doppler radar investigations, testing for deformity and distortion of optical surfaces in conjunction with interferometric techniques, and various other laboratory studies in the infrared spectra. The block diagram of Model C948, in the C900 series, is shown in Fig. 3-9. The diagram generally represents the working scheme of all C900 series systems, except those provided with optional accessories.

EXCIMER LASER SYSTEMS

Excimers are rare-gas halides which are stable in an excited state in an electric discharge tube and dissociate immediately after they have produced a radiation. Examples of excimers are: ArF, ArC1, KrF, KrC1, XeF, XeBr, etc. They usually emit in the ultraviolet with high intensity in the wavelength range between 1,930 angstroms for ArF and 3,540 anstroms for XeF. Other excimers emit between these two limits in general, although other wavelengths of other types of excimers are also reported, but they are commercially less important; an example of such an excimer is

NeF emitting at 1,080 angstroms, overlapping the longer x-ray wavelengths.

Excimer lasers are mixed in the electron discharge tube or just before being introduced into the discharge cavity. As the high voltage is applied across the tube, the gas plasma becomes excited and radiates. Subsequent to the emission of radiation, the gas is discharged into the atmosphere, contaminating the air at the flue. Provision is now being planned to recover the expelled gas for reuse. Because the halogen gas is chemically reactive, all inside wall surfaces of the container as well as the internal surfaces of the circulation conduits must be passivated to prevent reaction with the halogen gas. Fortunately, fluorine is now available commercially in a mixture of helium in the 1:20 radio; this mixture is then diluted to 0.2 percent fluorine in the excimer material. There are other mixtures, such as $Ar-Kr-NF_3$ in the ratio 1,300:130:1, respectively. The latter mixture has produced 1.5 joules at an efficiency of 15 percent. The excimer lasers operate either pulsed or continuously.

It is reported that KrF excimer laser developed by GTE Sylvania has produced 40 watts, emitting in the ultraviolet, and operating at a pulse repetition rate of 1 kilohertz. The gas flow proceeds under a pressure of 15 psi, and the laser system has achieved an efficiency of 0.4 percent; this is comparable with the efficiency of most excimer laser systems. A hydrogen thyratron firing at the leading end of the pulse provides the full energy of the pulse at the given rate. The applications of excimers include uranium enrichment, laser-induced photochemistry, isotope separation, optical pumping of tunable dye lasers, purifying silane (SiH_4) used in the production of solar cells, and possibly it may replace, in some future date, the current nitrogen laser pumps.

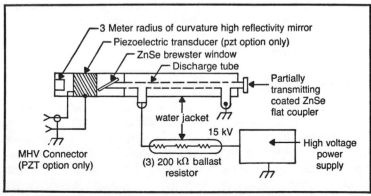

Fig. 3-9. Block diagram of Model C948 Spectra-Physics CO_2 laser system.

APPLICATIONS OF GAS-LASER SYSTEMS

While all gas lasers can be used for a variety of applications not having specific requirements, the lasers can be categorized to enable the reader to obtain a clearer understanding of the purpose and the capability of different general types of gas-laser systems. The applications given below are only representative and it should not be construed that the systems described in the ensuing sections are functionally confined to only the applications as given.

He-Ne Type Lasers

Because a He-Ne laser system produces a narrow, coherent, and intense ray of red light, its general applications include alignment of parts of a large mechanical system, alignment of structural beams, bridges, tunnels, and building sections. The beam can be used for civilian and military metrological measurements, such as measuring distances, surveying, areas to be enclosed by walls or other surroundings, and for aerial and fiberoptic communications.

Other applications include aerial pollution measurement and control systems, spectroscopy of certain chemicals, experiments in physics laboratories, and measurement of speed of light, and Doppler effect. Using krypton or a mixture of krypton and argon gases, underwater measurement and sea-level measurements are easily achieved. As radiant beams of high illumination and penetration, these systems are used in the study of shallow-water contents and ground characteristics. In biomedical work, argon laser is generally used in coagulating and "welding" bleeding organs, retinopathic surgery, removal of birthmarks, drilling minute holes in the tympanic wall for easing the internal pressure formed by ear infection and thus alleviating the pain due to pressure. The He-Ne laser is also used in directing the invisible infrared laser radiation to the area of treatment in various parts of the human body.

Molecular Lasers

The most important molecular laser is the carbon dioxide laser. The radiation from the CO_2 system is used in precision processing of industrial materials. The processing consists of cutting, drilling, and welding heavy metallic materials and parts; etching and marking thermoplastic materials, resistor trimming of microelectronic devices, optical radar and communications, and spectroscopy are also included in its applications. Other applications cover infrared beacons and scanners, Doppler measurements, medical surgery of benign and cancerous structures in the human body, removal of warts from the skin, and in general surgery of the profusely-bleeding body organs. In the dental field, the CO_2 laser has found much use in inhibiting caries in the enamel of the teeth by "brushing" the teeth with the laser beam before any disorder has set in. It is expected that in the near future, the laser beam will also be utilized in the drilling of surface enamel areas where incipiant caries are indicated for restorative work. It is also anticipated that some day in the near future, the carbon dioxide laser will be used for drilling through the gingival tissue of the teeth for the treatment of the root canal, where dental infection is set in. The process can lleviate the presently time-consuming and costly method of approaching the dental canan through the upper surface of the enamel of the infected tooth. Other applications of molecular lasers will be taken up with discussions of pertinent systems.

Control Laser's CO_2 Laser System

A powerful CO_2 system manufactured by Control Laser Corporation possesses certain unique features different from most conventional CO_2 lasers, as illustrated in Fig. 3-10. A mixture of CO_2 gas, nitrogen, and helium is mechanically pumped into the four-glass-tube discharge cavity impressed with a high voltage. The voltage energy raises the nitrogen atoms to a high-quantum state, motivating them to fast vibrations. The energy of the vibrating atoms is transferred to the vibrating CO_2 atoms, which are then

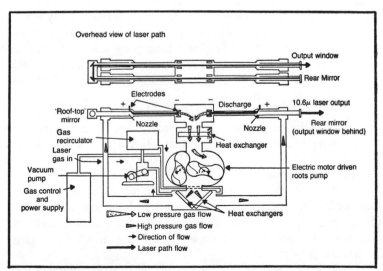

Fig. 3-10. The schematic diagram of the gas mixture flow through the CLC carbon dioxide laser.

excited to higher-quantum levels and upon relaxation emit a laser radiation at 106,000 angstroms and TEM_{oo} mode. Since some thermal energy is also released during the transition, it is conducted by the helium atoms to the heat exchangers provided in the system, as the gas tranverses the optical cavity.

The emitted photons from the CO_2 gas oscillate between the two feedback mirrors in the optical cavity and cumulatively produce additional photons of the same wavelength and phase as the exciting photons. The rear feedback mirror is curved and the output mirror is flat and transparent to infrared radiation. Since the discharge cavity is 7 meters long, it is folded to reduce the size of the laser system. The diameter of the beam emerging from the optical cavity is 17 millimeters at $1/e^2$ points and its divergence is 1.2 milliradians.

The lasing mixture is circulated through the optical cavity by means of a blower and is cooled by means of heat exchangers, which are in turn cooled by water flowing through them at a rate of 35 liters/minute and at a temperature of 20°C. During each circuit of the gas mixture through the system, a small amount of it is extracted and passed through a catalytic converter to partially recover the gases and then is fed back to the discharge cavity to conserve especially the costly helium gas.

The CO_2 laser system is powered by a 380 to 425 Vac, 3-phase, 50/60 Hertz, and 40 kVA power source. This produces a laser output power of 2 kilowatts Cw at maximum setting at the panel controls. The output power stability of the system is ± 5 percent. At this high power, the applications of the system cover all types of materials processing, such as cutting, drilling, and welding of metals, and high-speed cutting of quartz tubing and dieboards for the packaging industry. Materials processed by the CO_2 laser are not susceptible to warpage or heat-affected zones because of the high-speed of laser-processing.

Questions and Problems

3-1. Which lasers are the most widely used among ion lasers? Are all lasers polarized internally? What types of polarization can be achieved from lasers in general? How does one produce such a polarization? Discuss.

3-2. What are ion lasers? At what mode do they usually operate? In what special ranges do they emit radiation? What is the TEM_{oo} mode? In an electric discharge tube, what types of ions exist when a high voltage is impressed across the tube? In what direction do they move in the tube?

3-3. In an ion laser discharge tube, what is the design of the electrodes? Why? What are optical feedback elements in such a tube? How are the optical feedback elements constructed? What causes cumulative excitation of atoms in the discharge tube? What is optical cavity? Discuss two types.

3-4. If the initial number of photons in the ion laser tube is 10^{19}, the ionization coefficient of the atoms is 4.5 and the space travelled in the ionzation of the atoms is 4 centimeters, what will be the cumulative number of stimulated photons?

3-5. What type of capillary bore is used in a gas discharge tube? What causes the erosion in the capillary bore? Which bore material is thermoconductive? With what types of lasers is such a capillary bore used? On what type of resonator framework is the plasma tube mounted? Why is that particular type of framework used? Discuss. In what power range do the gas lasers operate?

3-6. Why is beam polarization preferred in a laser tube? What relation does polarization have on the control of laser power? How does one obtain low beam divergence from a gas laser tube? Why does a laser beam diverge as it leaves the exit port of the plasma tube? What measures are available to reduce beam divergence from a plasma tube? Discuss.

3-7. If the diameter of a He-Ne laser exit port is 2 millimeters, what will be the beam diameter of the laser beam at a target distance of 200 meters? Can the diameter of the beam at the target area be reduced by use of optical elements? If so, what optical elements can be used?

3-8. If the diameter of an optical aperture is 4 millimeters, and the diameter of the incident beam at the target 50 feet from the optical aperture is 10 millimeters, what is the beam divergence in radians?

3-9. What is a multiline operation in a plasma tube? How is it achieved? What types of gases are used to produce multiline emission in a plasma tube? What is the relative wavelength range from such a plasma tube? What can one achieve by changing the resonant-cavity mirrors in a plasma tube? Discuss.

3-10. How is a single-line operation achieved in a plasma tube? What is the advantage of a single-line operation over the multiline operation? At what points is a Gaussian laser beam waist measured? What percent laser does this relation represent? What is the polarization ratio in this plasma tube?

3-11. What is a molecular laser? What is the most commercially important molecular laser? Up to what maximum power can be achieved from this laser system? What is this type of laser used for? In medical work, for what type of tissue does this laser have better compatibility? What does TEA-type operation impart to the laser output? What type of gases do TEA lasers optically pump?

3-12. What are the applications of TEA lasers in industry and medical field? What is the purpose of using a flowing gas in a molecular laser? Can molecular lasers be tuned? If so, how? What is the purpose of the use of ZnSe Brewster windows and feedback mirrors? What is the advantage of a sealed-off CO_2 laser system over the flowing-gas-type system?

3-13. What are the applications of Spectra-Physics Model C900H series lasers? What advantage does it possess when applied to range-finder applications? How is air-pollution detection achieved with this type of laser system? What is the relation of the length of the optical cavity to the output laser power? Discuss.

3-14. What is an excimer laser? What range of wavelengths do excimer lasers emit? Give some examples of excimer lasers. Which one of these lasers has the most application in industry? How much power can be obtained from excimer lasers? What precautions are necessary in using excimer lasers? Why? Discuss.

3-15. A certain electron in a plasma tube is travelling with a speed of 1.5×10^{10} centimeters per second. If this electron energy is completely converted into a photonic energy, what will be the frequency of the photon? What will be the wavelength of this photonic radiation? In what spectral range will this photon radiate?

3-16. What is the difference between a spontaneous emission of radiation and stimulated emission of radiation? How does each of these radiations occur in a lasing medium? Does a laser beam contain both spontaneous and stimulated emissions? Explain.

3-17. What is the percentage content of the gases in a He-Ne laser tube? From what gas is laser radiation emitted in a He-Ne laser tube? What is the purpose of helium in a neon laser plasma? Draw an energy level diagram for a He-Ne laser mixture and explain the mechanism of laser emission.

3-18. Which of the lasing elements has four-level energy state? Is such a lasing element preferable over the three-level energy state laser? Discuss the advantages of one over the other. Give some applications for a He-Ne laser system. Give examples of important applications of molecular lasers. Which types of lasers can be utilized in medical instrumentations?

Chapter 4
Solid-State Laser Systems

A solid-state laser system contains, for its lasing element, a ruby, Nd-YAG, Nd-glass or the like. This category of lasers does not include the semiconductor diode lasers. Solid-state lasing elements are fabricated into solid cylinders of various lengths and diameters; for example, a nominal size of the laser rod would be about 8 millimeters in diameter and up to 80 millimeters long. The rods are optically transparent and the ends are cut flat and parallel to each other. The end surfaces are polished very highly and coated with a reflective material, such as silver, gold, or MgF_2. One end of the rod is 100 percent reflective and the other end is 40 to 50 percent light transmissive. These laser elements are optically pumped (illuminated) by a high-intensity flashlamp or krypton-arc or tungsten-halogen lamp. Certain of these lasers operate in the pulsed mode and others operate in both pulsed and continuous-wave modes. They are cooled either by air or tap water circulating through the laserhead, which includes the flashlamp.

In all solid-state laser elements, the excitation to emission occurs in the dopant, for instance, in the chromium dopant ions of ruby, and in neodymium ions in the YAG lasers. The energy of radiation from the flashlamp is at least equal or greater than the energy of the photons produced in the respective dopant. The excited atoms are raised to a higher than normal quantum state (energy state) from which they return to the ground state in steps, emitting photons of wavelengths characteristic of the dopant. The greater the energy applied to the dopant from the optical pump the greater is the intensity of the emitted radiation; this stimulating energy does not alter the frequency of the radiation from the particular dopant. Because the photons in the lasing cavity are produced by equal-energy photons, any two photons in the cavity are of the same phase, frequency, amplitude, and direction. When the energy from the optical pump is not sufficient to excite the dopant atoms to radiation, the energy in transition may dissipate in the form of heat or photons. This condition elevates the temperature of the laser rod; the elevated temperature in the rod tends to reduce the photon emission. To overcome this condition, the lasing rod is cooled either by circulation of air or by tap water through the laserhead.

RUBY LASER SYSTEMS

A ruby laser system consists of a ruby rod, a flashlamp which is housed together with the rod in the same container, a cooling system, and a power supply. A ruby rod is made of aluminum oxide (sapphire) containing about 0.05 percent chromium oxide, which provides the lasing action in the rod when illuminated with a flashlamp emitting at about 5,000 angstroms; the rod radiates principally at 6,943-angstrom wavelengths. Since the ruby rod has great affinity to absorb energy from blue-and-green wavelength light, and since xenon radiation contains these wavelengths, a close optical coupling between the ruby and the xenon flashlamp is achieved. The optical pump cavity, also known as the oscillator cavity, provides optical pump reflection from all sides of the container so that a relatively full energy from the optical pump can be absorbed by the ruby rod. The ruby rod, the flashlamp, and the feedback mirrored ends of the ruby rod constitute the optical resonator, in which the excited chromium ions produce the laser action. The photons thus produced oscillate between the mirrors for the amplification of the stimulated radiation. A schematic diagram of the operation of a ruby rod (solid-state laser) is shown in Chapter 1, Fig. 1-16.

It must be pointed out here that energy can never be created nor destroyed; it is only transferred from one form or state to another. Thus, an atom in a neutral ground state cannot do work; that is, it cannot radiate just by remaining at a neutral or ground state. The atom must gain energy externally in order to become activated to perform some function, such as to radiate. This activation may be achieved by thermal agitation, by an electric force, or by a light-radiation energy absorbed by the atom. When any one of these phenomena occurs, the atom gains energy and becomes excited. An excited atom must regain its original state by giving off the energy it gained. This energy may be used up by driving the excited atom from one position to another, such as in the electric discharge tube. Or, the energy of excitation may dissipate itself in the form of heat, or optical radiation from the atom.

In Fig. 4-1, a graphical representation is made to show the energy-transition states in an excited ruby atom located in an optical cavity. The ground level is denoted by L_1, the intermediate level is denoted by L_2, and the top level, which represents the energy state to which the atomic energy is raised is denoted by L_3. The xenon flashlamp emitting a blue-green illumination has raised the Cr^{+3} ions in the ruby to level L_3, from which the ionic energy returns to a metastable level L_2, giving off a red fluorescent emission, which is not a laser radiation. The energy state of the ion then makes a transition back to the ground state. This transition results in the stimulated emission of red radiation at 6,943 angstrom wavelength. As shown, the flashlamp radiation energy is greater than the energy emission from the ruby rod. This diagram is known as a three-level ion stimulation scheme.

One of the earliest solid-state laser systems manufactured by Hughes Aircraft Company is shown in Fig. 4-2, in which the first ruby laser system is improvised, by the author, to operate as a laser welder and driller. The system operates in the pulsing mode and emits 1.4 joules per pulse; only three or four pulses per minute were possible with the system, because of the time it took for the capacitors to fully charge. In spite of the slow pulsing rate, I have produced thousands of welds in Kovar sheets ranging in thicknesses from 1 mil to 3 mils. The equipment is cooled by circulating air from a pressurized cylinder at the rate of almost one-half cubic foot at a

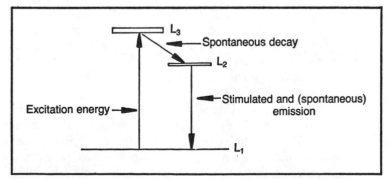

Fig. 4-1. Simplified energy transition levels from Cr^{+3} ions of ruby.

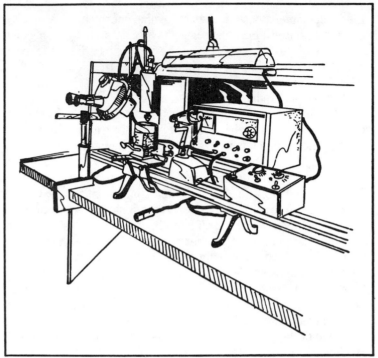

Fig. 4-2. The first ruby laser and power supply.

pressure of two atmospheres. In the drawing a binocular microscope is shown positioned in the anterior aspect of the laserhead mounted vertically on an iron stand. On the right, a timer is mounted on a 1-meter long optical bench for timing the charing of the capacitive network, and a heated platform on which some types of specimens could be heated to aid the laser welding of thicker materials is positioned directly below the exit port of the laserhead. A power supply with a voltage regulator is located on the right side of the laserhead. Although the system appears to be somewhat crude, many delicate operations could be performed with it, for example, welding of external leads to an integrated circuit chip. A simplified schematic circuit diagram simulating the circuit for this laser system is illustrated in Fig. 4-3.

It will be noted from Fig. 4-3 that the laser operates on 115-volt alternating current, whose voltage is amplified by the variable step-up transformer T and then applied across a rectifying bridge B, the output of which is fed to the variable capacitive RC network CN having branches 1, 2, 3, and 4. Each branch of the network could be made to provide a capacitive charge of 200 microfarads, so that if all the branches are closed, a total capacitance of 800 microfarads can be obtained from the system to energize the flashlamp. This particular circuit shows a water-cooling system to acquaint the reader how the water-cooling operates, whereas the system shown in Fig. 4-2 is aircooled.

To operate the laser system shown in Fig. 4-2, the cooling air is turned on and regulated to the desired pressure. Then the main switch (S) is closed and the voltage (V) in the pulse-forming RC network is regulated by means of the upper right-hand control knob to obtain the desired voltage (kilovoltage) as displayed on the square meter shown on the left. Before the first pulse is triggered, it was desirable with this equipment to let the system warm up for about a minute. The specimen to be welded or drilled is placed on the platform directly under the laserhead, and is positioned with respect to the focus of the converging lens located at the terminal portion of the laserhead, as shown.

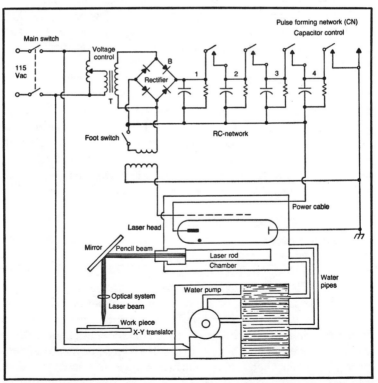

Fig. 4-3. A simplified schematic circuit diagram improvised for a laser welder.

The laser beam was focused by trial and error for the particular thickness of the specimen, by moving the laserhead up or down until a small dent was obtained when the laser was triggered by a hand-held switch. Later on, in the investigation, a lens holder was improvised from the empty tubing cap of a metallurgical polishing paste; in this cap, a lens of 10-millimeter focal length was disposed and cemented on its periphery. The lens holder then was inserted over the protruding exit port of the laserhead. In this arrangement, when the lens holder was rotated clockwise or counterclockwise, the lens within it could be respectively moved up or down for focusing the beam on the specimen.

The preceding description is given so that in the event an experimenter wants to set up a welding or drilling laser system, the parts are available from any electronic or scientific laboratory or store at a reasonable cost. The weld shown in Fig. 4-4 is made with the laser system shown in Fig. 4-2, indicating that regardless of the crudeness of the laser welding or drilling setup, one could obtain good work using personal prowess and manipulation technique. A BRH-approved pair of goggles should be used at all times. For experimental work, a laser system not to exceed 1-joule of energy should be used for purposes of safety if the experimenter is a beginner.

The cross-sectional view of a weld made with the laser system shown in Fig. 4-2 is given in Fig. 4-4. This view delineates the penetration of the beam into the lower layer of the two nickel sheets. The thicknesses were 3 mils each. The weld is sectioned at the middle of the nugget, polished, and etched with nital (nitric acid and alcohol mixture) to show the weld profile as well as the microstructural pattern. A 10-mm focal-length biconvex lens was used, with a laser energy of 1 joule at 4 millisecond duration.

ND-YAG AND ND-GLASS LASER SYSTEMS

As referenced earlier, meodymium-YAG is a laser rod having an active medium of trivalent neodymium ions (Nd^{+3}) in the host material, which is yttrium-aluminum-garnet of the purest quality obtainable. The content of Nd^{+3} in the host is about 3 percent, and possesses broad absorption bands for high efficiency of emission and for effective optical coupling with the pump energy from the flashlamp. Some authorities advocate the production of a high-frequency coherent emission from the YAG would be more efficient laser generation when it is produced at a lower frequency and then frequency-multiplied. Still others believe that rods of larger diame-

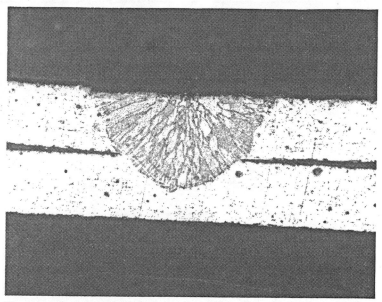

Fig. 4-4. Cross-sectional view of a laser weld.

ter and greater length will emit high output energy. However, when the latter scheme is used, the quality of the laser beam will be sacrificed. Furthermore, it is difficult to produce optically acceptable larger rods. Accordingly, the preferred method perhaps will be to start with the optically finest quality laser rod of standard size to eliminate oscillator-amplifier aids by use of additional laser rods.

The optical energy transmission from the optical pump to the Nd-YAG laser rod can be explained with four-level energy-transition states, in which the active medium is the trivalent neodymium ions (Nd^{+3}). These ions, when illuminated by a quartz-tube flashlamp or a tungsten-arc lamp, are raised to level L_4, shown in Fig. 4-5, because of the blue-green wavelengths of the xenon flashlamp being compatible with the neodymium ions and are easily absorbed by them. The excited neodymium ions cannot remain long at level L_4 state, and thus return in a few microsecond period to the next level L_3, the metastable level, in fast relaxation, from which they fall to the quantum-limiting level L_2, radiating a quantum of energy (photon) and then relaxing down to the ground level L_1.

As the energy transition to level L_3 occurs, a spontaneous emission of luminescent radiation takes place followed by both spontaneous and stimulated emissions between the levels L_3 and L_2. In the last transition, the dominant emission is the stimulated type

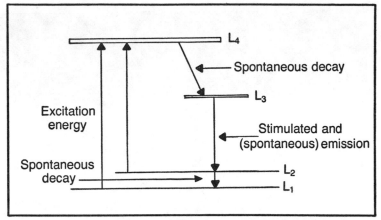

Fig. 4-5. Energy transition levels of Nd+3 ions.

which decays as the energy is transmuted to ground state at level L_1 in fast relaxation mode. The excited atom regains its original, neutral state, to be excited again for the next cycle. The process continues until the flashlamp illumination is cut off.

The dominant radiation from the Nd-YAG rod is in the infrared spectrum, at a wavelength of 10,600 angstroms. The power output of this laser ranges from less than 1 watt to 18 watts in the TEM_{oo} mode, and up to several hundred kilowatts/cm^2 peak power in the pulsed mode for nanosecond durations. The laser beam can be frequency-doubled, tripled, or quadrupuled using KDP crystals, respectively in wavelengths of 5,320, 3,540, and 2,660 angstroms.

The common method of optical configuration is TEM_{oo} mode, which produces a Gaussian output beam with low beam divergence; this mode gives the most uniform beam profile, with the exception that the energy that can be extracted from such a design is limited to the size of the rod. Increasing the rod volume has its limitations, too, that it gives rise to increased beam divergence. Thus, in order to achieve high power and low divergence from the Nd-YAG rod, it is necessary to cascade several rods together and to optically pump each rod separately, as will be discussed in a later section.

Nd-glass lasers operate only in the pulsing mode, as in ruby lasers, but the quality of the Nd-glass radiation is superior to Nd-YAG. Although the pulse repetition rate is slow, the energy achieved from it is equivalent to that from ruby laser. The laser rod emits principally at 10,600 angstroms in the infrared. Both a flashlamp and a krypton or a xenon-arc lamp can be used for optically pumping the glass rod.

Q-SWITCHING OF A LASER BEAM

A ruby or Nd-YAG laser may be equipped with a Q-switch. A Q-switch is an optical shutter used for increasing the peak power of the laser pulse with extremely short pulsewidth. The letter "Q" stands for "quality factor" of the resonant cavity. Q-switching may become necessary with some lasers in order to control the resonance in the optical cavity in such a way that the counteraction between the optical illumination and the laser action that exists in the cavity may be eliminated. During Q-switching, when the "shutter" is closed, the excited population of the atoms is in process of increasing cumulatively, and the atomic excitation in the optical cavity is made nonresonant during optical pumping of the lasing element; this action maximizes the population of the excited atoms at the high-energy level. When the Q-switch shutter is suddenly opened, the stored energy of the excited atoms at the high-energy levels become suddenly stimulated to emission in the shortest time (about a few nanoseconds). The stored energy then bursts out in a giant pulse from the laser element (rod) with a laser peak power in gigawatts/cm^2, in a time measured in nanoseconds. Such an action can also be achieved in other solid-state lasers, such as Nd-glass and similar rods. A method of Q-switching of a laser beam is illustrated in Fig. 4-6.

The laser storage time in the laser rod is equal to the round-trip time of the laser light within the rod; this time is equal to $c/2L$, in which c is the speed of light and L is the length of the cavity; in this case, it is equal to the length of the ruby rod. If external mirrors are used, then L will be equal to the distance of separation between the two mirrors. This mode of operation provides laser pulses of less than 0.1-microsecond duration at pulse repetition rates up to 10,000 hertz. There are other ways of accomplishing the Q-switching action or cavity dumping, but I prefer the method described, because the Kerr cell is easily available at most physics laboratories and the cost of the Q-switch setup is reasonable.

The Nd-YAG or Nd-glass lasing elements provide the highest output of laser radiation among solid-state lasers at room temperature, the amount of emission being dependent on the efficiency of coupling of the optical-pump illumination with the Nd^{+3} ions. The effectiveness of the optical pumping is a function of the active surface area, which is determined by the geometry, size, and the purity of the rod material. The directionality or coherence of the emission from the active element is also a function, to some extent of the resonant cavity. While increasing the length or the diameter

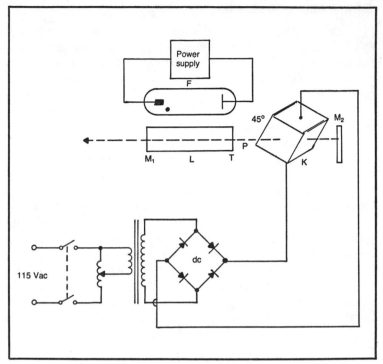

Fig. 4-6. Q-switching a laser beam, using a Kerr cell.

of the laser rod can increase the emission, the scheme has the limitations as determined by the following factors:

■ The optical-pump heat concentrates at the center of the rod and limits the emission.

■ The central portion of the rod with the elevated temperature may also produce a series of lens effects which retard the pumping effect and reduce the radiation emission.

■ When the rod length exceeds a certain threshold, a condition of spontaneous avalanche of photons occurs erratically which adversely affects the directivity of the emitted radiation from the rod.

■ The metastable quantum state can only function while the thermal effects have not reached the core of the rod; in the event they reach the core, the condition distorts the optical path.

■ An attempt to increase the emission from the rod by increased geometrical size and configuration may lead to the cracking of the rod, unless proper cooling measures have been taken.

Thus, the preceding limitations should be overcome before the oscillator material can be used as an amplifier.

ALEXANDRITE VIBRONIC LASERS

The energy of stimulated emission generally occurs in the form of photons. One of the first solid-state lasers that radiated with photon emission is the ruby. Akin to ruby, recently a new type of laser source has been developed and classified as solid-state vibronic laser, commercially known as alexandrite laser. The radiation from this laser is due to *vibrational quanta*, known as *phonons*, and is intimately related to photonic emission. This phenomenon, first put in practice by Bell Laboratories in 1963, was accomplished by the use of nickel-doped magnesium fluoride ($Ni:MgF_2$). Further developments of the laser material employed cobalt or vanadium as the dopant material in hosts of MnF_2, ZnF_2, $KMgF_2$, etc. These lasers were optically pumped by flashlamps and operated at cryogenic temperatures.

In 1973, Allied Corporation of Warren, New Jersey, developed a chromium-doped beryllium-aluminum oxide ($BeAl_2O_4$) lasing material, which was called alexandrite to operate at room temperature. This material emitted 6,804-angstrom-wavelength red light, but unfortunately did not find much commercial use. The threshold pumping intensity was relatively low and was found to be a function of the reflectivity of the feedback mirrors. Further investigation by Allied Corporation resulted in a longer-wavelength laser material emitting at 7,260 angstroms. Thus, a new vibronic lasing material (alexandrite) was on its way to a successful commercial application.

Concurrently with the above achievement, the Lincoln Laboratory of MIT reported the development of $Co:MgF_2$ laser, which could be tuned from 16,300 to 20,800 angstrom range. Later, using cerium-doped YLF($LiYF_4$) the laboratory team produced 3,250-angstrom radiation by optically pumping the crystal with 2,490-angstrom illumination from a krypton fluoride laser.

The Allied alexandrite can operate similar to the three-level transition ruby and as a four-level, tunable, vibronic laser at low pumping threshold. It emits a 6,804-angstrom-wavelength radiation at room temperature. As the temperature is increased, the effective emission cross-section increases and the terminal level population makes a transition with shortest wavelength photons, as shown in Fig. 4-7, which depicts the laser emission is the maximum with high initial-level population and minimum with low terminal-level population. Thus, with an increase in temperature of the lasing crystal, the performance will be enhanced for wavelengths exceeding 7,300 angstroms between the red and infrared spectral range.

The chromium content in alexandrite varies from 0.01 to 0.4

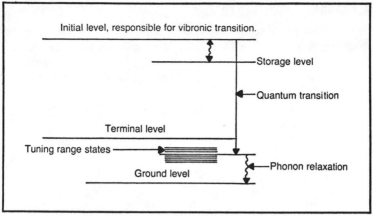

Fig. 4-7. Chromium quantum-energy levels in Alexandrite crystal.

percent, in which a percentage of 0.1 is equivalent to 3.51×10^{10} chromium ions per cubic centimeter of the crystal. The dimensions of the rod range from 5 to 9 millimeters in diameter and 8 to 10 centimeters in length. The rod can operate either Q-switched or pulsed in the stimulated state and in the continuous-wave mode in the vibronic format. In pulsed mode, it can operate either as a 3-level or 4-level laser, and in the continuous mode it operates as a 4-level vibronic device. The material has best performance when pumped with a laser-light source.

The radition from alexandrite can be frequency-doubled with angle-tuned KD*P to operate in the ultraviolet region of the optical spectrum, at which point it can be continuously tuned between 3,600 and 4,100 angstrom wavelengths. Both ruby and alexandrite have similar continuous-wave thresholds; however, in alexandrite the emission power increases as the optical power is increased because of its vibronic kinetics, unlike ruby.

LASER ENERGY AMPLIFICATION

Several methods of amplifying the laser beam are available. They are: Removal of the central portion of the rod by drilling it out so that the concentrated heat at the center can be carried away by circulation of air or deionized water. However, drilling a bore through the rod is a very time-consuming and costly procedure. Rods with square cross-sectional dimensions are also produced which have reduced the thermal effects, lens effect in the center of the rod, and have afforded a large exposure area to the optical-pump illumination. The drawback to such rods has been the difficulty to obtain optically flat and parallel surfaces with homogeneous rod material. Thus, it would seem that the ideal lasing element for producing amplification of the laser beam would be one that would eliminate principally the thermal effects, lens effects, and would be easily compatible with the optical-pump radiation. Such characteristics have been obtained by the use of thin lasing plates arranged parallel to each other at Brewster angles to reduce extraneous reflections, as shown in Fig. 4-8, or in a zigzag manner at 45° angles with respect to the axis of the optical beam, as shown in Fig. 4-9.

In the configuration shown in Fig. 4-8, the plates are arranged at a 57° to 60° angle, known as the Brewster angle, between the parallel mirrors M_1 and M_2. The mirror M_1 is fully reflective and mirror M_2 is coated only partially to permit the transmission of the amplified laser beam to the exterior of the resonant cavity. The laser disks are made of silicon glass containing 3 percent neodymium. The two flashlamps L_1 and L_2 furnish the pumping illumination in the internally reflective oval housing H. For the pulsed mode, the flashlamps are xenon type and for the continuous-wave mode krypton- or xenon-arc lamps are used. The system in Fig. 4-8 can be cascaded to produce cumulative amplification.

The oscillator-amplifier design shown in Fig. 4-9 has oval lasing disks arranged in zigzag manner at 45° angles with respect to the optical axis of the amplifier. This design does not eliminate interface reflection losses. However, it has the advantage of utiliz-

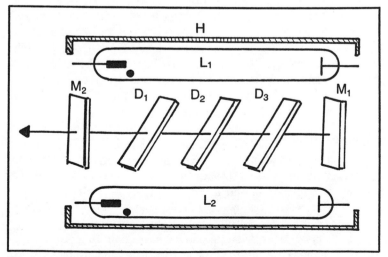

Fig. 4-8. Laser disks arranged in parallel and at Brewster angles.

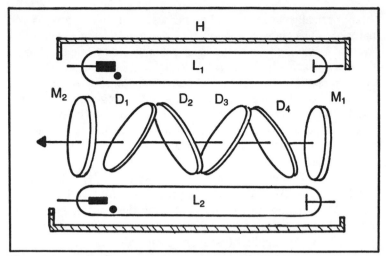

Fig. 4-9. Laser disk amplifiers arranged in zigzag patterns.

ing the secondary emissions cumulatively in the Fabry-Perot or resonant cavity. The lasing elements are included in an oval resonant cavity to utilize all the reflections from the walls of the reflective housing H.

Possibly the best arrangement among the oscillator-amplifiers is the one developed by International Laser Systems, Inc. In this oscillator-amplifier configuration, the laser amplifiers are of modular type, so that several modules can be cascaded with the basic oscillator-amplifier system to obtain a large output power. The basic system, shown in Fig. 4-10 consists of a Nd-YAG laser rod having a diameter of 6.3 millimeters and length of 57 millimeters; the oscillator-amplifier is immersed in a liquid-filled, close-coupled, optical pump cavity. The laser rod is illuminated by means of a flashlamp, and the optical feedback is accomplished by means of a rear spherical mirror coated 100 percent for full reflection and an output mirror coated for 50 percent transmission. A frequency double (KDP) Pockels cell disposed between the rear mirror and the Nd-YAG rod doubles the frequency of the rod emission, emitting a green light at 5,320 angstroms. The latter light makes an efficient optical pump for raising the excited Nd^{-3} ions to beyond the threshold frequency of the laser system. A dielectric polarizer located betwen the Pockels cell and the laser rod linearly polarizes the laser before it exits from the system.

The basic laser system shown in Fig. 4-10 operates Q-switched at pulse repetition rates of up to 20 pps and produces 0.1 to

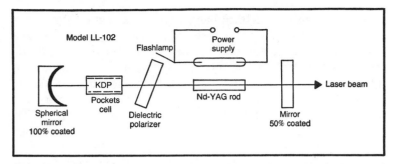

Fig. 4-10. The basic oscillator-amplifier system manufactured by International Laser Systems Incorporated.

1.2 joules per pulse. When the basic system is cascaded with Nd-YAG amplifiers, shown in Fig. 4-11, the capability of the amplifier increases to 2 joules per pulse at 10 pps. Various wavelengths, from infrared to ultraviolet, can be obtained from the cascaded configuration by adding other optical elements, such as prisms or etalons. With the use of a beam expander, up to 200 millijoules per pulse TEM_{oo} at 10,600 angstroms can be achieved, or in a frequency-doubled operation, up to 60 millijoules per pulse at TEM_{oo} mode can be obtained. This system is operable at a high repetition rate of 400 pps and at low insertion loss. The extinction ratio is 100:1, that is, the ratio of the transmitted light when a modulator is "on" to that when it is "off". Some of the applications of the system are: holography, high-speed photography, timing chemical reactions, and investigations requiring precisely-controlled coherent laser pulses.

PULSED ND-YAG-AMPLIFIED LASER SYSTEM

For obtaining the highest possible power from a Nd-YAG laser in a single unit, the Control Laser Corporation (CLC) has developed an oscillator-amplifier laser system, Model 438, generating 400-

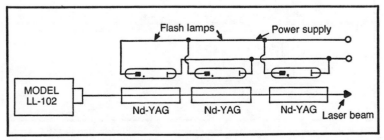

Fig. 4-11. ILS cascaded oscillator-amplifier.

watt laser radiation at 10,640-angstrom wavelength. Operating in pulsed mode, the system is capable of producing 29 joules/pulse at 0.65-millisecond pulsewidth, with a pulse-repetition rate of 100 pulses per second. The diameter of the output beam is 10 millimeters and the beam has a divergence of 10 milliradians. Each of the laser oscillator-amplifier heads is optically pumped with a krypton-arc flashlamp, whose lifetime is 10^6 pulses at the rated energy. The schematic diagram of the optical train with the amplifier is illustrated in Fig. 4-12.

The optical subsystems of the Model 438 Nd-YAG laser system are arranged in the optical axis of the laser beam and are sequentially mounted on an optical rail. The laser resonator consists of a Nd-YAG oscillator having a rear mirror of 100 percent reflectivity and a front mirror of infrared-transparent glass of partial transmissibility. A shutter is located between each mirror and the laserhead. Following the front mirror is a laser-beam amplifier similar to the laser oscillator, and is followed by a mechanical shutter. Both the oscillator and the amplifer heads are optically pumped by two krypton flashlamps. Each of the laserheads is enclosed together with its respective flashlamp in an elliptical cavity plated with nickel-gold for maximum reflectivity and durability.

The output power of the oscillator is fed to the Nd-YAG amplifier, which doubles the output to 400 watts CW. The radiation passes through a mechanical shutter, expanded in the upcollimator, and then is made to impinge on a dichroic mirror positioned at 45° with respect to the optical axis of the beam. The reflected beam

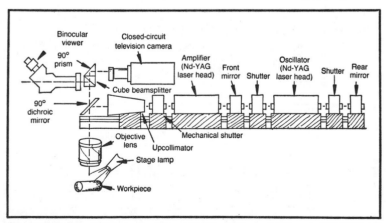

Fig. 4-12. Schematic diagram of the optical train for double-headed CLC Model 438 Nd-YAG laser system.

from this mirror becomes incident on a focusing lens which focuses the beam on the workpiece.

The light from the stage illuminator reflects from the specimen and passes through the dichroic mirror to impinge on the cube prism, which splits and reflects a portion of the reflected beam to the binocular viewer and the remainder to the closed-circuit television camera. The specimen and the incident light beam are displayed on the television screen.

The laser system is powered by a 22-Vac, 3-phase, and 45 kVA power source, and is provided with a high-voltage pulse-forming network charged through two silicon-controlled rectifiers (SCR), one at each high- and low-side of the line. They operate alternatively and produce a total of 18 kHz sawtooth wave. The SCRs automatically regulate the line voltage, so that a uniform laser power can be obtained. The optical cavity is cooled by water circulating through it at 15 gpm and at a maximum temperature of 80°F. The system applications cover cutting, drilling, welding, and heat-treating metals. The machine is also capable of cutting and drilling plastic materials and textiles.

BOOSTER-DISK AMPLIFIERS FOR FUSION WORK

At the Rochester Research Laboratory where atomic fusion research is being investigated, the researchers have produced energies in excess of 10^{10} joules/cm^3. The heat produced in the system plasma exceeds 1-million degrees kelvin, whereby the reaction gives rise to neutrons. The oscillator in this system is a modelocked tunable phosphate glass of high gain. The main amplifiers are 90-millimeter-diameter rods of maximum allowable lengths; they contain booster-disk-amplifier mirrors, as shown in Fig. 4-13. Each booster disk of the amplifier-oscillator is optically pumped from its back surface and the beam reflects from the rear mirror before exiting from its 170-mm-diameter aperture. The amplified laser beam emerging from this system proceeds to the next amplifier disk, which further amplifies the beam, so that the cumulative output of the entire system aggregates to 30 terawatts.

LASER FREQUENCY MULTIPLIERS

A laser-frequency multiplier is a harmonic generator which increases the frequency of the fundamental laser beam and proportionally shortens its wavelength. Solid-state lasers and dye lasers are frequently frequency-doubled, -tripled, or even -quadrupled by

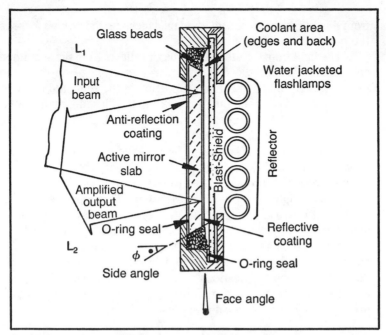

Fig. 4-13. Booster-disk amplifiers for atomic fusion work.

the use of nonlinear crystals, such as KDP (potassium dihydrogen phosphate), KD*P (potassium d-deuterium phosphate), lithium iodate, KPB (potassium pentaborate) and a number of other suitable crystals for optimum performance which are under consideration. For example, to double the frequency of the Nd-YAG laser of 10,640 angstrom wavelengths a crystal of KD*P is used which doubles the frequency and shortens the wavelength to one-half that of the fundamental radiation beam. The frequency-doubled wavelength is in the visible spectrum at 5,320 angstroms. If it is desired to obtain an even shorter wavelength, the harmonic wavelength 5,320 angstroms is shortened to 3,550 angstroms by the use of a second harmonic generator or frequency multiplier. The last wavelength is in the ultraviolet spectrum. Frequency multiplication is a direct function of input power. With dye lasers, a frequency conversion technique can extend the tuning capabilities of the laser system. The technique consists of frequency doubling the fundamental beam of the dye laser and mixing it with the primary beam (fundamental beam) to increase its energy, especially in the ultraviolet spectrum.

One manufacturer employs lithium iodate crystal, temperature-controlled in a temperature-stabilizing oven, to frequency-double the Nd-YAG laser beam. The crystal is angle-tuned and is disposed within the temperature-controlled oven, which is located in the optical axis of the fundamental beam. This system attains efficiencies as high as 30 percent, while mixing a 10,640-angstrom beam from a Nd-YAG laser with a 5,600-angstrom beam from a rhodamine 6G dye laser beam has produced up to 40 percent efficiency, with an emission of 30 millijoules. Conversion efficiencies to cover between 2,000 angstroms (ultraviolet) to 7,000 angstroms (near infrared) have also been achieved by stimulated Raman scattering action in a high-pressure hydrogen cell.

Another company employs a CD*A crystal doubler, angle-tuned at 82°; this system produces 150 millijoules of green laser from Nd-YAG fundamental beam operating at 500 millijoules per pulse. The company reports that this crystal can be operated without a thermally-controlled oven. Other types of crystals are also manufactured for frequency multiplying. One of these types is KBS ($KB_5O_8.4H_2O$); it is used for phase-matched frequencies at 1,860 angstroms in the ultraviolet spectrum. Thus, complete systems for converting the frequencies of Nd-YAG, ruby, dye lasers and other lasers are available, using one of the optical pumps of Nd-YAG, excimer laser, and nitrogen laser. The harmonic lasers emitting at 5,320 and 3,550 angstroms are excellent optical pump sources for frequency multiplying dye lasers and for mixing with the dye laser output to generate both ultraviolet and near-infrared wavelengths. The use of fourth harmonic wavelengths (2,660 angstroms) will not be a reliable optical pump, but the scheme possesses the ability of producing copious ultraviolet radiation that can be used in medical treatment as well as biological investigative instrumentations. The sizes of the KD*P and KDP crystals are nominally 14-mm square and 25-mm long, housed in a temperature-controlled oven. These crystals are angle-tuned externally to the resonant cavity, using a thumbwheel.

Questions and Problems

4-1. What is a solid-state laser? Name several solid-state laser elements. What is a host material? What is a dopant? Give the percentage of dopant in ruby and that in Nd-YAG. Draw a diagram of energy transition states for ruby and for Nd-YAG.

4-2. What is the reflective material at the polished ends of the solid-state laser element? How are the solid-state lasers optically pumped? What optical pump is used for pulsing-mode operation? What optical pump is used for the continuous-wave mode operation? What is the reason for the choice for these optical pumping devices?

4-3. A certain lasing element receives an optical-pump illumination to excite the element below the threshold energy; what type of radiation is emitted from the element? The optical-pump energy is increased to above the threshold excitation energy; what type of radiation is emitted? Does the higher optical pumping energy produce higher frequency in a dopant? Does it produce higher intensity? Explain.

4-4. Explain why any two photons in the optical cavity are of the same phase, frequency, amplitude, and direction? What is a phonon? How is it produced in an optical cavity? What does an increase in phonons in the optical cavity give rise to? How does one overcome the condition of phonon increase in the optical cavity? Explain.

4-5. What wavelength of radiation is produced from a ruby laser? Approximately what wavelength must a flashlamp emit in order to stimulate the ruby rod to laser radiation? What does an oscillator cavity provide to the ruby rod? What do the polished and mirrored ends of the ruby contribute to the process of laser emission? Can energy be created? Can it be destroyed? Explain.

4-6. Draw a simplified diagram of a laser system operating in the pulsing mode and label the essential parts. What does artificial heat do to the specimen to be welded by a laser beam? How can one determine how much artificial heat would be necessary for a given weld condition? Does this situation also hold true for drilling a hole in the specimen? Explain.

4-7. Why should a laserhead containing the laser element and the flashlamp be cooled? What is the relationship of cooling a lasing element to its radiation emission property? Can a laser system be operated without artificial cooling? What type of laser system does not need any cooling? What type of laser system requires cooling? Explain.

4-8 .What types of laser systems can be operated in the Q-switched mode? What types of laser systems cannot be Q-switched? What does Q-switching mean? How is it produced? Draw a diagram of a simplified Q-switching system. Does Q-switching a laser beam increase its energy? Its power? What transformation occurs to the linewidth of the radiation?

4-9. What is the meaning of "laser storage time"? What is the significance of $c/2L$ with respect to the optical cavity?

4-10. What is a Nd-YAG rod? What does it contain for its active medium and at what percentage? What is the host material in this rod? How does Nd-YAG achieve effective optical coupling? What relation has the length of Nd-YAG have on the emission output from it? What will become of the quality of laser if the rod length is increased beyond a standard length? Explain.

4-11. In a four-level energy transition diagram, in what form does "fast relaxation" emission occur? What type of optical pump is used to raise the active element in the Nd-YAG rod to the top excitation level? At what state does emission of laser radiation occur in the diagram? Does the laser emission transition fall back to the ground state after emission of a photon or photons? Where does spontaneous emission on the curve occur?

4-12. What range of power output is achieved from a Nd-YAG rod when it is operating in the TEM_{00} mode? What does this mode produce with respect to divergence? How can one obtain a uniform beam profile? When the rod is operated in the pulsing mode, approximately what peak power can be expected from it? Increasing the length or the diameter of the Nd-YAG rod increases the power output from it, but what disadvantages are encountered in doing so?

4-13. List the disadvantages of an increase in rod diameter and length. How do you overcome these disadvantages? Give several examples. In overcoming the disadvantages listed, what other drawbacks become existent? How do you then ideally produce laser radiation from the rod in the most advantageous manner? Explain.

4-14. What is fundamental laser-beam amplification? What methods can be used in amplifying a laser beam? Which of the methods given in the text is the most effective way of amplifying a laser beam? Explain why? Are the amplifying elements made of the same material as that producing the fundamental laser beam? Could these elements be made of different types of lasing materials? Explain.

4-15. What is a frequency multiplier? How does it achieve the muliplication of the frequency? In a given single laser beam, how many times can it be frequency-multiplied? What becomes of the wavelength when the beam frequency is multiplied? Does the power of the beam increase? Does the energy of the beam increase? What are the applications of a frequency-multiplied laser beam? What is a harmonic generator?

4-16. What types of crystals are used to frequency-multiply a fundamental laser beam? Can all these crystals be used interchangeably for any given laser element? What is frequency-mixing? How does it differ from frequency-multiplication? Which of these two methods produces increased power? Is frequency multiplication a direct function of input energy? Explain. What are the two laser beams that enter into the process of frequency mixing?

4-17. What effect has frequency conversion technique on

tuning of the laser beam? What influence has the stimulated Raman scattering action on the conversion efficiencies of the beam? The use of a fourth harmonic laser pump energy increases what type of radiation in the electromagnetic spectrum? What are the nominal dimensions of frequency-doubling elements KDP and KD*P?

4-18. What are vibronic lasers? Is emission from vibronic lasers stimulated, vibrational, or both? What is alexandrite? Which firm discovered the vibronic lasers? Why were those lasers by the first discoverer not practical? At what temperature did they operate.

4-19. Which company discovered or developed the first practical vibronic laser? What was the composition of this laser? At what temperature did this material operate normally? What threshold pumping intensity did this product possess? Who developed 7,260-angstrom-wavelength vibronic radiation?

4-20. Can a vibronic laser be tuned? To what wavelengths can it be tuned, if such is possible? What optical gain can occur if the temperature of operation is increased in a vibronic laser? What is the chromium content of alexandrite? How does alexandrite differ from ruby, since both materials contain chromium in varied amounts? Can ruby be substituted for alexandrite? Discuss. Can alexandrite be frequency-multiplied? How? Discuss.

Chapter 5
Diode Laser Systems

Diode lasers are similar to semiconductor light-emitting diodes (LEDs), in that both types have n- and p-type active layers positioned together to form a pn junction at which the light is emitted. The difference of the two types is that a LED is electrically driven at low current level and emits an incoherent, visible light, while the laser diode is operated above the threshold current of the diode and emits a coherent laser light. Some diodes operate in the continuous-wave mode at 7,800 to 8,500 angstrom wavelengths and others operate in the pulsed mode at wavelengths between 8,000 and 9,050 angstroms. The diodes that operate at continuous-wave mode are ideal for communication purposes. The pulse diodes can be used for a variety of applications, and because they are unable to withstand continuous operation without becoming heated, they are usually manufactured with heat sinks for the dissipation of the excess heat.

The types of laser diodes that are in commercial use are: gallium arsenide (GaAs), gallium-aluminum-arsenide (GaALAs), gallium-aluminum-phosphide (GaALP), gallium-indium-aluminum-arsenide (GaInALAs) and others. The wavelength range of these diodes varies from 7,800 to 300,000 angstroms, although the diodes in the last wavelength range is not in common use, because they have to be cooled at liquid-nitrogen temperatures.

Diode laser are used in applications requiring portability, narrow bandwidth, and high efficiency. Among these applications are those for military service where high-power pulsed lasers are extensively used in electro-optical systems; these include missile guidance, fuzing, and weapon simulation such as training soldiers in the field. In commercial applications, GaAlAs diodes find many uses, such as optical scanning, pollution detection, fire detection, videodisk playing systems, rangefinders, and in aerial or fiberoptic communications. Because the diodes operate in the continuous-wave mode, they can be used to modulate high-frequency digital and analog systems.

STRUCTURE OF DIODE LASERS

There are a number of methods of fabricating GaAs diodes and their variations, each method being proprietary to the manufacturer of the diode. One of the simplest ways of constructing a diode is to sandwich GaAs active material between two layers of GaAlAs chips, and then to cleave the chip at the GaAs layer to form two perfectly smooth surfaces. These surfaces are then placed face to face at about 1 micron distance to configure a Fabry-Perot optical cavity. Since the index of refraction of the GaAlAs is smaller than that of GaAs, the latter achieves a 30 percent reflectivity to form the "end mirrors" of the active cavity. The union of the two surfaces is known as the pn junction, formed by p-active material with a hole concentration of 10^{19} holes per cubic centimeter, and an n-type active layer with a carrier concentration of 10^{18} carriers per cubic centimeter. The p-active side acts as a positive electrode and the n-active side acts as a negative electrode. When this junction is forward biased with a current through it, the current flows from the n-type layer to p-type layer and emits a light radiation. As the forward current is increased across the pn junction to exceed a threshold value (about 100 milliamperes ordinarily), the emission becomes a laser radiation.

The efficiency of a diode emission can be measured by the number of photons produced at the junction divided by the number of electrons that have passed the junction to produce the photons. Thus, the relation may be expressed as:

$$N_q = \frac{P_t}{hc/\lambda} \qquad \textbf{(Equation 5-1)}$$

where, N_q is the number of photons (quanta) produced, P_t is the total laser power emitted at the junction, h is Planck's constant equal to 6.625×10^{-34} joule-second (6.625×10^{-27} erg-second), c is the speed of light equal to about 3×10^{10} centimeters, and λ is the wavelength of the radiation in angstroms. In solving a problem with this equation, all linear quantities should be converted into centimeters.

The number of electrons N_e that pass the junction per second is given as:

$$N_e = \frac{I}{e} \qquad \text{(Equation 5-2)}$$

where, I is the current in amperes and e is the electron charge equal to 4.8×10^{-10} electrostatic unit.

The external efficiency of the quantum emission is the ratio of the number of photons produced to that of electrons that have passed the pn junction in the same period, and is given by:

$$Q_{eff} = \frac{N_q}{N_e} \qquad \text{(Equation 5-3)}$$

$$= \frac{P_t \times e \times \lambda}{hc \times I} \times 100 \qquad \text{(Equation 5-4)}$$

where, Q_{eff} is the external efficiency of the quantum emission, given in percentage.

Since the electrical power input to the diode is equal to $I \times V_i$, where V_i is the input voltage in volts, we may rewrite Equation 5-1 and obtain:

$$P_{eff} = \frac{I \, hc/e\lambda}{I \times V_i} \qquad \text{(Equation 5-5)}$$

where, P_{eff} is the power-utilization differential efficiency in the diode, and I/e is the rate of photon emission per second.

A schematic diagram of a diode laser is shown in Fig. 5-1 and the diode itself is shown in Fig. 5-2. As will be noted, the emitted beam is not collimated due to diffraction of the beam as it exits from the pn junction. In the active surface GaAlAs, the peak emission wavelength can be controlled by varying the proportion of aluminum in the active formula. Thus, in a diode, the elements forming it may be varied in concentration to produce a desired wavelength range. Because semiconductor diodes can be mass-produced by conventional methods, their low cost of manufacture makes the use of these diodes very attractive in many applications.

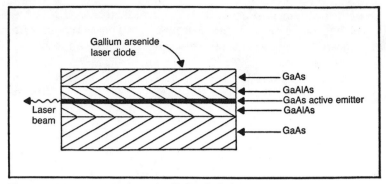

Fig. 5-1. Schematic diagram of a GaAs diode laser.

A diode laser with a GaInAsP active medium has been developed by the Mitsubishi Electric Corporation of Japan emits at a low threshold current of 20 milliamperes, yielding 3 to 5 milliwatts of laser power, depending on the method with which it has been fabricated. The crescent-configured active area of the diode is approximately 2 micrometers on a side and is inset in the InP as its cladding. As threshold current is exceeded, the output of the diode increases linearly up to 5 milliwatts. The device has a modulation bandwidth of 1 gigahertz, with a lifetime in excess of 1 million hours, as reported.

GENERAL CHARACTERISTICS OF A DIODE LASER

Table 5-1 gives some of the principal characteristics of a diode laser that are ordinarily required to be known before the incorporation of a diode in a particular system. There are other characteristics or parameters that also are important and they are given in the manufacturer's technical brochure for each diode.

DIODE LASER APPLICATIONS

The applications of diode lasers are numerous, therefore, only

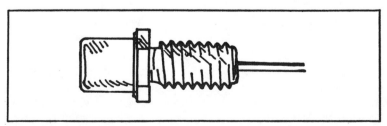

Fig. 5-2. A diode laser.

Table 5-1. Characteristics of Diode Lasers Chosen at Random.

Type of Diode	GaInAsP
Emission Wavelength	1.27 μm (12,700 angstroms)
Spectral Width	10 angstroms
Output Power	5 to 7 milliwatts
External Differential Efficiency	0.25 mW/mA
Threshold Current	100 mA
Forward Voltage @ 100 mA	1.3 volts
Reverse Voltage	2.0 volts
Beam Divergence	10 × 30 degrees
Operating Temperature	20° to 50°C
Risetime of Output	0.5 nanosecond
Forward Current	300 milliamperes
Storage Temperature	70°C max.

(This diode operates with a heat sink at temperatures as high as 55°C.)

a few important applications will be taken up. Since a laser system incorporating a diode laser can be made compact, small, and portable, the principal applications for such a device would be in a rangefinder for both industrial and military uses, a compact pollution-detection instrument that can be carried from one place to another for measuring the pollutants issuing from a factory, fire detectors for both homes and military installations, burgular-alarm detection systems, laser illuminators of targets, security surveillance systems,and above all for training soldiers in the field of marksmanship.

In the pollution-detection system, the technique consists of monitoring a long path in the atmosphere through which the laser beam travels, integrating the pollution content along the entire path, and then displaying the pollution concentration at the ambient conditions. As the beam is projected, a portion of it is sampled (reference beam) by a small computer located in the system and this beam intensity is compared with the intensity of the beam after having been absorbed partially by the pollutants in the atmosphere. An energy integrator in the system compares the returned beam with the reference beam as sampled and produces an error signal. This signal is converted into a direct readout of the pollutant concentration in the path of the laser beam. By this scheme, pollutant concentrations as small as one part per billion can be determined.

Another firm manufactures a system which identifies and measures the quantity of the pollutant expelled into the atmosphere from the factory stacks. The detector system consists of a transmitter provided with a lithium niobate crystal emitting a narrow laser beam. The beam is projected to the pollutant particles and retroreflected to a telescope mounted on the pollution-detection system. The retroreflected beam is fed into a computerized analyzer, which both analyzes and measures the pollutant content. The analyzer can separate the pollutant content into its different constituents that make up the pollution and can tune to the particular pollutant for measurement of its concentration. It is reported that the Environmental Protection Agency has been using this system to monitor the effluents from different stacks of companies and to instruct them to take proper measures to correct the pollutant condition.

One other company has developed a road visibility sensor to be installed on roadways, highways, or long bridges to monitor the atmospheric visibility that may become diminished by dust, fog, snow, and smoke, all of which affect the view of the driver. The system comprises a transistor provided with a laser diode, which projects a modulated 1,000-hertz laser beam into a 1° beam and transmits it to a receiver located about 250 feet away, with its detector system facing the transmitter beam. The laser diode uses about 5 watts of its rated 25-watt power, which is stabilized by the power monitor. The system is adapted to furnish compensatory power as the device ages. The modulated laser pulses are projected to the receiver, whose lens forms a 1.5° field of view, and an optical filter blocks out the background noise (radiation) from the pin-diode photodetector.

The pulsed laser beam from the transmitter is divided into two channels. One of the channels receives an amplified laser signal with a gain of 50, the other receives the remaining part of the laser signal without amplification. The high-gain portion of the detector responds to weak signals corresponding to severe humidity and for conditions of the road. The two signals are fed parallel to a visibility level detector, from which they are fed to the logic circuit for further processing and displaying the visibility levels.

A guidance cane for use by the blind consists of a set of GaAs diode lasers which are designed to warn the blind user of any hazard he might encounter ahead of him has been developed by Bionic Instruments, Inc. The cane is provided with a transmitter near its crook section and contains three infrared laser diodes connected in series with each other. The diodes act as three light probes, respectively projecting a beam forward, downward, and upward. The reflected beams from objects ahead of the blind are detected by three respective photodiodes located in the receiving circuit about nine inches below the transmitter. The information received through the beam from each direction stimulates the blind to take proper action. For example, when there is an object ahead of the blind user a poking signal is sensed by his fingers, and an auditory tone signal informs the user that there is an object either below or above the projected beam. The diode emits 100-nanosecond pulses at 9,000-angstroms at a rate of 40 pulses per second. The cane is about 50 inches long and the sensing circuit and the guidance system are battery-operated; the cane weighs about 1.5 pounds.

Gallium arsenide laser diodes have found another use in correcting errors on a typewritten paper. The device was developed and patented by myself and consists of a hand-held stylus and a power supply, which readily mounts on a side of the typewriter. The stylus has a coniform erasing head with an aperture for the exit of the laser beam, which is produced by an array of gallium arsenide diodes epitaxially formed on a chip. A beam integrating element directs the laser beam on a planoconvex lens which focuses the beam within the coniform stylus head. The diverging beam from the focus passes through the aperture of the stylus to its exterior divergently. The diameter of the aperture is such that the divergent beam passing through it just covers a typewriter-type size area.

For correcting an error character, the tip of the stylus is placed perpendicularly on the character and a pulse of about 1-joule laser is triggered on the character either automatically or by the use of a thumb switch at the end opposite to the exit aperture. One pulse is sufficient to remove the character. The reason the character does not burn is that by diverging the beam from the focus its intensity is reduced just enough to oxidize the black typewritten character. The use of the diverging beam has dual functions—one for complete coverage of the error character and the second is for safety purposes, because as the beam diverges from the exit port its intensity is reduced as the square of the distance from the focus. A beam-to-character relation is given as:

$$d = \frac{D \times s}{S}$$ (Equation 5-6)

where, d is the diameter of the incident beam on the error character, D is the diameter of the lens optical plane, s is the distance between the laser-beam focus in the coniform section and the tip or exit aperture of the stylus, and S is the distance between the optical plane of the lens and the laser-beam focus, as illustrated in Fig. 5-3.

The diameter d of the laser beam can be adjusted internally within the coniform section by the use of a small screwdriver to move the lens holder within the stylus forward or backward, so that

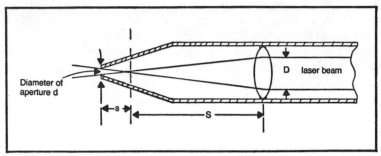

Fig. 5-3. Graphical representation of the laser beam within the stylus.

a smaller or a larger character can be respectively accommodated at the exit port of the device. Naturally, for different-size characters the laser beam energy must be adjusted from the power supply housing by the use of a knob located externally to the power-supply housing.

Questions and Problems

5-1. What is a diode laser? What is the difference between a diode laser and a LED? How is light emitted from a diode laser? From a LED? Give examples of diode lasers. At what wavelengths do cw diode lasers operate? At what wavelengths do pulsed diode lasers operate? What is the purpose of a heat sink?

5-2. In what applications are diode lasers used? What characteristics of diode lasers make them suitable to these applications? Are radiations from diode lasers visible? How does one know that a diode laser is emitting laser radiation? Is the radiation from a diode laser hazardous to the eye? Explain.

5-3. Describe the structure of a diode laser. What is a Fabry-Perot cavity? What is a p-type active layer? What is an n-type active layer? What is the hole concentration in a p-type active layer? What is the carrier concentration in an n-type active layer? What does increasing the voltage across a diode do to output laser power? Explain.

5-4. If the total laser power emitted from a pn junction is 2 watts and the wavelength of the emitted laser radiation is 9,000 angstrom, what is the number of photons produced in the emission?

5-5. A certain diode laser is forward biased with a current of 20 amperes, how many electrons have passed across the pn junction in 2 seconds? How many electrons would have passed across the junction if the current was reduced to one-half? If the current was sustained for 4 seconds, how many electrons would have passed across the pn junction?

5-6. Define the external efficiency of quantum emission. If 2 amperes have passed the pn junction for one second and 2×10^{16} photons have been produced during this period, what is the external quantum efficiency of the emission?

5-7. Is the emitted laser radiation from a diode laser collimated? In what form is it emitted? Explain. How can one control the peak emission wavelength in the active surface of GaAlAs? Prior to the incorporation of a diode laser in a given system, what characteristics of the diode should be known? How can you obtain these characteristics? Explain.

5-8. What is the approximate beam divergence of a diode laser? What is the range of emission wavelengths of GaAs diode laser? What is a threshold current of a diode laser? What is the threshold of GaAs? At what temperature range can a diode laser operate?

5-9. How can a diode laser be used in a fire detection system? How can it be used in a burglar alarm system? Show by a diagram, how can a diode laser be used in a security surveillance system?

5-10. What is a pollution-detection system? How is it constructed? How does it operate? Does such a system require a retroreflective mirror? Can it be used without a retroreflective mirror? If so, how? Explain how the concentration of pollution in the atmosphere can be measured. What is lithium niobate used for with respect to pollution-detection system?

5-11. Describe the operation of the ILS pollution-detection system which is designed to operate on roadways. How far is the detection effective in this system? What type of photodetector does this system use? What section of the detector system is used for severe humidity and fog conditions?

5-12. What is a guidance cane for a blind? How does it operate in use? What is a laser eraser? Generally speaking, how is it constructed? How does it operate? Why does it not use the focus of the beam for removing the error character? What safety features does it possess?

5-13. A certain laser eraser has a lens with a principal plane of 8 millimeters, a focal length of 12 millimeters, and the distance between the focus of the beam and the exit port and the stylus is 0.6 centimeters, what is the diameter of the beam at the exit port? Give the answer in millimeters.

Chapter 6
Liquid Dye Lasers

Although powerful and coherent lasers were in existence for some-time and some of them could be tuned a small range, it was not until the dye laser was developed that the tunability of the laser through the broadest spectral range was enhanced, especially in the visible region of the electromagnetic radiation. In a dye laser, the active medium is an organic dye in solution, and it is optically pumped by a flashlamp, Nd-YAG laser, excimer laser, nitrogen laser, broadband dye ions, or by radiation from the harmonic beams of a solid-state laser. Lasing action occurs by the absorption of the radiant light by the excited dye molecules and resulting in the emission of radiation characteristic of the particular dye lattice structure.

Dye lasers are produced in two modes of operation—in con-tinuous wave mode and pulsed mode. The continuous-wave (cw) dye lasers are optically pumped by an ion laser, such as an argon or krypton laser, while the pulsed dye lasers are pumped by Nd-YAG laser, excimer laser, nitrogen laser, or by a coaxial flashlamp. It is possible to obtain higher laser-output radiation with pulsed lasers than with cw dye lasers. Thus, a broad range of laser wavelengths can be obtained from the pulsed lasers, by using various optical elements in the path of the emitted laser beam; such elements are an etalon, prism, birefringent filter, and the like. Pulsed dye lasers can also be frequency-multiplied because of their high output laser power. On the other hand, the cw dye lasers are commercially useful because of their having narrower linewidths and high stability than pulsed laser wavelengths. The applications of dye lasers include holographic data storage, spectroscopic studies, initiation of chemical reactions, materials research, dissociation of chemical bonds, isotope separation, and as sources of ultraviolet radiation for medical and dental treatments.

CONSTRUCTION OF DYE LASER SYSTEMS

The following information covers both continuous-wave and pulsed dye lasers.

Continuous-Wave Dye Laser

A cw dye laser system consists of a capillary tube (T), Fig. 6-1, containing a flowing dye solution (L), which is illuminated by an argon ion laser flashlamp (F) energized by a high-voltage power supply (HV). One end (M_1) of the capillary tube is 100 percent reflective and the other end is provided with a Brewster window (B). The resonant cavity is completed by means of the output mirror (M_2) which is 40 to 50 percent transmissive. An etalon (E) is positioned between the output mirror (M_2) and the Brewster window (B), for tuning the laser beam. The dye solution is continuously pumped by the electric pump (P), through the capillary bore. The dye solution can be either cooled by having a cooling jacket around it or the dye storage tank may be cooled by running water around it. The dye solution may be any one of the dyes selected from Table 6-1.

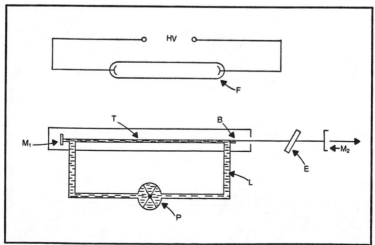

Fig. 6-1. A simplified view of a cw dye laser.

Table 6-1. Typical Characteristics of Dye Lasers.

Laser Output	1 watt and up
Beam Diameter	0.5 mm
Beam Divergence	0.8 to 2 mrad
Optical Pump	Ion laser (argon)
Tuning Range	3,900 to 10,000 angstroms
Beam Linewidth	0.05 nm to 40 GHz Variable

As stated earlier, the principal use of the cw dye laser is in Raman spectroscopy, since the beam may be tuned to suppress fluorescence and to isolate the tuned beam. The etalon (E) can select a single longitudinal cavity mode rejecting other modes. If the length of the cavity can be made variable, very high resolution can be obtained over a narrow range of the laser-beam spectrum.

A schematic diagram of a commercial cw dye laser is shown in Fig. 6-2. In this figure, the dye solution constitutes a flat cell through which the dye solution flows continuously, while the optical pump, such as an ion laser, illuminates the flat dye cell D. In this case, the resonator cavity comprises the dye-cell and mirrors M_2 and M_4, the foci of which are located at the center of the flat section of the dye cell D. The optical pump mirror is designated by M_1 having a short focal length; the 100 percent reflective mirrors M_2 and M_3 oscillate the photons, the M_3 further reflecting the emission to the output mirror M_4, which is partially reflective and through which the emitted dye laser beam projects to the exterior of the system. An etalon or a birefringent filter E tunes the laser beam.

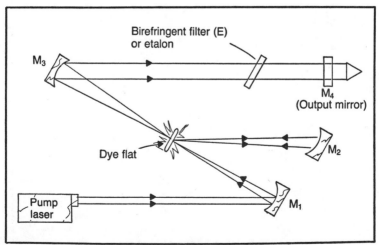

Fig. 6-2. A commercial version of cw dye laser (simplified).

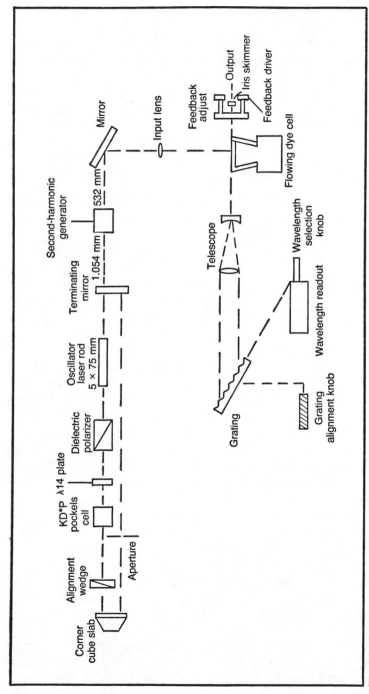

Fig. 6-3. Schematic diagram of a pulsed dye laser.

95

Pulsed Dye Lasers

As mentioned earlier, pulsed dye lasers possess peak output power much higher than cw dye lasers, but the average power is much less. Thus, pulsed dye lasers will achieve a broader range of wavelengths and their output power is sufficiently high to be used for frequency-doubling and for production of tunable power outputs.

A pulsed dye laser schematic diagram is shown in Fig. 6-3, in which a cuvette or dye cell is used instead of a flowing jet of the dye solution, as in the cw dye laser scheme. The resonant cavity is formed by a 100 percent rear reflecting mirror and a 50 percent transmissive output mirror. The tuning is achieved by means of a birefringent element B.E. A Fresnel lens may also be used in place of a spherical rear mirror M_1 for wavelength selection. This type of laser arrangement can be utilized to frequency-double the beam by the use of a frequency-doubling element, as described in a preceding section. Tuning range can thus be extended into the ultraviolet at the shorter end and into the infrared at the longer-wavelength end. Pulsed dye lasers are also used in physics experiments involving molecular spectroscopy because of the broad linewidth offered by them, and for measuring decay time of rapidly occurring fluorescence.

Another scheme of utilizing pulsed dye lasers is to synchronously pump the dye laser, using beam-directing optical elements, and by extending the dye-laser cavity to the length of the optical pump, which may be an ion laser. This scheme can achieve a very high peak power with short pulses, especially when the dye solution is optically pumped by means of a nitrogen laser.

CHARACTERISTICS OF DYE LASERS

Present-day dye-solution lasers are more efficient, achieve broader tuning ranges, easily cooled because of the flowing jet of the solution, and their lifetime is much longer than that of the liquid lasers which were used during the early days of investigative work. The performance of the dye depends on the excitation pump quality, the types of resonant-cavity optical elements that are used, and the type of solvent of the dye. If a beam dispersing element is used in the resonant cavity, the linewidth can be decreased with increased intensity, whereby the system can be tuned over its entire gain spectrum.

Dye solutions operating at the ultraviolet range have some limitations in their quantum absorption, because of the molecular bond dissociates in the high-power pump illumination. Dyes operating in the visible spectrum also decompose but not as fast as those in the shorter-wavelength range, as in the ultraviolet range. Thermal problems in the dye may also cause the dye molecules to go into reaction with the molecules of the solvent (host) or with dissolved oxygen in the solution, resulting in the decomposition of the dye molecules. For this reason, the dye solution in operation must be sustained at room temperature and not too much above it. See Table 6-2.

DISSOCIATION OF DYES BY USE

Laser dyes dissociate photochemically during their operational life, and the rate of failure depends on the type of optical pump used. Flashlamp pumps deteriorate the dye faster than the laser pumps, especially when the dye and the pumping illumination are not compatible. Ultraviolet illumination causes further deterioration of the dye by bleaching it at times. Increasing the volume of the dye solution increases the life of the dye; however, the character of the solvent will also affect the life of the dye solution. When the ultraviolet light is filtered, the dye life increases with an increase of excitation energy within certain limitations. The purity of the dye and the clarity of the solution also enhance longer life to the dye solution. As it was stated earlier, operating temperature influences the life of the dye material; as the temperature increases, the tendency of the dye solution to deteriorate increases. On the other hand, overcooling the dye solution will also affect its life adversely. The most favorable temperature at which a dye solution should be operated is at or near room temperature, between 18° to 24°C. Bubbles that form during the operation of the dye solution can act

Table 6-2. Examples of Dye Solutions and their Excitations.

Laser Dye	Wavelength Angstroms	Solvent	Optical Pump	Operational Mode
P-Terpenyl	3260 - 3580	Ethanol	KrF	Pulsed
Coumarin 440	4200 - 4570	Ethanol	Nitrogen	Pulsed
Coumarin 481	5000 - 5400	Ethanol	Nd-YAG	Pulsed
Fluorescein 552	5380 - 5730	Ethylene Glycol	Argon	Continuous Wave
Cresyl Violet	6500 - 6960	Ethylene Glycol	Argon	Continuous Wave
Oxazine 750	7490 - 8250	Ethylene Glycol	Krypton	Continuous Wave
IR-140 (C10$_4$)	8580 - 10,300	Dimethylsulfoxide and Ethylene Glycol (1:3)	Krypton	Continuous Wave

There are dozens of other dyes that operate in pulsed and continuous-wave mode; these are just a few selected specimens. See Exciton technical data.

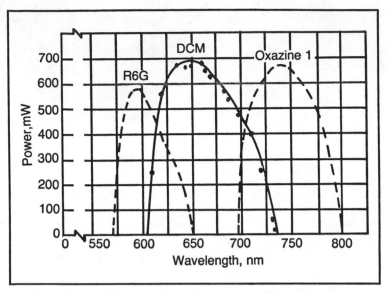

Fig. 6-4. Spectra-Physics dye laser performance, with power versus wavelengths.

adversely to dye operation but can be eliminated by filtering the solution continously; bubbles also reduce efficiency of the laser output. For the foregoing reasons, in using dye lasers, the manufacturer's instructions should be strictly followed.

WIDE-RANGE TUNABILITY DYE LASER

A new dye laser having a broad tuning range of 6,050 to 7,340 angstroms and using a DCM dye has been recently developed by Spectra-Physics of Mountain View, California. The unit operates with high efficiency in both continuous-wave and mode-locked formats and is optically pumped with high-power ion lasers. Its peak conversion efficiency is 34 percent, and covers the visible spectral ranges obtained with Rhodamince 6G and Oxazine 1, as illustrated in Fig. 6-4. It has shown good dye stability for operations exceeding 220 watt-hours when pumped by a laser beam of 5,145-angstrom wavelength.

This dye system has been tested with the Spectra-Physics synchronously-pumped dye laser (mentioned earlier) and also with the synchronously-pumped, cavity-dumped (SPCD) dye laser. Excellent results were obtained using peak powers as high as 520 watts at 3-picosecond pulses, with a repetition rate of 82 megahertz. The SPCD mode of operation also produces 13-picosecond pulses, with peak powers of up to 2.8 kilowatts sustained at 800-kilohertz pulses. The pulsewidths in these experiments were measured with Spectra-Physics Model 409 Scanning Autocorrelator provided with a suitable KDP crystal.

DYE LASER MIXING

A simplified method of mixing a dye laser beam with the harmonic from a Nd-YAG laser is shown in Fig. 6-5. In the figure, the YAG harmonic wavelength of 5,320-angstrom beam is bent from a 45° mirror M_1 and is projected on the dye cell containing, for example, a solution of rhodamine 6G for pumping it. The dye laser beam is expanded by the beam expander B.E. and then projected on the grating after passing through the etalon, which is used to narrow the bandwidth.

The beam returns from the grating, passes through the dye cell and the output mirror (O.M.) and falls on a second beam expander, which is used to match Nd-YAG harmonic beam diameter. The two beams are mixed in the mixing crystal and projected as an amplified laser beam tuned by the grating to any desired wavelength.

LASER-BEAM SHARING

One of the latest innovations in the laser field is a laser-beam sharing facility that uses high-power tunable laser radiation. In this facility, a frequently used laser radiation is distributed through optical channels to various research centers for individual laboratory use. The purpose of such a system is the efficient utilization of costly-produced laser beams in concurrently varied experiments in different research or materials-processing centers of the facility to eliminate unavailing downtime of system operation. The laser beam

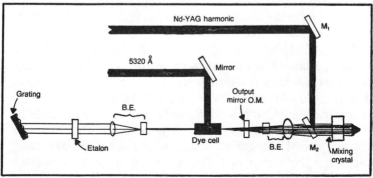

Fig. 6-5. Beam mixing in a tunable dye laser.

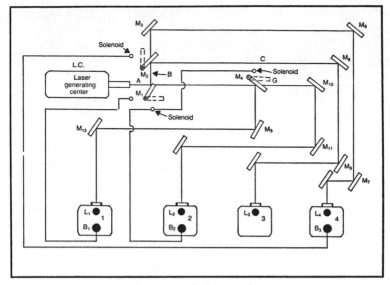

Fig. 6-6. Laser-beam sharing among four research centers.

in the system may operate in either the pulsing mode or in cw format.

One method of distribution of the laser beam consists of generating a high-power laser beam of specific type and splitting it by means of dichroic mirrors into the required number of channels, each channel serving a particular research or industrial production center. The beam channeled to the center can be tuned, frequency-multiplied, or even split into various beams for different applications. In a more sophisticated method of distribution, the main trunk of the laser beam is shared wholly by one center at a time through the programmed use of a computer, in which case the beam is available to only one center at a time. The combination of the two methods is generally used by laboratories such as Sandia, Livermore, and similar facilities.

A simplified beam-sharing method is illustrated in Fig. 6-6. In the figure, a laser beam (A), projecting from a tunable dye-laser radiation, is generated at high power at the main laser center (L.C). The mirrors M_1, M_2, and M_4 are coated 100 percent with a high-reflectivity material, such as MgF_2, and each mirror is rotatable by means of an electromagnetic solenoid (not shown). The remaining mirrors M_3 and M_5 through M_{13} are stationary and have 100 percent reflectivity. The numerals 1 through 4 are separate laboratory centers, in each of which a particular research or investigation is conducted. Any one laboratory can use the beam independently of the other centers. The red lights L_1 through L_4 indicate the beam is in use in another station.

In operation, for instance at the laboratory No. 1, the operator presses a button B_1 located on the laser control panel. This action energizes the solenoid at S_1 of mirror M_1, opening the path of the beam to mirror M_4. The beam then reflects from M_4 to M_5 and M_{13}, from which it propagates and enters the laboratory No. 1. Similarly, by pressing the button B_2, the mirrors M_1 and M_4 rotate by means of the respective solenoids and open the path of the beam G. The beam G then reflects from mirror M_{10} and M_{11} and enters the laboratory No. 2. The laboratory No. 3 does not have a button since the optical path is normally available to it. Finally, when the operator in laboratory No. 4 presses the button B_3, the mirror M_2 rotates, and the beam B reflects to M_3 and to M_6 and M_7, and enters the laboratory No. 4. It will be evident from Fig. 6-6 that when one laboratory is using the laser beam, the other laboratories cannot share it at the same time in this particular system of beam sharing.

In another arrangement, the mirrors M_1 through M_4 can be made 50 percent transmissive, in which case each of the examplary laboratories, as shown in Fig. 6-6, receives a laser beam at all times but at one-fourth the energy of the original intensity of the beam at A. In such an event, the maximum laser output is generated at the laser center L.C. Each laboratory is equipped with means to vary the incoming beam intensity at will.

In case the laser beam projecting from the laser center L.C. is invisible, such as if it is emitted by CO_2, Nd-YAG, or Nd-Glass laser, a beam of red He-Ne laser can be combined with the invisible beam before it emerges from the main center L.C. The scheme of mixing the two beams, visible and invisible beams, is shown in Fig. 6-7.

If the mixed laser beam is to be employed in spectrographic or interferometric work, the red He-Ne light may be filtered out with an optical filter at the laboratory where the invisible beam is to be utilized. Furthermore, if a frequency-doubled or frequency-tripled laser beam is required, it may be obtained using a KDP crystal at the work area. Or, if double the laser-beam intensity is required, a second CO_2 or Nd-YAG laser unit can be arranged in the same manner shown in Fig. 6-7, using an additional dichroic mirror in the principal axis of the projected laser beam.

A more elaborate and sophisticated beam-sharing facility built at Sandia National Laboratories operates by means of a computer-programmed laser generator, in which either a tunable dye laser or a

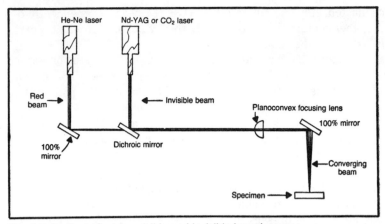

Fig. 6-7. Method of mixing visible and invisible laser beams.

frequency-doubled Nd-YAG laser can be used. The dye laser generates 1.5-microsecond 5-joule pulses which are tunable from 3,900 to 7,500 angstroms at a repetition rate of 10 hertz, employing various dye combinations. The Nd-YAG laser operating frequency-doubled produces 1.5-microsecond 1-joule of laser energy at 5,320 angstroms and at a pulse repetition rate of 1 hertz. Both of these lasers are principally used in the diagnosis of gas-combustion environment where different, evolved gases are analyzed. Other areas of research and study include Raman scattering measurement, diagnosis of pollutant emissions, measurement of efficiency of fuel combustion, and investigation of substitute fuels for a given operational system. As studies progress at this facility new applications of the system usable by various outside institutions are expected to evolve.

Questions and Problems

6-1. What is a dye laser? How does it differ from other types of lasers already studied? Why is a dye laser tunable? What optical elements are used to tune a dye laser? How does the laser action occur in a dye solution?

6-2. In what modes do the dye lasers function? What types of optical pumps are generally used for exciting the dye in the pulsing mode? What types of optical pumps excite the dye to continuous-wave mode? Explain.

6-3. What is frequency multiplying? What optical elements are used in frequency multiplying a dye laser radiation? What is the commercial use of continuous-wave dye lasers? What are the applications of pulsed dye lasers?

6-4. How is a simple dye laser system constructed? What modifications can be made to this system to give it more flexibility of use? What does an etalon do in an optical cavity? What other optical element can do the same function as an etalon? What are the differences of uses?

6-5. Does the laser energy increase by converting a continuous-wave dye laser emission to a pulsing mode? Which mode of operation is apt to achieve broader range of wavelengths and output powers?

6-6. What is the advantage of a flowing jet of dye solution over the static dye solution? How does the flowing jet-type operation affect the life of the dye solution? What type of optical arrangement can extend the operation of the dye laser to the ultraviolet region of the spectrum?

6-7. On what factor does the performance of a dye solution depend? What does a beam-dispersing element in the resonant cavity do with respect to the linewidth of the spectrum and the intensity of the emission? Is it disadvantageous from the standpoint of lifetime to operate a dye laser in the ultraviolet region of the spectrum? Discuss.

6-8. What effect does thermal conditioning a dye resonant cavity have on the lifetime of the dye solution? What are the effects of dissolved oxygen and impurities on a dye solution? How can these effects be corrected? Discuss.

6-9. How are the laser dyes affected photochemically during operation? Which types of optical pumps affect this condition more severely? What does ultraviolet illumination do to the lifetime of a dye solution? In what manner does ultraviolet bring about the condition, in your last answer? Discuss the mechanism involved.

6-10. How does the character of solvent affect the lifetime of a dye solution? Does cooling increase the operational life of a dye solution? At what temperature should a dye operate normally? What does overcooling a dye solution do to the lifetime of a dye? How do bubbles in a dye solution affect the laser emission? How can the bubbles be eliminated from the solution?

6-11. State and discuss some of the applications of dye lasers that operate in the pulsed mode. What are some of the applications of the cw dye lasers? If the laser dye energy is frequency-multiplied and mixed with the fundamental laser beam, does the energy increase or remains the same? Explain.

6-12. How can one obtain a wide visible spectral range using only one type of dye? In what modes can such a system operate?

What type of optical pump is necessary to operate this system? What results are obtained when such a system is operated with a synchronously-pumped, cavity-dumped laser? Are the results obtained significant? If so, in what way? Discuss.

6-13. What is meant by dye laser mixing? What is the function of Nd-YAG in dye laser mixing? Which harmonic wavelength of Nd-YAG is used in this process? What is the function of an etalon in dye laser mixing? Why is a second beam expander used in this process? How is the amplified laser tuned to a desired wavelength?

6-14. What is laser beam sharing? What types of laser radiations can be shared? Why should a laser beam be shared by different laboratory work stations? What are the advantages of laser-beam sharing? Can visible or invisible laser beams be shared? Approximately how many laboratories can be channeled with the laser beam? Discuss.

6-15. Draw a simplified laser-beam sharing diagram. Can all existing laboratories in the facility share the laser beam at the same time? Individually? Discuss how this can be accomplished. Why are dichroic mirrors used in a laser-beam sharing system?

6-16. Can a laser beam that is invisible be made visible to be shared by different laboratory work centers? What method is used to convert the invisible laser beam into a visible beam? Discuss. If the laboratory is not equipped with apparatus to convert the invisible laser beam into a visible laser beam, what other method can be used to utilize the invisible laser beam as if it is visible? Draw a diagram showing the mixing of two invisible laser beams and making them visible at the work area without frequency-multiplying.

Chapter 7
Industrial Applications of Lasers

Materials processing lasers cover the operations of cutting, drilling, welding, scribing, trimming, annealing and hardening. There are a large number of laser types that can perform one or more of these operations; some do more effectively than the others. For the majority of processed work, lasers serve as sources of intense thermal energy. In order to effectively transfer this energy to the material being processed, a close compatibility must exist between the laser beam and the material being worked upon. This property is mainly dependent on the wavelength of the laser beam used for the particular work in hand. For instance, a high coupling efficiency of a certain beam with the object being processed can perform the work with lower laser energy than one that emits an unsuitable wavelength but possesses high laser energy. We have already learned about lasers emitting different wavelengths, power outputs, and their modes of operations. In materials processing, we shall have an opportunity to apply all this knowledge selectively to diverse modes of utilization on different materials of industry.

There are several types of lasers that can be used in materials processing. They are: ruby laser, Nd-YAG laser, Nd-glass laser, CO_2 laser, and argon laser. The first three lasers are optically pumped and the other two are pumped electrically by passing a current through the gas enclosed in an electric discharge tube. Ruby lasers emit red rays in the visible and are optically pumped with a xenon flashlamp. They operate in the pulsed mode and their energies vary from less than a joule to several hundred joules per pulse of several millisecond duration. Nd-YAG and Nd-Glass lasers operate in the infrared in both pulsed and cw mode; they are pumped by xenon, krypton-arc lamp, or by tungsten-halogen arc lamp. A carbon dioxide laser emits in the infrared and is pumped by passing an electrical current through it; it can operate both pulsed and in cw mode. The argon ion laser is operated by passing through it a high-density current to ionize the gas; it emits radiation in the blue spectral region in the cw mode, although it can be cavity-dumped, when needed, using accessory optical elements.

LASER CUTTING AND DRILLING

Laser cutting and drilling can be performed on metals, plastics, ceramics, textiles, cloths, and even glass when its surface is coated with a radiation-absorbing material such as carbon or soot. For cutting or drilling, a long focal-length lens is used in order to produce a narrow kerf and to reduce the tendency for the cut or the drilled hole from becoming bevelled. To correct or avoid the latter situation, a gas-jet assisted laser beam can be used, the gas being either an inert gas, such as helium or argon, or a reactive gas such as oxygen. The inert gas is employed when the material is prone to burn or oxidize; such materials are cloths or plastics. Oxygen is used to obtain exothermic reaction with metals to produce a clean-cut kerf and rapid rate of cutting or drilling. A gas-jet-assisted cutting or drilling scheme is shown in Fig. 7-1.

For drilling or cutting, a ruby laser, Nd-YAG laser, or a carbon dioxide laser can be used either in the pulsing mode or in the cw format. Of the three lasers, carbon dioxide laser yields the highest depth-to-diameter ratio (as much as 250:1) in most metals, using a gas-jet assist. Q-switched high-power CO_2 laser may also be used; however, short-time pulses from the Q-switched beam will be less effective in removing the metal from the cut area than when longer-pulse lower-energy pulses are used. This is because the longer pulse delivers more energy to the work area than when a shorter pulse is used. When high-power and longer-time pulse is used, the laser energy will be partially wasted. Furthermore, when a short focal-length lens is employed, the kerf size will increase and the cut or drilled hole will have slanted configuration.

The hole drilling mechanism consists of elevating the temperature of the surface to be drilled by incident laser beam at a rate approaching 10^{10} degrees kelvin per second, vaporizing the hole area to a depth of several microns, and melting the metal below the vaporized layer. The molten mass in the hole forms an enormously high pressure resulting in the expulsion of the molten and vaporized material in a plume. This process continues until the remainder of the material in the processed hole is ejected from the hole; all this action occurs in the course of a fraction of a second. The plume thus formed also removes any debris due to solidified particles at the edges of the hole, leaving behind a clean-cut aperture. Cutting materials with the laser beam also undergoes the same procedure, and when the process is oxygen-jet assisted, cutting rates can rapidly increase, depending on the thickness and the type of material is cut. Figure 7-2 illustrates the configurations of laser-drilled holes.

The laser energy required to drill a hole in a given material may be given as:

$$H = \pi r^2 \, t \, \rho \left[m(T_f - T_a) + L_n + L_v \right] \quad \textbf{(Equation 7-1)}$$

where, H is the laser energy in joules required to drill a hole or cut a mass equal to the hole volume, r is the radius of the hole in centimeters, t is the depth or thickness penetrated in centimeters, ρ is the density of the material in gm/cm^3, m is the specific heat (thermal capacity) of the material in cal/gm/°C, T_f is the tempera-

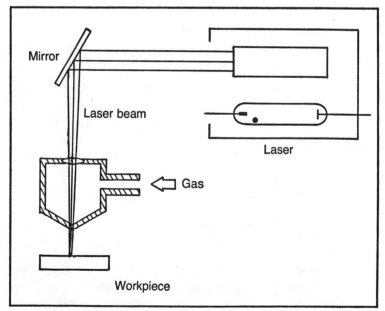

Fig. 7-1. Scheme for cutting with a gas-jet-assisted laser beam.

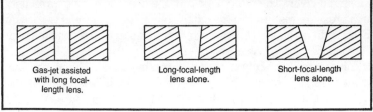

Fig. 7-2. Hole configurations by different drilling methods.

ture of fusion of the material in °C, T_a is the ambient (room) temperature usually taken as 20°C, L_h is the heat of fusion of the material given in cal/gm, and L_v is the heat of vaporization of the molten material in cal/gm.

As an example, let us solve a problem using a sheet of zinc for rilling with a laser beam from a Nd-YAG laser system. Assume the following parameters for the problem:

ρ = density equal to 7.133 gm/cm³,
t = thickness equal to 0.5 millimeters,
r = radius of the hole equal to 0.5 millimeters,
m = specific heat equal to 0.0915 cal/gm,
T_f = temperature of fusion equal to 906°C,
T_a = ambient (room) temperature equal to 20°C,
L_h = heat of fusion equal to 24.1 cal/gm,
L_v = heat of vaporization equal to 425.6 cal/gm, and
H = is the laser energy in calories required to remove the hole material.

Thus, substituting the numerical values for quantities in Equation 7-1, we have,

$$H = 3.1416 \times 0.05^2 \times 0.05 \times 7.133 \, [0.0915(906 - 20) + 24.1 + 425.6]$$
$$= 3.14 \times 2.5 \, 10^{-3} \times 5 \times 10^{-2} \times 7.133 \, [80.9 + 24.1 + 425.6]$$
$$= 2.8 \times 10^{-3} \, [530.6]$$
$$= 1.84 \text{ calories}$$

or, Joules

$$= 1.84 \times 4.186$$
$$= 7.70 \text{ joules.}$$

In the preceding problem, the heat dissipation by conduction, reflection, and diffusivity was not considered. Assuming that there was a loss of 60 percent at room temperature, then the energy needed would be:

$$\text{Joules Needed} = \frac{7.70}{100 - 60} \times 100$$
$$= 19,25 \text{ joules.}$$

If the pulse duration in this operation is 0.006 second, and the system operates with one pulse per second, the wattage rating of the laser system would be:

$$\text{Joules} = \text{Watts} \times \text{Seconds}$$

$$\text{Watts} = \frac{\text{Joules}}{\text{Seconds}} = \frac{19.25}{0.006}$$

$$= 3208 \text{ watts, or } 3.2 \text{ kilowatts.}$$

LASER SCRIBING SEMICONDUCTOR WAFERS

Epitaxially deposited microcircuits on semiconductor wafers, such as silicon dioxide, sapphire, or ceramic, are separated one from the other by scribing the wafer between the separate circuits. As many as several hundred microcircuits can be deposited on a nominal-size wafer of 20 by 40 millimeters in area. The usual method of scribing a wafer is by the use of a diamond scriber; however, a diamond scriber produces residue on the wafer that must be cleaned thoroughly before use of the wafer. Otherwise, any particle of the residue that may lodge between the microcircuit components may eventually cause the malfunction of the circuit. For the latter reason, laser scribing is found to be clean, fast, and accurate. After scribing the wafer, the individual microcircuits are separated by breaking the wafer at the junctions of the scribed lines. The wafer is then mounted in a header or holder and leads are bonded to the circuit terminals to external Kovar leads, which transmit the external current to the circuit for its operation.

With a diamond scriber, usually deep lines are drawn between the circuits, while with a laser scribing a fast pulsing current is used to make fine, closely arranged holes in the wafer while the wafer is moved at an adjusted rate under the laser beam. These holes are as deep as ⅔rd of the thickness of the wafer, and the microcircuits are separated by the usual method of breaking the wafer into chips at the scribed lines. The wafer can be accurately lined under the laser beam converged by a long focal-length lens so that the kerf is narrow and the hole deep. With laser scribing, as fast as 15 to 20 centimeters per second can be achieved, thus making the production throughout very high and reasonable in cost.

In selecting an optical lens, it will be desirable to select a lens with long focal length. The laser beam should be spatially filtered and collimated before it is incident on the focusing lens. This procedure will yield clear-cut and sharply scribed holes. An example of the scribed wafer is illustrated in Fig. 7-3.

In scribing, it is necessary to select a laser-beam-focus diameter that will yield the narrowest kerf in the wafer. This can be determined by the following expression:

$$d = \frac{2S}{a} \sqrt{\frac{1.7\lambda}{\pi}} \qquad \text{(Equation 7-2)}$$

in which, d is the diameter of the incident beam focus on the wafer, S is the distance between the optical plane of the lens and the focus of the beam (focal length), a is the diameter of the laser rod, and λ is the laser/beam wavelength. All dimensions, including the wavelength, should be given in centimeters.

LASER TRIMMING OF RESISTORS

Laser trimming of resistors is the process in which the resistance of a thin-film resistor in a microelectronic device is accurately adjusted to meet tolerance. Since it is difficult to precisely vapor-deposit resistors (usually in microhms) in wafers, they are fabricated with lower resistance than the device is intended for operation and then an increment of the resistor is removed to increase its resistance to the tolerance desired. There are other methods of resistor trimming, but the method designed for laser trimming has greater flexibility, accuracy, and speed of production. The trimming can be performed either manually or by means of automatic, computerized laser machines. With the latter process, the production rate increases and the cost of fabrication is reduced to profitable levels.

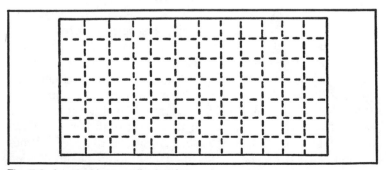

Fig. 7-3. A typical laser-scribed wafer.

In laser trimming, illustrated in Fig. 7-4, the resistor R_4 to be trimmed is made a leg of a Wheatstone bridge arrangement, in which the bridge is driven by a dc current. The resistor is positioned at the focus of the beam converged by a long focal-length lens L, and the laser trigger circuit is connected through a relay R to the bridge so that when sufficient material is removed by laser from the resistor film, the bridge becomes balanced and no current flows through it. This condition causes the relay R to open, thus cutting off the laser beam from the resistor material. The adjustment of the resistor value is made by inserting the required resistance value R_3 in the bridge circuit leg which is equal to the required resistance and is in the compensating circuit of the resistance to be trimmed. Both thin film and thick film resistors can be trimmed by this method.

LASER WELDING OF MATERIALS

Welding materials with a laser beam requires more precise control of the input laser power than it is necessary for drilling. Accurate positioning of the specimen with respect to the laser beam is also important, although the same system that is used for cutting and drilling can be used for welding, too. A typical welding machine is shown in Fig. 4-3 in a schematic form. In a system of this type, the welding technique has to be established by trial and error for different types of materials to be processed. However, there are several rules that should be adhered to in welding any type of material. These rules may be given as:

■ The laser system must generate sufficient laser energy for welding a given specimen.

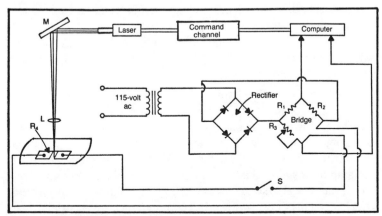

Fig. 7-4. A simplified resistor trimming scheme.

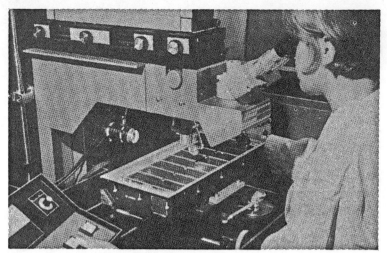

Fig. 7-5. A commercial laser welder and cutter.

■ Close contact with the faying surfaces must be maintained at all times.

■ The wavelength of the laser beam must be compatible with the material being welded.

■ A pulsed mode of operation is usually better than continuous-wave type.

■ The pulse shape of the laser beam must be controlled precisely from weld to weld.

■ The focus of the beam must be adjusted to the thickness of the material; thicker materials require larger focus size and therefore higher laser power.

■ A stabilized flashlamp energy should be used to produce uniform laser pulses.

■ Unless the system operates automatically by a computer control, safety goggles should be used during processing of the material to eliminate eye hazard.

The operator may establish other rules for the effective and safe operation of the system under his control.

The important components of a laser system are a source of alternating current, a step-up transformer, a rectifying system, a pulse-forming network, (for pulsed lasers), a lasing element with a flashlamp enclosed in the same reflective chamber, a cooling system, and an optical system for controlling the beam profile projected to the specimen being processed. A commercial laser system which can perform both welding and cutting manually is shown in Fig. 7-5.

The laser welder-driller shown in Fig. 7-5 is a Nd-YAG laser designed and manufactured by Holobeam, Inc., for welding, drilling, and scribing parts at production speeds of up to 100 firings per minute. It operates in the pulsing mode with pulsewidths from 1 to 6 milliseconds. It can weld sheet stock up to 0.05-inch thick using a beam focus size varying from 0.001 to 0.06 inch, and can drill holes from 0.0005 to 0.06 inch in diameter. The system operates from a 220-volt, 60-ampere, and 50/60 Hz, single-phase power source. It is cooled by tap water running at a rate of 1 gpm at 20 psi.

To weld a material with any given laser welder, electrical parameters must be chosen so that the laser output at the given focal area is sufficient to melt the two parts being welded to practically the same diameter as the beam focus, in order to obtain an intimate joint. The two faying surfaces must be in good contact with each other, with minimum or no air space between them so that the radiant heat will be completely absorbed by the two faying surfaces. To establish an intimate contact, a pressure can be applied on the upper part against the lower part by means of a jig, or a continuously moving transparent plastic tape can be used for sheet materials. If the welding is performed manually, that is not by automatic machine, a pair of tweezers may be used to hold the upper sheet or part tightly against the lower part being welded.

The operating electrical parameters are chosen from a prepared chart, which gives the proper voltage to be used versus the thickness of the particular material. An exemplary graphical representation of voltage versus thickness is shown in Fig. 7-6. All

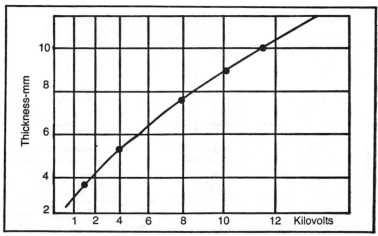

Fig. 7-6. Voltage versus thickness of nickel sheet.

electrical parameters, such as voltage, current, and capacitance can be set by means of control knobs located on the instrument panel. If the laser unit is water-cooled or air-cooled, the cooling system may also be adjusted to the proper cooling range, before starting the machine.

When the materials to be welded are thin, for example, from a fraction of a mil to several mils, a short focal-length lens, such as 10 to 15 millimeter focal length should be used in order to produce a large focus area. With thicker materials, such as 1 millimeter to several millimeters of thickness, a long focal-length lens should be used because a short focal-length lens may not drive the laser beam deep enough into the material; however, the focal area should be large enough for the material to join effectively. This means, the laser power should be raised to compensate for the larger area. With a given, properly scheduled electrical parameter condition, the distance between the lens and the workpiece influences the charac-

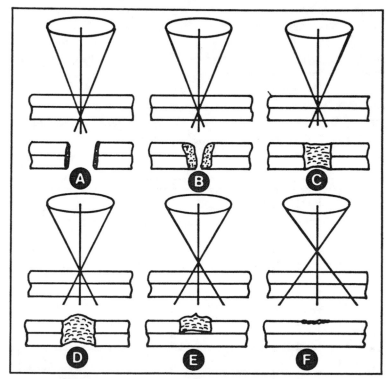

Fig. 7-7. Diagrams showing the configurations of focal spots obtained with varying distances between the lens and the specimen.

ter of the weld that can be obtained. This statement can be illustrated by the diagrams shown in Fig. 7-7, in which when the focus of the beam is below the thickness of the material to be welded, one obtains a hole, as shown in (A). As the focus is raised slightly but still halfway of the thickness of the lower sheet, a weld is obtained with a hole in its center, as in (B). When the focus of the beam is exactly at midway of the two sheets being welded, a properly structured weld is produced, shown in (C). As the beam focus is raised so that the focus of the beam is incident on the surface of the top-sheet material, a convex weld with an apex in its center is formed, shown in (D).

As the focus is continued to be raised so that it is above the upper sheet, a slight fusion of the upper layer occurs with no effect on the bottom layer, shown in (E). When the beam focus is further away from the upper sheet, the heat from the beam causes slight heat-affected area, and the laser beam dissipates away in air by reflection from the surface (F), the reflection originating from the diverged portion of the beam incident on the material. Consequently, these indications are evidence to the fact that the lens-specimen distance relationship is critical. This condition may also vary from one operator to another; that is, one operator may correctly focus the beam while another may not. Any incorrectly welded nugget can only be seen by metallurgical sectioning of the weld nugget, as shown in Fig. 4-4.

ENERGY USED IN WELD FORMATION

For welding any two pieces of metal together, the temperature of the weld area must be raised to the melting point of the metals in union. If the two metals are similar, there is not much problem to weld them together. However, if the two metals are of different materials, then a compromise of the laser energy must be made so that each metal will melt and join together. Furthermore, which metal is on the top also enters into the compromise. For instance, if the top metal has a lower melting point or is thinner than that of the lower metal, the laser energy may vaporize the focus area of the upper sheet without significantly affecting the lower metal. Or, if the condition is reversed, then higher energy must be applied to the upper layer in order to transmit the heat to the lower layer. Other characteristics of the metals, such as thermal conductivity, diffusivity, latent heat, etc., also enter into the proper welding of the materials, as it will be shown in an example.

Assume that the following parameters were given for welding two sheets of metals of the same kind together:

Material	-	Stainless Steel
Material Thickness	-	1 millimeter (t)
Weld Diameter	-	1 millimeter (d)
Material Density	-	7.87 gm/cm^2 (ρ)
Melting Point	-	1539°C (T$_f$)
Heat of Fusion	-	65 cal/gm (L$_h$)
Specific Heat	-	0.11 cal/gm/°C (m)
Room Temperature	-	20°C (T$_a$)
Optical Loss	-	20 percent

Assuming no vaporization, Equation 7-1 becomes,

$$H = \pi r^2 \, t \, \rho \, [m(T_f - T_a) + L_h] \qquad \textbf{(Equation 7-2)}$$

The volume of material in two thicknesses of the sheets to be welded is as follows:

$$
\begin{aligned}
\text{Volume (V) in cm}^3 &= \pi(d/2)^2 \times t \times 2 \\
&= 3.1416 \times (0.1/2)^2 \times 0.1 \times 2 \\
&= 3.14 \times 0.0025 \times 0.1 \times 2 \\
&= 1.57 \times 10^{-3} \text{ cm}^3.
\end{aligned}
$$

The weight W of steel of density 7.87 gm/cm^3 is:

$$
\begin{aligned}
W &= \text{Volume} \times \text{Specific Gravity} \\
&= 1.57 \times 10^{-3} \times 7.87 \\
&= 1.235 \times 10^{-2} \text{ gram.}
\end{aligned}
$$

Calories required to raise the temperature of 1.235×10^{-2} gram of stainless steel of specific heat 0.11 cal/gm/°C will be:

$$
\begin{aligned}
\text{Calories} &= 1.235 \times 10^{-2} \times 0.11 \\
&= 1.36 \times 10^{-3} \text{ calories.}
\end{aligned}
$$

The heat H required to raise the temperature of 1.235×10^{-2} gram of steel to its melting point is:

$$
\begin{aligned}
H &= 1.36 \times 10^{-3} \times (1539 - 20) + 1.235 \times 10^{-2} \times 65 \\
&= 1.36 \times 10^{-3} \times 1519 + 65 \times 1.235 \times 10^{-2} \\
&= 2.06 + 0.83 \\
&= 2.89 \text{ calories.}
\end{aligned}
$$

The last quantity given in joules J will be:

$$
\begin{aligned}
J &= \text{Calories} \times 4.18 \\
&= 2.89 \times 4.18 \\
&= 12.0 \text{ joules.}
\end{aligned}
$$

WELDING TECHNIQUE DETERMINATION

When a laser system is sold to a customer, the welding technique for different materials and thicknesses are usually included in the operating instruction manual. However, the customer sometimes may want to weld materials other than those given in the instruction manual. In such an event, the operator of the system can prepare his own welding techniques chart by making firings of the laser beam using a given focal-length lens, and electrical parameters. The chart can be made from a table in accordance with Table 7-1.

In Table 7-1, the electrical parameters have been set for four thicknesses, and the one to be made by the operator may include eight or ten thicknesses. The more parameters are included with smaller increments of changes the more accurate the welding technique will be. For example, instead of making capacitance changes in increments of 200 or 100 mfd, the changes may be made in increments of 50 mfd, etc. When such a table is completed, graphs may be made with voltage versus thickness, capacitance versus thickness, etc., so that when a given thickness material is to be welded, the technique can be taken right from the chart. Of course, such a chart can only be used for the material tested.

LASER MICROSOLDERING SYSTEM

A laser-soldering system developed by Apollo Lasers, Inc. is the latest innovation in laser applications in materials working. The

Table 7-1. Laser Feasibility Test Firings for Kovar (Lens Focal Length is 20 mm).

Thickness in Mils					Voltage in kV				Capacitance in μF				Weld Size in Mils*	Energy Input in Joules**	Laser Output in Joules†	Remarks	
1	2	3	4	5	1.1	1.2	1.5	1.8	200	400	500	600				Weld	Hole
X					X				X								
X					X					X							
X					X						X						
X					X							X					
	X					X			X								
	X					X				X							
	X					X					X						
	X					X						X					
		X					X		X								
		X					X			X							
		X					X				X						
		X					X					X					
			X					X	X								
			X					X		X							
			X					X			X						
			X					X				X					
				X			X				X						
				X			X				X						
				X			X					X					
				X				X				X					
X					X					X							
X						X				X							
X							X			X							
X								X		X							

Notes: (*) Measure weld size with microscope and place across appropriate X.
(**) Calculate input energy in joules and place across appropriate X.
(†) Calculate output laser energy using Equation (3-1) and place across appropriate X.
Any variation of this table may be tried for other electrical inputs and laser outputs.

Fig. 7-8. Laser microsoldering system (Model LMS-1) manufactured by Apollo Lasers, Inc., an Allied Company.

system consists of a 20-watt flowing-gas CO_2 laser emitting at 10,640 angstroms. Since this radiation is in the infrared spectrum and invisible, a 1-milliwatt He-Ne laser source, provided in the system, projects a red-light beam which accompanies the CO_2 laser beam and is focused jointly through a 2.5-inch focal-length lens on the workpiece. The workpiece is moved under the incident beam either manually or by means of a computer-programmed micro-processor in the X-Y direction. The solder used to join the electric leads to the copper pads or to ceramic flat packs is an Alpha Metals RMA-341 solder in the form of a paste containing 60Sn.40Pb solder particles with an organic or acid flux. The laser-soldering system is shown in Fig. 7-8.

In operation, the specimen to be soldered is mounted on the X-Y translator, and the He-Ne laser beam is focused on the copper pad where lead soldering is to be performed. The copper lead is held either flat on the pad or at a 45° with respect to the pad, and the fluxed solder is introduced by means of a syringe between the lead and the pad. The CO_2 laser power is set to a nominal 18 watts and a pulsewidth of 200 milliseconds, although other settings are also possible depending on the lead dimensions and whether the lead is bare copper or coated with tin or solder. It is also found that if a lead is provided with an insulation cover, the latter does not have to be stripped prior to soldering. The heat from the laser beam burns the insulation and melts the solder to bond. A cross-sectional view of a soldered lead is shown in Fig. 7-9.

Physical tests performed on the solder joints have shown high peel strength. The cross-sectional views of the solder joints examined under a binocular microscope at 5 and 10 magnifications have shown no voids or discontinuities; a very uniform solder flow and wetting characteristics have also been observed. It is also found that the laser-soldering of microcircuit leads is 5 to 10 times faster than hand-soldering. The process can be automated to obtain faster and low-cost performance from the system.

The laser-soldering system operates with an input power of 115-Vac, 60-Hertz, and 20 amperes. It can also operate on 220-Vac, 50-hertz power source. The laserhead is cooled by circulating tap water flowing at a rate of 0.5 gpm (gallons per minute). The carbon dioxide gas mixture consists of 6 parts CO_2, 18 parts nitrogen, and 76 parts helium; the mixture consumption is one cubic foot per hour.

LASER ANNEALING AND HARDENING METALS

Parts that require hardening or softening in only one section without affecting other sections are difficult to process with conventional methods, which require the heating or cooling of the entire

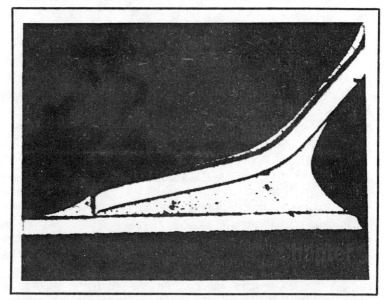

Fig. 7-9. Cross-sectional view of a solder-joined lead to a pad (magnified 75×).

part at the same time. For such operations where a specific portion of a part is to be hardened, for example, such as the cutting edge of a knife or the teeth of a gear, without hardening the remainder of the part, a laser hardening technique can be used very conveniently. The laser beam can be accurately directed at the spot or area in consideration, and following the exposure of the area to the beam, the area can be cooled immediately to harden it, without affecting the remaining sections. The cooling may be achieved by immersing the entire part into cold water or oil or by spraying the area by means of a "quick-freeze" type can spray.

Using the same technique, parts that have sections that require annealing without affecting the remaining section can be annealed by playing the laser beam on it and letting the section cool slowly by itself. In this method, cw, Q-switched, or frequency-doubled Nd-YAG laser would be very suitable. Or, cw argon can be used for fine and thin materials, such as in microelectronic devices.

Questions and Problems

7-1. What is the difference between a laser welding system and a laser drilling system? How does a technique of welding differ from drilling? Discuss. Which technique is more critical and why? What types of lasers can be used for welding procedures?

7-2. What types of lasers operate in the pulsed mode? What types of laser operate in the continuous-wave mode? Which operating mode can deliver more power to the welding area? Can continuous-wave laser beam be used for welding? Discuss.

7-3. What type of gas can be used in cutting or drilling plastic materials? What type of gas can be used in cutting metals? What is the function of the gas used for cutting metals? Can inert gases be used for cutting metals? If so, why are they used in cutting metals? Discuss.

7-4. Which type of laser yields the highest depth-to-diameter ratio? Can Q-switched laser be used for welding? Which operating mode, Q-switched or pulsing mode, can deliver more laser power to the weld area? When does one use a short focal-length lens? When does one use long focal-length lens? Discuss.

7-5. For drilling thick materials, which type of lens is used? In drilling thin materials, which type of lens is used? Discuss why different lenses are used for thin and thick materials. Can one use gas-jet in drilling holes? Is laser energy to drill a hole the same as that for welding the same-diameter area? Discuss.

7-6. Does heat of vaporization enter into the welding of materials? What is meant by fusion temperature? What is specific heat? What is density of a metal? How is heat content per gram of a given material determined? What is the difference between a calorie and a joule? How are they related to each other?

7-7. A certain metal has a density of 7.56 gm/cm³, and a specific heat of 0.105 cal/°C. If 1 cubic millimeter of this metal is to be raised to a temperature of 60°C from room temperature, how many calories will it require?

7-8. A certain metal has the following parameters: $\rho = 4.5$, t = 0.5 millimeter, r = 0.5 millimeter, specific heat is 0.109 cal/°C, vaporization temperature of 906°C, heat of fusion of 24.1 cal/gm, heat of vaporization of 425.6 cal/gm. What energy in calories is required to vaporize this metal? How many joules equivalent to the heat required you calculated is necessary?

7-9. What is laser scribing? What procedure is used to scribe a semiconductor wafer? What is the advantage of laser scribing over diamond scribing? What approximate focal-length lens should one use for scribing a 1-millimeter thick wafer? Why should a laser beam be spatially filtered for scribing a wafer? How does one separate the individual microcircuits on a sapphire wafer?

7-10. What should be the focal length of a lens if the diameter of the laser rod is 8 millimeters, the diameter of the focal spot on the wafer is 0.5 millimeter, and the laser-beam wavelength is 5320 angstroms?

7-11. What is meant by laser trimming of resistors? Why should resistors be trimmed? Discuss. What type of resistor materials can be trimmed? Discuss the simplified method of resistor trimming, by drawing a diagram of the procedure.

7-12. State six rules that are essential to follow in welding metal or plastic materials. Name the least number of components that are necessary in a laser welding system. What lasing elements can be used for welding? What electrical parameters are controlled in setting the system to do certain welding? Give an example for establishing electrical parameters for welding a given thickness material.

7-13. Draw diagrams showing different configurations of focal spot area, using different lens-to-specimen distances. Explain what takes place in the specimen when the lens-to-specimen distance is altered. How can the quality of weld nugget be determined? Discuss.

7-14. If two similar-material metallic sheets are of the same thicknesses, where would you focus the laser beam for welding them? If the upper sheet is thicker than the lower sheet, where will you focus the laser beam? If the upper sheet is thinner than the lower sheet, where will you focus the laser beam? Discuss.

7-15. In paragraph 6 of this chapter, if the melting point of the metal given in the problem is 1240°C, its specific heat is 0.09 cal/gm/°C, density is 4.56 gm/cm^3, and the volume of the metal to be welded is 1.28×10^{-3} cm^3, how many calories will be required to fuse the metal?

7-16. What is meant by annealing a metal? What is meant by hardening a metal? Why does one use a laser beam to anneal or harden a metal, while other established metals are existent? Can you anneal a silicon wafer? Can one weld broken weldable filaments in an electric light bulb without breaking the glass bulb? Explain how.

7-17. If the diameter of an incident laser-beam focus is 0.2 millimeters, the focal length of the lens is 16 millimeters, and the rod diameter is 8 millimeters, what will be the wavelength in angstroms of the laser beam to produce the 0.2 millimeter-diameter focus on the specimen?

7-18. What are some of the advantages of laser-soldering microelectronic devices? Could laser-soldering produce less heat-affected zone on the microcircuits than hand-soldering? How, explain. Can any other type of laser besides CO_2 laser be used in soldering microelectronic devices? Explain what other types can be used?

7-19. Explain why Apollo laser system uses solder paste rather than the usual solid metal. How can soldering schedules be established? Why is He-Ne laser beam employed in conjunction with a CO_2 laser? Can an insulated copper wire be soldered to the pad of a microelectronic circuit? Is laser-soldering performed pulsed or continuous wave? Would Q-switching improve laser-soldering in any manner? Explain.

7-20. Draw a diagram showing how the CO_2 and He-Ne laser beams are combined and projected on the focusing lens. Show how both beams can be in focus at the same focal spot.

Chapter 8
Metrological Measurement Systems

Lasers can also be used in alignment of structures, surveying lands, finding distances both in civilian and military fields, quality control, guidance systems in trenching and mining, and a variety of other measurement devices. Such measurement and gauging instrumentations have been possible because of the monochromatic and unidirectional properties that can be achieved with a laser beam. Formerly, such alignment and distance measurements were performed by strings, tapemeasures, and by triangulation methods, which are time-consuming and do not yield accurate measurements.

Lasers used in metrological work are He-Ne lasers, GaAs lasers, Nd-YAG laser usually in frequency-doubled mode, and ruby laser in certain types of applications. The construction industry and the military use the greatest number of laser metrological systems. In marine applications, the laser beam can be used as beacon to delineate areas around a central point. In industry, among other applications such as measurement of surface flatness and parallelism, laser-beam systems are being used for measuring parts to determine tolerance, measurement of flow rates, for alignment of one structure with respect to the other in an electromechanical equipment, and to accurately align the walls in tunnel digging, with the laser beam being sustained as the central reference line. The many military applications of metrological systems will be taken up under Chapter 14, Military Applications of Lasers.

LASER ALIGNMENT SYSTEMS

As stated earlier, one of the general applications of lasers is the use of aligning equipment in the construction industry for digging tunnels, aligning sewer pipes, and providing a reference plane for a variety of structural components. The beam is also used for alignment of building walls and their angular relationship to the building under construction.

A laser alignment system consists of a cw laser-beam unit with a telescope, both of which are usually mounted on a tripod for field use, and a retroreflector located at a remote location for the alignment of the laser beam with respect to the particular structure along the path of the laser beam. The laser beam in most cases is from a He-Ne laser unit and is collimated so that it can be projected to reasonably long distances without significant attenuation by the atmospheric contaminants. The laser power from the unit is about 0.5 milliwatt or less, which is sufficient for most alignment applications. The target could be a simple retroreflector, or a photosensor whose output is transmitted back to the laser system for becoming processed for digital display.

In operation of the laser system, the collimated pencil beam is projected to the target, and all structural parts are aligned with respect to the laser beam, since it is the most accurate straight line that can be obtained for this purpose. Unless the earth on which the laser unit is positioned is moving, the laser beam retains its position and direction over long distances in both the horizontal and vertical planes. On some laser systems, which employ a photodetector as the target, an automatic indicator on the laserhead, next to the telescope, indicates when the beam is accurately centered to the target and when it has deviated during the course of operation, so that adjustments can be made by the operator.

A number of manufacturers are producing laser alignment equipment, and among them are: Jodon Engineering, LaserElectronics, Nippon Electric, Oriel, and others. In order to determine which firm has the type of alignment instrument suitable to one's particular purpose, it is best to write to them to obtain their technical or sales brochure from which to make the selection. Spectra-Physics is one of the world's largest He-Ne manufacturers and furnishes He-Ne laser systems for the production of sewer-pipe alignment systems. The instrument shown in Figs. 8-1 and 8-2 uses a Spectra-Physics laser and is a portable and very versatile alignment device. Figure 8-3 shows a different alignment system.

Fig. 8-1. Alignment unit mounted on a trivet.

LASER GAUGING INSTRUMENTS

A unique gauging instrument developed by Systems Research Laboratories, Inc. is designed to measure dimensions of manufactured parts with an accuracy of ±0.15 percent. The instrument is also suited for on-line production inspection for quality control of manufactured parts. Tradenamed LaserMike, the applications of the device include dimensional inspection of machined parts or formed or cast parts, extrusions, wire, extruded profiles, and similar parts made of metal, glass, or plastic. In operation, the part to be gauged is placed in the path of the ribbon-like laser beam and its dimensional profile is displayed on a digital readout in inches or centimeters. The readings can be taken, with a repeatability of ±0.1 percent, at a rate of 10 readings per second. The company manufactures several different models, one of which, Model 1150E is illustrated in Fig.

Fig. 8-2. Alignment unit mounted on a tripod.

Fig. 8-3. Another commercial alignment system, formerly manufactured by Spectra-Physics.

8-4. This instrument is an indispensable tool in quality assurance procedures.

LASER RANGEFINDERS

A rangefinder is a device for measuring range or distance of objects or targets located at any distance from the instrument. The scheme uses a laser beam, such as from a He-Ne laser, a GaAs laser,

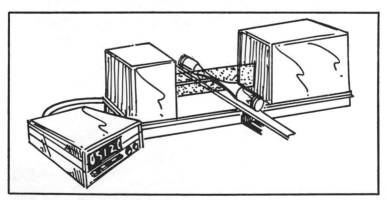

Fig. 8-4. LaserMike Model 1150E.

or any other solid-state laser, such as a ruby or a Nd-YAG laser. To measure the distance, the laser rangefinder transmitter projects a pencil-beam at the remotely-located object or target, and after receiving the reflected beam from the object the computer circuitry in the system analyzes the retroreflected beam and converts the time of travel of the beam into a distance readout. Since the distance travelled by the beam to and from the target is twice the actual distance to be measured, the computer also compensates for this by dividing the time of travel by 2. In addition to measuring, most rangefinders can also compute the azimuth or elevation angles of the target. Range accuracies to a few centimeters can be made up to 2 to 3 kilometers, depending on the pulse rating of the system and on a atmospheric conditions.

A simplified diagram of a typical rangefinder circuitry scheme is shown in Fig. 8-5, in which a modulated laser beam is projected from the transmitter to a target whose range is to be measured. At the instant that the laser beam leaves the transmitter, a portion of the beam is sampled by a silicon photodetector, which starts the counter to count the time pulses. When the laser beam is retroreflected from the target and is received by the receiver photodetector, the latter immediately transmits a pulse to the counter, which stops instantly. The distance then is computed by the system by the number of pulses that have occurred during the roundtrip of the laser beam and the total pulse duration. The summed-up numerical value of the counter is automatically divided by 2 and the result is displayed in actual distance units.

A very simplified equation for determining the distance measured by a rangefinder may be given by the following expression, which neglects a number of finer points for simplicity:

$$S = \frac{N \times C}{2 \times N_c} \qquad \textbf{(Equation 8-1)}$$

where, S is the target distance in centimeters, N is the number of pulses counted by the counter during the travel of the laser beam to and from the target, N_c is the counter frequency per second, and C is the speed of light equal to approximately 3×10^{10} centimeters.

As an example, a rangefinder, operating with a clock frequency of 100 MHz, projects a laser beam at a retroreflector (target). If the counter counts 8×10^2 pulses, what is the target distance, neglecting the risetime of the pulse?

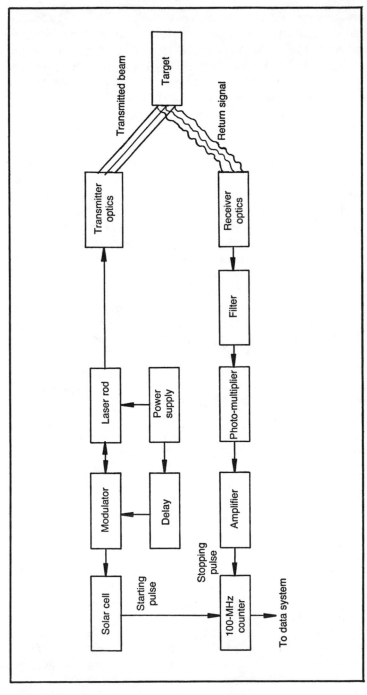

Fig. 8-5. A block diagram of a typical rangefinder showing arrangement of important components.

Substituting numerical values in Equation 8-1, we have:

$$S = \frac{8 \times 10^2 \times 3 \times 10^{10}}{2 \times 10^8}$$

$$= \frac{24 \times 10^{12} \times 10^{-8}}{2}$$

$$= 12 \times 10^4 \text{ cm, or 1.2 kilometers.}$$

A military rangefinder is shown in Fig. 8-6. It is reported that this system can also be used as a target illuminator.

AERIAL POLLUTION MEASURING SYSTEMS

A pollution-measuring system using a carbon dioxide laser, developed by General Electric Company, consists of a transceiver and a retroreflective target positioned at a remote area. The system integrates the pollution concentration along the entire path of the laser beam to the target, and displays the average of the pollution content on an instrument panel at the transceiver end. The transmitter of the system projects a laser beam to the target and the returned beam signal is compared with a reference laser signal, resulting in an error signal. The error signal is then converted by the computer of the system into a degree of pollutant concentration along the beam path. As reported, pollutant concentrations down to 14 parts

Fig. 8-6. A military rangefinder/target designator (Hughes).

per billion (ppb) of ethylene gas and 19 ppb of ammonia gas, which are commonly found in effluents from factory flues, have been recorded. Since carbon dioxide laser emits the harmonic wavelengths 95.050, 105,320, 106,750, and 107,190 angstroms in prominent amounts and since different wavelengths have affinity to be coupled with specific gases, the system can differentiate any one of the pollutant gases within its range of detection.

Another company manufactures a laser road-visibility sensor system having a transmitter and a receiver positioned 250 feet apart on the side of a freeway, bridge, or other roadway, to monitor the atmospheric visibility near-ground level to notify the drivers. The atmospheric pollutant in this particular case consists of a mixture of smoke, dust, fog, or snow in states where snow is prevalent during the winter months.

LASER MAPPING OF THE SEA FLOOR

A Nd-YAG laser system is being used to sound and map the sea floor by Royal Australian Navy. Both the primary radiation of 10,640 angstroms and the frequency-doubled 5,320-angstrom wavelengths are being directed to the sea surface from an airplane. The 10,640-angstrom infrared radiation is mostly reflected from the surface of the water, while the green 5,340-angstrom beam traverses the water and is reflected from the sea floor back to the receiver of the sounder, and the delay between the two beams determines the depth of the sea or ocean floor. It is reported that depths to 30 meters have been thus measured with a resolution of one meter. The principle of measurement of the sea floor is similar to that of a rangefinder, with the exception that here there are two laser beams projected to the target, and one beam reflects from the surface of the water and the other reflects from the sea bottom. The computer of the laser system subtracts the distance of plane-to-water surface from the total distance of plane-to-sea floor, and the remainder is the depth of the sea floor from the surface of the water. Putting this relation in a simplified equation form, we have:

$$D = F_1 - W_s \qquad \text{(Equation 8-2)}$$

where, D is the depth of the sea floor from the surface of the water, F_1 is the distance between the plane and the water floor, and W_s is the distance between the plane and the water surface.

However, the distance F_1 is equal to:

$$F_1 = \frac{N_1 \times C}{2 \times N_c} \qquad \text{(Equation 8-3)}$$

$$\text{and, } W_s = \frac{N_2 \times C}{2 \times N_c} \qquad \textbf{(Equation 8-4)}$$

where, N_1 is the number of clock pulses received by the counter with respect to the sea floor from the airplane, and N_2 is the number of pulses counted with respect to the water surface from the airplane.

Combining the Equation 8-3 with Equation 8-4 and substituting them in Equation 8-2, we have:

$$D = \frac{N_1 \times C}{2N_c} - \frac{N_2 \times C}{2N_c}$$

$$D = \frac{C(N_1 - N_2)}{2N_c} \qquad \textbf{(Equation 8-5)}$$

Example: A depth sounder on an aircraft operates with a 100 MHz clock frequency. If the distance between the water surface and the aircraft is equivalent to 0.5×10^2 clock pulses and is further equal to 3/5th of the distance between the sea floor and the aircraft, what is the depth of the water?

Let surface-to-aircraft distance be equal to D_1, then we have:

$$D_1 = \frac{0.5 \times 10^2 \times 3 \times 10^{10}}{2 \times 10^8}$$

$$= \frac{1.5 \times 10^{12} \times 10^{-8}}{2}$$

$$= \frac{1.5 \times 10^4}{2}$$

$$= 7,500 \text{ cm, or 75 meters.}$$

Let sea-floor-to-aircraft distance be equal to D_2, then we have:

$$D_2 = 75 \times 5/3 = 375/3 = 125 \text{ meters.}$$

The water depth D_3 is:

$$D_3 = 125 - 75 = 50 \text{ meters.}$$

PRECISION AUTOMATED TRACKING SYSTEM

The Precision Automated Tracking System, developed by GTE Sylvania, is a mobile laser tracking and ranging system, shown in Fig. 8-7. PATS provides space-position information on a wide variety of vehicles and targets in real time. The target equisition is

Fig. 8-7. PATS with laser optics mounted atop.

performed either manually or automatically. In the manual mode, the operator manipulates a joystick and locates the target on the screen of a television mounted on the system. He then triggers the laser beam and locks the system on the target. The retroreflected laser beam from the target triggers the automatic tracking section. In this mode of acquisition, the angular rate for either the azimuth or elevation is 100 milliradians per second. In the automatic mode, the angular rate rises to 500 milliradians.

Upon locking the system on the target, the automatic tracking system takes over, and all the target data are multiplexed and displayed on plotters and CRT readouts in real time. The system measures azimuth, elevation, and range automatically. This is performed by transmitting 100 pulses per second from a Nd-YAG laser transmitter to the target and measuring the angle of the retroreflected beam and its round-trip time. The pulses are 15-nanosecond durations each, which also trigger an internal counter in the range computer. The counter stops when the returned laser signal from the target de-activates it; this action instantly gives the target range. The laser and the optical system are incorporated in one unit, and the unit is automatically driven by the locked-on servo system.

The servo system sustains the laser beam locked on the target, so that continuous space information is fed to the system. The tracking of the target is achieved with an accuracy of ±0.01 percent for target ranges of 200 to 30,000 meters for azimuth and elevation. The range accuracy is ±0.01 meters for target ranges of 200 to 10,000 meters, and ±1 meter for target ranges of 10,000 to 30,000 meters. The target range, as in a rangefinder, is measured by one-half of the transmission-reception time. The system operates from a 208-volt, 3-phase, and 30-kW power source. A schematic block diagram of PATS is shown in Fig. 8-8. It must be emphasized here that the transmitted laser power in PATS is automatically maintained at an eye-safe condition as specified by U.S. Government standards, for the safety of the operator and other attendant personnel.

LASERS IN HOME USE

A low-power laser beam can be used in a burglar alarm system to protect a house from burglars or other criminals. A He-Ne unit of about 0.5-milliwatt power emits a red radiation to circle the configuration of the house by means of folding mirrors. The beam is brought back to a photodetector, such as a silicon or cadmium sulfide detector, located in the receiver circuit, where the detector signal is amplified into an electrical energy, which may be fed to a relay to turn on the alarm system. The beam retains the relay continuously open. When the beam is interrupted temporarily by being crossed by a person, the relay closes and in doing so it energizes the alarm system. The relay then must be set back manually.

A similar arrangement can be made at the periphery of a swimming pool, so that when a child accidently walks near the edge of the swimming pool, the beam becomes interrupted, turning on the alarm. The laser beam can be split into two beams running parallel to each other at a distance of 6 to 10 inches apart. Either one of the beams can be made to energize an alarm when the beam is interrupted.

A LASER POISON-GAS DETECTOR

Because the modern chemical-warfare agents are often odorless, colorless, and tasteless, considerable difficulty is experienced in detecting them. However, scientists at the Los Alamos National Laboratory have developed a laser detection system for spotting minute concentrations of nerve gas or skin-blistering gas to give advance warning to moving troops. In operation, the system projects a beam of Nd-YAG laser of 1-nanosecond pulses to the speci-

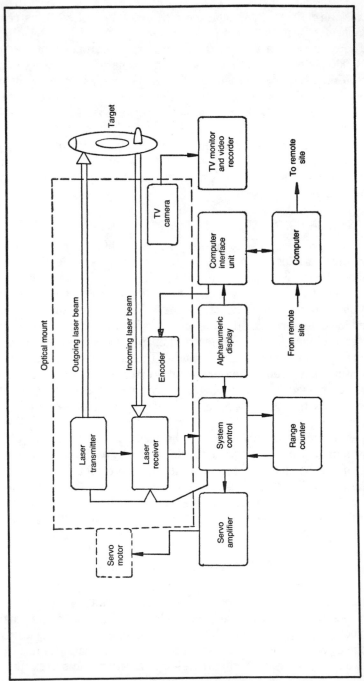

Fig. 8-8. The schematic block diagram of PATS electrical circuit.

mens of the gases to be analyzed. This action produces a plasma, which breaks down the gas molecules into their element forms. These elements then are identified and their origin characterized.

It is reported that the system was originally developed to detect very minute quantities of beryllium dust in air breathed by workers machining beryllium for weapon components. The exposure tolerance of workers exposed to the beryllium atmosphere given by the Federal Standards is 2-micrograms of beryllium dust per 8-hour shift. The laser system can detect two parts per billion of beryllium dust in air. The procedure is said to be rapid and accurate, in contrast to conventional time-consuming methods. The laser system's capability of detection of atomic emissions from phosphorus and chlorine that are found in chemical warfare agents makes the laser system an indispensable tool in advance toxic-gas detection during a chemical warfare.

A LASER ENGRAVER/MARKER

The Holobeam Corporation has developed a cw Nd-YAG laser system which is upcollimated and then deflected by two galvanometer mirrors projecting the beam on the workpiece to be marked. One mirror moves the beam in the x-axis and the other moves it in the y-axis. A flat-field lens of 100-mm focal length focuses the beam on a plane surface of 70-mm diameter, and the mirrors deflect the focus in the x and y axes to engrave characters or symbols set by the microprocessor program, as a uniform focus is maintained on the workpiece. The memory capacity of the system is 16,000 16-bit

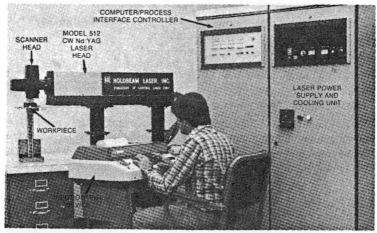

Fig. 8-9. View showing the operator entering instructions.

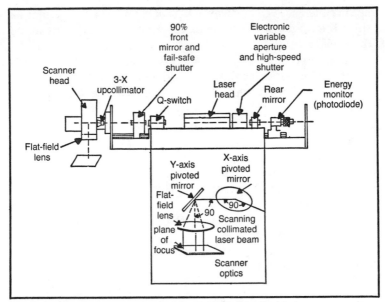

Fig. 8-10. Physical arrangement of the InstaMark optical train.

words, with provision for expansion to 32,000 16-bit words. The unit is fully interlocked for protection against mulfunctions due to electrical or cooling systems. The InstaMark engraver is shown in Fig. 8-9, and its operational scheme is shown in Fig. 8-10.

FINGERPRINT-DETECTION LASER SYSTEM

A latent-fingerprint-detection system developed by Control Laser Corporation uses an argon laser with variable wavelengths from 5,145 to 4,579 angstroms, suitable to cause fluorescence in many materials prone to fluorescence under a blue or ultraviolet light. The system, shown in Fig. 8-11, consists of a Control Laser LPD Series 550 argon laser emitting an output of up to 25 watts,

Fig. 8-11. Fingerprint-Detection Laser System LPD Series 550.

136

with a stability of 1 to 2 percent, depending on the model, and has an E-polarization ratio of 100:1. The beam is transmitted through a 1-millimeter-diameter optical fiber of 6-meter length.

Unlike a conventional fiberoptic waveguide that is provided with an output lens for delivery of the laser energy to the point of interest, the present optical fiber contains an optical element at its proximal end that provides a continuously diverging laser beam through the fiber. This design permits the beam to diverge as it emerges from the exit aperture of the optical waveguide, so as to cover any practical size area to be illuminated. To operate the device, the specimen is merely irradiated with the argon beam and the fluorescent print then can be photographed in color, as desired.

The divergent laser beam has three principal advantages—(1) it offers safety to the operator by preventing an accidental manual exposure to the beam; (2) the beam can be made to cover any-size fingerprint to a luminescing material by merely change of distance between the specimen and the exit port of the stylus provided at the distal end of the optical fiber; and, (3) the divergent characteristic of the propagating beam eliminates the need for an additional lens at the tip of the stylus.

Because of the long length of fiberoptic cable, a complete flexibility of movement of the cable is achieved within the work area. The cable core is made of fused silica with a low-refractive-index silicon polymer cladding and obviates any stray radiation from the cable. To enhance physical strength to the cable, which has a bend radius of 9 inches, a Dupond Tefzel outer jacket covers the entire length of the cable. The tensile strength of the cable is given as 500 kilopounds per square inch. The system is powered from a 3-phase, 180-280 Vac, and is cooled by water flowing at 5 to 6 gpm and 45 to 60 psi, respectively.

A high-speed fingerprint-detection and identification system has been developed jointly by Ontario Provincial Police and Xerox Research Center of Canada. The system utilizes a continuous-wave argon laser emitting at 5,145-angstrom wavelength, with an output power of 1.5 watts. The laser beam is expanded to an area of 65 square centimeters to fully cover the fingerprint area. The illuminated fingerprint luminesces with a yellow-green color when fresh. It fluoresees orange when the print is several months old. The fluorescence of the print is due to the inherent constituents of the palmar sweat, and thus no chemical sprays or powders are required to bring about the identifiability of the fingerprint.

The fluorescence induced by the argon laser on the fingerprint may be photographed in color if it is taken against a dark background. Unfortunately black-and-white photographs cannot be taken because of the interference by background luminescence. The observed pattern of the fingerprint is said to have sharp ridges which do not deteriorate in time even when exposed to severe humid environment for several weeks or months. The method is applicable to the detection of fingerprints on plastic, metal, wood, checks, cloth, glass, and paper.

In line with the fingerprint-detection system, the MIT has developed a rapid printing machine, tradenamed Laserfax, for transmititng fingerprint facsimile. The system is being manufactured by Harris Corporation for use by the Associated Press to transmit high-resolution (285 lines.in.), 8 by 8 inch fingerprint cards to any location remote from the system in less than one minute, the speed of transmission depending on whether the information is transmitted on telephone lines, microwave links, or through satellite communication channels. This system uses a low-power He-Ne laser system, which scans the fingerprint card, converts the optical signal from the print into digital form.

A receiver at the remote station decodes the transmitted signals and feeds them to a second He-Ne laser system whose light beam is modulated and scanned over a sensitive, dry-process film and prints on it the exact copy of the fingerprint with pertinent information. It is thus seen that a system of this type speeds up the transmission and identification of the fingerprint and has become an essential adjunct to other forensic methods now in general use.

SUPERMARKET CHECKOUT LASER SYSTEM

The first grocery supermarket checkout system using a laser beam was put in operation in 1974. The system employed a beam of He-Ne laser radiation to scan a series of bar codes, known as Universal Product Code (UPC), affixed on the merchandise instead of the price label. The codes consisted of the name and the price of the merchandise, in addition to the information for maintaining records of inventory and disbursals. A facsimile of the UPC symbols is shown in Fig. 8-12.

Since the inception of the laser checkout system, there have been many improvements by several companies that principally produce the system. In general, the checkout system consists of a cash register, a code-scanning window that is located at the terminal section of the counter which carries the grocery items on a

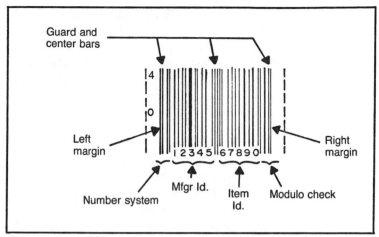

Fig. 8-12. The UPC symbols with explanations.

motorized belt, a grocery-price display window on the cash register and a slot through which the printed identification and the price list emerge as the checker operates the machine.

The code-scanning laser system (see Fig. 8-13) comprises a 1-milliwatt He-Ne laser unit, which produces a narrow beam and projects it to the scanning window over which the merchandise is pulled by the grocery checker, with the UPC symbols facing the window and the scanning laser beam. The scanning beam is actuated by means of a scanning mirror which oscillates the beam over the UPC bars. The reflected diffuse beam form the code bars becomes incident on a photodetector, such as a silicon detector, which converts the incident beam into electrical signals. The logic decoder receives the electrical signals and decodes them and transmits them to the cash register for printout as well as to the memory storage section of a computer located in the system. In this way, all checkout calculations are performed speedily and accurately, and the customer is handed out the slip having the printed information consisting of the name and the price of the merchandise together with the purchase date.

The decoding is done in accordance with the beam intensities received by the logic decoder. These intensities vary in accordance with the thickness of the UPC bars, the thicker and darker bars reflecting less laser intensity than the lighter bars. The decoder signals further vary with time of scan in milliseconds, the wider bars being scanned for relatively longer time than the thin and lighter-shade bars. Thus, the logic system converts both the intensity and duration of the scanned beam on the UPC bars into the alphanumeric print, which is shown on the checkout slip and is also permanently stored in the computer storage section. The overall function of the laser-scanned checkout system is to calculate the total price of the merchandise, maintain inventory control, accounting, disbursing, and to keep records in a systematic manner.

Questions and Problems

8-1. What are metrological measurement systems? What types of lasers can be used in the instruments? Can pulsed lasers be used in metrological systems? Can a continuous-wave laser be used in a metrological unit? On what principle does a metrological device using a continuous-wave laser beam operate? On what principle does a pulsed laser beam operate in a metrological device?

8-2. What is a laser alignment system? What principal components does it contain? How does it operate? How is it applied to alignment operation? What accuracy can one obtain from an alignment instrument using a laser beam? Discuss.

8-3. What is a laser gauging instrument? What does it gauge? How is it made? How does it operate in gauging a part? What accuracy can one obtain from it? How does it produce a ribbon-like laser beam? Discuss. (There are two ways of obtaining ribbon beam.)

8-4. What is a laser rangefinder? What types of lasing elements does it use? Which of the lasing elements used in a rangefinder is the most powerful? Which type of laser beam is eye-safe to use? How does a rangefinder obtain its data for yielding the range information? Can a rangefinder measure angular attitude of a moving target? How? Explain.

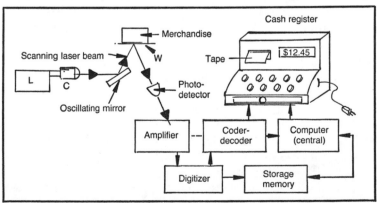

Fig. 8-13. A simplified functional diagram of the UPC scanning laser system.

8-5. Explain the operation of a simple rangefinder. How far should the laser beam travel in order to yield range information? What is a receiver photodiode? What is its function in a rangefinder? If the rangefinder does not operate pulsed so that no pulses can be counted to determine distance, then how can one obtain range data form a continuous-wave laser system? Explain.

8-6. A certain rangefinder counter operates on 98 MHz and during its operation the counter has counted 6.8×10^3 pulses. What is the distance measured by the rangefinder?

8-7. If a rangefinder operates on 100 MHz counter frequency and has measured a distance of 4 kilometers, how many pulses has the counter counted during a 4-kilometer travel of the laser beam? What is the pulsewidth of the system?

8-8. What is an aerial pollution-measuring system? How is it constructed? How does it operate? What laser element can be used in the construction of a pollution-detection or measuring system? Do laser wavelengths play any role in the measurement of pollution content?

8-9. How does laser-road visibility sensor differ, if any, from a pollution-detection system? What are the atmospheric pollutants that are measured or monitored by the sensor? How far does the system project its beam to integrate the air pollutant content?

8-10. What is a sea-floor mapping system, using a laser beam? How many laser beams does it use? If more than one beam is used, are the beams split from the fundamental beam? How can the system receive two sets of data during mapping of the sea floor? Discuss.

8-11. If the distance between the water surface and the air-craft is 80 meters, and the depth sounder operates at 100 MHz for 1.5×10^{-3} second, what is the depth of the water?

8-12. If a depth sounder operates on 100 MHz and its counter has counted 2×10^4 pulses for a round trip of the laser beam from the ocean floor, what is the depth of the water, if the ratio of water-surface-to-aircraft distance to ocean-floor-to-aircraft distance is 2:3?

8-13. What is precision automated tracking system? How is it principally constructed? What is a transceiver? How is the laser beam aligned with respect to the flying target? How is the laser beam locked on the target after acquisition? What does the system measure? How does it measure?

8-14. What is the accuracy of acquiring target range by PATS? What is its tracking accuracy? What laser element is used in

PATS? Does it operate pulsed or in continuous-wave mode? How does it measure range? Discuss.

8-15. Give two applications of laser metrological function in use for homes. Discuss two home devices and their operations for home use. Can a laser beam be used for interoffice communications?

8-16. What laser system does Control Laser Corporation use for fingerprint detection? In what wavelength range is the laser radiation? What polarization ratio does the laser unit possess? How is the laser beam transmitted to the specimen? Is the output beam converging type or diverging type? Give reason for your answer.

8-17. Where does the waveguide contain its optical element? What type of lens is it, converging or diverging? What advantages does the optical element at the proximal end of the cable have? What characteristics of the cable provides flexibility of use and high tensile strength? How is the system used to detect fingerprint? Discuss.

8-18. Describe the construction and operation of the Ontario Provincial Police fingerprint-detection system. How does the MIT fingerprint-facsimile transmission system operate? What is a supermarket checkout laser system? How is it generally constructed? How does it operate? Discuss. How does this system differ from conventional grocery checkout systems? What is its overall function? Discuss.

Chapter 9

Aerial Laser-Beam Communications

The laser beam's high coherence and directionality makes this radiation a useful tool for communicating information data through the atmosphere with privacy and security. It is almost impossible to jam the data being transmitted through the laser beam by any known means. Because of the extremely wide bandwidth of laser radiation, up to 10^7 discrete conversions can be executed simultaneously. The laser beam can be modulated by frequency, amplitude, phase, and polarization formats using analog or digital transmission mode, with efficient use of transmission power. Image transmission is also possible by scanning the image by intensity-modulation format. The transmitted beam can be locked on the receiver, whereby the communication cannot be interrupted if the transmitting station or the receiving end is in movement, such as on the sea between the ships, between a ship and the shore, or between an aircraft and a ship or shore.

Several manufacturers are producing aerial laser communication systems for special use in the construction industry and in military field applications. On a clear day, a well-collimated laser beam can be transmitted several miles and to shorter distances when the atmospheric conditions due to fog, mist, rain or smog does not permit the penetration of the beam for more than a few hundred feet.

There are several drawbacks to this type of transmission through long distances. The transmitted beam attenuates due to

143

contaminants in the atmosphere, such as carbon dioxide, sulfur dioxide, water vapor, and varying temperatures of the air, the latter causing aberrations and dispersion of the beam. These disadvantages are further intensified by the fact that the beam-energy level must be at low hazard or no-hazard grade for eye safety, thus resulting in a limitation of distance to which the laser beam can be transmitted without significant attenuation. The wavelength of the laser beam is also of concern because the beam must be compatible with the receiver detector to couple with it; this wavelength is determined by the modulation speed of the transmitting system. Because the modulators must operate with wavelengths in the visible spectral range for high efficiency operation and for beam visibility to the communicating parties, the power of the radiation runs low, thus limiting the distance to which the laser beam can be projected. In most aerial communication systems, He-Ne laser is used for its high visibility and meeting the safety regulations.

Argon or krypton laser can also be used, but the beam visibility of these lasers is low. For high-power transmission, either Nd-YAG or carbon dioxide laser will be desirable but both the beams are invisible, and it is very difficult to modulate a carbon dioxide laser beam. Frequency-doubled Nd-YAG at 5320-angstrom level would be a satisfactory candidate but its power has to be considerably attenuated prior to projection to the receiver. All these schemes indicate that aerial transmission of information data must be restricted to relatively short distances. Possibly, the latter characteristic is one of the several reasons why aerial communicators have not become as popular as fiberoptic communication systems, whose applications are now spreading all over the world. On the other hand, space communication, which is a different subject from our present study, will have greater advantage over the atmospheric communication, since space may be considered almost vacuum and transmission problems are greatly diminished.

HE-NE COMMUNICATION SYSTEM

An aerial communication system using a He-Ne laser unit and manufactured by Metrologic Instruments, Inc. is shown in Fig. 9-1. The communicator consists of a transmitter and a receiver. The receiver may be positioned at any distance within the range of the system either directly across the source of the beam or after the beam has been reflected from several mirrors, which means the beam can be carried around corners before becoming incident on the photodetector of the receiver.

The transmitter contains a He-Ne laser tube, which is modulated by voice at a modulation level of 50 percent, with a maximum input signal of 2.0 volts at a bandwidth of 125 kHz. It operates from a 115-volt alternating current source. The voltage is amplified and rectified to a voltage of 5000 volts dc. This voltage starts the discharge through the He-Ne tube and then becomes stabilized down to 2,800 volts, which is the operating voltage of the tube. The system consumes about 25 watts in operation. All voice data are converted into electrical analog signals and modulated in the transmitter before being transmitted through the air to the receiver.

The receiver contains a photocell (phototransistor) which receives a modulated laser beam from the transmitter and converts the light beam modulations into electrical signals, which are amplified to drive a speaker located in the receiver. The electrical signals thus produced are directly proportional to the laser beam level. The signals are demodulated in the photocell and are fed to an amplifier, from which they are transmitted to a speaker provided with a variable volume control. Since the amplifier output is 300 milliwatts, the level of laser power is ample to produce a sound of adequate listening level. Although there is a slight divergence of the beam during its projection through air, the photocell area is large enough to gather the entire beam to sustain the full beam power of

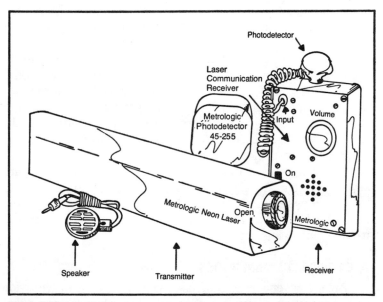

Fig. 9-1. The Metrologic Instruments sound communication system Model ML-868.

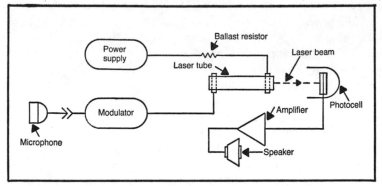

Fig. 9-2. A simplified block diagram of the laser communication system (Metrologic).

the incident modulated laser light. The receiver upper frequency is limited to 15 kHz, which is adequate for normal voice levels; however, if the operator desires to operate the system at higher frequencies, the photocell may be replaced by a phototransistor, although this will reduce the area of light reception at the photosensor. In the latter event, the beam must be collimated to a small diameter. A block diagram of the communicator is illustrated in Fig. 9-2.

In the operation of the communicator, the audio signals are fed into a crystal microphone which is connected to the modulating circuit through a 0.047 mfd capacitor. The modulator circuit amplitude-modulates the audio signals, which are fed into an amplifier. The amplified modulated signals are then led into the laser tube biased with a 4.5 mA current, so that the laser output from the tube is a modulated light. The (laser) light is projected out of the output mirror of the tube and propagated into air with slight divergence, which, for small distances, such as 40 to 50 feet lengths, is practically insignificant. If voice has to be transmitted to more than one receiver, not to exceed two because of the laser-beam power limitation with this instrument, the modulated laser beam can be split by means of a beam splitter into two 50-percent levels and directed by means of first-surface mirrors to the receivers at the two different locations.

LASER DIODE COMMUNICATORS

Among several brands of laser communication systems for aerial data transmission is a hard-held laser communicator provided with a GaAs laser diode for furnishing the signal light for modulation. The unit operates in the infrared and is frequency-modulated by the input voice signal. Its communication range is 3 kilometers but this range can be extended to 6 kilometers during clear weather. It has a beam divergence of 2 degrees and operates from a 6-volt battery source. Its application is for outdoor field service.

One other brand is a binocular system, in which one ocular transmits the voice data through the laser beam and the other receives the beam from another unit located at the specified location. A photodetector in the receiving section demodulates the incoming signal and feeds it to an amplifier for energizing the acoustical section. The system uses a GaAs laser diode which receives the modulated electrical signals from a microphone located on the hand-held unit. The operator listens to the incoming message by means of earphones connected through a cord to an output jack from the acoustic section. The laser-beam divergence of the system is variable from 2 milliradians using 20× collimator to 4 milliradians using a 10× collimator. The transmitter of the unit operates from a 60-volt variable voltage battery source, and the receiver operates on the 9-volt section of the same battery source.

A laser communicator developed by Holobeam, Inc. uses a time-code modulation technique and transmits digital data. The unit employs a GaAs laser diode having a transmission capability of 75 meters in air. Because the laser diode has a high divergence, 300 milliradians, the beam is collimated to 1-milliradian divergence prior to transmission from the transmitter. Since a GaAs laser is sensitive to temperature changes, the manufacturer employs a thermal control loop comprising a regulator, a modulator, and a thermistor. The thermistor monitors the ambient temperature and thereby controls the regulator output level. The unit operates from a 28-volt dc power supply.

ARGON LASER COMMUNICATOR

The Lockheed Missiles & Space Division has developed a laser communicator that is capable of transmitting 300 megabits per second through an argon laser beam. Its range is about 1.2 miles through clear atmosphere, although ranges farther than the specified range have been obtained with it using special techniques. The laser beam of the unit is frequency-modulated and achieves high rate of transmission. This rate has been made possible by employing a microwave transmitter to drive the optical-section frequencies. This combination makes the output beam less susceptible to atmospheric disturbances. Since the silicon photodiode of the receiver is compatible with the wavelengths from the argon laser, the accuracy of the system is significantly enhanced.

ND-YAG LASER COMMUNICATOR

Space communication method being akin to aerial laser communication scheme, the United States Air Force has developed a preliminary laser communicator link that transmits high rate data in gigabits. As was mentioned earlier, this type of communication offers complete security because of the impossibility of jamming the laser beam. It is reported that 14 television broadcasts can be transmitted with very high resolution with this system. The laser beam employed is a frequency-doubled Nd-YAG radiation emitted at 5,320 angstroms, which is in the green spectrum and, therefore, is very penetrating through the atmosphere. The transmission can be carried out between satellites or down to earth.

The Nd-YAG laser is optically pumped by means of a flashlamp containing vapors of potassium and rubidium emitting in the yellow and deep red, respectively. The output from the laser rod is 200 milliwatts in the green spectrum. The optical pump is supplemented by the radiation from the sunlight, which pumps the Nd-YAG laser when the metal-vapor optical pump is off. The system is said to be operable modelocked at 500 megahertz for a period of 18 months. At the receiving end, a photodiode, which has an efficiency of 20 percent for green light detects the radiation from the frequency-doubled Nd-YAG laser. The receiver, of course, can be located on another satellite or on a ground-based station or on shipboard.

Questions and Problems

9-1. Why should a laser beam be used in aerial communication? What characteristics of a laser beam make it adaptable to this type of application? Discuss. In what different formats can a laser beam be modulated? Which format is the most popular commercially? Discuss.

9-2. What are some of the applications of aerial communication by means of laser beams? Can aerial communication be carried out between two or more stations? Explain how this can be accomplished. Can aerial communication with laser beams be jammed? Give your reasons.

9-3. Is there any distance limitation in aerial communication? How can one increase the distance communicated with a given laser system? Are there any drawbacks to laser communication through air or space? Would a high-power laser system overcome these drawbacks? What role does the wavelength of a laser system play in the aerial communication? Can any laser wavelength be used for this purpose?

9-4. Which of the laser systems among He-Ne, argon, krypton, or GaAs lasers can be used for long distance communication? Which of these systems would you employ for communicating to a distance of 15 miles through air on a clear day? Can you use carbon dioxide laser beam for communication? If so, how? If not, what are your reasons for the disadvantage, if any, of this laser system?

9-5. If you were using a Nd-YAG laser for communication, at what mode or format would you use it? Will aerial attenuation prevent Nd-YAG from being used for long distances? If so, what are some of your reasons? What are two harmonics of Nd-YAG laser? Which one is the most powerful of the three types of its wavelengths?

9-6. If the communication is being carried out with the beam making several bends, what type of reflector would you use? Will the incident beam on the photosensor at the receiver end be expanded due to divergence? How would you correct this situation if it occurs? Will bending the laser beam with mirrors affect the signal resolution? Discuss.

9-7. What percent modulation does the Metrologic Instruments laser communicator have? Can it be increased? How would you increase the modulation level of this device? Do you use any repeaters in this type of communicator? What does the phototransistor in this system do to the transmitted signal? What does the phototransistor do to the communicated signals? Are the signals analog or digital?

9-8. What is the difference between amplitude modulation and phase modulation? Which one is preferable over the other in aerial communication of voice? How can modulation take place in a He-Ne laser tube? How can modulation be achieved by means of a GaAs laser diode? Can you modulate CO_2 laser? Discuss.

9-9. If GaAs laser diode operates in the infrared spectrum, can it be used in aerial communication? Is it amplitude-modulated or frequency-modulated? Why? Discuss. What is the communication range of a GaAs laser diode? What is the beam divergence of GaAs laser diode? If GaAs laser is temperature sensitive, what should one employ to overcome this drawback? What does Lockheed employ to transmit 300 megabits per second? What is its range? What modulation does it use?

9-10. Why does one employ microwave transmitter to drive the optical frequencies of a communicator? What is the advantage of this scheme? The U.S. Air Force laser system that transmits gigabits uses frequency-doubled 5,320-angstrom wavelengths. What type of laser is used in this system? How can one optically pump this laser? In what spectrum is the beam output from this communicator? Why is this chosen? Discuss. What is the fundamental wavelength of this laser system?

Chapter 10
Fiberoptic Communications

Light-carrying characteristics of glass and transparent plastic fibers were known for over fifty years. The fibers were assembled coherently into bundled which transmitted an image from one end of the bundle to the other end. However, it was not until the discovery of the laser beam, which provided a high-intensity light in the smallest area possible, that the application of glass and plastic fibers become very popular for transmission of data and voice from one place to another. The distance through which the communication can be achieved varies from a few feet to thousands of feet, using booster links along the entire transmission line. The transmission line may be a single optical fiber or a number of fibers which are not necessarily arranged in the cable into a coherent bundle unless a visual image is being transmitted from a station to another station. The distance to which such images can be transmitted is generally small, depending on the intensity of the image at the transmitting end.

Data and voice travels in an optical fiber in the form of a modulated light. The spoken words, for example, into a microphone are transformed into electrical signals which are used to energize a light source, such as a GaAs diode or He-Ne discharge in a tube and to modulate the light beam. The modulated light beam is fed into one end of an optical fiber (fiberoptic) cable, to couple the light from the source to the fiberoptic line. The choice of GaAs diode or He-Ne laser tube is for their high-intensity light, efficient coupling properties with the fiber, and their capability of becoming modulated by the modulated electric current passing through them. Furthermore, these laser sources can transmit high bandwidth data through the fiber, and have long operational lifetimes.

A fiberoptic laser communication system consists of a transmitter, a fiberoptic transmission line, and a receiver at the point where the message is to be received. The transmitter consists of a microphone or an electrical data source which is provided with means to modulate the data and to feed the modulated data to an amplifier to increase the signal intensity. The modulated current is coupled to a light source to modulate its emission. The light is coupled through a link to the fiberoptic bundle whose light coupling surface is highly polished to reduce absorption and attenuation of the light entering the fiber bundle. The light traverses the fiber bundle and becomes incident on the photodetector of a receiver. The photodetector converts the modulated light into electrical signal, which is amplified in the receiver amplifier and then applied to a speaker, or to a data bank for storage for later use. As in electrical wires, signals travelling through a fiberoptic line do attenuate, and this attenuation increases with distance.

FIBEROPTIC CHARACTERISTICS

All optical fibers designed to transmit optical signals consist of a central core of high index of refraction and a peripheral thin layer, known as cladding, which is made of an optical material of lower index of refraction than the core material. The modulated light travels through the optical fiber in a zigzag path, that is, it reflects from one wall of the fiber to the opposite wall a great many times before the light reaches the distal end of the fiber, where the fiber is coupled to a photodetector. In some types of fiber, the loss of intensity of the light passing through it is smaller than in some other types of fibers. These losses are expressed in decibels per kilometer (dB/km) of the fiber length, and vary from 0.25 dB/km to several hundred dB/km. For short distances, such as 25 to 50 meters, high losses are not significant, but for long distances, such as 50 kilometers or over, low-loss fibers are usually used in order to conserve the optical signal intensity during its transmission through the fiber.

Types of Fiberoptics

Types and grades of optical fibers now in commercial use are varied and numerous. There are those that transmit infrared light, those that transmit visible light, those that transmit ultraviolet light, and those that transmit almost all spectral rays from ultraviolet to infrared. Most grades of fiberoptics transmit visible light, and those that transmit in the invisible spectrum are made of special grade glasses and are more costly. Quartz glass and sapphire are used for either infrared or ultraviolet transmission, and ordinary glass and plastic fibers are generally used for transmission of visible light.

There are three general types of fiberoptic materials: (1) silica core with plastic cladding or step refractive index profile type, (2) doped silica core with doped silica cladding, and (3) graded index profile, which consists of a doped silica core with radially varying dope level. The first type has the greatest attenuation and the last fiber has the lowest attenuation characteristic. Plastic fibers are generally made of acrylic core and plastic cladding of lower index of refraction, and glass fibers are made of high refractive index glass core with cladding of low index of refraction. The purpose for the differences of the indices of refractions between the core and the cladding is to cause the light through the fiber to totally reflect as it traverses the fiber. If the core and the cladding material are of the same material and index of refraction, the incident light on the fiber entrance surface will also pass out of the fiber without becoming reflected, the same as when the ray hits the cladding at an angle smaller than the critical angle. The diameters of these fibers vary from 10 microns to 1 millimeter for data transmission; other sizes are also prevalent. For transmitting images, the smaller the fiber diameter the more resolution of the image at the transmitted end (distal end) will be.

Signal Attenuation Through Optical Fiber

It has already been stated that an optical signal travels through an optical fiber by total reflection and that there is a loss of signal intensity during its travel from the signal source to its destination. Figure 10-1 illustrates in a very simplified manner how this loss can occur and how it can be bolstered by means of a repeater or repeaters along the fiberoptic line. As can be seen, the loss is due to several factors, such as the angle at which the signal enters the optical fiber, the length of fiber traversed by the signal, absorption by the fiber due to impurities in it, such as traces of Mn, Co, Fe, Cr, etc., the index of refraction of the core material, connection losses, and the reflection losses at the entrance aperture of the fiber. The entrance aperture determines the light-gathering characteristic of the fiber—the larger this aperture is the greater is the light

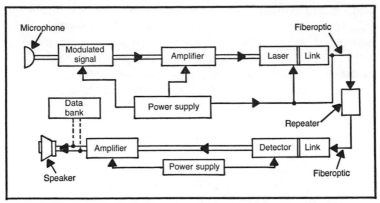

Fig. 10-1. Scheme showing a very simplified arrangement of a fiberoptic transmission line.

gathered at the fiber cross-sectional surface. However, for image transmission, the greater the light-gathering aperture the smaller is the image resolution at the distal, receiver end of the fiber. For this reason, fine diameter fibers are used for image transmission while relatively large-diameter fibers can be used for voice and data transmission. The total transmission attenuation in a fiberoptic cable is measured in dB, as mentioned earlier, and may be expressed as follows:

$$I_t = I_o - (L_1 + L_2 + L_3 \ldots L_d) \qquad \text{(Equation 10-1)}$$

where, I_t is the total attenuation in dB, L_1, L_2, L_3 etc. are the fiber-to-link losses, and L_d is the fiber-to-detector linkage loss, all quantities being given in dB.

Since the light-intensity loss in transmission through a fiberoptic cable is given in dB/km, one can determine in designing a transmission line with a fiberoptic cable what initial light intensity will be needed in order to obtain an adequate amount of light energy at its destination for activating the photodetector of the receiver. For an equal transmission distance, the optical cable has the advantage of lower signal attenuation than metal cable of equivalent diameter. Furthermore, the fiberoptic cable is lighter and less costly than the metal cable, in addition to offering immunity to interference by radio waves and security in transmission against interception by unauthorized parties.

Numerical Aperture

The numerical aperture (NA) of a fiber is the ability to capture the maximum amount of light incident on the fiber cross-sectional surface, and is numerically equal to the product of the index of refraction (n) of the transmitting medium and the sine of angle ϕ between the entrance angle of the light ray and the normal (perpendicular) to the entrance surface of the fiber. Given in an equation form, we have:

$$NA = n \sin \phi = \sqrt{N_1{}^2 - n_2{}^2} \qquad \textbf{(Equation 10-2)}$$

where, n is the index of refraction of the air equal approximately to 1, n_1 is the index of refraction of the core material, and n_2 is the index of refraction of the cladding of the fiber. For efficiency of transmission through the fiberoptic, the refractive index n_1 must be greater than the refractive index n_2. In addition, the angle at which the beam reflects within the core is of great concern and is called the critical angle of the beam. The larger the critical angle the greater is the transmission of light through the fiber. This relation is illustrated in Fig. 10-2.

In Fig. 10-2, an incident light ray making an angle θ_1 with respect to the central axis of the core reflects from the interface at the cladding to the other interface of the cladding opposite to it, making an angle of θ_c with the normal N. This angle, θ_c, is known as the critical angle. Any light ray that is incident at the core-cladding interface at an angle equal or greater than θ_c totally reflects in the fiber and is transmitted to the other end of the fiber. However, any ray of light that enters the core and makes an angle θ_s, which is smaller than the critical angle, passes out of the cladding, as shown. The light beam that is trapped in the core travels through the fiber by reflection from one interface to the other within the core until it reaches the terminal destination, where a photodetector will couple with it.

The critical angle may be expressed by an equation as follows:

$$\sin \theta_c = \frac{n_2}{n_1} \qquad \textbf{(Equation 10-3)}$$

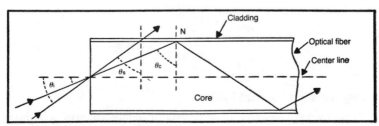

Fig. 10-2. Illustrating the critical angle.

Illustrating Equation 10-3 with a problem, we may assume: A fiber has a core index of refraction of 1.546 and a cladding index of refraction of 1.450. A laser beam becomes incident on the entrance surface of a fiber at an angle of 20 degrees. (a) What is the critical angle in the core? (b) What is the numerical aperture of the fiber? (c) What is the angle of refraction in the core?

Substituting numerical quantities of the indices of refractions and equating them to the critical angle, as given in Equation 10-3, we obtain:

$$\text{Sin } \theta_c = \frac{n_2}{n_1}$$
$$= \frac{1.450}{1.546}$$
$$= 0.9380$$
$$= 69.7°$$

The numerical aperture of the fiber will be:

$$NA = \sqrt{n_1{}^2 - n_2{}^2}$$
$$= \sqrt{2.39 - 2.10}$$
$$= \sqrt{0.29} = 0.54$$

The angle of refraction in the core will be:

$$n_1 = \frac{\sin i}{\sin r} \qquad \textbf{(Equation 10-3)}$$

where, n_1 is the index of refraction of the core, i is the angle of incidence, and r is the angle of refraction in the core.

From Equation 10-3, we have:

$$\sin r = \frac{\sin i}{n_1}$$
$$= \frac{\sin 50°}{1.546}$$
$$= \frac{0.7660}{1.546} = 0.5 \text{ approx.}$$

therefore, $\qquad\qquad$ r $=$ $\quad$ 30°

Packing Density of Optical Cable

The packing density of a fiberoptic cable determines the amount of light that can be transmitted through the cable. It is the ratio of the total area of the core plus cladding to the total area of the core in the cable. Figure 10-3 A shows a single fiber with its core and cladding, and Fig. 10-3 B illustrates the total number of fibers in a cable and the respective core and cladding areas. For example, let us assume that the diameter of the fiber is D and the diameter of its core is d. If N number of fibers make up the cable, and the total area of the core is designated by A_c and the total area of the bundle is designed by A_b, then we may equate the following expression:

$$A_c = \frac{Nn(d)^2}{4} \qquad \textbf{(Equation 10-4)}$$

and the total fiber area will be:

$$A_b = \frac{Nn(D)^2}{4} \qquad \textbf{(Equation 10-5)}$$

The packing density of the cable will be:

$$P_d = \frac{Nn(d)^2}{4} \div \frac{Nn(D)^2}{4} \text{ or, } \frac{A_c}{A_b} \qquad \textbf{(Equation 10-6)}$$

$$= \frac{Nn(d)^2}{4} \times \frac{4}{Nn(D)^2}$$

Cancelling the equal quantities from each side of the equation, we have:

$$P_d = \frac{d^2}{D^2} \qquad \textbf{(Equation 10-7)}$$

where, P_d is the packing density of the fiberoptic cable.

From these equations, it is readily seen that the smaller the diameter of the fiber the closer are the fibers and thus more fibers can be packed in a given cable. If such a cable is transmitting images, then the resultant images will be sharper and have greater resolu-

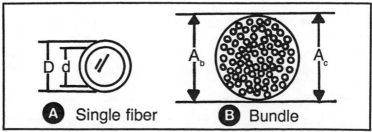

Fig. 10-3. View showing the cross-sectional areas of a single fiber and a bundle.

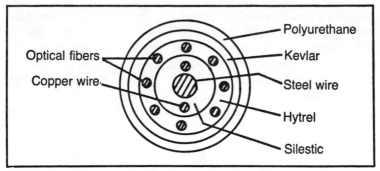

Fig. 10-4. A figurative design for a communication cable.

tion. Furthermore, by packing smaller-diameter fibers in a cable, the flexure of the cable can be made in a smaller radius and the breakage of fibers will be less than when large-diameter fibers are used. Diameters of such fibers range from 30 microns up, depending on the function they will perform and the corners around which the cables will be bent during installation.

Fibers for use in communication lines where repeaters are used and the cables are stressed by pulling on them, the structure of the cable may be represented by a nominal design as shown in Fig. 10-4, which may or may not be the exact construction of any one commercial cable. The scheme only gives an idea about the constituent parts of the cable and their relative positions in the cable. For instance, for stressing the cable by pulling on it during installing the communication line underground, a steel wire of the same type as the piano wire may be included in the center of the cable and embedded in a silestic material. About the silestic material could be positioned a plurality of fibers for transmitting the data. At least two copper wires may be included in the substance of the cable for conducting the electric current to the repeaters. These elements may be further surrounded by hytrel, and kevlar, which prevents the cable from being chewed on by rodents in the ground. Finally, another layer of polyurethane may be cladded for a durable construction. As stated above, the relationships of these elements to each other with respect to their positions may be different in cable constructions of different manufacturers, since each one will have its own proprietary cable construction and method of fabrication.

FIBEROPTIC LASER SYSTEMS

There are many different fiberoptic laser systems employed commercially. The field in which these systems are employed comprise the industrial applications, medical and dental instrumentations, military utilization in underwater and surface communications, and in atomic fusion and nuclear operations where fiberoptic visualization of nuclear reactions are performed for sake of personnel safety and high visual accuracy. In the newspaper industry, the information and image transmission through fiberoptic cables has become a commonplace because of the accuracy and speed with which such operations are accomplished at low costs.

In general industry, the most important application of fiberoptic cables is data and voice communications. Portable laser equipment for materials processing constitutes, although small, another important phase of the fiberoptic utilization. Welding, drilling, or annealing of parts or structures that cannot be brought under the laser head of a stationary laser processing system can be conveniently and efficiently accomplished by the use of optical waveguides made of fiberoptic material. An optical waveguide is a fiberoptic cable of about one to two meter length and is provided at its proximal end with a coupling that attaches the cable to the laserhead. At its distal end, the cable is fitted with an optical system for focusing the laser beam to the area of interest. In microelectronic industry, the waveguide is used to solder leads to printed circuit boards or to bond the integrated-circuit external leads to the header. The annealing and hardening functions of the laser beam have already been discussed; but, for microscopic areas where a very fine heat spot is necessary, the fiberoptic waveguide can perform very admirably.

For medical and dental work, special fiberoptic cables have been developed whereby surgery of profusely bleeding organs can be performed with great ease and flexibility of use of the cable. Gastrointestinal tracks are examined with the light transmitted through an optical cable and treatment is administered with the laser beam conducted through the same cable, such as in cauterizing ulcers in the stomach or in pyloric region. Thus, fiberoptic waveguides are routinely being used in the surgery of all parts of the body, as will be discussed under medical instrumentations. A waveguide developed and patented by Laserkinetics Corporation delivers both laser radiation and gas for anesthetizing the area to be treated or surgically removed. Carbon dioxide laser is also used in medical surgery using a fiberoptic waveguide.

In the military field, optical fiber cables are employed in communication. The present metallic signal conductors are being replaced by fiberoptic cables especially on ships, aircraft, and underwater communication operations. In this system, gallium arsenide diodes or He-Ne lasers of 0.5 to 1.0 milliwatt output are employed for transmitting data and message up to 10 kilometers without the use of optical links or repeaters. The transmission losses in these cables vary from one to several dB/km; fibers with higher dB losses for short distances are tolerable, because the attenuation in short distances becomes insignificant.

The light-emitting diodes (LEDs) have played great roles in data transmission through fiberoptic cables. Because they are efficient in high emission of radiance relative to their small sizes, coupled with their property of being capable of becoming modulated, high bandwidth information data can be transmitted in a narrow spectral width with almost insignificant dispersion during transit. Furthermore, the LEDs are reliable in their transmission of modulated data at many megahertz levels. Both laser diodes and LEDs are in considerable field use at present.

TRANSMITTER CHARACTERISTICS

A transmitter for a fiberoptic communication consists of a data receiving section, which may be a crystal microphone or a digital or analog source of signals, a modulating circuitry which modulates the input data and feeds it to an amplifier. The amplifier amplifies the input signal and transmits it to a light-emitting device, which may be either an ion gas laser or any one of a variety of semiconductor diodes, such as a gallium arsenide (GaAs) diode, gallium-aluminum-arsenide (GaAlAs), gallium-aluminum-phosphide (GaAlP), gallium-indium-arsenic antimonide (GaIn-As-Sb) and a number of others. These diodes are good optical data carriers as are the helium-neon, argon, and krypton lasers, and do not require circulating air or liquid cooling agent, since they are built with heat sinks which are sufficiently thermal conductive to dissipate the small amount of heat produced during the operation of the diodes. For remote communication, He-Ne, ruby, Nd-YAG, and CO_2 lasers are used with special high-power circuitry. When repeaters are used along the transmission line, the diode lasers will operate admirably. LEDs are used because of their small size, low cost, and high radiant intensity; they can emit up to 100 w/cm^2, and more, and are easily controllable by varying their input current to obtain the desired output radiation within their power limitations. The diode laser can produce more output power than LEDs, thus coupling more radiant power to the optical fiber cable.

A diode laser is principally an optical amplifier, its two active

160

surfaces forming a Fabry Perot cavity. The light-emitting diodes operate below the threshold current, and when this current is increased beyond the threshold level, a stimulated radiation in the form of laser occurs. Modulation is achieved by modulating the bias current through the diode. For most communication purposes, GaAs diode laser is specified. It is recently reported that a diode laser made of neodymium-aluminum borate developed by German scientists emits at 10,600 angstroms when optically pumped by 8000-angstrom krypton ion laser radiation. The efficiency of radiant emission of a diode laser is usually greater than other types of solid-state or gas lasers. This efficiency may be calculated by dividing the number of photons produced at the pn junction by the number of electrons that have passed the junction per second. In an equation which includes the wavelength, we may equate the quantum emission efficiency of the diode as:

$$Q_e = \frac{P_t \times e \times \lambda}{hc \times I} \qquad \textbf{(Equation 10-8)}$$

where, Q_e is the quantum emission efficiency of the diode pn junction, P_t is the total power emitted, e is the charge of the electron in esu, λ is the wavelength of the emitted radiation, h is Planck's constant equal to 6.625×10^{-27} erg-second, c is the speed of light, and I is the current in amperes.

When transmitting optical data to long distances, it is not always necessary to make the fiber cable out of a single strand for reasons of economy and at times for boosting the light intensity along the line. However, at every connection of the fiber, there is always some attenuation of the transmission light. When the attenuation is very high, then repeaters can be placed at various junctions of the fibers forming the continuous transmission. A repeater comprises a receiving transducer which receives the laser signal from the preceding cable, amplifies it, and then feeds it to a transmitting transducer containing a laser diode which is coupled optically to the following fiber cable. In such a system, metallic electrical wires carrying direct current follows the fiber cable often within the same cable sheath, as illustrated in Fig. 10-4. Thus, the amplification of the laser radiation comes from the electric current that energizes the laser diode. This latter device is more fully discussed in the chapter on security surveillance systems.

RECEIVER CHARACTERISTICS

The receiver of a communication system consists of a photodetector facing the distal end of the fiberoptic cable; this detector transduces the incoming laser light to electrical signals for the associated electronic circuitry. The photodetector most often used is either a silicon PIN diode (p-layer-intrinsic-n-layer) or an avalanche photodiode in the spectral range of 7,500 to 9,500 angstroms, because the PIN diode has a quantum emission efficiency of 50 percent. Because these diodes are temperature-sensitive, consideration should be given to the provision of a heat sink to endure environmental, thermal conditions. This is especially important when high-speed operation is necessary and consequently the diodes must be biased up to 50 volts; for the latter type of operation, avalanche diode is specified. The photodetector must match the optical design to reduce the detector capacitive effect and noise due to photons (phonons). Using wavelengths from an infrared source, it appears that in the region of 8,200 and 10,600 angstrom wavelengths the fiber attenuation is a minimum; where each signal channel has its own optical cable and receiver, this could help eliminate additional coupling losses.

SELECTION OF FIBEROPTIC CABLES

In selecting an optical fiber for transmission cable, consideration should be given to the determination of the length of the cable. If the length will be one or two meters, then the light attenuation problem will resolve itself immediately to insignificance. The next step then is to choose a fiber of large diameter which is capable of transmitting the power necessary, such as in medical surgery, materials processing, or process monitoring. For long cables, transmission of power and spectral bandwidth may become limited unless low-loss fibers are used. Thus, the determination of fiber diameter, length, and transmission losses must be made before installation of the cable. For short-length transmissions, high-loss cable may be more practical because of the low cost of the fiber and its high efficiency of light-coupling property resultant from its large numerical aperture.

Bandwidth decreases with length of the fiber and beyond 500 yards it tends to decrease as the square root of the length. Data transmission rate is also adversely affected unless an optimum-diameter fiber is considered for the work in hand. Among the cables most prescribed is the step-graded-index cable; because it is a low-attenuation fiber, high-volume data transmission through it may be achieved. This fiber has about 50-micron-diameter core and is used for telecommunication. Its attenuation factor is less than 5 dB/km at near infrared range (about 8000 to 9000 angstroms), and possesses high optical bandwidth. The minimal bend radius of the cable can be increased by increasing the number of fine fibers, instead of using fewer fibers of larger diameters.

Questions and Problems

10-1. What is fiberoptic communication? How can voice be transmitted through a fiberoptic cable? How does a laser beam take part in the transmission of sound through a fiberoptic cable? What types of laser beams can be employed in transmitting sound signals through the optical fiber?

10-2. How does sound couple to a fiberoptic cable? Explain the principle involved. What does a fiberoptic communication system consist of? State the principal subsystems and their functions. How is modulation accomplished in the transmission of sound through fiberoptic cable? Can digital and analog data be transmitted through the fiberoptic cable? Discuss.

10-3. How are optical fibers spliced in a fiberoptic communication system? What is a link? Do data signals through the optical fiber attenuate during transmission? What causes the attenuation? In what measurement unit is attenuation expressed? What does an optical fiber consist of? What relation has the central part of the fiber to the cladding? Which has higher index of refraction, the core or the cladding? Why? Explain. Does attenuation increase or decrease with increase of distance?

10-4. What grade of fiberoptic materials are commercially sold? Which grade is the best for voice communication? Is high attenuation of signal in short distances significant? Would you use very low-attenuation fibers for short distances? Why? Explain. What types of fibers are used to transmit infrared or ultraviolet radiations? Is attenuation in a fiber dependent on wavelength?

10-5. What is critical angle with respect to a light beam through an optical fiber? Should the critical angle be large or small in order that the optical fiber be able to transmit the light through it? To what factors are the losses due in an optical fiber? What is an optical aperture as applied to a fiberoptic cable? How does image resolution vary with greater optical aperture?

10-6. What is the advantage of using a fiberoptic cable instead of metallic wire cable? What is meant by dB/km? What is the range of dB/km in fiberoptic cables? What is numerical aperture in an optical fiber? With what property of the optical fiber does numerical aperture vary? How is critical angle related to the index of refraction of the core material? Discuss.

10-7. A certain optical fiber core has an index of refraction of 1.564 and cladding index of refraction of 1.483. What is the numerical aperture of the fiber? If the refractive index of the transmitting medium is 1.120 and the sine of angle ϕ is 30°, what is the numerical aperture of the fiber?

10-8. If the index of refraction of the core of a fiber is 1.588 and the index of refraction of the cladding is 1.462, what is the critical angle of the optical fiber? If the core index of refraction is equal to that of the cladding, what will be the value of the critical angle? Will light travel through such a fiber?

10-9. What is packing density of an optical cable? If the diameter of an optical fiber is 0.02 millimeter and the diameter of the cable is 4 millimeters, what is the packing density of the cable? What is the cross-sectional area of the optical fiber?

10-10. If a fiberoptic cable is transmitting an image, what type of fiber would yield the maximum resolution? To obtain flexure of an optical cable in a small radius, what relative size fibers are used? Give the equation for the total area of the core in a multifiber cable.

10-11. Give several military applications of fiberoptic communication systems. What are the commercial applications of fiberoptic cables? Name them. Are optical cables air-cooled or water-cooled? What type of cables are water-cooled? For what purpose is a fiberoptic cable used in microelectronic industry?

10-12. Can fiberoptic cables used for communication be used in medical instrumentation? What type of fiberoptic material is used in medical surgery? For gastrointestinal visualization, can ordinary fiberoptic cable for data transmission be used? What is coherent fiberoptic cable? Can image be transmitted through a coherent fiberoptic cable? How? Explain.

10-13. Can GaAs diode emission of 0.5 to 1 milliwatt be employed for communication to a distance of 10 kilometers? Does one have to use optical links along the transmission line? Is the attenuation high or low in this type of communication cable? Can light-emitting diodes be used for this transmission distance of 10 kilometers? Can light transmission from LEDs be modulated? How? Explain.

10-14. What does a fiberoptic transmitter consist of? Name its parts and the function of each. What types of laser diodes can be used in fiberoptic transmission systems? What types of lasers are usually used for remote communication? Can CO_2 laser be modulated? What one drawback does CO_2 have in fiberoptic communication? Discuss.

10-15. What is threshold current? At what level with respect to threshold current do LEDs operate? At what level with respect to threshold current do laser diodes operate? What is the wavelength range of GaAs diode? What is quantum efficiency of a diode? Explain.

10-16. In a given laser diode, the number of electrons that have passed the pn junction is 4.2×10^{18}, and the quantum efficiency with which the photons are produced is 52 percent. How many photons are produced in the process?

10-17. What are repeaters? When are they used in a fiberoptic transmission line? Do repeaters boost the photonic energy or do they just sustain the photonic energy at the initial transmission level? How do repeaters receive their operating energy?

10-18. What is the function of a photodetector at the receiving end of a fiberoptic transmission line? What type of detector is at the receiving end of the fiberoptic transmission line? What percent quantum efficiency does a photodetector at the receiving end have? What is the purpose for providing each signal channel with its own optical cable? Discuss.

10-19. In designing a fiberoptic communication system, what considerations should be given to the selection of a fiberoptic cable? Discuss. Does an optical waveguide have larger or smaller diameter for laser-power transmission for materials processing or medical surgery?

10-20. If the bandwidth decreases with increase of length of the optical fiber, in what relation does it decrease when this length is exceeded 500 yards? In a long-distance transmission cable, how is the cable protected from the environmental degradation or attack? How can the tensile loading on the transmission cable be reenforced? Discuss.

Chapter 11
Principles of Holography

Holography is the process by which a three-dimensional recording of an object is made by two split laser beams on a photographic film or plate. The split beams are expanded sufficiently to cover both the object to be holographed and the photographic plate. The resulting hologram is a superimposition of the wave patterns reflected from the object and the wave patterns of the laser beam direct from the source. The two superimposed waves interreact and produce a latent image in the photographic plate. This image is invisible to the eye in the developed film or plate until the plate is illuminated from the back with an expanded beam of laser radiation. When visualized in this manner, the latent image appears as a real image of the object in three-dimensional form. This image can be observed from either side of the plate, with the laser beam illuminating it from the opposite side. If the hologram is cut into several pieces, each piece still will show the entire image.

The wave patterns on the hologram consists of both the amplitude and the phase variations of the light from the object, while the ordinary photographic plate senses only the amplitude (intensity) of the reflected light from the object; the photographic picture is two dimensional. The two split laser beams replace the eyes, in holography, and record on the plate every point, direction, and latitude of the object to impart to the hologram the three-dimensional view of the object. Actually, when two split beams become superimposed on the photographic plate, the wavefronts from each of the beams interfere, that is, reciprocally interact with each other to result in a modified wavefront which produces the latent image in the photographic plate. Both the phase fronts and their intensities are recorded in the plate, thus utilizing the wavelength, intensity, and phase content of the incident laser beam. This phenomenon will be further explained step by step so that the reader will fully understand what light-wave interference is and how it is employed in a hologram.

COHERENCE OF LASER BEAMS

Light travels through space (atmosphere) by transverse vibration, which in effect is a sinusoidal wave characterized by its amplitude and wavelength. In its travel, both the amplitude and the wavelength remain unchanged. As an example, let us assume a single waveform as illustrated in Fig. 11-1. Any point on this waveform executes a sine wave as the ray propagates forward, with a constant wavelength along its travel. Both the crest and the trough of the wave are equal in size but are opposite in direction. The height of the crest or trough is the amplitude of the wave and any two consecutive, respective points designate one wavelength.

Suppose now, two waves, illustrated in Fig. 11-2, of the same monochromatic light are travelling in the same direction, with similar amplitudes and phase formats. Since both of the two waves are traveling with the same speed and wavelength, and are executing the same peak and trough within the same period, the two waves are said to be in phase and, therefore, are temporally coherent. They are also laterally coherent. Thus, two light waves propagating in the same direction with constant wavelength and constant phase difference (zero in this case) are coherent and characterize a laser beam in out discussion.

On the other hand, if two light waves propagating in phase in

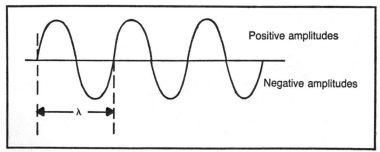

Fig. 11-1. A light wave executing a sine-wave pattern.

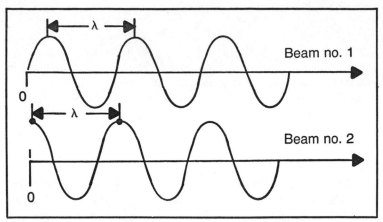

Fig. 11-2. Temporally coherent light waves.

the same direction have different amplitudes, their amplitudes add both above the zero line and below the zero line, so that the resultant of the amplitudes is greater than any one of the two amplitudes; the light intensity increases. This effect is known as constructive interference, as shown in Fig. 11-3. When the upper or positive amplitude and the lower or negative amplitude are of different magnitudes, as shown in Fig. 11-4, then the resultant amplitude, in either upper or lower amplitudes, is smaller and is equal to the difference of the two amplitudes; the light intensity in this case diminishes, and the effect is known as destructive interference.

When two light beams are out of phase 180 degrees, and are superimposed on each other, if the amplitudes are equal, then the two amplitudes (positive and negative amplitudes) cancel each other's intensity, reducing the light intensity to zero, as illustrated in Fig. 11-5. This phenomenon is important to remember when considering interference of light waves superimposed on each

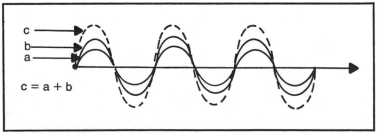

Fig. 11-3. Illustration of constructive interference.

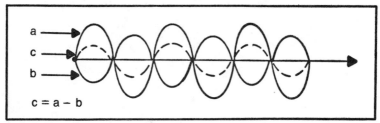

Fig. 11-4. Illustration of destructive interference.

other, forming interference fringes of light and dark lines, by which various spectroscopic analyses and measurements can be carried on.

MICHELSON INTERFEROMETER

A practical application of interference phenomenon is employed in a Michelson interferometer. This instrument, shown in Fig. 11-6, is used to measure distances in terms of the wavelength of light. Measurements are also made of the quality of optical elements, such as lenses, prisms, and mirrors. The index of refraction of optically transparent materials are also determined. The principal components of the instrument are mirrors M_1, M_2 and a beamsplitter, B. The light source S projects a beam of light (He-Ne laser beam in this case) to a beamsplitter B, which partially transmits the beam to mirror M_2 and partially reflects it to mirror M_1. Mirror M_1 is adjustable so that its distance from the beamsplitter B can be increased or decreased. The two beams from M_1 and M_2 return to the eyepiece E. If the M_1 and M_2 are equidistant from B and are distanced an integral number of full wavelenghts, the two beams will constructively interfere and a bright field will be produced at the eyepiece E. If the distance between C and E is increased, for example, by a quarter wavelength ($\frac{1}{4}\lambda$), the optical path for beam 1 will increase $\frac{1}{2}\lambda$, which condition will result in a destructive interference, and a dark field appears at eyepiece E. The angular

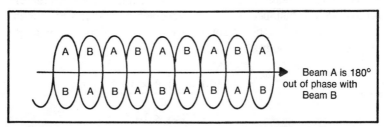

Fig. 11-5. Interference of phase difference by 180 degrees by two waves.

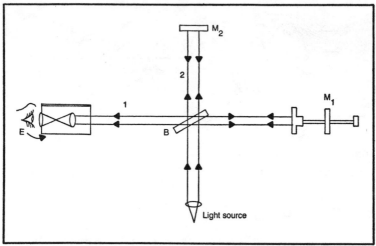

Fig. 11-6. The Michelson interferometer.

positions of the mirrors M_1 and M_2 are such that a field containing bright and dark fringes is thus prevalent. These fringes may be counted as the mirror M_1 is moved, and the count N may be translated into distance by means of the following relation:

$$D = n\lambda /2 \qquad \textbf{(Equation 11-1)}$$

and,
$$\lambda = 2D/N \qquad \textbf{(Equation 11-2)}$$

or,
$$N = 2D/\lambda \qquad \textbf{(Equation 11-3)}$$

The original Michelson interferometer used as a light source the red light from a cadmium-vapor lamp of 6438.47 angstroms. However, a gas ion laser of today, such as a He-Ne laser, is more intense and, therefore, the mirrors M_1 and M_2 can be separated one from the other up to 200 meters and minute differences along this length can be easily measured. The wavelength λ is 6328 angstroms.

Example: A 6,328-angstrom laser beam from a He-Ne laser unit is used as a source of illumination for Michelson interferometer to measure the distance between two given points. If 400 fringes have been counted as the mirror M_1 is moved, calculate the distance between the two points.

$$
\begin{aligned}
D &= N\lambda/2 \\
&= \frac{400 \times 6328 \times 10^{-8}}{2} \\
&= 2 \times 6328 \times 10^{-6} \\
&= 0.01265 \text{ cm.}
\end{aligned}
$$

Example: In a measurement with Michelson interferometer, 240 fringes were counted and the mirror M_1 was moved 0.006 cm; what wavelength laser beam was used?

$$\lambda = 2D/N$$
$$= \frac{2 \times 0.006 \times 10^8}{240}$$
$$= \frac{12 \times 10^5}{240}$$
$$= 5000 \text{ angstroms}$$

HOLOGRAPHY PROCEDURES

There are several ways of making holograms. They are: single-beam holograms, double-beam holograms, single-exposure holograms, and double-exposure holograms. While they are intended to serve the function of making three-dimensional images of a given object, each method may also be used to bring about a particular purpose. We will discuss a few to give the basic principle of producing a hologram. In the instrumentation of holography, a principal procedure that is of great concern is the stabilization of the table on which the holographic process is being performed. Although the time of exposure is short, nevertheless a slight movement either by the object of the photographic plate may spell failure. For this reason, vibration-isolated tables are manufactured by various laser companies and some of the tables are of reasonable cost, so that the final achievement will well be worth the initial investment of such a table. If a vibration-isolated table is not available, the table on which the work will be performed can be stabilized by packing sandbags at its legs. Of course, a location should be chosen where ground vibration from passing cars will be practically absent. Also, the work can be carried out either in a photographic dark room or in a lighted room where all holographic materials should be enclosed in light-tight enclosures. Fast-exposure films or plates can be procured from an Eastman Kodak sales store prevalent in most cities. Together with the above implements, a photographic dark room with processing solutions must also be available. The lighting in the dark room will be prescribed by the sales brochure of the photographic plate.

Single-Beam Hologram

This type of holographic process can be performed both with white light or a laser beam expanded to the size of the film or plate.

The laser source, the reflecting mirror, and the object may be arranged as shown in Fig. 11-7. As the laser beam leaves the laserhead, the beam may be either expanded by means of a beam expander or by the use of a biconcave lens. The mirror must be large enough to receive the oncoming laser beam and should be located at such a distance from the object that when the beam becomes incident on the object it covers both the photographic plate and the object under it. Another mirror or a shiny surface may be placed under the object so that the laser beam will reflect from its sides unto the plate. The laser-beam intensity could be either 0.5 milliwatt or 1.0 milliwatt. After the preliminary setup is made to adjust the laser beam with respect to the film position and the object, the exposure time may be about one second with the 0.5-milliwatt laser beam. If the laser beam power is 1 milliwatt, the time can be one-half.

If the holographic setup is not arranged in a dark room (photographic processing room), then the setup should be covered with an enclosure having a slit to introduce the film holder, as in a camera. When all light from the laser beam, mirror, and the film is sealed off by means of a two-inch tape affixed to the enclosure at its periphery, and an exposure shutter is attached to the proximal end of the beam expander, then the cover of the film holder may be pulled through the slit in the enclosure up to the upper margin of the holder and left there preparatory to exposure. Now, the exposure trigger may be pressed and it automatically will shut off the laser beam from the film. The cover of the film holder may then be pushed back to tightly

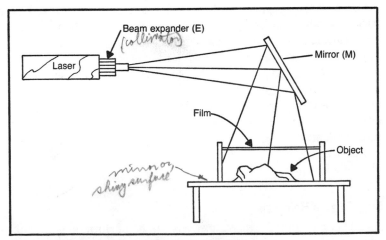

Fig. 11-7. Single-beam retroreflection hologram.

172

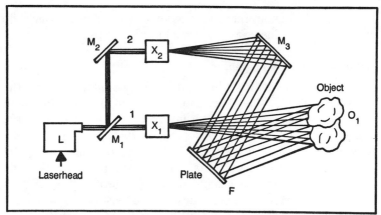

Fig. 11-8. Double-beam holographic setup.

seal it against light. The film holder then is removed, and the film is processed conventionally. If the holograph does not have sufficient contrast or is too dark, it may be reduced by immersing it in Kodak reducing solution until a desired contrast is obtained. The film is then washed in running water for at least five minutes and then dried before examining it with an expanded laser beam.

Double-Beam Hologram

The double-beam hologram is the most common process of making a hologram of an object. The instrument setup is shown in Fig. 11-8. As the laser beam projects from the laserhead, it becomes incident on mirror M_1, at which it splits into two beams of preferably equal intensities. The beam 1 proceeds to the beam expander X_1 and beam 2 reflects from a second mirror M_2 and proceeds to the beam expander X_2. The expanded beam from beam expander X_1 projects on the object O_1 and diffusedly reflects on the film F. The expanded beam from beam expander X_2 proceeds to mirror M_3, reflects from it, and becomes incident on the film F; this beam is the reference beam, and the beam 1 is the recording beam to interfere with beam 2 or reference beam. Thus the wavefronts of the reference beam and the recording beam become superimposed on each other in the film emulsion and form the latent image of the object. It is sometimes preferred that the lengths of the beams 1 and 2 be equal from the source to the film. But, this rule cannot always be followed, and the hologram is produced just as effectively. The hologram then is viewed with an expanded laser beam projected on it at the same angle as when the beam produced the hologram. The viewer observes the hologram from the side opposite to that to which the laser beam is incident, as illustrated in Fig. 11-9.

Double-Exposure Hologram

This hologram is made by exposing the photographic film to the recording beam of the object in one position and then making a second exposure with the object in a modified position. When the film is developed, dried, and observed, the two images will be seen superimposed, one image being slightly in a modified shape. If the exposure is performed with great care, measurements can be made which will determine the change in the object size or shape. Such a hologram is usually made in medical work to observe the healing of the treated parts along the entire treatment period; therefore, this subject will be taken up more fully in the chapter on medical instrumentation by means of laser beams.

POINTERS TO OBSERVE WHEN MAKING HOLOGRAMS

First of all, when considering the making of a hologram of an object, the least costly laser system should be chosen; this is a He-Ne laser operating in the TEM_{00} mode (Gaussian mode). In order to eliminate blurring in the finished hologram, the table on which the procedure is being carried out must be stabilized to a motionless state. To shorten the exposure to a minimum to eliminate movement of the setup, either a higher-level laser source should be used or a film with fastest emulsion must be employed for the hologram. If stabilization offers no problem, such as when a professionally constructed holographic table is used, longer expo-

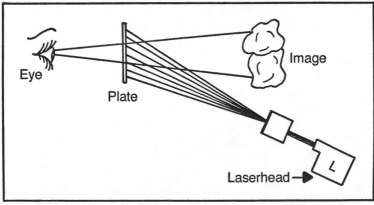

Fig. 11-9. Reconstructing the holographic image.

174

sure times up to 15 to 20 seconds may produce holograms with better resolution of the diffraction fringes that form the latent image; the laser power then should be reduced. The maximum emulsion resolution is characterized by the smallest fringe spacing. The contrast of the holographic film can be controlled by using an optimum filter for the work under hand. Negatives can be made from the positive or direct-exposure holograms, and copies of the positive hologram can be made from the negative hologram. In reconstructing a hologram by transmitting a beam of leaser through it and observing the image from the opposite side of the film, the observer should never look in the direction of the transmitted beam, even though the hologram may act as a filter to some extent. Safety goggles should be used as deemed necessary.

Questions and Problems

11-1. What is a hologram? How is the latent image formed in a hologram? How does a hologram differ from a photograph? What do the two split laser beams record on the photographic film in making a hologram? What does one mean by saying interfering of wavefronts? What intensities are recorded in the plate?

11.-2. What is coherence? Define amplitude and wavelength of a beam. When are two beams said to be in phase? If two beams are travelling in the same direction and have the same phase, with their amplitudes in coincidence, what happens to their intensities?

11-3. When two light beams are out of phase by 180 degrees, and have the same wavelengths, what becomes of their intensities? Explain. When two beams are split from a fundamental beam and are retarded quarter wavelength one from the other, draw a diagram showing where the two beams are located with respect to each other.

11.-4. What is a Michelson interferometer? How is it constructed? How does it measure distance? How does it measure flatness of an optical surface? What are interference fringes? What importance do they exhibit in distance measurement?

11-5. If a light beam of 6328-angstrom wavelength is used in measuring a distance between two points 0.048 cm apart, how many fringes has been counted to obtain this result?

11-6. How many ways are there to make holograms? Explain what each method consists of. When does one employ a double-exposure hologram? When does one use a single-beam hologram? Can one use two beams from two different laser sources to make a hologram? Under what conditions can a hologram be made with two beams projecting from two different laser sources? Should the wavelengths from two different laser sources be the same in order to be able to make a hologram? Explain.

11-7. Explain how a single beam of laser can produce a hologram in one exposure. Could this hologram be observed by reflected light on it? What intensity laser beam should be used for this type of holography? Should this type of holography be carried out in a dark room? If the film does not have sufficient contrast in its image, how can the contrast be improved?

11-8. In a double-beam hologram, should the reference and the recording beams be equal in length before they impinge on the photographic plate? Draw a diagram and explain how the holographic setup is arranged. Can a hologram be inserted into a picture frame and observed by shining white light on it? How can a double-beam hologram be framed and observed just by looking at it as if a framed picture is being observed? Explain.

Chapter 12
Military Applications of Lasers

The application of lasers in the various branches of the military has become an essential implementation of strategic armament. Every tactical technology now being used in the military is provided with laser in some form or another. Because a laser beam has high degree of directionality, weapon systems are now equipped with highly developed instruments for aiming both light and heavy artillery and directing missiles to their destination with pinpoint accuracy. In communication, the laser beams are used between any two or more installations, on shipboard, and on strategic aircraft. Monitoring ocean floors and communicating with submarines are every-day operations. The weapon simulation systems using laser beams are aiding the military to train soldiers in combat simulations, and almost eliminating the use of live ammunitions for training soldiers in marksmanship, thus reducing the cost of such maneuvers to armed services.

Two types of lasers are being projected for the military services. One of these is a nondestructive type, in which the laser beam is being used as a guidance implement, for rangefinding, tracking flying aircraft, and in battleground simulation on land. A destructive type of operation, which has not been actively put in service, is one that uses high-power laser equipment to project lethal laser beams at the target to destroy it swiftly and instantly. This is accomplished by directing a powerful pencil beam of laser at the strategic points of the target and deactivating the function of the system. Other devastating laser-beam weapons are also in development whereby a direct hit at the warhead will destroy or put it out of function instantly. Already, it has been shown that laser beams can penetrate steel, titanium and other hard metals to depths of more than a centimeter. They can cut and drill softer materials such as aluminum or magnesium alloys, that are used in aircraft structures, to depths of several centimeters under controlled process conditions, although with targets in air such controls are not yet practical. Techniques are also being developed together with systems to implement the equipment in the most efficient and skillful military science. In addition, to military implementations, high-energy laser beams are being developed and investigated for peaceful applications, such as for producing nuclear energy by atomic fusion and to translate this energy into electrical energy for civilian as well as for military utilization at a lower cost than it is possible at the present time.

The lasers employed in military applications include solid-state lasers, ion lasers, liquid dye lasers, semiconductor lasers, and excimer lasers. Among these, the most destructive type of lasers are the molecular or CO_2 lasers, Nd-YAG lasers or glass lasers, and excimer lasers. The other types are used in various other strategic implementations such as rangefinders, target designators, missile guidance systems, soldier training, weapon aiming, communication, monitoring warfare chemical reactions, and security surveillance systems. We shall study some of the systems representative of each category to complement our knowledge in laser instrumentation in military applications.

LOW-POWER LASER APPLICATIONS

The following describes the military uses of low-power lasers.

Rangefinders

Rangefinders are instruments using laser beams to measure distances. This is generally accomplished by projecting a pencil beam of laser, usually in the visible spectral range, to a target or object at a distance, and capturing the reflected beam in a component circuit in the system for timing the travel of the beam to and from the target and calculating the distance. The measurement is made easier by projecting a pulsed laser beam, whereby a counter in the rangefinder counts the pulses from the time the laser beam leaves the instrument to the time of its return from the target. The total number of pulses that are counted are divided by 2 by the internal computer and the result is translated by it into meters, feet, or inches, as the instrument is calibrated for.

Example: A rangefinder operates with a clock frequency of 100 MHz and the counter has counted 3×10^3 pulses. What is the distance measured by the rangefinder?

$$\text{Range} = \frac{3 \times 10^3 \times 3 \times 10^{10}}{2 \times 10^8}$$

$$= \frac{9 \times 10^{13} \times 10^{-8}}{2}$$

$$= \frac{9 \times 10^5}{2}$$

$$= 4.5 \times 10^5 \text{ cm.}$$

$$= 4500 \text{ meters or } 4.5 \text{ kilometers}$$

All categories of the lasers already stated in the preceding paragraph can be employed in a rangefinder. That is, solid-state lasers, gas lasers, liquid dye lasers, and semiconductor lasers. Among the gas lasers, He-Ne lasers are the best, for moderate distances, to employ in a rangefinder because they possess very narrow and intensely red, visible radiation, and they can be operated either continuous-wave or pulsed. Semiconductors and liquid dye lasers are also used but due to their limited intensity the range that can be measured is also limited. Carbon dioxide has the highest available power; however, it operates in the invisible infrared spectrum for which a suitable photosensor has not as yet been developed. A laser with high power and operable in both the continuous-wave and pulsed modes is neodymium-YAG, which is in extensive use in the construction of military rangefinders.

A rangefinder consists of three principal components—a transmitter, a receiver, and an electron signal processing section which displays the range in digital form. To fully discuss the construction and operation of a rangefinder, we shall take up a commercial rangefinder, as shown in Fig. 12-1, and discuss how it is constructed and how it determines the distance. Assuming that this rangefinder emits a 5-milliwatt He-Ne laser at 6,328-angstrom wavelength. The rangefinder is mounted on a tripod having a telescope for locating the target. The system operates with a clock frequency of 100 megahertz (MHz), and contains a counter which can count the pulses of lasers to and from the target. The pulsed beam of leaser is projected to the target from which it reflects to a photodetector in the receiver. The detector consists of four quad-

Fig. 12-1. A commercial rangefinder for military use (courtesy International Laser Systems, Inc.).

rant active areas and a middle zero area. When the retroreflected laser beam arrives at one of the quadrants, a signal known as error signal is developed. This signal is due to the motion of the target with respect to the beam first projected to the target. The error signal is amplified and fed to a servosystem for activating it. The activated servosystem directs the rangefinder back to the target by rotating the rangefinder on an axis toward the target. When the target is again acquired, the retroreflected beam falls on the zero circular area, and the servosystem momentarily returns to its quiescent operative state. Since the target is moving, another error signal develops and the servosystem again moves the rangefinder axis into position with respect to the target. This process continues rapidly, depending on the speed of the target, and maintains the rangefinder locked on the target until it disappears from sight. It must be emphasized here that this is an automatic rangefinder, and that not all rangefinders operate automatically; some operate manually.

During the travel of the laser beam to and from the target, the range counter begins to count the pulses from the first time the first pulse leaves the transmitter. Upon return of a first pulse to the receiver and hence the counter, the counter stops counting. The counter processor integrates all the pulses during a round trip, divides it by 2, and multiplies it by the speed of light (about 3×20^{10} cm). The result of this calculation is displayed on the data readout system in digital form. This result is the momentary distance of the target and changes as the target moves away from the rangefinder. If the target is stationary, then the servosystem takes no part in correcting the error signal (distance), because the incoming signal is on the zero signal area. The purpose of the servosystem is to maintain the rangefinder continuously locked on the moving target.

One manufacturer's rangefinder using a GaAs laser diode measures ranges from 50 feet to 10,000 feet against a cooperative target. A cooperative target has a reflector to retroreflect the projected laser beam to the receiver of the rangefinder. Therefore, such a target can deliver a greater amount of the projected laser beam back to the receiver, and this is why the system can measure longer distances using a relatively small-power laser radiation from a diode. This system operates in the infrared at 9,040 angstroms. The beam divergence is 5 mrad at the exit port and varies to 50 milliradians/within the range of the rangefinder. It emits about 5 watts and operates at 2,000 pps with a pulsewidth of 40 nanoseconds. Its logic is the first pulse. The receiver detector is an avalanche photodiode with a sensitivity of 10^{-9} w/cm^2. Its optical aperture is 5 inches with a field of view of 5 mrad. The rangefinder operates from a current source of 24 Vdc at 27 watts.

Another rangefinder which can operate as a target designator uses a Nd-YAG laser, which is Q-switched and its energy is dumped in short, intense pulses at the target. The retroreflected signal from the target is received by a silicon diode, such as a PIN diode or an avalanche diode, and the beam's round trip is counted by the computer counter and is transformed into digital data. The divergence of the laser beam is about 3 mrad and can be increased by an increase of beam diameter by the use of a beam expander and collimator. The avalanche detector is smaller than the PIN diode but operates with a practically noise-free gain and is about 100 times more sensitive than a PIN diode, although more costly. The optical system of the receiver is a three-element lens array to reduce spherical aberration, using a filter to control background radiation.

In many types of military weapon systems, the laser rangefinders are standard equipment. The rangefinders are usually mounted on tanks and other moving vehicles, and the reflected laser-beam information is transmitted to centrally stationed computers which then give command as to next movement in the tactical operation. This type of rangefinders may employ Nd-YAG, carbon dioxide, or CO laser. When the data transmission is from a satellite to a submarine, a krypton or xenon laser operating at the green wavelength is preferred.

The MIT Lincoln Laboratory has developed a CO_2 laser radar that possesses 10,000 times more accuracy than a microwave radar in both angular and Doppler resolution. It is reported that the system accuracy is about 14 inches at a distance of 50 miles. The system operates at 10 kHz frequency with a 50-microsecond pulsewidth. The retroreflected laser beam from the target is received by a Hg-Cd-Te detector at the front end of the receiver. The optical system can distinguish 2.5 centimeters at a distance of 5.6 kilometers, because the attenuation is very small, from ¼ to 2 dB/km. It provides high signal information from the target in its acquisition.

Laser Target Designators

A target designator pinpoints the target for delivering laser-guided weapons to their targets. The target designator/illuminator may be built as a separate unit or it may be incorporated with a rangefinder. The target designator is mounted on an airborne aircraft to provide precise designation of either a stationary target or an airborne target in any day or night operation. The system may also be made for hand-held purposes for laser-guided bombs or missiles. This system uses a Nd-YAG laser emitting at 10,640 angstroms in the infrared or 5,320 angstrom, frequency doubled. Target designators, when used with a rangefinder, provide a laser beam which is steered by a mirror system in pinpointing the target and maintaining a slew rate. Several companies are now manufacturing target designators. Among them are: Allied Chemical, Cilas, ILS, Ferranti, Kollsman and others. Each manufacturer has his own proprietary system structure, but principally all designators operate on the same basis.

Laser Rifles for Weapon Simulation

The military is also using laser-equipped rifles for training soldiers both in the field and indoors for marksmanship. A rifle for this purpose developed by the International Lasers Systems, Inc. is now being used under the tradename Lasertrain, shown in Fig. 12-2. The rifle uses a beam from a GaAs diode laser which provides an effective means of developing rifle marksmanship at low cost. The laser-beam transmitter is mounted on the barrel of a rifle and boresighted to the rifle. The laser output simulates bullets and when the rifle trigger is squeezed a single pulse is projected to the target, which is configured to simulate a given distance ranging from 25 meters to 300 meters. Hits are displayed on the target.

The laser system is powered with a rechargeable battery located in the gun stock. When the target is hit, a rifle-like sound is produced by an electrical component built into the console, which also has a volume control for the audible rifle sound. A memory bank stores up to eight rounds of hit and can recall either each hit individually or all the rounds simultaneously for displaying the firing pattern on the target screen. The laser storage power provides about 2000 rounds (flashes) per full charge of the rechargeable battery source.

For battlefield maneuvers, each soldier is equipped with a battleground outfit, which includes a Model FS-101 weapon fire simulator, and helmet with PIN diodes, and a uniform containing detectors at the arms, body, and legs. When any one of the detectors is hit by a laser beam, the soldier is informed by an audio alarm that is provided in his helmet. This action simultaneously disables the soldier's rifle, thus simulating a battleground hit received by the soldier, who is then taken out of the battleground as casualty. As the soldier is hit, an electronic signal is transmitted from the helmet to a remotely-located intelligence station, where the computers pro-

Fig. 12-2. Soldier with complete battleground outfit.

Fig. 12-3. A battleground scene, with a soldier using a GaAs weapon simulator.

cess the signal and cancel out the soldier. A battleground scene is shown in Fig. 12-3.

Other military weapons, such as machine guns, tanks, cannons and other artillery, located either on land or on shipboard, are also being equipped with simulating laser systems for practicing battle-ground maneuvers both on land and on sea. On these weapons, the laser system operates at 3,000 hertz and is pulse-coded to identify the casualty.

In addition to ground and sea laser weapon simulators, air-to-air gunnery systems equipped with laser simulators are also being developed. The transmitter in this gunnery simulator is provided with a laser diode and effectively simulates a machine gun firing at ground-located targets or flying banners with retroreflectors. The battlefield gunnery may be accomplished at any area in the city or outfield air space. The GaAs laser transmitter system is bore-sighted with a fixed sight on the aircraft. The system consists of the transceiver and the electronic control units. The hits from the aircraft are detected by an avalanche photodiode in the receiver and displayed to the pilot. The receiver counter counts both the rounds fired and hits scored, and the information is instantly available to the pilot. The system described can be used in air-to-ground simulations as well as in air defense weapon simulators.

HIGH-POWER LASER APPLICATIONS

The following describes the military uses of high-powered lasers.

Directed-Beam Laser Rifle

A directed-beam laser rifle developed by Laserkinetics Corporation is a rifle-configured device containing six solid-state laser elements arranged between alternately positioned fiberoptic coniform amplifiers, which are used to intensify the radiation from the largest cone to the smallest cone located at the distal end of the optical amplifiers. Each laser element is individually pumped, as shown in Fig. 12-4, by xenon flashlamps energized by a capacitive network charged by a rechargeable battery located in the stock of the rifle. The energizing dc current is amplified by means of a vibrator and the amplified current is smoothed out by a capacitor-resistor device prior to being fed to the RC network. The laser elements may be either ruby rods or Nd-YAG rods operating in the pulsing mode.

In the system, the laser rods are designated by 1, 2, and 3, with intervening fiberoptic cones 4, 5, and 6. The lasing elements are illuminated by the flashlamps 7, 8, 9, and 10. Each fiberoptic cone receives the laser radiation at its base, converges the beam to its small-diameter end and transfers the beam to the adjoining laser element, so that the last fiberoptic cone receives the radiation from the last laser rod 3 and converges it to a pencil beam preparatory to its projection from the rifle. The numeral 11 designates a glass envelope which surrounds the lasing elements and the fiberoptic cones; this envelope serves to contain a circulating fluid through it to cool the lasing elements during operation of the device. The device contains a trigger at the usual position of a rifle and when it is squeezed, a pulse of xenon light energizes the lasing element, while at the same time the trigger also turns on the cooling fluid to the lasing cavity.

As a directed-beam rifle, the system's effective range is approximately 200 meters with a nominal power supply. As a metal

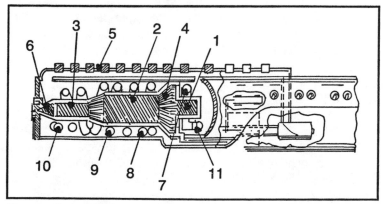

Fig. 12-4. Directed-beam laser rifle system.

processing device, it can drill, cut, and weld metals up to several millimeters in thickness. As a low-power laser generator, the rifle can be used in a battlefield training program, the same as the Lasertrain already studied in the previous paragraph. In marksmanship or battlefield operational mode, it will be preferable to use Nd-YAG rods at a low power, between 0.5 to 1 milliwatt level. Because the latter laser emits in the infrared and is invisible, it provides eye safety to some extent. Goggles must be used at all times with this type of laser rifle.

Free-Electron Laser System

A laser weapon system reported to have been developed by the U.S. Defense Department is a high-energy unit provided with a free-electron producing system which bombards the lasing element to excite it to emission. The laser generator is said to possess an emission efficiency three times more than an equivalent laser system and having more lethal striking power. The free electrons are accelerated spirally at relativistic undulations for acquiring their excitation energy. This system is capable of tuning continuously from ultraviolet to infrared spectrum, and will be eventually used on satellites, aircraft, and naval ships, as defense against enemy attack during wartime. The nature of the lasing element has not been given in the report.

Target-Penetrating Laser System

A penetrating laser-beam system that has been developed for the U.S. Army consists of a unit containing a source of cw CO_2 laser beam and a pulsed Nd-YAG laser beam. The cw CO_2 laser beam is employed to melt the surface of the target and simultaneously the pulsed Nd-YAG laser beam is injected to expel the molten metal from the focal cavity. In this process, the time of penetration has been reduced 90 percent over the time it would take for the CO_2 laser beam alone to penetrate to the same depth, according to the report. On an unpainted surface, the scheme has doubled the penetration depth, and on painted steel surface the penetration time is only one-fifth that on the unpainted surface. The cavitation of the beam focal area occurs as the molten metal is ejected by the pulses from the Nd-YAG laser; the depth increases with the sustained laser power. The coupling efficiency of the laser-metal surface also increases when the focal surface is roughened by painting or by irradiation with the cw laser beam.

Aluminum surfaces are very hard to penetrate because of their brightness and the high conductivity of the aluminum metal. However, when the surface is first irradiated with a pulsed power of 2.5 kW/cm^2, it is found that the cw CO_2 laser beam can drill a hole which cannot be accomplished with either the cw CO_2 laser beam or the pulsed Nd-YAG beam alone. These investigations are indicative of the success of combination of the cw and pulsed laser beams, which are available in the present laser systems with improved techniques.

It is also reported in the literature that extremely high-power laser beams have been produced that would be useful in military applications; however, because of their classified nature the laser elements and method of their application have not been disclosed. It can be conjectured that a laser system of this magnitude would be capable of producing megajoules of laser energy preferably in the pulsed mode. Such a beam can be produced with exit apertures of up to several feet in diameter, collimated, and then converged to a diameter suitable to drill or destroy the area of the focus instantly. Such an energy can be made equal to the energy of an atom in explosive transmutation.

SECURITY SURVEILLANCE SYSTEMS

A security surveillance system, as the name implies, is a laser-beam-aided equipment for detecting unlawful happenings at private or strategic military grounds. It can be made to produce an alarm or a display on the system instrument panel informing the authorities of an intrusion to the grounds or an escape from the grounds so that corrective measures can be applied immediately. While such a system is routinely used in and around certain military installations, it can also be used to protect any civilian property against vandals, thieves, arsonists, and other criminals. Such systems have been in use for sometime in the past using ordinary white light and detectors; however, their use has not been very reliable because the system has been tripped by the passage of a dog, cat, cow, or even a bird across the beam, signalling the central station of an event that is of no significance. With the advent of laser beams, this situation has changed considerably and new equipment has been developed to meet the improved techniques now in use. The main advantage of the present system is that the beam can be invisible and of high intensity, so that it can be transmitted along a longer periphery of a secured area. The system is adapted to

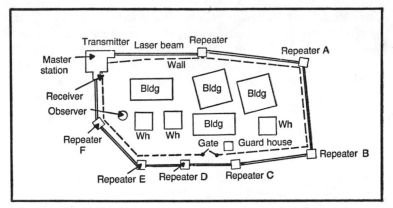

Fig. 12-5. A security surveillance system using electronic repeaters.

indicate the location of the event, with fewer failures by accidental beam interruption.

Since there are many variations of security surveillance systems, only a few representative types will be taken up here to give the various principles of operations. One type is an intrusion-detection system and consists of a transmitter section and a receiver section, both having been incorporated in the same unit. The transmitter projects a laser beam through several isolated photosensors and the beam returns to the receiver after travelling along the perimeter of the secured area. The location of intrusion is determined by the particular photosensor that has been activated by the interruption of the laser beam. Another type projects a number of laser beams, split from the same laser source, around the secured area and the determination of location is made by the particular beam intercepted. This determines whether the unauthorized person is escaping or entering the area.

Still another type of security system consists of a segment-locating alarm system, shown in Fig. 12-5. The laser beam, after having been projected from the transmitter located at the central station, passes through a series of repeaters during its travel around the perimeter of the protected area. When a person interrupts the laser beam in one of the segments located between two repeaters, the repeated that is closest to the central station produces a coded signal characteristic of that particular repeater. This signal crosses any other repeater on its way to the receiver without affecting the laser beam. The signal is decoded at the central station to indicate which segment has been intruded by the unauthorized person. This indication is immediately followed by an audible alarm to alert authorized personnel both at the station and outside of the station. Upon completion of the event, the system is reset to a quiescent operational state. Since a repeater is the most important component of the system in determining the location of the interception of the laser beam, we will discuss it in a simplified schematic diagram, shown in Fig. 12-7.

The repeater, shown in Fig. 12-6, is provided with a receiver transducer which is fed continuously with a laser signal either from the central station or from the preceding repeater during its quiescent operation. The transducer output is partially coupled to a ramp generator and partially to an OR gate logic circuit, which transmits its output to a transmitter transducer containing a GaAs laser diode. The output signal from the ramp generator is coupled to a signal-level-detection circuit in which this signal is compared with a present dc voltage from the power supply. When the two signals, the reset signal and the reference voltage signal, are equal, an output pulse is produced which is fed through a pulse shaper to the OR gate. The resultant output of the OR gate is coupled to the transmitter transducer which produces a laser pulse from the GaAs diode. In this manner, the repeater is sustained at a normal operational state until an interruption of the laser beam occurs.

When an interruption in the laser beam between the repeaters A and B occurs, a segment-identifying pulse is produced, which, when transmitted to the receiver of the central station the location of the intrusion is immediately identified. The remaining repeaters also operate in the same manner with the exception that each

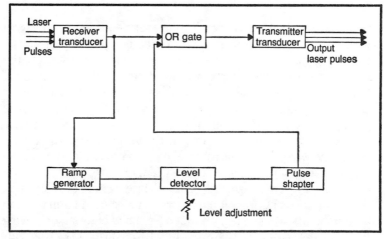

Fig. 12-6. Block diagram of a simplified repeater system.

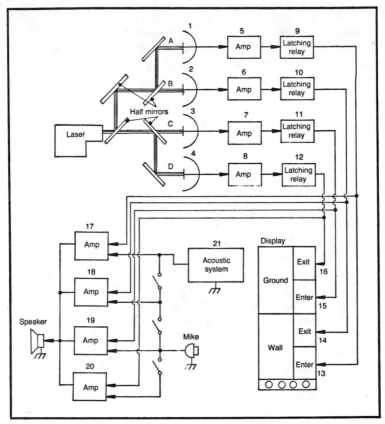

Fig. 12-7. Block diagram of a large-facility surveillance system.

successive repeater produces its own segment-identifying signal with a pulse time greater than that of the previous repeater. The increasingly longer pulse time from one repeater transducer to the other is characteristic of that particular repeater, and the location of the intrusion is determined by the segment preceding the longest pulse-time signal received at the station by the repeater. This system, of course indicates only an interruption in a particular segment in the entire perimeter of the secured area and cannot determine whether the unauthorized person is escaping from the area or entering the area of secured facility.

A comprehensive security surveillance system developed by the Laserkinetics Corporation secures the facility in a manner to determine whether the unauthorized person is entering or leaving the facility. The system, shown in Fig. 12-7, consists of a transmitter, a receiver, and a display panel, which are located at a centrally selected station. The transmitter projects a laser beam from either a He-Ne or Nd-YAG laser. This beam is split into four equal-intensity beams by means of three beamsplitters. Two of the beams are projected along one side of the protective wall of the facility and the other two are projected along the opposite side of the wall, each beam separated apart at a suitable distance. The beams are carried around the perimeter of the facility by means of front-surface mirrors. After circling the perimeter of the area, the beams return to the respective receivers at the central station by way of four photodetectors, one detector for each beam. The output of each photodetector is amplified by the respective amplifier and fed to the adjoining latching relay to sustain it open-circuit during the quiescent operation of the entire system.

When a person attempts to enter the facility over the wall, the laser beam C, for example, becomes momentarily interrupted, and no laser light falls on the photodetector 3. When this occurs, the normally open latching relay 11 is no longer biased by a current through it and thus closes by its spring action. The closure of the latching relay 11 turns on a light on a display panel, at the central station, indicating the word "ENTER" and simultaneously turns on the sound alarm to notify any authorized person to rush to the area of entry for taking corrective action. As the alarm is turned on, talking words "ENTERING" also are broadcast on the speaker. If needed, instructions can be given to the guards, if there are any, on a microphone connected to the display circuit. When the intrusion event is over, the system is reset to its quiescent operational mode. If repeaters are used, they operate in the same manner as those described in a previous paragraph.

The Air Force Systems Command, Hanscom, Mass., has developed a laser security surveillance system, designated Intrusion Detection and Identification System (IDIS), which detects and identifies the location of the intrusion. The equipment, shown in Fig. 12-8, resembles a traffic signal light and comprises six transmitters located within six traffic-light tubes positioned one foot apart on a six-foot-tall post. Each transmitter contains a GaAs laser diode emitting at 9050 angstroms and a convex lens to direct the laser beam to a respective photodetector of a receiver mounted on a companion post positioned up to a distance of 500 feet from the transmitter.

In operation, each of the six pulse-coded laser beams is transmitted to its respective photodetector. The pulses are coded

½-watt each and operate at a repetition rate of 1000 pulses per second. When an intruder crosses one or more of the beams, a number of coded pulses from each of the beams that is interrupted are nullified and the photodetector located in the path of the interrupted laser beam detects the missing counts, which are then

Fig. 12-8. The U.S. Air Force's portable laser security surveillance system (Laser Fence).

decoded in the counter of the receiver and thus the location of the intrusion is identified. The Laser Fence, as it is named, operates from either a battery-power supply or from an ac power source furnished by the secured facility.

A more elaborate laser fence that monitors and detects the activity along the border between any two countries is proposed by Laserkinetics Corporation. This system consists of a number of detectors positioned along the entire length of the border to monitor the day-and-night activity of the traffic along the border, and transmits intelligence signals to the central station located 50 to 100 miles apart to display the activity on a huge display panel at the main station. Recorders continuously register the time and location of any intrusive event that may occur at each 24-hour period. Each station contains a transmitter, receiver, pulse counter, decoder, and information-charting equipment that not only contains the events occurring with the station's nearby area but along the entire border. The system is complemented by an alarm system which goes on during emergency for alerting the border patrol stations. It uses an infrared laser beam for high power and personnel security.

Questions and Problems

12-1. Why are laser beam systems used in military applications? What are some of the applications of laser systems in military? What type of laser beams can penetrate ocean floors? Discuss them in terms of their wavelengths.

12-2. What are two categories of laser beams that are used for military use? Discuss two types of devastating laser-beam weapons under development. Discuss the mechanism of leaser-beam penetration into thick or hard metals. Can a laser beam fuse an atom to expel its energy? Is it being done now?

12-3. Name the types of laser systems that are used in military service. Which lasers are the most destructive? Which lasers are used for metrological applications? Are the latter type lasers eye-safe? What are excimer lasers and how are they used in military?

12-4. What is a rangefinder? How does it operate to measure distance? Can either cw or pulsed laser beam be used in a rangefinder? How is the distance measured with a pulsed laser beam? How is a distance measured with a continuous-wave laser?

12-5. Which solid-state lasers can be used in a rangefinder? Which semiconductor lasers can be used in a rangefinder? What type gaseous lasers can be used in a rangefinder? Which type is the safest to use from safety standpoint? Which type can measure longer distances? What is the drawback concerning CO_2 lasers in ranging? Which high-power laser is now being extensively used in a rangefinder?

12-6. If a certain rangefinder operates with a clock frequency of 98 MHz and its counter has counted 2×10^3 pulses during a beam's roundtrip, what distance will the rangefinder measure?

12-7. A rangefinder has measured a distance of 6 kilometers in 10^{-5} seconds. What is the clock frequency of the laser system? Using this rangefinder, what will be the time in seconds to measure a distance of 4 kilometers?

12-8. Of what parts does a rangefinder consist? What process takes place in the transmitter prior to the projection of a laser beam to the target? What is the function of a receiver in a rangefinder? How does a counter in a rangefinder start and stop during measurement of range?

12-9. What is a servosystem? If it is installed in a rangefinder, what will be its function? For what type of targets would one provide a servosystem in a rangefinder? What is a quadrant? How is it used in a rangefinder? Discuss.

12-10. What is an error signal? How is it developed in a rangefinder? Is the error signal responsible for the measurement of range? What is the function of an error signal? Do all rangefinders develop error signals? Can error signal be developed with a stationary target? Discuss.

12-11. Does the rangefinder give a constant range for a moving target? What is a cooperative target? Are longer or shorter distances measured when a cooperative target is used? If a rangefinder barely measures the distance of a target having a cooperative target means, can such a rangefinder measure the distance when the cooperative target means is removed? Discuss.

12-12. How does laser-beam divergence affect the measurement of long-distance targets? What is one remedy that can be used to aid the accuracy of measurement in such a situation? How does the magnitude of pulsewidth of a laser beam affect the accuracy of measurement of target distance?

12-13. What is a target designator? Can a target designator measure the range of a target? What type of photodetector is used in a rangefinder? Which detector is more sensitive than a PIN diode? From where do centrally stationed computers obtain their information to give command for the next tactical operation? What type of laser does this type of rangefinder use?

12-14. What is Hg-Cd-Te element? What system uses it and for what purpose? At what frequency does it operate? How small a distance can MIT Lincoln Laboratory's laser radar distinguish? What type of lasing element does it use? What type of detector can couple readily with this type of lasing element? Discuss.

12-15. What is a laser illuminator? What is the function of a target illuminator? Is a target designator mounted on an airborne aircraft the same as a target illuminator? At what wavelength ranges does a target designator operate? What companies produce target designator?

12-16. What are weapon simulation rifles used for? How are they used? From what source does a laser system used on a simulator obtain its electrical energy? Does such a rifle use pulsed or cw laser? Describe a soldier's outfit for laser reception in a battlefield simulation exercise. If a soldier equipped with the laser outfit is hit by a laser pulse, how does he know he is hit?

12-17. In an air-to-air combat simulation, how does a laser transmitter operate? How does a pilot sense that he or his aircraft has been hit? What kind of detector is used in this operation? Discuss.

12-18. What is a directed-beam laser? Don't all laser systems have directed beams? What type of rifle is Laserkinetics Corporation directed-beam device? How does it operate? What type of power supply does it have? How is amplification of laser intensity achieved in this rifle? Can this rifle be used for soldier marksmanship training? If the device can weld, isn't it harmful in soldier training? Explain how it is done.

12-19. What is a free-electron laser system? How does such a system differ from all other types of laser generators? How efficient is a free-electron laser system relative to Nd-YAG laser? How do free electrons obtain their energy? What is the tuning range of such a laser system? Discuss.

12-20. How does U.S. Army's target-penetrating laser system operate? Does it operate more effectively on rough surfaces than bright surfaces? There are two types of lasers in this system. Which of the laser systems produces cavitation? Which of the laser systems produce melting of the focal area? Is CO_2 laser beam more penetrating than Nd-YAG laser beam? Discuss.

12-21. Which surface is more easily penetrated, a painted surface or an unpainted surface? Is it easier to penetrate an aluminum surface than a steel surface? Is the combination of two penetrating laser beams more effective than when each is used alone? Which of the beams operates pulsed? Which beam operates cw?

12-22. What is a security surveillance system? What does the system consist of? How does it achieve its effectiveness as a security system? Which of the surveillance systems studied in this chapter is the most effective? Which of the systems is the most practical? Enumerate some applications for a security surveillance system? At what institution will such a system show its effectiveness the most? If the laser beam has to be bent at corners, wouldn't the intruder attempt to first break the reflector or repeater? How should they be protected from the intruding vandal?

12-23. What is a repeater? How is it constructed? How does it work? Does a repeater re-inforce the intensity of the transmitted laser beam or does it produce its own laser beam? What is a transducer? In a system using repeaters, how can one determine the location of intrusion? Explain the entire mechanism.

12-24. Which of the security surveillance systems studied can indicate the location of intrusion as well as the direction of movement of the intruder? How can this be accomplished? Draw a diagram and locate the laser beams on the diagram, in your explanation.

12-25. What is a Laser Fence? How is it constructed? How does it operate? How far apart are the laser beams projected from the transmitter to the receiver? What is the advantage of such an arrangement with respect to intrusion? What type of laser source is used in this system? At what repetition rate does the system operate? Why is this repetition rate chosen in the system?

12-26. From the discussion given in the text with regard to the security surveillance system used for monitoring the activity at the border of two countries, draw a diagram showing the arrangement of the detectors, monitoring devices, display devices, and the alarm system. This could be a block diagram if preferred.

Chapter 13
Medical Applications of Lasers

During the past few years, the investigations and applications of lasers in medical work have been accelerated because of the tremendous benefit of the laser beams in medical instrumentation on various body organs and tissues. The types of lasers used in this work comprise the ruby laser, Nd-YAG laser, CO_2 laser, argon and krypton lasers, and a number of others about which we shall learn as out study progresses. The most common practice in laser instrument is the surgery of profusely bleeding body organs and the treatment of retinitis, and eye disease in advanced diabetes. To date, the manipulations in surgery and treatment with laser beams have been confined in hospitals and medical institutions, where the new methods of treatment, the types of compatible laser wavelengths and surgical techniques are being investigated. The findings of the investigators have disclosed that different laser wavelengths have different effects on the body tissues, so that existing lasers can be classified in accordance their surgical benefits and radiation treatments.

In considering the lasers in accordance with their behavior on different body tissues, it has been found that the ruby laser beam is very effective in attaching a detached retina in the eye, because the radiation from it is readily absorbed by the retinal tissue. Since the radiation from ruby laser is visible, it can be focused through the lens of the eye precisely at the spot on the retina that has become loose. The ruby laser beam, however, is absorbed only weakly by the blood cells. Thus, when operating on an organ with highly concentrated blood vessels, the radiation beam from argon is used, since it is found to be very effective in coagulating the blood cells as well as fine blood vessels. The argon laser can be employed both cw and pulsed, and where only a single pulse can accomplish the desired treatment, the argon laser beam is prescribed.

While CO_2 laser is being employed in the surgery and treatment of a variety of organic and tissue disorders, its application is confined to surgery where healing time is not of serious concern. Moreover, the CO_2 laser beam in the long wavelength spectral range is easily absorbed by the transmitting and focusing optics; therefore, special quartz or phosphate glass elements are employed for this purpose. Fortunately, CO_2 laser radiation is also used very effectively in the surgery of skin blemishes, abnormal growths in oral tissues, in the removal of esophageal ventriculi, and other gynecological disorders, as we will presently study them. It is the most powerful laser beam to be used in the surgery of ophthalmological pathology, hematological abnormalities, benign tumors, cancerous growths, polyps and nodules in the esophageal cavity, brain tumors, disorder of the kidneys, liver, and pancreas. For gastric and intestinal ulcers, and bleeding tissues, an argon laser beam is being used. Nd-YAG is also a good candidate for the treatment of some of the diseased tissues. Apparently, some of the medical surgeons prefer the use of Nd-YAG laser beam over the CO_2 laser because the treatment with CO_2 laser takes longer time to heal. With all these applications of the lasers in the medical field, it is now up to the laser industry to design and develop medical instrumentation systems that can be employed with the ease and flexibility of the conventional scalpels and electroprobes. Since it is the focus of the laser beam that is capable of cutting, cauterizing, and bonding delicate tissues together, a laser beam conduit provided with a variable-focus lens system capable of performing medically acceptable functions is direly needed.

TREATMENT OF DETACHED RETINA

An argon laser system for the treatment of retinopathy, a pathological deterioration of the retinal membrane due to advanced diabetes, has been developed jointly with the scientists at Stanford Research Institute and Coherent, Inc. The output of the laser unit can be varied continuously from 0 to 1 watt, and the beam can be transmitted through a reflective optical waveguide into a microscope, with the beam pointed at the patient's eye. The surgeon places a contact lens over the cornea and adjusts the focus size of the beam directed to the retina. The focus diameter can be varied from 50 microns to 1 millimeter and the laser power is adjusted just to bond the detached retinal tissue to the choroid layer underneath it. More than 120,000 patients have been treated to date with this procedure. Since this treatment requires high skill and knowledge of laser power and its usage, the physician applying this treatment to the diabetic patient must be first well trained in the art of handling laser beams.

OTOLOGICAL LASER INSTRUMENT

The Eustachian tube of the ear at times becomes constricted due to nasal sinus inflammation or rhinal infection. This condition stops the passage of air to and from the inner ear, resulting in the distention of the eardrum and causing much discomfort and pain. The physician ordinarily pneumatizes the Eustachian tube, relieving the pressure on the eardrum. However, this treatment is only temporary and the pressure builds up again in the inner ear, until the condition in the Eustachian tube is healed. To avoid the pressure in the middle ear (due to accumulation of inflamed matter), the author has proposed, in his previous laser book, the puncturing of the eardrum with the use of an argon laser pulse, which cauterizes the periphery of the punctured hole and the patient is relieved of further pain due to pressure; the treatment is also painless and does not require the patient to have it done in a hospital.

Recently, both Stanford University medical professionals and those in Munich, Germany, have developed the instrument to routinely puncture the tympanic membrane for relieving the pressure as well as aiding the expulsion of the pathological matter, if it exists, from the inner ear into the ear canal, from which it is removed either naturally or by the physician. The patient who has undergone this treatment may further be treated by the physician for healing the sinus or rhinal infection, by administering antibiotic drugs or by mechanical instrumentation at the physician's clinic.

UNIVERSITY OF CINCINNATI RESEARCH EFFORT

Dr. Leon Goldman, MD, the director of the Laser Laboratory, University of Cincinnati Medical Center, also known as the forefather of laser instrumentation in medicine, has been using laser beams routinely for the removal of cancerous tissues, nodules, and other malignant growths from patients that otherwise have not been able to find relief by conventional methods. In this and other investigations with laser beams, it was found that ruby, Nd-YAG, argon, or CO_2 laser beam is equally effective in the removal of black-colored malignant growths. Comparative treatment with a ruby pulsed laser and cw CO_2 laser on skin melanoma indicated that both laser beams were effective in treating the disorder, but the areas treated with CO_2 laser beam healed more slowly. These patients were previously treated with conventional methods and found no relief. The laser radiation treatment was effective and painless, and the tissues healed normally in due time.

BLOODLESS SURGERY ON LARYNX

A team of surgical specialists at Boston University have reported their removal of horny growths, polyps, and nodules from human vocal cords. According to the report, the surgery on these abnormalities has been very successful and reasonably bloodless. In addition, these structures have been healed promptly and no damage has occurred to the vocal cords. A 14-year-old boy has undergone a similar surgery on his vocal cords by the removal of a huge tumor. The boy had undergone a number of previous unsuccessful operations by conventional methods. Subsequent to the healing of the surgery, the boy has regained his voice for the first time in his suffering life.

BRAIN SURGERY WITH LASER BEAM

Another medical team at the University of Pittsburgh has been operating on various types of malignant growths in the brain by the use of appropriate laser beams selected from tissue-compatible laser wavelengths. Their method consists of destroying the cancerous tissue with the laser beam and then removing the remaining mass by the use of a conventional scalpel. The report further states that patients with Parkinson's disease (shaking palsy) which is a disorder of the nervous system with progressive destruction of the brain and nerve centers for coordination of muscular movement, have been aided with the treatment using laser beams, eliminating surgical probing by former methods.

REMOVAL OF SKIN DISORDERS

At the University of Cincinnati, the ruby laser has been in routine use for its excellence in the absorption of its wavelengths by skin blemishes, such as birthmarks and tattoos. The laser beam is injected into a thin layer of the skin to vaporize the dark dye pigment of the tatto beneath the skin. In the removal of warts, a beam from a carbon dioxide laser is used. These skin blemishes that occur on any part of the body, such as the face, arms, legs, or chest, are readily reached by the laser beam for treatment; it seems that the beam transcends the treatment usually applied from an x-ray or radium source.

COOPER MEDICAL LASER COAGULATOR

The treatment of internal, bleeding organs has become possible by the use of an endoscopic laser coagulator formerly manufactured by Spectra-Physics and recently by its subsidiary Cooper Medical Devices, Inc., San Leandro, California. This device employs an argon ion laser for its higher compatibility of absorption by blood cells and is used for the coagulation of internal bleeding by various organs, such as the esophagus, stomach, and gastrointestinal tract. The blue argon laser beam is accompanied by a low-level white light for visualization of the structures to be treated. The laser waveguide consists of a quartz optical fiber which first directs the light to the affected site and then transmits the coagulating argon beam. This combination permits the diagnosis of the lesion followed by the laser treatment almost simultaneously. The optical conduit that contains the quartz fiber also conducts, peripherally to the fiber within the conduit, a jet of carbon dioxide gas that expels the blood from the affected site preparatory to the treatment by the argon-ion laser beam. Although the radiation from a Nd-YAG laser can also be used in this process instead of argon laser, it has been found that the Nd-YAG laser beam of equivalent power level penetrates about four times deeper into the lesion area, and consequently it would be more damaging to the tissues underneath the lesion, as reported by the manufacturer.

A SURGICAL LASER WAVEGUIDE

A laser waveguide developed by Laserkinetics Corporation is designed for use by both medical and dental professionals. The patented waveguide, shown in Fig. 13-1, includes a combination of wavelength-compatible optical fibers located centrally to the conduit. Peripherally to the fiber is a tubular space provided for the conduction of gaseous media necessary for cooling or local anesthesia. Because of the selective use of the optical fibers, degradation and solarization problems have been minimized.

The device can be connected at its proximal end to any source of laser beam and gaseous media; at its distal end it is provided with

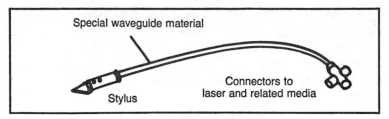

Fig. 13-1. Laserkinetics waveguide for medical and dental instrumentations.

an optical system for controlling the focus of the laser beam and the control of gaseous flow. For surgery, the fingertip pushbuttons provide the necessary gas preparatory to the treatment. The selected laser beam is readily conducted to the affected site at any focus diameter manipulated by the position of the laser pushbutton. The stylus offers the ease of operation of a mechanical scalpel. Up to 100 watts or 80-joule pulses can be easily obtained from the optical waveguide. The power and energy of the instrument can be increased by the increased diameter of the fiber cable.

HANFORD MEDICAL LASER PROBE

A Nd-YAG laser probe developed by the Hanford Laser Laboratory consists of a fiberoptic conduit with radiation-transmitting capability of 80 percent and a beam divergence of 10 milliradians can deliver 200 watts to the site of surgery of profusely bleeding body organs. It achieves a focused power density of 700 watts/mm^2, using a 50-mm focal-length lens. To aid the aiming of the invisible 10,600-angstrom radiation from a Nd-YAG laser, a beam from a He-Ne laser unit is directed through the same 50-mm focal-length lens to localize the focus of the Nd-YAG laser beam. The probe is used for removing tattoos, black-colored tumors, birthmarks, and similar anomalies.

DESTRUCTION OF TUMORS IN AUSTRALIAN TESTS

The test conducted at the University of Adelaide, Australia, with a dye solution selectively absorbed by cancer cells and then irradiated by a laser beam of 6,200 to 6,400 angstroms appear to be quite effective in destroying the cancer cells. The method consists of injecting the dye medium into the cancerous site and then treating the area with the laser beam to activate and accelerate the destruction of the cancer cells. The dye apparently aids both the effective absorption of the laser radiation by the cancer cells and in the destruction of the cancerous tissue.

DOUBLE-BEAM TECHNIQUE FOR CANCEROUS TUMOR

A fiberoptic bronchoscope that can conduct simultaneously a carbon dioxide laser beam and an argon-ion laser beam is found to be very effective in the detection of carcinous tumors and their destruction. As the carbon dioxide laser beam cuts the affected tissue the argon laser beam cauterizes it. The detection of the tumor is aided by a krypton laser beam transmitted through the same bronchoscope. A fluorescent dye is injected into the tumor through the blood stream preparatory to its incision. The dye fluoresces and localizes the tumor.

MEDICAL LASER SYSTEM

The medical profession has been encumbered by the lack of versatility of laser equipment that would offer the flexibility of an electrosurgical scalpel with added utility. This shortcoming had deterred the more rapid advance of the medical and dental instrumentations whereby the laser would become a commonplace in many of the medical professionals' clinical offices. Steps have been taken to connect a laser waveguide to the existing laser system, but the resultant function of the equipment has still precluded the many applications of laser beams as medical tools in the hands of the medical men. These problems possibly have been partially alleviated by the development of a medical laser system that can be employed both as a medical instrumentation device as well as a dental office instrument. This system, designed and developed by my organization contributes great versatility and effectiveness to the use of laser beam in the medical clinic. The system is shown in Fig. 13-2.

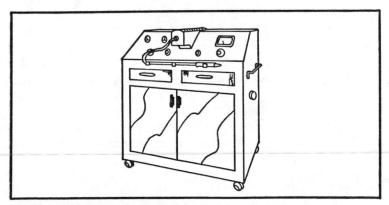

Fig. 13-2. Laserkinetics medical instrumentation laser system.

The new medical unit consists of a portable cabinet that contains three different laser generators, which can be selected by means of a series of buttons on the cabinet instrument panel. For instance, for surgery of a mass of tissue from the body, the surgeon presses a button to adjust a carbon dioxide laser generator with respect to a folding mirror positioned 45° with respect to the generator beam to direct the beam to the exit aperture. The flexible laser waveguide shown in Fig. 13-1 may then be connected at its proximal end to the exit port of the system. While using the waveguide, as the physician may require a cauterizing beam, he presses a second button on the instrument panel to position an argon ion laser beam with respect to the waveguide. The required power of the laser beams can also be controlled by two knobs on the control panel. The cabinet, provided with rollers under the system, can be moved from one office to another by just pushing it.

HOLOGRAPHIC APPLICATION IN MEDICAL WORK

Nearly 10,000 corneal transplants are being made annually in the United States, as reported. While the procedure is said to have become a routine matter, removal of the sutures from the eye has been somewhat a problem because of the precarious nature of the healing of the sutured sites under the bandage. In order to eliminate premature removal of the sutures, which condition is said to cause astigmatism, and longer retention of the suture subjects the eye to infection, the Johns Hopkins University Hospital has developed a holographic procedure whereby the sutures can be removed at a favorable healing time.

It is reported that the technique devised by the Johns Hopkins investigators permits the physicians to determine the strength of the transplanted cornea preparatory to the removal of the sutures. The technique consists of making a hologram of the lateral view of the cornea with the use of a He-Ne laser, as shown in Fig. 13-3. Two beams split from a primary laser beam projecting from the laser source are brought to incidence on a photographic plate to form an interference pattern of the lateral portion of the sutured eye. Any abnormal deformation of the eyeball compared with the expected configuration of the structure indicates incomplete healing of the cornea. The technique of producing the hologram is identical with that we have already studied in Chapter 12.

BREAST CANCER DETECTION

A double-beam holography system developed by a scientist at

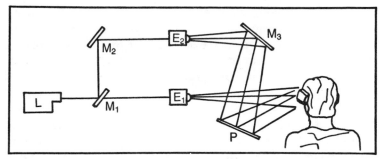

Fig. 13-3. Holographic method of determining the time for removal of sutures.

the university of Queensland, Australia, is reported to detect early stages of breast cancer. The method consists of taking two holograms of the breast a small exposure increments apart on the same photographic plate, thus superimposing the latent interferometric images in the photographic plate. The fringe patterns thus formed represent a minute displacement of the breast skin due to blood circulation. A disruption of blood circulation in this displacement and hence a change in fringe patter is said to attest to incipient cancer formation in the breast thus holographed.

RADIOREFLEX TREATMENT OF REFERRED PAIN

It is well known in the medical profession that pain due to the disorder of the internal organs of the body at times appears remotely from the ailing organ and centers in areas beneath the skin. These areas are known as reflex or referred-pain areas, the pain radiation through the nerve channels to the nerve endings in the skin. For example, the pain from a disorder of gall bladder or liver may appear in the right-shoulder area, an inflammation of the spleen may radiate pain to the left-shoulder area, and the pain from a decaying tooth may occur in the temporal region on the same side where the tooth is located, as illustrated in Fig. 13-4. Such pains have been alleviated by the use of needles embedded in the referred pain areas; this practice is prevalent throughout the Orient and is known as acupuncture treatment. The scheme is being used in a number of medial centers in the United States and in Europe.

Recently, the practice of acupuncture has been supplanted by laser irradiation scheme, which consists of exposing the reflex pain area to a narrow beam of He-Ne laser. Since the human skin cells are relatively transparent to the 6,328-angstrom red wavelengths of the He-Ne laser, perceptible treatment effects have been obtained at laser-power levels from 1 to 60 milliwatts.

In the treatment, the laser radiation is transmitted through a glass-fiber waveguide provided with a stylus at its terminal end. The beam is projected to the exterior of the stylus through a 1-millimeter-diameter exit aperture and directed to the reflex-pain area by placing the terminal point of the stylus on the skin and irradiating the area with a nominal 2-milliwatt laser beam for a period of several seconds up to 60 seconds. The beam can penetrate the skin to a depth of 3 to 10 millimeters, depending on the texture and color of the skin. The pain disappears almost instantly, according to the practitioners, who are investigating the use of the laser treatment on larger areas as well as on the primary pain centers. The treatment is painless and produces no perceptible damage to the skin.

PHOTORADIATION THERAPY FOR CANCER

A team of researchers at the Rosewell Park Memorial Institute in Buffalo, New York, have developed a technique for a cancer therapy using laser radiation that sensitizes the irradiated malignant tumor cells and shrinks and kills the cancerous tissue cells. The affinity of the tumor cells to become sensitized for selective absorption of the laser beam is achieved by the use of an organic chemical known as hematoporphyrin (HPD), initially used as antidepressant in Europe. This compound, when injected into the blood stream, aggregates the tumor cells without affecting the normal cells.

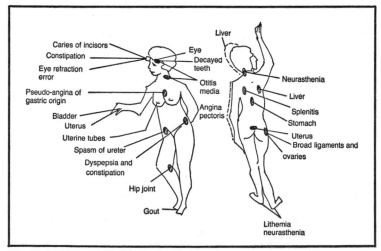

Fig. 13-4. Diagram showing referred pain areas.

In the present technique, the red radiation from a ruby laser is used and, as the investigation advances, other types of laser beams, such as those from a Nd-YAG, argon, excimer, or mixed CO_2-He-Ne laser, may be found more effective in accordance with their compatibilities with the type and texture of the cancerous cells irradiated. For instance, the Swedish researchers have discovered that a continuous-wave CO_2 laser could cause explosion of the ear labyrinth cells during an otological surgery, while the same type of surgery in the United States employing a modified laser technique has not experienced cell explosion or damage to the contiguous normal tissue cells, the laser power used being 20 watts precisely timed to 15-millisecond bursts.

At the Rosewell Park Memorial Institute, 150 patients have been initially tested with a ruby-laser beam and in approximately 75 percent of the cases thus exposed to the radiation the tumor tissues have shrunk 50 percent or more. In some patients, the malignant cells have completely disappeared, making the patients tumor-free for four years as of this writing. In hopeless cancerous cases, the irradiated cells have shrunk sufficiently to be removed by conventional surgical method. Nearly 20 medical centers around the world are engaged in testing the photoradiation technique on cancer patients. It is believed that early diagnosis of tumors and their early treatment with the laser beam will eventually conquer the disease in the patients.

A case of lung tumor reported by Japanese surgeons has been cured by introducing a thin coherent fiberoptic cable into the patient's lung through an incision made in the patient's chest. The operator could actually see the tumor through the optical cable and direct the beam accurately to the carcinous growth to kill it.

GENERAL COMMENTS

It should now be evident that the advent of the use of laser beams of various wavelengths in medical instrumentation has opened many new avenues for the physician to employ the beam almost the same as the conventional scalpel in a number of medical cases. The appearance of a laser system for surgical use in every surgeon's office has not made much headways because of the lack of properly designed equipment and its high cost. However, since the industry has foreseen the need and the potential applications of the laser beam for numerous types of maladies and disorders of the superficial and internal body structures, it should not be surprising to see, in the near future, in the market various types of medical instrumentation systems and devices using laser beams. It is expected that the newly formed medical society in conjunction with the laser industry will give the impetus to the realization of the medical instrumentation systems appearing in many of the surgeons' clinics as adjunct to their present medical equipment. We have seen that laser treatment has definite future in the medical field and to that end much effort will be initiated among the industrial laser companies.

It must also be pointed out here that the intent of this chapter is not to instruct the reader how to administer laser treatment to patients, but to point out that there are various applications of the laser beam to alleviate the suffering of the human society, and to emphasize the fact that there is a dire need for the development of properly designed medical equipment using various types of lasers intended to varied types of ailments. In the design stage and development of such equipment, the cooperation of both the laser physicist and the surgeon is unavoidable and essential.

Questions and Problems

13-1. What types of lasers are used in medical instrumentation work? Which lasers are used for cutting tissue? Which lasers are used for cauterizing? How do wavelengths of laser radiations affect different tissues in the body? If the laser radiation is invisible, how can the surgeon employ the beam in his work? Explain.

13-2. In operating on an organ with highly concentrated blood vessels, what type of laser beam is used? In what mode is that beam used? Where healing time is not of serious concern, what type of laser is used in surgery? What type of fiberoptic cable can conduct CO_2 laser beam? What type of fiberoptic cable can conduct ultraviolet laser beam? What is the most powerful laser beam used in general surgery of the body?

13-3. What is the treatment for detached retina? What is the cause of detached retina? What type of waveguide have Stanford University scientists developed? Why did they choose the type you mentioned? How many patients per year are being treated for retinal detachment?

13-4. What type of laser beam does the otological instrument use? Is this laser system operating pulsed or continuous wave? What is the purpose of using a laser beam on the eardrum? How painful is the treatment on the eardrum with the laser? What is the procedure in the laser treatment on the eardrum? Explain.

13-5. What types of laser beams are used at the University of Cincinnati for the removal of cancerous growths? Which of the laser beams is the most effective? Using the most effective laser beam, does the treated site heal very quickly? Is this type of operation painful? Explain.

13-6. How does University of Pittsburgh treat Parkinson's disease? State the procedure they use. What university appears to have specialized in removing horny growth, polyps, and nodules from human vocal cords? How are skin blemishes treated, and with what type of laser beam? Where is it being done? How does the procedure compare with x-ray or radium treatment?

13-7. What is a laser coagulator? For what body structure is such a device used? What laser beam has the greatest compatibility of absorption by the blood cells? Why does a waveguide conduct a gas in addition to a laser beam? Can Nd-YAG laser beam be used where argon-ion laser is prescribed? Explain.

13-8. How does Laserkinetics waveguide transmit ultraviolet radiation as well as infrared and visible radiations through it? Explain. What other substance does this waveguide conduct through it and for what purpose? How is the laser beam controlled through this waveguide? What other materials are controlled through the waveguide? Discuss.

13-9. What is Handford medical probe? How does it operate? Why are two lasers used in this device? What is the function of the beam from each laser source? What power is used in the device?

13-10. Explain the destruction of tumor by the use of a dye and a laser beam in the Australian tests. What wavelength laser beams are used in this device? What is the apparent function of the dye in this treatment?

13-11. What is double-beam technique for removal of cancerous tissues? What types of lasers are used in this technique? What is the function of each of the laser beams in this treatment? How can the power and energy of the instrument be increased?

13-12. What would be an ideal medical laser system for an average surgeon's office? What sort of flexibility of use of the equipment would you recommend? How would you implement such recommendations? How many laser radiations can be obtained in a Laserkinetics medical laser system? Explain.

13-13. How can holography be used in medical work? Describe the application given in the text respecting the use of holography. What type of laser beam is used in the holography described in the text on eye sutures? How is the eye prevented from being injured by the laser beam? Discuss.

13-14. How do Australian scientists detect incipient breast

cancer? What is the essential scheme in this technique that permits detection of the incipient cancer? What type of laser beam would be the most suitable for this type of diagnosis?

13-15. What is meant by referred pain? Where does referred pain of a decaying tooth appear? To what area of the body does pain or disorder of the hip joint reflex? What is acupuncture? What is radioreflex treatment? What type of laser beam is used in radioreflex treatment?

13-16. What laser-power level is used in radioreflex treatment? At what diameter of the beam the treatment is administered? To what depth can the beam penetrate in an ordinary white skin? Does color of the skin affect the penetration? Is the treatment painful? Is it harmful to the skin? Discuss.

13-17. What is photoradiation? What does it do to cancer cells which are injected with a solution of hemotoporphyrin? If the cancer cells are light, what type of laser beam would be more compatible with them? If the cancer cells are dark, what type of laser beam would be compatible with them? Discuss the latter two questions on the basis of knowledge gathered earlier on the absorption characteristics of laser beams.

13-18. In the present technique, what type of laser is being used? Should the laser beam continuous or pulsed? Discuss your answer. About what percent of the patients treated for cancer have obtained success with ruby laser beam? What type of fiberoptic cable was used by Japanese surgeons to see the tumor in the lung of a patient? Discuss.

Chapter 14
Laser Applications in Dentistry

Following the discovery of laser radiation in 1959, considerable experimentation was carried out by various biomedical institutions. During the decade following the discovery, the investigations were generally centered on the enamel of the tooth, because of its easy accessibility and its susceptibility to become carious. Since the ruby laser followed just after the gaseous He-Ne laser, and because of the availability of much higher laser power from the ruby laser, the investigations on the tooth enamel started with the ruby laser. It was soon found by various investigators in different parts of the continent that pulsed ruby laser could vaporize the dental enamel. When a laser pulse of 5 to 20 joule energy was focused on a 1-millimeter-diameter area on the enamel for a few milliseconds the focal area was vaporized to a depth of several microns. Greater focus areas with higher proportional energy levels could be vaporized with the laser, so that drilling into the enamel was easily achieved.

As long as the laser beam was directed and remained on the enamel, drilling of the enamel to a few millimeter depth would produce clear-cut depressions or craters. Amorphous enamel areas, indicating incipient carious condition, would be subject of formation of larger craters with an equivalent energy that would produce only smaller craters on the normal enamel. However, when the laser beam penetrated the enamel and reached the dentin, the area drilled contained a dark residue by the oxidation of the organic substance in the dentin. Furthermore, experiments conducted on teeth in vitro showed that when the beam penetrated to the pulpal cavity (within the dentin) it coagulated the pulp substance. It was then though that the effect of the laser beam on the dental pulp was irreversible and would not be desirable. Accordingly, drilling of the teeth for the removal of carious matter did not seem to be advantageous with the use of a laser beam. Thus, the direction of investigation was shifted to the study of the effects of a laser beam on the enamel itself.

It was also determined during those years that the absorption characteristics of different parts of the tooth vary with the constituent of the particular part to be lased (irradiated with laser). These characteristics further varied with the type of laser beam, radiation energy, and the wavelength from the laser source, if it contained harmonic wavelengths. The focus size and hence the distance between the focusing lens and the material lased also entered into the absorption properties of the material. The water content of the tooth structure was also a factor in the destructive energy threshold of the laser radiation; the water absorbed some of the radiant heat for dehydration before the laser beam could affect either the enamel or the dentin. While dentin contains about six times as much water as the enamel, the comparative hardness of the enamel required as high or higher energy to be penetrated to the same depth as the dentin. The vaporization of the water content within the dentin would at times induce pressure or even mechanical stresses in the contiguous structures. Both the carbon dioxide and the ruby lasers produced similar effects on the dental structure irradiated. Repeated pulsing of the laser beam on the same spot caused deeper and deeper penetration.

STRUCTURE OF THE TOOTH

Teeth are the hardest bones in the body. They are chiefly composed of mineral substances, such as calcium, magnesium, phosphorus, fluorine and other minerals in trace quantities (see Fig. 14-1). The teeth are embedded in the alveolar processes of the upper and lower jaws. The alveolar processes contain sockets for each tooth and are lined with a tough membrane called periosteum, which, with the aid of softer gums, attach the teeth to the sockets and provide nourishment to the teeth from the blood vessels within the tooth.

Each tooth consists of three sections: a crown, which is the uppermost part of the tooth and is made of enamel; a root, consisting of one or more fangs; and, a neck, which occupies the region

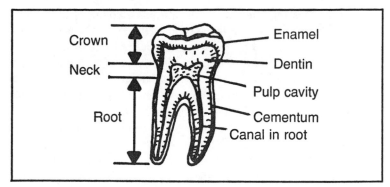

Fig. 14-1. The structure of a tooth.

between the root and the crown. The tooth substantially consists of a dentin which is softer than the enamel, and is attached to the enamel by means of cementum, which interfaces the dentin, enamel, and the gums. The dentin has a central cavity containing pulp, which is saturated with blood vessels and nerves, and a canal through which the blood vessels carry nutrition to the tooth.

The enamel is the part of the tooth that is exposed and is used for mastication of food. Caries of the tooth generally starts in the enamel, if the gums are healthy. If the gums are receding, due to malnutrition or a disease, the caries may also develop at the gumline of the tooth or in the dentin. When calcium metabolism suffers, the condition may cause the disorder of the alveoli and the adjoining tooth. Disease of the gums may also affect the health of the tooth by permitting the passage of bacteria from the mouth to the root canal, infecting the tooth. In the sections to follow, emphasis will be directed to the sustenance of a healthy gumline as well as an enamel, and to reduce incipience of caries, using laser beams as preventive dentistry.

EFFECTS OF LASER RADIATION ON HARD DENTAL TISSUE

While the ruby laser radiation (6,940-angstrom wavelengths) uncovered the first indication that the enamel surface can be treated with the laser beam to inhibit the surface against decay, a disadvantage of the radiation was that it produced a diathermal action in the enamel, causing a partial absorption of the radiation by the pulpal substance in the dentin. Since ruby was the first laser utilized for the investigation of the enamel characteristics, in interaction with the radiation, a laser radiation with increased effectivity of absorption in the enamel with lower energy density was essential for an improved method. Such a radiation was the further discovery that a long-wavelength carbon dioxide laser beam possessing higher absorption properties utilized by the enamel would be preferable.

The carbon dioxide laser radiation has a fundamental wavelength of 106,000 angstroms and is found to be more efficiently absorbed by the enamel, lessening the tendency to injure the pulpal substance. Carbon dioxide laser produces a continuous-wave radiation; however, the radiation can be converted into a pulsing mode, and controlled energies from a low power to a very high-power level can be achieved with it. Furthermore, the experiments with the carbon dioxide laser have indicated that the color or shade variation of the enamel surface from one tooth to another is not of consequence because the absorption behavior of the enamel toward carbon dioxide laser wavelengths remains constant. Thus, the beginning of a new era for preventive dentistry using laser radiation was well in view.

In-Vitro and In-Vivo Instrumentations

As early as 1965, various investigators had determined that the surface of the dental enamel could be affected by a laser radiation to increase the resistance of the enamel to caries. To substantiate this effect, the investigators have covered the surfaces of human enamel specimens with a radio-opaque material, leaving bare areas for exposure to the laser beam. After exposure to the radiation, the specimens have been immersed in a demineralizing solution consisting of hydroxyethylcellulose and lactic acid buffered by a solution of sodium hydroxide to a 4.5 pH, and left in the solution from 5 to 14 days. During the interim of every several days of test, the specimens were examined microscopically for evidence of lesions characterized by white spot formation at the exposed areas. When the white crystalline formation appeared on the specimens they were sectioned, microradiographed with soft x-rays, and the sections were examined with a microscope at medium magnification. The areas that were not lased (not exposed to the laser beam) indicated demineralization, while the areas exposed to the laser beam showed only a slight effect by the solution.

Since there was some disparity in the natural discoloration of the enamel surfaces from one specimen to the other, and only about 20 percent of the laser energy was absorbed by the specimens using the ruby laser, a more consistent procedure of achieving constant results was necessary. About this period, the use of carbon dioxide laser was becoming very common among biomedical researchers, and it was tried in place of ruby laser. It was noted that the carbon dioxide laser was less amenable to different colors or shades of the enamel surface and that its diathermic effect was far less significant on the dental pulp under the enamel. Thus the use of pulsed carbon dioxide laser beam was preferred to the ruby laser, because a lower level of laser power could be used with decreased absorption by the pulpal substance. The reason for this was the smaller penetration of the radiation in the enamel substance.

After exposure of several specimens to the carbon dioxide laser beam, in the manner described in the preceding paragraph, the specimens were sectioned and examined. No subsurface demineralization was observed. The surface structure alteration was increased with increase of laser energy density. These experiments proved that carbon dioxide laser radiation was more efficient in achieving surface transformation to increase resistance to decay than the ruby laser. All the experiment, with the exception of a few in-vivo instrumentation, were made on enamel of the teeth in vitro. Thus, the inhibition of caries by means of scanning the enamel with a laser beam had been initiated on a small scale.

Laser-Induced Inhibition of Caries

Stern and Songnnese were among the earliest investigators and advocates of laser-induced inhibition of caries. They showed experimentally that when the enamel surface of a normal tooth was "laser brushed", the resistance against demineralization of the enamel when immersed in a demineralization solution was increased. Such an experiment would also attest to the fact that the enamel could be affected by acid-causing environ. The technique in the experiment consisted of providing a window in a gold bridge, with the test enamel disposed in the window. A small area below the gold plate was provided to serve as a microbial accumulation site for both the lased and unlased specimens during the entire period of four weeks for inducing a carious condition. After the test period, the specimens were examined microradiographically as well as by means of a scanning electron microscope. The unlased specimens showed white lesions characteristic of incipient caries. They were then convinced that "laser brushing" the enamel would definitely induce resistance against caries.

Recently, "laser brushing" is accomplished by the use of a carbon dioxide laser beam transmitted through a single or multiple optical fibers made of either quartz or fluorite glass, which is transparent to infrared radiation of the carbon dioxide laser. At the distal end of the fiber cable is a stylus containing an optical focusing doublet (lenses). A laser energy varying from 10 to 30 joules per square centimeter is focused to a test site of one or two millimeters in diameter and the beam is scanned over the enamel for up to several seconds. The scanning is done manually and takes as much time as is necessary to cover the entire test area. To perform this procedure in vivo, the areas continguous to the test site are covered with a non-laser-transparent foil so that the surrounding soft dental tissue will be protected from stray radiation.

A Laser Waveguide

A biomedical laser waveguide, developed and patented by the author's staff, consists of a fiberoptic cable enclosed in a plastic tubular sheath, one end of which is connected to the laser source and the other end is provided with a stylus for administering the laser beam. The cable within the sheath is surrounded by a tubular space through which a gaseous material, such as an anesthetizing gas used during surgery or an inert gas can be transmitted to the area of interest. A variable-focus optical system directs the laser beam either focused or defocused, the focused beam being used for cutting or welding and the defocused beam for laser brushing the teeth. The waveguide is not in commercial use yet, but it will be when the dental instrumentation system now under development becomes commercial. It is believed that while the laser instrumentation system will not entirely replace the present mechanical dental instruments, it will be an important adjunct to dental treatment implementation, when dental professionals are trained to implement the procedure skillfully to dental patients. The training will have to come from dental institutions.

Laser Drilling of Enamels

Dental drilling of the enamel will probably be rejected by some dental professionals, by the use of laser beams, because it is a new procedure and the results have not been seen by such professionals. However, since ultrasonic cleaning of teeth has now been adopted by many dentists and is in extensive use in dental offices, in spite of the initial resistance against its application as a dental cleaning instrument, the application of laser beams in dental clinics will soon become commonplace. The first use of laser drilling possibly will begin with the tooth whose nerve plexus is infected and the dentist will ordinarily deaden it by use of a mechanical instrument and medicinal aid. In such an event, the use of a laser beam would seem very plausible, since not only the cavity will be cleaned thoroughly by the inert gas mentioned in the preceding paragraph of this chapter but also it will be sterlized by the coagulative action of the laser beam.

One other advantage of the use of a laser beam in drilling the enamel would be for incipient caries to remove the superficial layer of the enamel. The cavity then may be filled with an inorganic substance or a mixture of inorganic and organic substances and the laser beam directed to the material to sinter or cure it. Upon completing the work, the fillings can be glazed with the laser beam to diffuse the material into the enamel as well as polishing the surface without the use of mechanical polishers. In any event, such instrumentation will require previous training by highly skilled professionals at academic level.

EFFECT OF LASER ON SOFT DENTAL TISSUE

The following describes the effects of laser on the soft dental tissue.

Effect of Laser on Oral Mucosa

The reference to oral mucosa here includes the gingiva, pulpal tissue, the cheek and tongue, and labial membrane. Since these tissues could be exposed unintentionally to laser radiation when the use of laser becomes routine in the dental office, tests were made to determine what effects the laser radiation would have on them. Early investigators employed rubber dams but the possibility of injuring the dental pulp still existed by the diathermous effect through the enamel. These precautions were useful and applicable to certain types of laser radiations while for others they were not necessary as long as the laser exposure did not last more than a fraction of a second. For instance, exposure of the mucous membrane to low-power laser radiation at a defocused state would not have any more effect on the mucosa, when infrared radiation from a carbon dioxide laser was incident on it, than a bowl of warm soup. However, the shorter-wavelength radiation, such as those from an argon laser, even when the radiation is of low power, could cause serious damage to the tissue. The gingiva from the lased side were compared with those of the unlased side of the mandible where the experimentation on the teeth had been conducted; no significant change on the lased side was observed.

In exposures of Caucasian skin to ruby laser, it was observed that the skin became inflamed with resulting exudate from the underlying cells. The platelets and leucocytes would stick to the wall of the capillary. The mass also contained agglutinated erythrocytes. All these led to the beginning of the present knowledge that a laser beam can cause photocoagulation of the blood cells, and when used under controlled conditions, the beam could "weld" tissues together, such as in welding loose retina in advanced diabetic patients. Thus, the effect of laser radiations on human body tissues is the same as for metals; high density radiation can produce a hole in metal sheet while a controlled radiation density can weld two metal sheets together when in contact with each other, as we have seen in an earlier chapter.

Therapeutic Action of Ultraviolet Laser

While a long-wavelength radiation from a carbon dioxide laser beam can cause severe thermal effects on the exposed soft tissues the short-wavelength radiation from an argon laser, such as an ultraviolet radiation, can produce therapeutic effects when the beam is used under strictly controlled conditions. For instance, in the years past, a medical doctor could treat the nasal cavities of a patient ailing with sinusitis or nasal polyps by the use of a mercury discharge tube emitting ultraviolet rays. The rays were also used to alleviate or cure mild cases of gingivitis. The energy from the mercury discharge tube was relatively smaller than that given off by a laser source. When the use of lasers become common in a dental office or in a medical clinic, a short-wavelength argon laser would seem to become very effective means of therapeutic treatment of gingivitis, because the laser beam can be focused or defocused to the site being treated. By increasing the energy density of the radiation, a defocused radiation would cover a larger area and the time of treatment would be reduced to a minimum.

DENTAL INSTRUMENTATION PROGRESS IN '70S

The following describes investigations into other uses of lasers in dentistry.

Root Canal Laser Instrumentation

While no literature has been available to the author at the time of this writing respecting the application of lasers to root-canal treatment, investigations at the author's activity are in progress along this direction. The discussion given here then would be presented as potential possibilities. As recognized by the dental profession, treatment of necrosis or suppuration at the root of a tooth is not as simple as drilling the enamel and filling it with a restorative material. Depending on the severity of the case, it may take as long as several weeks to completely drain the root (usually by an endodontist) and sterilize the cavity prior to closing it with a filling material and then crowning the tooth. Frequently, antibiotic tablets are also administered by mouth during the extended period. The work is ordinarily time-consuming, delicate procedure, and requires special knowledge and experience. The treatment site aches, at times, until the cause of suppuration is removed and sometimes the nerve at the root is killed to abate aching.

A new laser instrumentation procedure advanced by the author is the use of the fiberoptic waveguide designed by the author. This waveguide is capable of delivering laser energy (preferably argon laser) to the treatment site either as a focused or defocused beam. With the instrument, the focus of the beam can be adjusted internally to the stylus, located at the end of the waveguide, to any diameter desired. When the point of the stylus is placed on the treatment site, the exact focus of the beam is achieved on the area to be treated. Because the operator or the patient cannot see the beam or any stray radiation from it, the device gives complete safety, since it cannot operate until the point of the stylus is disposed, on the treatment area.

The root canal treatment is performed as follows: the beam focus size is adjusted to about 1 millimeter and a pulse of the laser beam is directed at the gingival area under which the infection has been localized with x-ray radiograph. A hole through the gingival mucosa to the root of the infected tooth is made, which action simultaneously cauterizes the periphery of the hole, providing access to the suppurated cavity. The hole is left open for a few days until all the infection has been drawn out either by means of an aspirator or by leaving it alone for nature to expel the matter to the oral cavity, where it is absorbed by a cotton pledget. The dentist may also prescribe antibiotic tablets for the patient to take daily until the infection has subsided as determined radiographically or visually. Upon complete drainage of the infectious matter from the cavity, the hole is left to close naturally. This procedure is expected to be painless, and time-saving to the dental practitioner. In order to put this procedure in practice, sophisticated techniques must be established and the practitioner trained prior to attempting the technique.

Materials Sealed in Enamel Using Lasers

The latest investigations on the treatment of carious enamel have uncovered the fact that after the enamel is drilled by conventional methods, the cavity may be filled with a tooth-colored paste of either organic or inorganic substance and cured in the cavity by means of a laser beam, preferably from an argon laser, followed by fusing the material to the enamel with a carbon dioxide laser beam and glazing it to obtain a continuous filling-enamel surface. When the incipient carious pits are noted on the enamel, the laser beam may also be used to seal the pits by diffusing the enamel material into the pits. As a last procedure, the laser beam may be defocused, the energy density increased, and the beam "brushed" over the enamel to inhibit it from further decay by acid-forming food agents.

Other Recent Research Results

More recent tests with lasers on the enamel in vivo or in vitro have confirmed the early reports of the enamel immunization against caries. The reports further state that because of the recrystallization and growth of the hydroxiapatite of the enamel, the process has enhanced the diffusion of fluoride from toothpastes or dental treatments in the dentist's office. Another study reported has shown that lasers irradiation of the drilled tooth surfaces may replace the present method of acid etching the surface for easy bonding of the resin filling of the tooth.

A still more recent study at the University of California at Los Angeles has reported a technique in which a laser beam from a Nd-YAG laser emitting at 10,640 angstroms is used on the enamel surfaces. Since the radiation wavelengths of this laser are not absorbed by the enamel as efficiently as those from the carbon dioxide laser beam, emitting at 106,000 angstroms, the tooth surfaces are coated with a radiation-absorbing material, such as an apatite or a carbonacious material, before the tooth is subjected to the Nd-YAG laser beam. Because of the high-energy emission from the Nd-YAG laser, the energy from it can be reduced to about one-tenth, reducing the tendency of pulpal absorption and increasing the safety of the process.

The dental engineering laboratory at the University of Utah has reported its engineering staff as having successfully sealed fissures with tooth-colored sealants, such as a phosphate mixture, using the heat from a carbon dioxide laser beam. They also determined that short-time exposure of the enamel to laser radiation of 1.5 joules or less would be tolerable without damage to the pulpal substance. Also, for pulse durations of 0.25 to 1.0 second, a laser energy density of up to 23.5 joules/cm^2 could be applied to the enamel. The sealing material, mixed with ethanol, is applied to the cavity with an airbrush, and sintered with laser beam at energy densities up to 50 joules/cm^2 using a germanium lens for focusing the laser beam.

APPLICATIONS OF LASERS IN DENTAL PROSTHESIS

During the past decade, laserwelding of dental prosthesis has progressed to a point that if properly designed laser equipment were available, the work possibly can be performed directly in the mouth when necessary. The advantages of laserwelding dental bridges are many. For instance, superior joints can be achieved with a laser beam. The time of welding or fabrication of a given part on the bridgework can be reduced many times. To join a broken gold, nickel, or stainless steel frame, no additional welding metal is required, as in torch welding, and the joining or welding work is simplified with the use of a laser beam. A typical welding procedure directly in the mouth is shown in Fig. 14-2. When drilling enamel

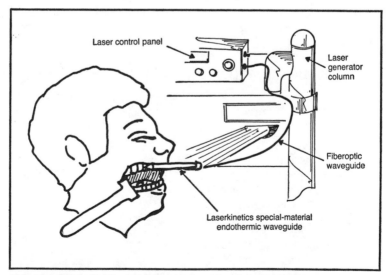

Fig. 14-2. Method of transmitting the laser beam to the teeth.

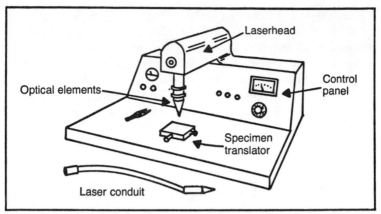

Fig. 14-3. Laserkinetics dental welding system.

with a laser beam becomes a routine procedure, this method will be the practical way to follow.

While commercial welders for welding exclusively prosthesis are not available, the author's firm has developed several years ago a microwelder that has successfully met the requirements for the ease of manipulation of the beam, offering flexibility of use in a dental office. The dental welding unit is shown in Fig. 14-3. Since the need for such a system is just beginning to appear, as laser knowledge in dental science progresses, this unit will soon be commercialized for routine application. The special waveguide will also serve to make surgical incisions in both dental and medical offices.

POTENTIAL CLINICAL APPLICATIONS OF LASERS

Many of the practical applications of lasers in preventive and restorative dental operations are already discussed in the preceding paragraphs. The general concept may be recapitulated here stating that when properly designed dental equipment is built so that the dentist can use it the same as any of the presently available conventional instruments, the potentials of laser applications will prove themselves as essential adjunct to present instruments used by the dentist, as follows:

■ The dental enamel will be treated with laser to induce inhibition against carious development and growth.

■ The treatment of the teeth with laser by "brushing" them with the radiation will facilitate the diffusion of the fluoride from dental treatment or the daily use of a toothpaste having fluoride, into the enamel to strengthen it.

■ The laser beam will seal minute holes or fissures due to incipient carious growth.

■ The laser beam will cure or harden the tooth-colored material filled in a drilled hole of the enamel in restorative treatment, and thereafter will fuse the material into the enamel and glaze it.

■ The incipient inflammation is the mucosa or gingiva could be treated with the ultraviolet beam of argon laser.

■ The photocoagulation property of the laser beam could be used for arresting the profuse bleeding of the gums after a surgery or extraction of a tooth.

■ Bleaching of the enamel with low-density laser beam would be possible.

■ Dental drilling of the enamel with laser in specific cases where the anomaly is superficial, rapid lasing of the area would be possible, to prevent heating of the tooth and hence avoiding damage to the pulpal cavity.

■ Dental prosthesis work would be performed both in vivo and in vitro conditions.

■ The possibility of root-canal treatment should not be overlooked.

COMMENTS

The experimental work discussed in this chapter is based on the investigative work and results obtained by a large number of workers in this field. Principally, the pioneering work has been done by Dr. Ralph H. Stern, School of Dentistry, University of California at Los Angeles, and his colleagues Dr. Harold F. Eastgate, Professor Johanna Vahl, Dr. Donald Rounds, and others as given in the accompanying references. The procedures given in the preceding discourse are only for purposes of information and not recommendations by the author for any one to implement or not to implement his dental investigative work with lasers. Nor does the author intend to prognostigate that laser instrumentation will eventually replace all conventional methods; however, it is believed, based on present knowledge, that radiations from various laser sources will eventually become very important and proper equipment designed to implement the radiation treatment will constitute indispensable dental tool for restorative and therapeutic dentistry in the dental professional's office.

References

Eastgate, H. F., UCLA Special Report on Laser Instrumentations, 1971

Stern, R. H. and R. F. Sognnaes, Laser Inhibition of Dental Caries in Vivo, Amer Dent Assoc, 85:1087-1090, 1972

Stern, R. H. and R. F. Sognnaes, Effects of Lased Enamel by CO_2 laser, J Dent Res, 51:455-460, 1972

Goldman, L. Dermatological Manifestations of Laser Radiation, Federation Proceedings, Suppl., 14, S-92, S-93, 1965

Bohm, R. L. and J. Webster, Laser Applications on a Durable Dental Sealant, OSA/IEEE Conference: Laser and Electro-optical Systems Feb 7-9, p-48, 1978

Gordon, T.E., Jr., and D. L. Smith, Laser Welding of Prosthesis, J Pros Dent, 24(4):472-476, 1970

Questions and Problems

14-1. Why was ruby selected to lase the enamel? Which mode was preferable, a cw or pulsed mode of laser radiation? Why was drilling the enamel with a ruby laser abandoned? Does absorption characteristics of different parts of the tooth vary? Does this characteristic vary with the type of laser wavelengths? Discuss.

14-2. What is the disadvantage of using ruby laser on the enamel? Is the pulpal substance affected when the enamel is lased? How does carbon dioxide laser differ in its action on the enamel from that of the ruby laser? What is the effect of laser radiation on the hard dental tissues? Discuss.

14-3. How does laser immunization against caries affect the enamel? What is the hardest substance in the tooth? How is dentin related to the enamel in the tooth? If the enamel is lased, does this affect the dentin or pulpal substance? What effect does irradiation of the enamel have on the pulp? What is diathermal effect by carbon dioxide laser? Explain.

14-4. Which laser was found to be more efficient in achieving dental surface transformation? What transformation occurs in the enamel to make it resistant to formation of caries? How is carbon dioxide transmitted to the tooth enamel, since it is invisible and ordinary glass materials absorb the radiation? Is the inhibition against caries carried out in vitro or in vivo?

14-5. What is a laser waveguide? How can it be used in the treatment of a tooth? What is the nature of the material in a waveguide for transmitting carbon dioxide laser? What is "laser brushing"? Can tooth enamel be drilled successfully with a laser beam? What is the controversy, if any, against using a laser beam for drilling enamel?

14-6. Should incipient caries be removed with the use of a laser beam? Why? Discuss. What is the effect of a laser beam on the oral mucosa, if any? How does skin react against a laser beam? What is photocoagulation? Would it be recommendable to photocoagulate any human tissue under any circumstance? Discuss.

14-7. How can ultraviolet rays be used in the treatment of nasal or sinus disorders? Can ultraviolet rays heal any disorder of the gingiva? What is root canal disorder? How is it treated at the present time? Can laser beams aid in the treatment of root canal disorder? How, explain? What possible manipulation is advanced in this chapter? Describe.

14-8. Can a tooth-colored material be filled in a drilled enamel and sintered by means of a laser beam? What type of laser beam would be recommended for this instrumentation? What materials aid the diffusion of fluoride from a toothpaste into the enamel? Is Nd-YAG laser beam as effective as carbon dioxide laser beam on the tooth enamel? How can its absorption by the enamel be aided?

14-9. What is dental prosthesis? Can lasers be of any service in dental prosthesis? What use does a laser beam have in dental prosthesis? Is the application of the laser beam accomplished directly in the person's mouth or outside of it? Is there any commercial laser system available at present for welding dental bridges? What type of laser system is in use at present? Discuss.

14-10. What are some of the potential clinical applications of laser beams? What is the most important factor that has retarded the advance of application of lasers routinely in the dentists' offices? Is it possible to overcome this difficulty in the future? Will laser brushing the enamel facilitate the diffusion of the fluoride from a toothpaste by daily use? Discuss.

Chapter 15
Atomic Transmutation with Lasers

Anything tangible or substantive on Earth is *matter* in one form or another. Matter consists of particles called elements, of which there are more than 90 on Earth, each element being different from the other in its characteristics and elemental weight. Matter may be a solid, liquid, or gas. For example, iron or copper is a solid element; the air we breathe consists of several gaseous elements, such as oxygen, nitrogen and other gases in trace quantities; and, mercury or bromine is an example of a liquid element. An element consists of atoms, the smallest particles into which an element can be divided. Thus, when we arrange the elements in accordance with their increasing atomic weights, from atomic weight 1 to the atomic weight of the 90th element or so, we find that each atom has a characteristic by which it can be identified; that characteristic is the atomic number. Thus, each atom has an atomic weight as well as an atomic number corresponding to its atomic weight.

An atom consists of a nucleus having positive charges called protons, surrounded by imaginary orbits containing negatively charged particles known as electrons. There are as many positive charges in the nucleus as there are negative charges in the orbits; thus, a normal atom at rest is neutral, because the negative and positive charges neutralize each other when the atom is at rest, doing no work. In the arrangement of the elements according to their atomic weights, as mentioned in the preceding paragraph, it is found that the atomic weight of an element corresponds to the number of positively charged protons and neutrons in the nucleus, and the atomic corresponds to the number of free protons or electrons in the orbits known as orbital electrons. Neutrons are neutral particles, and for simplicity of explanation we may consider them to be a combination of protons and electrons tightly held together in the nucleus. With the latter consideration, then, we may state that there are as many electrons in the atom as there are protons. In the study of laser radiation, we will be concerned only with the orbital electrons and their activities under the influence of an external energy such as electrical current or optical radiations. The nucleus will take part only in our study on atomic fusion reactions.

In the generation of a laser radiation, all the nuclear structure remains stationary, but the orbital or extranuclear electrons are in motion in all directions as they receive energy from an external source, such as from an electrical field in an electron discharge tube, and optical energy such as light from a flashlamp. When the electrons receive energy, their respective atoms are raised to an excited state. Since an atom in an excited state cannot remain excited permanently, it tends to regain its original neutral state. In doing so, the electrons return to their stationary states in the atoms. In returning to the atom, the energized electrons radiate, giving off quanta of light, called photons. This light could be either a noncoherent radiation or a coherent laser radiation, as we shall study them in the ensuing discussions. The intensity of the photons will depend on how much energy is expended in their radiation. The greater the radiation energy, the shorter the wavelengths of the radiation; and the smaller the energy expended by the electrons in producing photons, the longer are the wavelengths thus produced. The energy relation is given as:

$$E = hc/\lambda = hv \qquad \text{(Equation 15-1)}$$

where, h is Planck's constant equal to 6.625×10^{-27} erg-second, c is the velocity of light equal to 3×10^{10} centimeters, v is the frequency of the photon, and λ is the wavelength of the photon. It is thus seen from this equation that the higher is the frequency of the photon the shorter is its wavelength, and vice versa.

STRUCTURE OF AN ATOM

An atom is the smallest particle of an element that can enter into a chemical combination. As stated earlier, an atom consists of a nucleus containing neutrons and protons, with the exception of hydrogen which has only one proton in the nucleus and one electron in its extranuclear orbit. The extranuclear electrons, or orbital electrons, are responsible for the atom to enter into a chemical reaction with another atom. The electrons that are located in the outermost orbit of the atom are known as valency electrons because they determine the type of atom and the number of atoms that can be attached to the atom in a chemical reaction. For instance, a sodium atom has one electron in its outermost orbit and a chlorine atom requires one electron to fill up its outermost orbit. Thus, in a chemical-reaction environment, these two atoms can combine to form a molecule of sodium chloride, the common table salt. The magnesium atom has two valency electrons at its outermost orbit and oxygen requires two electrons to fill its outermost orbit; thus, an oxygen atom combines with a magnesium atom to form a molecule of magnesium oxide. And, other atoms similarly combine with each other in accordance with their valency electrons.

There are certain gases, such as helium, neon, argon, krypton, and xenon, which we have had occasion to study, are known as inert gases, because their outermost orbits are completely filled and thus they cannot enter into chemical reactions with any other atoms. However, in our study of lasers, we have had occasion to encounter chemical structures such as excimers, which are molecules of inert gases in combination with halogen atoms, such as chlorine, fluorine, bromine, etc. These chemical combinations can only occur under the influence of electrical fields. When the electrical field is removed, the atoms in combinations separate one from the other. For instance, the excimer laser argon fluoride (ArF) is formed when the two gases are in an electric discharge tube impressed with a high voltage, since the excited inert gases possess strong affinity for halogens. In this combination they produce laser radiation of high intensity, but as they are driven out of the discharge tube by means of a mechanical pump the combining bond between them dissipates and they regain their elemental forms.

When an atom is excited by means of an electric field or by means of an optical energy from a flashlamp, its extranuclear electrons rotate with higher speeds at larger orbits around the nucleus due to centrifugal force. Some of the electrons in rotation become driven outside of the nuclear influence and become free electrons. As we already know, an excited atom is an unstable atom and tends to regain its neutral state by acquiring electrons. Thus, electrons accelerating toward the nucleus of the atom radiate as they become located in the orbits, thus expending their energy. If the expended energy is relatively high, the photons thus produced have high frequency and short wavelength; those electrons that radiate with medium energy (less than the high energy) produce photons of low frequency and long wavelength. Still other electrons that may return to the atom may not have sufficient energy to radiate light and their energy dissipates in the form of thermal radiation. Thus, the radiation electrons may produce emissions of wavelengths from ultraviolet to infrared, depending on how much energy is involved in the radiation process of the individual electrons.

NUCLEAR TRANSMUTATION

While almost all our study laser radiations involve extranuclear energy transmutation, since laser radiations are being investigated to transmute the nucleus of the atom in order to abstract energy from it, some background of this knowledge should be injected into our study in order to understand the mechanism of the reactions. When the nucleus of an atom is involved in a chemical reaction, then the atom either disintegrates or integrates with another atom or a part of another atom. This is known as nuclear transmutation. Nuclear transmutation may be either natural, such as radioactive from radium or artificial such as by nuclear bombardment with neutrons or other atomic particles, with which we are not particularly concerned in our study of laser radiations. However, in order to form a foundation toward the explanation of atomic fusion with the use of laser radiations, we may take up some phases of the nuclear reactions related to the mechanism of atomic fusion. As an example of artificial transmutation, we may take up the following reactions: When, for example, lithium of atomic weight 7 is bombarded with high-speed deutrons (nuclei of heavy hydrogen), the lithium nucleus splits into two alpha particles (nuclei of helium atoms) and a neutron. This reaction is accompanied by a considerable amount of energy. This type of reaction is called atomic fission and simulates on a minute scale the chemical reaction occurring in an atomic bomb, in which the atoms disintegrate to give off tremendous amount of energy confined in them. The simple reaction for our example of the lithium atom may be given as follows:

$$_3\text{Li}^7 + {_1\text{H}^2} \rightarrow {_2\text{He}^4} + {_2\text{He}^4} + {_0\text{n}'} + \text{E}$$

An alternate reaction that may take place and in that reaction the original lithium atom becomes a beryllium atom of atomic weight 8, in which a neutron is also released with high energy. The reaction for this is:

$$_3\text{Li}^7 + {_1\text{H}^2} \rightarrow {_4\text{Be}^8} + {_0\text{n}'} + \text{E}$$

in which, the subscripts correspond to the atomic number of the atom and the superscripts correspond to the atomic weight of the atom. In the reaction $_0n'$ represents a neutron and E is the released energy.

The second reaction corresponds to a nuclear fusion, which we will study in the following sections, because the reaction is concerned with very high-energy laser beams. In our study of laser-aided atomic fusion, the energy released is to be used for peaceful applications, such as generating electrical energy.

In the investigations of atomic fusion with the aid of lasers, the purpose is to fuse atoms together by means of the thermal energy from laser radiations and to produce in the process the energy E on a commercial scale for furnishing cities and states with electrical power at reasonably lower cost than that at present. Whether such an undertaking will yield immediate results is a conjecture, but the concept appears to be feasible, dependent on the specific target to be discovered and the improvement of the technique of the present methods. The concept of extracting the latent energy from the atom has been investigated several decades ago and has been carried through to this date. It is anticipated that with the present knowledge of technology such a project will become a reality with the use of laser radiations. Whether we will succeed this time with the aid of lasers is to be seen. Billions of dollars have been expended for the research and development of equipment for this purpose. There has been some encouraging progress and the process technique has been altered from time to time as new advances in the knowledge by different institutions are brought into view.

The initial concept of the fusion process was dependent on the compression of the target to pressures in tens of hundreds of atmospheres to increase the target density and then to radiate it with terawatts of laser power to implode the target to release its energy in the form of heat. This heat then would be utilized to convert water into steam to operate electric generators and develop electrical power. The process consisted of compressing a pellet of deuterium and tritium to heat it to millions of degrees to cause nuclear combination and to form a heavier element, helium for instance. During this process, the energy released per atom of helium formation, and energy of 6.5×10^{11} joules is expected to be released theoretically. If this process is successful, it could also be applied to trigger atomic explosion someday. Of course, the amount of energy given off in this transmutation will depend on the type of atom used as the target and on the design of the laser equipment that can generate the necessary energy.

Recent candidates for fusion work are excimers and free-electron lasers. The excimers were already mentioned earlier as being efficient laser sources with maintainability of high population inversion (emission), especially when operated with an electron-beam excitation pump. The KMS Fusion, Inc. advocates the use of free-electron beam laser because it is tunable and could function at the level of optimum wavelength for interaction with the fusion target, with an efficiency in excess of 20 percent. The laser pulse from the free-electron interaction with a microwave beam transmitted in a direction within the reasonant cavity opposite to that of the electron beam is expected to yield the maximum radiation necessary in the fusion effort. However, the situation of the free-electron in this case is far from having been perfected at this writing.

FUSION INVESTIGATIONS BY VARIOUS INSTITUTIONS

One of the earliest investigators of the fusion effort is KMS Fusion, Inc., which was employing a Nd-YAG lasing element frequency-doubled, that is, at a frequency of 5320 angstroms. By bombarding a deuterium-tritium pellet with a laser power of 0.5 terawatt at 150-picosecond pulses, KMS has produced 5×10^4 neutrons. They have improved their techniques and increased this yield to 7×10^7 neutrons by the use of Nd-YAG laser at 10,600 angstroms; this time they have compressed the target to 5 grams/cm^3. The estimate is that the target should be compressed to 1000 gm/cm^3 in order to obtain from it a significant amount of energy. The Lawrence Livermore Laboratory has exceeded the KMS yield by producing 7.3×10^9 neutrons by impressing a 26-terawatt laser energy at 95 picoseconds. Recent tests have produced 30×10^9 neutrons. Reviewing the equation of lithium fusion with deuterium, one can immediately see what these figures of neutron yield represent.

At the Los Alamos Scientific Laboratory, carbon dioxide laser is used for fusion work. At this writing, they have produced 1.07×10^4 joules of energy. Under construction is also another fusion facility, Antares, which is projected to yield 100 to 200 terawatt power from their laser installation. The University of Rochester Laboratory for Laser Energetics (Fig. 15-1) has a laser facility under construction that is expected to produce 3×10^{13} watts from a series of Nd-YAG lasers. The British Atomic Weapons Research

Fig. 15-1. View of Rochester Laboratory for laser energetics, showing 24-beam, 12-terawatt Omega Laser system.

Establishment also has a fusion facility operating at a smaller scale. The latest concept in atomic fusion effort is the inertial confinement process in which short-wavelength high-density energy from light-ion laser drivers is in the projection.

PHOTON-ATOM INTERACTION

The interaction of photons with atoms in the excited states can be explained in the light of quantum energy transfer when an excited atom is irradiated with a high-intensity illumination, such as that from a flashlamp or an arc lamp. Since a quantum of energy hv cannot be destroyed, this energy must be expended in some form when it is incident on the excited atom. In an excited atom, the extranuclear electrons are in rotation in larger orbits than their normal orbits and when an electron encounters a quantum of energy from a photon, the excited electron is incited to resonance by the photon so that as the electron moves toward the nucleus of the atom it radiates with a quantum energy equal to that of the photon it encounter with it. Now, there are two photons of the same frequency. These photons undergoing the same type of photonic reaction with other electrons from excited atoms produced two additional photons, making the total four photons. The process continues as long as the electrical field is sustained and more atoms become excited and give rise to additional photons. This action complemented by the resonant cavity feedback mirrors increases to a threshold state whereupon the generated photons become ejected from the resonant cavity in an avalanche of stimulated radiation from the output mirror; this emission is, of course, the laser radiation. The cumulative action of photon formation can be further explained by means of an equation as follows.

Referring to Fig. 15-2, let us assume that a uniform optical radiation is sustained in the optical cavity included between the two mirrors M_1 and M_2, and let us further assume that N_1 is the number of photons, emitted from the flashlamp, incident on the lasing element per second, and N_2 is the net number of photons emitted by the lasing element per second as the result of incidence of the irradiating photons on it. In this stimuated radiation, let us suppose that the number of stimulated photons produced per centimeter path is a, then in an increment of dx in the radiation path the number of photons emitted will be a×dx. Thus, the accumulated photons within the entire path will be N_2a×dx. Putting this relation in an equation form, we have:

$$dN_2 = N_2 a \times dx$$

where, dN_2 is the number of photons produced in the increment dx, and

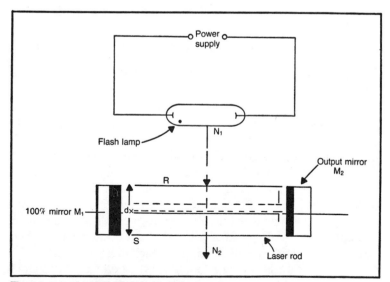

Fig. 15-2. Interaction of photons with atoms.

$$\frac{dN_2}{N_2} = a \times dx \qquad \text{(Equation 15-2)}$$

Integrating the Equation 15-2 from one plane R of the lasing element (laser rod) to the opposite plane S, we obtain,

$$\frac{dN_2}{N_2} = a \times dx + K$$

where, K is a constant taken as the exponent of the natural logarithm base e and is equal to $\log_e$ of N_1.

When K is equal to 0, then N_2 becomes equal to N_1; and the expression can be equated to,

$$\log_e N_2 = ax + \log_e N_1$$

where, $\quad \log_e N_2 - \log_e N_1 = \log N_2 / \log N_1$

hence, $\qquad \log \dfrac{N_2}{N_1} = ax$, and $\dfrac{N_2}{N_1} = e^{ax}$

or, $\qquad\qquad N_2 = N_1\ e^{ax} \qquad$ **(Equation 15-3)**

where, a is the coefficient of stimulation for the lasing element, and x is the distance between the two sides of the slab of the lasing element.

Since the number of photons N_2 stimulated per second is directly proportional to the intensity I_2 of the emitted radiation, we may write

$$I_2 = I_1 \times e^{ax} \qquad \text{(Equation 15-4)}$$

where, I_1 is the intensity of the stimulating radiation (from flashlamp).

From a study of Equation 15-4; it will be apparent that increasing the resonant cavity length, as represented by the quantity x, the emission intensity should increase. This relation is true to a certain threshold level of length, as determined by the tolerance of C/2L frequency of the radiation, and beyond which increasing the cavity length actually decreases the emission. This decrease would be due to capricious heating of the lasing medium, optical lens effect, and erratic thermal stability of the resonant system. The equation implies, however, that optical amplification can occur resultant from negative absorption of optical energy, which must be equal to or in excess of the threshold energy of the emitting element. Of course, the excess energy that is not utilized in the stimulated emission will expend in the form of thermal radiation, which condition will elevate the temperature of the resonant cavity unless compensated for by the circulating cooling medium. Finally, lasing elements which follow the four-level stimulation graphs, such as Nd-YAG and Nd-glass, will respond more readily to the irradiating stimulus than those operating on a three-level excitation states; the latter type of lasing element would be a ruby laser, or other fluorescent solids.

LASER FUSION PROGRESS TO DATE

Under construction at this writing is the NOVA facility at Lawrence Livermore National Laboratory. When completed, it is expected to produce 2×10^5 joules and a power density of 100 terawatts/cm^2 from its Nd-glass laser. The ANTARES facility at the Los Alamos National Laboratory, on the other hand, also under construction, will develop 4×10^4 joules and a power density of 60 terawatts/cm^2 from its CO_2 laser facility. Both facilities have projected their goals to eventually lead to nuclear weapons simulation, the electric-power generation being their secondary objective. Furthermore, the requirements for military application studies are less stringent than those for peaceful, civilian applications. The Sandia National Laboratory is also actively investigating the capabilities of a light-ion, pulse-power driven with an objective to achieve 3.5-megajoule, 100-terawatt laser output power within the next three years.

To date, the frequency-multiplied Nd-glass of NOVA is the preferred candidate for weapons physics research work. The radiation has high affinity toward coupling effectively with the fusion target material, and its spatial and temporal characteristics are readily controllable. It is also possible to convert the shorter-wavelength (harmonic) radiation from this system into longer-wavelength x-ray radiation to radiate the target pellet to cause implosion. It is manifest that the other two laboratories, Los Alamos and Sandia, are in accord with the concept. The CO_2 laser facility of ANTARES produces copious amounts of hot electrons of several-hundred-kiloelectron volts which tend to decrease the absorption efficiency of the radiation by the target material.

There are other approaches to effectuate target fusion, such as by the use of krypton fluoride and xenon chloride, as studied earlier in this book. Because of their (excimers') short wavelengths, normally in the ultraviolet spectral range, their coupling efficiency with the target capsule is very favorable. Another approach is the use of heavy-ion accelerators in conjunction with the concept of converting their radiation into long-wavelength x-rays prior to driving the fusion material. With pulse driver energies from CO_2 laser, energies to one megajoule is estimated to perform the expected fusion operation.

The conversion of Nd-glass radiation to short wavelengths (harmonics) approaching x-ray wavelengths is achieved by the use of optical apertures as large as 74 centimeters in arrays of KDP frequency-multipliers are used at both NOVA and University of Rochester's laser facility. Experiments at these facilities have shown that by converting the infrared radiation of 10,500-angstrom wavelengths to the 3500-angstrom ultraviolet wavelengths produces target absorption of the energetic radiation up to 90 percent at power densities of 10^{14} to 10^{15} watts cm^2. The x-ray conversion efficiencies of the shorter wavelengths also increase up to 50 percent; this action considerably reduces the hot-electron production as the side effect. As stated earlier, CeF and KrF radiate in the ultraviolet spectrum and their harmonic wavelengths can be used as optical drivers. These advancements have been complemented by improvements in damage-resistant optical coatings, in lithium, fluoride spatial filters, optical surface accuracies within one micron, alignment to 20 microradians, increase in damage threshold by us of Al_2O_3-SiO_2 and SC_2O_3-MgF_2 for shorter wavelengths, and efficient phase conjugation in ultraviolet range has been achieved.

Questions and Problems

15-1. What is an atom? A molecule? A neutron? Extranuclear electron? What is atomic weight? What is atomic number? In an atom, what does correspond to the atomic number of an element? What does atomic weight of an atom correspond to? What is an atom at rest? Discuss.

15-2. If an atom has 5 neutrons and 4 protons in its nucleus, what is its atomic number? How many extranuclear electrons does it have? What is its atomic weight? Look up in the table of elements at the back of the book and name the atom or element.

15-3. When an atom loses an electron from its extranuclear orbit, what becomes of the atom? Does it gain any charge? Is the charge, negative or positive? If an atom has lost two electrons in a chemical combination to another atom, what is its valence?

15-4. If one or more electrons are rotating in an orbit higher than their normal orbit or orbits, what is the atom said to be? If one of these electrons moves back to the normal orbit, what does it yield? What is a quantum of light? What is a photon? What is a free electron? Explain.

15-5. Do gases, such as neon, argon, krypton, helium, and xenon have any valence? If so, what is it? If not, how do they enter a chemical reaction with halogens? Is an excimer one of the products of the reaction of the inert gas with a halogen? When an excimer dissociates, what does it yield?

15-6. What positions do the extranuclear electrons take when an atom becomes excited? What positions do they take when that atom returns to the ground state? When the atom returns to the ground state, what happens to the energy expended during the return? If two atoms radiate, in which the emission is due to an electron falling back from a higher energy state than that of the other, which one of these atoms will radiate with a higher frequency?

15-7. Can a nuclear reaction occur the same as chemical reaction between extranuclear electrons of the atoms? How, if so, and under what conditions? In a nuclear reaction, what structural part of the atom becomes larger or smaller? Can nuclear reactions produce and radiation? Discuss.

15-8. In the nuclear reaction where the lithium atom has split into two alpha particles, what is the reaction called? When lithium reacts with a deuterium atom, and becomes a larger beryllium atom, what is this reaction called? Where can such a reaction take place? Discuss.

15-9. In experiments with atoms and high-energy laser beams, what does laser beam do to the target atom? What type of reaction is this? If the desired reaction took place, what is the expected end result? What is the purpose of compressing the target atom in a nuclear reaction?

15-10. What company was one of the earliest to investigate atomic fusion with a laser beam? What type of pellet (target) did the company use? How were the neutrons given off in the reaction? At what pressure was the target atom when the company produced 7×10^7 neutrons? What is the estimated compression value to completely cause a fusion reaction?

15-11. The Lawrence Livermore Laboratory has produced 7.3×10^9 neutrons. How much laser energy was impressed on the target atom and for how long? Has LLL improved on this yield of neutrons? By how much? What type of laser source did Los Alamos Scientific Laboratory use in producing 1.07×10^4 joules of energy?

How much laser power does LASL expect to produce in the near future for atomic fusion?

15-12. What is inertial confinement process, as related to atomic fusion? If an energy of hv is incident on an excited atom, what becomes of its extranuclear electron that receives the energy? How does photonic energy transfer occur to the excited atom? What role do the optical cavity mirrors play in the emission of a radiation from the cavity?

15-13. If the photons oscillate between the feedback mirrors in the resonant cavity, how long does this oscillation occur before a laser beam projects to the outside of the cavity? What is the diameter of the beam with respect to the cavity bore diameter? Does the output mirror influence the diameter of the issuing laser beam? Discuss.

15-14. If the number of photons N_2 stimulated per second is directly proportional to the intensity I_2 of the emitted radiation, and the radiation has travelled an increment of 10^{-2} millimeter with an intensity of 10^{16} photons, what current is necessary to produce this radiation, if the coeffiency of stimulation is 0.402?

15-15. What laser power is NOVA projected to produce when completed? What laser energy is ANTARES projected to produce? What are their goals? Which laboratory is engaged in the investigation of light ions for the production of laser power? Which method is preferred among the three activities?

15-16. How are x-ray radiations produced from laser radiations? What significance do x-rays have in the driving of atomic fusion processes? What one disadvantage does CO_2 laser in atomic fusion effort? What excimers are also good candidates for fusion work? How much energy can heavy-ion accelerators produce in their role for atomic fusion? Discuss.

15-17. What wavelength-range harmonics approach x-ray wavelengths? How are they produced? What optical process should infrared radiations undergo to increase their coupling efficiency with the atomic target? What affect do the shorter-wavelength harmonics of infrared radiation have on the hot-electron production? What improvements in optical elements and their threshold characteristics have been brought about in advancing the progress in atomic fusion effort? Discuss.

Chapter 16
Laser Systems and Characteristics

In this chapter, the basic laser systems and components that were studied in the preceding chapters will be taken up with respect to their construction, operation, and system characteristics. The discussions will include the solid-state laser systems, ion lasers, semiconductor lasers, excimers, tunable dye lasers, and laser systems accessories. The schematic circuit diagrams of some of the basic laser systems will also be taken up with the view of discussing the hardware design and development to complement the reader's knowledge concerning the laser systems. With this consideration, it is expected that a thorough knowledge of laser technology together with system parameters will form the basic background education of the reader in this branch of the profession.

SOLID-STATE LASER SYSTEMS DESIGN

The solid-state lasers include those systems that contain crystalline rods doped with chromium, neodymium, tellurium, lanthanum, or similar lasing elements. These lasers are excited to emission by high-intensity illumination from a flashlamp or an arc lamp, and can be operated in continuous-wave or pulsed mode. They are the most powerful laser generators in the class of solid lasing elements. These systems generally consist of a laserhead containing the lasing element, a flashlamp to illuminate and excite the lasing element to laser radiation, a cooling system to sustain the lasing element within the threshold emission temperature, a power

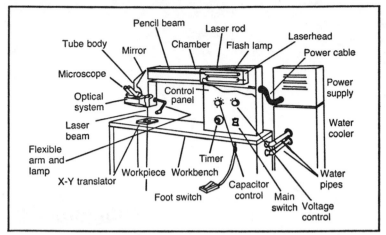

Fig. 16-1. Schematic of a laser welding system.

supply to energize the flashlamp, and a console with an instrument panel having control devices for adjusting the power to the flashlamp, the flow of the cooling medium to sustain a constant temperature, and in the case of pulsed radiation to control the pulsing rate of the laser beam (see Fig. 16-1). Other accessories, such as an x-y-z translator to position the specimen with respect to the laser beam focus, beam collimators, spatial filters, beam-wavelength selectors, and the like will also be discussed with relation to the specific laser system.

Since Nd-YAG laser, or Nd-glass laser, is the most powerful laser in this category, our study will be directed to a system containing a Nd-YAG laser rod in the laserhead. In the fundamental-mode operation, the beam from the laser has a Gaussian profile and operates at TEM_{oo} mode, emitting at 10,640 angstrom fundamental wavelength. The beam can be frequency-doubled or tripled by means of a KDP crystal. However, the fundamental mode does not yield the full power because the output aperture is smaller than the rod diameter. Therefore, one method of overcoming this disadvantage is to use multiple oscillator-amplifiers in series with the primary beam. Because the latter arrangement is complicated and costly, the next best scheme is to use an unstable resonator consisting of a diffraction-coupled output mirror. This type of resonant oscillator yields high pulse energy and low beam divergence. The beam profile resembles a donut, but further design improvements in this scheme have overshadowed this profile, which is supplemented by a near-Gaussian beam.

Table 16-1. Nd-YAG Laser Specification (Nominal).

Material	Nd-YAG Laser Rod
Output Wavelength	10,640 Angstroms
Power Output (Nominal)	50 Watts up; cw or Pulsed, TEM$_{oo}$
Beam Diameter	2 to 10 millimeters
Beam Divergence	0.2 to 3 milliradians
Pulse-to-Pulse Energy Stability	± 2 to ± 8 percent, long to short wavelength (10,640 to 2660 angstroms)
Peak Power Stability	± 5 percent
Optical Pump Lamp	xenon, nitrogen, krypton arc, etc.
Flashlamp Trigger (Nominal)	2 to 12 volts, 50 ohms, risetime variable from 3 to several hundred nsec.
Nominal Power Supply	208 Vac, 3 phase, 50/60 Hertz, 5 kW
Cooling (When Used)	2 GPM, Clear Water, at 15° to 35° C
Dimensions (Nominal)	50 Wide, 50 High, 60 Deep (all centimeters)

The parameters given in Table 16-1 are only nominal; there are a great many variable ratings of the laserhead, depending on the manufacturer's design and construction of the system. These figures are shown only to give an idea to the reader what the specification of a typical Nd-YAG system would be. A Nd-YAG laserhead is shown in Fig. 16-2.

ION PLASMA LASERS (GAS LASERS)

Gas lasers may be categorized into atomic, molecular, and ionic lasers, although the differences may not warrant their classification. Generally, an atomic laser refers to He-Ne type, molecular laser defines a carbon dioxide laser, and ionic laser refers to argon and krypton types (see Table 16-2). The most common types of gas lasers, as we have already studied, are the He-Ne, argon, krypton, xenon, nitrogen, carbon dioxide, and excimer lasers. Since space does not permit to take up them all individually, only a representative type, an argon ion laser, will be discussed to acquaint the reader of the ion laser characteristics.

Many of the commercially produced ion lasers are either argon or krypton, because they can produce wavelengths from ultraviolet,

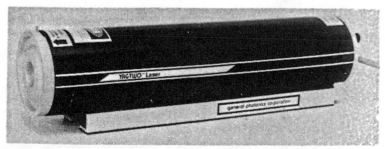

Fig. 16-2. General Photonics Nd-YAG laserhead.

Table 16-2. Specification of an Argon Ion Laser (Nominal).

Beam Diameter	0.9 to 1.33 millimeters
Beam Divergence	0.6 to 1.2 milliradians
Cavity Mirror Configuration	Flat High Reflector, Long Radius Beam
Cavity Length	0.6 to 1.5 meters
Mode-Spacing (Longitudinal - C/2L)	100 to 235 MHz
Plasma Tube Bore	Beryllium Oxide, in better made systems.
Polarization	Partial to Vertical (Y)
Optical Noise	1.0 to 1.5 percent rms
Current Control Stability	± 2 to ± 3 percent
Laserhead Size	Variable, with different brands.
Input Voltage Range	120/208 Vac, 3 phase, 50/60 Hz
Maximum Current	20 to 38 amperes (variable)
Laserhead Weight	Nominal 25 Kgm, variable
Cooling Water Rate	2 to 3 gallons/minute

through visible, to the infrared range at high power levels. They can be made with low optical noise and high optical stability to operate in the cw mode or in the pulsed mode. In the cw format, they can emit from one watt to several kilowatts, and in the pulsed mode they can produce up to several megawatts at up to 20 or more nanosecond pulses. Argon lasers emit both blue and green wavelengths, from 4,579 to 5,145 angstroms, respectively. The commonly used wavelengths are 5,145 and 4,880 angstroms. When driven by high current level outputs, the argon laser becomes doubly ionized and can lase in the ultraviolet at as short as 3,300-angstrom wavelength, and by changing the feedback mirrors they can produce through visible to 10,090 angstrom wavelengths in the infrared. The krypton laser also operates indentically to argon and its prominent wavelengths are 6,471 and 6,764 angstroms. The 6,471 angstrom wavelength emission gives off strong red lines which are most frequently used. Figure 16-3 illustrates a single-line ion laser arrangement.

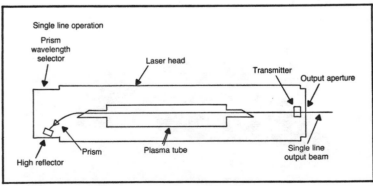

Fig. 16-3. A simplified scheme of single-line ion laser.

In Fig. 16-3, an ion laser with Brewster windows and external mirrors is illustrated. A prism is used at the rear window for selection of wavelengths. If the prism is removed from the cavity and the rear mirror is made parallel to the output mirror (transmitter), the system operates multiline, and the spectral lines can be separated by means of an external prism into the component lines, as shown in Fig. 3-5. However, any single line (color wavelength) that is selected by means of the internal mirror (Fig. 16-3), its intensity can be much greater than the identical spectral line selected from an external prism. The reason for this is that the internally selected single line is amplified in the resonant cavity prior to its emission from the exit port. Because of the Brewster-angle windows in the system, the emitted radiation is highly polarized.

While such a system has a very narrow linewidth, its coherence length is relatively short and cannot be used for holographic or long-path interferometric work. The coherence length can be extended by the use of an etalon between the rear mirror and the Brewster window of the plasma tube. This provision can increase the coherence length up to 100 meters, over which distance the beam wavefronts are sustained constant in phase, which condition is essential for making accurately recorded holograms in a photographic plate.

TUNABLE DYE LASERS

Dye lasers consist of solutions of organic dyes in methanol, ethanol, or any other high-molecule alcohol. Dye lasers are tunable across a broad range of spectra from ultraviolet through visible to infrared. They are optically pumped by an excimer, nitrogen laser, or by the harmonic wavelengths of dye lasers, or by Nd-YAG or Nd-glass lasers. The optical pump for a liquid dye laser is either a linear tube or a coaxial tube, the latter coupling the light more efficiently. The illumination from the pump can also be directed axially to the dye solution, especially in frequency-doubling the dye solution, or transversely to the axis of the dye resonance cavity. Tuning for pulsed lasers ranges from 1,900 to 11,700 angstroms, while for cw lasers it ranges from 3,500 to 8,000 angstroms nominally.

Selection of a dye depends on the tunable spectral range desired from it, and the choice of optical pump depends on the coupling efficiency of the pump with the dye solution. Also, the choice of a particular type of optical pump is further dependent on whether the

Fig. 16-4. Spectra- Physics synchronously pumped dye laser system

emitted dye laser is pulsed or continuous. Dye lasers can be frequency-doubled or tripled by the use of KDP (potassium dihydroxyphosphate) or KPD (potassium pentaborate) crystal. Much higher peak powers can be obtained by the use of pulsed optical pumps than those of cw type; accordingly, pulsed dye lasers can be frequency-multiplied, increasing their range of tunabilities.

Figure 16-4 shows the Spectra-Physics synchronously pumped dye laser. In this system, an ion laser is mode-locked with its output projected to a dye laser. The resonant cavity of the dye laser is expanded to make it equal to the length of the ion laser. Because the dye laser is gain-modulated in this system arrangement it becomes mode-locked and pulse-operated at tunable pulses as short as 50 picoseconds and at peak powers up to several hundred watts. The matching of the ion and the dye laser cavity lengths synchronizes the circulating light in the two systems; this means that each exciting light pulse from the ion laser and the light pulse from the dye laser traverse the dye stream at the same time. This synchronous process produces frequency-doubling of the dye laser and its operation in ultraviolet wavelengths. A schematic operational diagram of the system is shown in Fig. 16-5.

A representative liquid dye laser specification is given in Table 16-3.

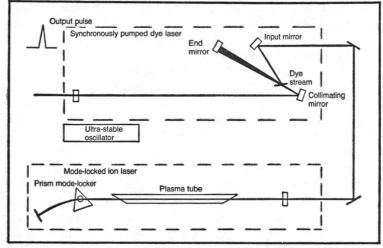

Fig. 16-5. Schematic of the Spectra-Physics synchronously pumped dye laser system.

It must be pointed out that there are hundreds of dye lasers whose parameters vary widely from one manufacturer's product to another. Each laser system comes with a data sheet on which the manufacturer specifies the characteristics of his dye laser, and gives the parameters in accordance with the type of dye and the design of the laser system.

HIGH-ENERGY EXCIMER LASERS

General types of excimer lasers were taken up in Chapter 3 and in this section, high-energy excimers will be emphasized. These lasers operate both continuous wave and pulsed. In the pulsing mode, they have produced up to 100 joules per pulse in varying pulse lengths measured in microseconds. Excimers are also considered for use in the atomic fusion work because of their spectral

Table 16-3. Nominal Specification for a Dye Laser.

Dye Material	Oxazine 1
Fundamental Tuning Range	6500 to 8000 angstroms
Linewidth	60 GHz
Beam Divergence	0.3 milliradian, and up
Beam Polarization Axis	Horizontal or vertical
Beam Diameter	0.60 millimeter and up
Tuning Resolution	12 GHz, nominal
Output Beam Mode	TEM_{00}
Cavity Mode Spacing	420 MHz
Input Power	115/230 Vac, single phase, 50/60 Hz

purity and high emission properties under high-pressure and high-voltage conditions. They are highly toxic and should be handled with special precaution to avoid breathing the gas, or having the skin of the hand come in contact with it.

High-energy excimers are pumped to radiation by two modes of excitation. One method is to use high-energy electron discharge through a high-pressure xenon gas to produce 1,720-angstrom radiation in the ultraviolet spectrum. This radiation is then coupled with an excimer, such as XeF_2 having a nitrogen-gas buffer, to dissociate the XeF_2 to its excited form XeF*. This form of excimer operates pulsed at high energy and is ordinarily used for military applications and for inertial confinement process in atomic fusion work.

The second method is the usual discharge-pumped mode, which is widely used in military communication between a satellite or land-based station and submerged submarines. Since these excimers emit in the blue-green spectral range of 4,500 to 5,300 angstroms, which have excellent ocean-water penetrating properties, they are the present candidates for communication and for detection of submerged enemy submarines. These lasers are also effective optical-pump sources for dye lasers emitting in the orange spectral region.

For satellite-to-submerged-craft communication, a land-based XeF_2 excimer emitting at 3,530 angstroms is Raman-shifted to a blue-green radiation, which is directed to a retroreflective mirror located on a satellite. The beam then is reflected into the ocean for exploring submerged navigating crafts, sounding the ocean depth, or for communicating with a submarine. Discharge-excited excimers can produce several joules of pulsed ultraviolet radiation, which is usually converted to a visible radiation for industrial applications.

The applications of excimer lasers include optical pumping of tunable dye lasers, isotope separation, multiphoton ionization and fragmentation of molecules, purification of certain organic chemicals, semiconductor annealing, laser-triggering of particle-beam fusion and the like. It has been reported that the excimer lasers may replace the nitrogen laser pump because of the high quantum-energy emission of the excimers, with short wavelengths and high frequencies. The excimer has proved itself to be a copious source of ultraviolet emission, and when sealed-off and well-designed excimer lasers are developed, they might become valuable medical tools in the clinic or in the doctor's office for the treatment of nasopharyngeal tract. A versatile nitrogen laser that can be used

Fig. 16-6. Nitromite LN-100 nitrogen laser manufactured by Photochemical Research Associates.

both as a source of laser emission and as an optical pump is shown in Fig. 16-6.

SEMICONDUCTOR LASERS

The semiconductor lasers, also known as injection lasers, are similar in structure to light emitting diodes (LED). The pn junction of the diode contains GaAs as its active element. When forward biased above the threshold, the diode emits laser radiation in a range between 8,000 to 9,040 angstroms. The semiconductor diodes can operate in cw mode or pulsed, and can be modulated by input analog or digital format (see Table 16-4).

Many of the applications of high-power semiconductor pulsed lasers are in the military field. They are used in weapon guidance systems, electro-optical communication systems, fuzing mechanisms, and target-ranging and acquisition systems. In the commercial field, the gallium arsenide derivative, GaAlAs, is used in optical scanning, videodisk lines, and fiberoptic communication systems, as we have already studied in Chapters 9 and 10. The diode lasers couple very well with the optical characteristics of fiberoptic cables in transmitting both digital and analog modulated signals. In these

Table 16-4. Characteristics of Gallium Arsenide diode (nominal).

Wavelength Range	7800 to 8500 angstroms CW 8000 to 9050 Pulsed
Operational Mode Pattern	Single Mode to Multimode, CW
Modulation Bandwidth	100 to 2000 CW
Pulses Per Second	500 and 20,000 nominal
Pulse Length	100 to 200 Nanoseconds
Spectral Linewidth	1 to 2 nm for CW and 3.5 to 4.5 for pulsed
Beam Divergence	125 to 400 nominal (mrad)
Peak Power	Variable, 1 watt to several hundred watts
Driving Current	100 milliamperes and up

Fig. 16-7. A GaAlAs Diode.

diodes, the peak emission wavelength can be controlled by varying the concentration of the aluminum content in the GaAl-As junction. A hybrid of GaAs diode, the InP-GaInAsP, is employed to obtain longer wavelengths extending into the midinfrared range. Since the laser diode is small, compact, and easily incorporated in electro-optical systems, and can operate at high repetition rates, it is becoming widely used commercially because the production of the device can be carried out at low cost in the same manner as nonlinear diodes. A commercial GaAlAs diode is shown in Fig. 16-7.

LASER SYSTEM ACCESSORIES

The following describes some of the accessories used with lasers.

Spatial Filter

When a laser beam is focused on a screen by means of a convex lens, a mottling effect will be noted around the focus of the beam. This effect is due to peripheral aberration in the focusing lens which prevents the formation of a sharp focus. The aberration can be eliminated from the optical field by the use of a spatial filter, which, in effect, is a metal sheet having a precisely drilled hole in its central area. The hole size varies from 5 to 50 microns and further varies inversely with the magnification power of the lens.

A spatial filter is usually mounted at the exit aperture of the laserhead. A commercial spatial filter is shown in Fig. 16-8, and a

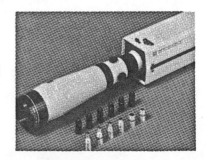

Fig. 16-8. Spectra-Physics spatial filter for laser beam.

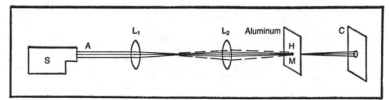

Fig. 16-9. The schematic of a commercial spatial filter.

schematic diagram of its construction is shown in Fig. 16-9. It will be noted in Fig. 16-9 that as the laser beam diverges from the focal waist of the lens L_1 a ghost-like peripheral beam, shown in broken lines, follows the fundamental beam and forms a fuzzy peripheral area around the focus. This fuzzy area can be eliminated by introducing a pinhole filter in the path of the beam and aligning the focus of the beam with the pinhole, which eliminates the extraneous, peripheral radiation. The thus "purified" beam upon converging to a focus on a specimen will have a very sharp focus. The beam then is said to have been spatially filtered.

The spatially filtered laser beam has wide application in microwelding and drilling holes in microelectronic devices, scribing microcircuits, and even in holography, in which it is essential that all cluttering from the laser beam be eliminated in order to obtain sharp interference profiles of the latent image of an object holographed. Of course, the spatially filtered laser beam must be expanded and collimated to cover the object being holographed, although collimation may not be necessary in all cases.

Laser Beam Expander and Collimator

Since the laser beam projecting from the source has a very small diameter, it is preferred that the beam be expanded and collimated if it is to be focused to a sharp point, or it is to be used in ranging or surveying systems. A collimated beam travels longer distances than a noncollimated laser beam. The method of collimation is given in Fig. 16-10, and a commercial collimator is shown in Fig. 16-11. It will take at least two lenses—one a concave lens to expand the beam and a second one a convex lens to collimate the expanded beam (see Fig. 1-12).

A beam expander and collimator is an optical device for expanding the input laser beam and then collimating it. Some types have also a spatial filter included in the same collimator, so that the output beam is free of extraneous beam abnormalities, such as aberration and other cluttering due to impurities and peripheral

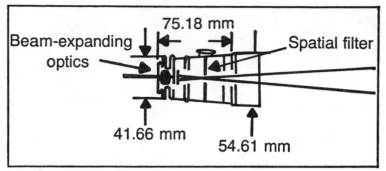

Fig. 16-10. A cross-sectional view of a spatial filter.

diffraction. The device can have expansion capability of 1 to 60 diameters through appropriate choice of lenses, with wavefront deformation less than λ/10 at wavelengths from 4,000 to 12,000 angstroms.

Mode Locker

Mode-locking is an optical technique for amplitude-modulating a laser beam at a frequency rate determined by the resonator modespacing or the length of the cavity of an ion laser. A series of high-peak and short pulses at a chosen frequency of modulation are produced to lock the phase and amplitude of the chosen mode. To reduce the intracavity losses to a minimum, the wavelength selection prism in the resonant cavity is combined with the model-

Fig. 16-11. A commercial spatial filter (courtesy of Spectra-Physics).

Fig. 16-12. Spectra-Physics Mode locker, Model 342-S.

locking. This system is modulated by an ultrasonic transducer bonded to the intracavity prism, and pulsewidths of up to several hundred microseconds have been obtained by this technique.

The application of the mode locker in conjunction with an ion laser is for synchronously pumping dye lasers to emission of tunable pulses of high peak power. The scheme is also used for obtaining low-noise radiation. A mode locker manufactured by Spectra-Physics is shown in Fig. 16-12.

Optical Power Meter

An optical power meter is an instrument for measuring laser power output, or its attenuation by optical elements at any distance from the source. A power meter manufactured by Jodon Engineering Associates, Inc. is shown in Fig. 16-13. The power meter measures laser power of wavelengths from 4,000 to 11,500 angstroms, with an accuracy of ± 5 percent. While it is calibrated to measure wavelengths at 6,328 angstroms, it can be adjusted to measure other wavelengths. The unit consists of an antireflection-coated lens with an effective aperture of 22 degrees and an acceptance angle of 20 degrees; an optical diffuser in front of a high-linearity silicon detector prevents high-intensity incident beam in random areas from driving the silicon detector into nonlinearity. The frequency response of the unit is flat from a direct current to 50 kHz for amplitude-modulated signals. The instrument has a direct-reading range of 0.020 to 100 milliwatts at 6,328-angstrom wavelength region. Other ranges are 1, 3, 10, 30, and 100 milliwatts full scale.

Dye Laser Amplitude Stabilizer

It is a well known fact that the output power of dye lasers varies

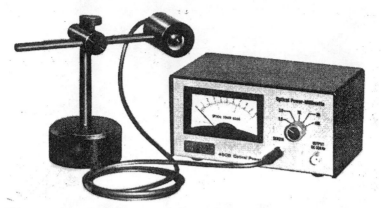

Fig. 16-13. The Jodan Engineering Optical Power Meter Model 450-B.

in course of time or during wavelength scanning. Thus, the dye laser application for certain operations becomes difficult and sometimes impossible. For this reason, a dye laser stabilizer developed and manufactured by Spectra-Physics precisely regulates the power output of all optically pumped dye lasers, and improves the long-term stability of the dye solution. It operates over the spectral range from 4,000 to 10,000 angstroms with a stability of ± 5 percent for any one-hour period at any selected power level from 30 milliwatts to 3 watts. The power level at which the user desires to operate the dye laser can be preset. The amplitude stabilizer is shown in Fig.

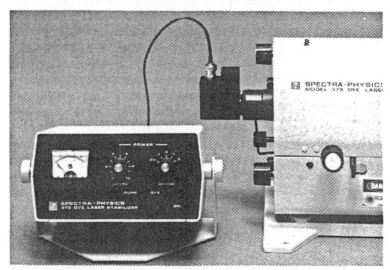

Fig. 16-14. The Spectra-Physics dye laser amplitude stabilizer.

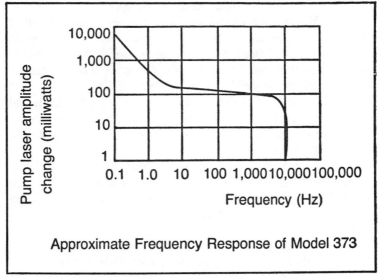

Approximate Frequency Response of Model 373

Fig. 16-15. Frequency response of the dye laser stabilizer.

16-14 and its frequency response graph is given in Fig. 16-15. The system operates from 115/230 Vac, 50/60 Hz source.

Dual-Axis Translation Stage

The dual-axis translation stage is used for accurately positioning specimens for laser processing under the optical head of the laser system. The stage is a useful tool when manual welding or drilling is to be performed on a part or component, since it can be stabilized securely on the stage, and displaced in two orthogonal directions for precise positioning. A commercial translation stage is shown in Fig. 16-16.

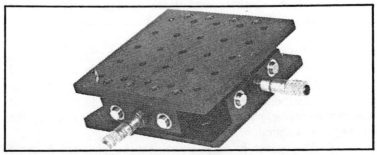

Fig. 16-16. Dual-axis translation stage Model 400, manufactured by Newport Corporation.

Questions and Problems

16-1. How does a solid-state laser system differ from other types of laser systems? How is a solid-state laser element excited to emit laser radiation? Describe a solid-state laser system, giving its various subsystems and their functions. Why doesn't the fundamental wavelength mode yield a very high power? Explain.

16-2. Design a solid-state laser system diagrammatically and assign numerical values to electrical parameters employed by it. Also, prepare a specification table giving nominal values to the system parameters.

16-3. Give a list of gas-type lasers. What are ion lasers? What are molecular lasers? What lasers can be made with low optical noise and high optical stability? In what range of wavelengths do ion lasers emit? In what range of wavelengths do the molecular lasers emit? Discuss.

16-4. In ionic lasers, are the mirrors always positioned parallel to each other in the Fabry Perot cavity? What arrangement of mirrors can be made in this cavity? If a single-line emission is desired, which arrangement will produce more laser power in that single line, an external prism or an internal prism? Explain, why? Draw a schematic design of an ionic laser, showing optical elements for selection of different spectral lines from a multiline laser system.

16-5. What are dye lasers? How do they operate? Give several types of operations. Can dye laser be frequency-multiplied? How? Draw a diagram, showing what optical elements are required for frequency multiplication. What is the tuning range for pulsed liquid dye lasers? What is the tuning range for cw liquid dye lasers? Explain.

16-6. On what factor does the choice of optical pump depend? What types of optical pumps can be used in exciting liquid dye lasers to emission? How can one increase the range of tunability of pulsed dye lasers? Draw a diagram of a liquid dye laser and label the various parts.

16-7. What is an excimer laser? How can an inert gas, such as krypton, combine with a halogen if it is chemically nonreactive? After emission of a laser radiation from a molecule of excimer, what becomes of the molecule? Can it be used again for laser emission? What is the range of excimer laser emission? In what mode do the excimer lasers operate?

16-8. Approximately what power can be obtained from an excimer laser? Can an excimer laser be used to optically pump other lasers? How, if so? Explain. How should one take special care in handling excimer lasers? What excimer laser emits 36,000 to 40,000 angstroms? What beam divergence do these latter lasers possess? What are excimer applications?

16-9. How do semiconductor lasers differ from solid-state lasers? What is a pn junction made of? If a semiconductor diode is operated above the threshold level, what radiation does it emit? If a semiconductor diode is operated below the threshold level, what radiation is emitted? What does a diode laser usually contain at its pn junction? What is the divergence of GaAs diode laser?

16-10. In what operational mode can semiconductor devices operate? If GaAs diode has aluminum in its active layer, what happens if the aluminum content is increased or decreased? In what field can diode lasers be used? Give a list of nominal parameters that the diode lasers do possess.

16-11. What is a spatial filter? How is it constructed and how does it operate? What is the application of a spatial filter? What is a laser beam expander? What is a laser beam collimator? Can a spatial filter, beam expander, and a collimator be incorporated in one unit? Show by a diagram how this can be achieved.

16-12. What is a mode locker? What does a mode locker do? How does a mode locker operate? What is the application of a mode locker? What is an optical power meter? Is an optical power meter the same as a radiometer? Describe Jodon's optical power meter.

16-13. What is a dye-laser amplitude stabilizer? What is it used for? Over what spectral range does a dye laser amplitude stabilizer operate? For how long does the stability of dye laser amplitude remain constant using Spectra-Physics stabilizer? At what laser power levels does the stabilizer operate? Explain.

16-14. What is a translation stage? How is it constructed? How does it operate? For what purpose is a dual-axis translation stage used for? Can one perform manual metal processing without a dual-axis translation stage? Explain how one can weld or drill a sheet of steel without the use of a translation stage. It can be and has been done.

16-15. In what operational mode do the high-energy excimer function? What power can they produce in the pulsing mode? What are they used for? How are high-energy excimers optically pumped? Which method of pumping produces the shorter wavelengths? In what spectral range do these excimers emit?

16-16. What wavelength excimers have high penetrating quality for ocean water? Could such excimers be used for optical pumping? What lasing material is Raman-shifted to result in blue-green radiation? For what purpose is a Raman-shifted radiation used for? Discuss the radiation's properties.

16-17. How are submerged marine crafts detected for communication with a land-based laser station? How can one produce pulsed ultraviolet radiation and then convert it to visible radiation? How are tunable dye lasers optically pumped? What is meant by multiphoton ionization and fragmentation of molecules? What molecules can be fragmented in this manner? Discuss.

16-18. Why can excimer lasers replace nitrogen laser pump? Discuss. If excimers can generate copious amount of ultraviolet radiation, what application would such radiation have in medical field? What type of sealed-off discharge device can be used both as an optical pump and as a lasing system? Discuss why?

Chapter 17
Selected Laser-Aided Developments

The innovative ideas that are presented in this section have been selected for the reader who has gained a basic understanding of laser principles and is capable of applying his knowledge to practice. The laser industry, technology, and the individuals now engaged in electro-optical profession will also benefit from the outcome of their development of the inventions delineated in this writing. While some of the ideas may have been already worked out using different techniques than those given here, the main purpose of their presentation here again is for the continuing need for fresh approaches and improved techniques that can be achieved by the use of laser beams. Furthermore, when such innovations are implemented using various types of laser beams they could be simpler, more effective, and at low cost, and compatible with the particular project approach. There is no better way of serving our country than applying inventive talents to the development and improvement of new and useful products. From this viewpoint, the author has also included a plan of approach with each new project proposed herein, as applicable.

AERIAL AND FIBEROPTIC COMMUNICATIONS

Field Communication System. A field communication system using a He-Ne laser beam of several milliwatt power that can transmit voice to a distance of at least 1 kilometer would be a desirable system for both civilian and military use. There are now on the market several different communicators, but due to their cost and bulkiness, their sales have not reached to normally dominant levels. A small, pocket-size laser communicator within a few hundred dollars cost level will be a good seller; a low-level GaAs diode light could be used. However, the alignment of the beam should be done with a telescope before the diode laser beam is turned on.

Portable Fiberoptic Communicator. A portable fiberoptic communicator that can be carried in the field or war zone for communication between two or three stations would be a novel and unique innovation that can be easily adapted to the use of metrological measurements in road construction and surveying land. The device should be low cost and flexible for varying environmental and communication conditions. Either a LED or low-power He-Ne laser may be used for the modulation of the spoken words in analog form. The device and its ancillary subsystems should be rugged for terrain application.

Laser Radar for Automobiles and Trucks. A low-cost laser radar that is permanently installed on a passenger car or a truck and having a display panel on the dashboard to indicate the distance of a car ahead as well as its speed is needed to save hundreds of lives annually being destroyed in serious accidents. When a car is detected within 100 feet ahead, a yellow flashing light should automatically appear in the rear of the car equipped with the laser radar, to warn other cars following it. The frequency of the flashing should increase as the driver decelerates his car.

Such a device or system should reduce the occurrances of many read-end collisions or telescoping of a series of cars due to sudden stoppage of the first front car. The Federal Highway Administration as well as the state Transportation Administration is highly interested in such a system, so that the development of the system may be subsidized by them. A green dye-laser beam or a krypton light may be tried for the purpose.

Visual Acquisition of Downed Airman in Water. A reliable laser system that can locate an airman downed in water is required. Such a system can be mounted on an aircraft to scan a minimum area of about 2 square miles from an altitude of 600 to 1,000 feet. A television camera-type scanner using a laser beam and an electronic locking mechanism to the object would be needed to achieve this development. A high visual contrast is needed between the target (airman) and the water. The system should be capable of acquiring the target both during daytime and nighttime. Start with the use of IR and UV laser beams.

AERONAUTICAL SYSTEMS AND DEVICES

Detector of Moisture in Aircraft Fuel. The aircraft fuel has an affinity for water, which may freeze when low temperatures are prevalent on the aircraft. Aircraft crashes have occurred due to the icing of the fuel filter. Develop a method of de-icing or preventing the formation of ice in the fuel carburetor or injection conduits. A low-cost laser device may be used which will constantly monitor the fuel flow at or near the filter. The laser beam will be sensed by a detector which will actuate the current to an enclosed heating member, thus maintaining a constant temperature above the melting point of the ice. The device must be accurate and reliable and should not overheat or spark at any point exposed to the fuel. Any malfunction of the device should be indicated at the pilot's instrument panel.

Laser-Aided Rocket Engine. A compact, high-power laser source that can be carried in a cruising spaceship and can create a new type of propelling energy to move the craft at speeds consistent with those of conventionally propelled crafts would transcend present methods. One way of accomplishing this achievement is to vaporize a quantity of mercury by means of the laser-beam heat and to pass the vapor through an electric field to ionize it into positive ions. The positive ions then can be made to be repelled by positively charged electrodes into space at high velocity because of the absence of drag, producing a forward thrust. Such a system would be an ion-driven engine of the future for rocket propulsion. The rocket must be launched into space by conventional methods.

Laser-Propelled Space Vehicle. When a nominal-power laser beam is focused on an object, it reacts explosively with the object, creating a pressure or thrust of several million pounds per square inch. Utilizing this thrust, a space or aerial vehicle could be propelled in space where rarefield atmospheric conditions exist. Such a system could have enormous potentialities because of the efficient usage of energy in such a medium.

ATOMIC FUSION AND DETONATION

Atomic-Fusion Initiator. Considerable amount of work is being carried out at present to produce fusion of two or more elements together in order to obtain the energy formed in the fusion reaction. Various types of laser sources have been tried to cause the fusion reaction. Among these sources are: excimers, CO_2 laser, frequency-doubled Nd-YAG laser, and free-electron lasers, emitting laser powers ranging to terawatts. The laser power is concentrated on a low atomic weight element, such as deuterium in combination with tritium, which combination is subjected to laser-beam energies under thousand atmospheres or over as available. While fission or fusion of atomic elements have been achieved by explosive methods, there is not as yet a practical method of fusion reaction under controlled conditions so that the energy thus produced can be utilized generally for civilian application. Therefore, development of a small-scale high-powered laser device which would produce a single or multiple pulses to ignite an atomic fuel to be used under controlled environments for production of thermal energy to be converted into electrical energy is direly needed.

One preferable method possibly will be the use of free electrons on grounded target elements to cause minute explosive reactions between the target and the electron beam. The heat developed in the reaction will range to millions of degrees per square inch sufficient to fuse even greater atomic weight elements than the hydrogen isotopes.

Shorter-Wavelength Implosion Driver. As discussed in the earlier part of the text on atomic fusion, the fusion reaction consists of the implosion of the target material. Thus, the latest investigations by several institutions lean toward the use of shorter-wavelength radiation beams produced preferably in the ultraviolet region of the spectrum. Both Livermore and Rochester laboratories have shown that increasing the frequency of an infrared beam to that dominant in the ultraviolet increases the target absorption of the radiation as much as 90 percent at power densities in the neighborhood of terawatts/cm^2. In this state of affairs, the production of hot electrons is decreased up to 100 times, improving the x-ray conversion efficiency to as much as 50 percent. It must be emphasized here that the higher the efficiency of x-ray conversion in the process the better is the drivability of the radiation to implosion.

In spite of all this progress in atomic fusion work, there is still a need for a continuous implosion process, whose intensity can be increased or decreased continuously at will; that is, the reaction process should be varied the same as an electric current can be varied in a conductor by the use of a variable resistor, such as a rheostat. Accordingly, a means should be developed that can continuously feed the target material to the implosion chamber and a high-power radiation applied to the flowing target material and continuously converting the material into thermal energy, which can then be absorbed by heat exchangers to produce steam to drive electric generators. The problem is unique but not unsurmountable.

DENTAL INSTRUMENTATION BY LASER BEAMS

A Laser System to Treat Caries. A CO_2 or Nd-YAG laser system that can be mass-produced at a low cost may become a standard equipment in a dental office. A frequency-doubled Nd-YAG may even be preferable because of its 5,320-angstrom wavelength which is in the visible spectrum and thus the focusing and defocusing of the beam is facilitated. This system should be provided with a laser waveguide having a stylus at its distal end and optical elements to manipulate the beam focus on the teeth. Since the energy of such a laser system should be reasonably high, in the range from 50 to 100 joules per square centimeter to penetrate the enamel of the tooth, a pulsed beam may be conveniently used.

Laser System to Drill Enamel. Drilling of the enamel by means of a laser beam has not been of much interest to the dental profession, because no laser equipment which is suitable for the procedure has been developed. The present laser instrumentation systems tried on the enamel on an experimental basis have been very costly and the results of the drilling have not shown any improvement or even any parity with conventional drilling instruments. One drawback has been the discoloration of the drilled hole by laser, because the control over the laser beam has not been precisely directed and therefore the laser beam has penetrated too far into the tooth, charring the organic material, such as that in the dentin and its pulp substance. Accordingly, a simple controllable laser system that can stop the drilling automatically before the beam reaches the dentin would be a very useful tool, since drilling can be performed without anesthetizing the roots and gingival area of the tooth. The beam should be delivered to the tooth through a laser waveguide provided with an optical control means at its stylus. Such a system may also be used for prosthetic restoration of the dentures.

Ultraviolet Laser Treatment System. An ultraviolet beam can be used to treat the gingiva of the mouth, because of the germicidal effect of the beam on soft tissues. Gingivitis is the disease of the gingiva (gums) which have been treated, in the past, with ultraviolet radiation emitted from a mercury-discharge tube. The beam from such a device has not been of high density and could not be varied in intensity by manually operated devices. Since any amount of ultraviolet usable on the gingiva now can be produced by an argon laser system and the beam can be accurately controlled by means of a stylus-provided laser waveguide, a low-cost and portable laser system for this purpose will be a very useful tool for any dental office. In addition to gingival treatment, the laser beam can be utilized to cure dental implant material or a restorative paste right in the enamel cavity that is drilled by means of a laser beam.

MEDICAL INSTRUMENTATION BY USE OF LASER BEAMS

Treatment of Nasal Passages with Ultraviolet Laser. Ultraviolet light is a strong germicidal agent as well as having healing properties. Prior to the discovery of laser radiation, nasopharyngeal specialists have employed a mercury electric discharge tube producing ultraviolet radiation to irradiate the nasal sinuses to treat the inflammatory condition of the mucus membranes lining these air cavities. The main disadvantage of the discharge tube was its inflexibility of use. The control over the radiation emission was also difficult, since the radiation intensity could not be varied in accordance with the dosage required. Because the laser intensity can be varied easily and accurately and the radiation can be delivered to any part of the nasal sinuses, a device operating with a laser beam will be a useful adjunct to the physician's instruments.

Develop an instrument that would be compact, small, and has great flexibility of use. An argon laser or a tunable dye laser in the ultraviolet range of emission and using an optical fiber conduit for directing the beam to the area of interest will be a practical medical instrument. Since the nasal passages also contain, when infected, copious amounts of streptococci and staphylococci which are found to be vulnerable to the ultraviolet treatment, the laser system emitting at wavelength ranges between 3,000 and 3,800 angstroms would be a desirable instrument for use in a medical clinic or in private doctor's office.

Otological Laser Instrument. The inflammation of nasal sinuses due to infection may cause the clogging up of the Eustachian tube which leads from the throat into the inner ear, interfering with the passage of air to and from the ear. This condition gives rise to a pressure to form in the ear, distending the tympanic membrane and resulting in great pain. To relieve the pressure and the ensuing pain, the physician neumatizes the Eustachian tube; however, if it cannot be neumatized due to advanced infection, the otologist punctures a minute hole in the tympanum and inserts a grommet for the free passage of air into or out of the inner ear. This relieves the pressure and the earache. The treatment is usually carried out in a hospital to restore normal hearing of the patient.

An argon laser beam or a frequency-doubled Nd-YAG laser of low-level power can be used for puncturing the hole. Develop a fiberoptic laser conduit provided at its distal end with a stylus having a long focal-length lens to deliver a single pulse of 5 to 10 joules to vaporize a small amount of the tympanic tissue to form an aperture of about one-half to one millimeter diameter. Since the laser beam will cauterize the periphery of the hole, no grommet will be needed. Furthermore, the optical fiber waveguide should have a central coherent bundle for the visualization of the tympanum by first transmitting a visible light to localize the laser beam focus. The waveguide must have an optical viewer located about six inches from the terminal point of the exit port. Such a waveguide may be attached to any existing argon or dye laser or usable power range.

Endoscopic Laser Coagulator. A practical endoscopic laser coagulant for the treatment of internal bleeding organs, such as stomach, intestines, duodenal ulcers, and for vernicular growth in the esophagus is direly needed. Such an instrument should be small, compact, and have good flexibility of use. For this instrument, an argon laser system can be used to furnish the radiation energy. When Nd-YAG or CO_2 laser is used for coagulating the ulcer or affected area, a He-Ne laser or other bright light should be used to provide localization of the lesion and focusing the invisible beam.

Thermal Imaging System Using Laser. At present, medical thermal imaging methods employ either an infrared device or liquid crystal spray in liquid form. However, the colors produced in the image are changeable in rapid progression as the patient's nervous condition changes. A thermal imaging system having a high sensitivity to colors and shades and using complementary laser beams compatible with the object texture or patient's skin would give improved imaging performance, which would make medical diagnosis more reliable. A television screen used with this system would air in more accurate diagnosis of superficial skin diseases and subsurface carcinomatous breast tissue. The patient should be scanned with a television color camera and viewed with a black-and-white television screen. The author's preliminary tests with such an arrangement have uncovered that fine definition together with high contrast of the skin blemishes and those anomalies occurring immediately below the surface layer of the skin can be distinctly delineated.

Acupuncture-Type Laser Treatment Instrument. Pain due to the disorders of many organs of the body travels remotely from the source of trouble and appears in an area adjacent the skin and remotely from the ailing organ. Since pain manifests itself due to the irritation of a nerve ending, nerve ganglion, or a nerve trunk, there are a number of areas on the human skin where pain from the organ appears. The condition is known as referred pain or reflex pain. One of the commonest pain of a decaying tooth appears in the temporal region. Inflammation of the gall bladder or liver produces a pain in the right-shoulder area. In angina pectoris, one form of heart trouble, the pain radiates to the left shoulder and down the arm to the fingers. The true acupuncture practice used in the Orient employs steel needles embedded in the skin where reflex pain occurs, and the practitioners advocate the presence of about 700 referred pain points in the skin. However, the latest method is the use of low-level laser radiation instead of needles. The treatment is fast and painless, as reported.

A portable laser treatment instrument may be developed that is small and compact, and uses the radiation from a He-Ne laser with an output of 2 to 4 milliwatts. The beam should be transmitted through a fiberoptic waveguide having a stylus at its proximal end and provided with a laser control means. No optical elements for focusing the laser beam is necessary, because the exit port of the stylus terminal may be made of a diameter of one millimeter or slightly larger for the delivery of the beam to the skin. The treatment time may be varied from several seconds to one minute, depending on the physician's dosage. It is possible that techniques may also be developed to use the treatment directly on the primary pain areas.

Skin-Wrinkle Removal with Laser Beam. The same laser-beam waveguide that is used for radiation treatment of referred pain may also be made with interchangeable stylus heads for the use of wrinkle removal from the face, forehead, and under the chin. The treatment could consist of separating the two sides of the wrinkle using metal probes and passing the laser beam from the He-Ne system over the line or fissure of the skin. The treatment may take a few seconds but should be continued for intervals of a day or so for a period of several weeks until the wrinkle disappears. The device should be small, portable, and of low cost, not to exceed about $200, and the waveguide preferably should be provided with coherent, flexible optical fibers, although not absolutely necessary.

A Fiberoptic Otological Examination Device. Develop a fiberoptic waveguide with coherent fibers using a low-level light such as that from a LED diode and having a observation optical device mounted at the proximal end of the waveguide for use to observe or examine the condition of the tympanic membrane or the foreign matter that might exist in the ear canal, causing pain or feeling of stuffiness in the canal. The device should be battery-operated, small, compact, and at a cost not to exceed $200. This is a needed household instrument as well as a medical clinic implement.

Other Laser Instrumentation Devices.

Neural Instrumentation—Develop a fiberoptic conduit which can be attached to a binocular microscope to weld nerve endings. The optical fibers should be coherent and flexible. A focusing lens should be provided at the distal end of the conduit for visualization of the nerve structure as well as focusing the laser beam, which may be from a ruby laser, argon laser, or even from a dye laser.

Port-Wine Mark Remover—A simple and compact laser instrumentation system that can be easily portable from one office to another in a doctor's office, for removing skin blemishes such as port-wine marks or small corns from hands or feet is needed. The laser beam can be transmitted through a fiberoptic waveguide provided wih a stylus at its distal end having variable-focus optical element.

Tunable Dye-Laser Device—A small, practical, and tunable dye-laser device that can easily be tuned to various frequencies that would be compatible with different tissue cells (easily absorbed by cells) would be a useful biomedical cell instrumentation probe, that can be used for synthesis, separation, and study of cells and collagens. Start with an argon laser.

Fallopian Surgery with Laser Beam. A laser waveguide that can transmit CO_2 laser radiation and is provided with a long stylus (about 20-cm long) having focusing optical elements and beam-control means would be a useful tool for the surgeon engaged in obstetrics and gynecology. The waveguide should be flexible and adapted to be mounted on any laserhead exit port for performing operation on female organs, such as unblocking fallopian tubes to aid fertilization in an infertile woman.

METEOROLOGICAL SOUNDING SYSTEMS

Sounding System for Shipboard Application. The military agencies will welcome the development of a meteorological sounding system for shipboard application, since the telemetering methods used at present cannot be employed under emission control conditions. The system should possess unlimited altitude capabilities and should use a completely passive means to obtain data. The system should operate reliably in all climatic conditions and at all temperatures. A laser beam, being highly directional and insensitive to jamming, would be an admirable candidate for this purpose.

Overpressure Detector. When the atmospheric pressure changes, certain meteorological changes occur, including a change in the density of the atmosphere. Since laser beams are sensitive to pressure changes, a laser system that can detect or sense overpressure or rarefaction of 0.01 to 10 dynes/cm² above the reference pressure would be suitable for this purpose. Such a device or instrument will be welcomed by meteorological instrument manufacturers as well as users. In developing this instrument, apply some of the principles already studied in the previous chapters.

Atmospheric Moisture Indicator. The meteorological instruments currently sold on the market measure all types of parameters and telemeter them to weather stations. However, it appears that at least one instrument is not capable of measuring humidity accurately. Thus, there is a need for a humidity sensor that would operate at ambient temperatures from 0°C to 60°C. This device should also measure the dew points from $-10°$ to $+30°$C, with high accuracy. The laser radiodiffusion principle should be tried for the development of this sensing meter.

Instrument to Measure Meteorological Parameters. An instrument which can make accurate and instantaneous measurements of atmospheric characteristics for altitudes from 100,000 to 200,000 feet will be an improvement over the prevalent instruments. The parameters considered must include small package size, about 20 to 30 cubic centimeters, a life span of 1 hour minimum, a response time of 10 milliseconds maximum, an output adaptable to telemetering techniques, a calibration accuracy of ± 2 to ± 5 percent, and a power capability of several milliwatts. Naturally such a device is to be used on a missile or other high-altitude vehicle, or rocket which is to be returned to earth by parachute.

In a rapidly-changing environment at high altitude, where the atmospheric medium is of extremely low density, the time lag to reach equilibrium is critical in obtaining accuracy. The rarefaction of air molecules at the high altitude must be considered. The greater mean free path of the molecules may exceed the size of the sensor, and thus counting of the molecules and measuring their mean kinetic energy would be a problem. In addition, the absorption of this energy in the projected laser beam and translated into a color-change device in a light-sensitive material would be a further problem to be resolved.

Cloud Height Measuring Instrument. It appears that the present ceilometers or radars are not adequate for measuring cloud heights accurately, and a need for a precision measuring instrument is evident for use by military operations and for commercial airlines. A pulsing laser beam projected to the clouds and the reflected beam received at the station projecting the beam is timed, similar to a laser rangefinder, and the distance is calculated by the instrument simultaneously. The cost of such an equipment could be from $10,000 to $15,000 and would be considered reasonable.

Device for Atmospheric Transmissivity of Light. The present system for obtaining transmissivity or visibility in air apparently are limited to 500 to 1,000 feet. Such short distances aggravate the problems of calibration and necessitate the lengthening of aircraft runways up to 15,000 feet. The cost of installation of a path of this magnitude will be considerably reduced, if accurate information respecting visibility is obtained. An invisible laser beam, such as that from a CO_2 laser or GaAs diode transmitting a pulsed beam through the proposed length of path may provide a solution to the attempted problem. If the atmosphere is partially filled with fog or mist, a green beam from either a krypton laser or dye laser may be tried. An error of 100 to 200 feet appears to be permissible throughout the 15,000-foot distance.

METROLOGICAL INSTRUMENTS AND SYSTEMS

Monitor for Aircraft-Fuel Contaminant. Contaminants in aircraft fuel adversely affect the fuel system in the aircraft, by plugging up the delicate fuel lines and valves. A laser monitoring device installed adjacent the flow of the fluid to monitor its flow during fueling would alert the attendant by some signal, such as sound or light signal, if the contaminant content exceeds 15 to 20 milligrams per liter of the fuel.

Underwater Missile Timing Device. Develop a rugged, inexpensive, and highly-reliable timing device for use with a torpedo or any underwater missile. Its accuracy may vary about ±1 percent without significantly affecting the short-period missile travel, which may be a maximum of 5 minutes. Existing electronic or mechanical timers are vulnerable to vibration, shock, and temperature. A laser-beam timer, using the usual clock frequency and operable from the selected frequency expiration would not seem to be infuenced adversely by deep sea environmental conditions. deep sea.

Quality Assurance Device. Present mechanical devices for measuring the various dimensions of manufactured products for controlling their accuracy of dimensions usually employ a micrometer. The use of such a device is slow and cumbersome when demand for rapid production and acceptance tests of the device are critical. A laser device that can be mounted in the path of the manufactured product moving on a continuous belt would measure the needed dimension and automatically throw out the part that does not meet the production standard would eliminate human error and increase production.

Laser Flow Meter for Corrosive Media. Apparently a need exists for a flow meter which may be used with high corrosive liquids, such as red fuming acid employed in the propellant system of a rocket. The device should be fast in its measurement of flow as well as viscosity of the material, with a resolution of 1 percent or less for flow rates up to 40 gallons per minute. While mechanical flow meters made of stainless steel are now in use, they do not seem to give the accuracy over the ranges set by the operator during the liquid flow. A laser-aided device that uses a two-beam technique whereby the interferometric shift of the liquid image fringes between the two beams located a known distance apart should give accurate and fast results.

Vibration Monitor. Develop an airborne vibration monitor for turbine engines that will forecast to the pilot any engine or component failure that is imminent during flight. A visible laser beam operating at high clock frequency may be made to develop a beat between the normal and abnormal operations of the turbine of the engine and the magnitude of beat difference analyzing the degree of malfunction which may lead to complete failure of the engine in time could be the starting point of such a development.

Aircraft-Wing Icing-Condition Indicator. The present icing-condition indicators integrate the differential pressure of heated impact tube with heated impact tube to icing. Such an instrument is said to be subject to excessive lag in indication. An instrument is needed which will indicate the approach of icing rather than after the icing has formed. In addition, the device should give indication to the pilot at all times the ambient condition tending to form icing, and at the same time should automatically de-ice the surfaces as the icing begins to form. Such an indicator should be independent of specific atmospheric characteristics not directly contributing to a condition of icing. Start with laser diode sensors with temperature and humidity-sensing characteristics. There are several such elements in use in other fields.

Ship Collision Preventer. Ship-to-ship collision, as in aircraft collision, occurs in the wide open sea every year, causing damages running to millions of dollars. A ship-collision-preventive system is direly needed. Such a system, regardless of size, could be installed on a shipboard to prevent collision before it happens. It should be reliable and practical. A green laser beam capable of penetrating and scanning an area of 2.5 to 3 kilometers in radius, 360° horizontally and 15° vertically should be tried. The system should be made to warn the captain of the ship to maneuver the ship to the right or left, depending on the forward attitude of the approaching ship. The maneuvers do not have to be coorperative between the ships if one is equipped with the sensing system and the other is not.

MILITARY SYSTEMS AND DEVICES

Aircraft Collision-Preventive System. At present, there are various types of aircraft collision-preventive systems or devices, but none of them is sufficiently practical or reliable for installation on any commercial, military, or private plane, as standard equipment. A system built at a reasonable cost for private planes, or one built for civilian or military planes, regardless of cost, that is reliable and accurate is direly needed. A blue or green laser beam can be used. The beam is projected to the oncoming plane detected by scanning it and then locking on it. This will be the reference point which will be displayed on the instrument panel in the cockpit. As the two planes are moving, the reference point will also move with respect to the image of the aircraft displayed on the same instrument, so that the pilot can maneuver his plane with reference to the "reference point" and evade the oncoming plane. A corresponding tactical system on the oncoming plane is not required.

An Identification Friend-or-Foe Laser System (IFF). The present radar, microwave, or infrared IFF devices do not seem to be effective and rapid in identifying an aircraft in flight. A reliable and accurate system using two laser beams to cooperatively complement each other's accuracy of signal acquisition will be a needed adjunct to the military tactical equipment. An ultraviolet beam from a dye laser or argon laser and a frequency-doubled Nd-TAG beam could be tried for this purpose. While the penetration of these beams through the clouds and rain will be limited, for clear sky the combination of the beams should give accurate results. The identification will be achieved by the differential absorption of the beams by the aircraft skin and the translation of the result into the standard skin texture of the friendly aircraft whose characteristics must be known.

Target Search and Acquisition System. The present radar-controlled systems are accurate in operation beyond certain height limit but they cannot acquire a low-flying aircraft information. A system using a powerful laser beam projecting divergently at about 10-milliradian angle at a target flying up to 10,000 feet above ground would be a useful military equipment. The ground-based laser system, after acquiring the aircraft, would lock on it and the divergent beam will be reduced to a collimated beam and then would acquire information regarding the speed, direction, and character of the target. A cloud-penetrating beam must be chosen from several that exist, so that the flying target at cloud height or beyond can be acquired.

Missile Velocimeter. At missile test ranges, the velocity of the missile at altitudes less than 1,000 feet cannot be accurately measured by radar. A laser system is needed that could measure altitudes of only several feet above ground. The proposed system should measure the velocity of the missile as well as its height from the ground. Since the height of the missile launched from the ground is constantly changing, the change in velocity may be translated to distance and the varying distance and the velocity of the missile can be recorded continuously.

Fiberoptic Coder-Decoder Device. A coherent and square cross section fiberoptic cable which receives coded image signals from a transmitter having a mirror scanning the cross-sectional proximal surface of the cable and transmitting dissected image signals would be a useful military communications system. At the receiving end, an identical scanning mirror decodes the dissected image signals into a recognizable information. The coded signals may also be stored in a memory device for future decoding.

Torpedo Recovery from Deep Water. In recovering an exercise torpedo, the location of the torpedo appears to be a major problem. Devices now in use give information only at 2,000 to 3,000 yards from the torpedo for a few days. Develop a method having a green-emitting laser which will reliably locate the torpedo to 5,000 yards and will be at a cost not to exceed $10,000. The green-light signals given off from the torpedo should persist for at least five days.

SECURITY SURVEILLANCE SYSTEMS

Portable Security System. A portable security-surveillance laser system is needed which can be easily moved from one place to another and can be set up in a short time, less than 10 minutes, around the area to be secured, especially where artillery is concerned. The setup should be invisible so that the device would not be vulnerable to artificial implementation or destruction by the intruding vandals. There are several types of surveillance laser systems; however, they are prone to detection by the intruder and optical jamming is not impossible, thus confusing the central station instruments. Infrared laser diodes enclosed in camouflaged containers would be the start of this laser system.

Home Security Sentinel. The present infrared, microwave, or acoustic home security devices or systems are too bulky and costly to be afforded financially by an average wage earner. A simple and easily installable device is required which uses invisible laser beams to protect a private home from intruders. The device should project split beams at various ground levels, whereby the intruder cannot jump over the suspected beam or crawl under it. The entire cost of the system or device should be within several hundred dollars. The consumer should be able to set it up himself and the beam from the system should not be dangerous to the user. An acoustic alerting device should also be provided with the system.

Portable Intrusion Alarm for Campers. An intrusion alarm that can alert the campers of any intrusion by human being or an animal into the area of camping by producing a loud alarm will be a useful device for campers on mountainous areas or deserts. Sensors located at strategic locations would alert the campers of the instrusion. A low-cost GaAs device with an alarm could be made in a compact package, using rechargeable batteries or dry cells.

Auto Theft Alarm. Develop a laser-beam fence that will be safe to the user as well as monitoring the safety of the car after the driver locks and leaves the car wherever it is parked. Any activity related to the breaking into the car would activate the device and sound a shrieking tone to alert the owner or the passerbys. The system can be made so that it will automatically reset itself when the owner leaves the car after parking.

Automobile Proximity Indicator. As most drivers have experienced, there is a blind area in the rear of each automobile. A car following in the rear at close range cannot be seen through the driver's rear-view mirror. An abrupt movement by the driver to change a lane may result in an accident if a car at close range is following him. A low-cost laser device to scan the rear of the car to alert the driver of an impending danger of accident is needed in every car. The device does not have to image the rear car on a screen. A flashing spot on the instrument panel would be sufficient to signal the driver that there is a car behind his car at close range.

UNDERWATER ACOUSTIC DETECTION

Fiberoptic Detection Cable. A lightweight, high-sensitivity fiberoptic interferometer which can replace the conventional piezoelectric transducers in the detection of sound waves converted into light waves in the ocean would be preferable to present techniques which are vulnerable to changing ocean environments. One of the two ways of accomplishing this would be to vary the delays from a blue or green dye laser, krypton laser, or He-Cd laser activating the optical elements mounted in the fiberoptic cable. The second method would be to measure the phase difference (the beats) of the optical signals between a control fiber channel and an acoustically-coupled channel.

Target Detection and Classification. When the presence of an unknown vessel in ocean is detected by a submarine the only method of identification appears to be to track the vessel for an extended period and to attempt communication. Of course, the ambient sea noise complicates the problem and affects acoustic transmission, causing confusion in identification and classification. New techniques and equipment are needed for long-range detection, localization, and classification of any underwater target. It seems the identification of the target is one of the essential and primary requirements of the new development system. Utilize a deep-sea penetrating beam for scanning and acquisition and a double-beam scheme for the identification. If a friendly submarine, project signals similar to sounds produced by marine creatures, from which sound coded signals can be extracted.

Torpedo Miss-Distance Indicator. When a submarine torpedo misses its target, torpedo pingers are used at present which are said to be unreliable and inaccurate, since such a technique depends largely on the torpedo that is launched. An accurate miss-distance indicator for torpedo-submarine encounter is needed. The accuracy of such a device could be 50 percent of target size plus the attitude of encounter. A gyro-operated laser beam scheme should be tried.

COMMENTS AND WARNING

Any type of laser beam radiation, direct or reflected, should be considered dangerous to the eye. In addition, the ideas or innovations listed are described herein require a working knowledge of laser systems and characteristics. These ideas are not for the amateurs or beginners, and therefore, such persons must be supervised by highly-versed laser professionals during development work. The laser worker must wear at all times safety goggles that are recommended by BRH or LIA as safe for the work in hand. As stated at the beginning of this chapter, it would be preferable that persons already in laser or laser-oriented industry or institution should attempt the challenge of the development of any specific item described. No responsibility is assumed by the author or the publishers of this book for any injury arising from the use of laser beams with which the innovator conducts experimentation. It is also assumed that the worker in any branch of laser technology would have a basic knowledge of electronics and related subjects. To be successful in achieving an innovative project discussed herein, the investigator should be well-versed with a variety of technologies involved in the project achievement. Laser and electrical safety as prescribed by the Bureau of Radiological Health and Laser Institute of America standards should be studied and followed.

Appendix A
Elements and Their Characteristics

Element	Symbol	At. No.	At. Wt.	Melting Point °C.	Specific Gravity
Actinium	Ac	89	227.00	....	....
Alabamine*	Ab	85	221.00	....	....
Aluminum	Al	13	26.97	660	2.70
Antimony	Sb	51	121.76	630.5	6.68
Argon...................	A	18	39.94	−189.2	1.27 g/l
Arsenic	As	33	74.93	814.0	5.73
Barium.................	Ba	56	137.36	850.0	3.50
Beryllium............	Be	4	9.02	1350.0	1.85
Bismuth	Bi	83	209.0	271.0	9.78
Boron...................	B	5	10.82	2300.0	2.54
Bromine..............	Br	35	79.91	−7.2	3.12 liq.
Cadmium.............	Cd	48	112.41	320.9	8.65
Calcium...............	Ca	20	40.08	810.0	1.54
Carbon................	C	6	12.00	> 3500.0	2.25 graph.
Cerium................	Ce	58	140.13	640.0	6.90
Cesium	Cs	55	132.81	26.4	1.87
Chlorine..............	Cl	17	35.45	−101.6	3.2 g/l
Chromium...........	Cr	24	52.01	1615.0	7.1
Cobalt	Co	27	58.94	1480.0	8.9
Columbium**	Cb	41	93.30	1950.0	8.4
Copper................	Cu	29	63.57	1083.0	8.95
Dysprosium.........	Dy	66	162.46	....	....

* Astatine
** Niobium

Element	Symbol	At. No.	At. Wt.	Melting Point °C.	Specific Gravity
Erbium	Er	68	167.64	....	4.77
Europium	Eu	63	152.00	....	....
Fluorine	F	9	19.0	−223.0	1.69 g/l
Gadolinium	Gd	64	157.30	....	....
Gallium	Ga	31	69.72	29.75	5.91
Germanium	Ge	32	72.60	958.5	5.36
Gold	Au	79	197.20	1063.0	19.32
Hafnium	Hf	72	178.60	1700.?	13.30
Helium	He	2	4.00	< −272.2	0.177 g/l
Holmium	Ho	67	163.50	....	....
Hydrogen	H	1	1.0078	−259.1	0.0899 g/l
Illinium	Il	61	146.00	....	....
Indium	In	49	114.80	155.0	7.28
Iodine	I	53	126.93	113.5	4.93 sol.
Iridium	Ir	77	193.10	2350.0	22.42
Iron (cast)	Fe	26	55.84	1275.0	7.85
Krypton	Kr	36	82.90	−169.0	3.7 g/l
Lanthanum	La	57	138.90	826.0	6.15
Lead	Pb	82	207.22	327.5	11.35
Lithium	Li	3	6.94	186.0	0.534
Lutecium	Lu	71	175.00	....	....
Magnesium	Mg	12	24.32	651.0	1.74
Manganese	Mn	25	54.93	1260.0	7.20
Masurium	Ma	43	....	....	....
Mercury	Hg	80	200.61	−38.87	13.59
Molybdenum	Mo	42	96.00	2620.0	10.20
Neodymium	Nd	60	144.27	840.0	6.95
Neon	Ne	10	20.18	−248.67	0.9 g/l
Nickel	Ni	28	58.69	1452.0	8.90
Nitrogen	N	7	14.008	−209.86	1.25 g/l
Osmium	Os	76	190.80	2700.00	22.48
Oxygen	O	8	16.00	−218.4	1.42 g/l
Palladium	Pd	46	106.70	1555.0	11.40
Phosphorus	P	15	31.02	44.1	1.8−2.2
Platinum	Pt	78	195.23	1755.0	21.45
Polonium	Po	84	210.00	....	....
Potassium	K	19	39.10	62.3	0.86
Proseodymium	Pr	59	140.92	940.0	6.50
Protactinium	Pa	91	....	....	....
Radium	Ra	88	225.97	960.0	5.0
Radon	Rn	86	222.00	....	9.73 g/l
Rhenium	Re	75	186.31	3000.?	20.53
Rhodium	Rh	45	102.91	1955.0	12.50
Rubidium	Rb	37	85.44	38.5	1.53
Ruthenium	Ru	44	101.70	....	12.20

Element	Symbol	At. No.	At. Wt.	Melting Point °C.	Specific Gravity
Samarium............	Sm	62	150.43	> 1300.0	7.7
Scandium	Sc	21	45.10	1200.0	2.5
Selenium.............	Se	34	79.20	220.0	4.5
Silicon.................	Si	14	28.06	....	2.42
Silver..................	Ag	47	107.88	960.5	10.50
Sodium................	Na	11	22.997	97.5	0.97
Strontium............	Sr	38	87.63	800.0	2.6
Sulphur	S	16	32.06	120.0	2.07
Tantalum.............	Ta	73	181.40	2850.0	16.6
Tellurium............	Te	52	127.50	452.0	6.24
Terbium..............	Tb	65	159.20	....	....
Thallium	Tl	81	204.39	303.5	11.85
Thorium..............	Th	90	232.12	1845.0	11.20
Thulium	Tm	69	169.40	....	....
Tin......................	Sn	50	118.70	170.0	5.7—6.5
Titanium	Ti	22	47.90	1800.0	4.5
Tungsten.............	W	74	184.00	3370.0	19.3
Uranium...............	U	92	238.14	< 1850.0	18.68
Vanadium............	V	23	50.95	1710.0	5.87
Virginium............	Vi	87	224.00	....	....
Xenon	Xe	54	131.30	−140.0	5.85 g/l
Ytterbium............	Yb	70	173.50	....	....
Yttrium	Y	39	88.92	1490.0	5.51
Zinc	Zn	30	65.38	419.4	7.14
Zirconium............	Zr	40	91.22	1700.0	6.40

Appendix B
Important Physical Constants

Electrical Units:—
 Charge (quantity):—
  Electronic Charge (e)............ $= 4.802 \times 10^{-10}$ e.s.u.
   $= 1.592 \times 10^{-20}$ e.m.u.
   $= 1.592 \times 10^{-19}$ coulomb.
  Coulomb (Q)...................... $= 10^{-1}$ e.m.u.
   $= 3 \times 10^{9}$ e.s.u.
   $= 6.28 \times 10^{18}$ electronic charges.
  Microcoulomb (μQ) .... $= 10^{-6}$ coulomb.
  Faraday .... $= 96,500$ coulombs.

 Current:—
  Ampere (I)............................. $= 10^{-1}$ e.m.u.
   $= 3 \times 10^{9}$ e.s.u.
   $= 1$ coulomb per second.
   $= 1.036 \times 10^{-5}$ faraday per second.
  Milliampere (MA).................. $= 10^{-3}$ ampere.
  Micro-ampere (μA).............. $= 10^{-6}$ ampere.

 Potential:—
  Volt (E or V)........................ $= 10^{8}$ e.m.u.
   $= 10^{8}$ gausses.
   $= \frac{1}{3} \times 10^{-2}$ e.s.u.
  Kilovolt (KV)........................ $= 1000$ volts.
  Million-Volt (MV).................. $= 10^{6}$ volts.
  Millivolt .... $= 10^{-3}$ volt.
  Microvolt............................... $= 10^{-6}$ volt.

Resistance:—

Ohm (R or r) .... = The resistance of a uniform column of mercury 106.3-cm long, at 0° C., having a mass of 14.452 grams.
= 10^9 e.m.u.
= $1/9 \times 10^{-11}$ e.s.u.

Megohm .... = 10^6 ohms.

Microhm.............................. = 10^{-6} ohm.
= 10^{12} megohm.

Capacity:—

Farad (C)................................ = 10^{-9} e.m.u.
= 9×10^{11} e.s.u.
= 10^6 microfarads.

Microfarad (μC)...................... = 10^{-6} farad.

Micro-microfarad ($\mu\mu$C) .... = 10^{-12} farad.

Inductance:—

Henry (L) .... = 10^9 e.m.u.
= $1/9 \times 10^{-11}$ e.s.u.

Millihenry.............................. = 10^{-3} henry.

Magnetic Units:—

1 line of force = 1 maxwell = 1 e.m.u. = 10^{-8} volt-second.
1 gauss = 1 maxwell/sq. cm. = 1 line/sq. cm.
1 gilbert = 1 gauss-centimeter.
Magneton (Bohr) = 9.22×10^{-21} erg per gauss.

Other Constants:—

Velocity of Light.................... = $\dfrac{\text{Electrostatic Unit}}{\text{Electromagnetic Unit}}$
= $\dfrac{\text{e.s.u.}}{\text{e.m.u.}} = 3 = 10^{10}$ cms/second.

Positron Charge (positive electron) = 4.802×10^{-10} e.s.u.
Positron Mass = 9.107×10^{-28} gram.
Electron Mass = 9.107×10^{-28} gram.
Mass of Proton = 1.672×10^{-24} gram.
e/m = 5.2741×10^{17} e.s.u. per gram.
Electron-volt = 1.59×10^{-12} erg.
1 erg = 0.629×10^{-12} electron-volts.

Gas Constant (R) = 1.9864 calories/degree/mole.
= 8.3136×10^7 ergs/degree/mole.
Avogadro's Number = 6.06×10^{23} per mole.
Planck's Constant = 6.625×10^{-27} erg-second.
Boltzmann's Constant = 1.3708×10^{-16} erg/degree.

Grating Space of Rock Salt (NaC1) = 2.8 A.U. (approx.)
Grating Space of Calcite (CaCO3) = 3.0 A.U. (approx.)

Appendix C

International
Weights and Measurements

─────────────────────────────────────

Units of Length

Angstrom Units	Microns	Millimeters	Centimeters	Inches	Meters
1	10^{-4}	10^{-7}	10^{-8}	2.5×10^{-8}	10^{-10}
10^4	1	10^{-3}	10^{-4}	2.5×10^{-4}	10^{-6}
10^7	10^3	1	1/10	1/25	10^{-3}
10^8	10^4	10	1	2/5	10^{-2}
2.54×10^8	2.54×10^4	25.4	2.54	1	1/39
10^{10}	10^6	10^3	10^2	39.4	1

1 light year = 5.9×10^{12} miles = 9.5×10^{12} kilometers.
1 kilometer = 10^3 meters = 10^5 cm. = 10^6 millimeters.
1 mile = 1760 yards = 5280 feet = × 63,360 inches.
1 yard = 3 feet = 36 inches = .9144 meter
1 foot = 12 inches = .3048 meter
1 inch = 2.54 centimeters
1 meter = 1.093 yards = 3.279 feet = 39.37 inches.

Units of Area

1 square meter = 100 sq. decimeters = 10^4 sq. cm. = 10^6 sq. mm.
1 square mile = 640 acres = 3,097,600 sq. yds. = 27,878,400 sq. ft.
1 acre = 4840 sq. yds. = 43,560 sq. ft.
1 sq. yd. = 9 sq. ft.
1 sq. ft. = 144 sq. in.

Units of Volume

1 cubic meter = 10^3 cubic decimeters = 10^6 cu.cms. = 10^9 cu.mm.

1 cubic decimeter = 10^3 cu.cms. = 10^6 cu.mm.

1 Cc = 10^3 cu.mm.

The weight of 1 Cc of water at 4°C. is 1 gram.

Units Of Capacity and Equivalents

1 liter = 1000 Cc = 1000 milliliters

1 Cc = 1 milliliter = 16.2 minims (drops)

1 Cc distilled water = 1 milliliter distilled water = 1 gram

1 gallon = 4 quarts = 8 pints = 128 fl. oz.

1 quart = 2 pints = 32 fl. oz.

1 pint = 16 fl. oz.

1 fl. oz. = 8 fl. drams = 29.57 mils = 29.57 Cc

1 fl. dram = 3.696 mils = 3.696 Cc

Avoirdupois

1 ton = 2000 pounds = 32,000 ounces = 907.2 kilograms

1 pound = 16 ounces = 453.59 grams

1 ounce = 28.34 grams

1 gram = 100 centigrams = 1000 milligrams = 15.43 grains

1 grain = .0648 gram = 6.48 centigrams = 64.8 milligrams

Units of Angle

1 circumference = 360 degrees = 2π radians =

$(2\pi r; r = radius)$

½ circumference = 180 degrees = π radians

¼ circumference = 90 degrees = $\frac{\pi}{2}$ radians

⅛ circumference = 45 degrees = $\frac{\pi}{4}$ radians

$(\pi = 3.1416)$

1 degree = 60 minutes = 3600 seconds = 0.01745 radian

1 minute = 60 seconds

1 radian = 57° 17′44.8″ = 57.2958° (degrees)

1 knot (nautical mile) = length of 1′ (minute) of arc on
Earth's equatorial surface.

Other Units Used in Book

Nanosecond	–	10^{-9} second	Megawatt	–	10^6
Nanometer	–	10^{-9} meter	Gigawatt	–	10^9
Microfarad	–	10^{-6} farad	Terawatt	–	10^{12} watts

Appendix D
Selected Sources of Laser Data

General Information

Japan's Progress in Diode Lasers, Hideya Gamo, University of California at Irvine, pp 57-59, also see pp 61-66, March 1982 LF

"Reading" Flames with Lasers, pp 33-34 February 1982 PH S

Laser Systems and Applications, Elion, H. A., Pergamon Press, New York 1967

Lasers (2nd Edition), Lengyel, B. A., John Wiley, New York 1971

Principles of Gas Lasers, Allen L. et al, Plenum Press, New York 1967

An Introduction to Lasers and Masers, A. E. Siegman, McGraw-Hill, New York 1971

Optical Instruments and Their Applications, D. F. Horne, Heyden & Son, Inc. Philadelphia, PA 1980

Free-Electron Laser Produced in Uniform Magnetic Field, S. K. Ride, Rice University of Applied Physics, 20 1, 41 September 1979

Resonant Laser Beam Choppers, Stanley M. Riech, Bulova Watch Company, Woodside, New York 1980

Laser Interaction and Related Plasma Phenomena, Helmut J. Schwarz et al, Plenum Publishing Corporation, New York 1981

Los Almos 72-Beam 100-TW Antares Projected for 1982, LF Staff, October 1978

Laser Assesses Weld Conditions, Laser Focus Staff, pp 30-36, April 1981 LF

Laser-Induced Damage in Optical Materials, Alexander J. Glass et al, Government Printing Office, Washington, D.C. 1978

Laser Safety Handbook, Alex Mallow and Leon Chabot, Van Nostrand, New York 1978

Power Transmission by Laser Beam, Bell Tel Labs, Jan & Mar 1979 LF

Infrared and Millimeter Waves, Kenneth J. Button, ed., Academic Press, Inc. New York 1981

Laser-Induced Chemical Processes, Jeffry I. Steinfeld, ed., Plenum Publishing Corporation, New York 1981
Materials Processing by Lasers
Laser Brazing to Join Small Parts, Charles E. Whitherell, Nov p-73 1981 LF
Lasers in Industry, International Resource Development, Inc., Norwalk, Conn. 1979
Metalworking with YAG, Simon L. Engel, December 1978 LF
High-Power Laser Welding, British Oxygen Company, August 1979 LF
CO_2 Laser Cuts Metals—and Costs (Everrett), November 1979 LF
Apollo Laser Machining Systems, Technical Publication, Apollo Lasers, Inc., Van Nuys, CA 1979
Laser Processing of Materials, Ebtec Corporation, Agawam, Mass., 1979
Laser Machining of Tough Materials, S. Rajagopal, pp 57-59, March 1982 LF
Biophysics and Medical Applications of Lasers, pp 95-97, February 1982 LF
CO_2 Laser Best Choice for Welding Titanium, September 1977 LF
Dual-Wave Annealing With Lasers, D. H. Auston, Bell Tel Labs, Murray Hill, (App Phys Lett 34 9, 558 May 1979)
Laser Metalworking Systems, Control Laser Corp., Technical Brochure 1979 Orlando, Florida
Lasers in Materials Processing, Daniel J. Gofgen, Optical Spectra May 1979
AVCO High-Power Metalworking Lasers, Staff of AVCO Everrett, Co., Somerville, California, November 1979
Infrared and Millimeter Waves, Kenneth J. Button, ed., Academic Press, Inc. New York 1981
Holographic Studies
Advances in Holography, N. H. Farhat, (Vol 1) Marcel Dekker, New York 1966
Principles of Holography, H. M. Smith (2nd Edition), Wiley-Interscience, New York 1975
Nonlinear Mixing and Holography, Amnon Yarif et al, Calif Inst of Tech, IEEE J of Qaunt Elec, QE 15, 4, 224 April 1979
Holographic Scanner Both Deflects and Collects, LF Staff, Newton, Mass. July LF
Laser Technology, Chapter 2—Laser Holography, H. M. Muncheryan, Bobbs-Merrill Publishing, Indianapolis, Indiana 1979
An Introduction to Interferometry, S. Tolansky, Wiley-Interscience, New York (1973.)
Applications of Holography, E. S. Barrakette et al, Plenum Press, New York 1971
Two-Photon Holography with a CW Laser, March 1981 LF
New Home Electronic Game Use Hologram for Scenery, Atari, Sunnyvale, CA. March 1981 LF
Laser Communications—Aerial and Fiberoptic
One-Megabit Fiber for Aircraft, LF Staff, October 1979 LF
Optical Waveguide Communications, R. L. Gallawa, U.S. Dept. of Commerce, Boulder, Colorado 1979
Principles of Optical Fiber Measurements, Dietrich Marcuse, Academic Press, Inc., New York 1981

Fiberoptic Links for Cables, Valtec Staff, Valtec Corp., Optical Spectra August 1979

Battlefield Fiber Network, Peter D. Steensma and A. Mondrick, ITT Defense Communication Division, Roanoke, VA 1979

An Introduction to Fiberoptic Sensors, Dynamic Systems, Inc., pp 112-115 February 1982 LF.

Detection of Ultrashort Light (Laser) pulses, Eric P. Ippen, MIT, Jan 1982 LF

Integrated Optical Lasers, USC Technical Paper, pp 78-80, January 1982 LF

Laser and Microwave Radar, Albert V. Jelalian, p-88, April 1981 LF

Optical Communications, R. M. Gagliardi et al, Wiley Interscience, New York 1976

GaAs Aerial Communication, Technical Bulletin, International Laser Systems, Orlando, Florida 1979

Optical Fibers for Long-Range Data Communication, ITT Staff Tom A. Eppes et al, Electronic Design, Vol 8, April 12, 1976

Tailoring Diodes to Match Fiber-System Requirements, LF Staff, March 1978 LF

Aging of Optical Waveguides, H. Liertz, June 1978 EOSD

Measuring Optical Index Profile, Dennis G. Leiner, March 1978 Optical Spectra

Optical Fibers for Transmission, John E. Midwinter, John Wiley & Sons, New York (1979)

LEDs for 32-Megabit for Communication, L. R. Dawson et al, Bell Tel Labs, Bell Systems Technical Journal, 59 2, 161, Feb 1980

Fiberoptic Sensors, Charles M. Davis, pp 112-115, February 1982 LF

Fundamentals of Optical Fiber Communications, Michael K. Barnoski, ed., Academic Press, Inc., New York 1981

Fiber and Integrated Optics, Daniel B. Ostrowsky, Plenum Press, New York 1978

Optical Waveguide Theory, H. G. Unger, Oxford University Press 1977

Fiberoptic Trunk for Cable TV, Robert Sturm and Otto I. Szentesi, March 1980 LF

Waveguide Harmonics, E. M. Zolotov et al, Zh Eksp Teor Fiz (Russian), Oct 1979

Laser Technology, Chapter 7, H. M. Muncheryan, Bobbs-Merrill Publishing Co., Indianapolis, Indiana 1979

Low Fiberoptic Losses at Long Wavelengths, p-70, April 1981 LF

Biomedical Applications of Lasers

Biomedical Applications of Lasers, Leon Goldman, M.D., Springer-Verlag, New York 1967

The Biomedical Laser, Leon Goldman Ed., Springer-Verlag, New York 1981

Lasers in Photomedicine and Photobiology, Pratesi/Sacchi, eds., Springer-Verlag, New York 1980

YAG vs Argon Endoscopy, Journal Review, November 1977 LF

Endoscopy with Argon Laser, Spectra-Physics Technical Brochure, Mountain View, California 1980

Medical Instrumentation, Leon Goldman, M.D., Med Instr J, 10 2, 125 Mar-Apr 1976

Holography in Medicine and Biology, G. von Bally, Springer-Verlag, N.Y. 1979

Surgery of Female Incontinence (Laser), Stanton/Tanagho eds., Springer-Verlag New York 1980

Laser Applications In Surgery, Richard Dwyer, M.D., Harbor General Hospital, Torrance, CA, January 1982 LF

Biomedical Laser Studies in Munich, Germany, October 1979 LF

Laser Destroys Dye-Containing Cells to Treat Cancer, LF Staff, December 1979 LF

Eye Safety Endoscopy, Chris Galacsik et al, University of Washington, Seattle, App Opt 18 11, 1816 June 1, 1979

Lasers Used in Diagnosis, University of Southern California, Cleo Report, January 1978 LF

Laser Technology, H. M. Muncheryan, Bobbs-Merrill Publishing Company, Indianapolis, Indiana 1979

Military Laser Systems

Directed Energy Weapons, Ruth Davis, October 1979 LF

Military Laser Systems, Technical Bulletin, Fraser-Volp Corp., Warrington, Penna 1979

Laser Weapons, Laser Focus Staff, pp 85-88, Jaunary 1982 LF

Army's Laser Battle Simulators, Xerox Corp., July 1979 LF

Hughes Laser Range Designators, July 1979 LF

High Precision with Laser Satellite Ranging, D. A. Byrns & G. E. Overstreet, GTE Sylvania, Ind Res & Dev, April 1980

Military Systems Technical Bulletins, Laakman Electro-optics, Inc., Dana Point, California 1980

Laser Systems for the Military, Laser Technology, H. M. Muncheryan, Bobbs-Merrill Publishing Company, Indianapolis, Indiana 1979

Directed-Beam Portable Laser System for Military, Dr. Arthur M. Muncheryan, Laserkinetics Corp., Patent No. 3,478,278 - 1969

Military Systems, Technical Bulletin, Davidson Optronics, Inc., West Covina, California 1979

Military Security Surveillance System by Laser, Laser Technology, Bobbs-Merrill Publishing Company, Indianapolis, IND 1979

U.S. Army's Laser Fence, Laser Technology, Bobbs-Merrill Publishing Co., Indianapolis, Indiana 1979

Directed-Beam Portable Laser System, A. M. Muncheryan, Pat. No. 3,404,350 - 1968

Information Processing with Laser Beams

Laser Transceivers for Satellite Communication, LF Staff, July 1979 LF

Undersea Fiberoptic Cable (Transmission), R. F. Gleason and R. A. Smith, December 1979 LF

Bettelle's Digital Optical Storage System, August 1979 LF

Optical Data Processing for Engineers, David Casasent, Carnegie-Mellon University, Pittsburgh, Penna, June 1978 EOSD

Lasers In Printing, Staff Members, Photonics Spectra, pp 52-54, Mar 1982 PHS

Blue-Green Eximers, Technical Articles, Naval Ocean Systems Center, San Diego, California, and Lawrence Livermore Laboratory, pp-53 to 58, Jan 1982 (LF).

New Recording Development for Optical Storage, LF Staff, August 1979 LF

Laser Engraves Printing Cylinders, B. C. Doxey, July 1977 LF

Kerr Cell Applied in Information Handling, S. M. Hauser and H. Quan, Opto-electronic Devices and Circuits, McGraw-Hill Book Company, New York 1964

Optical Storage Media, Bell Laboratory Report, p-33 PH S, March 1982

News Phototransmitter Employs He-Ne Laser, LF Staff, November 1979 LF

Optical Automation Methods, RAI Seminar Management, OAM-CNP-04, Cincinnati, Ohio 1979

Digital Signal Processor, Cliff Morgan, November 1977 LF

Transmission of Images Through Optical Waveguides, Lev A. Rivlin and Alexander T. Semenov, p-82 February 1981

Gasdynamic Laser, S. A. Losev, Springer-Verlag, New York 1981

Adaptive Optical Systems, James E. Pearson, p-53, September 1981 LF

Lasers for Atomic Fusion Research

Plasma Fusion Research with Lasers, Staff of Industrial Research and Development Magazine, April 1980

Fusion Driven by Neutral Particles, Occidental Research Corp., Irvine, California, February 1980 LF

Electron-Beam Heating for Fusion, James Benford, July 1975 EOSD

Los Almos Laser Fusion Program, LF Staff, November 1979 LF

Transmutation of Superheavy Elements by Laser Fusion, S. M. Ayub, Oct 1980 LF

Raman Compression of KrF Laser Pulses, Lawrence Livermore Laboratory, January 1979 LF

KMS and LLL Use Frequency-Doubled Glass for Fusion, February 1980 LF

Laser Interaction and Related Plasma Phenomena, Helmut J. Schwarz et al, Plenum Publishing Corporation, New York 1981

Laser Fusion Effort by Various Research Centers, Laser Technology, H. M. Muncheryan, Bobbs-Merril Publishing Company, Indianapolis, Indiana 1979

Laser Fusion Reactors, S. L. Aladel et al, University of Wisconsin, Nuc Tech 43 1, 5 April 1979

Laser Fusion Progress and Goals, pp 65-87, January 1982 LF

Laser Applications in Entertainment Field

Holograms in Displays, LF Staff, July 1977 LF

Electro-optic Effects in Entertainment Park, LF Staff, October 1979 LF

Recent Achievements in High-Power Lasers, LANL, pp 53-56, Febraury 1982 LF

A Simple Low-Cost Scanner, Jim Godwin, Spectra-Physics Laser Systems

Division Technical Data, Eugene, Oregon 1982

Lasers Illuminate Fashion Shows and Rock Group, LF Staff, July 1979 LF

Laser Graphic Displays, Laser Displays, Inc., Boston, Mass. 1979

British Holographic Systems for Light Shows, LF Staff, 1977 LF

Light (Laser) Shows in London, LF Staff, December 1979 LF

Laser Interaction and Related Plasma Phenomena, Helmut J. Schwarz et al, Plenum Publishing Corporation, New York 1981

Laser Research and Development

Doppler-Free Spectra from Dye Laser, L. M. Humphrey et al, Bell Tel Lab October 1979

Measuring Atoms Velocity with Dye Laser, C. Y. She, Colorado State University August 1979

Double-Quantum Saturation Spectroscopy with Lasers, Erhard W. Weber, December 1979 LF

Research and Fiberoptics, Paul H. Endland, Photodyne, Inc., Westlake Village, California April 1980

Laser Research in China, Staff of Spectra-Physics, Inc., July 1979 LF

Infrared and Millimeter Waves, Kenneth J. Button, ed. Academic Press, Inc. New York 1981

Mapping Air Pollutants with Laser, D. C. Wolfe and Robert Byer, Stanford University, California October 1979

Laser Calorimetry, Richard J. Becherer and Franc Grum, March 1980 LF

New Laser Fusion Results at Plasma-Physics Meeting, March 1981 LF

Martial Atmosphere is a Solar-Pumped Laser, March 1981 LF

Laser Interaction and Related Plasma Phenomena, Helmut J. Schwarz et al, Plenum Publishing Corp., New York 1981

Temperature Profiles at a Chemical Laser Nozzle, P. J. Marteney, United Technology Research Center, East Hartford, CT 1979

Laser Cold Processing of Semiconductors, Quantronix Corp., Smithtown, New York December 1979

A Primer on F-Center Lasers, Technical Staff, Burleigh Instruments, Inc. Burleigh Park, New York September 1978

The Excimer Age: Lasing with the New Breed, David L. Hiestis, June 1979 Optical Spectra Magazine

Vibronic Alexandrite Lasers, Brian E. Newman, Los Alamos National Laboratory, pp 53-56, February 1982 LF

Abbreviations

LF - Laser Focus Magazine

Rev of Sci Instr - Review of Scientific Instruments (Physical Society)

Bell Tel Labs - Bell Telephone Laboratories

App Phys Lett - Applied Physics Letters

EOSD - Electro-optical Systems Design

Calif, Inst of Tech - California Institute of Technology

Med Instr J - Medical Instruments Journal

Ind Res & Dev - Industrial Research and Development (Magazine)

Nuc Tech - Nuclear Techology (Magazine)

LLL - Lawrence Livermore Laboratory (Berkeley, California)
MIT - Massachusetts Institute of Technology
J of Qunat Elec - Journal of Quantum Electronics
LANL - Los Almos National Laboratory
PH S - Photonics Spectra (Formerly, Optical Spectra Magazine)

Appendix E
Laser-Oriented Manufacturers

Advanced Kinetics, Inc.
1231 Victoria Street   Phone - (714) 646-7165
Costa Mesa, California 92627
Mfg - pulsed lasers, detectors, power supplies, interferometers, spectrometers.

American Laser Systems, Inc.
106 James Fowler Road   Phone - (805) 967-0423
Goleta, California 93017
Mfg - Laser communication systems, modulators, silicon detectors, power supplies.

American Optical Corporation
10 Optical Avenue   Phone - (603) 352-3202
Keene, New Hampshire 03431
Mfg - laser systems, optical components, beam expanders, beam splitters, lenses.

Apollo Lasers, Inc.
6357 Arizona Circle   Phone - (213) 776-3343
Los Angeles, California 90045
Mfg - ruby, glass, YAG, CO_2 lasers; photodiode detectors, radiometers, holography.

Ardel, Kinamatic Corporation
125-20 18th Avenue   Phone - (212) 353-3600
College Point, New York 11356
Mfg - optical mounts, translators, optical benches, He-Ne lasers.

Atomergic Chemetals Corporation
100 Fairchild Avenue   Phone - (516) 822-8800
Plainview, New York 11803
Mfg - Birefringent windows, infrared windows, ultraviolet windows, laser crystals.

AVCO Everett-Metalworking Lasers
32 Cobble Hill Road   Phone - (617) 389-3000
Somerville, MA 02143
Mfg - Carbon dioxide lasers, metalworking systems, metal surface treatment, etc.

Barnes Engineering Company
30 Commerce Road   Phone - (203) 348-5381
Stamford, CT 06904
Mfg - photon detectors, collimators, infrared radiometers, spectrum analyzers.

Bausch & Lomb, Inc.
820 Linden Avenue   Phone - (716) 385-1000
Rochester, New York 14625
Mfg - diffraction gratings, grating monochromators, laser safety goggles.

BOC Ltd, Industrial Power Beams
7 Royal Oak Way South   Phone - (03272) 4813
Daventry, Northants, UK
Mfg - CO_2 lasers, Nd-YAG lasers, beam expanders, radiometers, Q-switches.

Bond Optics, Inc.
Etna Road   Phone - (603) 448-2300
Lebanon, New Hampshire 03766
Mfg - beam splitters, etalons, filters, lenses, mirrors, prisms, windows, laser rods.

Broomer Research Corporation
23 Sheer Plaza   Phone - (516) 249-1544
Plainview, New York 11803
Mfg - thin-film coatings, optical filters, etalons, lenses, mirrors, polarizers.

Burleigh Instruments, Inc.
Burleigh Park   Phone - (716) 924-9355
Fishers, New York 14453
Mfg - Fabry-Perot interferometers, mirror mounts, power supplies, piezoelectric/translators.

Cleveland Crystals, Inc.
19306 Redwood Avenue   Phone - (216) 486-6100
Cleveland, Ohio 44110
Mfg - optical components, KDP group, Q-switches, polarizers, waveplate retarders.

Coherent, Inc.
3210 Porter Drive   Phone - (415) 493-2111
Palo Alto, California 94304
Mfg - pulsed CO_2 lasers, He-Ne lasers, radiometers, detectors, collimators, dye lasers.

Control Laser Corporation
11222 Astronaut Boulevard   Phone - (305) 851-2540
Orlando, Florida 32809
Mfg - Nd-YAG lasers, holographic equipment, collimators, etalons, expanders.

Daedal, Inc.
P.O. Box G   Phone - (412) 744-4451
Harrison City, PA 15636
Mfg - beam positioners, optical benches, optical mounts, motor-driven stages.

The Ealing Corporation
22 Pleasant Street   Phone - (617) 655-7000
St Natick, MA 01760
Mfg - laser monitors, safety goggles, collimators, detectors, attenuators, filters.

Eastman Kodak Company
343 State Street   Phone - (716) 325-2000
Rochester, New York 14650
Mfg - laser dyes, Q-switch for ruby and Nd lasers, optical materials, lenses, phosphors.

EG&G Inc.
35 Congress Street   Phone - (617) 745-3200
Salem, MA 01970
Mfg - detectors, radiometers, flashlamps, krytrons, thyratrons, pulse selectors.

Edmund Scientific Company
1776 Edscorp Building   Phone - (609) 547-3488
Barrington, New Jersey 08007
Mfg - Lenses, mirrors, gratings, fiberoptics, optical benches, flats, mirrors, goggles.

Hughes Aircraft Company
6155 El Camino Real   Phone - (714) 438-9191
Carlsbad, California 92008
Mfg - He-Ne lasers, power supplies, collimators, interferometry, CO_2 and military Lasers.

Infrared Optics, Inc.
5 Jean Court   Phone - (516) 694-2977
Farmingdale, New York 11735
Mfg - beam expanders, splitters, filters, coatings, lenses, mirrors, wedges, domes.

IntraAction Corporation
766 Foster Avenue   Phone - (312) 595-3770
Bensenville, Illinois 60106
Mfg - acousto-optics modulators, mode lockers, Q-switches, deflectors, beam generators.

ITT Corporation
7635 Plantation Road   Phone - (703) 563-0371
Roanoke, Virginia 24019
Mfg - all types fiberoptics, fiberoptic components, communication systems, connectors.

Korad/Hadron, Inc.
2520 Colorado Avenue   Phone - (213) 829-3377
Santa Monica, California 90404
Mfg-pulsed lasers, holography, mode lockers, mirrors, Q-switches, photodiodes.

Karl Lambrecht Corporation
4204 North Lincoln Avenue   Phone - (312) 472-5442
Chicago, Illinois 60618
Mfg - beam splitters, collimators, filters, coatings, polarizers, waveplates,
radiometers.

Laserkinetics Corporation
1735 N. Morningside Street   Phone - (714) 637-4683
Orange, California 92667
Mfg - developers of medical and dental laser systems, communication
systems, military.

Lasermetrics, Inc.
111 Galway Place   Phone - (201) 837-9090
Teaneck, New Jersey 07666
Mfg - modulators, Q-switches, polarizing prisms, optical elements, translators.

Lexel Corporation
928 East Meadow Drive   Phone - (415) 494-3241
Palo Alto, California 94303
Mfg - argon and krypton lasers, holographic systems, power meters, mode
lockers.

Lumonics Incorporated
105 Schneider Road, Kanata   Phone - (613) 592-1460
Ontario, Canada K2K 1Y3
Mfg - gas lasers, markers, detectors, power meters, energy meters.

Metrologic Instrument, Inc.
143 Harding Avenue   Phone - (609) 933-0100
Bellmawr, New Jersey 08033
Mfg - He-Ne lasers, collimators, filters, optical benches, holography,
radiometers.

Molecron Corporation
177 North Wolfe Road   Phone - (408) 738-2661
Sunnyvale, California 94086
Mfg - pyroelectric detectors, Nd-YAG and tunable dye lasers, radiometers, etc.

Newport Research Corporation
18235 Mount Baldy Circle   Phone - (714) 963-9811
Fountain Valley, California 92708
Mfg - optical tables, vibration isolators, beam positioners, laser kits.

Optical Coating Laboratory, Inc.
15251 E Don Julian Road   Phone - (213) 968-6581
City of Industry, California 91761
Mfg - silicon photodiodes, beam splitters, beam expanders, lenses, polarizers.

Owen-Illinois, Inc.
P.O. Box 1035   Phone - (419) 247-8364
Toledo, Ohio 43666
Mfg - Nd-glass rods, disks, Faraday rotators, samarium filter tubes, clad rods.

Phase-R Corporation
Old Bay Road   Phone - (603) 859-3800
New Durham, NH 03855
Mfg - tunable dye and nitrogen lasers, expanders, optical benches, flashlamps.

RCA Corporation
New Holland Avenue   Phone - (717) 397-7661
Lancaster, PA 17604
Mfg - helium-cadmium lasers, semiconductor lasers, detectors, transceivers.

Space Optics Research Laboratories
7 Stuart Road   Phone - (617) 256-4511
Chelmsord, MA 01824
Mfg - Fourier lenses, infrared components, parabolic mirrors, mounts, interferometers.

293

Spectra-Physics, Inc.
1250 West Middlefield Road   Phone - (415) 961-2550
Mountain View, California 94042
Mfg - He-Ne lasers, Ar lasers, Krypton Lasers, radiometers, splitters, expanders, etalons.

United Detector Technology, Inc.
2644 30th Street   Phone - (213) 396-3175
Santa Monica, California 90405
Mfg - silicon photodiodes, radiometers, positioning devices, photometers.

Valtec Corporation
99 Hartwell Street   Phone - (617) 835-6082
West Boylston, MA 01583
Mfg - custom fiberoptic cables, telecommunications, industrial and medical illuminators.

WEC Engineering, Inc.
86 Woodbridge Road   Phone - (617) 369-4183
Carlisle, MA 01741
Mfg - laser systems, amplifiers, beam expanders, modulators, mounts, radiometers.

Index

8137